Begin by Loving Again

My Safari from Farm Girl
to Missionary Doctor
to Wife and Mother

Dorcas L. Stoltzfus Morrow, M.D.

with portions by Theodore E. Morrow

Cover and internal design and layout by Alice S. Morrow Rowan

Produced by Not Forgotten Publishing Services
not.forgotten.publishing@gmail.com

The Lord will fulfill his purpose for me;
Thy steadfast love, O Lord, endures forever.
Do not forsake the work of thy hands.

Psalm 138:8 RSV

Begin by loving again
Begin by loving again
When all that once mattered
Seems ruined and shattered
Just begin by loving again

From a song by Theodore E. Morrow

For Dad and Ted

Contents

Foreword

On June 15, 2014, Dorcas and I ate dinner in the dining room at Landis Homes with the daughter of a preacher who many years earlier had preached during the week of evangelistic meetings that were held every fall at Dorcas's home church. It was at one of those meetings that Dorcas became a Christian. "I never thanked him," she said, "because I was so bashful."

Near the end of our meal that day, Dorcas took a minute to thank this woman for her father's significant influence in Dorcas's life. Then, as we were preparing to leave the table, the woman said to Dorcas, "Did you ever hear what my dad said about you one time when he came home from visiting your family? He said, 'She wants to be a doctor, but she won't make it.'" This story was greeted with joyful laughter around the table, because Dorcas did indeed go on to become a doctor, and not just a doctor but a missionary MD, surgeon, OB-GYN, and later, in her fifties, a psychiatrist—and more, far more, than she had ever dreamed. Ironically, she probably would not have had the courage to do any of it without the faith sparked in her by this man's preaching, even though at the time he could not imagine what she would go on to do with it and because of it.

Alice S. Morrow Rowan, Editor
Not Forgotten Publishing

God bless you, Anna with Jacob and Don
for your friendship with Dorcas
and your kindness to me.
♡ Alice Morrow Rowan

THe Story OF MY Life

By

Dorcas Stoltzfus

CRADLE

LMS

Preface

My sister Dorcas Stoltzfus started writing her autobiography in the fall of 1948 when she was a high school student at Lancaster Mennonite School. On the cover she wrote "The Story of My Life" and drew a cradle, a building marked with "L.M.S.," and a person walking on a path toward L.M.S. The booklet has twenty pages. Six of these are photos and the rest are typed text. This project was a school assignment, and she did a lot of digging to find information about our ancestors. After three pages of this information, she wrote about our parents, her childhood, her school days, her favorite things, and her ambitions (which were "somewhat akin to that of a new automobile just rolling off the assembly line, if it had the ability to think; it would probably be wondering who would be its owner and where it would [be] privileged to go to"). In conclusion she wrote, "I have been impressed for some time with the need for workers in God's harvest field and if God ever leads my life that way I want to follow Him all the way, wherever He may lead me."

Dorcas graduated from L.M.S. in 1951; from Eastern Mennonite College in Harrisonburg, Virginia, in 1956; and from the Woman's Medical College of Pennsylvania in Philadelphia in 1960. She worked a variety of jobs in the summers and over Christmas holidays to help pay her tuition. During a year of internship at Chester County Hospital in West Chester, she was asked by the Eastern Mennonite Board of Missions and Charities to serve at Shirati Hospital in Tanganyika. During her years overseas she wrote many interesting letters to her parents and siblings. I'm not sure if she had in mind that these might someday be helpful in writing her autobiography. I don't remember that she asked us to keep her letters, but we did. She typed and edited many of them and they are included in this book.

The story of the life of her husband, Ted Morrow, is woven into the book beginning in Part One, about Dorcas's life prior to their marriage; continuing in Part Two, about Ted's life prior to their marriage; and culminating in Part Three, about their marriage, Ted's passing, and Dorcas's life after Ted.

In an outline of her life written in 2000, Dorcas states, "I want to do some writing . . . about my childhood, my family and many things I have experienced. God has led me and provided so many good things that I did not expect would ever happen when I was younger. I want to leave a record that my family and friends can enjoy." After her retirement, Dorcas and Ted took some classes at a community college and did some writing, but there was always work to do both inside and outside the house. As the years rolled by, Ted developed more health issues, and Dorcas did not have much time or energy to write her stories.

After Ted's death on January 25, 2004, Dorcas moved to Landis Homes. She quickly joined several writing classes and began writing about her life and Ted's life. She continued this work for nearly a decade. But in a letter written on September 21, 2013, she shared that she was "getting less able to write because the proper words don't come to me and my ability to work on the computer does not work as well as it used to." In the fall of 2014 she decided it was time to proceed with publishing. Though she was not able to hold the printed book in her hands before her Lord and Savior took her home on Friday, August 7, 2015, she knew the book had been completed. A final chapter, "Saying Good-bye to Dorcas," was added after her funeral, and now the story of Dorcas's life that she started writing as a child and wanted so much to share with you is in your hands.

Anna Mary Stoltzfus Groff
August 28, 2015

Part One
Dorcas Leah Stoltzfus:
The First Forty-Three Years

My Call to Become a Doctor

When I was growing up, we always went to a church service on Sunday evening, alternating between Millwood one Sunday and Maple Grove the next. The evening often included Young People's Bible Meeting. Several of the young folks would be asked to answer a question about the Bible, then several older folks would give short talks on some assigned topic, which I guess was meant to help us learn to speak in public. Sometimes a visiting minister came and preached for us. I enjoyed that. And occasionally we had a really special treat, such as a missionary speaker. I can remember hearing a number of missionaries, such as Amos Swartzentruber and my uncle D. Parke Lantz from Argentina; Clinton Ferester, Dr. Noah Mack, Dr. Merle Eshleman, and Dr. J. Lester Eshleman from Tanganyika; and Dr. Jonathan Yoder, who served in India and later Nepal.

One particular summer evening—it may have been the summer after seventh grade, when I was going on fourteen—the guest speaker was to be Dr. Jonathan Yoder. Our family had an extra reason for looking forward to this service: Dr. Yoder was a distant relative. His grandmother was a daughter of Tennessee John Stoltzfus, which would make him a second cousin to my dad, but we had not met him before. We were eager to hear about his work, and of course we wanted to say hello to him afterward.

It was a gorgeous evening, not too warm. It must have been in June, when the days are really long. I remember sitting maybe halfway back on the left side with the ladies. The sun had come so far around us to the northwest that it was shining through the windows behind us from the cemetery side of the building. And because the service began at 7:00 P.M. and lasted a bit over an hour, we had sunshine streaming onto our backs most of the evening.

The building was not full but there was a nice-size group present. We began by singing several rousing missionary songs:

- "At home and abroad on life's battlefield, brave soldiers are needed. . . ."

- "From Greenland's icy mountains, from India's coral strand. . . ."

- "There's a call comes ringing o'er the restless wave, 'Send the light.' . . ."

- "Speed away! Speed away on your mission of light to the lands that are lying in darkness and night. . . ."

- "Far and near the fields are teeming with the waves of ripened grain. . . ."

- " 'Tis the harvest time, 'tis the harvest time; to the fields I must away. . . ."

- "Rescue the perishing, care for the dying; Jesus is merciful, Jesus will save. . . ."

Then one of the ministers read a Scripture passage, led us in prayer, and finally introduced Dr. Yoder.

Dr. Yoder began by expressing that he was grateful for meeting with us because his grandmother had been from Millwood and he was eager to meet some of his local cousins. He spoke easily about India and it was clear he enjoyed the land and the people. I remember him saying, "I enjoy my work. I am eager to go back, and I would really be disappointed if I could not go back." I don't remember if he included an actual sermon in his presentation, but God used what he said to speak a clear message to my young heart.

A significant part of that message came via the story that Dr. Yoder told about Dr. Ida Scudder. It went something like this:

Ida Scudder's grandfather, her father, and four of her father's brothers were missionary doctors in India. Ida, who had five older brothers and no sisters, was born in India in 1870. Their family began a much-needed furlough in 1878. Her father, Dr. John Scudder Jr., went back to India two years later while her mother, Sophia, stayed with the children on their Nebraska farm for two more years. Then Sophia returned to India, leaving Ida with an uncle's family in Chicago. Ida was distraught by her mother's departure but slowly adjusted to living with her uncle's family—until her uncle decided to go on a mission to Japan a year later. But then evangelist Dwight L. Moody invited Ida to attend the Seminary for Girls that he had founded in Northfield, Massachusetts. Ida enjoyed her life at Northfield very much. She made many friends and could be described as the "life of the party." She joined some of her friends in planning to attend Wellesley College after graduation.

Then came a decisive cablegram from her father in India, reporting that Ida's mother was ill and needed Ida's help. Ida was eager to see her mother, but she did *not* want to go to India to do so! Her friends tried to discourage her from going, but after a sleepless night and some prayer, she decided she would go to help her mother for a short term. She had no intention of becoming another Scudder missionary! She traveled with her brother Harry and, once in India, applied herself to household duties, garden work, and teaching school girls so that her mother could get more rest. Within weeks her mother began to look better, her color improved, and she felt better too.

Suddenly, one memorable night, Ida was confronted by three situations of desperate need in which she was unprepared to provide the requested assistance. It was through these dramatic encounters with three needy fathers, and then with her Lord, that Ida came to know, and accept, that God had a special plan for her life. Two versions of her biography show some differences in the story, but basically the facts are these:

1. Ida was sitting at her desk in her room one evening when she heard footsteps on the veranda. She looked up to see a very tall, fine-looking Brahmin gentleman approaching. When Ida went to the door and asked if she could help him, the man said that his wife, a lovely young girl of only fourteen years, was dying in childbirth and the barber woman (midwife) could not help her. He asked Ida to come and help his wife. Ida explained that she knew absolutely nothing about midwifery but her father was a doctor and when he returned from the village he would gladly come to help.

Well, the man drew himself up and said, "Your father would come into my caste house and take care of my wife? Never! She had better die than have anything like that happen." Ida continued to try to persuade him. Her father returned and Ida explained the situation to him. Together they pleaded with the man to let them come together to see his wife, with Ida offering to assist her father so that he would not need to touch the young mother. But the Brahmin gentleman turned away, apparently believing that Ida was simply refusing to help his wife.

As Ida watched him go into the darkness, she turned to her father and asked *why* the man had refused help from Dr. John, especially because Dr. John was trained and Ida was not. So Dr. John gently explained to Ida that it was because of the rules, the customs, and the caste system that forbade a wife to be looked upon by any man except those in her own family. There were *no* exceptions for any reason. There were many classes in the caste system, and people were not permitted to marry someone outside their own class, or even to have contact with other classes. At the bottom of all of these castes and subcastes was a large group known as "untouchables," who were doomed to the "unclean occupations" such as sweeping, filth removal, leather-working, and so on.

2. Ida returned to her desk but her thoughts were in turmoil. How could an upper-class Brahmin who obviously loved his beautiful child bride not accept help from Ida's father, who was a trained physician? Then she heard footsteps on the veranda again. Assuming that the Brahmin father had changed his mind and was ready to receive help from Ida and her family, she jumped up quickly from her seat. But the one who approached was a Muslim man in a long white coat. He promptly requested help for his wife, explaining that "she has had other children, but this time the little one does not come. There is no one to help her but an ignorant, untrained woman. I am afraid she is dying."

Ida was struck by the coincidence of the two needy women in labor. The Muslim man went on to say, "I have heard there is a doctor here who came from America not long ago." Ida assumed that a Muslim would have no caste system to worry about, so she led him to meet her father. But this man also said that only the men of her immediate family ever entered a Muslim woman's apartment, and he was asking for Ida's help because she was a woman. Ida explained that she knew nothing about midwifery, and the man rejected the offer for Dr. John and daughter Ida to come together, saying, "She had better die than have a man come into the home."

3. By this time Ida was quite distraught and frustrated. She was unable to concentrate on her books, and her thoughts were quite scattered. When she suddenly heard footsteps again, she ran to the door, hoping that the Muslim man had returned. But no, this time it was a high-class Hindu man whose family Ida knew. His wife too was having a difficult labor and he begged Ida to come, saying that if Ida did not come his wife would die. Again Ida tried without success to convince the man that she had no midwifery training, that there was nothing—*nothing at all*—that she could do. And she repeated her plea that her father, a doctor, would gladly provide help if the man could accept it. But he refused, just as the others had, and vanished into the darkness.

Ida finally went to bed, but not to sleep. She was so aware that three women, one a mere child, were dying because there was no woman doctor to help them. She spent much of the night in anguish and prayer. She struggled with not wanting to spend her life in India. Afterward, she wrote this in her diary:

My friends were begging me to return to the joyous opportunities of a young girl in America, and I somehow felt that I could not give that up. I went to bed in the early morning after praying much for guidance. I think that was the first time I ever met God face to face and all that time it seemed that He was calling me into this work.

Early in the morning I heard the "tom-tom" beating in the village and it struck terror in my heart for it was a death message. I sent our servant, who had come up early, to the village to find out the fate of these three women, and he came back saying that all of them had died during the night. As the funerals passed our house on the way to the burning ghat, the wails from the people made me very unhappy. I could not bear to think of these young girls (and young women) as dead.

Again I shut myself in my room, and I thought very seriously about the condition of the Indian women and after much thought and prayer, I went to my father and mother during the morning and told them that I must go home and study medicine, and come back to India to help such women.

As Dr. Yoder finished telling us how Ida Scudder became willing to be a doctor and help India's needy people, especially the women, I sat on my bench and did not miss a word he said. And I began thinking to myself, "Well, if these people are too superstitious and too bound by their caste system to accept help from a male doctor for their women in labor, then—there should be more women doctors!" It was as clear as crystal to me. And then, just as clearly as if it had been spoken into my right ear, I heard an inner voice say to me, "Well, what about you? Yes, you too could become a doctor to help sick people."

In amazement, I responded silently, "Me?!? It takes a lot of money, and a lot of brains, to become a doctor. I'm just a chubby farm girl. And I'm not sure I have either—enough money or enough brains—to become a doctor—let alone both!"

Dr. Yoder went on to say that Ida Scudder did return to the United States and several years later became a doctor as she had promised. She then returned to India, where she helped many needy women, sick children, and blind men. Later she also developed a broader vision: she felt that she must help women to get an education instead of being married as young girls, and what better way was there than to develop a medical school in which to train women to become doctors and to assume leadership in order to deal with the caste system and oppression of women in India. The result of her thinking was the Christian Medical School for Women in Vellore, India.

Dr. Yoder then said something else that stuck with me: "Maybe God is speaking to someone tonight about preparing to become a missionary in some overseas country. If He is, I urge you to follow his call, wherever He takes you."

Soon the meeting was over. I sat and watched until Dad got close to Dr. Yoder and met him. Then I made my way over to the men's side, where I finally shook Dr. Yoder's hand and shyly introduced myself by pointing out who my dad was. I don't know if he realized that we were part of the Stoltzfus "Freundschaft."

You are right if you assume that I, being my usual quiet and shy self, did not tell anyone right away about the conversation I had with God that evening while Dr. Yoder was speaking. But some months later I decided that I was ready to share this experience. I decided to tell my dad's uncle D. Parke and aunt Lillie Lantz, who were serving in Argentina with the Mennonite Board of Missions and Charities (MBMC, now the Mennonite Mission Network), based in Elkhart, Indiana.

After I had finished writing my letter, I put it in an envelope and addressed it to Argentina. I then asked Mother for a stamp to put on it. That request created a temporary impasse. I didn't want to share my letter—not because there was anything bad in it, but because it was just so personal to me. Well, she insisted that she would not provide a stamp if she could not read my letter first, so I eventually handed over my precious letter, and after she had read it, she did put a stamp on it, and in due time my special letter was delivered to Argentina.

Within a year or two I began talking about going to high school. When I was asked why—because I already had working papers that excused me from going to school—I merely said, "Oh, to find out what I don't know!" In no way was I ready to share with anyone else the conversation that God and I had on the evening that Dr. Yoder spoke at Millwood. It was all so very precious and personal to me. Others might not understand my dream; they might even laugh at me, a farm girl, thinking I could become a doctor and a missionary. But even though I tightly guarded my dream, I never gave up on it—not even when I had so many opportunities to forget about going to high school and college. ✝

Mother and Dad

My roots are deeply intertwined with the lives of my parents and my Stoltzfus and Lantz ancestors, plus several school teachers and Sunday school teachers. So let me begin my story with my parents.

My father, Christian G. Stoltzfus, was born on October 7, 1900, the youngest child of Ezra Stoltzfus and Leah Lantz Stoltzfus. He grew up near Gap, a small town founded in 1701 in eastern Lancaster County, Pennsylvania. It is probably best known for its town clock, still located on a tall tower beside Route 41, where it overlooks the railroad in the gap in the hills and the broad valleys to the north and south. Route 41 comes up from the south and runs into the well-known Route 30, the Lincoln Highway, which crosses the entire country from east to west.

My mother, Elizabeth S. Stoltzfus, was born May 20, 1905, the youngest child in the family of Daniel S. Stoltzfus and Susan Stahl Stoltzfus. She grew up on a small "farmette" in Chester County known as Frog Hollow, less than a mile from the farm where she was born. Frog Hollow sat beside the Mercer's Mill covered bridge, which spans the east branch of the Octoraro Creek, not far from the small towns of Atglen in Chester County and Christiana in Lancaster County. A small stream that descended from the Bailey and King farms up the hill ran behind the farm's buildings. The children of these neighboring families enjoyed playing in the meadow and the creek with the Stoltzfus children.

Both families attended Millwood Amish Mennonite Church in Gap from 1882 and Maple Grove Mennonite Church in Atglen from 1909, so I suppose Christ and Lizzie were acquainted as young people, although Dad was four and a half years older than Mother. As a child I went with my parents to Maple Grove one Sunday and to Millwood the next Sunday, just as my parents and grandparents had done. The Millwood congregation was formed in 1878 when some families withdrew from the Amish to become Amish Mennonites, with Gideon Stoltzfus, my great grandfather, as their minister. Four years later, in 1882, they voted to build a meetinghouse. Work began immediately and the frame building, 50 by 36 feet, was built at a cost of $2,300 and dedicated on October 3, 1882. In April 1906, Sunday school was begun at the Sadsbury Quaker meetinghouse near Christiana. These meetings alternated with the biweekly services at Millwood, following the Amish tradition of having church services every other week. The Sunday school was well received, and folks appreciated the use of the English language. When the owners of the Sadsbury meetinghouse chose to stop renting their building in 1908, the families decided to construct a meetinghouse of their own. The 40-by-56-foot Maple Grove building cost $2,500 and was dedicated on August 7, 1909. The pulpit platform was originally built eleven inches higher than the floor level, with two steps, but some felt that was too modern, so the platform was lowered to seven inches with only one step. Except in cases of renovations and repairs, services were held at each meetinghouse biweekly, alternating from week to week.

For many years Dad's mother experienced medical limitations, so he stayed close to home and postponed courting activities until after her death on December 1, 1925, when he was twenty-five. How long he and Mother courted I do not know. Mother's parents had suffered financial hardship when a mysterious barn fire destroyed their threshing rig, a severe loss from which the family probably never fully recovered. When Mother was only twelve years old, her father died after abdominal surgery. He was billed for use of the operating room and for eighteen days of room and board—at $1.00 per day. His total bill was $53.50! He was discharged to his home on April 10, 1918, and died the following day. He was forty-eight. Grandma Susan had a public auction to sell the Frog Hollow place, which was rather isolated despite its scenic location beside the covered bridge. It was close to good neighbors, but moving to town brought easy access to trolley transportation, grocery stores, and so on. There they lived in a small house above the Strasburg Road that looked out over the old railroad freight station and downtown Gap.

Mother was the youngest child in the family. Her brother Lloyd was two years older. Two of her siblings, Anna and Marcus, had died at four years of age, in 1902 and 1905, of diphtheria. Her three other siblings—"Lomi" (Salome), "Minnie" (Minerva), and Ammon—had married and left home before their father's death. At some point Mother dropped out of school and did housework to help support her mother. She had learned early to work hard, to save her pennies, and to "hoe her own row." She was always thrifty and saved her money as well as belongings that might be of use at some future time. Her sister Salome had married Sam Smoker on February 19, 1913, and promptly started having a family that grew to include six boys and six girls. Mother took her few belongings to Lomi's house and became her "live-in maid." She washed many stacks of dishes by herself and did whatever else was waiting to be done. When she turned fourteen she moved in with her mother after beginning a job at the Christiana silk mill. There, in addition to earning more money, Mother enjoyed working with "the girls," and she rode the trolley to get there, which made for a cheap and convenient commute.

When Mother was seventeen, her mother died. The Gap home was sold and Mother's sister Minnie and her husband, Chris Fisher, who had lived in the Gap house with Mother and Grandma Susan for a time, moved to a house in Millwood on the corner between the Millwood schoolhouse and the Millwood church. Mother moved with them. She now had to walk more than two miles to Gap to catch the trolley to work, but she did not seem to mind it, especially after her cousin Vera Stahl from nearby Ephrata, who also worked at the silk mill, came to room with her. Such good times they had together! I can remember multiple occasions when our families got together and Mother and Vera talked in Pennsylvania German about the fun they'd had as young women. The "Pennsylvania Dutch" would fly and I would hang out in the kitchen too, immensely enjoying their stories and laughter. Mother and Vera may have stopped working at the silk mill for the same reason— to get married to their beaus early in the winter of 1927–1928. (Vera, who was five years older than Mother, married James S. Weaver on November 18, 1927, a month before Mother's wedding.)

In February 1927, Mother and her friend Marian Kennel (Zook) agreed to travel to Venice, Florida, with three of the King sons to work for several months. The men had gotten jobs in a construction project designed to attract more tourists to Venice. They lived in a tent community, and Mother and Marian did the cooking, shopping, and laundry for the crew. Dad and Mother had been seeing each other for a while before this, and while Mother was in Florida, Dad got a bit lonely for her, so he wrote her a letter, which was no small task for him, and asked her to marry him. Somehow his letter never reached Mother and she was left wondering why he had not written to her when it was his turn. She kept waiting for a letter and did not write again to him.

Mother returned from Florida with mixed feelings and somehow kept her distance from Dad. Then a number of the young folks, including Dad, were invited to Ontario, Canada, to attend a wedding. After he got there, Dad found out, to his surprise, that Mother had come to Canada too. So he made sure he got to talk to her, and was relieved to discover that the reason she hadn't written back was that she had never gotten his special letter and, yes, she still cared about him too. They quietly began making wedding plans in the fall of 1927. Dad was twenty-seven years old and Mother was twenty-two. In that era, a wedding was supposed to be kept secret until the young couple went to the ministers to discuss their plans. The news was then "published" at the end of the church service two weeks before the wedding date. Preparations such as the sewing of new dresses did begin before that, but there were no engagement announcements and photos in the local paper.

One evening after church, Dad's good friend Elam King asked to talk to him. They went outside and Elam said, "Say, you and Lizzie are planning to get married this winter, aren't you? Well, Sarah and I are getting married too. Why don't you get married soon? Then the four of us can go on our wedding trip together." Elam's mother, Katie Stuckey King, was from Ohio, so Elam had many relatives there who could provide meals and places for them to sleep. Dad talked the idea over with Mother. They both liked it but agreed to consult Mother's sister Minnie, because both of Mother's parents were deceased, and Dad's father, because Dad's mother was deceased. Both families gave their approval. Mother and Dad then visited the ministers and arranged to get married on Saturday evening, December 17, 1927. The wedding would be at Maple Grove because the Sunday service would be there the next morning and they would therefore save coal by not having to heat Millwood for just a Saturday evening wedding.

It was Minnie who made the announcement of her younger sister's marriage. Mother and Minnie were especially close, even though Minnie was nine years older. When Minnie died more than four years later, reportedly of pneumonia and influenza, on March 31, 1932, leaving behind three daughters and a son between the ages of six and twelve, Mother reached out to help those motherless children, even though by then I, at almost six months of age, was demanding my share of her attention too. Mildred and Mary Fisher lived with us for a year or so and attended Salisbury High School at White Horse from our home. Carl Fisher spent at least one summer on our farm as well. And when Roberta Fisher, who had just turned eighteen, was preparing for her wedding to Sylvester Blank, Mother planned and hosted a surprise wedding shower for them.

In the days of Mother and Dad's wedding, though specific invitations were sent to the guests of a wedding reception, it was assumed that the members of a congregation were welcome to attend any wedding service held at their church. Thus a sizeable audience assembled at the Maple Grove Mennonite Church by 8:00 P.M. on December 17, 1927, to show their support for Mother and Dad as they began their new life together. I am not sure who provided the sermon, but in that era the Bishop was expected to perform the ceremony, and the bishop at Millwood and Maple Grove was John A. Kennel. I have no idea where Mother and Dad spent their first night as husband and wife, but I doubt it was in an expensive motel. It could be that they spent some time together afterward, then went back to their own beds to sleep.

Mother's sister Minnie prepared food for the "small" reception, which was held on Sunday, the day after the wedding, at Minnie's home at Millwood, just north of the church where the road bends left to head for Millwood School and Byerstown. Minnie doubtless baked pies and cakes, and prepared some chickens or turkeys she had killed, as well as canned pork or beef plus potatoes, and several vegetables and side dishes for the bride and groom, their attendants, and the siblings and their spouses and children, which added up to thirty-one adults plus probably ten children. Bishop Kennel and his wife were also present, as were Elam and Sarah King, the couple who had invited Mother and Dad to go along with them on a joint honeymoon trip to Ohio. Elam and

Sarah had been married on November 24, 1927, Thanksgiving Day, by Bishop John S. Mast at the Conestoga Mennonite Church, because Sarah's family lived near Morgantown.

The day after the reception, Monday, December 19, 1927, the two couples left to travel in Elam's car to Ohio, where Elam introduced

Sarah to many of his relatives. Mother and Dad made many new friends, and both couples had a wonderful time. They remained friends after their joint honeymoon and often visited each other in the early years of their married lives.

Rhoda King, Elam and Sarah King's daughter, told me that the two couples were gone for six weeks. So I guess by the time Mother and Dad got back home there was a lot to do. In late winter 1928 they moved Grandpap (Dad's father) off the 107-acre farm on Hoffmeier Road that he had bought in 1904 when Dad was only four years old. Grandpap then lived by himself on the farm known as the Umbletown place, which was over the hill and down the other side, until his death on September 20, 1944. According to her diary, Mother continued to live at her sister Minnie's house until March 16, 1928, when she moved onto the farm with Dad, who already lived there. They proceeded to set up housekeeping and to start all the "spring work."

The stock market crash in 1929 and the Depression that followed affected our family as it did so many others. Dad usually hired one man to help him operate our big farm. Mother sometimes helped with the milking, but she was usually busy with the housework, heating water and washing clothes in the springhouse, keeping her potato yeast alive from one baking day to the next, baking her own bread and sticky buns, caring for the garden and truck patch, canning vegetables, and helping with butchering and processing the meat. You name it, I think she did it! And all without indoor plumbing or running water, with only a hand pump in the summer kitchen and no electricity.

Mother was a fairly tall, well-built woman, but she was thin if she was only 200 pounds. Dad was average height and sometimes weighed less than 125 pounds. Both Mother and Dad worked hard. I think Mother was not in a hurry to have children, because of the Depression, for one thing, so it wasn't until several years of marriage had passed that it became clear someone was preparing to change this married couple into a family. I don't know how often Mother went for prenatal care, because it was still during the Depression, and I think Dad tried to provide proper care for the mother-to-be. There was no resident physician in Gap at that time, so they went to Doc Steffen in Atglen. I know they were seen by Dr. Steffen several days before the delivery, because years later, after I had my own M.D. degree, Mother told me that three days before my birth, Doc Steffen had told her to expect a "dry birth" because she had been leaking amniotic fluid for two or three days. I don't know when her labor contractions actually began; I probably forgot to ask her because I was thinking about the complications that could have happened. It must have been a rather difficult labor, because Mother was not eager to have another child for several years.

I finally made my appearance at 6:30 A.M. on Sunday, September 20, 1931. My birth suite was in the big southeast guest bedroom of our farmhouse. I think there was at least one other person present, probably a friend of my mother who was a noncertified "nurse midwife" who mainly assisted the doctor, cared for the baby, and stayed with the family for a week or so after delivery to help with whatever was needed.

I'm not sure if the hired man milked the cows by himself that morning or if Dad went back and forth to the barn. They may have asked a second man to help out that day. Mother and Dad were both understandably tired after the long labor, but they were happy too. After all, I was their first child. After having some breakfast, they both got some needed sleep. That was one occasion when Dad missed the Sunday morning church service, and all because of me!

After Sunday dinner, Dad went to Mother's secretary desk, opened it, and sat down. He pulled a penny postcard out of a pigeonhole, found a pen, took the top off the ink well, and sat in silence for a few minutes. He then dipped his pen into the ink and laboriously wrote this message to his sister Mary and her husband, Ezra Nafziger:

September 20, 1931

Dear Uncle Ezra and Aunt Mary:

I just wanted you to know that I actually arrived this morning, at 6:30. Mom and Pop are both pretty tired and, well . . . maybe I am too. But they hope you will soon come to see us all. And please bring along my cousins David and Gene. I am eager to meet them. Pop says to bring along your milk container too.

Sincerely,

Then Dad signed my name: Dorcas Leah Stoltzfus.

I was more than four years old before I had a sibling. Paul was born at 6:00 on a winter evening, two days before Christmas 1935. He weighed eight and three-quarter pounds. I remember his birth very well.

Dad told George, the hired man, to milk the cows, all twelve or fifteen of them, by himself. (I'm sure we did not yet have DeLaval milkers then.) Mother was upstairs in the big spare bedroom with the doctor and the home nurse and I was downstairs in our big kitchen. I guess Dad was looking after me but also checking on how Mother was doing with her labor upstairs. On one of his trips downstairs Dad asked me to do something for him. I agreed, so he helped me to put on my coat and cap and told me to go to the barn and tell George that I had a new baby brother. It was after dark and we had no electric lights, so I headed for the barn with our flashlight. The gate to the barnyard was open, so I entered and walked under the forebay, past the horse stalls and the heifer pen to the door to the cow stable. This was a big sliding door and to open it I needed to raise the latch and push the door to the left at the same time. I tried several times without success, so I finally stretched up on my tippy toes to the latch hole and yelled as loud as I could into it, "Hey, George, I got a baby butter." Well, George heard me. He came and opened the door to let me in. He tried to sound surprised by the news about my "baby butter," and as I grew older I was occasionally asked how my "baby butter" was doing.

Three years later, on December 5, 1938, Mother was again in the big spare bedroom. I don't remember what time or on what day of the week Nathan Elam was born, but I do remember that he had dark hair, and lots of it—so much that he would perspire around his neck despite the winter weather. Within a few weeks, Mother trimmed his hair to make him more comfortable. I was more than seven years old when Nate was born and I enjoyed helping to dress him and combing his thick hair. He also had not one but two cowlicks on the back of his head and I experimented with parting his hair on each side of his head. I think he ended up using the right side for his part.

Nate was an active baby. He began walking by nine months. Dad's cousin Nora Stoltzfus came to visit us one day when Nate was still a toddler and found him parked on the kitchen table eating a slice of bread. He had climbed up onto a bench, then onto the table, and then had helped himself to the slice of bread. Nora had brought her camera along and took his picture to prove it. When he was a teenager, Nate could always be counted on to fix himself a slice of bread with jelly or peanut butter to munch on as he headed toward the barn to milk the cows after supper.

It wasn't until I was twelve years old that my parents finally gave me a sister, Anna Mary. Because of the age difference, it took us a while to get acquainted. One of my earliest memories of her was talking to each other in Pennsylvania Dutch at bedtime when she was just starting school and I was in high school. I soon went off to college, then to medical school, then to internship in West Chester, and finally to Africa. While I was in college and medical school, we got to spend some scattered summers together. After I got married and was living in Philadelphia, we had easier contact by phone and visiting. But our friendship really began to flourish after I moved to Landis Homes in 2004.

My mother gave birth to one more daughter after Anna Mary. I share about Ruthie in detail later in the book. ✣

My Early Childhood

One of my earliest memories is of me sitting either on Mother's lap or beside her on a bench near a window at Maple Grove Mennonite Church on a Sunday morning. The sunshine was streaming in and Mother was giving me a snack, maybe a soda cracker or a pretzel stick. I remember her offering me a snack during church only that one time. I'm not sure if that means she did not offer me snacks very often, or if it means I was getting old enough to sit through church without having a snack. I was probably three years old, or maybe had just turned four, because I am certain it was before my brother Paul was born, three months after my fourth birthday. Once Mother had baby Paul to take care of during church, I got to sit with Dad on the men's side. Maybe some little girls would not have enjoyed that, but I did not mind sitting with Dad in church.

Another very early memory is of the morning I saw Grandpap do something quite unusual. By then he was living on the farm just over the hill, and he usually came over to our place to help Dad with the easier chores, such as driving a team of horses to mow the hay, or running the cultipacker over a newly plowed field. When Grandpap came to our place, he almost always drove his light blue Whippet sedan and parked it at the end of our driveway, across from our mailbox. But this time, as I watched from our front porch, I saw Grandpap coming down the dirt road beside the apple orchard walking beside his black horse, Frank. They turned into our lane, came past the house, and went down to the barn. I still do not know if Frank was needed to do some work that day, or why Grandpap walked him to our place. Guess I never will know why, but I must confess that it still "wonders" me sometimes, as we Pennsylvania Dutch would say.

Frank was an old horse and I guess Grandpap was rather attached to him. Frank had the lower level of Grandpap's barn pretty much to himself, although sometimes Dad kept some heifers there and Grandpap let them graze in his meadow. When Frank was there, he could wander about in the meadow too. Well, a little stream ran through the meadow from a spring at the upper end, and near the barn there was a sharp bend in that stream with a steep bank of four to five feet. Though no one witnessed what happened, Frank apparently slipped down the bank into the creek and was unable to get back up on his feet. So Grandpap and Dad and George—and me to watch, of course—went to see about Frank. I must say that although I remember seeing Frank in the creek, I cannot remember exactly how they got him up onto his feet again. But he did get out of the creek somehow. And I guess he went to "horse heaven" at some point after that.

I clearly remember the days of flashlights and kerosene lamps and lanterns. Every evening I went to our outhouse down at the corner of the yard before going to bed. Our outhouse provided two places to sit, plus the old Sears catalog to use as wiping paper. I don't know if there was any fancy toilet paper available in those days, but I'm sure my parents would not spend money on unnecessary "luxuries" when the Sears catalog came for free! Anyway, I sat down on one of the sitting places and put the flashlight beside me. And don't you know it: that flashlight somehow rolled right down through the other opening into the privy! And its light was still shining from the privy. So I finished my business, then went and told Dad what had happened. What do you think he did? No, he didn't scold me or accuse me of being stupid or careless. Instead, he went to the springhouse with a lantern and collected a hoe and a garden rake, then went to the outhouse, where he "went fishing." Fortunately the flashlight was still shining, so he knew where to "fish." After he had collected the flashlight, he took it to the springhouse and washed it with some soapy water. We continued to use that flashlight for a long time. After all, money was scarce in those Depression days.

Speaking of kerosene lamps, I remember a time when Uncle Earl Howe was visiting us and reading the newspaper that Grandpap subscribed to. When he finished, he folded it up and laid it on the kitchen table near the lamp. As he laid the paper down, the air moved enough to make the flame flicker a bit. I noticed this, so I picked up the paper, then laid it down, but a bit too quickly and the flame went out! Well, I was rather embarrassed, but I guess I was at least being observant, and learning a little about physics at an early age.

As I got bigger, Dad let me tag along as he milked the cows and worked around the farm. That way, Mother could get more done in the house while I enjoyed being outside with Dad. I especially enjoyed riding with him in the old International pickup to deliver the cans of milk to the Aristocrat Dairy milk truck at Gap. Of course I was supposed to stay in the cab while Dad unloaded the milk cans. But one day I experimented with the emergency brake while Dad was unloading the cans, and suddenly the truck began to drift forward down the small incline. Dad quickly jumped into the cab and stopped the moving truck. He of course knew what I had done and warned me never to do that again. But the real punishment was that he did not take me along to deliver the milk for a whole week! That really made a lasting impression on me.

One evening Dad and I were walking to the house after the milking was done. It seems like it was a fall evening, but not cold, and I was maybe four or five years old. As we walked up the sidewalk near the house, the full moon was shining brightly down on us from far above the pear tree. I looked up at the friendly moon and said, *"Hallo, Moon! Du bist so gros als die sun, gel du bist!"* ("Hello, Moon! You are as large as the sun, aren't you!") Years later, of course, I learned that the sun really was bigger, but the moon was closer to us, so they could sometimes look as if they were similar in size.

One day I was out in the meadow with the cows, who were busy munching the grass, when a small airplane flew overhead. Of course we did not see many of these in those days. I looked at that small airplane flying up so high and thought, there must be a very small man in that airplane to fly it, because it looked much too small for someone like my dad to get into!

One summer day my Mother packed a picnic basket with sandwiches and other goodies, then packed the family into the car. We drove east on the Lincoln Highway, all the way into Philadelphia, and went to the zoo. Dad parked the car in the east lot, facing the river, and Mother carried the lunch basket. Dad paid for our tickets and we headed up the sidewalk on the right. We saw some animals outside and others inside. When we got to the far end of the zoo, we stopped at the picnic tables and ate our lunch. As we walked back toward the main gate, we saw some very big animals, including an elephant and a giraffe. Some children were riding the elephant, and I wanted to ride it too, but my parents did not agree. Dad said if I wanted to ride a pony, he could probably arrange that after we got back home.

And true to his word, Dad spoke to Mr. Umble of Sunnyside Farm, just outside of Gap, after we got home. Some days later I got to ride their pony on their big lawn. I don't remember if my brothers got pony rides too. I do remember that we made repeat visits to the Philadelphia Zoo for a number of years after that. Later, when I was living in the Germantown area of Philadelphia, I again visited the zoo, after it had an elevated train (a monorail) for traveling from one end to the other. ✞

Dad's Little Helper

It was a warm, sunny day in early September. We had finished our noon meal and Dad was planning to sow winter wheat. That meant loading up the stone wagon with seed and fertilizer and hitching the mules to the seed drill.

Let me explain what the stone wagon was. It was a wagon used primarily when we picked up loose stones from a field after the ground was prepared for planting. The flooring of this wagon consisted of loose planks about three inches thick. When we had filled the wagon with stones, we would haul them off to the woods or to a designated "stone pile." The floor planks could be turned edgewise to dump off accumulated dirt and small stone chips after we had unloaded the bigger stones and rocks.

We were still feeling the effects of the Depression, and Dad could not afford a truck to carry loads so, well, sometimes he used the stone wagon, with its three-inch-wide iron wheels. For a number of years Dad also used the family automobile to haul our cans of milk to the Aristocrat dropoff depot in Gap. And he "broke in" our new 1937 Plymouth automobile by hauling the milk cans in the trunk after he had fastened some old leather straps to the inside frame to tie around the cans to keep them from falling out. Some years later he got an old International pickup truck, but it was rather contrary about starting, even if he parked it on the grade to the barn bridge and let it coast downhill in a sometimes futile attempt to make it go.

But back to the stone wagon. That afternoon Dad pulled it out of the wagon shed and hitched a team of horses to it. He then carried several bags of seed wheat from the granary floor of the barn to the wagon. George, the hired man, hauled out several bags of fertilizer. Dad then brought out another team, the mules Mollie and Toby, and hitched them to the drill. Then Dad led the way out the lane, up the country road to the top of the hill, and halfway down the far side of the hill. I sat on a bag of wheat on the stone wagon while George stood as he drove the horses. We followed Dad as he turned up the back lane on the left to go to the back field. When we got to the field, George helped Dad fill the drill with the fertilizer and wheat, then tied the lead horse to a small tree at the end of the lane with a short rope. While Dad was busy sowing in the field, George walked back to the barn to clean out the ditches where the cows had made their deposits. He also prepared the stables with fresh bedding and chow for the cows to enjoy during the evening milking procedure.

Meanwhile, I sat on the wagon and inspected the world. I watched a greenish-yellow bird singing a scant ten feet above me. It almost sounded like it was singing "meow." I watched as Dad made his rounds, back and forth, through the field with the drill. On every fourth round he would come back to the stone wagon for more seed and fertilizer. Finally, the sun was getting low in the western sky, and the air was getting noticeably cooler. Dad was getting closer to the woods, and I could not see him very well as he got further away from me. I wondered if he would finish sowing the wheat or if the darkness would force a halt to his work.

I also wondered how Dad would get both the drill team of mules and the stone wagon and its horses back to the barn by himself. Somehow the idea came into my four-year-old head that maybe I could be Daddy's helper by driving the stone wagon team for him. And in my childish faith I asked Jesus to make it happen.

When Dad came up to the wagon and said it was time to quit and go home, he indicated that he would return later for the stone wagon team. But I said in my matter-of-fact way, "Why? I can sit on the stone wagon and hold the reins and we can follow you and the drill team. I already asked Jesus to help me."

Well, Dad thought about that for a minute or two. I frankly don't remember if he made any further verbal response to me, but I had my answer when he unhitched the stone wagon team and brought them around behind the drill team. He carefully spread out several empty burlap bags near the front of the wagon so I could sit down without danger of picking up any splinters from the rough planks. He then gave the reins to me and showed me how to hold them gently but snugly in both hands. He then stepped forward in front of my team of horses and behind the drill team of mules. He picked up the reins to his team, looked back to see if I was ready, then said, "Giddyap," and we started walking down the back lane. We went up to the top of the hill on the country road and Dad pulled more tightly on his reins as we started down the hill, so I pulled more tightly on the reins for my team too. We all got back to the barn safe and sound, just as it really began to get dark.

I suppose that George and my mother both asked Dad some questions as to why he had let me hold the reins to bring home the team of horses and the stone wagon even if Dad and the drill mules were walking just in front of us. After all, those mules could be a little ornery sometimes, especially Toby! But I think Dad wanted to respect my childhood faith, and I believe he felt that because I had asked Jesus to help me, well, surely Jesus would honor my faith and protect all of us in this venture. ☩

Dad Makes a Surprise for Me

Dad didn't believe in wasting things. After all, he farmed during the Depression and money was scarce. He often took eggs and freshly churned butter to the store to exchange for the few staples we needed, such as flour, sugar, and sometimes raisins or a small wedge of cheese from the big round wheel that was parked on the counter. Dad and Mother used things until they were completely worn out. So, when one of the two pear trees outside our kitchen died, Dad did not cut it off just above the ground and recycle the whole tree for firewood. No, he had something different in mind.

Several weeks after the tree died, Dad brought out his short ladder and his handsaw from the shed. He propped the ladder against the dead tree, climbed it, and proceeded to saw off the limbs that were about fifteen feet above the ground. The tree was not very tall, maybe twenty-five feet. He stopped sawing as each limb began to droop, then carefully sawed a little more until the limb was severed.

After the upper limbs were cut off, Dad came down several steps on the ladder and deliberately cut off another limb, but this time, rather than saw right next to the trunk, for some reason he cut the limb about six inches away from the trunk. He didn't tell me why he had cut this one differently. Dad then proceeded to saw the main trunk in a transverse fashion, and when he finished I noticed that the trunk and the stub of the limb now formed a V-shaped notch.

Dad still didn't explain anything to me as he came down the ladder. He just asked me to help him take the smaller branches out to the woodpile behind the springhouse. And believe me, I obliged without question! Dad could be so mysterious at times, and he was especially so now when I wanted to know why he had left the trunk of the dead tree standing in the yard, and why he had cut the trunk and the last limb in that particular way, with the notch between them. Dad was not ready to explain it to me yet. He just picked up his ladder and saw and took them back to the shed. He was always very particular about putting things back where they belonged when he finished using them, so he could find them the next time he wanted them. And that was the end of his work on his project, whatever it was, for that day.

Several days later, Dad went into the shed again, and when he came out he brought along the ladder and a twelve-foot length of used galvanized pipe. Of course I watched every move! He parked the ladder against the tree stump, grabbed the pipe, climbed up the ladder, and rested one end of the pipe in the notch of the stump. Then he climbed down, moved the ladder over, and leaned it against the living pear tree, which was about eleven feet away from the dead stump. He took the other end of the pipe, climbed up the ladder, and easily pushed that end of the pipe into a notch on the pear tree. Well, even though I was only four or five years old and had little idea what a horizontal bar twelve to thirteen feet above the ground could be used for, I was starting to get the picture.

Dad headed off to the shed again, with me trailing close behind. He soon located a piece of wood about two feet long, one inch thick, and six inches wide. Next, he pulled out his brace, fitted a one-inch drill bit into it, and proceeded to drill two holes into the board about an inch and a half from each end. By now I had a pretty good idea that he was making a swing—for me—and I could hardly wait.

He took the drill bit out of the brace and put them away. He looked around for a while and eventually said, "Well, I still need something else. I thought I had it here, somewhere." I watched anxiously as he kept looking. Finally he pulled some rope out of a box and said, "Yes! Here it is! I thought I had some old hay rope left in here."

He untied the knot that held the roll of rope together. He then threaded one end of the rope through one hole in the board and pulled it far enough to thread it through the other hole. He put his arm through the roll of rope and carried the board in his hands as we walked back toward the house. When we arrived at the trees, he pulled about twelve feet of the rope through the hole that had the shorter length of rope through it. Next, he parked the ladder against the pipe rail and climbed up holding the board. He swung the shorter length of rope over the rail and tied it around the longer length with a secure knot. (I have to wonder if he used a square knot or if it was some other special knot that farmers used.) Then he measured out the amount of rope needed to support the other side of the board and used his trusty pocketknife to cut it off from the remaining roll of rope. He adjusted the rope to make sure the board would be fifteen inches above the ground, then tied the same knot as he had on the first piece of rope.

Now the swing was ready! Dad gave me a push, then another push, and another, on my new swing. Mother came to the porch to see what Dad had made for me and to watch me swing for a few minutes before she announced that it was time to come inside for supper. Even though I was only four or five years old when Dad made that swing, I can still feel my happiness that he had done this for me, and that he sometimes pushed me on the swing. Dad had lots of other things to do on the farm, but because I was small and did not know how to swing myself, he often took the time to push me when he was coming to the house at mealtime.

Then Dad thought of a way to make those swing times even more special for both of us. He would begin by saying "Genesis," then give me a push. I would repeat, "Genesis." Then Dad would say "Exodus" and give me another push, and I would repeat, "Exodus." We could continue like this for a long time, and that is how I learned the books of the Bible before I started going to school. (I suspect Dad also thought that if he wasn't just swinging me and entertaining me when there was so much work to do but was also doing some constructive teaching, well, then his pushing me on the swing wasn't just idle play!)

With time the grass under the swing was replaced by a firm cake of hard dirt. And yes, I learned to swing by myself. I think that swing survived as long as we lived on Grandpap's farm. We moved to a smaller farm when I was twelve years old. The swing—and the shed, the chicken house, and the pig pen—has long since disappeared from the old farm, along with the tall maple trees and the grape arbor in the yard. Over the years other things appeared, such as several huge Harvestore silos, a heifer barn in the meadow (which no longer grazes cows), and a large cow shed that housed fifty cows. (All of our cows had individual names, such as Snow Ball, because she was almost completely white, and Flossie, whose hide had large black patches with small white "dividers" between them. Dad originally had only Holstein cows, but later he got one Guernsey cow to help raise the butterfat content of our herd.) The milk house had a huge milk tank. Now the triple-decker barn is no longer stuffed with loose hay and straw, and its granaries are empty too, except for dust and cobwebs. I guess no one needs a big barn anymore, especially if he has a big implement shed to house five tractors plus. Now the big hay wheels wrapped in white plastic are stored outside, arranged in rows behind the shed.

But some things haven't changed, much. I can still pretty much go through the books of the Bible like Dad taught me, although I tend to say a lot of them in groups of four or six, to get the correct sequence. I clearly remember when I first attended the Coatesville Mennonite Church's Bible school (I was between six and eight years old) and the teacher said something about memorizing the books of the Bible. Well, I promptly piped up and said, "I already know them!" She was surprised but gave me a chance to demonstrate that I really could recite the books of the Bible.

Yes, I have so many memories to think about! And so many experiences to thank God for. ✞

The Lost Ball

It was a beautiful spring day on the farm. I was maybe seven or eight years old. I was not occupied with any chores and there was no one to play with, because my brother was four years younger than me. Dad was out with the horses, ploughing to get the fields ready to put in corn. And of course I wasn't keen on hanging around the house, where my mother might find something for me to do!

So I decided to play with the old yellow ball I had found somewhere. Why I didn't play in the yard, or in the open space between the house and the barn, I really don't know. Maybe I just wanted to be by myself. Or maybe I wanted to be out of sight. Anyway, I went down to the springhouse at the corner of the yard and let myself out into the meadow. The grass had already grown rather tall for my short legs, and my shoes got damp from the dew. I suspect that the cows had not yet been turned loose into the pasture to start trimming the grass and to find some garlic to eat so that the milk would have that unpleasant springtime aroma.

I walked past the house where the pigs lived and along the orchard to the foot of the meadow hill, where I started to play with the ball. I held it in my up-turned right hand and threw it up into the air. Then I tried to catch it as it came back down. Sometimes I caught it, but more often, of course, I missed it.

I began throwing it higher into the air so that I might have a little more time to catch it. Well, don't you know, one time when I threw the ball harder and higher, it went back over my head and I lost sight of it, so I didn't see it come down. I looked toward the hill to the south but did not see any yellow ball in the knee-high grass. I turned toward the orchard in the east, but no ball did I see. I turned further to my left, toward our big house, and then toward the big triple-decker barn, which stood to the north. I still did not see my ball. I turned further, toward the west, where I could see Grandpap's sawmill parked in the middle of our meadow, and still did not see any ball. I kept turning around, and the grass got tramped down where I was standing. But I still did not see my ball anywhere.

Now I was getting a little worried. After all, we had just come through Depression times and toys were rather scarce. And I wanted to play ball. Suddenly, an idea popped into my mind: I could pray and ask God to help me find my ball. I decided to try it. Whether I prayed aloud or silently, I do not remember. I was used to hearing Dad pray aloud, but Mother did not, so I don't know whose example I followed. But I closed my eyes and I prayed. And when I opened my eyes, there was my ball, about one foot in front of me in the grass!

I was so happy to find my ball. It was a very intimate and precious experience to have God answer my prayer for help. For many years I kept that very personal experience all to myself. I'm not sure if I remembered to thank God that day for answering my prayer. I think I probably did not play much more ball that day. But I will always remember the thrill of finding my ball, and I will always feel that warm sunshine on my back as I walked my ball back to the house that beautiful spring day. I could still take you to the spot, or very close to it, where I found that ball sixty-five years ago! ♱

Five Years at
Gap Centralized School

In our small town of Gap, when I was a child we did not know about kindergarten, so my parents did not have to worry about which preschool program to send me to. They probably could not have afforded it anyway. And they certainly were satisfied to care for me at home. Their major decision was about *when* I should start school. I'm sure they did not discuss this concern with me. Maybe they thought I was a bit small for my age, or maybe they wanted to keep me with them for an extra year. At any rate, instead of starting me to school when I was almost six years old, they waited until I was two weeks shy of my seventh birthday, in 1938.

I was eager to go to school. I enjoyed having Dad tell me Bible stories. He also read to me from the book *First Steps for Little Feet,* by Charles Foster, and with his repeated reading of my favorite story, about the birth of Jesus, I came to memorize it. Then I could open the book to the proper pages and "read" the story myself! I clearly remember that my parents felt I should take a nap on the Sunday afternoon before my first day of school. So I did go to bed, because I did not want to mess up my first day. Whether I actually slept or not I do not remember. Mother also took time to braid my long hair that night so that the next morning she could just comb the top, put a barrette on each side behind the ear, and pin my braids around my head.

On Monday morning, Mother prepared a lunch for me, because that was before students could buy lunch at school. What she put in my lunch box that day I do not remember, but my usual lunch included a bologna sandwich, a sticky bun, an apple, and maybe a cookie or two. After we ate breakfast, Mother washed her hands and took off her apron while Dad put the milk cans into the trunk of the family car. Then we all got into the car, including little brother Paul, and headed for Gap.

Dad drove into the schoolyard of the Gap Centralized School in front of the east door, which had *BOYS* carved into the stone above it, and the three of us got out. Dad then drove on to the Aristocrat depot and unloaded his cans of milk. Meanwhile, Mother, in her protective way, took Paul and me with her to one of the adults who were standing among the children at the tall swings near the doorway. The lady introduced herself as Mrs. Trout, the first grade teacher. Mother and Mrs. Trout chatted for several minutes and Mother gave my lunch box to Mrs. Trout. Then Mrs. Trout extended her hand to me and said, "Dorcas, welcome to first grade. I hope you have a wonderful year with us." Several other first grade students arrived, so Mother and little Paul went over to the street to wait for Dad's return from the milk depot while I stayed near Mrs. Trout.

Suddenly there was a loud noise. Oh! It was just the bell announcing that it was time for school to begin. The door opened and more teachers came out and helped the students to line up two by two with their teachers, beginning with first grade and continuing through eighth grade. We then marched up the steps, entered the school building, and walked up a half-flight of stairs to the hallway, where we all stopped and were silent. We faced the US flag and said the Pledge of Allegiance, though at the time I did not yet know it by memory, so I just stood still and watched and listened. We sang a song that was new to me too. Later I learned that many of the songs we sang at our morning assembly were written by Stephen Foster and told about life in the deep south as experienced by black persons in the days of slavery— something that was new to me as well.

Finally Mrs. Trout led us into our classroom, the first room on the left. Then she unobtrusively stepped into the cloakroom at the front of the room and parked my lunch box on the shelf above the coat rack. She let us choose our seats, so I selected one near the window, three rows from the front. She made sure she had all of our names on her list. Then she asked us to tell her what we expected school to be like. Next she told us to look at the blackboards on the front and hall sides of our classroom and pointed out the ABCs that were written in both capital and small letters at the top of the boards. She explained that in order for us to read, we first needed to learn these letters. She asked if some of us already knew our ABCs, and though some of us did, others did not. She then asked if we knew how to count, and more of us did, but some did not.

Then that loud bell rang again. Oh! It was time for recess, or to go to the bathroom, which was located in the basement. I soon learned to enjoy recess as the time to go down the slides or ride the swings or play tag.

The next time the loud bell rang it was lunchtime. The other students marched into the cloakroom, got their lunch boxes, and returned to their desks to eat. But when I looked for my box, I did not see it, or at least I did not recognize it as mine. I think I was looking for a rectangular blue box with two handles near each end that could be folded together to carry the box when the lid was closed. But the only box I saw remaining on the shelf was more of a green color. Mrs. Trout came back into the cloakroom with me to check on the box and encouraged me to open it. What I found inside looked like what Mother would have packed for me, so I had lunch after all. I took that green lunch box home that afternoon and Mother confirmed it was my box. I used it for several years, until they got me a bigger one that had a thermos so I could take along some milk to drink with my lunch.

When the last bell rang at 3:00 P.M. and it was time to go home, some of us went out through the big front door, which faced north, toward the highway, and were shown how to form three lines. One line went west along the highway to lower Gap, another went east along the highway and up Gap Hill, and our line went north along Route 897 toward Millwood and White Horse. I don't remember that any of our students came to school on a bus. Most of us walked, but a few got rides, like I did with my dad when he took the milk to Gap in the morning. But in the afternoon I was expected to walk home.

Most of the children in our line were Amish, and we again walked two by two, always with the same partner and in the same order from front to rear. Some of the older students were safety patrols; they got to wear a special belt with a medal on it to show their authority and their responsibility for the rest of us as we walked along a major roadway. Our line had maybe fifteen or so children, many of whom left the line at the road to Millwood, leaving five of us to walk another half-mile to the second big turn in the road, where several children went to the small house on the left, the oldest boy went straight ahead to the farm on the knoll, and I turned into the dirt road to the right and walked another half mile to Grandpap's farm in the hollow on the right. It was more than 1.6 miles altogether—a rather long walk for a little girl. I'm guessing it was about 4:00 when I got home. Mother asked me how school went and I told her. I suppose I was rather tired by then, after my long walk and all. But I'm sure I was ready to go back to school in the morning.

I usually got to school a bit early, because I got a ride with Dad. I sometimes played outside with other students and sometimes stayed indoors and looked at our small supply of library books—maybe fifty for our classroom. One morning while I was inside, Mrs. Trout went out into the hallway for something and suddenly fell onto the floor. One of the other teachers immediately called for her son Bill, who was the principal of our school and our eighth grade teacher. I can still see his tall frame come flying down the stairs at the girls' end of the building and to her side. Turns out she had broken her hip and was unable to teach for a number of months. I don't remember who took her place, but I did miss Mrs. Trout. She did eventually return to the first grade classroom, but not until after I had moved on to the next grade. After I was in high school and had a driver's license, my mother and I once stopped in to visit Mrs. Trout, who lived at the foot of Gap Hill, near the school. We were warmly received and had a nice visit. I think she had retired by then. (Speaking of broken bones, I was probably still in first or second grade when one of the little boys broke his arm. I was naive and thought it was broken *off*, because he had it in a splint or a cast under his clothing for a number of weeks, so I did not notice that it was still attached!)

For second grade I moved across the hall, where Mrs. Esther Groff became my teacher. She too was well-liked. I remember her assigning our seating arrangements, which was a small inconvenience for me because the seats in the back of the room were a bit larger and higher than those in the front, so my feet did not reach the floor. But that was part of my education: I often had to sit in such chairs, and still do sometimes! The advantage was that I was closer to our classroom library, and I did check out some books. I remember that Mrs. Groff wrote a list of words on the blackboard each week that we copied into a lined notebook to study for our weekly spelling quiz. I was a pretty good speller, and one time I won a spelling bee for our classroom of second and third grade students. My prize was an unruled tablet with a nicely colored picture of a dog outside his doghouse on the cover. I treasured it for a long time.

I was delighted that I got to be in Mrs. Groff's room for third grade too. She always read a story from the Bible when we returned to our classroom after lunch. I was especially pleased when she read a story I was already familiar with, which was fairly often. It was a time for us to unwind from our play before resuming our schoolwork.

Every week it was possible to pay a nickel and order a popsicle for the following week. When the popsicles were delivered and eaten, everyone checked their popsicle stick very carefully, hoping it had *FREE* written on it so that we could claim a free popsicle for the following week. It was a real treat when I was given a nickel to order a popsicle. One fall I had outgrown my shoes and had to go to school in my bare feet for maybe a month, until my parents had enough money to buy me new shoes. Of course I got teased about my "chocolate toes."

It may have been when I was in third or fourth grade that the school held an assembly and showed us the movie *Pinocchio*. Well, I had never seen a movie before and I did not feel that this one was quite true to life. I probably did not tell my parents about it, however, because I did not want them to scold me for seeing it.

In fourth grade my teacher was Miss Caldwell, who later in the school year became Mrs. Barley. She had a reputation for being quite strict, and I can still see her applying a wide wooden paddle to a boy while he stood in front of the class. She hit him several times, until he stopped mocking her. It was in her classroom also that during the winter months we were allowed to put our milk and cold drinks on the ledge outside the window after we arrived at school to keep them cold until lunchtime.

I vividly remember the cold winter morning with snow on the ground when Dad could not get his pickup to start so he could haul the milk into the depot. I put on my boots, coat, mittens, cap, and scarf and started to walk to school. It was windy and cold and I was chilled to the bone, it seemed, by the time I got out to Route 897, and I still had three quarters of the way to go. Part of the time I walked backward, to keep the wind out of my face. I had been clearly taught never to accept a ride from a stranger, so I refused the first offer despite being so cold. As I crested the top of the grade but was still less than halfway to school, I heard a

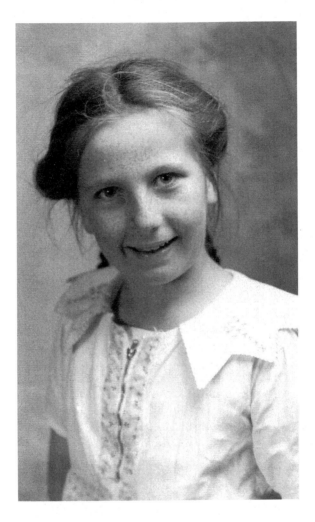

sound and recognized the school bus returning from its run to White Horse with the high school students. Though I did not know this driver by name, I felt that, as a school employee, he could be trusted. He stopped the bus beside me and invited me in, and I gladly accepted his offer. I was still cold when I got to school, and I can remember Miss Caldwell taking me behind the piano and helping me remove my wraps, then my shoes and stockings, and then putting some warm water into a basin to warm my feet. She also put my shoes and stockings on the steam radiator to warm them up before I put them back on. So I learned she had a caring heart despite a sometimes stern exterior.

I moved upstairs for fifth grade. Miss Worst was my teacher. She was a younger lady who loved to teach and related well to her students. She often came out to the playground and played softball with us girls at noon, and we loved it. After the bell called us to leave our game, she too would read to us from the Bible. She would let us rest our heads on our desks as she read if we wished to. She also read to us from other books, such as the *Legend of Sleepy Hollow, Evangeline,* and *Hiawatha,* and then asked us to write a synopsis of the story.

I remember that during fifth grade the school had one or two assemblies in which they featured a movie. By now students were permitted not to go if they so wished, so I skipped these movies and stayed in the classroom. The problem with that option was that there was no adult supervision and some Amish boys also chose not to go and they were not above teasing me at times. So again I was torn between wanting to do what I knew my parents would want me to do, which I also basically wanted to do, and feeling uncomfortable about the resulting teasing and badgering by several of my classmates. It was this dilemma that caused me to hope that I could instead go to a Christian school, where hopefully I would not have to confront such difficult decisions. Again, so far as I can remember, I never told my parents about this situation.

During the spring of 1943, while I was in fifth grade, our family moved to a smaller farm on Gap Hill. Now Dad could park his pickup with the milk cans beside the highway at our farm and the Aristocrat milk truck would stop there to pick them up. So brother Paul, who was in first grade, and I no longer got a ride to school in the morning. But it was not nearly as far, and it was downhill on the way to school. More than once, though, we got a late start and would hear the warning bell ring as we were running down on the cinders beside the highway in our attempt to arrive at school before the tardy bell rang. ✞

Changes at the New Place

As I mentioned previously, our family moved to a smaller farm in the spring of 1943. That meant a lot of things were different and we had to make some changes, such as walking to school in the morning rather than getting a ride from Dad. Also, we had a smaller herd of cows, maybe only ten or twelve to start with. And for a year or two at least we had no DeLaval milking machine like we had at Grandpap's farm, so seven-year-old Paul and I helped to milk the cows by hand. I didn't mind milking my several assigned cows every morning and evening. Initially, Dad put a milk cooler in the old springhouse beyond the barnyard, but later he built a cement-block milkhouse nearer the barn. That new milkhouse was equipped with a pulley hoist system so that he could attach two hooks onto the handles of the milk cans and lift the can out of the cooler without straining himself. (Dad appreciated that feature because he did have a "rupture" that sometimes interfered with his work.) We children, who were shorter than Dad, could hoist a full milk can out of the cooler too. We would tip the can a bit and roll it out the door onto the concrete platform, then onto the pickup truck, with no need to pick up the full can, because the platform was built high enough to be level with the pickup bed.

We had no tractor either, because Dad had sold his McCormick-Deering 10-20. He had kept only one team of two horses, Mike and Roy, so they were kept busy that first summer. When it came time to cut the wheat with our binder, well, Dad knew he couldn't ask faithful Mike and Roy to pull the binder by themselves. So he talked to a neighbor who had a Farmall A, which, granted, was not a "big" tractor, but it did do the job. By the next year, Dad had bought himself a new John Deere H tractor with a two-way plow attachment. I enjoyed plowing with that machine. But I enjoyed working with Mike and Roy too, cultivating corn or mowing the long grass in the upper meadow. I was eleven years old, Paul was seven, and Nathan was four that first summer on our new farm.

I took responsibility for mowing the yard, just as I had done on Grandpap's farm from the time I was probably seven or eight years old. But our new yard was more of a challenge, with a steep bank out front and plenty of uneven places. I helped in the garden too, and sometimes in the house as well. But I really preferred outside work, whether it was making hay, setting up wheat shocks, hoeing the corn, or digging out

thistles in the meadow with a shovel. And yes, I was around to watch the big Romley Oil Pull tractor pull the threshing machine and straw baler along the lane to thresh our wheat. I took a big container of mint tea (we called it "meadow tea") out to the crew in mid-morning and again in the afternoon. I helped "some" in the kitchen too, setting the table and so on while Mother and a friend of hers fixed the noon meal for the whole crew of hungry men. Mother was always relieved and glad to see all the machinery and men go out the lane when the threshing was finished, but I really enjoyed seeing them come!

Soon after we moved, Dad hired several carpenters to remove the old wooden porch floor outside the kitchen. They built a lovely sun porch that connected the kitchen to our wash house to the south. And they added a door to the west to provide easier access to the garden. These renovation projects were done over a period of years. We soon got a bathroom upstairs, plus a new entrance to the bedroom above the kitchen. Then the stairs that went up to that bedroom from the kitchen were removed, giving us more room in the kitchen, plus an extra-large window overlooking the garden to the west. Several years later we got an early version of storm windows for our house. Later we added asbestos siding to cover the old clapboard. Eventually we got new wall cabinets in the kitchen too. Finally, a powder room that opened into the sun porch was built in a corner of the living room. Beside the powder room we put a coat closet, next to the door that opened into the kitchen.

Dad also made some changes in the barn. An early change was adding a second floor by making an opening for two big doors and putting heavier planks on the floor. He also installed under the roof a track for the hay hooks to run on for unloading loose hay. After several years that track became obsolete, along with the hay loader, when men came to our fields with a baler to bundle up the hay and straw. Bales took up less space in the barn and were easier to handle, especially after the invention of the bale and grain elevator, which Dad soon got.

Dad later had a bigger job done on the barn. He took out the front wall of the cow stable and eliminated the forebay, which made room for several calf and heifer stalls. Mike and Roy had separate stalls at one end. I think it was before my second year of high school that Dad decided to get another DeLaval milking machine. By then, I think, our barn had stalls for eighteen cows.

Later, after Dad decided to stop raising pigs, he converted the hog shed into a shed for one of our John Deere B tractors by taking out the end wall and putting up a big sliding door to close the opening. We also built a cement-block "three-car garage"—not for three cars but for our one car, a 1937 Plymouth; our one pickup, a 1938 Chevrolet; and our second John Deere B tractor.

Well, as the old song says, "The times they are a changin'." Well, yes, things do change. But duh! Without change, what kind of boring and mundane life would we have?! ☩

We Go to a New School

As I have already explained, I enjoyed my years at Gap Centralized School a great deal. I was curious and enjoyed learning, but I was troubled by the assembly programs that featured a movie and by the "plain" boys who stayed behind in the classroom and teased me while the teacher was absent. So I began looking for a way out of this dilemma.

A couple of years earlier a Christian day school had opened some miles away, between Atglen and Cochranville. It was supported by families from my home churches (Millwood and Maple Grove) and I think my dad had actually helped dig the foundation of the building with his two-wheeled dirt scoop. I began talking up the idea of going there to school. Granted, we had just moved onto our smaller farm and there were plenty of things to spend money on, like making all those improvements and renovations. But my parents listened to my ideas and checked out what the cost would be. They also learned that other children from the Gap area were students there, so transportation would be available. So they signed us up to go to West Fallowfield Christian School.

School started right after Labor Day. At 7:15 A.M. Paul and I grabbed our lunch boxes, marched down the lane, and stood by our mailbox. Soon a brown General Motors van swung off the Lincoln Highway and onto the "Old Highway." It stopped beside us. Elva Engel was the driver. She was one of our mother's friends from their single days, so we knew her and her three daughters. The van was nothing like our modern vans with all their elaborate extras. It was more like what we called a panel truck, except it had windows all the way around and a door behind the front door on the passenger side for access to the back area. It also had two rear doors that opened out, but we used only the side door. Several students got to ride in front on the bench seat with Elva, but the rest of us filled up the rear. How many of us there were altogether I don't remember, but it was probably more than a baker's dozen.

It may be that the van originally had an upholstered seat behind the front seat, but the back area was now equipped with wooden benches, three rows, I think, or maybe even four. They were all attached to each other by their support boards at each end. They had no backs—and no seat belts! But we were just children going to school. And we were going "the long way around the barn" too. Yes, we went all ten miles to Coatesville and then out Walnut Street to the top of the hill to pick up some cousins. Then we circled around the southern side of Coatesville to the Strasburg Road and went west to Parkesburg, where we turned south on Route 10 toward the Highland Road, where we again went west, to Route 41, where we made a short jog to the left and arrived at school just before 9:00 A.M.

The school building was almost new and it was nice but not elaborate. The main floor had two classrooms partially divided by a hallway to the front door, which faced Route 41 and was seldom opened. The hallway served as an entrance to the lower grades' cloakroom and had doorways to the upper grades' classroom and to the basement. Each classroom also had a main entrance to the east. In Paul's and my classroom the seats faced the blackboard on the east wall, and there were windows along the north wall and partway along the west wall. The upper-grade classroom had windows to the south and west, and their seats faced the blackboard on the wall to the north. Their small cloakroom was in the corner of the classroom. The building had a complete basement with a boys' restroom in the southwest corner and a girls' bathroom in the southeast corner. The furnace and coal bin were tucked behind and beside the stairway near the north wall, leaving a big open room in the basement that often rang with the clatter of roller skates when the weather was too rainy or too cold for us to play outside.

Our teacher was Miss Vera Stauffer, and Miss Marian Messner taught the upper grades. One of the first items of business that first day was the assignment of our desks, and we were given some textbooks, of course. If I remember correctly, there were six rows of seats. Paul got a seat at the end of the second row. I was assigned to the third seat in the last row, beside the windows of the north wall. There were four of us in the sixth grade: Ada Nancy King (later Smoker), Leon Mast, me, and I don't remember who the fourth person was.

It was different for me to be in a classroom with six grades of students, including my brother! I got to watch some of the older students help the younger ones with their work. I don't seem to remember a lot about what I learned in sixth grade, except that I did become aware of a need to be more assertive sometimes. One day the student who sat behind me opened up the window about halfway and the raw, chilly wind from the northwest blew directly across me. I became uncomfortable, so at recess time, when most of the students were outside, I lowered the window to only an inch or so. But when the other students came in from recess, the same student promptly opened the window way up again. I lowered it again at noontime, but it was raised again that afternoon. So I sat there and shivered, and said nothing to the teacher. By evening I was really feeling miserable. I did not sleep well that night, and by the next morning I had a full-fledged cold with a stuffy nose and a nasty cough. I ended up missing two days of school, which of course ruined my perfect attendance record. I had seldom missed a day of school before that. ✞

I Embark on a New Life

When I was a child, despite living on a farm where the cows expected to be fed and milked every morning and evening, and where the hired man expected to have some weekends off, my parents made sure we got to church every Sunday morning and often on Sunday evenings too, especially if we had a visiting speaker. So church attendance was a regular part of the week for me, just as daily Bible reading based on the International Sunday School Lessons was an integral part of our daily routine. Dad was the leader for these daily devotions. He also led us in meaningful prayer. Mother gave silent support, but I know she prayed in private. (I clearly remember that at least once I came into the house, probably after school, and found her kneeling in silent prayer by the overstuffed chair in our living room. I stayed quietly in the kitchen until she was finished.) So, as a child I expected to become a Christian and a member of the local Mennonite church when I got older.

Every year in November our congregation had an annual Bible instruction meeting that covered Friday evening, three sessions on Saturday, and three on Sunday. That same month we also had a week of evangelistic meetings. The speakers included Clinton Ferster, William H. Martin, and in later years Amos W. Weaver and John F. Bressler. Our family attended these meetings as frequently as we could.

When I was still in fifth grade and in public school, I felt an inner tugging in my heart to make a public commitment to Christ. But I hesitated to do it. After all, I was still rather young—just eleven years old. And if I had suddenly appeared with a prayer covering on my head at a public school, where no other students wore one, I would doubtless have invited unwanted attention and more teasing. I felt it would be easier to make that decision if I was attending a Christian school. But of course I never admitted my thoughts and concerns to anyone else—until now!

During that same year I had found a form inside my Sunday school quarterly inviting the reader to ask Jesus into his or her life and claim salvation by signing the statement and indicating the date of the transaction. So I cut out the form, signed it, put the date on it, and pasted it into the Bible that Dad had given me several years previously. But I told no one else about this piece of paper, and my inner uncertainty continued. Did signing a piece of paper make me a Christian? Then I heard about Romans 10:9–10: "If thou shalt confess with thy mouth the Lord Jesus, and shalt believe in thine heart that God hath raised him from the dead, thou shalt be saved. For with the heart man believeth unto righteousness; and with the mouth confession is made unto salvation." Thus I came to understand that to become a Christian meant not only to believe in Jesus in my heart, which was rather easy, but also to make a verbal confession to others about my inner belief in Jesus and to make a public commitment to live for Him.

Though I did not discuss with my parents my thoughts about becoming a Christian, I think I did pray about it. And I did talk to my parents about my desire to attend a Christian school. God heard my prayers. When our annual evangelistic meetings came around in the fall of 1943, I felt I was ready for the next step.

The speaker for our evangelistic meetings that fall was Martin R. Kraybill from Elizabethtown. The services began on a Saturday evening in November and went through the following weekend. Martin's sermons were easy to understand, and he often included a story or two to get the attention of the children.

As I remember it, only Dad and I went to the first Sunday evening service of the week while Mother stayed home with my two younger brothers and my baby sister, who was barely four weeks old. For some inexplicable reason I entered the church from the front, hung my coat in the front anteroom, and entered the auditorium from the front. I sat down on the far end of the front bench, by the outside wall, by myself. That evening, Martin chose to preach from a familiar text, Romans 3:23: "For all have sinned and come short of the glory of God." Martin emphasized that he had at one time lived without God but had come to realize that he was a sinner and had yielded his life to God. "I wouldn't want to live without God for a single minute," he said. I realized that I was a sinner too, living without God. When Martin gave the invitation, we sang several verses of "Just as I Am." He then invited us to stand to sing a last verse and asked anyone who wanted to accept Christ to remain standing while the others sat down.

I remained standing. Martin did not notice me, but some other people did. As soon as the service was over I went out the front way, got my coat, and went out to the car and sat down in the back seat to think about what I had done. Dad soon joined me in the back seat. He told me how happy he was with my decision.

The next morning, Mother fixed my braids a bit differently on my head, then pinned one of her coverings onto my hair. It was a bit large for me, but I wore it until we went to Hager's department store in Lancaster and got a covering that was a better fit. I also worked at putting my hair in a bun and using big hairpins, but I had thick, long braids so it took some time and practice to learn a new hairstyle. Meanwhile, we went to the evangelistic services as often as we could. And Martin made sure he got to talk to me, with Dad, one evening after the service. He affirmed me in my decision. He also emphasized the importance of daily

Bible reading and prayer to growing as a Christian. I don't think I said very much, although he may have asked me several questions just to be sure I understood what my decision meant.

As I remember it, there were maybe fifteen or so young people who "stood for Christ" during that series of meetings. Afterward, we attended instruction classes that met during the Sunday school hour in the minister's anteroom. In addition to learning about Christian doctrine, we also heard about the rules and disciplines of the Mennonite Church. And in early spring we received water baptism as new members of the church. I regret to admit that, except for one or two, I really do not remember who was in that baptismal class with me.

I got to hear Martin preach occasionally thereafter, when he was invited back by our congregation. I vividly remember the time he spoke from Exodus 14 about the fear of the people of Israel when they had departed from Egypt and were being pursued by Pharaoh to the sea. The people cried out in terror and asked to return to slavery in Egypt! But Moses said,

> "Fear not, stand firm, and see the salvation of the Lord, which he will work for you today; for the Egyptians that you see today you shall never see again. The Lord will fight for you, and you have only to be still."
>
> The Lord said to Moses, "Why do you cry to me? Tell the people of Israel to GO FORWARD." Exodus 14:13–15 RSV

Martin emphasized that the message of Moses to Israel was for us too—that we need to go forward and grow in our walk of obedience to God. That message was especially meaningful to me.

At some point later, perhaps when I was in high school, I did communicate to Martin that I felt God wanted me to become a doctor and perhaps serve as a medical missionary. To me it all seemed rather unattainable at the time. I believe Martin prayed for me over the years and knew about my steps toward practicing medicine. Part of the process of applying to serve overseas with the Eastern Mennonite Board of Missions and Charities (EMBMC; known since 1993 as Eastern Mennonite Missions, or EMM) was to meet with one of their committees of ministers (for them to check out my doctrinal beliefs). Well, I relaxed a bit when I saw Martin sitting at the table. He told the group that he had known me for eighteen years—ever since I had made my public commitment to Christ. I still thank God for him, and for my parents, some special relatives, and other friends who supported me in my dream to become a doctor and prayed often for me along the way and while I was overseas. ✝

Learning in the Big Room

In the fall of 1944 I moved into the "big room" at West Fallowfield Christian School with the older students, who were in the 7th, 8th, 9th, and 10th grades. Again we went to school in the brown General Motors van. Both rooms had new teachers that year. The lower grades were taught by Miss Caroline King, and Miss Barbara Garber taught the upper grades. Miss King also taught the music classes for my room, because she was well trained in music and really made it interesting for us.

During that year there were several episodes in which I was subjected to teasing. I was shy, not at all assertive, overweight, short, and had lots of freckles, so I just assumed that people had adequate reasons not to like me and to tease me. Though teachers never discussed these situations with me, they dealt with them in ways that made things more pleasant for me. As usual, I did not discuss this issue with my parents. After all, I had asked to go to this school, and it was better than public school in a number of ways, at least for now.

When eighth grade arrived, there were several significant changes for me. First, I now had a man for a teacher whereas before I had always had a women teacher. John F. Bressler was an excellent teacher who had a profound influence on me. I came to admire him a great deal. Another change was that because Mr. Bressler lived near Lancaster and commuted every day, it was arranged for my brothers and me plus several cousins to ride along to school with him in his black 1937 Buick with the separate black "suitcase" on the back bumper. We arrived at school about a half hour before class began so that Mr. Bressler could have some time before school to take care of assorted projects, such as firing up the coal furnace when the weather got cool.

I clearly remember the day he taught me to think before I spoke. It was a sunny autumn morning with a nip in the air. We arrived at school about twenty minutes before class was to begin. I put my lunch box in the cloakroom while our teacher organized his books on his desk. Then, as he turned toward the inside door that led to the basement, I asked, "Are you going to fire up the furnace this morning?"

"Well, yes," he said, turning back to me. "Do you think I don't need to?"

"No, it's not cold," I said in a matter-of-fact tone.

Soon another student came in and hung up her coat in our six-by-six-foot cloakroom. As she came out she shivered and asked, "Why is it so cold in here?"

"Oh," Mr. Bressler replied, "I was going to fire up the furnace, but Dorcas said it wasn't cold in here." With that he headed downstairs and got the furnace going, while I wondered why I had offered such a dumb opinion anyway and wished I could find a hole to hide in.

Mr. Bressler would sometimes have us do "mental arithmetic." Of course that was before someone invented adding machines and calculators. Or he might send four or five students to the blackboard and have them write long columns of numbers for us to add. The goal was to be the first to finish with the correct answer. I never won that contest, but I did learn what Joe's secret to winning was: he would add the right column in his head as the numbers were called, and when we were told to go ahead and add, he would immediately write down the sum for the first column and jump to the second column, and win.

It seemed as though Mr. Bressler could expound on anything and everything! He would stretch our vocabulary by using big words. One day I asked him what a certain word meant. He replied, "Well, I could tell you what it means, but go look it up in the dictionary. Then you might even remember it!" He had such a wry sense of humor. One day he said he was an anencephalic, so we asked him to spell it. Then we went to the dictionary and discovered that it means "without a brain, or with only a partial brain." He laughed at our naiveté, but we knew he was just teasing us.

Mr. Bressler enjoyed reading all kinds of books. One day when he had no particular project to work on, he began reading the Bible at Genesis, chapter one. He said he read through the whole Bible that day, though to me that still seems impossible. He encouraged us to read, and he added books to our small library. I can still picture the metal bookcase that was about the size of a nightstand. Each side was open and accommodated probably four books. It stood on a pedestal with a four-footed base. Its top was flat and unadorned, but the books within it were a treasure of historical fiction that dealt with the discovery of our country—from the days of King Ferdinand and Queen Isabella, who finally agreed to finance Christopher Columbus's trip to the west in search of a route to the east, to Ponce de Leon and many others who opened up our vast country. History became more interesting as I read the whole series in sequence during my eighth-grade year.

In the decades since I attended that school, it has grown from two classrooms for ten grades to nine classrooms for eight grades and a kindergarten, and it is expanding still. And sometimes I wonder, if I visited that school now and went to the library, would I find that bookcase with its books somewhere, maybe parked in a corner? I wonder how many other students read that set too. I don't remember the author or the title of the series, but I do remember the joy of reading all those books and developing a great appreciation for the early settlers who helped to make our country what it is today.

Mr. Bressler was a man of his word; when he made a promise, he intended to keep it. After he had taught at our school for two years, he stopped teaching to spend more time with his wife. But he was sometimes invited back to the school. One time, at the end of a talk he gave at the weekly chapel service for the older students, he asked us to pray for his ailing wife. "Last night she had a really bad spell," he said.

Mr. Bressler attended our Christmas program that year. I was glad to see him again, and though I was still a rather bashful teenager, I spoke to him afterward and thanked him for arousing my curiosity and desire to learn about a variety of things. Whether I told him about my dream to become a doctor I am not sure, because it was such a deeply personal thing for me. But I'm sure he knew that he had been an important teacher to me, and that I was no longer waiting for others to tell me what to do or even to push me in a certain direction. Now I was developing some goals of my own and forming ideas about how to achieve them, because he had encouraged me to ask questions and think for myself. ♱

My Special Sister, Ruthie

There was another important event during my eighth year of school. It began on a Sunday afternoon in September 1945 with a visit by our family to one of Mother's favorite first cousins. Among their children was a daughter who was several months older than me (I had just turned fourteen). As we were outside talking, out of the blue she asked if I knew that my mother was expecting another baby. Well, I had to admit that I knew nothing about it. As I said earlier, Mother was a fairly tall, large-framed woman who was thin if she weighed two hundred pounds, and with her loose dresses and aprons, any increase in girth was not conspicuous. No, my parents had given me no clue about the impending addition to our family. And I decided not to let on that I knew anything about it. I guess I figured that if my parents could keep a secret, well, so could I!

It was probably six weeks later that my brothers and I arrived home from school and found that our new sister had arrived. It was November 7, 1945. Anna Mary was only two, so she was doubtless at home, and a friend of Mother's was there too when Ruthie was born with the assistance of Dr. Beacher. We "oohed" and "awed" as we looked at her sleeping in the basinet. Our next project was to choose a name for her. Some of us, including me, wanted to call her Ruth Ada, but others liked Ruth Esther, and they won. While she was still a baby we often called her by both names, Ruth Esther, but later we lapsed into calling her just Ruthie.

Mother was now being kept busy with two little people. She quickly realized that Ruthie needed "special care." The first clue was that Ruthie did not nurse very well. Mother had nursed all of us for a number of months, but Ruthie needed so much encouragement, and it was impossible to know how much she had taken in. At some point Dr. Beacher told my parents he suspected she was a "mongoloid baby." In those days, very little was known about what caused this condition, but one theory was that the thyroid gland was not producing enough hormone to produce adequate growth.

We now know that it is caused by a chromosome abnormality known as Trisomy 21, and the current name is Down syndrome. It occurs more often in children of older parents and usually affects their last child. Physical markers include short stature, a single crease in the palms of the hands (most people's palms have three creases); narrow, slanted eyes; variable degrees of mental retardation; and slow physical development. Ruthie's eyes had that typical slant and that fold of skin on the inner side, and she had a small mouth with a protruding tongue, and a single crease across the palms of her hands.

Mother soon discussed with Dr. Beacher the situation of Ruthie not nursing well and they agreed to try cow's milk. But Ruthie did not tolerate that. Mother then tried several store-bought formulas and finally settled on Similac, a liquid preparation that was added to water and put into sterilized bottles, then heated, cooled, and stored in the refrigerator until it was feeding time, when it was warmed again. It was such a laborious process compared to today, when you wash the bottle, run in warm tap water, dump in a scoop of Similac powder, put the nipple on, shake it good, and feed the baby. Feeding Ruthie was so time-consuming. Many times when I arrived home after school, my first task was to try to get baby Ruthie to take two ounces of formula, which often took at least thirty minutes. But eventually, after a number of months, she learned to eat some table foods and developed a better appetite.

Ruthie was also slow to reach those baby milestones like sitting up, crawling, and walking. It seems to me that she was going on three years of age before she walked by herself, and then she really learned to get around! She loved to go for rides in the car with us. As she got older, she learned that if the window in our Chevy pickup truck was completely open, she could get up on the running board, hike her one foot inside, pull the rest of herself in, and sit on the seat to wait for someone to come take her for a ride. She also was "double-jointed" in her hips. She could sit on the floor with her legs extended in front of her and then swing them around herself in a full circle and lie down on her abdomen with her legs extended behind her without flexing her knees or rolling onto her side. I'm not sure I've ever seen anyone else do that.

Ruthie never learned to talk with words, but she could surely communicate her wishes and feelings to us with her grunts and verbal outbursts. I remember a Friday evening when I arrived home from high school, where I was a dormitory student. I came in with my suitcase and walked through the living room to the stairs, where Ruthie was sitting on the bottom step. I proceeded to go around her, as though I was in some kind of a hurry, but she let out a loud "eeeeoh!" So I did a hasty backup down the stairs, parked my suitcase on the floor, sat down beside her, and talked to her for several minutes before I went upstairs.

Ruthie was an important member of our family, and she enjoyed us too. She seemed to know that we accepted her as she was. But she knew that some people would stare at her because she was different, and then she would get tense and noisy. So, when Ruthie was maybe five or six years old, Mother decided to stop taking her to church. Instead, Mother would stay at home on Sunday mornings and have dinner ready when the rest of us returned from church. Then, in the evening, someone else would stay at home with Ruthie while Mother went along to church with the rest of the family. Nate especially was often ready to stay with Ruthie on Sunday evenings.

Ruthie could tolerate some group gatherings. I know we took her along to some family reunions. I specifically remember several Stahl reunions that Ruthie attended. She enjoyed watching other children playing on the swings and the merry-go-round; she would stand quietly on the fringes of the group and watch the others having a good time. I stood nearby to monitor the situation while Mother visited with her cousins from the Ephrata area and Snyder County.

In time my parents discovered some other families with children who were like Ruthie or less severely handicapped. They also discovered that there was a "special" school, the S. June Smith Center, in Lancaster for these "special" children. Here they were taught basic skills such as brushing their teeth, dressing themselves, and going to the bathroom. Ruthie attended this school when she was eleven to twelve years old. This is documented in Mother's diary, where she reports that she and Anna Mary attended a picnic at the school on June 6, 1957. Not only did the children learn new skills, but their parents also learned what to expect of their children and how to teach them. Several parents carpooled to take their children to school. It was certainly a benefit to both the children and their families.

As Ruthie grew older, she remained short—yes, shorter than me! But she developed very good physical strength, and if she set her mind on doing something different than what I had in mind, well, she really made me work to convince her otherwise. ☩

Mother Encounters Depression

With all the extra work that caring for Ruthie required, Mother was not getting enough sleep. She was also struggling to understand why our family should have a child with such special needs. She did not easily share her feelings, but she did sometimes wonder aloud what she had done wrong. Had she committed some sin to cause her baby to be like this? Was God punishing her? I'm sure Dad tried to comfort her. In his family there was an aunt, Katie Stoltzfus, the youngest child of his paternal grandparents, who was also limited in some manner. Whether it was limited intellect, speech, mobility, or some combination I do not know, but she lived, I think, into her late teens. Aunt Katie's oldest sister, Lizzie S. Zook, lived to a month shy of ninety years and was alert until suffering a severe stroke a week before her death in 1950. When Aunt Lizzie saw Ruthie as a baby, she took a long look at Ruthie's hands and commented that they looked like Katie's, so maybe Katie had Down syndrome too. At any rate, I think Dad was perhaps more prepared to accept a child with limitations than Mother was.

Mother and Dad must have talked about Mother's feelings. Whether they talked to Dr. Beacher about them I do not know. At some point they did talk to Mother's older brother, Ammon Stoltzfus, and his wife, Lillie, about Mother's situation. Uncle Ammon and Aunt Lillie had twelve children (a number of whom were married). They arranged for Mother and Ruthie to live with them for several months. During that time, Anna Mary, who was more than two and a half, stayed with one of Dad's cousins; and as soon as school was over, Nate, who was seven and a half, went to stay with Dad's foster sister near Spring City for the summer months of 1946.

That left Dad, ten-and-a-half-year-old Paul, and me, going on fifteen, at home to run the farm and take care of ourselves. At that stage I was a better farmer than a housekeeper! We milked eleven cows by hand, so I milked my three cows every morning and evening. I helped with haymaking and other farm chores as well as pulling the weeds in the garden, and I mowed the lawn, including the rather steep banks by the old highway, with our trusty old push mower. ✝

My New Role at Home

I don't remember how much Dad told Paul and me about these arrangements before they went into effect. I do know they meant an adjustment for me, but I don't remember that I complained about becoming a housekeeper during Mother's absence. I recognized that she was not her usual jovial self and needed some relief from all her household responsibilities and child care. I was willing to help out as well as I could, with my limited knowledge of cooking. I was more experienced with cleaning and laundry chores. I must thank my dad for his patience with me in this new role, for I do not recall that he ever made negative comments about my "cooking" or menu selections, even though I served up a very simple and repetitious fare.

Fortunately I enjoyed making meatloaf and potatoes in various presentations—mashed, plain cooked, raw fried, or even scalloped sometimes. Our electric stove had a timer for the oven, so I could put in several casseroles and set the timer to start while we were at church so that the main dishes were ready to go on the table soon after we got home.

I frankly don't remember if we had our usual big vegetable garden that year or not, because Mother did most of the garden work, with Dad plowing the garden in the spring and helping with the planting. But I always enjoyed almost every vegetable that arrived on our table, so I assume I fixed some fresh vegetables for our meals that summer too. Mother did not grow spinach, broccoli, or Brussels sprouts, and not much cauliflower. But we did enjoy sweet corn, green and yellow wax beans, peas, lima beans, and asparagus from our garden.

Mother hadn't trained us to expect dessert after every meal, though we often had fruit pies or cake on Sundays and when we had company. She also made a variety of puddings. Sometimes she made a yellow cake without any frosting if it was just for us. I'm sure I did not attempt to bake any pies or cakes while Mother was gone. But I probably did make homemade ice cream in our eight-quart freezer a number of times.

I nearly served a disaster one evening. I tried to make tomato soup from scratch. I cooked the tomatoes and let them cool. I'm sure I did not know enough to cut up some scallions and green peppers to add some flavor to my bland concoction. Then I added some flour and milk and heated the soup not quite to boiling. I then poured it into a serving container and waited for Dad and Paul to come for supper. Fortunately either they were a bit late or I was a bit early. Anyway, a few minutes later I noticed that the white flour had settled to the bottom, so I quickly returned the uncooked mixture to the soup kettle and heated it some more before they arrived. I doubt that I got any raving compliments for my "cooking," but as I said, Dad was very patient and never complained.

We saw Anna Mary at church on Sunday mornings and she seemed to do well with her temporary family. Dad, Paul, and I often went to visit Mother and Ruthie on Sunday afternoons, and we could see that Mother gradually was not as sad and quiet. We were told that she was sleeping better too. Ruthie did not need as many feedings at night and was gaining weight. The nieces were happy to entertain her and to help care for her. Another important factor for Mother, I think, was that Uncle Ammon's family enjoyed many good times together, and I'm sure that helped to raise Mother's spirits.

Sometime in August 1946, Dad and I went to see the local officials about getting working papers so that I could stay out of school that fall to help at home. It was no big deal to complete the papers. Before we finished, though, one of us—I do not remember if it was Dad or me—asked if I, because I would not be fifteen until September 20, 1946, would need any further papers to stay out of school permanently. The answer was a firm "no." But I was thinking to myself, "Well, but I really do want to go to high school—sometime."

When Labor Day came, Nate returned home so he could go back to school with Paul. Now I had lunches to pack. I also had to be sure that the boys had proper clean clothes to wear to school.

Mother continued to show improvement, even though there were no medications to treat depression in those days. But less responsibility plus help in caring for Ruthie and repeated affirmation that she was a good mother and that God was not angry at her, all in a happy environment where people enjoyed a good laugh, were all the therapy she needed at that time.

As I remember it, the year when I was not in school (1946–1947) was the same year we did not have a farmer renting the farm that had been Grandpap's place. Grandpap had died in September 1944, and afterward Dad had bought the farm at public auction. For a year or so he rented out the double farmhouse but grew corn and hay in the fields and kept some heifers in the meadow. That farmwork was in addition to our small dairy and the maybe twenty acres we were farming on Gap Hill.

I clearly remember we had corn standing in the "long field," which was maybe a half-mile long, on the top of the hill at the farm that had been Grandpap's. Dad and I had our routine for harvesting that field. After the milking and breakfast were over, my brothers would head off to school with John Bressler. Dad would take care of the cows, then place the cooled cans of milk on our 1936 Chevy pickup truck and park it beside the highway so that the Aristocrat milk truck driver could pick the cans up. Dad also emptied out the manure gutter into a wheelbarrow and dumped the contents onto the manure pile out in front of the barn—where it was visible to all passers-by!

Meanwhile, I would harness up our bay horses, Mike and Roy, hitch them to the corn wagon, and head for the corn rows. I would go up the old Lincoln Highway, turn left along the upper border of our lower meadow (between the old and new highways), and stop by the new highway until it was safe to cross over. I would then follow the dirt road down the hill, past the old house where Grandpap had lived. Further down the hill I would pass the old store building, then the open wagon shed with its long corn cribs on two sides, then just beyond it the old barn. Next we would clatter over the small wooden bridge above the gurgling stream into the "flats," a narrow valley with an old, forsaken house at the corner of the meadow. Right behind the old house was a forlorn country road seldom traveled except by Andy Diener's cows, who walked up this track to the Dieners' back meadow. (Andy's farm and Grandpap's farm had initially been a single tract of land that was purchased from members of the William Penn family and later known as the McIlvaine tract.)

This trail to the isolated back meadow of the Diener's farm also went hard by another lonesome building that for many years had been the Umbletown schoolhouse. My dad got all of his education there, and when he finished eighth grade the school closed, because in 1915 the big new Gap Centralized School, with six classrooms, had opened beside the highway at the foot of Gap Hill.

Mike, Roy, and I would continue across the flats and up the hill to the top, where we would enter the long field and turn to the left. We would go to the last corn row that had been shucked, which Mike and Roy would straddle. They would then stop when I said, "Whoa."

I would tie the reins around one of the upright posts on the front of the wagon, then jump off and begin shucking the next row of corn. I would remove the husks from the ears, then throw the ears into the corn wagon, which was maybe five or six feet wide, with a high board on the left side to keep the corn from flying over the top and into the field. When I had shucked two rows of corn, I told Mike and Roy to move ahead. All it took was a little whistle through my pursed lips. They also knew when to stop, at a wagon's length, without me saying, "Whoa."

After a while, Dad would arrive, and then we would each shuck and husk one row. We did a fair amount of talking while we were at it, about a variety of things. As a child and teenager I always found it easier to talk to Dad than to Mother, but eventually it became easier for me to talk to Mother too. What specifically Dad and I talked about I don't remember these seventy years later.

By noon we would reach the woods at the far end of our two rows of corn, and we would be rather hungry. So Dad would drive the team along the edge of the corn to a tree, where he would fasten Mike's bridle by a rope to the tree limb so that the horses would stay put until we returned. Then Dad and I would walk back to the west end of the cornfield and drive home for lunch in our 1937 Plymouth sedan. Mike and Roy would have to wait until evening for their supper.

After lunch we would shuck two more rows of corn on the right side of the field. When we had finished shucking our four corn rows for the day, we would sometimes both go down to the farm buildings and shovel the corn into the corn crib together. But other times Dad would drive back home to get ready for the evening milking while I shoveled the corn into the crib by myself.

I vividly remember one beautiful fall evening when I had finished unloading the corn from the wagon. Mike and Roy and I had started home. As we passed the farmhouse and the orchard's few remaining apple trees, I looked westward beyond the meadow hill and toward Gap, and saw a gorgeous red-orange sunset unfold before my eyes. It was just awesome! And I can still remember that I asked God to let the end of my life be as beautiful as that sunset. Looking back seventy years later, I can see clouds of disappointment and depression in my life, plus attempts to serve God by my own effort. But I can still see that sunset as an ideal of what God wants to do in me and through me.

Dad and I followed this routine for several weeks as the corn rows got less and the corn crib got fuller, until finally two of Uncle Sam Smoker's sons arrived with their Silver King tractor and corn picker, plus a second Silver King tractor and wagon to drive alongside the corn picker to collect the corn. Mike and Roy got the day off as Dad used our John Deere H tractor and our hay wagon with sideboards on both sides to collect the corn as it was picked lickety-split. And would you believe it? They finished that remaining half-field of corn in the space of a day!

Another thing I remember from that corn-picking day was Dad driving our "tricycle" tractor and collecting the corn when unexpectedly his front wheels dropped into a big groundhog hole. He tried to back out but couldn't do it. Trying to go forward did not work either. So the cousins unhitched one of the Silver King tractors and produced a chain from somewhere, and maybe a shovel too, to make the far side of the hole bigger. We did rescue Dad's tractor from the groundhog hole, and finished picking all our corn, all in the same day!

I am not sure how long Mother and Ruthie stayed with Uncle Ammon's family, but it seems like it was well into the fall before they came home, maybe in October or early November. In any case, they were home for Thanksgiving, and Anna Mary came home from our cousin's place, and Nate from Dad's foster sister's home. Finally our family was reunited, and it felt so good. The major outdoor farmwork was done, so I could spend more time in the house with Mother and Ruthie, and I was glad that Mother, who seemed to have made a good recovery, promptly assumed responsibility for most of the meal planning and

preparation. She also seemed more comfortable in caring for Ruthie as we shared the household chores.

A highlight for me that winter was the fact that, because I was not going to regular school, I was able to go to the Millwood Bible school for two weeks in early January. Friends came from eastern Lancaster County to attend, but there were also many young folks from the Hagerstown, Maryland, and Chambersburg, Pennsylvania, areas. The students who came from a distance often received room and board from local families. The school's teachers included John E. Lapp, Elias W. Kulp, Harvey Shank, and J. Z. Rittenhouse. In addition to studying the Bible, I also learned some Mennonite history. Everyone enjoyed the music class at the end of each day, and many lifelong friendships were established. ✝

The School Dropout
Goes to High School

After attending Bible school at Millwood, I began thinking more about going to high school, so I spoke to Dad about it and he agreed to discuss it with Mother. I figured they might agree for me to go to the local school again, though I really preferred a bigger school with better-trained teachers. So I decided I would not push for the bigger school at that point.

When I mentioned to some of my Sunday school girlfriends that I wanted to go to high school, they looked at me rather strangely and asked, "But why? You have your working papers already. You don't need any more education!" I was not ready to tell them that I wanted to go not only to high school but also to college and even to medical school because I wanted to become a doctor. No way! I would not risk the chance that they might laugh at me, a farm girl thinking she could become a doctor—and a missionary! Frankly, that goal seemed unreachable even to me. But I knew God was telling me to "go for it!" So my response to my friends and their questions was, "Oh, I just wanna find out what I don't know!"

Like many teenagers, I had developed a real inferiority complex. I felt that I was too fat and too short and had too many freckles, so why would anybody like me? I did not like myself a whole lot either. I was very shy and quiet too. But, well, on the positive side, I knew how to work, and I especially enjoyed outdoor farmwork and milking the cows. Mowing the yard and working in the garden were not bad either. But the housework, cooking, and cleaning were just "not my cup of tea!"

When the 1947–1948 school year began, I found myself at the West Fallowfield Christian School again, in ninth grade. As I mentioned earlier, Mr. Bressler had resigned because of his wife's health problems, and I missed him. The school board had interviewed other prospective teachers and then hired a young single man to be our teacher. What his teaching credentials were I do not know, but he wore a plain suit and had some musical ability. To protect his identity, I shall call him Frank.

It soon became clear that Frank, a rather slender man, was not particularly skilled at handling discipline problems, and some of the older students soon found a variety of ways to create trouble for him. Things kept getting worse, and among the students there was little respect for Frank as our teacher. Sometimes a school board member or parent would come and sit in the classroom to help maintain order. My response to all this was to feel like I was wasting my time in a school where I was not getting a very good education—though I did read and appreciate a number of the classroom's library books.

Finally a new teacher arrived, maybe in the early spring of 1948, and Frank was released. Our new teacher was Floyd Sieber, who was waiting with his wife, Alice, and their two children to get visas to go to Argentina under the MBMC. Earlier, Floyd had worked at a children's home, so he knew how to handle children. Also, he was a tall, well-built man who immediately took charge of the classroom. He assigned us special projects in biology. He also gave us a Bible word or theme each week and expected us to find verses on that topic, to memorize the verses we had found, and then to recite them the following week. I wish I had kept a record of those themes and memory verses, but I know I learned a lot of Scripture in those few months.

Floyd also took time to play with us after lunch. We would play softball for maybe an hour, until Floyd said we were finished. Then we would return to the classroom and hit the books for the rest of the afternoon. Now school was really fun, and everyone knew Floyd was in charge.

After Floyd came and emphasized Bible memory work, I began to spend more time reading my Bible. I began to think and pray seriously about going to Lancaster Mennonite School the following year. Finally I wrote a short note and gave it to Dad in the kitchen one evening. This is basically what I said:

> Dear Dad,
>
> I believe that God wants me to become a doctor for Him, so I want to give my best to Him. Can you help me get the education I need to do this? Our school does not have science laboratories and lacks well-trained teachers. So I'd like to go to a better school.
>
> Dorcas

On the last day of school that year we had a picnic for everyone and finished with a softball game. The field south of our ballfield was newly plowed and ready to plant. That day I hit a ball through our grassy right field and down the smooth field for my only home run ever! That same day I also hit a single but was tricked by the first baseman, who hid the ball from me in his glove and told me I could step off the base. When I did as he suggested, he tagged me out! I never forgot his sneaky trick.

By the end of that school year I had learned a lot about how God works things out in ways I could not have anticipated. In the end, it was a school year with a lot of good lessons for me. I thanked God for arranging it that way. I was especially happy to get to know Floyd and his family, because Floyd was a really good teacher, and because his wife was a first cousin of my mother. ☩

Lancaster Mennonite School

During my first year at Lancaster Mennonite School (LMS) I lived with five other girls in a third-floor room at the Weaver residence. Four other girls lived in the other third-floor room, and we all shared one bathroom. Imagine ten girls sharing one shower every morning! Breakfast was served at 6:45 A.M., and I promptly decided that this was too early for me, because chapel did not start until 8:30 A.M. Meanwhile, the school was building a much-needed dormitory for girls.

I enjoyed the library and read quite a few books, including several biographies of physicians, and classics like *Les Miserables* and *Crime and Punishment*. One of our assignments in sophomore English, taught by Lois Garber Keener Kauffman, was to write our autobiography. I believe she gave us the chapter headings. I still have that booklet.[*]

As the spring of my sophomore year rolled around, the doctors who were caring for Mother said she should have a hysterectomy and some repair work done. She was admitted to Lancaster General Hospital (LGH) on a Friday for preoperative tests. So I gathered up all my textbooks and notebooks and took them home with me that day because, whether prepared or not, I was again in charge of "keeping house." That meant fixing meals, taking care of Ruthie, doing the laundry, and so on. I think Anna Mary stayed with a cousin's family, and Paul and Nate helped with the milking and barn work. I had learned a little about doing housework two years earlier, when Mother and Ruthie were with Uncle Ammon's family. I did get to study a bit sometimes. Mother was in the hospital for probably ten days and wasn't supposed to do much at first when she came home. Fortunately for me, my brothers finished school at West Fallowfield in May, and by then Mother was able to do more things around the house, so I returned to LMS as a day student after missing three weeks. I finished the year with acceptable grades, but I suspect the teachers cut me a break on some of the homework assignments and lab work that I had missed.

I remember seeing a letter sent to my parents by Noah Good in which he complimented me for my efforts to complete my schoolwork and continue my education during the period of Mother's surgery and recuperation. He probably did not know that this was the third time I could have quit school and given up on my dream to become a doctor. The first time,

---

[*] This is the booklet that Anna Mary refers to in this book's Preface.

of course, was when I dropped out after eighth grade for a year while Mother recuperated from her first bout of depression after Ruthie's birth. The second time was when I was in ninth grade and our new teacher was unable to discipline the students and I felt like I was wasting my time—until a real teacher came in and taught us to study and do projects and made school a lot of both learning and having fun together.

But I persevered, and all along I clearly knew that *if* I ever was to become a doctor, I needed to complete high school, then get a college degree, and finally complete medical school. But few people knew *why* I wanted to go to school, and frankly that inner call to become a doctor was too personal and precious for me to share it with people who might not understand it or, worse, even laugh at the idea of a short, chubby, freckled farm girl becoming a doctor, of all things!

The next year I got to live in the new dorm, which was really nice, with spacious rooms. That was the year I signed up for a course in church history taught by Amos W. Weaver. There were only five or six of us in the class, but it gave me a lasting interest in learning more about my roots as a member of the Mennonite Church and the Stoltzfus family.

There were many fine teachers at LMS. Lois Garber Keener Kaufmann, who made the *Tale of Two Cities* come alive, was a treasure; with a twinkle in her eye, she took a personal interest in each student. She also tried to teach "her girls" how to become young women and to navigate the pitfalls of dating. Clarence Keener had an answer for every situation. And Harvey Bauman was the teacher who loved to ask questions and make his students think hard and deep.

Once a year the students were given the opportunity to complete "criticism slips." These were pages filled with blocks about three inches wide and a half-inch high with the name of a student printed in each block. We were invited to write compliments or suggestions for each of our fellow students. Some blocks I left blank because I did not really know these people. When I received my own stack of "crit slips," some were helpful, but others were rather harsh. I'm not sure if faculty looked over the slips and removed the inappropriate ones before giving the rest to the named student. I also do not know where such a practice came from, or whether it has perhaps by now been discontinued. Anyway, I slowly did develop good friendships with several girls, but there were some things I just would not discuss with them either.

During my senior year at LMS, John Mumaw, president of Eastern Mennonite College (EMC, now Eastern Mennonite University), came to visit and interview prospective students. I spoke with him and, as it turned out, was the only student from my class of 1951 who enrolled at EMC the following September. Many of my classmates did follow me to college in subsequent years.

Finally, graduation day arrived; however, the weather was rainy and thus unsuitable for gathering outdoors by the Mill Stream. But the

Brunk Brothers revival tent was parked across the street from East Chestnut Street Mennonite Church in Lancaster City, so we moved the ceremony there. The platform was packed with fifty-one graduates plus dignitaries. For the day program I sat by the middle aisle, but for the graduation ceremony itself I was told to go to the outside end of the back row. When everyone else sat down, I remained standing—with no chair to sit on! Lawrence Brunk quickly appeared beside the platform with a chair. He warned me not to look down at the ground until the program was over. When I finally looked, my chair's legs were one inch from the edge of the platform, which was at least six feet above the ground and had no protective railing. But George Brunk had preached the graduation sermon, and we had all graduated into life after high school. ✝

Unpleasant Childhood Memories

Among the many memories of my childhood are some that I did not think about, much less share, until 2001, when I began writing a letter I gave to my son before his first wedding. Other memories came back to my awareness as I continued to write about my life after moving to Landis Homes in 2004. I have decided to share these stories in the hope that they will be of value to others who have had experiences similar to mine, and in the hope that they will not try to hide their pain for most of a lifetime, as I did.

Among the earliest of these memories are some disturbing dreams I had when I was perhaps six to eight years old. In the only one I remember vividly, I was out in the field behind the barn and someone or something was chasing me as I ran as fast as I could toward the barn. I finally made a tremendously long jump down a long slope and landed by the chicken house in the safety of the yard between our house and barn. After having such annoying dreams several times, I prayed in my bedroom one evening by myself and asked God to stop them—and they did stop for a number of years. And when I again experienced such dreams, they were not as distressing to me as they had been before.

Another memory concerns one of the extra men whom Dad sometimes hired to help with the harvesting and haymaking. One sunny mid-afternoon when I was four or maybe six years old, Mother asked me to take a two-quart jar of cold mint tea and a tin cup out to the hill field where Grandpap, Dad, and one of his helpers were loading loose hay onto the hay wagon. I approached another worker, Bill, who was raking hay into windrows while Dad and his crew worked at the far end of the field. After Bill finished the tea, he came close to me and said he wanted to show me something. He then opened the corner of his broadfall trousers and showed some of his pubic hair to me. He did not actually expose his genitalia, but he did say he might show me more another time. I innately knew I did not want to see more, and I was relieved that Dad and his crew were again headed our way with the hay wagon. I do not remember if Bill told me not to tell anyone else or to keep this as our secret, but he may have. Maybe this was the beginning of my keeping things to myself instead of telling my parents. Anyway, it was anywhere from fifteen to thirty years later, after Bill and his family had moved to another community, that I learned he had been arrested for inappropriate sexual contact with young children. I was amazed that after all those years that forgotten episode came back to me so vividly, and I belatedly thanked God for protecting me from Bill's evil designs against me.

A more traumatic event was my unfortunate introduction to "sex play" when I was eight or nine years old. A boy about my age invited me upstairs to play when I was visiting with my family. He asked me to get into his bed so that he could lay on top of me. I did not want to do it, so he said he would not like me anymore if I didn't let him do it. Finally I let him do it, but I did not like it at all. And I was not disappointed that we did not often visit that family after that. I was too embarrassed to tell my mother about it, and I don't think I ever did. In fact, it was many years before I told anyone about it.

When I was maybe eleven years old, a different, older boy wanted to lay on top of me. Again I refused, and he too threatened not to like me anymore if I did not cooperate. He had another boy with him. I felt trapped. What was I to do?

Another incident occurred when I was thirteen and needed to go to the bathroom during class. The girls' bathroom was in one corner of the basement and the boys' bathroom was in the next corner, only fifteen feet away. As I walked across the open basement to the girls' room, an older boy from another classroom came out of the boys' bathroom and headed toward the stairs to return to his classroom, or so I thought. Instead, he stepped behind the furnace and hid in the coal bin. Then, when I exited the girls' room and walked around the furnace toward the stairs, he came out and ran up the stairs behind me, reached his hand up under my dress, and touched me where I did *not* want to be touched. I was too shocked to scream or yell. I just hurried up the stairs and quickly but quietly went to my seat. Did I tell the teacher what he had done? No, I never told anyone—until now—and I had not thought about it for more than forty years until I began writing this chapter. I do not think that boy had ever once talked to me, but he must have been pre-occupied with sex and with bothering younger girls. I do wonder now, what if I had reported him to the teacher? Would he have been disciplined in some way or maybe even been expelled from school?

After each of these incidents I would wonder, why do boys do these things to younger girls? Why do they take advantage of girls in this way? Do I have a sign on my back that invites them to pick on me? Later, as I would ponder these episodes, I would wonder, why did God make boys different from girls? And why did God make sex anyway?

When I was in seventh or eighth grade in school, I was still milking three cows each morning and evening and spending several hours in the barn, so I sometimes observed when a cow was in heat and saw how the bull could serve her needs. Eventually Dad decided that it was safer to get the services of an artificial inseminator and sold the bull to the stockyard. We also had chickens, sometimes pigs and ducks, and usually a dog as part of our animal population. And for a number of years we had two horses. So, animal sexual activity was observed as part of the normal routine, not to be laughed at or ridiculed. Still, I did not see any good reason for human sex, and wanted no part of it.

It was hard for Mother to tell me about menstruation. She had a little old booklet written by Lydia Pinkham about a variety of women's health matters and some home remedies. One day when I was around twelve years old, she brought out this booklet when we were upstairs, opened it to the section about menstruation, and told me to read it. So I read it. Wow, that stuff surely was news to me! Then I looked at some adjacent articles and kept on reading until Mother came back to see if I had finished the specified article. I gave the booklet back to her and, well, that was that! I don't remember us having any further discussion about the "purpose" of menstruation.

So I tried to figure things out for myself. I did not like being a girl for boys to take advantage of, and being a man was clearly not an option either (although as a little girl I had once naively asked my dad if I would be a man like him when I grew up, and frankly I was rather disappointed when he said, "No, you will be a woman like your mother"). So I concluded that, although I appeared to be a girl, I would consider myself to be some sort of sexless "it" rather than a he or a she.

It should not be a surprise to anyone that I, with this assortment of childhood experiences, was not at all interested in boys while I was growing up. Instead I sometimes tried to compete with them, such as in softball games. Mostly I was quiet around boys and did not seek to be friends with them. And I clearly did not dream of someday getting married and becoming a mother. After all, I believed that God wanted me to train for overseas missionary service, so I needed to stay focused on going to high school and then to college and medical school. I could not afford to be distracted by boys and derailed from my personal goals in life. That basically was my attitude for more than twenty-five years.

At one point during my junior year of high school I spoke to a teacher, who was also a pastor, about my struggle to develop a meaningful devotional life. I also mentioned to him, without offering details, a little about my struggles with sexuality. One day a bit later, I came into the dorm after class and found our housemother sitting where she often sat, in the receptionist's alcove by the front door. She invited me to come in and sit down too, so I did, wondering what she was up to. I was rather shy and had not talked a lot with her before. She lost little time in getting to the point, which was, "I am wondering if someone has hurt you or taken advantage of you in some way. Maybe you could talk about it and let me try to help you with it." Well, I was clearly not prepared for this, so I just stared at the floor and said nothing. Part of my silence was because we were sitting in a rather public area, whereas her room with the door closed could have provided some privacy. But I also probably was just not yet ready to "spill my guts," even in a private setting. Without warning, I did not have time to sort through my feelings and think about what to say. I also did not feel I knew her well enough to trust her with my dark secrets. At that point I had not yet established many meaningful friendships with adult women, including my mother. So the housemother had little chance of getting me to open up and talk to her that day.

If I could talk to her now, however, after learning a lot more about myself and being more willing to share my feelings, I would first apologize for not being receptive to her offer to hear my hurts and help me find some healing and growth. I would also thank her for her efforts to help us girls grow into mature young women and prepare for the days of dating, courtship, and marriage. I would tell her that although I did not receive from her all that she tried to offer me, when I was in my mid-thirties I met a woman named Betty who mentored me and led me to accept myself as a woman, as a daughter in the family of God, and as one who could even ask God about finding a marriage companion, which at that time seemed far out in the realm of possibility. With Betty's help, I did come to believe that God could do that even for me. And in his good time, God did exactly that. ✞

Eastern Mennonite College

I still remember my first trip to Eastern Mennonite College in Harrisonburg, Virginia, in September 1951. Dad's cousin Nora Stoltzfus, who had never married, lived in Gap and enjoyed doing things for people. She offered to deliver me to EMC and invited Mother and my brother Paul to go along. We took most of a day to get there, with several stops for gasoline, as we followed Route 30 to Chambersburg and then Route 11 through Hagerstown, Martinsburg, Winchester, and numerous smaller towns before we reached EMC around 4:00 P.M. We were directed to the women's dormitory, which I quickly learned was not yet completed; the first, third, and fourth floors were still large open spaces. But the second floor had accepted its first residents the previous winter (January 1951), and the basement contained a kitchen and dining room plus several small classrooms.

Arlene Krupp, another freshman, who knew her way around, led us to my new abode. When I opened the door to room 21 (the third door on the right on the long hall, facing Mount Massanutten and the east), my first thought was, "Oh! This is a really small room compared to the dorm rooms at LMS!" In fact, it seemed rather crowded, even with bunk beds. Nora, Mother, and Paul got to sleep in the dorms that night and left after breakfast the next morning to return home. Arlene continued to show me around the campus for several days, until I knew where things were.

We had several days of freshman orientation before we registered for our classes. Then, on Friday afternoon, we girls were asked to climb aboard the college's three-ton 1936 Chevrolet truck, which was equipped with four benches, one along each outside sideboard, facing the middle, and the other two situated back to back down the middle of the truck's bed. The photo of our freshman class of 1955 shows thirty-nine females and thirty-two males. It was no problem for us girls to seat ourselves on the back of the Chevy truck with our sleeping bags while our food supplies and some of the faculty ladies went in separate vehicles. Meanwhile, the boys went off in a different direction with some of the male staff members.

We took the first major road to the right in Park View, went up over the hill and down to the west (toward Sparkling Springs and West Virginia), and soon found ourselves in a large green pasture, where we unloaded and parked our bags beneath a spreading oak tree, then got involved in some team sports. Later we had a satisfying meal of baked beans, potato salad, and hot dogs that we cooked over a fire. As the sun dropped toward the west, we played some get-acquainted games. Then Miss Evelyn King, our dean of women, led us in prayer time. Afterward, someone stirred the fire's embers with some more sticks and brought out the marshmallows. The stars and then the moon made their appearance. Eventually we opened up our sleeping bags, climbed inside them, and went to sleep. There were no restrooms nearby, nor was there a stream in which to wash our hands, but somehow we did take care of our basic needs. The next morning, after we'd had a hearty breakfast and done some more exploring of the territory, our trusty Chevy truck returned at around 9:30 and transported us back to EMC. The showers were busy for a time after our return. That camping trip was only the first of a number of outings, some of them also overnight events, to visit various scenic spots in the Shenandoah Valley and along the Skyline Drive, and to the array of caverns in that area of Virginia.

I enjoyed these and other social outings, as well as sports, with the girls, but I did not really socialize with boys except if I knew them quite well or was related to them—although my science classes had mostly male students in them. I was not into fancy clothes or stylish shoes, but I did soon recognize that if a lady was wearing black nylons, which we had been required to wear in high school, I noticed it; but if a lady wore lighter hose, I did not notice! So I stopped wearing black nylons!

My roommate, Catherine (Kitty) Roth, arrived at midday on Saturday. She did not need freshman orientation like I did, because she had spent her last two years of high school and her freshman year of college at EMC and thus already "knew the ropes." I vividly remember my first meeting with Catherine. I came up the stairs in the girls' dorm after the noon meal and opened the door into our hallway, and here comes a girl in a hurry. She was shorter than me, with wavy brown hair and glasses, and just as she was about to push her way out the door, I pulled it away from her. Well, we didn't quite collide, but we did meet in a hurry! She stopped and briefly introduced herself before rushing off to rejoin some of her family for the weekend. After she returned it didn't take long for us to get acquainted, and we had lots of good times together. Catherine had a keen sense of humor and could shoot back a quick answer for almost anything I could ask her, and with time I increased my ability to respond to her too. We often had a tit-for-tat exchange of comments during the evening as we studied together.

Catherine's mother had supplied her with small jars of fruit snacks to enjoy occasionally. I clearly remember the evening she decided to open a jar of cherries. I was already in my pajamas and my hair was hanging to the floor as I sat on it to eat my cherries. We were exchanging our rejoinders as we ate and of course we were laughing. I actually stretched out on the rug beside our bunk beds as we continued our verbal sparring. I then sat up in front of the bunk, completely oblivious to the fact that the "free time" after our study period was now over and it was supposed to be "quiet time" for our evening devotions. Suddenly there was a knock at our door, and then Evelyn King opened the door, poked her head inside, and said, "Excuse me but could you girls lower your voices a bit?" She then pulled the door shut without waiting for us to think up an excuse or an apology. I quickly looked up at Catherine from my seat on the floor and said in a distressed tone, "Well, how much lower does she want me to get?" So of course we had another siege of laughter before we managed to subdue ourselves.

Because many students liked to put a name on their dormitory door, we decided to name our room too. Both of us knew some German and we were both short (less than five feet, to be exact, and admittedly a bit chubby too) so we decided on "Klein Aber Klug" (little but smart). When people asked us what it meant, Catherine would say, "Well, I'm the short one and Dorcas is smart." But I would say, "No, both of us are short and both are also intelligent and clever!" I guess that sounds rather cocky and presumptuous now, but it was good for some laughs.

I remember the day when "shorty" me went to pull something off the high shelf in my closet and somehow my bottle of shampoo came along down. I desperately tried to stop it between my back and the side wall of the closet, but it careened on down and landed in one of my bedroom slippers. This was before the days of plastic bottles, so the bottle broke and poured out the shampoo into my slippers. Oh well, at least my slippers did not smell like feet for a while!

Soon classes began. For me they included general biology, English composition, a study of Mark's Gospel, second-year German, and trigonometry. EMC had some excellent teachers, who expected good work from us, and I quickly realized that my old high school study habits would not be adequate for college if I wanted to be a good student.

As a freshman, I started off with D. Ralph Hostetter in biology. The first semester we studied plants and, frankly, I wasn't terribly interested. In our lab workbooks we had to make drawings of various plants and label the parts. I was not much of an artist, and when I labeled the parts, I even misspelled some of the words. I clearly remember that I wrongly spelled *chromosome* with an *n* in the place of the second *m*, and that word came up in many labels. And of course our student assistant in biology lab, Herb Minnich, caught each misspelling with his red pencil. So I was shocked into reality when I got a D in biology for the first semester. The second semester was more interesting and I managed to get a B. Professor Hostetter also took us on a walking field trip over the hill behind the administration building. We walked beyond Astral Hall and up the steps erected over the fence and into the neighbor's meadow, where we walked down the hill and saw a variety of plants and flowers, including a persimmon tree. Professor Hostetter was well known for his Avian Society, and many of us went along with him on Saturday hikes to see a variety of birds in their natural habitat. He freely admitted that he always expected his wife, or someone other than himself, to drive the car so that he could devote his complete attention to watching for birds and other wildlife.

M. T. Brackbill, a poet who sometimes shared his poetry with us, was another unforgettable teacher. His humor and enthusiasm bubbled over frequently in class. But his age sometimes caught up with him too. I remember the day he wanted to explain the proof for some mathematical theorem but finally said, "Oh, I can't put it together for you now, but just take my word that it is so!" I also treasured his Astral Society, in which we met by the planetarium up on the hill to look at the stars through a telescope built by a former student. As a society and under his leadership, we also gave some choric readings for the public. I still smile as I relive his renditions of Charles Dickens's *Christmas Carol* from memory. As a sophomore I was in his physics class. Not the best student in math, I often did an extra problem or two for our homework assignments, just to get more practice. The student assistant who corrected our papers that year was Clarence Rutt, an upper-class premedical student.

In English composition class, Hubert Pellman assigned us to write a number of papers and at least one story. We also had to give a speech, and for me this was much more difficult than writing. I remember that I began my speech by talking about walking up the hill behind the administration building to think about my speech. After I finished, I was asked to explain why I had begun it as I had. I said it was just a crutch to help me get started, even if it seemed irrelevant to them. I often waited until the last day to write my assigned papers and therefore handed in what was merely a draft version, which later I would rewrite and return as a considerably improved version. Many years later I have finally learned to revise my writing as I go; thus I present a better version the first time.

I had studied German under Noah Good for two years in high school, so I signed up for second-year German under Ernest G. Gehman. At that time, German was required for premedical students. In the class there were twelve to fifteen students, most of whom were inclined to ask the teacher questions about his experiences in Germany, so we did not get into the classwork until the period was nearly over. Professor Gehman would then try to cover the lesson quickly by keeping us for several minutes after the first bell rang. We were therefore sometimes tardy for our next classes. One day a student even got him to give us a demonstration of yodeling, which he did while standing behind a curtain with his back to us.

All freshmen were required to take a Bible course. Most of us took an inductive book study of the Gospel of Mark taught by Paul H. Martin.

As we learned to divide a passage into segments in an attempt to grasp the full content of the assigned portion, some students began referring to our tall, slender professor as "Segments Martin." It must be said that his teaching was thorough.

By the end of my first year of college I knew that my study habits needed to improve even more if I was to get into medical school. So, for my sophomore year I made a weekly schedule. I blocked out each hour of the week—when I had classes and lab periods and when I would study for each course. I did leave a little free time. I learned to study Latin vocabulary before I went to bed. And I got up at 6:00 several mornings each week—and that was *early* for me—to do my physics problems. My hard work paid off, with acceptable though not outstanding grades.

As a sophomore I had Henry D. Weaver Jr. for general chemistry. He was a young man who really knew his subject. He also enjoyed working with his students, but he soon went off to Goshen College in Indiana, so Vernon Schmid taught me physical chemistry in the spring semester of 1954. Grace Lefever, who taught high school chemistry, stepped in to teach organic chemistry in my junior year, and qualitative and quantitative analysis in my senior year. I came to admire her not only as a teacher but also as a friend and role model.

I had only one class—either general psychology or introduction to sociology—taught by Daniel W. Lehman, but he had an unforgettable style of teaching. He always came striding into the southwest classroom on the first floor of the administration building just before the tardy bell rang. He would be singing an old hymn in a lusty and enthusiastic style, and of course we were all expected to join in. Then he would "take the attendance roll." At the beginning of the year he assigned each of us a number for our name, in alphabetical order. After we sang together, he had us each say our number, to see if every number was present. At the beginning of the course he gave us a schedule of when we were to have each chapter in our textbook studied. And even if our class discussions lagged behind that schedule, he sometimes gave us a pop quiz on the material we were supposed to have learned already. Some of us objected that this approach was unfair, but Professor Lehman did it his way. For these quizzes he would read aloud the questions, sometimes twenty or more, which we were to write down followed by our answers. One time he said we would correct our papers in the next class session, and although a student tried to suggest that it was a better learning process to correct our papers and recognize our mistakes immediately, Professor Lehman was not convinced to change his teaching methods.

One year I asked to take Latin under Miss Dorothy Kemrer and the only other student in the class with me was Stanley Yake. I'd had one year of Latin in high school and although it was not required in the premedical curriculum, I felt that Latin would be useful to me in learning medical terminology—and it was.

During my sophomore year I roomed with Amy Beiler, an Amish girl from Ohio. A special event that year was a weekend visit to her home and the opportunity to observe more closely the simplicity of the Amish lifestyle. This included sleeping in the unfinished attic on mattresses that were stuffed with corn fodder. It was a bit crunchy when I moved around, but I slept anyway. We attended an Amish church service at a home in Apple Creek. I really admired Amy for coming to college to train to be a schoolteacher, but it must have been very hard to leave her family and her Amish friends to come to such a different environment. In retrospect, I suspect she may have been homesick sometimes, but I cannot remember that she ever verbalized such feelings to me.

After two years of college I was running low on funds, so I dropped out for a semester to earn more money by picking potatoes and working in a nursing home. A friend and I also went by Greyhound bus to Batavia, New York, to visit Catherine Roth and to meet her parents before they left for a two-year term of service in Germany. Catherine had taught school in Ohio the previous year and had met Ted Morrow and his family a few months prior to our visit, so we met the Morrow family that weekend, as well as a number of the Alden Mennonite Church folks. The five of us young people (Ted, his sister Pinky, Catherine, my friend Erma Lapp, and I) also enjoyed a Saturday trip to Niagara Falls.

When I returned to EMC for the next semester, I had two room-mates, Mary Gehman and Edna Wetzel. I took physical chemistry and an extra Bible course that semester. In my last two years I took several other elective courses, such as music appreciation with J. Mark Stauffer and the history of social work with Paul Peachy. I thus got to study with several other teachers whom I otherwise would have missed.

A favorite teacher among pre-med and nursing students was the pre-med student advisor, Daniel B. Suter, who taught the advanced biology courses, including vertebrate anatomy, physiology, embryology, and histology. In anatomy class we each had our own dogfish shark to dissect over a period of many months, and those fish remains became increasingly oily and unattractive with time. We made our drawings in our lab books and enjoyed working together in our small laboratory in the back of the administration building's basement, which also served as our lecture hall. In histology class we worked with tissue specimens and prepared our own slides to study under the microscope. In physiology class we did experiments with frogs and learned to measure their leg-muscle contractions in various test situations using an activated tuning fork to provide the time measurement—if everything went as planned. This did require *some* manual dexterity! But in the midst of all the work we did in that small room, we also had plenty of good conversation with Professor Suter. He was also sponsor of the Premedical Society and brought in a variety of doctors to speak at our monthly meetings. He organized some field trips, to Dr. Samuel Bucher's clinic in Harman,

West Virginia, and to medical schools in Charlottesville, Virginia, and Washington, DC, where some of our EMC graduates were students. Even though EMC was a small school, our premed graduates had a reputation of doing well in medical school. Professor Suter had a sense of humor; the one-liner I remember is, "Did you realize that when we got married, a suture married a fissure?" He was a Suter/suture and his bride was a Fisher/fissure!

In my junior year I roomed with Edna G. Detweiler. Edna became a special friend. She maintained contact with me, and many other people, for many years. A number of times I went with her and her parents to the Worcester Mennonite Church in Pennsylvania. That year, along with studying, I also prepared and submitted applications to three of the Philadelphia medical schools: the Hahnemann Medical College, the University of Pennsylvania School of Medicine, and the Woman's Medical College of Pennsylvania. The application for Woman's Medical College asked for an essay explaining why I wanted to be a doctor. I remember writing a full eight-and-a-half-by-eleven page, perhaps on both sides, to answer that question. I do not remember exactly what I said, but I probably wrote about Ida Scudder being called to help the neglected women in India, where the caste system did not permit them to accept help from male physicians. I may also have mentioned my own desire to help underserved people in some neglected corner of the world.

That summer, 1955, I had interviews at each school, and I clearly remember one question I was asked at Hahnemann. After we had talked about the students I already knew at Hahnemann and about which other schools I had applied to, one of the doctors asked, "Now, tell me, which school would you really most like to go to?" That question surprised me, but I tried to answer it carefully. I supposed that the quality of education did not vary greatly from one school to another, but the Woman's Medical College had three attractions that the others did not have: its alumni included several Mennonite women whose names I recognized; the classes were small, with fifty-one students in each; and all of the students and many of the teachers were women, so I would not face competition or comments from male students who might question a woman's place in medical school.

For my senior year at EMC I requested permission to move out of the dormitory. Initially my request was denied. But I discussed it with a couple of friends, and we learned that Mollie Kauffman, widow of Daniel Kauffman, was building a house with a walk-in basement apartment to rent out while she lived upstairs. The three of us—Martha Bender, an Amish girl from Kalona, Iowa; Edna Hoover from near Ephrata, Pennsylvania; and I—got approval to live there. As it turned out, the apartment was not quite ready when the school year began, so we lived in the Sarcos' garage for several weeks while Mollie lived in the house with her daughter and the rest of the Sarco family. Meanwhile, I had purchased a three-speed bike, which was state-of-the-art in that day, and had equipped it with a metal basket attached to the handle bars. Thus I was ready to go grocery shopping in Harrisonburg every week.

The three of us got along quite well, although we did not have exactly the same preferences when it came to food (one of us was really into "natural" foods), and our styles of food preparation were different too. We tried having one person cook supper for a week and another do the dishes while the third had that week off. But we found that we each preferred to do our own dishes and then have two weeks off. We really did get along OK. We even had a fourth lady with us for several months in the spring semester. During that period I slept on the sofa in the living room because the bedroom accommodated only three people. It was a good senior year together. I also enjoyed spending time with Mollie Kauffman as she shared stories of her earlier life while making rugs out of colorful old dresses on the big loom in her front room.

A major highlight of college occurred in the fall of my senior year. I was accepted by the medical school of my choice: Woman's Medical College of Pennsylvania, in October 1955. The next goal was to finish it—successfully. But first came graduation from college. It was a bit hard to separate from classmates who had become my good friends but would now be scattered across the United States and into Canada, and even into foreign countries. Graduation was made even more special for me by the fact that Dad's aunt Barbara Lantz was able to attend the commencement ceremony. A highlight of the week was a lovely tea to which the graduates and their parents were invited. It was hosted by President and Mrs. John Mumaw. The faculty met with us on the lawn. I invited Aunt Barbie to go along and introduced her to several faculty members who had known her brother, D. Parke Lantz, and his wife, Lillie Lantz, from their days in Argentina.

I do not remember much about the commencement ceremony or who the guest speaker was. But I had reached a milestone, and my family and Aunt Barbie were there to congratulate me. Now it was time to go home, to earn as much as I could over the summer, and then to head for medical school in Philadelphia in the fall. ✞

Medical School

Preclinical Years

During the summer of 1956, before I began medical school, I worked at Weaver's Poultry to earn money for school. I also made a trip into downtown Philadelphia, to Williams, Brown & Earle, and bought a used microscope for about $100. (I used it for two years in histology and pathology, rented it to another student for two years, then sold it, through the school, to another student for more than I had paid for it. Yes, prices were going up in those days too!) I also checked in at the Woman's Medical School office and got information from Miss Huston about where I might rent a room in a nearby home. I settled on a small bedroom in a row house on Tilden Street owned by Miss Iona Becker, for which I agreed to pay $6 per week.

That summer I also got a letter from an upperclassman at the school that told me about the life of a medical student and what to expect. And just before classes were to begin, the school had a Sunday afternoon open house for the new students and their parents. My parents came with me to see this special place from which I hoped to graduate as an M.D. in four years.

After the open house my parents dropped me off at my room and went home. I had brought mainly summer-fall clothes because the closet in my room was quite small, and I was only fifty miles from home, so I could shift clothes from home to school as the seasons changed. My room had a twin bed, a secretary desk, one straight chair, a rocking chair, and a dresser. It had one window that looked out onto the back alley. I had brought along a small Zenith AM-FM radio that I had found in a pawn shop and parked it on the desk. That radio became an important companion to me throughout my four years of medical school. Every day, after I got home from dinner at 6:00 P.M., or later, it supplied me with the evening news. I would silence it at 7:00 P.M. and study until 10:00, when I would listen to Fibber McGee and Molly on WQXR, a suburban New York City station, before turning it off again and studying for several more hours. On Saturday evenings I listened to WQXR's classical music program during my scheduled break from studying.

On my first day of medical school I left the house at around 8:00 and briskly walked the five blocks to school with my red briefcase, my checkbook, and writing supplies. We had already been told that the freshman and sophomore students were to turn left upon entering the building while the upperclassmen went to the right side to work with the hospital patients. So we walked past the faculty offices on the first floor, piled onto the elevator, and went to the fourth floor. We then walked timidly down the hall, looking for our classroom on the left. Miss Menough, the administrative assistant for the anatomy department, was watching for us and greeted us warmly. We soon learned that she did not mind answering our questions, and she was quite helpful to us in sundry ways as we began our new role as freshman medical students. She also taught us what syringomyelia (a neurological disorder with which she was afflicted) is all about.

We went into the classroom and chose our seats. I sat beside the window overlooking Henry Avenue. The seats were wooden and rather tall for my short legs, so I sometimes put the toes of my shoes on the book shelf of the chair in front of me rather than letting my feet dangle—so much for the inconvenience of being less than five feet tall!

The front of the classroom consisted of pairs of blackboards across the entire width of the room. The lower blackboard of each pair could be filled with diagrams before class, then pushed up as the other blackboard was brought down to be filled up with additional drawings for us to copy. I again realized that I was not a very good artist and had limited ability to copy what was before me.

At 9:00 A.M. Dr. Hartwig Kuhlenbeck came in and introduced himself as our professor of gross anatomy. He was a slender, reserved, elderly gentleman with a German accent. He began by giving us a few preliminary instructions: There would no smoking by the students in the classroom or in the cadaver room, although we learned later that the professor himself might occasionally smoke his pipe in gross lab, and it was a pleasant change from the aroma of formaldehyde. Everyone was to sign out a box of dry bones to take home and use to make drawings. Students should assemble themselves in groups of three or four for gross lab.

Within ten minutes, Dr. Kuhlenbeck was into his lecture. As he paced back and forth across the front of the room, we scrambled to get out our notebooks and pens. His first lecture was, I think, about the skin—and why not? Isn't it the outside of the body that we see first? I began to take notes, but he spoke rather fast and my writing degenerated into a scrawl. After a few weeks I learned to use some shortcuts for long words, and eventually I decided to rewrite my notes at home in the evening so that I could study them and check them for accuracy.

After an hour or more of lecture, Professor Kuhlenbeck took us to the gross lab, where we met his assistant, Dr. Max Levitan. We stood near the entrance as Dr. Levitan reminded us to always show respect to the human body, because these cadavers had once been living members of the human race just as we new medical students now were. We

were also told that some persons had specifically donated their bodies to science so that, by dissecting them, medical students like us could learn anatomy, the bedrock of our medical training, to prepare us to offer healing to those afflicted by various illnesses.

As we students, mostly strangers to one another, wandered into the room of thirteen tables arranged in two rows, we saw the yellow, tarp-like cloth wrapped around each cadaver. I finally found myself at the far end of the room, at the last table, with three other students. We introduced ourselves as Signe, Vija, Dorcas, and Pinsky. We were then instructed to unwrap our cadaver and inspect the exterior of the body. The odor of the preservative was unpleasant initially, but with time we got used to it. Before we left the lab for the day, we were told to buy a long white lab coat to use only for gross lab and to keep the coats in our lockers beside the elevator when we were not using them.

I had brought a packed lunch (a sandwich, some fruit, a cookie), so I headed for the lunchroom, but wow, the cloud of cigarette smoke was overpowering! This was before awareness of the cancer danger from cigarettes and secondhand smoke. So I was exposed even though I never smoked. After eating my lunch, I stopped by the small bookstore-in-a-closet to the side of the lunchroom to buy *Gray's Anatomy* and a histology textbook.

That afternoon we met Dr. E. Frances Stilwell, our histology professor. After her lecture, she took us into the histology lab at the end of the hall, where we each picked a high stool and a cubicle for our microscopes. In this lab we looked at slides of tissues taken from many organs and structures of the body and tried to draw what we saw. As I've said, I was not a very good artist, but I worked at it. Later, in neuroanatomy class, we worked on drawing cross-sections of the brain and spinal cord at different levels. We then assembled the drawings and used colored pencils to show the pathways of the various nerves, beginning with the brain and moving down the spinal cord, showing where they crossed over to the opposite side. It was a major project, and I felt I had really achieved something when it was completed!

So that was our routine: gross lab lecture and dissection in the morning, histology lecture and slide drawings in the afternoon. We got out early on Wednesdays, but we had class on Saturday morning. And of course we had exams, about every three weeks, in each course. In the second semester we started work on physiology (how the body works) and embryology (how the fetus develops) both of which I found more interesting than my other classes. We also studied biochemistry, which again meant a lot of memory work, which was *not* my forte!

One Saturday afternoon I arrived back at my room and found Martha Bender, one of my roommates from my senior year at EMC, in the living room. I was so surprised to see her. Though I had planned to study hard for my Monday morning biochemistry exam, I instead went with Martha by bus to Center City to visit the Preston Maternity Center. Martha was considering training in nursing or midwifery and wanted to see what Preston had to offer, so a nurse showed us around. Most of the babies were delivered by midwives, and if an episiotomy was needed the repair could be delayed by a day or more until a doctor came in to do the stitching. As it turned out, Martha later went to Riverside Hospital in Newport News, Virginia, for nursing training.

After we left Preston that day, we rode a trolley to the end of the line in West Philadelphia and sat on it until it went all the way back to Center City. Martha spent the night with me and we went to church at Diamond Street Mennonite the next day and had dinner before she left. I then belatedly began to study for my exam. My normal weekend study routine was to rest with some classical music as my "Sabbath" on Saturday afternoon, then study Saturday evening, go to church on Sunday morning, and resume my exam preparation after lunch and study until 10:00 or 11:00 P.M. That Monday morning I knew I was not well prepared for the biochemistry exam, but I did the best I could. Later, eight or ten of us were called before Dr. Phyllis Bott, head of the biochemistry department, who thoroughly castigated us for our poor showing on the exam. We were made to feel as though we had not even tried, and she even said, "After all, we didn't ask you to come here!" Well, as I recall, that is the only exam I ever flunked in medical school!

It was perhaps early in my sophomore year that, as I mentioned earlier, I learned to rewrite each day's lecture notes that same evening. In this way I could not only check them for accuracy but also print them much more legibly. The notes were then much more useful to me in preparing for exams. I studied hard in medical school but this did not come quite as easily for me as it did for some of my classmates. Eventually I teamed up with Agnes Cornesky to review for exams. She would have me memorize facts and formulas for bacteriology and biochemistry (which I did not like to do) and then explain them to her in my own words until they made sense to her. This review plan worked well for both of us. And we both graduated in June 1960 and became competent physicians, if I do say so myself!

Clinical Years

At last the preclinical years—with their long hours of lab work, of peering into the microscope, doing gross anatomy dissection, watching autopsies, doing physiology experiments on dogs and checking petri dishes for microbe colonies—were over. The long lab coats were gladly discarded. Several of our classmates were no longer with us. One had departed by Christmas of our freshman year; no one knew whether she had dropped out or been asked to leave. Another classmate dropped out after her sophomore year to care for her newborn twins for several years before completing her medical studies. Another was asked to repeat a year. And two girls transferred in from other schools.

Now when we entered the building, we turned right and went down the hall into the hospital. And we now wore white skirts and short white jackets with our name tags on them. We carried our leather bags containing the instruments needed to do a physical examination. We were now assigned to work with real patients instead of practicing on our classmates. We would take our patients' histories for our supervisors to check over, and we would do a complete physical exam on them. We accompanied the resident physicians and staff doctors on daily rounds. We were also called on by nurses to start IV (intravenous) fluids, to insert NG (nasogastric) tubes, and so. We were on call every second night and every second weekend when we were working with in-patients, and we often did not get home before 9:00 P.M. on our nights off. Would you believe that the novelty of hearing our names paged on the public address system soon wore off and it became too intrusively frequent to be a welcome sound to our ears? We did look forward to spending time in the outpatient clinics, where we did not have night call duty.

In our senior year we rotated to other hospitals, such as Philadelphia General Hospital and Germantown Hospital. Woman's Medical College had a rather small hospital and did not have interns, so we senior students got a lot of hands-on experience. We charted our patients' histories while the resident wrote up the physical exam. We assisted in surgery too, mainly holding the retractors and maybe cutting off the ends of sutures used in the operation.

We had regular lectures late in the afternoon during our clinical years, but we were glad not to have as many exams. We were kept busy. Some of our clinical assignments were more interesting than others. Most of our professors and teachers were really good and made their material interesting. I especially enjoyed working with the professors and resident physicians in Obstetrics-Gynecology (OB-GYN). I remember how impressed I was when Dr. Elizabeth Laufer, one of the OB residents, complimented me on the running notes I took on a patient in labor who had some complications. I documented the various events that culminated in a Cesarean section and the birth of a healthy infant for the pleased mother and OB staff.

During the summer before my senior year, I received a ten-week externship at the Eastern Pennsylvania Psychiatric Institute (EPPI), which was next door to the medical school. It offered a good stipend and was a great introduction to working with psychiatric patients. There were five or six of us Woman's Medical students at EPPI that summer; some worked with outpatients, but I worked with inpatients under the supervision of their resident-in-training. I did several admission histories and interviewed the patients regularly to monitor their progress. Thorazine had just become available to treat schizophrenia. I enjoyed listening to case presentations and various group discussions. I explored the Institute's library and did some reading. (Years later I would return to psychiatry after spending my earlier years in surgery and OB-GYN.)

During medical school, we students had a couple of major decisions to make. Where did we want to do our internship? Did we want a rotating internship, in which we would spend time in all of the major specialties? Or did we want a straight internship in the specialty we already planned to pursue? Because I felt I would be serving overseas and need to treat a variety of medical conditions, I easily opted for a rotating internship. I visited LGH, where a number of EMC graduates had interned. There I met only staff physicians and none of their interns or residents. The stipend was the standard $200 per month, plus room and board. And the interns were expected to work every other night and on alternate weekends from Saturday morning to Monday evening. I then scheduled a visit to Chester County Hospital (CCH) in West Chester. After I met the administrator and learned that the stipend was $350 per month and that the on-call schedule was every third night and third weekend, one of the current interns, Dr. Robert Hanna, was invited in to meet me. The administrator then excused himself and let the two us talk privately in his office. Dr. Hanna freely shared his happiness with his internship at CCH and answered several questions for me. Afterward, I submitted my application to be matched for a rotating internship at CCH. Some weeks later, when the results arrived, I was pleased to learn that I was going to CCH, which was only about twenty miles from my home.

The other major decision was whether I wanted to take the national board exam or the Pennsylvania state board exam to practice medicine. The national exam was given in three sections: after the second year of medical school, after the fourth year of medical school, and after the internship. It was longer than the state exam, requiring two days for each section. And the cost was considerably higher. The state exam was given all at once over two days near the end of the internship, with one major medical specialty examined in each portion of the test. I opted for the state exam, to be given in Philadelphia in June 1961. By the time the exam was over, I felt it was mostly a requirement for licensure in Pennsylvania and not really designed to eliminate candidates from medical practice. The questions on the OB-GYN exam in particular were straightforward and I felt I knew the correct answer in every case. Though I was not completely confident in some of the other specialties, I did feel I had done my best and was not worried that I had failed any of the exams. Some weeks later I received a letter stating that I had been approved to practice medicine in the state of Pennsylvania.

As our senior year in medical school drew to a close, we had to face a number of final exams. Some of them were written, but others were oral exams. I vividly remember what urology professor Dr. Stanford Mulholland said when I entered the room: "Well, I will try one more time and see if *you* can answer my question correctly." I sat quietly and waited. Then he asked, "What is a hydrocele?" I drew in a deep breath, then slowly said, "A hydrocele is an enclosed sac attached along the spermatic cord and filled with clear fluid." He was satisfied with my answer and soon excused me. Next I faced one of the OB staff and was asked what should be done if a patient has just delivered her infant and continues to bleed excessively. I gave an answer, but afterward I remembered that I had left out an important part, which left me feeling rather unhappy and concerned about what my final OB grade would be. But the following day, all of us senior students were relieved to learn that we had passed our exams.

The next thing on our schedule was an overnight bus trip to New York City. We could take along a family member or friend, so I invited Esther Stover to go with me. After lunch we had the afternoon free to shop or see the sights. Esther and I met up with Mabel Herr, who was living in New York City at that time, and she took us to some of the Mennonite worship centers in the city, then to Chinatown, and then to the tip of Manhattan, where we hopped onto the ferry and rode past the Statue of Liberty to Staten Island. I was very impressed that the fare was only a nickel per person one way. When we got to Staten Island, we went through the turnstile, turned around, put in another nickel, and rode back to Manhattan. We had a lovely buffet meal at our hotel and then walked a short block to Radio City, where *Pollyanna* was playing. We found our seats, up in the balcony, before the previous show was finished. Thus we saw Pollyanna fall out of the tree before we saw the beginning of the movie. But it was a delightful story, with many good moral themes in it.

The next morning our bus took us northwest into the New York countryside to visit the Lederle Company, where they showed us their production lines for an array of vitamins and pharmaceuticals. At the end of the tour, they provided each of us with a box of samples of some of their products. After lunch, the bus took us further west, to Suffern, where our destination was atop a hill that looked like a big, upside-down ice cream cone with a narrow road curled around it. Our bus seemed to have difficulty climbing that road, so some of us got out and walked the rest of the way. When we got to the top, most of our group ordered alcoholic beverages, but some of us instead drank sodas as we sat on the veranda until dinnertime. After dinner, we climbed back into our bus, and most of our group slept during the long ride back to Philadelphia. So now you know a little about how the drug companies try to woo doctors into prescribing their particular drugs for their patients! They provide not only drug samples but also meals and entertainment (though perhaps there is more government control of some of these methods nowadays).

Now the only thing left was to have our graduation ceremony and receive our diplomas. The ceremony was held in an auditorium at the University of Pennsylvania. The speaker was a well-known OB-GYN doctor. We then marched forward to receive our diplomas and our hoods. Afterward, we met out front with our families and friends to receive their congratulations and be photographed. My group—which included Helen King from Virginia and Edna Detweiler from Sellersville, Pennsylvania—then went to a park in Germantown for a picnic, where I received gifts and good wishes. My great aunt Barbie Lantz, who had been so supportive of me, did not feel able to come from her home in Warminster, Pennsylvania, but she sent along her good wishes. ✝

My Internship Year at Chester County Hospital

I could now enjoy several weeks at home before my internship started. I probably mowed the yard and helped some in the garden. I maybe even volunteered to cultivate some corn with our John Deere B tractor. I kept my medical texts and black bag packed and ready to go. The day soon came for me to begin my role as a new and still very inexperienced doctor.

My internship year began on Friday, July 1, 1960. Dad must have driven me to West Chester, because I had not yet purchased my own set of wheels. I'm not sure if I arrived the afternoon before or checked in that morning. At any rate, I unloaded my books and belongings at a house several blocks from the hospital, where I was to live with three of the nursing school instructors. After I got my first paycheck, I bought a 1951 two-tone Chevrolet from a friend. Then I could easily go home on the weekends when I wasn't on call.

The first person I met when I arrived at the hospital was Charlotte, the switchboard operator, and she promptly told me how to get to the medical library for our intern orientation meeting. There I was introduced to Adam Brown, a graduate of a Nashville medical school, and John Hesson, who came from the West, maybe Missouri or Kansas. Also present were two other men (Igor Islamoff and Dr. Nabi, the latter from Pakistan or Africa) who had already completed their internships and were there to do more surgical work. One day Dr. Nabi invited me to come with him to the library, where he pulled a spool of thread, a straight needle, and a patch of cloth from his pocket. He proceeded to thread the needle and push it through the cloth; then he showed me how to tie a square knot. I don't know if my dad ever used a square knot when he was working around the farm, such as when he tied my new swing to the pole in the trees in front of our house, or when he spliced together two heavy ropes. But as an intern I learned how to make a square knot that does not slip like a granny knot often does.

There were four or five of us "house staff." The hospital had also hired some residents from the Philadelphia area to "moonlight" so that our on-call schedule—every third night and every third weekend—could remain intact.

We were given our on-call assignments for the month of July, and I started on Monday, July 4. As other holidays came along, for some strange reason my name landed on Labor Day and Christmas (though not Thanksgiving, because I had a trip planned with my parents). I don't know who made the schedules, but eventually I asked why I was "privileged" to work all the holidays and the men got off. After that I finally got several holidays off.

The first clinical service I was assigned to was the emergency room. The nurses in the ER were very helpful, but I felt very "green" facing an array of medical problems. One evening, for example, an ambulance squad brought in an accident victim and, before we could examine him, a middle-aged member of the squad collapsed onto the floor and died of an apparent heart attack! This was before modern resuscitation methods were available to restart a heart quickly. I also vividly remember a family from Ohio that was in a car crash on the Pennsylvania turnpike and the car burned. The rear passengers got out safely, but the mother, who was sitting in the front passenger seat, died several days later from her burns, and the driver did not get out of the car alive. One of the woman's sons was in the military and overseas. The Red Cross called to ask if they should help the son come home, and I said, "By all means; she will not likely survive."

I don't remember how many beds the hospital had—maybe two hundred. Two house staff were assigned for each night. Until midnight, both of us accepted calls, one in the ER and the other in-house. Then one person took all calls from midnight to 4:00 A.M. and the other from 4:00 A.M. to 8:00 A.M. That way we each got some uninterrupted sleep.

Our night calls included patients who did not have a private obstetrician. I used to have a notebook with a record of all the babies I delivered that year, but in one of my downsizing blitzes I unfortunately threw it away. My memory, however, is that I delivered around one hundred babies during my internship year. And I really came to enjoy working with the OB-GYN staff, and with the mothers and babies.

Initially when I was on night-call duty I was told that I could sleep up in a tower where the male house staff also slept during their hours on call. Well, it was not private enough up there for my taste. I could always hear when the phone rang for someone else, and overhear that person's side of the conversation. I also did not enjoy taking a shower in male quarters. I don't remember who I shared this with, but maybe it was Charlotte. In any case, at some point I was offered an empty room in the student nurses' dormitory, and that suited me just fine, even if I did have to walk outside for a hundred feet or so on my way to and from the hospital during the night.

I don't remember much about the medical service but one day as I admitted a man and took his history, I learned that he was a heavy smoker. In those days we were not so aware of the health consequences of heavy smoking, but I did comment to him on the financial costs—about $200 a year in 1960. He was taken aback, and some days later when I happened to see him again he said, "Hey, Doc. Guess what: I've quit smoking. I can use that money for other things—for my family."

I also spent two months working in surgery and found it very enjoyable. Most of the surgeons were very competent and enjoyed teaching the house staff. One day I was with Dr. Tyson as he was performing thyroid surgery and he decided to quiz me about something—maybe where the nerves go around the thyroid gland. Anyway, I hedged a bit and admitted my limited knowledge. He responded, "Doctor, don't you know that our hospital protocol says that if the surgeon becomes unable to complete the operation, the assistant is expected to complete the procedure?" My calm reply was, "Well, I guess they forgot to show me that page when I asked to come here as an intern!" After we had completed the procedure, the male nurse anesthetist approached me and said with a chuckle, "You gave him the right answer!" I assisted Dr. Tyson with many more major surgeries after that as well.

The pediatrics department was rather small and I was not keenly involved in it. I was put off that the chief of pediatrics would countersign each of my orders, even if it was only for some routine lab work. But I was pleased when a lad of maybe five or six years came in for an inguinal hernia repair. His mother had signed a permit to repair a hernia on one side. After completing the patient's history, I examined him and discovered that he actually had a smaller hernia on the opposite side too. So I called his surgeon, then got his mother to sign a new permission form to repair both hernias.

In addition to having rotations in the major specialty fields of medicine, I got to spend a month in the laboratory, where many medical tests were done to clarify patients' state of health and treatment needs. I spent another month in the X-ray department, looking at many X-rays with the radiologist and following the technician to see how the X-rays were made. I also spent a month with the anesthesia staff, learning how they evaluated a patient prior to surgery and sitting with the anesthetist when anesthesia was induced and during the operation.

My room in the house I shared with several of the nursing school instructors was at the back of the house on the second-floor. Middle-aged Miss Wildonger was in the room across the hall. Miss Arabella Coble, matriarch of the nurses, was the oldest—probably in her seventies—but still quite spry and jovial. Miss Noga, who was in charge of the maternity unit, was younger, built tall and large, and what she said was what went. Nancy Maxton, who was quite young, completed our group. We got along well and even went to a Phillies game together at Philadelphia's Shibe Park.

So it was a good year with lots of new friends and good experiences in caring for a diverse group of patients. ✝

Trip to Colorado

My yearlong internship officially ended on the last day of June 1961. Interns did not typically get a vacation, but I asked for two weeks off to travel with my parents and sister Ruthie to visit Dad's uncle D. Parke Lantz and his wife, Lillie, in Sarasota, Florida. I agreed to work two extra weeks in July 1961 to make up the time.

Uncle Parke and Aunt Lillie had served four terms in Argentina (from 1921 to 1946) with the MBMC, and had assisted in Spain during two of their furloughs. They had also worked in a Spanish mission in Chicago for several years before retiring to Sarasota in the early 1950s. In 1947 they attended a Lantz family reunion hosted by Uncle Parke's younger sister, Barbara Lantz, but otherwise we did not see them very often.

Dad had never been to Florida and we were all looking forward to the trip, but several weeks before our planned departure we learned that, due to Uncle Parke's fragile health, the MBMC had decided to transfer them to La Junta, Colorado, where they could receive needed nursing care. Aunt Lillie had been diabetic for a number of years and used insulin, and Uncle Parke had become unable to walk and needed an indwelling urinary catheter. We decided to visit them anyway, for what would doubtless be the last time.

We had invited Anna Mary to go along with us, but she was a senior at LMS and felt she should not take off two weeks of school. So, reluctantly we went without her. Ruthie was a good traveler and seemed to enjoy the trip despite her severe Down syndrome. We tried not to take her into public places, where she would feel uncomfortable when strangers stared at her.

When we studied maps, we noticed that La Junta is at about the same latitude as Lancaster County, but the altitude is higher. We decided to go in November anyway and hoped we would escape any snow or bad weather. We also decided to stick with our plan to visit Dad's cousin Aquila Stoltzfus and his family on the northwestern tip of North Carolina. They were having special services at their church that week and we planned to attend the Friday evening service.

Mother's diary shows that we began our trip at noon on Thursday, November 3, 1960, and spent our first night at Harrisonburg, Virginia. I attended the premedical students' monthly meeting at EMC that evening and spent the night with Pinky Morrow. The next morning we visited Pinky's parents before heading on to North Carolina. Before we got to Mountain City, Tennessee, we stopped along a country road, where I pulled out our Coleman one-burner gas stove. I had placed a tin sheet around three sides to improve the heat by shielding it from the wind. (Later models of Coleman camp stoves have two burners and adjustable metal wings on three sides to do what my metal sheets did for our stove.) Because there was no picnic table nearby, I parked the stove on the ground behind the car, then opened a can of vegetable soup and heated it for our supper. It was dark when we finally pulled into the yard of the Big Fork Mennonite Church an hour later and joined in their service. We spent the night with Aquila and his family and had a lovely visit with them the next day before leaving after the noon meal. We headed south and west across the mountains toward Knoxville and found a motel near Concord, Tennessee.

On Sunday morning, November 6, we located the Concord Mennonite Church, where Dad's great-grandfather Tennessee John Stoltzfus and five of his children had lived. Dad and I went in for Sunday school while Mother sat in the car with Ruthie. Then I sat with Ruthie while Mother went to the church service. William Jennings, the pastor of this church for many years and a well-known Mennonite evangelist, preached that morning. Afterward, the David Yoder family invited us to their home for dinner before we continued our journey, and my parents accepted. We spent Sunday night in a motel in western Tennessee.

Monday, November 7, was Ruthie's fifteenth birthday. We spent the day driving north into Kentucky and west across the Mississippi River into the rolling hills of Missouri. That night we stayed in an "old-time motel" at Lamar, Missouri.

On Tuesday morning we were on the road by 7:10 Eastern Standard Time. As we progressed into Kansas, the countryside became more flat. This was the prairie, with its forlorn windmills and rolling tumbleweeds that crashed onto our 1957 Ford without causing any damage. We must have covered about five hundred miles of open country that day. We met little traffic and saw very few people, but we passed through an occasional small town with its tall grain elevators.

After we entered Colorado, we began to see more hills, and at 6:00 P.M. we finally reached the town of La Junta. We contacted Pastor Paul H. Martin, who told us about a local motel that provided cooking facilities. Despite its small size, the room with two double beds was adequate for our short stay. After Mother fixed a simple meal, she and Dad made a brief visit to Uncle Parke and Aunt Lillie to let them know we had arrived. I stayed at the motel with Ruthie.

Tuesday, November 8, was also a special day, because it was Election Day and John Kennedy and Richard Nixon were in a tight presidential race. Our room had a TV, so I watched the election reports that evening until Mother and Dad returned and got ready for bed. I knew the results would not be finalized for a number of hours because the race was so close, so I soon went to bed with Ruthie. On Wednesday morning, Nixon was shown on TV decrying the election outcome.

Dad and Mother went to visit Uncle Parke and Aunt Lillie that morning, then found a store and bought some groceries. Mother and I went to visit Aunt Lillie in the afternoon while Dad stayed at the motel with Ruthie. On Thursday morning, Dad and I went together to visit Uncle Parke. That afternoon, Mary Petersheim invited Mary Erb and I to go for a drive to the west, to the Spanish Peaks. We stopped at a town at the base of the mountains and enjoyed a "spot of tea," drove south to the next town, and completed the triangle on our way back to La Junta, a trip totaling a hundred miles of open space in our country's western plains.

Meanwhile, Mother, Dad, and Ruthie went to the turkey processing plant to see a man they knew, Paul Hershey. They also called on J. W. and Salina Shank, who had served in Argentina with Uncle Parke and Aunt Lillie. Dad and I visited Aunt Lillie that evening while Mother stayed with Ruthie at the motel. Thus it went, with each of us taking our turn staying with Ruthie at the motel the next day as well.

We had planned to leave La Junta on Saturday, November 12, so we checked out of the motel that morning and loaded everything into the car. As we drove up to the hospital for the last time, I told Mother and Dad that I would stay with Ruthie in the car while they went in together first to say good-bye to Uncle Parke and Aunt Lillie. When they returned, I went in by myself. I don't remember what I shared with Aunt Lillie, but I clearly remember talking to Uncle Parke about my sense of being called to serve somewhere overseas as a missionary doctor, and that I had already made contact with both the MBMC at Elkhart, Indiana, and the EMBMC at Salunga, Pennsylvania. He affirmed me in this call. He also offered some precious advice: that a missionary is more effective when he or she cultivates a "teachable spirit" and is gentle in interpersonal relationships. I thanked him for his encouragement and for his prayer support. I always felt that Uncle Parke was a real prayer warrior on my behalf, especially after I first revealed to them my sense that I had been called, before I even began high school. Uncle Parke's younger sister, Aunt Barbie Lantz, was another precious relative whom I knew really prayed for me as well.

As we headed east from La Junta across Kansas, I watched the evening sky get darker while the sun got lower behind us in the southwest. I watched the shadow of our car get larger on my left and then—behold! The sun was shining beneath and beyond our car—making a complete shadow of it run along right beside us! It was fascinating to watch the dusky sky rise before us like a dark wall while the sunlight was still beneath and beside us. It was a very beautiful, long twilight.

It was dark when we arrived in Newton, Kansas, and found a nice motel, where we got two rooms that shared a bathroom. It was much more comfortable than our cramped motel in La Junta. But the back parking lot was very well lit and the motel's windows seemed to let in all the light, so Ruthie thought it was daylight and not the time to sleep. I put her into the double bed with me, but she climbed out, so I put her back in and put my arms around her. But though she was shorter than me, she was a strong sister, so I closed my hands around her and tried to keep her in the bed. I'm not sure who won that tussle or who fell asleep first. I do know that we were both rather tired the next morning. That was the only problem we had with her the whole trip.

On Sunday morning, November 13, we drove to nearby Hesston College to attend its worship service. Dad and I went to the Sunday school class, then I sat with Ruthie in the car while Mother attended the worship service with Dad. Don Augsburger preached that morning. Afterward, when Mother and Dad returned to our car, an older couple was with them. Mother introduced them as John and Florence Cooprider Friesen. They were inviting us to have the noon meal with them and Mother wanted to know if I wanted to go. I recognized their names and knew they had served as missionaries in India under the MBMC. I also knew that Mrs. Friesen was a medical doctor, and perhaps also a graduate of Woman's Medical College. But I was unsure whether Mother and Dad wanted to go with them, so I tried to punt the decision back to them. I would have enjoyed spending some time with the Friesens, but we declined their invitation.

In retrospect, I don't know if my parents knew that the Friesens were missionaries and that Mrs. Friesen was a doctor. I don't know how much they spoke together before coming out to our car. Did the Friesens know that I too was a doctor? Was it just standard practice for them to invite visitors to share the noon meal at their home on Sundays? Maybe I was thinking about getting on to Kalona, Iowa. This was just another situation when *if* I'd had more time to think the situation through, I might have responded differently. It was too awkward to discuss the invitation in front of the Friesens, and I somehow felt that Mother preferred not to go but wanted me to make the decision. A week earlier, when we were at Concord, Tennessee, she and Dad had decided to accept a dinner invitation without consulting me, and I had been OK with that. So why did they put the decision in my lap this time? Basically, Mother was the decision maker in our family, and Dad had little problem with following her wishes, except when she was depressed.

So we had lunch elsewhere, then drove northward into Missouri. At Cameron we found an "old-fashioned motel," as Mother wrote in her diary. She was "glad to get out of that noisy place." It seems I was not the only one not impressed by that motel, for I don't remember anything at all about it.

On Monday, November 14, we kept going north and got to Kalona by early afternoon. Twice we stopped by the home of Chris Nafziger, but they were not there. Chris had family members in Ontario as well as in Lancaster County, so it was disappointing not to make contact with them. We did have a very nice visit with my EMC friend Martha Bender's parents and her sister Elva. The Benders were very special people. Martha's father, Harvey Bender, was a man of God who shared his faith with others. He corresponded regularly with some prisoners. Eventually the Amish church wearied of his witnessing and made things unpleasant enough that he became a member of the Mennonite Church, though he really would have preferred to remain with the Amish. He had two single daughters, Elva and Martha, plus some married children. After a delightful but all too brief visit, we got back on the road and headed east toward northwestern Illinois.

We crossed the Mississippi River and continued east in Illinois for thirty miles to the city of Sterling, where Dad had a cousin on his maternal grandmother's side named Leslie Breitweiser. He was a cousin to Uncle Parke and Aunt Barbie Lantz too. We had a nice visit with him and his family that evening, and later they showed us to a motel where we spent the night.

On Tuesday, November 15, we awoke to rain and thunder. Even after the rain stopped, the weather was cloudy all day. Sterling, Illinois, was one hundred miles west of Chicago on Route 30 and the toll road and turnpike system that would take us to Goshen, Indiana, and onward to Scottdale, Pennsylvania, and home. I knew that our route went through Wheaton, Illinois, and I wanted to show my folks the Wheaton College campus, where I had attended a Christian Medical Society convention in late December 1959. (At least a thousand medical students and doctors from all over the country and from many foreign countries had participated, and there had been excellent speakers, such as A. W. Tozer.) I drove us around the campus, then got back on the main street to continue eastward toward Chicago.

Before we could get out of town, a driver behind me stepped on the gas to pass me and hit our left tail light. I stopped and so did the other car. The driver apologized, saying that she had just recently bought the car and was not yet accustomed to its faster response to the gas pedal. We exchanged the pertinent information. At that point we were not aware of any damages or injuries aside from the broken left tail light.

We proceeded on to Goshen without further incident. First we visited Mae Hershey, widow of T. K. Hershey. Mae was a cousin of Dad's; they were both descendants of Tennessee John Stoltzfus. The Hersheys had also been missionaries in Argentina with J. W. Shanks and Uncle Parke and Aunt Lillie, so Mae appreciated hearing about our trip to Colorado. We then went to the home of Levi and Fanny Peachy Miller. Fanny was another good friend of mine from EMC days. She took us to meet Levi's parents that evening. Dad also telephoned another Levi Miller, whom he had known from his youth, when Levi lived in Lancaster County and traveled around with the same group of young people. We spent the night with Fanny and Levi.

On Wednesday, November 16, we drove to the Scottdale area. We went to the motel at Laurelville Mennonite Camp and fixed our evening meal. Then Mother and I drove north to Greensburg Hospital and paged Dr. Eva Stremp, a good friend of mine from Woman's Medical College. Eva was on call, so we waited a while until she appeared. We talked and compared notes on our internships and our thoughts about what would follow. She wanted to get some training in surgery, and I was not yet clear about where I would be going after internship. She showed us around some areas of the hospital. We finally got back to Laurelville at about 11:00 P.M. As expected, Ruthie and Dad were not yet asleep, because Ruthie was waiting for Mother and me to come to bed too.

On the morning of Thursday, November 17, we stopped at the home of Ted and Catherine Morrow in Scottdale. Ted was at work at the Mennonite Publishing House, but Catherine wanted us to stay for lunch. She was kept busy with three preschoolers: Joey was four-plus years of age, Alice was just about to turn three, and Mary was going on two. Ted did come home for lunch. Mother and I washed the dishes afterward, before setting out on the final leg of our trip. We arrived home at Gap at around 6:00 P.M.

As I wrote earlier, Mother had done some traveling in her youth—working in Venice, Florida, one winter and in Wildwood, New Jersey, for a summer, and going to Ontario, Canada, for a wedding. But Dad had not really traveled except to attend the same wedding in Canada. So this two-week trip to Colorado to visit Uncle Parke and Aunt Lillie was a special trip for all of us. And I still wish Anna Mary would have gone along. ✢

Preparation for Overseas Service

My internship officially ended on June 30, 1961, but I owed CCH two weeks for the trip to Colorado, and I had also arranged to have two weeks off to prepare for my next assignment. So after the internship "ended," I returned to the hospital for four more weeks before I said good-bye to all my friends there.

The first thing I had done after graduation from medical school was spend several days in the school's library researching sources for a special project of Dr. Oesterling, one of the biochemistry professors. I had worked as a student monitor in the library some weekends during my senior year, and that had led to the research job.

When I finished that project, I traveled to the Christopher Dock Mennonite High School campus in Lansdale, Pennsylvania, to attend the annual meeting of the MBMC for several days. I enjoyed the sessions, met many old friends, including a college roommate, and made some new friends too. I had submitted an application to the MBMC, because it was still unclear to me where or with which mission board God was leading me to serve. I had also signed up for lodging with a family for several nights. I was pleasantly surprised to discover that my roommate was the wife of Dr. H. Clair Amstutz, a well-known Mennonite physician who also wrote medical articles for one of our Mennonite publications. He was unable to attend the mission meeting. The next morning, as we were getting dressed, she said, "I can't wait to tell my husband that I slept with another doctor last night!"

I had also submitted an application to the EMBMC before I started my internship. And I had written a letter to my great aunt Barbie Lantz to tell her about these steps I had taken. One morning less than a month after my graduation from medical school, God had silently taken Aunt Barbie to be with Him. I went with my family to her funeral in the chapel at Christ's Home in Warminster, where Aunt Barbie had worked from late 1915 until her death. After her body was laid to rest in the Christ's Home cemetery, a number of her female colleagues escorted us to the building where the single ladies lived, on the second floor, above the boys' kitchen and dining room and the main office. They took us to the room that had been home to Aunt Barbie and invited us to take whatever we wanted of the things she had left behind. She had a secretary desk, which contained some recent letters and some books and other reading material. Her favorite poem, "Have You Considered Him?" was hanging in a frame inside the door. I don't remember what things my parents selected to take home, but I do remember that I timidly approached her desk and looked through the letters, and when I saw the one I had so recently sent her, I quickly returned it to the pile and stepped back from the desk. I guess my first thought was gratitude to know that she had received my last letter, and I'm sure she spoke to God about it. Afterward, however, I wished that I had kept it for myself. I don't know if the Christ Home ladies retrieved the letters before the desk was accepted by one of my uncles.

The ladies then took us to the attic, where a closet contained some of Aunt Barbie's clothing. Because Aunt Barbie was short and built somewhat like me, I did look closely at her dresses and selected two of them. One was a flowered blue dress with long sleeves that she had worn the last time she visited us. The other was a summer dress, violet with small flowers and short sleeves. I kept those dresses for many years and wore them on special occasions in memory of her. But finally, before my move to Landis Homes, when I felt pressured to downsize, I parted with them, and now I wonder why I did not keep them. I guess this is just another example of the fact that when I make a decision without really thinking through the results beforehand, afterward I often end up wishing that I had done things differently. When I mull over a situation first, I can then speak or do what I really want, and feel satisfied afterward with the outcome.

At some point after I had submitted my applications, I was invited to the headquarters of the EMBMC for an interview with some Lancaster Conference ministers and bishops. As I mentioned earlier, Martin Kraybill was one of those present and he informed the group that he had known me since I made my public commitment to Christ when he was conducting evangelistic meetings at my home church. I was asked about my stance on the matter of plain dress. I replied that it was not a problem for me, that in fact I had worn my plain attire during medical school when I was not wearing a white uniform. But I also said that I did not see plain attire as essential, especially for those of non-Mennonite backgrounds, and I would hesitate to push for adherence to this way of dressing.

As the months of my internship rolled by, I was asked by my colleagues and friends what I was planning to do afterward, and I kept saying that I was not sure yet. Then, in the early spring of 1961, I got a letter from Elkhart, Indiana, telling me that the MBMC was in need of a doctor in West Africa. The position was described as new medical work in a needy area, and they asked if I was available. Well, this put me in a quandary, for inwardly I was hoping that I might serve with the EMBMC, for several reasons. For example, it was based in the Lancaster Conference, which was my home area, whereas Elkhart was five hundred miles to the west. Also, I had a hunch that some of the home folks would be less supportive of me if I were serving with the western board, which some perceived to be less conservative than the Lancaster Conference. But because Uncle Parke and Aunt Lillie Lantz had served in Argentina for many years under the Elkhart mission board, I was open to considering it as a second option. I had attended some of the Elkhart board's meetings, such as an annual board meeting at nearby Maple Grove Church in 1947, and its missionary conference at Laurelville in the late 1950s. But when the letter inviting me to go to West Africa arrived, suddenly I was not at all sure that this was what God wanted me to do. Perhaps I thought God would send me as he had sent Ida Scudder, to India, where women were not permitted to receive medical examinations and care from male physicians because of the country's caste system. After all, the Elkhart board had been sending missionaries to India since 1899; the first had been Jacob A. Ressler and Dr. William B. Page and his wife, Alice Thut. So I began to really pray that God would show me more clearly what his plan was for me.

Meanwhile, I had heard nothing whatsoever from the EMBMC. I continued to pray, but I don't remember discussing this situation with anyone else, not even my parents. Several weeks passed and I felt embarrassed that I had not yet responded to Elkhart. I finally sat down and worked at composing a letter. It was one of the most difficult letters I had ever written, because I was not at peace about it. But I let myself be pressured by the medical needs of West Africa and the fact that there was no doctor yet for this new medical program. I did want to be of help, but I was concerned that I had just completed my internship and was not very experienced in the practice of medicine, especially in the treatment of parasitic infestations and tropical illnesses. Maybe I was too ready to help despite not being adequately trained to deal with the particular medical situations I would encounter. Anyway, I finished my letter by saying that I was willing to do what I could in this needy area of Africa. I read it over several times and made some changes before I made a final copy and put it in an envelope.

The next morning I sealed the envelope, put it in my coat pocket, and walked up to the hospital. I opened the front door and walked over to the big mailbox in the foyer. I was ready to pull the letter out of my pocket and put it in the box when an inner voice said, "Leave it in your pocket." So, I did. Later that morning when I checked my own mailbox, I found a heavy envelope from the EMBMC, and immediately I heaved a big sigh of relief that God had stopped me from mailing that letter to Elkhart. God wasn't late! I waited to read my Salunga letter until I had finished work for the day and was back in my room. ✝

Mother Is Depressed Again

Mother had made a good recovery from her bout of depression and had done well since then in caring for Ruthie's needs. In the spring of 1949, when I was a sophomore in high school, she had tolerated major surgery without incident. And she continued to do well during my four and a half years in college and during my four years of medical school.

A number of weeks after we returned from Colorado, Mother revealed that she was not sleeping well and was sometimes awake for several hours during the night. So Dad took her to Dr. Beacher and he discovered that she was having pain in her neck and left shoulder. He examined her and diagnosed it as a whiplash injury from that bump to our car some weeks earlier. I do not remember what he prescribed for her. Did we have muscle relaxants back then? I do remember that Mother was also seen by a doctor in a small town northwest of Lancaster, because I drove her there a time or two. I don't know whether he used "talk therapy" or medication or both.

I know that Mother was depressed for quite a while after that, and somehow I was a contributing factor. I was an intern trying to figure out what I would be doing the following year, and Mother apparently had her own dream, that I would be a doctor on Gap Hill and that she would set up one of our front rooms as my office. A mutual friend relayed this information to me some ten years later, and I was aghast at the very idea, for I had never in my wildest dreams thought of opening an office on Gap Hill. Mother clearly knew of my call to be a medical missionary, but I guess in her depression she was hoping that I would stay nearby to be *her* doctor.

When I received word from the EMBMC in the spring of 1961 that they had a need for me in Tanganyika, I did not hide my plans from my parents. Dad was very supportive, but when Mother was depressed she wanted to lean on someone. I clearly remember an episode, maybe in July 1961, when Mother was again leaning on me as she said, "The people at Salunga probably don't even know I'm sick or they wouldn't ask you to go to Africa." I replied as gently as I could, "But Mother, I have told Paul Kraybill about your illness." She did not say any more, but she continued to be depressed. Meanwhile, I packed my barrels and went to Tanganyika in October 1961.

Maybe that sounds like I was running away from Mother's illness and problems. Anna Mary had just graduated from LMS in 1961 and was still living at home. Brother Paul was married and living nearby. Brother Nate was married and living on what had been Grandpap's farm, the farm where I was born. So it was basically Dad, Anna Mary, and my brothers who had to deal with Mother's illness in my absence. And Ruthie needed supervision too. So Anna Mary helped out a lot at home the first year I was in Africa, but at some point she needed a change of scenery, so she got a job at Ezra Martin Meats in Bridgeport. ✠

My First Safari to East Africa

I was scheduled to leave by plane for Africa in mid-September 1961. But several days before our planned departure, I was informed that my medical degree and credentials had not yet been approved by the Tanganyika government, which was necessary for me to practice medicine in their country, so the mission board had not yet received clearance for me to go. Well, it was no problem for me to find more things to do while I waited. During that time I visited at least one school to share my story about my call to become a doctor and go to Africa.

Several weeks later, on Monday, October 1, 1961, I received a blue airmail letter from Dar es Salaam that said my credentials had been approved. When I called Paul Kraybill with this information, he told me that Harold and Connie Stauffer would be flying to Nairobi, Kenya, on Thursday of that week en route to Somalia and he asked if the mission board should get me a seat on the same flight. I knew both Harold and Connie from my days at LMS as well as from my orientation in Salunga, so I eagerly said yes! I would *not* have enjoyed making my first overseas *safari* (trip) by myself (though I did eventually fly across the Atlantic alone four times during my second tour of overseas service).

Despite the short notice, I was able to charter a Blue Line bus in West Chester to take many of my relatives and friends along to New York to see me off. We met the bus at Maple Grove Mennonite Church on the morning of October 4. We stopped to pick up another cousin at the end of a nearby farm lane, and two more friends at the Speedy King Laundry on the Lincoln Highway in Frazer. We ate our packed lunches in the bus on the New Jersey Turnpike and arrived at New York's Idlewild Airport by 4:00 P.M.

The driver took us to the proper terminal and we all went inside. We found a counter for checking in my luggage, except for my carry-on stuff. A lightweight suitcase carried most of my clothes and my compact but trusty Hermes Rocket typewriter. I also checked in a small bag that held my shoes and additional clothing. I would have to make these supplies suffice for a number of months until my barrels arrived, so I had tried to plan carefully. I carried on a briefcase that contained my essential books, a purse with a long shoulder strap, and my Argus C4 camera, also on a strap that crossed from my right shoulder to the left side of my body. In addition, I carried on another camera, with its strap riding over my left shoulder, for LeRoy Petersheim, who

had gone to Tanganyika before me and asked me to bring a few things along for him. So I was "loaded," with my purse and one camera on my left side, my briefcase in my right hand, and the other camera on my right side.

I quickly found Harold and Connie Stauffer sitting with some of their family members and friends. It was soon time to say our good-byes and find our seats on the BOAC (British Overseas Airways Corporation) plane. BOAC served most of the world except for areas of the USSR, China, and the northern countries Norway, Sweden, and Denmark. Their fleet included the Jet-Prop Airliner, the Comet 4 Jetliner, and the Rolls-Royce 707 Jetliner. We flew on a Jet-Prop (also sometimes known as a Prop-Jet), which I think was the first of these three planes to be built. It looked like a large propeller plane, with its engines mounted above and to the front of the wings, and its propellers were visible. I am unsure how many passengers it could carry, but it had a center aisle with three seats on either side and maybe twenty-five to thirty rows of seats. In our row I was assigned to the seat nearest the window, Harold curled his long body into the middle seat, and Connie sat in the seat beside the aisle. The space between my seat and the seat in front of me was not so great, even for my short legs, so I'm sure it was uncomfortable for a tall man like Harold.

Soon one of the flight attendants gave us instructions about the seatbelts, oxygen masks, and other safety precautions, and the location of the restrooms. This was all new to me as it was my first flight in a big plane. My only other plane ride had been as a teenager, when a cousin

took me for a ten-minute ride in his biplane that had two seats open to the wind and scenery. But now I was flying in a real passenger plane.

Harold soon told me how concerned he had been when he saw a bus filled with people wearing Mennonite garb pull up outside the terminal. He was a quiet man and had not wanted a lot of fuss made about their departure. He had wondered if the people on the bus were coming to give him and Connie a surprise farewell. But when they saw me with the folks who had been on the bus, they figured it was my relatives and friends, so Harold relaxed. No one at the EMBMC had told them I would be joining them, so they were surprised anyway.

We took off from New York at around 8:00 P.M. It was dark, of course, but the lights of New York City and Long Island were something to see, as were the areas without lights, which were bodies of water. Our seats were a bit behind the doorway through which we had entered the plane, so we were well behind the wing and could "sight-see" at times. Our row was situated between windows, so by either leaning forward or reclining our seats we could see out. I explored the materials in the pocket on the back of the seat in front of me and appropriated a folder that showed the BOAC air routes to many parts of the world. According to this folder we were traveling at 415 miles per hour at nineteen thousand feet.

At 9:00 P.M. the airline staff served us a tasty dinner that included chicken and sweet potato. It was somewhat like a TV dinner but the food was in containers that had straight edges at least an inch high. We each lowered a platform from the seat in front of us to hold our trays. After dinner I was able to relax and dozed off.

The next thing I knew it was getting light outside, but my wristwatch said it was only 2:30 A.M.! I decided not to change the time on my watch until we got to our final destination. I opened the window screen in front of us and watched as the daylight got brighter, and by 3:00 (according to my watch) we had a beautiful sunrise above all the clouds. (We were fortunate to be on the right side of the plane as we flew eastward.)

By 3:20 the crew arrived with breakfast—scrambled eggs, bacon, and cereal. I wasn't really hungry after our late dinner only six hours before and not enough sleep. An hour later, at 4:30 my time, we landed at Glasgow in "Scottish weather—mostly rain" and went through customs. We had already lost five hours. The weather was much better— clear sunshine—as we flew over England at 23,000 feet. We touched down in London at 11:45 A.M., local time. There we changed planes, so we had to accompany *all* of our luggage, not just our carry-on bags, on a cart to the new departure terminal and check it in before we went to a restaurant for our noon meal. Afterward they took us in a bus to the boarding area. They were most considerate of our weariness. We took off again at 3:40 P.M. and traveled at 315 miles per hour at 19,000 feet over mountains of clouds on our way to Rome. I slept much of the way and missed my opportunity to look down on Paris.

We arrived at the Rome airport at 7:00 P.M. British time and took off again at 7:45. At 4:25 A.M. local time we touched down in Khartoum, Sudan, and was it ever *hot*—even at such an early morning hour. I stayed on the plane. We had lost two more hours. We took off again at 5:10 A.M. and continued southward to Entebbe, near Kampala, in Uganda, arriving at 8:40 A.M. Here I saw an elderly white male, perhaps from Great Britain, barking orders at a younger black man, and I hoped that foreign domination of African countries would soon cease.

We took off again at 9:30 A.M. and flew eastward. Despite some cloudiness on the way, I got a glimpse of the vast expanse of Lake Victoria glowing in the sunshine as we completed our journey to Nairobi. We landed on Friday, October 6, at 11:00 A.M. local time, seven hours later than the time at home; we had lost five hours flying from New York to London and two hours flying from London to Nairobi. We had been in the air for a total of twenty-two hours, made four stops lasting three-quarters of an hour to an hour each, and changed planes once.

In Nairobi, Connie and Harold and I parted company. They had been directed to stay at a hotel for several days until their flight would leave for Somalia. I, meanwhile, had been instructed to go by cab to the Church Missionary Society (CMS) guesthouse, although I had no reservations, to see if they could accommodate me until I could make connections to Tanganyika, perhaps going by train to Kisumu and then by lake steamer to Musoma. But, well, God had a better plan all figured out.

When I had collected my luggage at the airport, I got a cab. The driver understood some English (which I learned after I used my one Swahili sentence, *Sifafamu Kiswashili bado,* which means "I do not yet understand Swahili"). He nodded when I asked to go to the CMS guesthouse, then took me there. Upon my arrival I asked if they had any space for me. They could accommodate me for Friday night but not for Saturday. When I went to pay the cab driver, he could not accept my US dollars, but he offered to drive me to a bank where I could exchange my dollars for East Africa shillings. I accepted. He then returned me to the guesthouse with my luggage and I paid him. A servant carried my luggage to my room. By now the noon meal was over but I was more tired than hungry anyway, so I gladly went to bed and slept soundly until 4:00 pm, when a tinkling bell announced that it was teatime. I quickly came to enjoy this African practice of afternoon siesta and tea. It is common for African folks who have a store or other business to close it down for an hour or more after the noon meal so they can rest. This African custom is especially enjoyable if it is "topped" afterward with hot tea, and maybe something in the other hand too (*chai cha mikone miwili* means "tea with a sweet treat in the other hand").

That evening after dinner, which was served somewhat later than I was accustomed to, I wasted little time getting back to bed. The next morning when I appeared for breakfast, I was surprised to see Don Jacobs and Hershey Leaman, who were also working for the EMBMC in Tanganyika. They were returning from Somalia, where their plans to work on a proposed agricultural project with Chester Kurtz and others had been dissolved by five days and five nights of rain with "wonderful" mud, washed-out bridges, and stuck caterpillar tractors. Don and Hershey had decided to postpone their project until January or February. They asked me how I was getting to Shirati, so I told them about the train-steamer idea. Well, their better idea was this: They both wanted to do some business in Nairobi, but they were not eager to stick around until the Tuesday evening train left for Kisumu (in more than three days) to connect with the lake steamer for Musoma. No, they wanted to get back to their families in Tanganyika (especially Hershey, whose wife was awaiting the birth of their first child), so why not see if the Missionary Aviation Fellowship (MAF) could fly the three of us there on Saturday afternoon? A phone call was made to MAF pilot Gordon Marshall. As it turned out, Gordon was to be on vacation for four weeks from the following Monday, but he agreed to deliver us to Shirati and Musoma that afternoon. What good timing for all of us!

On Saturday morning, Don and Hershey took me and my luggage to the New Stanley Hotel, where I waited for them to take care of their business in Nairobi. I parked myself on a bench on their outside patio and wrote my first letter home to my parents. That letter was handwritten, because I was not about to dig out my Hermes typewriter and peck away on it in a public area of downtown Nairobi. I knew that Dad would *not* enjoy reading my handwriting, but I figured they would be glad enough to get this letter and know that I was almost "home" to Shirati. Besides, it was Dad's sixty-first birthday and I wanted to let him know that I remembered that. I also told them about the flights and about the sights I saw on the way.

It was early afternoon when Don and Hershey showed up at the hotel with Gordon, who drove us out to the Wilson Airport, where the MAF parked their Cessna airplane. Gordon carefully checked everything, including our weights and the total weight of our luggage. We then taxied out to the runway, obtained clearance from the control tower—and by 1:30 P.M. we were off. The sky was clear, but we still bobbed around some. It was so neat to be flying nearer the Earth instead of nineteen thousand feet up, often above the clouds. Now I could see mountains, lakes and rivers, tea plantations, villages, houses, herds of domestic animals, and even people. We flew about three hundred miles in an hour and fifteen minutes, arriving at Lake Victoria and Shirati by 3:00 P.M. By car that trip would have taken all day, in dry weather, over mostly dirt roads. Around Nairobi, the ground had been rather dry and brown, but the rolling hills in this area of Tanganyika were vivid green because of the recent "short rains."

Gordon buzzed around the houses on the hospital compound to tell them to meet us at the airstrip. We had arrived at the end of siesta time. The mission vehicle was out on safari somewhere and the only vehicle available was an old Ford truck, or lorry, with a badly worn seat for the driver and an upside-down five-gallon plastic bucket for the passenger to sit on. So this ancient lorry came chugging down to the airstrip to meet us, with Dr. Lester Eshleman at the wheel. His wife Lois followed on her bicycle, and various local people from the nearby villages also came out to see who had arrived. Hershey's and my luggage was placed in the back of the lorry, and I accepted the passenger seat in the cab. Don and Gordon took off for Musoma to deliver Don to his family so that Gordon could fly back to Nairobi before dark. (Soon after I arrived at Shirati, that ancient Ford lorry was completely retired, and some of its truck bed was later used in a construction project at the hospital.)

After the lorry arrived on the compound, my luggage was delivered to the nurses' house, where I was to occupy the third of four bedrooms. We were then summoned to the home of Dr. Lester and his wife for *chai* (tea) to celebrate my arrival and the return of Hershey, whose wife, Norma, was so happy to have him home again. Lois told us that she had been aroused from her siesta sleep that day by a dream in which she saw a great bird using its beak to carry three people in a large *shuka* (cloth), like a stork delivering a baby. What a premonition of our arrival!

Before we had finished our tea, Dr. Lester invited me to go with him the next morning to see the hospital wards before the Sunday service.

Naturally I agreed. After the tour, I went to church with Dr. Harold Housman and he translated some of the sermon for me. After the service, he introduced me to a number of people by saying, *Jina lake ni Daktari Stoltzfus.* I began to say the same thing when I met someone new. Dr. Housman soon told me, "I use third person when I introduce you, but you should use first person when you introduce yourself, like this: *Jina lango ni Daktari Stoltzfus.*" That was my first lesson in Swahili.

The next day, Monday, Dr. Lester (who preferred handling surgeries while Dr. Housman treated the medical patients) took me along with him on his rounds. First we went to the maternity ward, where I noted the wooden delivery table and the small wooden baby beds (doubtless constructed by local carpenters). There we visited with the mothers and their infants. I was also introduced to the adult men and women patients in the hospital. But the first patients I was asked to care for were those in maternity, and that was fine by me. I needed a little time to get oriented before I accepted a lot of responsibility. I also wanted time to study Swahili. Dr. Housman and his family were preparing to go on furlough in six weeks, so I felt pressure to pick up some of his workload too.

So, here I was, in a very different world where I needed to learn a new language and become familiar with many new people. I knew I would come to see the strengths, and a few of the foibles, of my missionary colleagues. I would also, I hoped, become an effective witness for Christ to the folks among whom I now lived in this corner of Tanganyika on the shores of Lake Victoria.

Meanwhile, back at home, Mother was getting more depressed and becoming unable to manage the household and supervise Ruthie, so in 1962 she was admitted to inpatient psychiatric care at St. Joseph's Hospital in Lancaster, then transferred to Philhaven Hospital near Mount Gretna. Electroconvulsive therapy was recommended, but Mother resisted that idea and Dad wouldn't sign for it if Mother was fighting it.

Although I was on the other side of the world, I was informed of the situation. I knew if I wrote to Anna Mary at our home address, Mother would want to read what I'd written, so I sent my letters with private feelings, questions, and advice about the family's dilemma to the home of a friend of Anna Mary's. I'm not sure how much input I actually provided to the decision-making process, but while Mother was at Philhaven in the early summer, Dad and my three other siblings agreed to submit an application for Ruthie to be admitted to the Hamburg State School for intellectually handicapped children. It was not an easy decision for them to make, but Mother's doctor felt it was too much to expect Mother to recover while continuing to care constantly for Ruthie.

I do not remember whether I shared with my Shirati missionary colleagues what was going on. I did update Paul Kraybill about Mother's illness when he visited Shirati early that year, but I did not write him any follow-up letters despite his invitation to share further developments with him. I guess I did not want to add to his load of responsibility and, yes, I must admit that I did stuff my feelings and got frustrated and depressed at times. But perhaps Paul understood better than I did the source of Mother's depression and the effects that her depression could have on me and my ability to be an effective physician and Christian witness at Shirati.

When the application to Hamburg State School was accepted and the admission date set, Anna Mary packed up Ruthie's clothes. Then, on Tuesday, July 24, Dad and Anna Mary delivered Ruthie to her new abode. Dad tried to explain to Ruthie what was happening, but he did not know if she understood why he was leaving her there among strangers. I'm sure it was hard for him and Anna Mary to say good-bye. Then Dad and Anna Mary went to visit Mother at Philhaven. Mother immediately asked, "Where is Ruthie?" Dad explained that Ruthie was now at Hamburg State School. I am sure that neither Mother nor Dad felt good about not being able to provide ongoing care for Ruthie. And I know that Mother missed Ruthie and was sorry that the rest of the family had decided to place her at Hamburg.

After several courses of in-patient treatment with different medication regimes, Mother was able to return home. We all made occasional visits to Hamburg to see Ruthie. As the years rolled by, it was hard to tell how much she remembered us, but it was always good to see her and to know she had friends there and was well cared for. Several times she had health problems but recovered. At some point she tested positive for Hepatitis B, which can be a problem at this type of school, where it is a big task to monitor personal hygiene and toileting habits. ✝

Letters from East Africa

My sister Anna Mary kept some of the letters I wrote to my family from Africa, but my dad held on to the rest of them. Sometime after his death in December 1985, his desk was moved to my brother Nate's house and put in his "Heritage Room" along with other records and treasures of our family. But the contents of the desk were not explored until mid-2008, when Nate and his wife, Esther, prepared to move into a smaller home and we siblings were asked to help sort through the things in the Heritage Room. Such fun it was, and so many treasures were found, including pages of information about our dad's father, and papers on which were recorded Dad's financial affairs from the time of his marriage in 1927. But I was most pleased to find many of my old letters from Africa, just where he had put them forty plus years before.

I have used those letters to write about my years in Africa. I am grateful to have them because I had forgotten completely about some of the events they describe. I share many of them here, though I have edited them somewhat in order to make sure that the material is presented in chronological order and to include background information so that my readers can better picture what I am writing about. I have identified people and told how they fit into my story, and I have deleted a few details, such as items I wanted my sister to send, or other personal comments. I have also deleted material that I have incorporated elsewhere in the book, to cut down on repetition. And I have removed the salutations and signatures from all of the letters, to save a little space and because most of them are identical anyway. But I have remained honest about my struggles and frustrations. You will discover in these letters that I was *not* a perfect missionary by any stretch of the imagination.

Because I am a medical doctor and was sent to Africa to work in a mission hospital, I naturally included in my letters some stories about my medical work. Some of you may be uncomfortable with my descriptions of medical situations. I have tried not to elaborate too much and to spare you the goriest details of the medical procedures.

I hope these letters will help you to understand better what is involved in moving to a new country, learning a new language, facing the different mores of a new culture, adjusting to a different climate, and accepting the fact that sometimes the host culture has some values that are superior to one's own and can teach one a few things. Also, remember that since I lived there in the early 1960s, Africa has made much progress, such as better communication through cell phones, and improved roads and transportation systems. May you find as much enjoyment in reading these letters as I found in rereading them and in the process reliving so many of the experiences I had in Africa.

Sunday, October 8, 1961

My first letter home was written in the hotel lobby in down-town Nairobi. The previous chapter shares what I wrote in that letter, and more. My second letter to my family was writ-ten in Shirati, and I have already shared some of its details, so this letter has been shortened and adapted to avoid repetition.

Greetings from Shirati for the first time. It is 10:30 P.M. and the genera-tor usually stops at 10:00 P.M. except if there is some medical situation at the hospital that requires electricity. So I am writing this by the light of a faithful old kerosene lamp.

So, the flight was pleasant the whole way. I was never "seasick"—not even en route to Shirati—but I did feel overfed. The return of Hershey Leaman and Don Jacobs to Nairobi when I had just arrived there was a Godsend, because I was not keen on traveling by myself, overnight, by train and lake steamer, in a strange land. Now I am here, away from America, sort of "dumped" beside Lake Victoria, and expected to take care of the sick when I'm just fresh out of internship.

I will be living at the nurses' house with Anna Martin from Paradise, Pennsylvania; Alice Reber from Illinois (she helped to care for Mother at LGH), and Elsie Cressman from Ontario, who works in the lepro-sarium but spends most of her nights here. Alta Weaver lives next door in a smaller house by herself. She hails from the Springville area near Ephrata, where some of Mother's Stahl relatives live. Our house has a rather large living room and a bedroom on each corner, plus a kitchen and bathroom in the middle of the back.

Tomorrow, Hershey and his wife, Norma, and I will go to Tarime to register as immigrants to Tanganyika. So long for now.

Saturday, October 14, 1961

Greetings from Shirati, where we are having a late afternoon thunder-shower. I understand that this might be the harbinger of the rainy sea-son, which can bring fresh vegetables and other garden produce to our kitchen table. The weather here is nice; it can get quite warm by 11:00 A.M., but then the breezes from Lake Victoria start to blow to the cast. This makes the indoor areas quite comfortable as the fresh air enters through the screens on our doors and windows.

On Monday, Hershey and Norma and I drove the thirty-seven bumpy, dusty miles one way to Tarime to register our presence in Tanganyika. We also wanted to apply for Tanganyika driver's licenses, but we discovered that Monday was a holiday, so our trip was useless. As we returned home, I saw more thin, poorly developed cows and goats.

On Tuesday afternoon we returned to Tarime, and this time we were able to do our business. Also, the mail normally comes into Tarime on Tuesday and Friday, so that is a big reason to visit Tarime on those two days. Hershey picked up the mail for the Shirati folks. There was nothing as yet for me, but it was only October 5 when I left the United States, so I'll just wait some more.

Now for a little geography lesson. Our elevation at Shirati is over thirty-seven hundred feet, just two hundred feet above Lake Victoria, which is two to three miles to the west. We have beautiful sunsets as the sun is slowly "swallowed" by the lake. We have significant hills and even low mountains to the east and north of us. Our Nyabasi mission station is fifteen miles east of Tarime and its elevation is a thousand feet higher, so their nights tend to be much cooler than ours.

Pastor Zedekia Kisare and his wife, Susanna, are visiting here at Shirati this week. Yesterday he spoke about his safari to the United States to visit the EMBMC and see how Mennonites live and work in eastern Pennsylvania. Today we had a preparatory service and feet washing, and tomorrow we will have communion.

As for me, I am studying Swahili a bit by myself—I now recognize a few words. The African nurses do speak English and are very helpful in communicating with patients when I make rounds. I really sleep during afternoon siesta, and I think I am partaking of too much food at meals. Besides the regular rounds in the maternity ward, on Wednesday I was asked to do a postmortem examination on a lady who had hung herself the previous evening. The findings were as I had expected, and I made a written report for the coroner's office.

Yesterday I helped a woman in labor by rupturing her membranes. She then promptly delivered a big (for here) nine-pound baby to the midwife. Then last evening a lady came in after delivering a four-pound five-ounce boy at home that morning. But she had failed to deliver the other twin and the afterbirth, and the twin's hand was protruding from her vagina. Well, this was a challenge, but I was able to return the hand, then turn the baby around until I could get ahold of both feet and pull out a stillborn little girl. I later had the midwife encourage the mother to come to the hospital next time *before* her baby is born; if she had come earlier this time, maybe we could have saved the second twin too. But the woman replied that her husband wanted her to deliver her children at home (partly because of the cost). So I see that we need somehow to help the husband understand the value of both prenatal care and coming to the hospital before there is an obvious problem with the birth of a baby.

Elsie Cressman has offered to take me along to her house beside the lake and near the leprosarium whenever I can take a day off to study

Swahili. So I will try to do that one day each week before Dr. Housman and his family go on furlough in about five weeks. I can see already that it will be hard for me to study Swahili when I am here on the compound and the phone can reach me at any time. Plus our nurses' house with its large living room seems to be a hangout place for people to talk, and that does not help me to learn much Swahili.

Tuesday, October 31, 1961

Greetings from Nyabasi this time. On Friday, October 20, Elsie Cressman, Alta Weaver, and I took Pastor Zedekia to Bukiroba, which is where they live. It is seventy miles from Shirati to Bukiroba, and six more miles to Musoma. The next morning we went to Musoma, which is a fairly big town with a large market and many shops, a Barclays Bank, a government hospital, and so on. I went to the bank and opened a checking account with my US traveler's checks. The exchange rate currently is seven shillings for one US dollar. Each shilling is worth one hundred cents, and twenty shillings are worth one pound. I also looked at a new bicycle. It cost fifty US dollars, so I will wait and think about it some more. Or maybe I'll look at something else.

It was nice to visit with the missionaries at Bukiroba (also known as Nyabangi): John and Catherine Leatherman, George and Dorothy Smoker, Phoebe Yoder, and Don and Anna Ruth Jacobs. After the Sunday service in their lovely brick church, our missionary group enjoyed a picnic atop the hill just behind the missionary houses, which has a lovely view of the Bukiroba station and, further west, the town of Musoma, situated in the arms of Lake Victoria.

We headed back toward Shirati by mid-afternoon but, sure enough, got into rain, and then more rain, and lots of mud on the dirt road. When we got to Utegi, we learned that the nearby river was overflowing its bridge, so we could not navigate the last twenty miles to Shirati. Elsie decided we would backtrack six miles to the Catholic mission at Kowak, whose folks sometimes brought patients to us for medical care. They treated us royally with overnight lodging and breakfast before sending us on our way on Monday morning. The roads were still muddy but the sun was out and the river was lower, and we got back to Shirati by noontime.

The old-timers around here are saying that the daily rains are more than usual. And the dirt roads are in bad shape. But in spite of the extra rain, the five nurses and I took off again this past Saturday morning and traveled to Nyabasi in Elsie's VW pickup. Despite some muddy places, we got to Nyabasi OK. There we picked up nurse Mary Harnish, who runs the clinic and maternity center, and school teachers Clara Landis and Martha Jane Lutz. Clara and Martha teach at Mara Hills School, a

school for missionary children located at Nyabasi, which is cooler and has less malaria than our area beside Lake Victoria. Some of our missionary children from Somalia come here to school also.

After loading our three passengers and their bags into the car, we headed on toward Kisaka. We first traveled a bit further east along the top of the escarpment, then made a sharp right turn and drove in low gear down the side of the steep slope into the Mara Valley. We then drove in a more southerly direction to the Mara River, where Clyde Shenk was waiting for us. He had already crossed the river, which was maybe twenty feet wide, in a dugout canoe. Yes, someone had made a canoe by hollowing out a tree trunk. It was perhaps fifteen feet long and two and a half feet wide and deep. Clyde and his African helper made several trips to transport us with our bags to the other side. The river was not terribly deep, and they used poles to touch the river's bottom and push the boat to the other side. The banks of the river were rather steep, however, so the tricky part was getting down into the dugout and out of it again at the other side. Obviously we left the VW on the Nyabasi side of the river and Clyde transported all of us to Kisaka in his Jeep pickup.

Our hostess at Kisaka was Velma Eshleman, a nurse who managed a small clinic. She had invited all of the single lady missionaries to Kisaka for the weekend, so there were also eight more ladies who had come from Bukiroba and Mugango. [*I did not list their names in my original letter, but they could have included Martha Myer, Laura Kurtz, Grace Gehman, Rhoda Wenger, and Phoebe Yoder.*] We had a wonderful time together. Some of us had brought along our tents to sleep in and, true to form, it rained on Sunday, so we did get wet and muddy. But we were glad to get back up the escarpment to Nyabasi without getting stuck in any mud.

When we reached Nyabasi on our return trip, the clinic worker was watching for us and promptly told us she had a bleeding maternity patient, so I saw her and decided she'd better go to Shirati Hospital. We had supper together at Mara Hills before the nurses left with the patient, and I stayed at Nyabasi for several days to get acquainted with their medical program and personnel. Meanwhile, the nurses got to Utegi, then had to wait an hour for the river water to go down, so they did not get to Shirati until 2:00 A.M. And then the patient did have surgery.

Tomorrow I plan to return to Shirati with Elam Stauffers. Elam is our bishop and he has been going to each mission station to give preparatory teaching for the ordination of an African bishop sometime this November. Do remember this important work in prayer, that God's man may be chosen.

It is now Wednesday noon, November 1, 1961, and I am back at Shirati. I traveled with Elam Stauffers and Robert Keeners. The river near Utegi was sixteen inches deep, but we got through OK—just in front of the next rainstorm! And your two letters were here to greet me. It sounds like you are kept busy. I do study some Swahili and I can recognize some words, but to respond in Swahili is completely beyond me. The good news is that they are planning to have a Swahili language school for us this December. I am really looking forward to that.

Saturday, November 4, 1961

Finally, I am sending you a typewritten air form letter. I have gotten a supply of East Africa air forms. I am sure these will be more legible than my handwritten ones, and I can get a lot more information onto them. I hope to send this letter along with Gordon, the MAF pilot, to be mailed later today in Nairobi. Gordon's base is in Nairobi and he flies out into Kenya and Tanganyika as needed. He comes to us at Shirati at regular intervals to take one of our doctors on medical rounds to our other stations.

Gordon came here on Wednesday afternoon by way of Nyabasi so that he could bring Simeon and Edna Hurst to Shirati. Simeon has had back surgery and does not enjoy long car rides on our dirt "turnpikes." Maybe he'd had enough of car travel back in the United States and Canada with the deputation visitors from Tanganyika several months ago. When Gordon left Shirati, Dr. Housman went along to Musoma and on to our South Mara station. Between these hops, Gordon brought a pa-

tient to Shirati and took Hershey Leaman to Musoma and back for some business matters. Then he took Elam Stauffers home to Musoma after Elam led yesterday morning's meeting about choosing a bishop.

Let me explain why we are so dependent on MAF at this time. The dirt road from Tarime to Musoma is actually closed for repairs due to the excessive rains. In good weather, Musoma is more than seventy miles or a two and a half hour drive from Shirati. But by MAF plane it is only fifteen minutes away. So the MAF plane is a wonderful link to our neighbors, and we do have airstrips at most of our stations, including Shirati, Nyabasi, Kisaka, Kenyana, Musoma, Mugango, and Masinono. Kenyana, located fifteen miles south of Kisaka, and Masinono, a rural area near Lake Victoria and a short hop south of Mugango, are not actually mission stations, but the local people appreciate a medical visit. Bumangi station is our other mission outreach and has a clinic with a dresser [*someone who works in the station but isn't trained as a doctor or nurse*] but no airstrip because of the hilly, wooded terrain.

Gordon is most accommodating in taking our mail to Nairobi to speed it on its way to you. He also brings along fresh vegetables and groceries for us. This time he brought big carrots and peas. Our diet is not too different from what we ate at home; the ladies bake bread, and meat is obtained by hunting trips to the *pori* (grasslands inhabited by large-herd animals—deer, giraffe, buffalo, and so on—and tsetse flies, which cause sleeping sickness and therefore prohibit many people from living there). Chicken, eggs, and fish are locally available. Cows and goats are in abundance and provide milk, but goat milk is rather hard for me to get used to. The cows and goats loiter on the dirt roads, ignoring car horns and sometimes almost being run down. Bananas and pineapples grow locally, doing especially well in the higher climate and heavier rainfall of Nyabasi. Papaya is another popular fruit; it looks like a cantaloupe and tastes good with lemon juice on it. Oranges are also readily available, and potatoes grow well in Nyabasi. We also get tomatoes, peppers, and some lettuce and celery. How did I forget to mention cabbage? Anyway, we get a variety of good food, also canned things, cold cereals for breakfast, or oatmeal and cream of wheat.

I did not aim to write a letter about food, but somehow it happened anyway! So, let me shift gears. Maybe this letter will arrive even before my last one of November 1, which probably went via Tarime and Musoma, and possibly Kisumu also, while this one will fly directly to Nairobi.

Anyway, Elam Stauffers and Simeon Hursts came here to teach preparatory to ordaining an African bishop. Elam has visited most of our stations. He has clarified the differences between the Tanganyika Mennonite Church (the church of Christ) and a political machine. Everyone here is very conscious of freedom as December 8, Uhuru (Independence) Day, approaches, when Tanganyika is to obtain complete independence. Although many do not understand the new responsibility of this step, they are eager to "have their say" and to help control the money. This attitude also creeps into the church, where each one wants to speak his opinion in choosing a bishop, and some backsliders would gladly make non-Christian choices. Therefore, the General Council drew up a wise procedure. After presenting pertinent teaching at each church, those members allowed to partake in communion would be permitted to suggest delegates for choosing the bishop. The number of delegates from each church would be a percentage of the membership. Twenty-one were chosen here at Shirati, not including the pastors and deacons. After the names were given, the ordained men went outside to decide if the suggested delegates were acceptable. When one was determined to be unacceptable, he was asked to pray at home and another name was given. These delegates plan to meet at a school near Bukiroba on November 20 to 22 for further teaching and prayer before nominating men for bishop. A three-quarters majority vote is required for the one to be ordained at a later date. Elam carefully explained that this process was planned by the General Council and was not just his way of doing things as a European when some Africans might want to do otherwise. So, do remember these 120 delegates as they meet in November for this important work.

Today is a special day in Tarime. Julius Nyerere, the political leader of Tanganyika, who will become prime minister next month, is visiting and Dr. Lester Eshleman has been invited to attend a special tea in Nyerere's honor.

A new part of my duties at Shirati beginning next week will be teaching nursing school students. The nursing school began last year with eleven students. The full nursing school course goes for three years. I have notes that Dr. Housman gave me for the courses he taught last year. My own medical textbooks and study materials are not here yet, so I must start with the notes that Harold prepared and a few British nursing textbooks that use different vocabulary for instruments and procedures than my US textbooks use.

Sunday, November 19, 1961

Greetings from a still-wet Shirati. Last night we got 2.48 inches, but we hear that some places along the coast have gotten pelted with 8 to 10 inches within twenty-four hours. Our soil is quite sandy, so you can understand why our roads and railroads are closed to traffic. Mombasa, the big port on the east coast of Kenya, where our barrels are shipped to, has communication with Nairobi only by air. Their railroad and main road, which are sand much of the way, are impassable. My barrels are expected to travel by rail from Nairobi to Kisumu on the northwest shore of Lake Victoria, and then by lake steamer to Musoma. So, despite my eagerness to have more clothing and my own medical books, the truth is that my barrels may not arrive for some months. This difficulty with traveling by land also causes problems with transporting food in some areas, especially in Kenya, where some food is being delivered by airplane and helicopter. Locally, the rain has prompted our church leaders to postpone the meeting scheduled at Bukiroba for the 20th to 22nd of November, when the previously chosen delegates were to receive more instruction on seeking the Lord's will in calling forth our first African Mennonite bishop.

This past week has been busy. Despite the rain and mud, the medical committee managed to get here by Monday evening, though some of them had been on the road all day and had gotten stuck in the mud four times. They had long sessions on Tuesday and Wednesday to plan some improvements in our medical care and facilities. They also spent time at the Nyabasi clinic, which has an active maternity unit too. Mary Harnish is currently the nurse in charge there, but she is due to go on furlough next month. The problem is, who will replace her? It had been planned that an African medical assistant, who is trained to diagnose and treat common diseases but is not equivalent to an M.D., would manage the clinic, and a midwife would care for the maternity patients. But the midwife was just discharged from Shirati after she admitted to immoral living. When she was interviewed, she admitted her wrong, but when asked what the church should do to her she said, "Just forgive me." They warned her but she remained unrepentant, so they told her not to return to work the next day. She plans to marry a young man who is not acceptable to the church leaders. She is a talented girl who was doing a good job in the operating room here. The church does have some say in these matters and has set up guidelines of conduct for the hospital employees. The other medical assistant also has been creating problems and has been accused of gross sin too, so perhaps he will not be approved to work at Nyabasi either. So maybe a nurse will go to Nyabasi—but who? We have Alice Reber and Alta Weaver in the nursing school, but Alice goes home in mid-summer. Elva Landis left here this past September, just before I arrived, and she hopes to get a year of midwifery training before she returns. Anna Martin is busy with maternity and hospital patients. Cora Lehman will soon arrive and after language school she may work in the nursing school to relieve Alice Reber. So who goes to Nyabasi? Pray about it, please. Anyway, the committee was kept busy. And then some of them traveled for two days to get back to Bukiroba. Normally that trip of seventy miles is completed in two and a half hours, but this was *not* a normal trip.

So this was the week for babies to arrive! On Tuesday night we had two maternity patients. The first mother had twins, which I had suspected. Both babies presented head first, and the mother sneakily delivered the first baby to the midwife after Anna Martin and I got tired of waiting and went to bed. Unfortunately, the umbilical cord to the second twin slipped down in front of the baby's head, and because it took more than an hour to deliver it, naturally the baby was stillborn. Then I waited an hour and delivered the first daughter of Joram, one of our middle school teachers, and his wife, to the joy of both parents and the three older brothers.

On Wednesday night the midwife on duty went into labor, so she asked an aide from the women's ward to give her an enema. After her membranes ruptured, she called Anna, who gladly delivered a healthy child as the climax to the mother's night of work in maternity!

And on Friday afternoon Norma Leaman went into labor. Dr. Lester thought her progress was a bit slow, so he called me to see her. The baby's head was crowning, so when I was ready, Lois Eshleman gave Norma some sedation. I then made an episiotomy, inserted forceps, and lifted out their husky eight-pound son, Lynn. I repaired the episiotomy, and mother and baby were transported to the nurses' house for several days of recuperation. Now our house has some baby noises.

On Thursday I spent the whole day at Elsie Cressman's house, which is three miles from Shirati, next to the leprosarium, and right by the lake. It has no telephone, and I studied Swahili all day, except for siesta time, in her comfortable hammock on the porch. It was so great to have a whole day to study without the many interruptions one has in the nurses' house. Granted, I occasionally checked on the fishermen in the lake, and I walked Lady, Elsie's dog, twice. Elsie got me back to the nurses' house too late to help with surgery for a wound from a spear that went through both walls of the man's stomach, but Dr. Lester did well without me.

Last evening we had a farewell party for the Housmans, with pizza, ice cream, and root beer. They will leave either Tuesday or Wednesday, spend several days in Nairobi, then visit in Ethiopia and Switzerland, and arrive home in the United States just before Christmas. Their departure will make for some living rearrangements here. Anna Martin from the nurses' house and Alice Reber, who lives in the small house with Alta Weaver, will move into the Housmans' house and employ the Housmans' cook. That will leave new arrival Cora Lehman and me in the nurses' house, plus Elsie Cressman, who sleeps here because the local folks do not want her to spend the night alone in the lake house. But she cooks there and has a nice quiet place away from the mainstream of Shirati activity.

Thursday, November 30, 1961

Greetings from Shirati, where the major news item is that we have had *no* rain to speak of for two and a half whole days! But I must admit that it is quite overcast this morning, so we may get more rain soon, whether we want it or not! No one has been off the Shirati station, except via the MAF plane, for the past two weeks. The water level of Lake Victoria has risen about a foot, which means the lake has expanded over the adjacent ground and extended its shoreline. And Lake Victoria was already not a little two-by-four-foot puddle.

I've made a copy of my Caltex East Africa map for your geography lesson. You can see that Lake Victoria is basically rectangular rather than round or oblong. The transverse line that runs below Entebbe on the upper left side of the lake and above Kisumu on the upper right side of Kendu Bay is the *equator*. But despite being so close to it (about 0.6 degrees or eighty to eighty-five miles south to be exact), we do *not* live in a steaming jungle, because our lake is 3,700 plus feet above sea level! There are delightful breezes off the lake from late morning until late afternoon, so the temperature is much more comfortable here than at home in July and August. The east-west distance from Kisumu to the western shore is about 160 miles. (How far would 160 miles take you across Pennsylvania?) From Kalamera on the right side of the bottom of the lake to the western shore is only about 120 miles. And from the southern to the northern shore is about 150 miles. So it is BIG. In fact, Lake Victoria is second in size only to Lake Superior in the United States. Maybe that position will change if we keep on having so much rain!

Now you can see the route of the steamer as it goes around the lake, south from Kisumu to Musoma and Mwanza, then northwest to Bukoba,

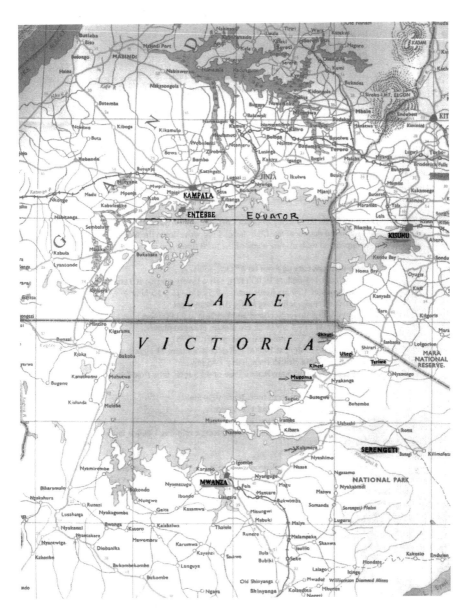

north to Entebbe, and east to Kisumu. It also provides service in the opposite direction. Notice that Shirati is just below the Kenya-Tanganyika border and just above the ferry that connects Kinesi to Musoma across the bay. The news is that the lake level has risen enough that neither the Kinesi ferry at Musoma nor the Kirumi ferry on the Mara River can load vehicles, because the ferries sit so much higher in the water than usual and cars can't drive off the approach without getting hung up on the edge with their front end dangling. I hope you can picture it because I'm not very good at drawing!

Maybe you have figured out that our post (mail) is, well, not getting through very often. You all are more lucky, because every time we learn that MAF is coming we suddenly write letters, whether inspired or not, and send them along to Nairobi with Gordon to be mailed. The last letter I got from home was written on November 3, four weeks ago, and arrived on November 13. I did get a note from Nate with a letter from Kitty Morrow on the 20th. MAF is due here again tomorrow, so we may get mail then. Airmail is normally flown into Musoma on Tuesday and Friday, then transported by truck to Tarime as soon as possible; that road has been open sporadically for the past month, but now that the ferries cannot run, what will happen? Sometimes we can get our mail at Musoma instead of waiting for it to get to Tarime and then trying to get to Tarime to pick it up. Our Shirati road is still impassable because of high rivers and washouts.

Harold Housmans got off as scheduled last week, on Tuesday, the 21st, and were to fly out of Nairobi on Saturday. They will be in the Lancaster area a lot, so when you get a chance to see them, don't miss it. He will do some work with Dr. Ripple, an eye doctor.

Jim Mohlers, Cora Lehman, and Helen Landis were late leaving New York; instead of leaving at 4:00 P.M., they left at 10:00 P.M. on a jet flying directly to London. They stopped in Zurich and Athens, got into Nairobi on Wednesday morning, the 21st, and came here by MAF on Thursday. Helen Landis went on to Somalia without getting to see her sister Clara, a teacher at our Mara Hills School. The Mohlers went on to Musoma and Bukiroba. Cora moved into our nurses' house with me. I am glad that she is here and that we have time to get acquainted before we go to language school.

On Tuesday, Cora and I went along with Elsie to her house by the lake. It was such a lovely day that I took a little break from studying to hoe some sand away from Elsie's young palm trees. The high water and the wind have made the lake rough, so it sometimes almost looks like the ocean. The sand has been slammed about ten feet closer to the house. The lakeshore used to be a hundred feet from the porch.

Language school is to start at Bukiroba this coming Monday and run for two weeks. December is a vacation month for school children here, so students from Mara Hills School at Nyabasi, the Morembe Middle School for Girls (grades 5 to 8) near Bukiroba, and the Alliance Secondary School for Boys near Musoma are having difficulty getting back home. Maybe some will travel to Shirati by tugboat; if so, we hope that some food and gas supplies will come too. And if the tug comes, maybe Anna Martin, Cora Lehman, and I will ride along back to Musoma to catch language school. Aside from the MAF, we are rather isolated at Shirati during this unusual rainy season. Everyone says they have never

seen rain like this before, and some think that Russia's bomb testing has caused atmospheric disturbances. But despite the hardship involved in getting food and the wrecking of homes, I wonder if the rain may be a hidden blessing in preventing large gatherings of people during the Uhuru Day celebrations on December 9, with their potential for excess.

The postponement of the ordination of an African bishop may also be God's way of showing that the church is not yet ready for this important step. Some of our pastors will enter Bible college, which opens at Bukiroba next February, and it may go better if no one has yet been singled out as bishop. The initial focus will be on learning the English language before getting into Bible study in English.

Friday, December 8, 1961

Greetings from Bukiroba. Yes, I am here for two weeks of Swahili language study. Cora Lehman, our newest arrival at Shirati; Anna Martin; and I flew to Musoma by MAF in fifteen minutes on Saturday, December 2, while Clara Landis and Martha Jane Lutz came overland by "taxi," which is the local term for an old bus. They traveled more than seventy miles on dirt roads and crossed the river on the Kirumi ferry. The other students in our Swahili school are Martha Myer, Mark Brubaker, and Jim Mohler and his wife. Anna Martin and several others are in a more advanced class taught by Don Jacobs while the rest of us,

beginners, are taught by Phoebe Yoder. Both are interesting and skilled teachers. We have our morning sessions from 8:00 to 12:30, with a half-hour break for tea at the home of George and Dorothy Smoker. The afternoon includes siesta, study, and going to Musoma for shopping and celebration. Evening class time goes from 8:00 to 9:30 P.M. But the really once-in-a-lifetime experience of this week is the fact that Tanganyika is receiving independence from Great Britain tomorrow, Saturday, December 9, 1961.

It is now Saturday. Yesterday was a *long* day. We had our two regular morning Swahili sessions. Then after our noon meal we spent the afternoon in Musoma at a large grassy meeting place where various tribal groups presented their dances and displayed their prowess. One man even picked up a large metal drum with his mouth and carried it around inside the circle of spectators. Most men wore animal skins, feathers, and face paint. The music makers' instruments included drums, bells, and flutes. The dancing was mostly rhythmic jumping up and down and slow marching around the leader, but some groups also made many body-twisting movements. Several groups carried their spears, shields, and long knives. The women wore colorful *shukas* (colorful four-by-eight-foot cloths that have many uses) and mostly kept an eye on their children.

This evening, after our Swahili class, we went back to Musoma for the Uhuru Day program. First, a number of middle school students (grades 5 to 8) presented skits about Africa and Uhuru. They also had two good bands with some marching and vocal music. There were some speeches, but I can't tell you much about their content because it was mostly in Swahili. The climax of the evening came at midnight, when the lights were turned off and the Union Jack flag of Great Britain was brought down. Then the new flag of Tanganyika was raised and the lights were turned back on. The flag's colors are green for the productivity of the land, black for her people, and yellow for the minerals and products of the earth—diamonds, gold, and so on. The crowd briefly stood in silent awe, then burst into loud cheers. This was followed by a fireworks display, though not as loud as what we hear in the United States. Then the crowd slowly dispersed and went home to savor the fact that Tanganyika was now an independent nation with Julius Nyerere as its prime minister to lead the people in this new adventure.

As for me, when I got back to Bukiroba I decided to light the kerosene lamp and tell you all about the Independence Day events, especially because I want to mail this letter in the morning with the new Tanganyika postage stamps on it, on the first day of issue. I am getting some pretty stamps here, and someday I hope to get them organized into my neglected stamp collection.

I should write a lot more about language school, but the other girls are in bed and it is 1:30 A.M., so I should stop the noise from my typewriter and sack in too. So good night and good morning from the land of Tanganyika, where everyone is rejoicing in Uhuru, which is the Swahili word for FREEDOM.

Thursday, December 14, 1961

Greetings again from Bukiroba. Time is passing so fast. The language school has been really great. As for independence, so far as we know, everything seems to continue much as before, without any of the violence and disturbances that occurred in nearby Congo. We thank God for peace.

Yesterday when we went to Musoma on business we noticed that there were two big red planes and a lot of people over at the Musoma

"airport" (actually it is a big grass strip without a lot of fancy facilities). So yes, we went to see what the attraction was and—would you believe it? We saw the Duke of Edinburgh—the husband of the Queen of England! He had been further south in Tanganyika to see our big game and the rains were bad down there too, so his big plane could not land there to pick him up. Instead a small plane picked him up and brought him up to Musoma, where he switched onto his own plane. It was a nonscheduled stop but many people were on hand anyway to cheer him and to see him pilot his own plane off our airfield! [*Somehow the news of his coming got around before the arrival of cell phones and computers! We just followed the crowd!*]

With all the other news last week I somehow forgot to tell you that some freight arrived from Salunga and my barrels are now at Bukiroba. But Martha Myer's one barrel that contains most of her clothing has not shown up yet. I really hope it is not permanently lost. I hope to receive my barrels soon, to have more clothes and my own medical books.

We girls have occupied the Leatherman house while they are on leave, and they have a 1961 *Laurel Wreath* [LMS yearbook], so Sis's (Anna Mary's) picture is in our house, and a 1961 *Shenandoah* [Eastern Mennonite College yearbook] is here too. Martha Jane Lutz and I are sharing a bedroom, and we find we have things in common. On Tuesday we girls from Shirati got some mail again, after none for twelve days. Cora was very glad to get her first mail since her arrival. And I got ten very welcome letters, which kept me occupied for more than an hour.

Another news item: tomorrow night the Tanganyika Mennonite Youth League begins its first big meeting at a school near here. They have been studying Genesis and Esther and will present skits, songs, and Bible quizzes on these two books. Some of our people know very little about the Old Testament, so this will introduce them. With their low but rising literacy rate and their background too often devoid of Christian upbringing, it is easy to understand this lack of biblical knowledge.

The news from Shirati is that it is still raining some, the rivers are still high, and the road to Tarime is still impassable, even by *piki-pik* (motorcycle). Shirati had more than twenty inches of rain in November. Without the MAF plane and Lake Victoria, Shirati would really be cut off. Petrol (gas) and diesel fuel plus food staples are brought by tugboat from Musoma, but that service is not always reliable either.

Thursday, January 4, 1962

Greetings in Jesus' Name in this New Year. Maybe Pauls shared with you about our Christmas celebration. It was different but nice nonetheless. Christmas trees and Christmas lights and Santa Claus are not commonly seen in Africa (except maybe in cities like Nairobi where more Europeans live), but our African church people do celebrate Christmas. Gifts and decorations are not so important, or available, to them. At Shirati, most of the village people have no electricity (though the hospital and nearby houses usually have electricity, by generator, during the morning work hours and again in the evening). Sometimes they will celebrate by presenting a skit of the Christmas story in church. They also enjoy writing and performing new songs.

Other times they have a fellowship meal. Instead of a casserole, most families bring some *ugali,* which is a thick porridge made from manioc root (also known as cassava, the source of tapioca), corn, or other grains. They often butcher a cow and provide pots of broth with one-inch cubes of cooked meat. Six to ten people will gather around a meat pot and a bowl of *ugali* after first washing their hands. They will then pull a bit of *ugali* from the bowl with their right thumb and fingers (they never use their left hand to eat!) and mold the *ugali* into sort of a spoon shape. Then they dip the tip of the *ugali* into the meat broth, being careful not to get their fingertips into the broth as they enjoy their meal. Their everyday diet has much less meat than ours does, but they eat a lot more fish because they are beside Lake Victoria. Their church buildings are simple auditoriums with mud-brick benches that usually do not have backs; they can eat inside the church by sitting on every second bench and facing each other across the empty bench in between and using it as a table. Thus they do not need a separate fellowship hall like we do. But sometimes for a special time of feasting and fellowship they make a *banda,* a temporary shelter built of sisal poles or whatever other green branches are available. Leafy branches, such as from the brightly colored bougainvillea bushes, are spread on top to provide some shade.

Early Christmas morning, some of our missionary group went caroling at the homes of our African pastor, the school teachers, and the hospital workers. I took along my *Tenzi za Rohoni* (a Swahili songbook) because I do not know the carols in Swahili by memory like I know them in English. The moon was full, so I did not need my flashlight to read the words—which reminds me that I was told that George Smoker, one of our veteran missionaries, said that a full moon at Christmas is a truly special event in Tanganyika, perhaps like a new cover of snow gives North Americans the joy of a "white Christmas." As we caroled that night and walked down the garden paths from house to house, some mosquitoes greeted us too. Yes, they were all set to get their Christmas feast a bit early, because they bit our bare arms, and we kept slapping at them as we sang in the beautiful moonlight.

[*The music of Christmas has always made the Christmas season extra special for me. As a teenager I enjoyed caroling with our youth group. And I have always enjoyed listening to Handel's Messiah during the Christmas season, wherever I have been. One year I was in Nairobi when the choir from the Kijabe missionary school presented their Christmas program. It was there that I heard "The Drummer Boy" for the first time. I will also never forget how Miriam Housman and her three children came caroling at each house one night after the generator had stopped but my lantern was still lit. They sang "The Friendly Beasts," which was also new to me. I can still see them standing outside my window with their flashlights.*]

Now let me backtrack to tell you more about the end of our two-week language school on Friday, December 15 at noon. That morning, during our tea break, we students sang our special adaptation of "Old MacDonald Had a Farm" with the new theme "Don and Phoebe Had a School." We reviewed some of the things we had learned, using some Swahili words. Part of it went something like this:

Don and Phoebe had a school, E I E I O.
And in this school we learned Swahili, E I E I O.
With a *Jumbo* [Hello] here and a *Kwa Heri* [Good-bye] there.
Here a *Jumbo,* there a *Kwa Heri,*
Everywhere a *Habari gani.* [How are you?]
Don and Phoebe had a school, E I E I O.

Dorothy and Anna Ruth were kept busy, E I E I O.
Filling our *tumbos* [stomachs] with food and *chai* [tea], E I E I O.
With a peanut here and a cracker there.
Here a peanut, there a cracker.
Everywhere a peanut butter cracker.
Don and Phoebe had a school, E I E I O.

There was at least one more verse, maybe two, which I can no longer recall. But I clearly remember that on the last refrain half of us sang the vowels as we do in English—*a* as in day, *e* as in free, *i* as in sigh, *o* as in toe, and *u* as in true—while the other half sang them as in Swahili, in which the vowel sounds are the same as they are in German, like this: *a* = *ah* as in *Pa, e* = *aa* as in *say, i* = *ee* as in *he, o* = *oh* as in *so,* and *u* = *oo* as in *who.* And we made faces at each other for not singing together. Well, everyone enjoyed our entertainment, and we students wished that our school could have lasted longer. But Christmas was coming and there was work to return to at our compounds.

That afternoon we had a final tea together up on the big hill overlooking the compound. I took some pictures of the rocks and the scenery overlooking Mara Bay and Musoma that I hope will turn out well.

Then that Friday evening through Sunday evening the first conference of the Tanganyika Mennonite Youth League was held at the Morembe Middle School for Girls, a Mennonite school located between Bukiroba and Musoma. In spite of the rain and muddy roads, about fifty young people assembled for a weekend of Bible study and fellowship. The previously announced books to be studied were Genesis and Esther, and the group enjoyed choosing two teams for the Bible quiz. A sword drill was also popular. It worked like this: Everyone held their Bible aloft while Scripture verses were identified on the blackboard and given verbally. Then, at a predetermined signal, the Bibles came down and the pages rustled until someone jumped up and began to read the verses. The youth groups had come from different areas and many of them had prepared special songs and a play to present to the entire conference. The plays were mostly based on the books they studied. One group gave a vivid portrayal of Haman's dealings with Queen Esther and the king. Official judges ranked each presentation on various points. I attended the Youth League events on Saturday afternoon and all day Sunday. On Sunday morning I enjoyed trying to understand some of the Swahili, and I did understand some of Elam Stauffer's talk about the different names of Jesus. But by Sunday evening I could think only about going to bed and crawling under the sheets to escape the millions of hungry mosquitoes—or so it seemed to me!

Also that Sunday evening I had my first taste of *ugali.* This batch had some sand added to it during the grinding process. My "broth" was mostly fat that, upon cooling a bit, solidified! The one piece of meat I got was good, however.

When we got back to Shirati, Gordon deposited a big sack of mail on our living room floor for us to sort and enjoy. That kept us occupied for several hours!

It is now Sunday, January 7. Last evening I had my third meal of *ugali,* and it was really good. It was a family meal rather than prepared for a large group, and the woman who made it is a fine cook. (Both the husband and wife are among the few rather obese Africans I have seen.) This *ugali* was hot and was served with a side dish of broth containing tasty chicken and onions—a really delightful meal that was completed by drinking tea with lots of sugar and milk, which I understand is British style—with some extra calories too!

It is now Monday morning. MAF came in on Friday, January 5, and brought us more Christmas mail. I was surprised to find none postmarked since December 15, which is about three weeks ago. I did get your letter of December 11 this time, whereas Paul's letter of December 12 came with the previous mail. It was a real surprise to get a lovely letter from Dad, so thanks to all of you for the letters. And forgive me for complaining when I ache to have more letters from home.

About the rains: they are still coming, especially in the Nyabasi area. And the road from Tarime to Musoma is now officially closed, with posts planted across the road. So our mail will fly into Musoma and eventually dribble on to Shirati, maybe by MAF.

Three to four weeks ago I sent to you by surface mail a book about the Uhuru Day festivities with some nice pictures and articles that I hope you will enjoy. More recently I also sent by surface mail three calendars with big pictures and Swahili Scripture verses—one for you, one for Pauls, and one for Nates. These are not fancy gifts, but they do let you know I am thinking of you all. I hear that the surface mail takes six to eight weeks to deliver, so it will be a while yet before you see it.

If you should ever wish to send me anything by parcel post, I am told that it should be tightly wrapped in paper, then placed inside a cotton bag or piece of cloth, which is then sewed shut all around before putting the package into a cardboard box and tying it up. I am told that people have a way of poking their hand inside a box that has developed broken corners during its journey, and if they catch ahold of some loose item, they will pull it out. But if everything is sewed up inside, they are less apt to pull anything out. Also, a package sent by parcel post may not weigh more than eleven pounds, and any package from a foreign country must have a tag from the post office declaring the contents of the package and its monetary value. I am *not* hinting that I am wanting a package, just offering general information in case you want to send something sometime.

Friday, January 12, 1962

Greetings in Jesus' Name. Here at Shirati we are having some nice warm, sunny weather. Locally our rainfall has decreased considerably; we had only five inches total in the whole month of December. But Nyabasi, which is fifty miles to the east and a thousand feet higher in elevation, is still getting a lot of rain. These days, LeRoy Petersheim gets stuck when he travels on the main road—all dirt, of course—with their tractor, no less, to try to get some necessary supplies and mail at Tarime. But few supplies are coming into Tarime from Kenya to the north or Musoma to the south, so they are probably as isolated as we are. The Shirati and Musoma-Bukiroba stations do have access to Lake Victoria, where boat transportation is sometimes available at Shirati and available several times a week at Musoma. It is also good to have radio communication with most of our other stations, plus with Gordon Marshall, the MAF pilot. (The African Medical and Research Foundation, or AMREF, has placed two-way radios in various mission hospitals in East Africa. These radios enable mission hospitals to contact specialists in various fields about urgent problems, such as needing to transfer a patient to Nairobi for special care. These medical specialists also sometimes come to the mission hospitals to provide specialist care and improve the expertise of the missionary doctors there. The AMREF also provides a mobile van equipped with instruments and medications for mission hospital staff to use to go out into the bush to examine and treat persons in scattered locations.)

We unexpectedly got another bagful of mail on Monday, January 8, just four days after the previous delivery. Getting two big deliveries of Christmas mail in early January was a real treat. Both batches included letters from home. And you will all be glad to know that, after sitting at Bukiroba for a month, my two barrels finally arrived by tugboat at Shirati pier, about six miles from Shirati station, on Saturday, January 6. The unpacking went a lot faster than the packing did! The contents had settled a little, but I did not find anything broken or obviously damaged by the long trip. It is so good to have more clothes to wear. And I am so glad to have my own familiar medical books to use to prepare my lectures for the nursing school classes.

Yesterday afternoon, quite unexpectedly, Gordon flew in by MAF from Nairobi and brought along some of our wholesale order of food items, such as dry cereals, salt, and tin cans of fruits and vegetables. So Dr. Lester hopped a ride to Nyabasi to check on the people up there, and I got up early and started this letter before I went to the hospital here to make rounds. Now I'll do a quick finale on the letter before they come back and Gordon heads off to Nairobi.

I suppose you get letters from me with a variety of postmarks in East Africa, but that does not mean I have set foot in all those places yet. It is just wherever the pilot happens to drop them off, mostly in Nairobi, I suppose.

Maternity has been busy this month and I have not gotten down to Elsie's house for the past two weeks to study Swahili. I am also staying nearby because the Robert Keeners are expecting an addition to their family soon and Dr. Lester has asked me to preside at the delivery.

Hershey and Norma recently received a large crate of supplies from the United States that included baby clothes and other supplies. We were recently served afternoon chai at their house, and with the chai we were also treated to good old Pennsylvania pretzels.

Sunday, January 21, 1962

Life here at Shirati continues to bring me a variety of work experiences. A pregnant lady was seen some weeks ago and felt to be carrying twins, so she came in about two weeks ago, before her labor began, and was given a place to stay in our maternity building. Last Tuesday morning she began to have good labor, but the midwife on duty did not notify Anna Martin or myself about it until that evening. Meanwhile, the mother delivered a seven-pound healthy girl at 5:30 P.M. She continued to have contractions and the second twin even changed from a breech to a head presentation. I was finally told about the unborn second twin, so I immediately went to check on her. I ruptured the membranes and could feel an inquisitive hand, which I replaced above the head, then soon delivered a seven-pound eight-ounce twin sister. Both babies are doing well. They are rather light-skinned and at this time their hair is fairly straight rather than kinky. I also communicated, via my translator, to the midwife that I did not consider twins to be a "normal delivery" and that I wished I had been notified earlier that this patient was in labor. Not only did this mother have three unnecessary additional hours of labor, but the second twin could have died from prolonged labor and prolapse of the hand as well as possible prolapse of the umbilical cord. Anyway, it all worked out well for this mother. I aim to help pregnant women understand the importance of prenatal care plus the value of shots for DPT [diphtheria, pertussis (whooping cough), and tetanus], polio, measles, and small pox for their babies. This month we have already had eighteen deliveries, with twenty living babies and two mothers who came in after delivering their babies at home. One mother came in with a laceration and some infection that required treatment; the other mother arrived five days after delivery with the afterbirth still not delivered, so I delivered that for her.

Several days ago I got to deliver another baby for missionary parents. Robert and Florence Keener had been here for two weeks awaiting the arrival of their child, and Robert was scheduled to return on Saturday the 20th to Musoma, where he is a teacher at the Alliance Secondary School for Boys. So I admit I gave the baby a hint or two to get on the way, and he cooperated by arriving at 9:30 P.M. on Friday the 19th, all eight and a half pounds of him, squalling and having a lot to say. If no food is available, he goes for his fist. His name is Jay Gordon, and his parents happily recognize these traits as being quite different from Debbie's behavior eight years ago. (Debbie was a Down syndrome baby who was very quiet and had to be coaxed to eat, just as was true of our sister Ruthie.) So baby Jay is a grandson of the Clayton Keeners and a nephew of Gerald Weaver, an LMS classmate. My first missionary baby delivery was for Hershey and Norma Leaman. Hershey is another LMS classmate, a son of Daniel Leaman, and a grandson of Martin Hershey.

Last weekend we had a communion service here. We have communion four times a year. On Saturday morning they had an "inspirational sermon," but I was busy at the hospital, so I missed that service. That afternoon we had a preparatory service: after the input by the ministers, we divided into small groups to share our testimonies and then washed each other's feet. Sunday morning we had a big crowd. We also had a baptismal service, which happens only once a year. Forty-nine persons, mostly young people, filled the two front benches. After each person gave a short testimony, each row was baptized, by pouring, by a team of pastors. Then followed a sermon and a short recess, during which all the non-Christians (meaning all nonbaptized persons, including believers who are still receiving catechism instruction) were excused. The rest of us then seated ourselves on every second bench. (These backless benches were low seats of sun-dried bricks topped by a layer of concrete.) The communion emblems were then served. A row of people would stand up and the pastor would pass through the adjacent empty row to give each individual the communion emblem. This seems to be more orderly than how it is sometimes done at home, where people crowd out into the aisles to receive the emblems. I noticed one thing in common with communion at home, though, and that is that even with the omission of Sunday school, the service tends to last until 1:30 P.M. And here the sunshine on the tin roof made it rather hot by early afternoon!

This past week also included some routine activities, like making hospital rounds and giving lectures to the nursing students. The nursing school was opened only a year ago, so for the first-year students I can use the lecture material prepared last year by Dr. Housman. But for the second-year class I have to prepare my own lectures. At least I now have my own familiar textbooks and notebooks to use instead of those strange British nursing texts! This past week the topic was skin conditions, and in this part of Africa that includes a lot of things that are uncommon in the States, such as leprosy, scabies (allergies), insect and animal bites, and so on.

Raymond Charles and Paul Kraybill arrived in Musoma on Saturday morning. Hershey Leaman and Dr. Lester Eshleman went down to Musoma on Saturday for some committee work. They plan to return here tomorrow evening, so that means meanwhile I do all the hospital rounds and answer all the calls. Mr. and Mrs. Orie Miller arrived in

Musoma on Saturday afternoon. We Shirati folks are looking forward to their being here this coming Wednesday evening and Thursday. I'm sure they are kept quite busy with everyone hoping to spend time with the deputation folks while they are here—a rare opportunity.

It is now Monday morning and we expect the MAF plane to come this morning, so I am finishing this letter first thing. It is almost 8:30 and I have all the rounds to do today. And I have not yet begun preparing my two hours of lectures for the nursing school tomorrow, so *Bas* ("Enough for now!" or "It's finished!" in Swahili). And I hope we get some post this morning.

Thursday, January 25, 1962

Greetings from Shirati, where the weather is somewhat warmer, though we have had one cool day in the past week, with 2.7 inches of rain. Four-wheel vehicles are getting in to us, but none of us has gotten out by car as yet.

This week has been busy—and not just because of the mission board visitors. Sunday night I was called out to see several patients, because Dr. Eshleman was not here, and neither was our right-hand staff nurse, who can diagnose and treat various problems. So I got maybe four to five hours of sleep. On Monday morning I finished rounds in only two and a half hours and went to work on preparing my lectures for nursing school. That evening, as I studied again, I developed a headache (very unusual for me), then felt nauseated, so I went to bed early despite the uncompleted lectures. At 12:30 A.M. I awoke and was still uncomfortable, so I went to the little room and had a very "adequate elimination" (as the British would say). I returned to bed but not to sleep, so I got up again and, without retching, simply returned all my undigested supper (soup) with some relief. On Tuesday I got up at 7:00 A.M., still nauseated and still having a headache. I had only a cup of tea for breakfast. Then, at the suggestion of my nurse colleagues, who can diagnose and treat many things in Africa (but not in the United States), I took four chloroquine tablets and went back to bed. That day I had no fever, but I had no energy either. I did try working on the lectures again that morning, but it was hard going with the headache. I had a bit of rice and a small carrot at noon, then went back to bed. A blood slide for malaria taken that afternoon was negative, but the mere thought of supper was nauseating, so I stayed in bed and took more chloroquine. Dr. Eshleman got back that evening from Musoma and agreed that I probably had malaria. So he gave me a sleeping pill, which worked until 12:30 A.M., when the wind and the rain came. Then the phone began to ring, but I ignored it. Finally I dozed off, to awaken at 5:00 A.M. as the generator came to life and the lights came on. My headache and nausea were gone, however, and I subsequently ate a healthy breakfast. So there you have the story of my first [*and only, as I can report more than fifty years later*] significant encounter with malaria. It certainly was not a severe or complicated siege, though it did slow me down for two days. But malaria can be lethal for children and persons who are in poor health. I later switched from chloroquine to daraprim as a medication to prevent me from contracting malaria again.

After breakfast, although still feeling weak and tired, I ventured out to the hospital to see a mother who had come in to have her first baby after bleeding at home for two days. She was very pale (anemic) and not in labor, so I ordered more blood for her, which she finally got three hours and six crossmatches later. I encouraged Dr. Eshleman to do surgery (a Cesarean section), even though I assumed that the baby was dead, and maybe premature too. This was her first pregnancy and I hoped to stop the bleeding and spare her life. Dr. Eshleman somewhat reluctantly agreed to do the C-section, and I scrubbed in to assist him. Even though I was still weak, I did *not* faint like some other staff members who reportedly have been "floored" at one time or another while assisting in surgery at Shirati. The next day the mother was still living but in need of more blood replacement.

[*Though we did provide blood transfusions for some needy patients, such as this very needy woman, we did not have a blood bank as US and other modern hospitals do. So, when someone needed blood, as this woman did, we asked the family to bring in their healthy adult relatives so that our lab people could test them to see who matched the patient's blood type. Then we explained to the prospective donors that we wanted to take some of their blood and give it to the patient, who had lost so much of his or her own blood. In this case, the process took three hours to type six relatives and draw a pint of blood from several of them to give to her. We could then do the surgery necessary to control her bleeding.*

If there were not many relatives available with the matching blood type, and if the nearby middle school was in session, we would sometimes send word to the headmaster to ask the oldest students to come and be tested to see if they were a match to give blood to the patient. We were able to save some lives in this way even without a sophisticated blood bank.]

By Wednesday evening I was feeling about normal but somewhat tired. Chloroquine has the undesirable side effect of inhibiting the ability to sleep, so despite the use of a sleeping pill (the second one in my life!) I did not get to sleep until after 2:00 A.M. last night. I am glad I encountered my malaria on Monday night instead of on Wednesday morning when the deputation folks—Orie Miller and his wife, Paul Kraybill, Elam Stauffer, and Pastor Ezekiel Muganda—began arriving. I had not met the Millers before but enjoyed getting acquainted with them at the supper table. Pastor Nashon Nyambok, the pastor here at Shirati, joined us for our evening worship, which was bilingual with Elam Stauffer translating. Orie told us about his visits to Ghana and Nigeria and about the growth of their churches. Paul told some about his trip with Raymond Charles and his understanding of the church here in Tanganyika—it's progress and it's growing pains. Pastor Ezekiel then spoke about the development of Tanganyika and its relationship to the white men who came in "to run things." Africans learned to obey and to say the expected things instead of honestly expressing their own feelings. Pastor Ezekiel showed how this behavior carried over into their relationships with the missionaries, whom they saw as whites with authority. So this meeting provided us with new understanding of each other as brothers and sisters and about the role that we missionaries have in *assisting* a young church—rather than being administrators who tell them one, two, three how to efficiently do the job. Elam then shared with us from Hebrews 2:14–18 as a meaningful closing meditation.

Raymond Charles arrived this morning (Thursday) and Orie Millers left after dinner. Paul Kraybill made himself available for private interviews, so we each had opportunity to share our thoughts and concerns with him. I shared about Mother's struggle with depression. Paul certainly is an understanding person who can see the larger situation as well. He invited me to keep him informed of her progress, or lack of it, as well. But I tend not to talk about Mother's problems with the folks here.

This afternoon at tea time, a number of English-speaking Africans were invited to join us. Then, at our regular Thursday 4:30 P.M. prayer meeting, Raymond Charles gave his testimony and a short message about his travels to visit Mennonites in various countries—Switzerland, Palestine, and Ethiopia. He also plans to visit India, Vietnam, and Japan. Raymond shared a brief history of our Mennonite origins in Switzerland.

Tomorrow morning, Paul, Raymond, Hershey Leaman, and Dr. Eshleman will go to Musoma for the church conference, which will include business talks to plan for the hospital's administration in the coming year; what all that entails I'm not really sure. But I will be here to do hospital rounds, answer other calls, and teach nursing school students, with no prospect of time to study Swahili.

Friday, February 2, 1962

This has been a really busy week. In fact, in some ways it seems like a long time since the EMBMC deputation folks visited Shirati, and it was only last week. They attended conference at Bumangi this week and are going to Nairobi today. Then they go to Somalia. Meanwhile, I hope to get this letter ready to go along to Nairobi. Somehow I have spent a lot of time in the hospital making rounds and changing some dressings, and it still seems there is more to do.

Today we admitted a young girl who is very withdrawn. She refuses to talk, keeps her eyes closed, and maintains a catatonic stupor position, that is, when I raised her arm into the air then removed my hand, she kept her arm suspended in the same position. She was lying on her bed and when I raised her head from the pillow, she kept her head in the air after I removed my hand. I did not see such catatonic states in my summer of psychiatric externship at Eastern Pennsylvania Psychiatric Institute in 1959. I have been surprised by the number of cases of mental illness and suicide that I have seen here in Tanganyika.

Night before last, around 11:00 P.M. a young man was brought to the hospital. He had been watching his goats when a leopard came by and decided a goat would make a nice dinner. The leopard apparently knocked down the goatherd and inflicted some scalp lacerations. As the young man's friends were bringing him to the hospital, he became restless and confused. I was unsure how much blood he had lost or if he had bleeding inside his skull too. I ordered some IV fluids and a blood transfusion for him. His condition continued to deteriorate, however, and he died at noon yesterday from what I assume was bleeding inside his brain. Well, did we ever have a loud wailing time afterward as family and friends announced his death! Fortunately we don't have a patient die at our hospital every day.

I asked permission to do a postmortem exam, but the family refused, thereby frustrating my intellectual curiosity but also sparing me the hard work of sawing through the skull with a rather dull saw on a hot afternoon. Perhaps if Dr. Eshleman had been here he might have attempted surgery. But I was not about to tackle brain surgery as my first major surgical procedure out here—especially because I had never seen that procedure done at home, much less helped to do one. Besides, many of the people I knew about who'd had such operations were not really helped and many of them died anyway.

Today James Shelly and Cora Lehman will try to go overland to Tarime—the first overland trip attempted by any of our Shirati folks in several months. Nyabasi is still getting some rain, but things are getting more dry around here. Next will come the work of repairing and rebuilding the roads. We surely have been glad for radio communication with our other stations at Bukiroba and Nyabasi, and glad of course for our regular contacts with the MAF plane and pilot during this unusual rainy season.

It is now Monday, the 5th of February. I had understood that the plane would probably come on Friday afternoon, so I was unprepared for its arrival at 10:00 A.M. I was in the midst of rounds and, in addition to this letter, several other letters were all ready to go but did not get off. Also on Friday Dr. Lester and Hershey returned from conference and reported that some discussions were not easy but, as hearts were melted in tears and prayer, God did work to bring about new understanding and new cooperation in the church.

After orienting Dr. Lester to some problems on the ward late Friday afternoon, I got to spend a wonderful weekend with Elsie Cressman in her house at the lake. Besides her nursing work with the leprosy patients, she also enjoys cooking (and eating!) and delivering babies. I was so glad for a change of scenery. The crashing water of the lake was so refreshing. The water is creeping closer to the house as the lake level rises. I really slept down there, away from the noisy telephone. On Saturday evening, Elsie and I went for a long walk and visited several villages. We then sat on some rocks overlooking the bay and enjoyed a picnic supper.

James and Cora got back last evening. They had gotten to Tarime and to Nyabasi without any serious road problems. There were "diversions" around several washed-out places, but they did not need to do any road building to get through. James reported some marked changes in contour at some places, especially at the rivers.

We are having warmer weather now, especially at noontime. With the breezes blowing toward the east from the lake and our screened windows open, it is really very pleasant indoors.

Thursday, February 22, 1962

Greetings again from Shirati. It continues to be busy around here. I am still trying to get the worms straightened out in my head—and if you can't decipher that, let me just say that I am working on my parasitology lectures for the nursing students. I postponed one lecture this week because I didn't yet feel ready to explain malaria and the mosquito cycle.

Enough about worms and parasites! This week has seen a variety of maternity cases. The first was a mother who delivered her baby at home but retained the placenta (afterbirth). I was able to deliver it without much trouble. Another mother came in with a marked curvature of the spine (scoliosis), but she nonetheless had a rather normal delivery, fortunately. She is much shorter than I am. Another mother came in with bleeding from the vagina, but I was able to increase the strength of her contractions and control the bleeding, so she delivered a healthy baby. Another woman came in looking as if she was ready to deliver a full-term baby. When her membranes ruptured, however, she released three quarts of amniotic fluid (the normal volume is only about a quart). Then I noticed that the uterus had decreased in size and was just above the belly button. So I realized that this was doubtless a baby with congenital defects of some sort. She went into good labor and soon delivered a three-and-a-half-pound baby who gasped for breath several times and had a slow heart beat for about an hour before passing. The baby's head was a little larger than normal. I asked the parents for permission to do a postmortem examination, and they agreed. I found some bleeding under the scalp and inside the brain, but the most interesting finding was in the heart. The normal heart has two small atria above the two larger and more muscular ventricles. The right atrium receives deoxygenated (venous) blood from the body, then sends it into the right ventricle, which delivers the blood to the lungs, where it is reoxygenated and returned to the heart through the left atrium, which sends the refreshed blood back into the body. This baby's heart had only one atrium for returning blood to the heart. The two ventricles each pump the blood through an artery into the lungs or to the rest of the body, and the blood is sent back into the heart through two veins. In this baby, there was no return vein from the lungs to the heart, nor was there a left atrium to receive the reoxygenated blood. This was a most interesting and unusual congenital failure in the development of the heart. It meant that blood could go toward the lungs to receive oxygen, but it could not return to the heart to be circulated to the rest of the body. This configuration of blood circulation was not compatible with life.

Forgive me if this is too technical and too medical for you. And do feel free to tell me when I get too detailed and too explicit in my medical descriptions! Otherwise, I will keep on writing about the things I see and do. But read what Psalm 139:13–18 has to say about our human bodies in the Good News Bible:

> You created every part of me; you put me together in my mother's
>   womb.
> I praise you because you are to be feared; all you do is strange
>   and wonderful.
> I know it with all my heart.
> When my bones were being formed, carefully put together in
>   my mother's womb,
> when I was growing there in secret, you knew I was growing
>   there—
> You saw me before I was born.
> The days allotted to me had all been recorded in your book,
> before any of them ever began.
> O God, how difficult I find your thoughts: how many of them
>   there are!
> If I counted them, they would be more than the grains of sand.
> When I awake, I am still with you.

Now, let me tell you about last evening. I was all set to write some letters when a man from Utegi, which is twenty miles east of here on the main road (just a dirt road) from Kenya and Tarime to Musoma and Mwanza, came in to Shirati and developed a broken axle on his lorry. He requested transportation back to Utegi. Jim Shelly agreed to take him and asked for some company, so Anna Martin and I went along. We left here at 7:30 P.M. and got back soon after 10:00, just in time to help eat some freezer-made ice cream instead of writing letters.

Did I tell you that there is a portable treadle organ in our big living room? Since the rains have stopped, the organ's keys have finally unstuck themselves, so I can amuse myself by pecking on it. It provides a little music when I get starved for it, when the generator is off and the radio and record player and Elsie's recorder won't play. I was so used to having good music available practically all the time when I was in my room at West Chester. Well, maybe I can get a recorder and/or radio at some point. They do have such machines for sale in Nairobi.

Pastor Nashon, our pastor here at Shirati, will soon be going to our bible college at Bukiroba. He is a mature and understanding man, but some feel he is too pro-missionary. Because we are no longer a mission and everything belongs to the local church, we have some growing pains too. Who will replace Pastor Nashon? The deacon, who is rather capable, has been accused of gross sin—perhaps unfairly by some who oppose him. In these days of newly achieved political independence nationally and new church status locally, some folks are using political methods to try to influence the church. So do pray that spiritual leaders will emerge to lead His people into greater spiritual maturity.

Sunday, March 4, 1962

Greetings on a lovely Sunday afternoon. *Kumbe* (Oh!), it is more than a week already since I last wrote you. Time just does keep going!

Last Sunday the Merlin Grove family, who are with EMBMC in Mogadishu, Somalia, came to visit us with Merlin's parents, who are visiting from Ontario, Canada. Merlin and his father brought greetings to the Shirati congregation at the Sunday morning service. Another special feature of the morning service was the dedication of two young children to the Lord; one was the first living daughter of a fine African teacher in our middle school—they have three boys—and the other was Hershey Leaman's son. As they stood up front and the parents read their statements presenting their children to the Lord, it dawned on me that both of these children were "my babies"—in the limited sense, of course, that I had escorted both of them into the world for their happy parents.

On Sunday evenings at 5:30 we have an English worship time at the nursing school. With all of the nursing students, staff nurses, school teachers, and missionaries in attendance, we have a nice-size group. Two weeks ago, the nine girls in our new group of students shared their testimonies, in English. Not only did they have a good command of the language, but their Christian testimony was sincere. Each spoke for three to ten minutes, with only a minimum of notes, and I was impressed.

Last Tuesday afternoon we received two visitors by plane—a father and son from near Lansdale, Pennsylvania. The son is in Mennonite Central Committee's (MCC's) Pax (Latin for "peace") service in the Congo, and the father, Ralph Hedrick, had flown out for a three-week vacation. His first two wives had died, leaving him with five children, so he'd gotten married again, to a girl I knew from EMC named Sarah Meyers. She stayed at home to be with the younger folks.

On Wednesday morning, the Groves left by car for Bukiroba and Musoma, and that evening the Hedricks left by plane for the same destinations. Dr. Lester came back from Flying Doctor Service (FDS) that evening, bringing along Velma Eshleman from Kisaka. On Thursday morning the Hershey Leaman trio went along with MAF to Nairobi. They were headed to Mombasa and the east coast for a month's leave—their first vacation in a year and a half. So people are coming and going nowadays at Shirati. Phoebe Yoder, Catherine Leatherman, and Pastor Zedekia from Bukiroba came in yesterday to help us enjoy a weekend fellowship conference with four guests from Kenya. Phoebe translated for me this morning and I really appreciated getting to hear everything that was said in church.

This coming week we are also expecting some medical visitors—doctors who are specialists in orthopedics (bones) and plastic surgery (burns), and an anesthesiologist (makes patients comfortable for surgery). Of course Dr. Lester's wife, Lois, who is a nurse, does a lot of our anesthesia work too. If you know Dr. Lester, you know he has been busy rounding up a lot of people with bone problems, from polio to club foot, burns, and so on, for these visiting doctors to see and treat for us. It will be a very busy, long three days for all of us.

Next weekend, Daniel Wenger and James Shelly will be winding up their three-year terms here at Shirati. Right now they are at Nyabasi trying to complete a new ward building for their clinic. They probably will not finish all the projects they could do, and they will be missed a lot—especially because we will not receive any replacements for them. They plan to leave for Nairobi on the 14th of March or so and then make visits in Somalia, Ethiopia, and Europe before arriving in the United States about June 1st.

When we learned that Catherine Leatherman and Dorothy Smoker were coming this weekend (they are both on the language committee),

Cora sent word by radio asking them to bring her a first-level Swahili language exam. They offered to bring me one too, but I declined: *Sina nafasi kujifunza Kiswahali kutosha* ("I do not have enough opportunity to study Swahili"). I have had two study days since New Year's, but I hope to get more study time this month. I think Dr. Lester will not be away so much this month, so maybe I can get more study days. Also, Elsie Cressman and I are wanting to go to Nairobi. I don't have a lot of money to spend, but I am curious to see what I might spend my shillings on, and we both are specifically interested in something that helps our legs go farther and faster than we travel now. We have some guests who came from Nairobi by bicycle, but that sounds like a *long* way to pedal, half of it over dirt and sandy roads, and there are hills too. Anyway, we want to have a look-see.

Friday, March 9, 1962

On Tuesday I scrubbed in (washed hands and arms, then dressed up in a sterile gown and gloves) to assist Dr. Lester with surgery on a man with a huge hydatid cyst in his abdomen. The cyst was filled with a "dishpan" of eggs with thin membranes and clear fluid. We could not remove the entire cyst, so we scooped out as much of its contents as possible, then placed a tube to the outside to encourage further drainage. This condition is caused by a parasite and can be treated only by surgery at this point. Maybe someone will find a medication to treat this problem.

Yesterday afternoon two doctors—a plastic surgeon (who treats burns and such) and an orthopedic (bone) surgeon—flew in from Nairobi. Both had been here last September and were eager to see the patients they had operated on last time. Last evening we made rounds on the new patients with these particular problems, then had supper together at the Eshleman house before returning to the hospital to study the patients' X-rays and prepare for their surgeries.

This morning we started by removing a kidney that had many stones in it from recurrent kidney infections. Kidney stones are rather rare here, so we were glad for the expert help. We also operated on some foot deformities—clubfoot and post-polio foot drop. The plastic surgeon applied skin grafts to several hands that were badly scarred by old burns. Tomorrow we have more leg (knee and hip joint) problems to repair and a leprosy patient with a bad foot ulcer to work on. The guest doctors also diagnosed a patient who has progressive paralysis and is unable to walk because of tuberculosis of the spine. We will start medication for the TB, and the doctors will return in three weeks or so to do spinal surgery and insert a bone graft. They say that spinal

TB is rather common here. Like many other things, I had heard about it only in books at home, but now I have seen it for real.

We stopped surgery at 4:00 P.M., had late tea, and went to the leprosarium to see some patients with foot problems due to chronic ulcers. After supper the orthopedist showed some slides of surgery on clubfeet and for chronic osteomyelitis (bone infection). The photos were very instructive. It is so helpful to have these specialists come see and help treat our patients who have special problems, because two heads are better than one in finding the best procedure for treating a given patient. I certainly need to learn all I can while I have access to these expert colleagues here at Shirati, before I transfer to Somalia, where such consultations will be less available.

Last week, Phoebe Yoder asked how I am progressing in my Swahili study, so I told her the discouraging fact that I have had only two days at the lake house since New Year's. She asked a staff nurse who knows English quite well to spend some time teaching me Swahili. He came twice this week and, after discussing my situation, read me a story while I picked out the unknown words and discussed the grammar. This could be a big help *if* I could do it daily and study vocabulary regularly; but the pressure of my hospital duties often demands more immediate attention of my time and concentration.

Bible college was scheduled to start at Bukiroba this past week, but at a recent committee meeting it was unexpectedly postponed until August. This unexplained move is a puzzle to some, but at least we Shirati folks are happy to have Pastor Nashon remain here as our spiritual leader. We welcome his stability, whereas others might make hasty and unwise decisions. He is working hard at learning English, because the Bible college classes will be taught in English, and several months of preliminary study of English will be required before the Bible courses begin. Pastor Nashon stopped by the other evening to chat with me and is really doing well with English. He often recognizes his own mistakes, such as in the tenses of verbs. I just wish I was doing as well in Swahili as he does in English!

It is now midnight but the generator is still running for some reason and I seldom waste any generator light by going to bed before it stops. And I can send this letter along with the doctors to Nairobi tomorrow.

Thursday, March 15, 1962

Greetings from Shirati, where the past week has been very busy. Last Saturday morning when the specialists were here Dr. Eshleman and I worked with them as two teams in the operating room. Dr. Eshleman helped with a hip operation and put on a hip cast while I helped the plastic surgeon repair the stump of a leprosy patient's foot. This week Dr. Eshleman did a similar operation, and we cleaned another leprosy patient's chronic leg ulcer, then applied a skin graft. These surgeries show the practical value of having experts come and show us how to treat more complex problems. We see such a variety of medical problems here, so it is really great to have such "graduate training" supplied for us on occasion by the AMREF in Nairobi.

The visiting specialists departed on Saturday afternoon. After they left I spent more than an hour cleaning and debriding a badly infected wound for a new admission instead of going to tea time. On Sunday morning I had barely sat down in church when I was asked to come see a maternity patient. A quick inspection revealed a prolapsed umbilical cord and a hand waiting to greet me, so I returned to the house, got into my "scrub" attire, and went back to work. A better inspection showed that the baby's back was facing the vagina and one arm was stretched upward behind the head. So I had to turn the baby ninety degrees to get ahold of a foot and deliver it as a breech with a single-foot presentation. That I could manage, but the problems were not over. The afterbirth was easily delivered and appeared to be intact, but the bleeding continued, so I gave her extra medication to contract the uterus. I also gave her two units of blood, but the bleeding did not stop. I eventually inserted some packing into the uterus, but all to no avail; she kept on bleeding until she had no more. She is the first mother I had die of delivery problems, but she probably will not be the last.

On Monday I got a new problem: a woman who had been in labor for a day and a half and then "got tired of it all and quit"! She finally came to us, and because she did not resume contractions even after I used some medication, I finally resorted to surgery that evening to relieve her of a baby who did not live. Later that evening another woman presented in labor. The baby was in distress with a slow heartbeat. This patient, however, responded to some stimulation, and I delivered a baby who is now doing fine.

On Tuesday morning at 5:00 A.M. I was called out for a lady who was three months pregnant and bleeding. I relieved her of the "products of conception." I found that the placenta had not developed normally. That afternoon, a mother came in with her child's buttocks presenting and the legs extending over the abdomen. Her contractions were not very strong all day, but after I finally decided to go home to bed, well— she finally decided to deliver her baby. By the time I got dressed and ran to the maternity ward, she had partially delivered, but before I could deliver the baby's arms, shoulders, and head, pressure had been applied to the umbilical cord long enough that its pulsations had stopped and the baby's heart had stopped too. Also, at some point the afterbirth had prematurely separated from the inside of the uterus, so the placenta was delivered immediately after the baby was born.

So, those were an eventful three days as far as our maternity patients were concerned. The midwife had two normal deliveries on Tuesday. From Sunday the 11th thru Tuesday the 13th, our maternity statistics were as follows:

6 full-term pregnancies: 2 were normal deliveries, 4 were not
3 babies and 1 mother died
2 mothers had abnormal presentations
1 mother had major surgery for delivery
1 mother miscarried at ten weeks of gestation

I think that some deaths could have been prevented if the mothers had arrived earlier for care. And if I had not gone to bed when the mother with the buttocks presentation was in labor, maybe I could have expedited the process and delivered a living baby. In any case, times like this, when so many maternity patients have complications, make it a little harder for me to enjoy obstetrics. But when things go well, obstetrics can be a joyful experience.

Let's change the subject. James Shelly and Daniel Wenger left us at 6:00 A.M. today to start a two-and-a-half-month journey to the United States via Somalia, Ethiopia, Palestine, and Europe. It was interesting to watch as they packed and sold things the last few days. Daniel sold some kitchenware and books that had belonged to his mother. Their house is a sight to behold, but fortunately several of our nurses know the disposal plans for the remaining things—clothing to leprosy patients, books to the Bible college and nursing school, and so on.

It's Sunday evening. We have visitors again—Bishop Elam Stauffer and Pastor Zedekia from South Mara, and Daniel Sensenigs from Ethiopia. They are visiting us before attending the Peace Conference near Nairobi sponsored by MCC and other Mennonite groups working in Africa. In our English service, Daniel spoke from Luke 2 about Jesus remaining in the temple while His parents started home, supposing Him to be with them. Daniel challenged us to take Him with us in all we do and not to take His presence for granted. The visitors go to Musoma tomorrow, so I will send this along with them to catch the Tuesday plane out.

Monday, March 26, 1962

Surprise! This finds me sending you greetings directly from Nairobi, the capitol city of Kenya and our favorite place to go shopping. But first I must tell you about the events of the past week at Shirati.

Although the week began with routine rounds and changing dressings on several infected wounds, it became a continuation of the complicated OB problems that I described last week. On Wednesday morning, Dr. Lester went on FDS by MAF Cessna Airplane and by noon the plane returned with two patients. One had delivered the first twin near Nyabasi several days earlier, but then had decided to bleed instead of delivering the other twin, so she was sent to me to receive blood and to deliver the other twin. On the plane for the fifteen-minute flight to Shirati she got better contractions, but the pilot got her to our airstrip and transferred her into our VW Microbus before she delivered the other twin, stillborn. The woman was quickly brought to our maternity ward, which was empty of patients and staff because I had discharged the last patient that morning. Simeon Hurst (one of our missionaries from Nyabasi), who had accompanied her from Nyabasi, soon located me. I promptly delivered the placenta but was surprised to see that it was a double placenta with an accessory lobe that had separated early, which explained why she was bleeding after the birth of the first twin. One does not usually treat a patient before getting a history of the symptoms, but fortunately this mother and the first twin are doing well.

The second patient on that flight had delivered a premature baby at Kisaka and perhaps had retained placenta tissue. At any rate, she had developed a fever with significant bleeding so she was transferred to me for further care. [*This patient likely survived because I made no mention otherwise.*]

Then, on Friday afternoon, I got another OB problem. I think this mother lived not so far from Shirati but had been in labor for two days at home and then had gotten tired and quit. She was unable to pass her urine and had a very full bladder. In fact, her abdominal contour presented as two mountains, one above and one below the umbilicus (belly button), which made me remember that old tune, "The bear went over the mountain . . . to see what he could see. . . . He saw another mountain. . . ," and so on. But this was *not* an amusing problem. I soon realized that she would not deliver this baby without surgery, and Dr. Lester was still on safari. He had gone south to Mugango and the MAF plane had gone elsewhere, so there was no way to get him back early to help me. So this mother was *my* patient and urgently needed expert help. Although she was not having contractions, she was quite uncomfortable because of the low presentation of the baby's head and her very distended urinary bladder. She also had painful leg cramps. I did not then have a suction cup to use on the scalp to pull on the baby's head. And I would not try using forceps beside the swollen vaginal tissues. That left me the option of a C-section. I consulted with our anesthetist, Lois Eshleman, then inserted a catheter to empty the bladder partially. Finally, at 10:30 P.M., I began the operation that I hoped would save the mother's life.

One generally does a C-section by making a vertical or transverse incision in the lower abdomen. But in this case I made the incision upward from the umbilicus. I entered the uterus and withdrew the infant by grabbing its legs. Maybe I should have worked faster, but I was still rather inexperienced at this. After closing the incision, I inserted an indwelling Foley catheter into the bladder. The patient then apparently threw a blot clot from her pelvis or leg veins into the lungs; this congestion of the lungs and poor oxygen exchange resulted in acute heart failure. Despite the use of intravenous digitalis and other efforts, the patient died one hour after the surgery was finished. So, as doctors sometimes say in such situations, "The surgery was a success, but the patient, alas, died." At least I had tried to help her, and I know she could not have survived without the operation.

That same evening, two children died. One had a respiratory infection that did not respond to our antibiotics. The other had complications following severe burns of his head and shoulders. The wailing of the mourners on Friday evening and Saturday morning was almost continuous. When Dr. Lester returned on Saturday at noon, I told him what had happened during his absence. I reported that the morgue was booming with business—the bodies of one adult woman and three children. But at least the wards were now fairly quiet after the previous night's activities. I explained that my first major surgical case was history, and I had lost two mothers with labor problems in less than two weeks after having lost none for a number of months. The loss of this last mother was even more tragic in that for two days she had begged to come to the hospital for help, but her elderly husband had procrastinated and said, "It is not our custom to go to the hospital for the birth of a child. Our babies can be born at home."

I was really tired after the short Friday night of making the decision to do surgery, then doing it; watching her die of pulmonary embolism and acute heart failure soon afterward; then hearing the wailing of the mourners. I did not sleep very well for the few remaining hours of the night. I made later morning rounds after packing some clothes for a short trip to Nairobi with Elsie Cressman, who had arranged for the two of us to hitch a ride with MAF. We picked up Don Jacobs at Musoma, and saw lots of elephants and other animals on the way to our final destination. We are staying at the CMS guest house, where I spent one night last October on my way to Shirati. Elsie knows her way around, so I follow her. I am glad to be in Nairobi for a short break, to see what the big city has to sell. Incidentally, *if* Nate has not yet taken any definitive action about shipping a recorder to me, please tell him to delay on that item while I check into what might be available here in Nairobi.

Thursday, April 12, 1962

The weather report for Shirati is sunny warm days, usually ending with dark clouds and rain coming from the east around sundown. Sometimes it is a short thunderstorm with driving rain; other times it is a steady rain that lasts all night. So people are busy digging and planting their gardens. This is what is usually called the big rains, but they are nothing like the floods we had several months ago. Cora and I planted corn, beans, cucumbers, and pumpkins the other evening. The rains are heavier around Tarime and Nyabasi, so sometimes the rivers near Utegi are impassable by car. Our driver went to Tarime last Friday and started back, but he sat by the river all night at Utegi and all day Saturday and into Sunday morning before he could get across with the very-low-slung Peugeot vehicle he was driving.

Yesterday a week ago "the boy" began working in our kitchen. (He is actually a married man, but the men who work in our homes are called boys. Is this maybe a carryover of the British practice of calling an African house employee a "boy" even if he is married and has a family?) His name is Eleazar and he used to work for Jim Shelly and Dan Wenger. Cora can converse with him fairly well, so she works with him to plan menus, purchase foods in the market, and so on. Frankly, I am glad she does it, for it would be quite a chore for me. Eleazar is an experienced cook and does fix good meals. But he is still preparing quantities to feed "growing boys" rather than "dieting girls."

My trunk finally got here last Friday after sitting at Bukiroba for about two months. Poor Cora has lived out of her suitcase since November 20, so she was pleased to get her barrels. As for my trunk that spent some time at Salunga and did not get some other items inserted to complete filling it, I was concerned about the "mobility" of the contents. Well, things did get rearranged, but much to my amazement there were no holes in the trunk, though it was battered. Best of all, the treasured motto I feared to unpack survived without any breaks or scratches, though there were a few loose edges, but some glue will fix that.

On Saturday, Elsie and Cora and I took off for Utegi at 3:15 P.M. to retrieve Cora's barrels. After wading through two rivers, we finally came to the last river. To paraphrase the old "polly wolly doodle all the day" tune, "I came to a river / and I couldn't get across / And I didn't jump on anybody / and think he was a horse. . . ." So I just sat with the VW pickup and our stuff and watched Elsie wade across the "bridge." The water did not reach to her knees, but she is much taller than I am and the water was quite swift. Her effort paid off, for she found a large lorry that was just ready to drive into Shirati. The agreeable Indian owner turned around and returned the mile to Utegi to pick up Cora's barrels. Meanwhile, I was fascinated watching people and objects cross the river. I saw several obedient donkeys cross with their masters, but the cow refused to follow the poor little calf that its owner rather brutally yanked across the river by pulling on its front foot. I saw one child carried piggyback while another was lofted onto the adult's shoulder and carried in a horizontal position like a log or a bicycle.

Elsie soon returned. This time she rode across the river in high style aboard a high cab-over-engine British lorry. Our mission accomplished, we turned around and went home. The lorry delivered the barrels to our front door and Cora unpacked. She had brought lots of stuff—Revere Ware, stainless steel "silverware," place settings for eight people, eight to ten new dresses, and so on. I sort of felt like I had not brought much along, but then I remembered that I had brought a lot of medical books. I am glad I did not put lots of money into expensive kitchenware. If I ever decide I need more utensils and equipment, I reckon I can buy it later here.

Well, the fellows I wanted to send this with left this morning because they decided to walk the twenty miles to Utegi instead of trying to go by bicycle this afternoon. So I will finish this letter later.

It is now Tuesday the 17th. Would you believe that I have not been asked to teach any classes for nursing school since I returned from Nairobi? That was more than two weeks ago. But at least I have gotten a day and a half each week for language study for the past two weeks. That is such a boost to my morale, especially after getting only two days for Swahili study in the previous three months. With such infrequent study days, I very quickly forget what I have "learned" before I get back to it again.

I have more responsibility in the hospital these days, but it is not so overwhelming at this point. Dr. Eshleman has been here most of the time since early March and that makes a real difference for me.

Sunday, April 22, 1962

Greetings at 4:15 P.M. here. The sky is very dark over the mountains to the east of us, and there is thunder, so we may get rain before sundown tonight. Cora just told me that our garden things are up, but I have not yet gone back to our garden to see for myself.

Wednesday was *some* day. First, I sent off some letters that morning. Then, soon after breakfast, I was called out to see Alta Weaver (from Ephrata), who had suddenly become ill at the nursing school, where she is the "sister tutor," or head teacher. She complained of severe chest pain and was very pale, so I asked several students to carry her on a bed to our nurses' house, where I also live. She has been in bed ever since but is more comfortable now. This appears to be a "heart attack," but it is hard to be sure because we do not even have an EKG (electrocardio-gram; abbreviated from the Dutch *Elektrokardiogramm*) machine. Maybe we can later send her by MAF plane to Nairobi for further tests and some expert advice on her care. Meanwhile, Alice Reber, the other teacher in the nursing school, is due to go on furlough in July 1962, so now she suddenly has extra teaching responsibilities when she is also preparing for furlough. And Alta doubtless thinks about the things she was planning to do and now someone else has to do them. So do pray for a speedy recovery for Alta, as well as wisdom and strength for those who are filling in the gap while Alta is unable to do the job.

On Wednesday afternoon the folks returned from Tarime with what seemed like a carload of mail, which landed in the middle of our living room floor to be sorted. I got three letters, including a special letter from Nate telling me that baby Leonard arrived on Monday, April 9, less than two years after Joyce was born on June 28, 1960. I had no clue he was on the way! But at least I now know to expect a new addition in Paul's family too. Maybe that information will come in the next post bag.

I got a package from Nairobi—a pair of strap sandals I had ordered—so now I have something besides the faithful brown oxfords to wear for knockabout. And two tapes of the EMBMC meeting came from Uncle Bill Hursts. Alta and I listened to parts of one tape on two evenings while other folks attended special Easter season services. We listened to more tapes (of Raymond Charles, James Stauffer, John H. Kraybill, and P. T. Yoder) on Wednesday afternoon to Thursday morning. Hershey Leaman took the other tape with the rest of the Thursday program. It is nice to listen to tapes whenever I wish—provided the generator is running. I can stop the tape if I get called out to the hospital, then let the speaker finish when it is convenient for me to listen again.

This afternoon I had a new experience. I had gone to the hospital to see a new patient and was talking to the staff nurse when suddenly things began to move. The windows rattled and the tin roof made a noise. It lasted only a few seconds and was not severe. This was the first time I have been shaken by an earthquake. One of the Africans said, "That is the way it will be when the Lord comes," but I thought, "Oh, much more than this little shake will happen when He comes."

Next time I should have lots to say about my first FDS. The plane will come on Wednesday morning and take me to Kisaka, on Thursday to Masinono and Kenyana, and on Friday to Bukiroba and Mugango. At least that is what the plans are as of now, but things can change.

I understand that the *Missionary Messenger* this month has some photos and an article about Shirati by Dr. Lester Eshleman that you might find interesting.

In my "spare time" I have done some carpentry work. When I was in Nairobi I bought a good claw hammer, and with my new hammer plus an old screwdriver I have removed the bottom of one wall of the

closet in my office and made two deep shelves instead of three shallow shelves. I let the shelves remain open to my desk instead of closing them as a closet with a door. This provides more space for my bigger medical books. I actually enjoyed pounding around a bit, especially because someone else is paid to clean up the sawdust! (I did, however, try to saw over the waste can most of the time to collect at least some of it!)

Saturday, May 5, 1962

I did go on FDS about two weeks ago, and it was true to the African pattern of being unpredictable and without regard for our well-planned schedule. MAF was due here on Wednesday morning, April 25, but arrived somewhat late at 10:30. The pilot took me to Kisaka as our first stop. Much like a consultant, I saw several patients in the dispensary while the nurse and dressers treated the "routine" problems. And I really slept during the afternoon siesta. Maybe the fact that Kisaka is a thousand feet higher than Shirati accounted for my good sleep. I saw more patients that evening, then wrote a letter to brother Nate.

The next morning the plane arrived at 7:30 (What time did he get up and leave Nairobi?) and took nurse Velma Eshleman, Erasto (an African dresser), and me thirty miles south and across the *pori*. The teacher of the bush school met us at the airstrip and helped us carry our supplies a half-mile to the site and get organized for the clinic. There were eighty students in his one-room school with a grass roof. The students had done most of the work of grading and preparing the airstrip before Clyde Shenk came out to "drag" it, probably by pulling a tree trunk behind his Jeep truck, to make the strip smoother. We found a partly built house nearby; the sticks were in place for the walls and the roof. Some grass had been put on the roof, but there was no mud on the walls. This was the site of our clinic that morning, so we had sunlight and shade with lots of ventilation. I saw thirty to forty patients. Some were quite sick with fever, possibly malaria, but others had perhaps "invented" a headache so they could see the doctor too. (Some of the latter I treated with vitamins.) I also saw a number of maternity patients. We took them out behind a pile of straw and spread a blanket on the ground for our examination table. At 1:15 we tried to close the box of medicine as we returned to the airstrip, but the people kept coming to ask for more. When the plane arrived, the box was closed—to the great disappointment of some!

The plane then took us to Kenyana, which is located midway between Kisaka and Masinono. We have a fine Christian family living at Kenyana. Naaman is a graduate of our Bible college at Bukiroba; his wife was also a student there. After our late noon meal of hominy grits and meat, we went to their little church, which was filled with patients. After eating our dinner in a house with a tin roof, we felt somewhat roasted, so it was very refreshing to work in this church with its grass roof. It was so wonderfully cool and comfortable in there, we could work fast. I saw the maternity patients and about half of the others while Velma and the dresser took care of the rest. We finished around 6:30 P.M. and were quite ready to call it a day's work.

Gordon, the pilot, had warned us that because of his busy schedule that day he might not be able to pick us up that evening to return to Kisaka, so we resigned ourselves to staying for the night as darkness came but no airplane. As we rested, we heard the chickens squawking outside as Naaman's wife worked to prepare supper. The "kitchen" was in a separate house where they built a fire in a pit using several big stones as a tripod to support the kettle, usually one kettle at a time, over the fire. The chicken and hot *ugali* tasted really good when it arrived at 9:30. After supper, the dishes were washed outside on a homemade stick table. Velma and I slept together on their bed—a wooden frame

with an animal skin and a blanket mattress, which was quite comfortable to us weary folks.

The next morning, Friday, we had *ugi* (porridge, which Africans often drink but we ate ours like hot cereal with milk and sugar) for breakfast. We also had hard-boiled eggs. Then we wandered toward the airstrip, where we waited in vain for the plane to come, so we finally returned to the house. After the noon meal I went to the church and slept in cool comfort on the mud-wall bench. At about 5:00 P.M. we heard a plane, but it was very high in the sky and *not* our MAF plane. We felt that our plane must have had some kind of trouble, so we had a "strategy meeting" and decided that if no plane arrived by 9:00 A.M. on Saturday, we would go overland to Kisaka by bicycle and/or foot. That evening, Namaan's wife heated some water and we took turns having a shower in their small bathhouse—so refreshing before we went to bed.

On Saturday morning we got up early and had breakfast. Again we saw no airplane, so we prepared to start walking. But before we got off, around 9:00 A.M. two young men came into the village on bicycles and said they were headed for Kisaka too. They offered to let us use their bikes and they would walk. Because we were three people for two bikes, Erasto offered to take me on the rear carrier of one bike and Velma would ride the other bike.

The grass was still quite damp as we began our journey. Kenyana lies fifteen miles southeast of Kisaka, with a significant hill to climb just before we would reach Kisaka. Sometimes the path was good enough

that we could ride the bikes. But if the path was muddy, we walked. And there were streams to cross. The first few were small enough that I could jump across them, but then we met a bigger one, so I gave up trying to protect my shoes and just stepped into the water with my shoes and socks on and got wet feet. We then came to a larger stream, and the only way to get across was to climb into a tree from the end of a limb, follow the limb to the tree trunk, then follow a second limb out the other side and down to the ground on the far side of the water. I was glad I did not have to carry a bike through that tree bridge! We had quickly realized that the men who had loaned us their bikes were making faster progress by walking than we were by riding and pushing their bikes!

We began to see our next challenge: the hill to Kisaka. Just then we heard a familiar sound: a plane. It was flying overhead, not extremely high, and going toward Kenyana. The sun was getting hotter and we went faster as we got closer to the hill. Eventually Velma and Erasto decided to walk and push their bikes up the hill. I was glad I had to carry only me up the hill. The plane soon returned overhead, flying toward Kisaka, but we were not sure if the pilot saw us. Finally we reached the top of the hill. Velma led the way down the trail to Kisaka and we followed. After only ten yards or so Erasto suddenly stopped and said, "I think we have a punch!" Sure enough, a tire was very flat, so we walked the rest of the way, downgrade this time, to Kisaka. We heard the plane leave from Kisaka and I wondered where he was going now—without me!

We were soon met by several young men who were coming from Kisaka to meet us. They looked at me, very red from spending all day in

the sunshine, and finally one of them said, "Well, I am not sure what kind of person you are, but for sure you are no longer a white person!" We all laughed as we hurried down the road to the Kisaka compound, where I pulled off my shoes and brown socks that had been white that morning. It felt so good to wash my dirty feet and lower legs with the garden hose, then enjoy tea and doughnuts before Gordon returned for me from Nyabasi. I climbed into the plane in my bare feet and flew back to Shirati, where Dr. Lester was expecting me but was taken aback when I climbed out of the plane all sunburned and carrying my wet shoes and socks in my hand! So that was my initiation into FDS!

Saturday, May 19, 1962

Greetings to you all again. I am still at Shirati, in case you were wondering whether I moved somewhere or got lost! Really, moving would not be a simple process on these wet days. But in spite of the rain, Dr. Lester and Hershey Leaman left here at 8:30 on Wednesday morning, headed for Tarime and Nyabasi. They waited for an hour to cross the river near Utegi, and then, when Hershey tried to cross, the car wanted to go sideways instead of forward. A car and a big lorry were previously washed off the same "bridge" and are still lying there as reminders of the power of water! Dr. Lester and Hershey then encountered MUD on the way from Tarime to Nyabasi—thick black sticky stuff. I remember clearly that I could hardly walk on that stuff when we were previously returning from Nairobi. Anyway, the men put ropes on the tires to increase the traction, and as the ropes wore through they put on more ropes. Because we pay carfare by the mile, the men were very happy that the speedometer is connected to the front wheels instead of to the rear ones, because the rear wheels did a lot of ineffective spinning!

After doing some business in Tarime, Dr. Lester and Hershey finally got to Nyabasi at 5:00 P.M.—a *long* fifty-mile trip. On their return trip, they again found an impassable river, so they backtracked on a long detour to get home. And would you know? They came home with almost *no* post. I got three air letters, but none from home. We got our last real mail on April 29, almost three weeks ago.

Granted, the poor delivery of mail is not all due to the roads being clogged by mud or high water. Some of it is related to growing pains in a young country where Africans are now working in positions formerly held by "Europeans"—mostly British persons. Some of the new personnel are doing an adequate job, but others are less successful. And the unaccustomed access to money brings with it the temptation to use it improperly and let the main task remain undone. Hershey and Dr. Lester found things somewhat deplorable at Tarime, where public employees and even police officers had been drinking enough that they could not manage their work in a responsible manner. Also, in Musoma as in other towns, people are striking for higher wages, just as in supposedly more advanced countries employees will rashly strike for more pay without realizing that a pay increase without an accompanying increase in productivity will only increase living costs. The typical African is not a keen businessman; most of the shopkeepers, contractors, and businessmen are Indians, from India, and Africans do mostly unskilled labor. So, as I started to say about Musoma and the strike, among other things, no one wants to load or unload the ferry, so no vehicles can cross the Mara Bay from Musoma to go to Tarime. But some people can hire a motor boat to cross the bay. No busses are running from Musoma to Tarime, so airmail that flies into Musoma sits there waiting for an eventual ride to Tarime. And maybe the Musoma post office is not sorting the mail, because the South Mara missionaries near Musoma are also feeling the delay in mail delivery. It seems that public utilities should settle their disputes without going on strikes and tying up this essential communication service.

Then, on Friday at about sundown, a car drove in from Tarime. Its driver said that one of the Europeans there was quite sick and needed a doctor, so Hershey and Dr. Lester took off on another safari. Why the sick man was not brought along in the car that came to request help, no one knows. The man had been treated for malaria without improvement, we were told. By the time the doctor arrived, several hours later, the man was feeling better and refused the invitation to return with the doctor to the hospital. So that was another exhausting *bure* (meaning "all for nothing" or useless trip), except that some post had dribbled into Tarime that day, so I finally got your EMC letter, and the May 1 jumbo edition, and one from Kathryn Hostetter in West Virginia. We "efficient" Americans can so easily get frustrated by such mismanagement of funds and energy, but I suspect that such experiences are part of the cost of learning and growing into mature nationhood. Similar things may sometimes occur in a young church and we may feel that unwise decisions are being made, but we should remember that this is God's church, not ours, and He will build it aright as we pray and concentrate on the job He asks us to do.

I began a letter to Mother a week ago, for Mother's Day and her birthday, and I hoped to send it out by MAF yesterday, but the plane did not come. Catherine Leatherman has been here for ten days and is eager to return home to Bukiroba, so we now expect MAF to come on Monday or Tuesday. Meanwhile I am cranking out a few more letters.

It is now Sunday afternoon. We planned an outdoor picnic for Anna Martin's birthday, but it rained, so we all went down to Elsie's house by the lake. Her house is now surrounded by water. Some of it is quite stagnant and we almost needed a boat to get there. But when we got inside her small but cozy house, we had a good time together. The lake level is now higher than it has ever been, at least in recent history. We are *not* having excessive amounts of rain here at this time, but large Lake Victoria surely is being enlarged from somewhere. Our pier at Shirati has been seriously undermined by the excessive water, which may make the pier useless.

Sunday, June 3, 1962

Hedwig Nacht, also known as Heddie, from Switzerland visited us two weeks ago. She had served as a nurse under EMBMC from January 1953 to 1957 but for health reasons had not returned to us. She stopped by now for several days while en route to another mission in southern Tanganyika. On Thursday she went along with Dr. Lester to Nyabasi "to visit" and got involved in some emergency surgery, without the equipment of an operating room. A mother had delivered a living child but the twin was lying in a transverse position, so Dr. Lester rotated the child and delivered it—stillborn. He then discovered that the mother had ruptured her uterus at some point, so he somehow repaired it from the vagina. Fortunately the mother and surviving twin were reportedly doing fine.

The next day, Elsie Cressman, Norma Leaman, several Africans, and I headed out to Utegi on our way to go south to Musoma. We met Dr. Lester and Heddie at the river several miles from Utegi and Heddie transferred to our vehicle. We also received some very welcome post from Dr. Lester, who then helped us push our vehicle through the river so that we could continue our journey.

The next major obstacle was how to get onto the Kinesi ferry so that we could cross the bay to Musoma. Lake Victoria has risen about five feet since the floods of last November, so most of the pier is under water. Some sturdy four-wheel-drive Land Rovers can manage to get onto the ferry. We parked our car and hired a canoe to carry us and our baggage the one hundred yards to the pier and the ferry. We had a pleasant one-hour ride across the bay. In the late afternoon the wind was strong enough to whip some waves up over the deck. It reminded me of going deep-sea fishing with Bucky.

At Musoma they had built up the pier, so we could step off onto dry land. We stopped at Elam Stauffers and heard about some thieves who took much of his wife's silverware and good dishes. The thieves cut holes through the screens to get in, and Elam and Grace's nice-looking brown dog, Buttons, did not bother to bark and merely tried to hide in the bedroom. Now her name is BB, for Bure Buttons (*bure* means "worthless" or "in vain"). Elsie and I were then taken to Bukiroba, where we had supper with John and Catherine Leatherman. (Catherine is a daughter of Henry Garber.) Elsie slept in the new house of Phoebe Yoder and Martha Myer, and I slept in the Smoker house with George and Dorothy. I discovered that George shares relatives with us. Uncle Ammon Stoltzfus's wife, Aunt Lillie, was a Smoker, and according to the 2009 Fisher book, George's father and her father were brothers. George and Dorothy had heard about my bout of malaria, which probably sounded worse than it was when the news circulated back to these veteran missionaries about my day and a half of mild indisposition!

On Saturday morning our staff nurse examined seventeen patients at the Bukiroba clinic while I saw several with somewhat unusual problems. This visit partially made up for the visits to Bukiroba and Mugango that I had missed the previous month when MAF gave us two extra days in Kenyana and we biked and hiked our way back to Kisaka.

On Sunday, Elsie and I were invited by the Robert and Florence Keeners for dinner at noon. Hershey Leamans were invited too, and the little boys had a good time. At five months, Larry Leaman is becoming a big boy. He pulls himself up and is ready to go crawling. Jay Keener is a big four-months-old chap with light hair. He must be like the Weaver relatives rather than the Keeners, who have lots of dark wavy hair.

On Monday morning we finished our shopping in Musoma, then after dinner at the Stauffers' we collected all our supplies, including four gas tanks for our houses' gas stoves, and boarded the ferry. There was no canoe waiting at the Kinesi end to transport Elsie, me, our male African escorts, and all our supplies to shore, but the ferry manager finally got a man to load all our supplies and us onto his canoe

and transport us to shore and our waiting vehicle. We traveled in the VW that Elsie used mainly for leprosarium work. Norma and Larry Leaman had arranged to return by MAF later in the week—and why not? It was such an easy fifteen-minute flight compared to hours of bouncing on a dirt road and waiting for a ferry.

We made good time until we reached Utegi and headed up the Shirati road. The rivers were still high and water was running over the bridges. We got through the bridge beside Utegi OK. But when we got to the second bridge, where Dr. Lester had pushed us through on Friday, the water was still high. And there was a new problem: the water was washing out the dirt at the far end of the concrete bridge, where there was a rather steep incline onto the dirt road above. How deep the water was, was hard to know. Elsie decided to find out. She drove carefully, keeping close to the upper side of the bridge, which had no side rails. We got to the Shirati end of the bridge and started up the springy, wet hill through the big hole of moving water, which was about the length of our vehicle. The bottom end of the hole was about a foot lower than the bridge's surface, and the rear engine sat down right in it. And there it stopped. So there we sat. What to do now? It would soon be dark.

Fortunately, some men came by and Elsie sent word with them to the Indian merchants at Utegi that we needed help. They came promptly and tried to get the engine to start, but without success. So they used the starter and the reverse gear plus human push power to get the VW back over the bridge to the side we had come from. We left our African men passengers to guard our vehicle and supplies while the Indian took Elsie and me back to Utegi, where we slept well that night in comfortable beds.

The Indian had a shop facing the street, and the family residence was in the back part of the same building. Behind the house was an enclosed courtyard lined with storage sheds and other vital facilities. When we awoke the next morning, we saw men carrying large sacks of flour (probably weighing two hundred pounds each) from a rear shed, through the family kitchen and living room, into the store, and out onto trucks. The store's floor was at the same level as the loading platform. You can imagine the commotion and dust all through the house and store. Later we were served rice and curry, which we ate with our fingers. Africans do provide spoons for eating rice, but we eat *ugali* with our fingers—after carefully washing our hands before we eat.

After our noon meal, a mechanic from Tarime worked on our vehicle. He removed lots of water and installed new oil and got it to run. Meanwhile, a lorry headed to Shirati attempted to cross the river at the same place where we had gotten hung up. He stalled on the same hill, and as he drifted backward, he slipped partly off the bridge on the upper side. So now the bridge was blocked. So how could we get home?

Well, there was another long way to go to maybe get to Shirati. It meant going northeast to Tarime and then northwest toward Migori (Kenya) until we met a country road that went south and finally connected us to the Shirati "turnpike." We went that way but encountered lots of mud and rain, and we had to have push help several times. It was a fifty-mile detour before we got back on the Shirati road. We finally arrived at Shirati at 11:00 P.M. on Tuesday. We were very tired and very dirty, having had no shower or change of clothes since Monday morning. But at least we got home before Dr. Lester was to leave on FDS the next morning. We two doctors had seen each other only coming and going for the previous two weeks.

Meanwhile, Mara Hills School for missionary children at Nyabasi was having an epidemic of measles, so Mrs. Eshleman has been there for more than a week, helping to care for the sick. And two Brethren in Christ missionaries from Rhodesia have been visiting Shirati, so we all were invited to Elsie's house by the lake for pizza last evening.

I had my camera along on some of these adventures, so maybe sometime you will see photos of all the water. Sometimes I wonder if I am a jinx for a safari, considering all the mud and water, and my first FDS with its long walk-bike ride to Kisaka. But frankly, I rather enjoy it.

Friday, June 8, 1962

On Wednesday I went along to Utegi with Simeon Hurst so I could drive our VW Microbus back to Shirati. Simeon had parked their Jeep at Utegi earlier in the week due to the high waters in the Mori and Merari Rivers, which made the bridges uncrossable.

Let me explain what these bridges are. Several huge concrete rings, maybe six feet in diameter and eight feet long, are placed transversely side by side in the roadway. Then the interval between the concrete rings is filled with small stones and concrete to a height above the top of the rings. There are no protective side rails along these narrow bridges.

This time the water over the Merari bridge was only two inches deep. The lorry that had backed off the bridge the previous Monday had been removed, so it was no problem to go *to* Utegi. Simeon came back with us to the Merari, where we prepared to cross by first off-loading all passengers. The bridge was fine, but the washed-out area at the far end was still a foot deep in water and very spongy. Our VW Microbus made it OK, but Simeon just managed to get the Jeep up through the muck, with his front end doing a brief lift job. The passengers then climbed aboard and the rest of the trip to Shirati was uneventful.

We enjoyed a visit from a nurse and a teacher—one a Lehman from York, Pennsylvania, the other a Miller from near Alden, New York—from the Brethren in Christ mission in northern Rhodesia. As for hospital work last week, Dr. Lester promptly left on FDS after I got back from my adventure with Elsie. He returned on Sunday but was quite tired, so he invited me to do some minor surgery.

A man had come in the previous week with a spear wound to his face and the tip of his thumb chopped off. It took an hour to get him to consent to the surgery; he thought it would hurt and that it could heal without surgery. His face had healed surprisingly well, but the thumb was a different story. He claimed that he had no money. I told him that the thumb would take very long to heal without surgery, that it would be tender for a long time if I did not work on it, but he kept refusing. I know that patients can be very reluctant to sign their name to anything, so I finally said, "All right, if you refuse to let us treat you the way we know is needed, then you can go home. You are only wasting time if you stay here and do not let us treat you." He agreed to go. Then I added, "But before you go I want you to sign a statement saying that you take responsibility for the outcome. Then, if the police need to investigate your case, they will know that you did not complete treatment." Well, he would not sign that release, but he did verbally agree to have surgery. (Our patients were not yet trained to provide written consent with their signature, and some even leave without paying their bills.)

I eventually had the man taken to our minor surgery room, where I used local anesthesia to numb the surgical areas. My assistant was Sospeter, our operating room worker who extracts bad teeth, opens abscesses, changes dressings, and administers some anesthesia. Sospeter sat by this patient and talked nonstop to him while I debrided the end of his thumb. I used some local anesthesia to numb his upper arm, carefully removed a nickel-size piece of skin, and attached it to his thumb with sutures. Sospeter's talking to the patient was the most important factor in my successful surgery, and he used the opportunity to witness to the love of God. I enjoyed doing the procedure, even though I did not do a speedy job. I clearly remembered watching a surgeon do a similar procedure in the accident room at Chester County Hospital the previous year when I was an intern just out of medical school.

Tomorrow Alta Weaver and Anna Martin will leave with Jim Mohlers, Mark Brubaker, and Grace Gehman for a month's leave. Some will climb Mount Kilimanjaro, so tonight the "veterans" want to show their slides to inspire the group. Alta is feeling much better these days and is eager to resume some teaching in July. She has been doing some desk work these past few weeks.

Friday, June 16, 1962

This has been a busy week. I had class with the nursing students every day for four days straight. I enjoyed telling them about mental illness—the symptoms, causes, and treatments. Mental illness is not common here, or at least not as recognized. I also went to the leprosarium three times this week to check on things there because Elsie is still in Nairobi for several weeks of eye care. The staff nurse seems to be doing a good job and has a good Christian witness, but some of the leprosy patients try him by not coming in at curfew time. Some even go off grounds at night for wild parties with dancing, music, and *pombe* (liquor).

On Thursday I spent most of the morning and all of the evening working on the tape that I am sending to you. I borrowed Anna Martin's tape recorder to make the tape, but I want to get one of my own at some point. I finished the tape just as the generator "retired" for the night. Then I packed my clothes for my Friday safari, and by 11:00 P.M. I had scratched out an anatomy quiz for the first-year students to take during my absence. When I did get to bed, the mosquitoes entertained me with lots of music and unappreciated attention. We really have had lots of mosquitoes lately, and many patients with malaria.

LeRoy Petersheim was here with a tractor and grader to work with Dr. Lester on extending the length of our airstrip, so I made fast rounds to see the urgent patients before my departure. We would be returning two patients, a man and a woman, to Nyabasi, and my vehicle's passengers would also include Deacon Zefania and Pastor Nashon, a young carpenter, a young dispensary worker, and the husband of the woman patient. I had previously told my passengers to be ready by 9:00 A.M., but I was not ready until 9:30, and several of the passengers straggled in after 10:00. I confess I let my frustration show. Later I apologized for my hasty words. We had a nice rain the night before, after no rain at Shirati for ten days or more. As we got near Utegi, it was apparent that they'd had more rain than we'd had. At the Merari River I tried to avoid the deep hole at the west end of the bridge, but I got caught on some rocks instead where the ground was higher. Some of the men tried to push our vehicle. Then a man with a Land Rover came along and helped us get on our way.

Several miles closer to Utegi I was unable to negotiate a muddy hill, so again the men pushed, and I gladly utilized their manpower. It took us two and a half hours to travel the twenty miles from Shirati to Utegi whereas under normal conditions we could do it in just over an hour. At one place we went through water that was almost two feet deep. Everyone who could waded through it, and the VW Microbus took the rest of us through to Utegi. There we had a lunch of tea with lots of sugar and milk, and *mandazi*, which resembles doughnuts and is very tasty.

The local people said that between Utegi and Tarime there had been lots of rain the night before. We found lots of mud because some big lorries had preceded us and thoroughly dug up the road, especially where the road crew had shoveled dirt into the previous ruts. This is accepted procedure and works fine in dry weather. But when rain follows promptly after the dirt is rearranged, it becomes a sticky, gooey mess. Then if the lorries come through and stir it around, you have a mess of a road!

We made slow progress for some miles until I reached the side road—more like a path—where the pastor, deacon, and dispensary worker were to spend the weekend with the Bukenya church folks. I suggested that the rest of my passengers get off and sit by the road while I took the others back into the grassy bush for a mile or two. I soon discovered that this small road was in much better shape than the main road, even though it was mainly grass and sometimes I was not sure where it was supposed to be. As I hurried back to the Tarime road, I saw some unwelcome black clouds, and sure enough we encountered rain before we got to Tarime. Fortunately I did not need push help from my passengers en route to Tarime.

At Tarime I collected the post and did business for various people. At 5:00 P.M. I was finally off for the last stretch of my safari. I accepted three hitchhikers to replace the trio I had left at Bukenya. They earned their ride on two miles of hills before we arrived at the Seventh-Day Adventist mission. Another man earned his ride on the way to the Catholic mission. I arrived at Nyabasi in time to tell Shirati by radio that I was there. After supper and a hot bath, guess what? I was ready to play Scrabble with the Mara Hills schoolteachers. And by some unusual good fortune, I even won!

On Saturday morning I made rounds. First I helped a mother complete the miscarriage of an early pregnancy. Then I examined a man who said his arm had gotten broken the day before, but I felt it was dislocated medially, so I tried to replace it, without success. I spoke to Dr. Lester on the radio that evening and he told me to give the patient a rather large dose of intravenous painkiller, then place him on the floor. A male dresser would then sit on the floor with his foot in the patient's armpit while the nurse and I pulled on the arm. After some trial and error and working up a good sweat, we finally got the right combination and the shoulder slipped into place with a welcome crunch. The patient immediately announced, "Ah, now it is fixed," and finished his supper before lying down to sleep. The medicine really did relax him. Once again, the radio contact between stations was very helpful in obtaining valuable information for a medical emergency.

Leroy came back with the tractor on Saturday and said that the road was really pathetic. He did lots of good Samaritan deeds with the tractor for folks mired in the mud. Today we had more rain. Tomorrow I am supposed to drive back to Shirati if . . . ?!

Wednesday, June 27, 1962

Greetings from Shirati, where it is raining again in what is supposed to be the dry season! "Old" missionaries say that one could count on the rains stopping by May 15th—but not this year! We had no rain at Shirati for ten to twelve days—just long enough to let the sun dry up the corn, which was sprouting little ears, and to let the bean blossoms wither. The rains resumed the night before I went to Nyabasi, which I told you about in my last letter. We have had almost daily rains ever since, with heavy thunderstorms the last two nights around 11:00 P.M. So the roads are not improving, nor are the rivers drying up. In fact, I think the rivers have been overflowing our two main bridges for most of the past three months. I do hope it is only a coincidence that the weather has been so unusual since I arrived here eight months ago!

Let me tell about the rest of my Nyabasi safari. I did not win Scrabble on Saturday night; in fact, I think I got the lowest score. But I did type out a whole letter to you as we played, and the letter got finished first, so maybe I was not concentrating on the Scrabble game. On Sunday morning I went with the teachers to the Mara Hills church service. It was Father's Day, so the children conducted the entire service as Leroy sat back and listened. The younger students conducted the devotional exercises and received the offering. An older boy, maybe in 7th grade, taught the Sunday school lesson, about "two kinds of fathers," based on the story of the prodigal son. I was impressed to see these students follow the example of their devoted missionary parents. The tall young "preacher" emphasized that parents who love their child will correct him and freely forgive him when he does wrong.

I ate the noon meal with the teachers and was ready to start home by 1:45 P.M. The weather was just as sunny and breezy and perfect as a day could be—the opposite of the previous day. It seemed like a good day to be drying hay, or some muddy roads, *if* there were not too many lorries between Tarime and Utegi. Well, the sun had nicely dried the top of the Tarime road, so I made fairly good time and got to the Bukenya trail by 3:30. I had asked the men to walk out to the main road by 2:30, but only one man had arrived, with a suitcase on a bicycle. We waited until the others arrived, by 4:30. When we reached Utegi, the men were ready for *chai*, so it was almost 6:00 P.M. when we headed down the Shirati "turnpike." The rivers were not so high, but my passengers still needed to help me up that muddy incline on the west end of the Merari River bridge (where last month Elsie and I sat and got water all mixed in with our engine oil). After that, I made good time and we got to Shirati by 7:15, without much night driving and in time for supper after the 5:30 English vesper service.

Now for a little geography lesson while I think of it. You have just had your longest day of the year, but here our days are a bit shorter. Remember that the Earth tilts northward, which lengthens your day. Also, the sun is quite far north of us now, so at noontime my shadow falls about four feet to the south. But would you believe that next December my shadow at noon will point about two feet to the north? Remember that the equator is some miles north of us. It crosses the northern part of Lake Victoria just north of Kisumu in Kenya, and south of Entebbe and Kampala in Uganda.

I am still doing hospital work. Just now we have two orphans in our maternity ward. The boy is about a year old. His mother came with him several months ago. She had surgery for breast cancer, which is rather rare here compared to the United States, but she had metastasis to her lungs and died last week. When she first came in, we put her son on powdered milk and had her stop nursing him. Her sister has not yet put together the money for the mother's care, so the son, Daniel, is still here. He may be a bit spoiled by the staff, who feed him and care for him, but we all enjoy him.

The other child, a one-week-old girl, arrived two days after her mother died at home of a postpartum hemorrhage. She seems to be quite healthy and hungry after a day and a half of proper feeding. This morning both children were hungry and squalling when I appeared for rounds, so I picked up the young lady. Well, Daniel was crushed and loudly wailed his protest, so I soon swapped children, and then the little one yelled at me. Such a *kilele* (noise)! Later, when I came to see a new patient, a lady was holding Daniel on the porch. I went about my business, then came out to return to the women's ward. But Daniel put up such a howl about my failure to greet him, so I returned and held him for a half-minute, then gave him back to the woman, and he was satisfied. Such a boy! We will certainly miss him when he goes home.

The MAF is expecting a new plane to come into service in Nairobi. I think it will accommodate more passengers and heavier loads. The current plane will then go to Ethiopia.

Friday, June 29, 1962

I want to tell you more about some events that happened before my trip to Nyabasi. Elsie Cressman was in Nairobi for eye surgery. She had a latent squint, which is a tendency of the eyes to cross. It causes lots of headaches, so they operated on the eye muscles. I tried to visit the staff nurse at the leprosarium several times a week during Elsie's absence. The leprosarium is several miles away and one day the only vehicle available was a Chevy van that Paul, the mechanic from Bukiroba, drove here when he came to work on our water pump by the lake. I arranged to ride along with him to the pump house and then to drive myself the other mile to the leprosarium. I had with me two boxes of bottles of various mixtures and sundry medicines. As I drove away from the pump house, I noticed that some spots looked really soft from the recent rains. I was OK until one box of liquid medicine slid off its position atop a tool chest and began to spill. I promptly stopped the vehicle. I lost only a pint out of a gallon and broke one tiny bottle, so I repositioned the boxes into more stable places and prepared to move on. Alas, I had stopped in a soft spot and my effort to get out of it only got me deeper into the mud hole. Fortunately a young boy came by. We tried putting some stones into the mud, but to no avail, so I sent him to report my *shida* (trouble) to the men at the pump house. After they got the pump working, they came and jacked up the van and got us out of the mud. I was able to deliver the medicines to the leprosarium in midafternoon instead of mid-morning, and the staff nurse was no longer on duty, so I missed talking to him.

Two days later I borrowed a bicycle and found that things were under control at the leprosarium. When I arrived, the staff nurse was in a committee meeting to arrange disciplinary action for some patients who had gone off grounds after dark one evening to attend a dance held in a nearby village following the death of an old man. It certainly means

much to Elsie to have a trained medical person there who can take charge of medical needs as well as share a clear testimony about Jesus to the folks in the community.

I mentioned the pump: we have had so much *shida* with it for several weeks. We were without water for a few days, except for the rainwater we collected off our roofs and into our rain tanks. Paul, the mechanic from Bukiroba, worked on the pump for several days, but as fast as he fixed one thing, something else went kaput. The day I got stuck in the mud was the same day Paul finally got the pump to work, and it has worked now for a week and a half. Meanwhile, it had been decided that the pump was too unreliable for our water needs, so Hershey went to Nairobi a week ago Tuesday to get another pump. He came back a week ago today with the new pump, materials to repair our radio station, and lots of post. I actually got four letters from home. And Elsie returned with Hershey from Nairobi. She had thought she would not get here until the MAF plane was scheduled to come, a week later.

Yesterday I went down to Elsie's house beside the lake by bicycle. I had to do some wading to get to the house. The lake water may be a bit higher than when I last visited her. Now when the afternoon breezes come in off the lake, the waves sweep right up to her front porch.

I told you last time about our two orphans here at Shirati hospital. Today we got another one. The baby was born at home ten days ago. Afterward the mother lost a lot of blood, so this morning the family finally brought them to us. The mother was in terrible shock, very restless, and her eyes were *white*. We started intravenous fluids and even got two units of blood for transfusions within two hours. We usually type and crossmatch the relatives' blood, and sometimes ask middle school students to give blood too. The mother died around noon despite our efforts. We asked the family what they had been feeding the baby and they said "cow's milk" and that they boiled it. I tried to explain that we preferred to have the baby stay with us for a while, to receive a powdered milk formula and vitamin drops and to be sure that the baby was doing well before it went home. We wanted to prevent malnutrition or severe diarrhea. The father seemed to understand our concerns for the baby, but the old women objected to our advice. The father permitted us to admit the baby to our "orphanage." This makes our third orphan admission within two weeks—the first orphans in the nine months I have been here. That also makes two mothers in one week who delivered at home and died of postpartum hemorrhage. This particular mother lived only two to three miles from the hospital.

If only these mothers would come in before delivery, we could save more of them, and their babies. It is such slow work to teach preventive medicine. And some family members get impatient if the sick person does not get well "overnight" after they have been sick for some days or in labor for a day or more. Just yesterday a girl came in with pus draining from her lower leg from osteomyelitis, an infection of the bone. She had been sick at home for seven months with terrible pain and inability to walk. She also has severe damage to her knee and probably will never walk normally again. These infections, if treated early, could sometimes be cured with penicillin. But the families wait and hope that the pain and deformity will go away. Therefore, one of our goals must be education, to help people understand the value of early treatment of illness.

Tuesday, July 10, 1962

Greetings from Kisaka this time. I am here on my second FDS. I hope it goes better than the first one, when I missed two days of my planned three days of visits. Nurse Alice Reber is traveling with me for a final tour to some of the stations before she goes home on furlough next week with Clara Landis, a teacher of the missionary children at Mara Hills School, and Mary Metzler, a nurse at the clinic and small in-patient ward at the nearby Nyabasi mission station, where missionaries Simeon and Edna Hurst also live. The Mara Hills School and Nyabasi station are about 1,500 feet higher than we are at Shirati, and we are 3,700 feet above sea level, so Nyabasi is much cooler than Shirati.

I was warned that I would have a different pilot this time. Gordon Marshall, our regular pilot, is very skilled and has run many errands for us missionaries (such as bringing us mail and food supplies) besides flying us around. Well, Gordon was scheduled for a well-deserved three-month furlough, so a substitute pilot, Graham, was hired to fill in. Graham was flying jet planes for the Royal Air Force in England before he agreed to hop little planes around the African bush. Also, MAF has just gotten a larger plane. The former plane could carry three people besides the pilot, and the suitcases and supplies went into the back of the cabin. The new plane, a Cessna 205, can carry six people in three rows, and the luggage and supplies go into a compartment beneath the cabin. The new plane also has a bigger engine, but the fuselage is built the same as their former plane. This plane can also carry more weight in the large fiberglass luggage carrier beneath the passenger cabin. This compartment seems rather low slung for our rural terrain. When Hershey Leaman saw the new plane with its large undergirth, he quipped, "It looks like it needs a Cesarean section!" These Cessna planes can do well in the bush country, especially when the pilot is familiar with bush conditions.

Well, Graham was more of a novice when it came to flying in the bush, as we soon discovered. I'm not sure we had a full load as we headed to Kisaka that sunny morning. I was seated in the front beside Graham and I wondered to myself why he did not circle the airstrip for a good look at its configuration. It looked like an enormous barn roof, with both ends much lower than its mid-portion, which ran to the left of the mission buildings. He headed for the west end of the airstrip and cut back the throttle. We suddenly bumped into some bushes and caught a lot of grass just before we bounced onto the airstrip. Slowly we found our way to the top of the "barn roof" and climbed out of the plane. Graham checked on the luggage carrier and found it had sustained a crack. What a shame to injure the new plane on one of its early flights. But at least no passengers were hurt.

We saw some patients at Kisaka and had a noon meal. Then Alice and a dresser from Kisaka and I were flown the few miles to Kenyana, where we arrived by 1:30 P.M. Graham inspected their airstrip, which was rather damp and soft from all the recent rains, and Kenyana is a flat lowland with a number of small streams. Graham asked Naaman to make sure that the local men cut the grass of the whole airstrip quite short before his next visit. He also told us that he would return at 5:00 P.M. that afternoon to pick us up. We found that many people had expected us to come that morning, so they got tired of waiting and went home at noon. But we did see twenty-some patients who had waited for us. Afterward, Naaman's wife had tea ready for us, and we walked out to the airstrip before 5:00 P.M. And we waited, and waited some more. Why was he late returning when he said he was only going to Nyabasi, which was only six minutes across the valley and over the escarpment from Kisaka. Time rolled by to 6:15 and dusk was approaching a bit early, hastened by the smoke from the numerous *pori* fires. I began to think about my previous visit to Kenyana, when I spent two nights there with a nurse and dresser waiting for the plane to return. This time I had no bedclothes or extra blankets with me. Naaman and his family had taken good care of us that first time.

Suddenly we heard the welcome drone of our plane. Graham explained that he'd had difficulty getting the engine to start until he located a loose connection to a sparkplug or some such thing that took him a long time to find and fix. We were all relieved to be on our way to Kisaka, so near by plane but so far away by foot.

I got the feeling that Graham suspects that my flying with him is an omen for trouble. He reminded me that he was with Gordon the time when I was left at Kenyana for two nights on my first FDS, and now, with this erratic rainy weather, the airstrips could quickly deteriorate, so he clearly warned me more than once that he does *not* want to take me to Kenyana again!

Well, need I say that we will all be glad when Gordon returns? I have not seen him flustered or unsure how to deal with a situation. But Graham is clearly in a new situation and often feels uncomfortable in this smaller plane and this different country. So your prayers for him would be most appreciated as he tries to work with us. Of course by the time Gordon returns on Sept 1, Graham will have gained lots of practical learning about flying in the bush and in a smaller plane, and hopefully he will also be more relaxed about transporting us around in this unfamiliar bush.

I will be at Bukiroba tonight and work in their clinic in the morning. Tomorrow I plan to visit the clinic at Masinono, south of Musoma. When I get back to Shirati, Dr. Lester and his family will fly along with Graham back to Nairobi and then go to Mombasa for their month's holiday. And I will be here as the solo doctor to deal with whatever medical problems my nurses and dressers refer to me.

This seems to be the time for changing people around to other positions of work. Yesterday Grace, one of our midwives, went to Nyabasi. Marshall, the staff nurse who worked in our dispensary, moved to Nyabasi last Saturday. Nurse Mary Metzler will be going on furlough; she will be replaced. But I could cry the blues a little that two of my dependable workers are leaving Shirati. They have been responsible for our dispensary and maternity units for some time. Fortunately, the remaining midwife, who has been in the operating room, is coming to maternity, where she will be quite capable. As for the dispensary, I now have only one dresser, whose English and medical training are both rather limited, so I should spend much time working with him. I hope to visit Nyabasi a time or two this month to see how Marshall and Grace are doing. Grace gets more maternity patients and more complicated cases at Nyabasi than we have at Shirati. Maybe the previous missionary nurses at Nyabasi developed better relations with the pregnant ladies so that they are more comfortable coming in when their delivery time has arrived.

So, if my letters get rather scarce during the coming month, just try to remember that I will be the solo doctor at Shirati for that whole time. At least I won't be scheduling a lot of elective surgery, and I pray there won't be much emergency surgery either! Fortunately, I think I won't be asked to present a lot of lectures to the nursing students during the coming month either.

Sunday, July 22, 1962

Greetings from Shirati in the name of our Lord and Master. First, let me finish telling you about my last FDS. I got to tell you about only the first of the three days. It was *not* a routine safari, for it featured a lot of "breaking in" of the new MAF plane and of Graham, our relief pilot. So let me tell you the rest of the story.

We did eventually get picked up late at Kenyana and got back to Kisaka the same day. The next afternoon, Tuesday, we expected to be flown to Masinono in South Mara, but Graham did not show up until 9:30 A.M. on Wednesday, so we missed our Masinono visit but got some extra rest. Graham explained that he had made two flights to Nairobi that day (he had originally been scheduled for only one) to get the storage carrier repaired or replaced. He also had to move all of the stuff from the external luggage carrier into the back part of the cabin. He asked them to check the engine too, because he'd had difficulty starting it the previous day. The mechanic said it was a matter of getting the new engine into efficient settings. So Graham finally took us to Musoma, and a driver there took us to Bukiroba, six miles to the east, where we had dinner and saw a few patients before we called it a day and went back to Shirati. Dr. Lester and his wife, Lois, and their children, Charlotte and Lynn, then flew off with Graham to Nairobi for their month's leave at the Mombasa shore of Kenya.

I have been kept busy here since the Eshleman family went on leave, but so far I have not been overwhelmed. Today the *Daily Light* reading, which we use at breakfast, said, "My presence shall go with thee, and I will give thee rest" (Joshua 1:9, Proverbs 3:6). I accept these promises as being for me, especially during the Eshlemans' absence. I used this portion of Joshua 1 in my testimony at East Petersburg just over a year ago. My task here still feels enormous sometimes, but God goes before me and will continue to lead me as I commit it all to Him.

When I become ineffective and unhappy, it is often because I am trying to do things in my own strength. So I have typed up today's portion of *Daily Light* and put it on my desk as a daily reminder to claim His presence and peace in all I do.

May I share with you the difficult task I had on Sunday two weeks ago? It was soon after I came back from FDS and Dr. Lester and his family left. In the afternoon a mother was brought in after delivery of a living child at home. But she could not deliver the second child despite her long efforts. I could see why: the baby was in a transverse position, with one hand presenting in the vagina. I tried to change the baby's position so I could pull on a foot, but with no success. So I sent word for Sospeter to come and give the patient some anesthesia (open drop ether). I knew that this baby had been dead for some hours and my goal was, first, to somehow deliver the baby and, second, to spare the mother's life. I knew that a C-section would have been easier for me, but it would have been tougher for the mother, who was already weary from the long labor and had lost an unknown amount of blood. Finally I was able to disarticulate both of the baby's arms at the shoulders so that they could be moved about more easily. I was then able to pull down a foot enough to grab the big toe with a forceps. I pulled on that toe until I was able to get a firm grip on the leg with my other hand. Finally I brought out the baby as a single-leg breech delivery. I don't know when I have worked so hard, and my fingers really cramped up on me. My anterior chest wall and the calves of my legs ached for several days from the various positions I had assumed during that exceedingly difficult delivery. Fortunately the mother has done fairly well despite the way I was forced to "treat" her. In retrospect, if I had known at the beginning how difficult the vaginal delivery would be, I would have gone for the C-section anyway. Meanwhile, our OB census is better this month—twenty deliveries in twenty days with two in labor today. I like it better this way, and so does the midwife.

Last Friday I had another first-time experience when I was called to court in Tarime to testify concerning my autopsy findings on a man whose body had been found near a *pombe* shop. These shops sell a "home brew of beer with a strong kick." The man had sustained head injuries, probably from a drunken brawl. Hershey, Norma, and Larry went along and did business in Tarime while I was at court. Then we all went on to Nyabasi to see how Marshall and Grace are doing running the clinics there. Currently there are no missionaries at Nyabasi, but both of these trained African nurses seem to be enjoying their work. Marshall had worked there previously, but Grace had never even visited Nyabasi before she came there to work. There are a missionary house and a guesthouse on the compound, so we occupied the guesthouse and Norma supervised the cooking. We made a fire in the fireplace and made baked potatoes (wrapped in tin foil) and roasted hotdogs (out of a can) for a real picnic supper. This safari featured dust and bumpy terrain, but *no* mud! While we were there, I missed seeing Alice Reber off from Shirati on Saturday for her return to the United States.

I suppose you heard about the stabbing death of Merlin Grove and about the injuries to his wife, Dorothy, as they were registering students for the new school year in Mogadishu, Somalia, on July 16. She had emergency surgery and was in serious condition but is reported to be improving. Merlin was director of our Somali Mennonite mission and appreciated by many people. Pray that God will bring glory to Himself through this pain and sadness.

Friday, August 3, 1962

Greetings from Shirati. I must warn you that the most recent news about me is that last night was one of those nights when I did not get much sleep. First of all, I took two chloroquine pills instead of the usual one to prevent malaria. I usually take one pill three evenings each week, but for some reason I had not taken any for four or five days. I was late getting in from the hospital several nights in a row and was tired, so I must have plain forgot the medicine and went to bed. When I realized yesterday morning that I was overdue, I took two pills, even though I knew that chloroquine can interfere with sleep, especially if I take it in the morning. So, when nighttime came, I could not sleep. I had other things on my mind too.

I was still awake at 2:00 A.M. when the phone rang and I was asked about a maternity problem. I went out to the maternity ward to see what was happening. The woman had been in labor for a while and was tired. I tried to stimulate her contractions, but without success, so I let her rest while I thought about what to try next. I finally decided to try a different procedure, one that I had seen Dr. Lester use several times but had not heard about in medical school. A symphysiotomy involves using local anesthesia, then inserting a scalpel where the pelvic bones join in front and carefully creating some separation of the anterior pelvis. The woman's cervix was already fully dilated, and after I performed the procedure, the mother was able, with several contractions, to deliver her son, who weighed seven and a half pounds. The baby's head was quite swollen, his heart rate was slow, and he did not make any respiratory effort. His birth was also made difficult because his face presented first, which requires a larger pelvic passageway to deliver the infant. Usually the back of the head presents first and the baby's chin flexes forward against his chest, which creates a smaller diameter than when the baby's head is extended toward his back. Fortunately the mother is making a better recovery than I had dared to hope for. And because of the procedure of enlarging her pelvis for this delivery, hopefully she can deliver a normal-size child the next time without difficulty and without the need for more surgery such as a C-section.

So, because of so little sleep last night and then my morning rounds, I really was hoping for a good siesta nap this afternoon. Well, do you think I got it? *Hata kidogo!* ("Not even a little bit!") I'm sorry but I got rather annoyed when the phone rang and I was told that a patient wanted to be discharged. I had already written the order on her chart, but the staff person had not bothered to check it. I later apologized for being so short. Then they called back because the patient wanted some *dawa* (medicine) to take along home. I said, "She does not really need it, but give her some multivitamins." I should explain that the person calling me was not the regular staff nurse, who is more efficient and respects our afternoon siesta time except for genuine emergencies. The phone rang several more times, so I finally stopped answering it. I did not learn of any urgent need for my services that whole afternoon.

I reckon that is a lot of depressing detail about the events of last night and today but, as some might say, "It's all in a day's work." I had similar exhausting workdays in medical school and internship before I came to Shirati just ten months ago. Looking back on it all, I am unhappy that I was so miserable yesterday, but I was really tired after almost no sleep for more than twenty-four hours, the two malaria pills instead of one that I took in the morning, and I was the only doctor covering the hospital while Dr. Lester and his family are on a well-deserved month-long vacation. I have covered three weeks without him but still have another week to go. Enough said!

Let's change the subject. This afternoon, Hershey Leaman heard by radio from Dr. Lester, who has just returned to Nairobi from the lovely shore of Mombasa on the Indian Ocean of Kenya! Hershey and his wife and son are leaving today for a week's leave in Nairobi. They will be getting company from Ethiopia—Calvin Shenk and his wife, Marie (who is Hershey's sister), as well as Janice Sensenig and two other ladies. Hersheys will meet them at the plane in Nairobi and later bring them all to visit us.

I got *no* calls last night, slept well, and do feel better! This letter will be going with Hershey to Nairobi.

Friday, August 24, 1962

The MAF plane with Graham as pilot brought Dr. Eshleman and his family back from their month's holiday, spent mostly at Mombasa. And somehow it had been set up that Graham would then take me for another FDS safari. This was a good safari in contrast to the previous one.

Graham had a less busy schedule, so he was more relaxed. But I was still tired from being the only doctor at the hospital for the past month. This was Graham's last scheduled time with us, and I look forward to having Gordon with us again.

On Thursday morning, Graham and I flew to Kisaka to pick up nurse Velma Eshleman. We then flew to Musoma. From there Velma and I drove twenty-five miles east to Bumangi and saw twenty patients. This was my first visit to Bumangi (which has no airstrip but does have adequate road access). We ate our lunch under a tree, then returned to Bukiroba to see patients at the Secondary School for Boys and at the Morembe Middle School for Girls. That evening we heard a speaker tell about the work of the East Africa Bible Society. Finally we got to bed.

On Friday morning, Graham flew us south to Masinono, where we saw a nice group of patients. We then flew back north to Mugango (about halfway to Musoma), where Laura Kurtz had fixed dinner for us. (This was also my first trip to Mugango.) Afterward, a mob of patients was waiting to be seen. It seemed that the dresser was inexperienced at screening out the more needy patients for the doctor to see while the dresser cared for the more common problems himself. So there was a mad rush as everyone expected to be seen by the doctor rather than let me be a consultant for the more serious problems. Velma finally brought order into the medley. When we finished with this group, we flew back to Musoma, then drove to Bukiroba for supper and bed.

On Saturday morning we flew to Kisaka and found some needy patients. One had a tubal pregnancy with bleeding, so I sent her to the Shirati hospital. It was nice to have the larger plane, but Graham still had to make one flight with four adults in addition to himself on Saturday morning, then another flight with two patients, two children, me, and himself on Saturday evening. We did not go to Kenyana this time (it may have been too wet to land there), nor to Nyabasi. I think Graham made some pleasant memories on this trip to contrast with his earlier memories of tight schedules, plane problems, the belly-flop landing, and so on.

The following Monday I went by car to Nyabasi for a medical visit. I took along Martha Jane Lutz (a teacher of missionary children at the Mara Hills School) and her cousin Anna Lutz, who is visiting from Somalia, where she is a nurse working under EMBMC. They had both visited us at Shirati over the weekend.

I am now writing from Eldoret, which is in Kenya about eighty miles northeast of Kisumu, along the northeastern shore of Lake Victoria. What am I doing here? Well, some of us girls are attending a Keswick Convention with a number of other missionaries, some African folks, and other interested Christians. It is a time for fellowship and Bible study. It reminds me of the Christian Medical Society meetings I attended while I was in medical school in Philadelphia. The theme is "All One in Christ Jesus," and the messages have been very practical.

There are six of us Mennonite women here: Elsie Cressman, Alta Weaver, Cora Lehman, and myself from Shirati; Martha Myer from Bukiroba; and Martha Jane Lutz from Nyabasi. We all traveled together to Nyabasi on Monday evening and spent the night with the Lutz cousins. The next morning, we took Anna Lutz to the station in Kisumu to meet her night train to Nairobi, where she would meet the MAF plane to Somalia. She has been helping to care for Mrs. Dorothy Grove since her injuries associated with the stabbing death of her husband, Merlin. Anna had come to Nyabasi to spend a month's leave with Martha Jane.

It was raining when we got to Eldoret on Tuesday at 7:30 P.M. We were late for dinner but they served us anyway. We then went to the conference's opening service. I did not sleep very well that night and felt nauseated the next morning, so I took extra chloroquine, stayed in bed, and slept until late afternoon. Then I was ready to eat again. I had been so weary from all the work of the recent weeks while Dr. Lester and his family were gone, but now I am feeling much better.

The elevation here is over six thousand feet, and it feels like fall at home. "Invigorating" is how I would describe the delightful weather. Lots of covers at night feels good, but the sun is warm in the daytime.

Our Convention is meeting in a government school. It has very nice facilities for many dormitory students and a large dining room. The meals are good, with a British flavor; frequent cabbage suits me, but puddings with raisins for dessert I can do without, and cheese with every meal! But I am enjoying being away and meeting people from other places and backgrounds. Our dorm room has eleven beds, so it is easy to wander into a variety of groups instead of having to stick together. Sis, you may remember Mr. Jury from Cochranville who came around to sell Raleigh products. He has a daughter living in Mwanza and I met her at the secondary school near Musoma two weeks ago when I was on FDS. Well, she and her husband are here too, so we are getting more acquainted. Many folks are from the United Kingdom— the "other side" of the Atlantic. I also met a lady from Lewistown, Pennsylvania; and a couple from Malvern is listed but I have not met them yet. It is interesting to watch the men play games on the green lawn in the late afternoon, but their games are admittedly "too British" for me. The Convention will go until Sunday afternoon.

Sunday, September 2, 1962

I have been back at Shirati for a week now, but let me say more about the Keswick Convention. It truly was a refreshing time for me, and the days went by rapidly. It was great to meet folks from many parts of East

Africa, plus others from Great Britain, Australia, Sweden, and even the United States. We could all share good fellowship together in Christ.

On Saturday afternoon an African brother from Uganda gave us a travelogue on his recent three-month tour of the United States. I was impressed by his remarkable insight into our American culture and our spiritual needs. He had previously studied in London for a year and said that the United States seemed to be ahead of Britain in technology and industrial matters, and generally seemed more prosperous. I'm not sure our British folks appreciated hearing the United Kingdom described as lower than the United States in some ways. But Great Britain is certainly much older that we are and can be proud of many older things. They are more sophisticated, formal, and proper while we younger Americans are seen as immature and brash, including our table manners. So I did try to be more "proper" at the table for the week at Eldoret. Elsie Cressman is a Canadian, so she can tell us Americans how we are supposed to hold our silverware and eat our food. I guess I just don't worry about it at Shirati or when I'm not in public places.

The last session of the Convention was on Sunday morning. It finished with a communion service at which Christians from many countries and churches shared the communion cup in honor of our Lord Jesus Christ. We packed our suitcases before dinner, then said goodbye to many new friends before we slowly headed down the road. We traveled about eighty miles south to a Church of God Mission, where Elsie knew a nurse. The nurse made supper for us and gave us a place to sleep. The next morning we loaded some extra baggage into the back of the VW wagon—a mother cat and three kittens. The mother was rather skittish, so we put a suitcase on top of the box she was in. We then drove to Kisumu, where I went window shopping while some of our group went shopping "for real." You see, I had carefully planned not to take a lot of extra cash along this time because I wanted to keep it available for my "big vacation" next month. I did order chicken with rice and curry for the noon meal, and it was really good. The Indian cooks used lots of spices in it and I really liked it—probably even more than a good hot hoagie.

Before we started off from Kisumu, Elsie looked into the cat box and said it was empty. So I looked around, and my eyes spied her sitting among the rest of the stuff in the car, but I did not enlighten Elsie. We had rain on both Sunday and Monday as we traveled. We got home at 8:30 P.M. on Monday, rather tired and eager to clean up and sleep. When we unpacked the kittens' box, it was empty too. We discovered that they had climbed into a duffle bag—I guess they wanted a softer bed! The mother cat was still with us too, so we put the four felines onto the back porch. Their fur is mostly black and they have rather long tails—not ordinary alley cats by any means! The mother cat will probably stay with me and the nurses in our house. Our cook wants one of the kittens, and the other two will probably go with Elsie to the leprosarium. This may be a rather long cat story, but I must say that the mother cat already caught a mouse in our living room, the night after she moved in. The next day she found her way to our attic, where birds and bats also live, so she may find more of her own food. If she is indoors when we are eating, she really knows how to beg for food. I wonder if I can teach her some manners, like keeping her paws on the floor rather than on my knees, and not jumping up on the chairs. Sorry this cat story got to be dominant and so long! Now I will shift gears.

Maybe you remember that long ago—in fact, a month after I arrived here—I wrote about the preparations made to choose an African Bishop, or maybe more, for the African Mennonite church. Careful steps were set out for those meetings, with delegates chosen from among members who may participate in communion. But after the initial step of choosing delegates took place at Bumangi last fall, the rest of the meetings were postponed because of the subsequent excessive rains and travel difficulties. The delegates received additional instructions about the qualifications for a bishop. Votes were then cast. Two pastors received fifty and sixty votes each, and another received four votes. Because the protocol indicated that a 75 percent majority was required before ordination could occur, the matter was rested until the next conference (in November 1962, I think). It will be a big step for the African Mennonite Church to select its first bishop, or bishops. The missionaries will then step back from leadership and decision making. Please pray that God will lead in this new step. Pray that everyone will seek God's will rather than promote personal desires or resort to political methods to select the man they prefer. This part of Tanganyika has many small tribes with their own languages and peculiar likes and ways of doing things.

Tuesday, September 11, 1962

Jambo ("hello") to you. I have been so busy the past two months, I think I forgot to tell you about our guests from the Persian Gulf. As a medical student I had heard Dr. Mary Bruins Allison speak at Woman's Medical College. A classmate of mine, Corrine Overkamp, is a member of the same evangelical church as Dr. Allison. I later met Dr. Allison at a Christian Medical Society convention at Sandy Cove in Maryland. She found my name in the alumnae bulletin. She had spent many years as a missionary physician in Kuwait in the Persian Gulf. Several months ago she wrote to me saying she was coming to East Africa and could she and her teacher friend maybe come to see us? I wrote back and invited them to come. They flew into Nairobi, then came overland by "taxi"—which looks more like an old bus than a fancy limousine. Some of these taxis

are rather rickety, especially on our dirt roads. Anyway, I made a medical visit to Nyabasi that day, then met our two guests at Tarime that evening. I also picked up Naomi Weaver at Utegi. Naomi is a nurse who recently arrived at Shirati and just finished three weeks of Swahili language class at Bukiroba.

We really enjoyed having these guests with us. I had read a book by Dr. Eleanor T. Calverley, whom I had met when I was a medical student. Dr. Calverley, like Dr. Allison, had spent many years in Kuwait. I learned from her book that things in Kuwait had changed a lot in the past twenty years since the discovery of oil, which brought sudden wealth and publicity to Kuwait. Dr. Allison had worked there in a mission hospital for a number of years, but now the mission hospital has competition from good government hospitals. Dr. Allison told me that local girls do not accept work as nurses, because they consider such work to be beneath them. So most of the nurses at the mission hospital are recruited from India. Also in Kuwait, the work of building up a Christian church goes very slowly. A Christian man is often exiled by his family and cannot find a woman to marry him. I mentioned Corrine Overkamp, with whom I was partnered in our biology class. I knew she was interested in going to Kuwait someday too.

We also had some visitors from Ethiopia: Calvin Shenk and his wife, Marie, who is a sister to Hershey Leaman. Their father is Daniel Leaman from Andrew's Bridge Mennonite Church, whose brother is Elmer Leaman. Calvin and Marie were accompanied by three ladies: Janice Sensenig, Alta Zimmerman, and Janet Shertzer. I had not previously met the last two, but I did enjoy getting acquainted with them.

Last time I wrote about the delegate meeting at Bumangi for choosing a bishop. Elsie Cressman was there and she felt that the presence of God was real in the messages given about the qualifications desired for this work. The importance of seeking God's leading was emphasized, with a reminder that Israel got the king they wanted but he was not God's choice for them! The group was urged to forsake personal ambition. When the votes were cast it was quite evident that while many desired God's leading and some frankly felt that this was *not* the time for God to choose a bishop, others seemed to be quite eager to get their own man in as bishop. It was decided to wait for several more months. Meanwhile, the group was urged to pray that hearts would bow to the will of God. There seemed to be a considerable feeling of alignment along tribal lines, specifically toward the Luo and Jita tribes. So do pray that there may be oneness in Christ.

Last week I was trying to get prepared for leave time, which included doing some mending, but the calls from the hospital kept me as busy as ever. I was even tempted to unhook the phone so I could work in peace, but I resisted that temptation. Then, on Thursday evening, Naomi came to the rescue and spent two hours ironing some clothes. And somehow I managed to be packed when the car arrived at 6:30 the next morning to take me to Nyabasi. Believe me, I wasn't in that big of a *shussel* [*Pennsylvania Dutch for "hurry"*]—*hata kidogo*. But Hershey has lots of work to do there, so I went along to see patients and make rounds with the staff nurses. Grace, the midwife who had previously worked at Shirati, had two recent deliveries that were not routine but still went rather easily. One was a frank breech, with both of the baby's legs up over its abdomen, so there was good dilatation of the uterine opening for delivery of the shoulders and head. The other was a hand presentation. Grace had been able to replace the hand into the uterus and then, like a miracle, the head came down into the cervix and the baby was delivered without any difficulty. Either one of these cases could have been difficult, but they were not. Thanks be to God!

I have had four patients with long labor and hand presentations at Shirati. The last was the most difficult, and I shall not object if I never have another that is as difficult as those I have already encountered!

Thursday, September 13, 1962

Greetings again from Nairobi. First, let me tell you more about our weekend at Nyabasi. We drove there on Friday morning. First I made rounds on inpatients. Then I saw outpatients, some before lunch and others after. I had visited the Mara Hills School previously, but this time I got to see inside their dormitories. They are really nice for children, with two single beds and one bunk bed so that four can live in one room. They have built-in dressers, plus four long dressers and cupboards.

I think it was an old-timer who said it has been twenty-seven years that the Mennonite missionaries in Tanganyika have gotten together once a year for several days of inspirational messages and fellowship. Some of our missionaries—such as our nurses at Shirati hospital and the staff at the Mara Hills School—do not often get to visit the missionaries at other stations as we doctors do, rather frequently. Last Friday we all gathered at Mara Hills. Some of the Shirati folks were delayed from leaving at 2:00 P.M. by a new admission who needed emergency surgery. They got off at around 5:00 P.M. instead.

The first meeting was on Friday evening, with an introduction to the weekend's general theme, from John 15—"I am the vine, ye are the branches"—and a time of fellowship and prayer for our work at the various stations. On Saturday morning, Simeon Hurst spoke from Jeremiah 17:5–8, 14. He clearly contrasted the green leaf of a tree planted by the water to the heath that inhabits the drought-stricken wilderness. That afternoon, George Smoker spoke from John 15:11—"that your joy may be full." On Saturday evening, Don Jacobs spoke from John 15:16—"I have chosen you . . . that your fruit should remain." I was especially impressed that he said we often are not satisfied by just abiding in Jesus. Instead we look for joy in other roots or vines, such as our work or a special position, and if these things are disturbed, we become unhappy and frustrated. I admit that I look for satisfaction in my work; I try to give each patient the best possible care with the available facilities. But frankly, I am often frustrated by my poor communication in Swahili with my patients. I can ask some simple questions and catch some of the answer, but I usually cannot really follow a longer conversation. In church I sometimes get an idea of the sermon's message, but other times I miss most of the content. Forgive me for complaining again about not getting more time to study Swahili. A more recent newcomer got two months of language study and passed her first test some months ago. It just seems rather unfair to me.

Back to the weekend at Mara Hills: it was so refreshing to hear a number of good sermons in English that I could really understand. It was such a spiritual feast for me. It also showed me how spiritually dry I am sometimes. Granted, I have my own daily Bible study, but I tend

not to share many of my thoughts with my colleagues. It was not easy to face up to my self-pity, but I thank God for His love and patience in dealing with me, and I want to be pliable to His leading. The enemy may present different temptations in this setting, and he can be quite tricky.

After the Sunday noon meal, the folks gradually thinned out, with many of the children remaining behind to begin their new school year. Some of us single women—Elsie Cressman, Cora Lehman, Martha Myer, Velma Eshleman, and I—also stayed behind to start our three-week vacation. We drove about two hundred miles into Kenya and spent the night at the Happy Farmer. The next day we reached Nakuru, then went southeast across the Rift Valley to Mount Longonot. We went partway up the escarpment on our left and stopped at the large Kijabe mission station, which included a primary and secondary school, and a hospital that looks out onto Mount Longonot on the right. In earlier years, before we developed our own school at Mara Hills, our Mennonite missionary children had attended school at Kijabe. There are also two guesthouses on the station grounds, but we made reservations at the Africa Inland Mission guesthouse in Nairobi for several nights. Miriam Leaman and a Sudan Interior Mission worker, both from Somalia, have joined us for the holiday. Mary Jane Zimmerman, a nurse from our mission in Ethiopia, is also with us. So, altogether we are eight women on vacation.

We eight ladies are *not* stuffed into a car! No, the Shirati VW Micro-bus seats all of us OK. This morning we went out to the Nairobi game park and explored the vast acres with a game guide. We saw an array of giraffe, lion, hippo, ostrich, wild pig, and members of the deer family. We got some photos, but some of the animals were rather car shy. A tele-photo lens might have enabled us to get better photos of these animals.

Tomorrow we will see how our Microbus accommodates all of the suitcases for all eight of us. It is 9:30 P.M. and because my Hermes typewriter goes into the bottom of my suitcase, I need to make my *kwa heri* to you and get to packing my stuff *sasa hivi* (right away). Tomor-row we will travel the main road to Mombasa at the Indian Ocean on the east coast. Some of the road nearer to Nairobi is tarmac, but I under-stand that when we get close to the Indian Ocean the road will be sand, just sand.

I look forward to living in a cabin right by the ocean where I can go swimming—except that I never learned to swim on our Lancaster County farm. At least I will enter the water and enjoy splashing around. And I intend to collect some sea shells.

Monday, September 24, 1962

Greetings from Mombasa, where we are having a wonderful time. We arrived a week ago Friday and gladly settled into our cabins (or grass-roofed huts for some of the girls). It is quiet and comfortable here. The dining area is not close to our sleeping quarters. We are near the beach and not far from the entrance to Mombasa harbor, so we can watch the big ships come and go, especially if Cora's binoculars are available.

Last Sunday morning we started out not knowing where to find a church, so Elsie asked and we got to an Anglican one (it's British but much like our Episcopal churches). The service was led by Africans in Swahili, with use of rituals—jumping up and down from the seats for the various hymns, Scripture readings, and prayer. The African pastor preached about Noah going into the ark and inviting us to Jesus, the ark of our salvation. After the church service was finished, our group met some of the local folks and were blessed that we fellowship with the same Lord Jesus. Several days later, some of the ladies came to our hotel one afternoon to get better acquainted and share more stories of God's goodness. Surely such "spontaneous" good relationships with newly found friends, especially friends from a different race, is a gift of God's love to His people.

You probably remember that one day last week had rather special interest for me. Someone in our group had brought along a copy of the Family Worship Guide (which the Mennonite Publishing House sup-plies to all of us), which included a list of all missionaries who have a birthday in September. Well, I was not forgotten! I was typing a letter when the girls sauntered across our porch singing "Happy Birthday." I even received a toy hedgehog, and in its paper bag it really looked like a baby of the real thing I had stepped on several nights before. I also got several inflatable balloons, a flute (which I have not yet learned to play), a handy mirror for travel, some talcum powder, and a wooden comb—quite an array of interesting things. Then someone brought in the sodas and ice cream. In all it was a pleasant surprise for me.

Yesterday we went into Mombasa to attend services at the Gospel Tabernacle. The pastor is an American named Mr. Lyons. He spoke from Acts 6 about Stephen being "full of the Spirit and of wisdom, of good repute." He challenged us to likewise be faithful and so glorify our Lord. Mr. Lyons also takes our barrels through customs and sends them on to Musoma. When we met him after the service, we were glad to hear that the June shipment from Salunga had been sent out just last week to Kisumu. So I should get my file cabinet soon after I get home from holiday. Mr. Lyons also told us that he had paid no duty on this last shipment, except for some truck tires. He surely gets special consid-eration for us. They have eleven services in that church every Sunday, in five tribal languages plus English, and Mr. Lyons takes his turn preaching in each one. There is also at least one African pastor. They surely make good use of their church building, plus they have services in the church during the week too.

I guess I had not explained to you that the City of Mombasa is actually built on an island. A long bridge connects the island to the mainland and Nairobi. We cross the harbor entrance by ferry to get to our hotel, which is along the coast just south of Mombasa. The ferry is quite efficient; cars enter on one side and form three lines on the deck while the walking passengers enter on the side deck. The ferry crosses the harbor with its platform slightly elevated and a chain across the end. When the other side is reached, the chain is removed. Then cars and people move off the ferry. The ferry does not turn around after unloading its cars and passengers. It just reverses its direction, and so saves a lot of time and energy.

The city of Mombasa is quite old. One day we visited the famous old Fort Jesus, which was built on the eastern shore of Mombasa Island about a hundred years after the arrival around 1500 of the Portuguese, who were looking for ports of call along the eastern coast of Africa on their way to India. Fort Jesus stands on a small coral elevation near the entrance to the harbor. The work of building the fort was begun in 1593; when it was completed I do not know. As photos show, it is tall and large. It faces the Indian Ocean to the east. We also visited the docks where the larger ships come in to leave their wares for folks like us. We peeked into a lovely German-African freightliner. It had several cabins that could accommodate a total of twelve passengers.

We also visited the old harbor in the Arab part of town. We had to go down a narrow one-way street between tall buildings to see where the Arab *dhows* (sailboats) come in. They have no cranes to lift their loads, so everything is carried or rolled up the steep incline to their warehouse. Believe me, that is real *kazi* (work) for younger men to do.

While we were walking in town and "window shopping" today, I found several *shukas*. This cloth that comes in many different colors is typically just over seven yards long and five yards wide, so if I were to buy more than one piece of the same design, I could have the local seamstress make me a new dress. So I did buy two *shukas* and will see what develops from that in the future.

On Monday morning we will break camp here and head for the big game in Amboseli National Park. On Saturday we are due in Nairobi, where I hope to find some letters. The following Tuesday we will hike back to Shirati and hopefully arrive before the Eshlemans leave on Friday for a twenty-four-day medical van trip into South Mara.

Wednesday, October 10, 1962

Greetings again from Shirati. It was actually rather nice to get home again on Wednesday a week ago today. We left Nairobi on Tuesday afternoon and spent the night at Nukuru. In addition to transporting five people in our VW Microbus with all our luggage and purchases, we also brought strawberries, some apples, and even two and a half pounds of some expensive peaches that we purchased for almost $1.00. The luscious big peaches were imported from Italy. So yes, we did do some splurging at that store.

On Thursday evening, Dr. Eshleman took time to make rounds with me before he left. The patient census had been quite high the past month, up to ninety-five patients in our 104-bed hospital, and that was with maternity being rather slow, with only nineteen deliveries. On Friday morning before 7:00, the Eshlemans left with the Chevrolet van filled with supplies for their twenty-four-day tour in South Mara. They took along tents for camping out, as well as food and cooking utensils, so it took much advance preparation. The van has a radio, so we can contact them from Shirati about their work or to seek advice on any problems we may encounter here. This van is one of two provided by AMREF for health care work in rural East Africa. The foundation really is very helpful; though it is not necessarily a Christian organization, it delights in assisting mission hospitals. The only charge for the use of the van is for the fuel consumed; the driver is provided and paid for by the foundation.

It is good to hear that Mother is busy canning peaches and freezing lima beans. If I were not so far away I would surely help you get rid of some of those garden goodies. The folks at Kisaka can grow lima beans, but it seems that Shirati is too dry to grow them.

The generator has stopped making electricity, but thanks to my kerosene lamp I can still see. I took time to trim the wick and wash the globe.

It was a year ago on the 4th of October that I flew away from you all one evening. I had my next noon meal in London and changed flights, and arrived in Nairobi late on the morning of October 6. The next day, Dad's sixty-first birthday, I was delivered to Shirati by MAF plane. Now, a year later, I have been invited to speak, in English, to the staff nurses and the nursing students who understand English. I have been given no guidelines for what I should speak about, and I have not done this previously, so I have decided to share with the group something of my background and how God led me here. This approach will be much easier than trying to prepare a sermon. As I have thought back over my first year here it has not seemed long at all; the time passed speedily. But when I thought about the usual five-year term before furlough and about seeing family and friends again, a year did seem longer.

We are having some nice rains nearly every day since Friday, so maybe we can put some seeds in the gardens. Right now we are rather dependent on tin cans, and that soon gets monotonous—especially when they add green color to the beans and peas. Today my cook, Eleazar, fixed some dried beans in a pot with potatoes and cut-up hotdogs. Fortunately it tasted much better than it looked—green juice plus blue potatoes and blue-green meat and beans! Saturday we hope to have a hotdog roast out on some rocks overlooking the lake. We brought the hotdogs with us from Nairobi.

Hershey plans to go to Musoma tomorrow by *piki-pik*, so I will send this letter along with him to go out to you.

Monday, October 29, 1962

Greetings from Shirati on a cloudy Monday morning. I wanted to get at this letter last night after supper, but instead several of us sat around and talked until I got too lazy to work on a letter, so I went to bed and read *Time* magazine for a while. I am still three issues behind on those that arrived while I was on holiday in Kenya.

Kumbe ("well"), I surely did not get far on this letter the other morning. Now it is Wednesday evening. But before I get into the events of this week, let me tell you about last week. I was perking along after the noon meal and had just settled down for an afternoon nap when I was roused by Dr. Lester's voice calling for his keys. You see, he had entrusted his keys to my care before they departed on the extended van trip I told you about in my last letter. I discovered that he and Lois had returned by lorry with a sick patient who needed emergency surgery. They had arrived early that morning at a clinic and waited for the crew to set up. Meanwhile, Dr. Lester had determined that this woman needed surgery, and that meant finding some sort of vehicle to take them to Shirati. The crew had traveled through mud holes until midnight, when they set up camp for the night. The Eshlemans were not eager for a one-hundred-mile ride through more mud on the back of a bouncing lorry, but they did it and arrived at Shirati at 2:00 P.M. As far as I know the surgery was successful. Afterward, Dr. Lester took time to check on several patients and have an early supper before climbing back into the lorry. Lois stayed at their house and began washing their accumulated dirty clothes. At least Lester got a more comfortable front seat on the way back, and they arrived at their destination at 10:00 P.M.

The next day, Thursday, I was very glad that Lois was at home, because an elderly man had come in the previous night with severe constipation, abdominal distension, and some vomiting. That morning he was worse, with severe vomiting, so I thought a colostomy might give some relief from his obstruction. But alas, the problem was in the small bowel and I could not correct it. In fact, some of the small bowel had "wormed" its way into the large bowel. At least he seemed more comfortable on intravenous fluids and without vomiting in his few remaining days. I was happy that Lois was there, not only to give anesthesia but also to give me suggestions and encouragement.

Something else happened on Thursday morning. While I was seeing patients, I was told that a Christian woman whose husband worked on our compound had died during the night and was being buried that morning. I went along with Anna Martin and Naomi Weaver to the funeral. We traveled by bicycle. I had never before attended an African funeral, so I was all eyes and ears. First some men dug a grave near the hut where the woman had lived with her husband. After the body was placed in the grave, a short service was conducted. A man read a Scripture portion, then the deceased woman's husband shared his testimony. Someone led us in prayer, then the men returned the dirt to the grave.

During the burial service, those present were generally quiet, except for groups of women who kept coming into the village, wailing as if they were announcing their arrival and sorrow. After the grave site was covered, a non-Christian son of the deceased mother began to wail. Some other relatives and friends had brought along their drums and costumes and began their funeral dances. They reminded me somewhat of the Uhuru Day dances I saw when Tanganyika received its independence last December. I wish I'd had my camera to get some close photographs, but I had left it in Nairobi to get some repairs. At some point, various members of the deceased's family brought out some of her earthly possessions and deposited them on the grave, "so that her spirit might leave the objects to join her body." Also, her family's cows were driven into the village to walk over the grave. So, between the lowing cattle, the wailing neighbors, and the beating of the drums, there was some noise after the burial. I appreciated the singing of Christian hymns, though many of them were sung in the Luo language, which I do not understand at all. Still, I appreciated the Christian fellowship with believers even without understanding the words.

This Monday afternoon my nap was disturbed again, before I actually started to snooze, when Dr. Lester and the van arrived at about 2:00. Instead of going to the Eshleman house, they came directly to the big house and proceeded to unload two barrels and a box for Naomi Weaver and a box for me. There was also a trunk for the hospital.

I suddenly forgot about having an afternoon nap. Instead I amused myself for a while by using my screwdriver and hammer to open the outer plywood box, then got into the two-drawer filing cabinet to retrieve the supplies that Nate had prepared for me. There was my blue plaid dress, my corduroy jacket, my desk lamp, and last but not least my tape player. Everything was intact and the tape player works fine. Now I have MUSIC IN MY LIFE AGAIN—that is, when the generator is on duty. The music is such a welcome change in my life, so many thanks to Nate for a job well done.

Sunday, November 11, 1962

Greetings to you all from Shirati on a beautiful moonlit Sunday evening. I think the full moon here is even more gorgeous than it is in Pennsylvania. If only we did not also have all these pesky mosquitoes scrounging around for a juicy meal, a walk outside about now could be the thing to do. Instead, I'll chatter to you a bit longer, then go to bed and read a while.

This past week has been another busy one. On Monday morning I left by MAF for a short FDS in South Mara. I went by car to Bumangi with Catherine Leatherman. We arrived after 4:00 P.M. to find that the patients had expected us to arrive in the morning. On Tuesday morning I traveled west and south to Mugango by car with the African staff nurse who works at Bukiroba. Things were better organized at Mugango this time. I saw a number of interesting patients but had no mob pushing at the door as happened the last time. I had dinner with Laura Kurtz, then stopped briefly at Morembe Middle School for Girls before seeing patients at Bukiroba. On Wednesday I returned to Shirati before noon. Dr. Lester had meanwhile spent a day and a half away at Nyabasi and Kisaka, so nurse Anna Martin had been in charge until I got back. She had been able to contact Dr. Lester by radio in case of emergency.

It is Tuesday evening and I did not get to finish this letter and send it off with Dr. Wood yesterday. He and another doctor came in on a two-engine plane to see some patients and do three operations between 10:00 A.M. and 2:00 P.M. After a late lunch at 2:45, they departed at 4:00 P.M. Their pilot had been leery of landing the large twin-engine Aztec on our "bush strip," but it seems he was agreeably surprised by its good condition—about 1,200 yards long with good drainage.

Other news: Lake Victoria continues to rise. Elsie Cressman is dreaming about going to Tarime tomorrow to get *gunias* (large gunny sacks) to fill with sand and place around her house where the waves are lapping at the foundation. I spent Saturday there with her, studying Swahili in the hammock on her front porch for the first time since June, and I can verify that the lake is very near the house. Elsie would love to have a retaining wall built between the house and the lake, but such projects require money and workmen and time. We have not had rain here for several weeks, but the lake is being fed from various rivers, and it definitely is not receding as of yet.

Now for another major news item to begin my second year at Shirati: I was told some information about Dr. Lester and Lois's twenty-four days on the AMREF van last month doing health work in South Mara. More recently, a shorter, weekend trip was scheduled to Utegi, plus a stop further south at Kinesi and Musoma, and I was to be the doctor this time—my first AMREF trip.

The van pulled in several days ago. On Thursday I began pulling out the clothes and supplies I would need to pack. Dr. Lester had arranged to give nurse Anna Martin and me more instructions after teatime about the innards of the van and how to utilize its supplies. As we approached the Eshleman house, we met flames flying out of the van's open back doors, and the driver was in the process of pulling things out. He told us he had been putting petrol into the generator when suddenly there was fire around him. We were able to move the burning van into a more open spot near our house and away from the doctor's house and the electrical wires. We got a bucket brigade going to carry water to the fire, and it was soon brought under control. Folks were arriving for the Thursday 4:30 prayer meeting, so we had quite a group of spectators, and the prayer meeting was cancelled. We managed to retrieve from the van some usable medication, a portable X-ray machine, and an examination table and chair, but Dr. Lester's personal tent was lost. Fortunately I had been slow in packing my own supplies for the weekend and had not yet put anything in the van. The chassis, cab, and engine of the almost new Chevy were not harmed, and on Friday afternoon, after all the damaged equipment had been removed, the "remains" were driven off to Nairobi. The vehicle was covered by insurance. The cause of the fire was uncertain, but the Foundation received this tragedy without placing responsibility on us. Dr. Wood said the fire could have happened for anyone. So my first van trip went up in smoke. [*And another such trip never did come my way*].

Friday, November 28, 1962

Greetings to you all from Bukiroba this time. I arrived here by plane this noon for FDS and saw a number of patients. Bukiroba is six miles east of the larger town of Musoma. Tomorrow we will drive nineteen miles further east to Bumangi, which, like Bukiroba, has no airstrip, but its road is quite accessible—if you don't mind sand, ruts, and dust.

The other Sunday was really busy. I made hospital rounds before church and found an orphan whose mother had died after delivering her daughter at home two days before. The baby weighed in at a *big* eight and a half pounds. I picked her up, calling her Susie, and tried to help her pull on the nipple of the bottle. She swallowed a lot of air and slowly poked along before she finally returned some milk with her burp. It was fun working with her, and now, a week later, she has reconciled herself to feeding herself three ounces of milk per feeding.

I next visited my pregnant patient who had come in with severe burns over both breasts from falling into her "kitchen stove" (actually an outdoor circle of stones on the ground) during an epileptic seizure. I discovered that her dressings were a mess, so I spent an hour getting her clean and fixed up. So I missed Sunday school, but I did catch most of the church service.

That afternoon I got a welcome nap and was ready to go to the English worship service when an OB patient arrived from Tarime Hospital. She had been in labor at home for three days without delivering the baby. Then the contractions had stopped and the father had finally brought her to the hospital. The mother admitted that her previous delivery by the village midwives had led to a destructive effort to remove the infant in pieces. Afterward, she'd had an infection that required vigorous treatment. Still, with her second pregnancy the father again neglected to get early treatment. The woman's pelvic bones were very small, even for a five-and-a-half-pound stillborn child, and the pregnancy had caused permanent injuries. If only she had come to us when labor began and received a prompt C-section delivery; the outcome would have been very different for both mother and infant.

After I finished what I could do for this patient, I discovered that my epileptic patient was bleeding again from the breasts I had dressed that morning—maybe as much as a pint of blood—so I applied new dressings with more pressure. So, this was not a pleasant day.

Let me give you an update on the patient whose breast I removed some weeks ago. She healed promptly and nicely, so I discharged her a week later. The biopsy report from Nairobi was not a surprise. It showed small cancerous growths inside the large cyst, so we will try to contact her and see if she will return to the hospital for reevaluation and further treatment.

Our census in the wards is still high; ninety-four patients this week means that nearly every bed is filled and elective surgery patients must wait their turn. In the past two weeks I have assisted on four hysterectomies (removal of the uterus) for fibroid tumors. Last week I also helped to remove a kidney stone from a ureter, which goes from the kidney to the bladder. I am glad to be assisting in more surgeries. I just wish it did not mean cutting back on my time to study Swahili. In recent months I have gotten only one day off to study Swahili at Elsie's house. I am also busy teaching classes to the nursing school students. The senior students just finished taking their final exams today. They will graduate next week as the first class from our Shirati nursing school.

We did not forget about Thanksgiving Day. We started by working as though it was a regular workday, doing surgery and teaching classes. But when 6:30 P.M. arrived, we all gathered on the Eshleman veranda for a real feast of roast chicken, candied sweet potatoes, dried corn, cranberry sauce, hot rolls, mince pie with ice cream, and coffee. After we had eaten more than enough food, we moved into the living room, where Norma Leaman provided music on the piano and we all sang a number of familiar Thanksgiving hymns. We even added several Christmas numbers before our hoarse voices finally pushed us to stop. It was a nice way to remember Thanksgiving Day and our Lord's blessings to all of us.

The following weekend was special too. Phoebe Yoder and Martha Myer live together in the newest mission house at Bukiroba. They moved in this past January and invited the Jim Mohler couple, the Maynard Kurtz couple, and us singles from the other stations to join them for a weekend "open house." We girls slept in the Bible college dormitory, which was quite comfortable. The weekend was most enjoyable, whether we were visiting, playing games, or just doing something different. On Saturday we had a mystery supper, which was quite interesting. One fellow ate his Jell-O and potatoes using a knife and a toothpick as utensils! On Sunday evening, we drove through heavy rain on the way home, but it finished before the water of the Mori River at Utegi became impassable. If we had arrived at Utegi a half-hour later, we may have been stranded there until the following morning. It was good to be back at Shirati!

Tomorrow is another safari, though I would be content just to stay put for several days at my homebase.

Monday, December 11, 1962

In my last letter, written on November 28, I told you about the woman who came in with severe burns around both breasts. She was also pregnant and near term when she came to us. We treated the burns. After two weeks, Dr. Lester was ready to put on some skin grafts, which he planned to do on Tuesday morning, but late on Monday afternoon the baby decided she was coming to steal the show! Because both mother and baby were so obliging, our surgeon and anesthetist proceeded with the skin grafts on Tuesday morning. The young baby was given tea to drink for several days, but her mother is now nursing her and she is gaining weight. The burn on the mother's one side reached right to the nipple but left it intact. On the other side, the burn surrounded the nipple but left intact the skin that the baby pulls on. The baby prefers the other side, for obvious reasons; she does not have to work as hard, and she gets more milk to boot. The mother is most cooperative and seems to really appreciate what we are doing for her. Perhaps as an epileptic she has been ostracized by her neighbors and family.

I mentioned baby Susie last time too. She was brought to us at two days of age after her mother died at home. She is *mtoto wangu*, "my baby." She is very cute and she gets held to eat. She drinks a bit and then settles down to sleep—if she is allowed to. But in another hour or two she wants to repeat the process, instead of finishing four ounces at one sitting. I manage to "waste" some time with her almost every day.

The Shirati staff began training students in our nursing school three years ago. Alta Weaver was sister tutor of the school. Nine students graduated from the first class. The graduation was held in the church on Friday afternoon. Mrs. Eshleman prepared the flower arrangements around the platform and placed a lovely palm leaf in the alcove for a beautiful background. Each graduate had a part in the program, and it seemed that they all felt it was a very nice and special day.

Tuesday, New Year's Day, 1963

Things have been rather busy here. For starters, our hospital received a rather unwelcome girl patient before Christmas. Her diagnosis was unclear but she had abdominal pain and fever, so she was admitted to the female ward and Dr. Lester considered doing exploratory surgery. After ten days she developed a rash that looked somewhat like chicken pox, but an alert staff nurse (Kefa) suspected that she may have had small-pox and promptly called me. Well, I had never seen smallpox but I was inclined to agree with him, so I ordered that she be moved into an isolation unit. I also called Dr. Lester, who soon came to verify our diagnosis. Fortunately our hospital had gotten a batch of smallpox vaccine a few weeks earlier, so on the following Monday morning we began scratching each available upper arm—on patients, relatives, school students, staff—on our compound. We also went to other schools in the area and did the same thing. Right now I am trying hard not to rub the itchy blotch on my own arm. We did about seven hundred vaccinations last week and have done more this week. The original patient has fortunately recovered well and her rash is fading. I forgot to ask to take a photo of her at the height of her rash. I got my camera back from repairs in Nairobi a week ago.

The hospital work just keeps coming. The Eshleman children—Charlotte and Lynn—are home from the Mara Hills School for the holidays, so I was asked to cover the hospital calls from the Sunday before Christmas through Christmas Day, the following Tuesday. But Dr. Lester got a different Christmas gift that morning: a man with acute appendicitis, which is very rare here. This man was an office worker from Tarime, so he may have eaten a more European-type diet, which would predispose him to a "new" illness that is quite common in the United States. He had been sick for several days and the appendix was severely inflamed by the time he came to us, but he recovered well after his surgery.

The following evening, Wednesday, I was asked to see one of our nursing school students, who was complaining of lower abdominal pain. How strange to have two patients with acute appendicitis in two days! The latter patient was treated more promptly, so she had less inflammation and made an uneventful recovery.

Amid the flurry of getting the smallpox vaccine out into the near-by communities, we did celebrate Christmas. We had invited guests to be with us, because we Shirati folks need to cover the hospital every day. Martha Jane Lutz, Miriam Buckwalter, and Edith Martin came from the Mara Hills School. Martha Myer, Grace Gehman, and Maynard Kurtz and his wife came from South Mara. They arrived on Monday afternoon and we had our Christmas dinner that evening by candlelight on the front porch of the Eshleman house. We had "ham without the squeal" because our hunters did not get a shot at a wild pig; they instead pickled the hind thigh of a wildebeest, and it made delicious meat. We also had peas, noodles, and cranberry sauce; and salad and fruit completed the meal. Between courses, thirteen-month-old Larry announced his readiness to go to bed, so Dr. Lester got out the vaccine serum bottle and jabbed some arms. Larry is rather uncomfortable just now. We later had a grab bag gift exchange and I got a lovely woven tray of colored grass, made in Uganda. We then just sat and talked and listened to some tapes of Christmas music. Afterward, I saw a sick patient and did not get to sleep until late—or maybe it was early in the morning.

Somehow I felt too tired to roll out of bed at 5:00 A.M. to go along caroling on Christmas morning, so I stayed in bed but did not go back to sleep. Later I helped with the nursing school patient whose appendicitis surgery we finished at 11:30 A.M. I then went to church and gave my Christmas offering. After a light lunch of soup and cookies, I again fell into bed and slept instead of going to the fellowship meal in the church at 3:00 P.M. I did get myself organized to go with the singles to Elsie's house by the lake that evening for games, supper, and reading aloud together Dickens's *Christmas Carol*. I got rather tired during the story, but was glad to hear it again; it reminded me of M. T. Brackbill reading it at EMC before Christmas. We got back to the compound around 11:00 P.M. On Wednesday morning, some of our guests left. I made rounds and found more people to vaccinate. That was my Christmas of 1962.

Saturday, January 26, 1963

Last week was a lost week as far as me doing anything at Shirati was concerned. I left here by VW Microbus that Monday morning at 7:30 to go to Musoma, where I had been summoned for a high court case. I arrived at Bukiroba at 11:45 and hurried to wash up and get into dress clothes. I had been told to arrive at the open-air pavilion on Monday morning, but when I got there they said my case would not be heard until Tuesday. I had actually planned to go to Musoma on Sunday afternoon, but there were rain clouds toward the northeast and Tarime all afternoon, so I delayed my trip and missed the rain, though I still drove through mud on Monday morning. I also had to contend with water in the vehicle's gas line. Dr. Lester had forewarned me about this problem and given me a short "mechanical engineering course" the evening before. I was able to remove the screw from the carburetor and clean out the water. I had brought along work clothes to Musoma, so I changed into them at the Stauffers' home before going shopping for various things that folks at Shirati had asked me to get for them. Then I took Martha Myer along to Bukiroba. Martha is now working in the bookshop at Musoma but still lives at Bukiroba. Grace Stauffer, Bishop Elam Stauffer's wife, is in charge of the bookshop, but they will soon be retiring to the United States.

On Tuesday morning I got into nylons, black shoes (flats instead of heels), a blue nylon dress, a bonnet, and a white wool dress sweater that I had bought in Nairobi. Again I went to the pavilion, and *kumbe!* (behold!)

it was deserted! Then someone reported that the prime minister of Tongaland had just been assassinated, so in sympathy Tanganyika had declared a national holiday. Maybe Tanganyika has more holidays than we do!

I went back to the bookshop, changed into more comfortable clothes, and found some work to do. The bookstore was not open for business but we assembled school supplies for our various primary schools. I sorted exercise books, Swahili readers, chalk, pencils, erasers, rulers, and so on. It was rather interesting, and five of us working together filled six orders by noon. Then Grace ordered a "half holiday" and Martha and I headed for Bukiroba. On the way I stopped under a shade tree for fifteen minutes to clean out the "screw." But every time I cleaned the screw and replaced it, more water flowed in with the gas. With two or three holes plugged, it sounded terrible and had no power, so I stopped again and tried to clean it.

That afternoon I got my one really good nap of the whole week. (I really miss my nap if I don't get it.) I also met Paul, an African mechanic, and asked if he would work on this miserable VW Microbus, so he did. He removed the gas, drained out the water, and readjusted the points. After that it started very well and idled properly for the rest of the week. That same afternoon, Martha and I found two rocks under a tree behind the John Leatherman house, so we each sat on a rock and studied Swahili. We were using a simple Swahili reader and really were amused by the story of the African who went on safari to see the world with his wife. They had amusing troubles on their safari too!

On Wednesday I again returned to the court and waited around almost all day for my case to come up, but it did not happen. The previous case dragged on and on. There were no waiting rooms or even vacant benches, so I leaned against a shade tree and waited, and waited some more. At one point I heard the judge say in an irritated tone, "Don't ask questions just to ask a question!"

Finally, on Thursday morning I was called as the first witness. Now I could really see the judge and lawyers in their formal attire of white bow ties, long black gowns, and wigs of white "hair" that apparently made them more capable of rendering justice. It took only about thirty minutes to answer their questions and "set straight" the lawyer who was defending the accused man. He tried to have me say that because I had found nothing wrong in the deceased man's chest or abdomen, I had then concluded that the man had died of head injuries. But the man had definite lacerations and bruises of the brain itself, which I had documented. I was finally excused from the High Court at 10:00 A.M. and, after having a cup of tea at Bukiroba, I departed for Shirati at 11:00 A.M.

Two new nursing school students traveled with me back to Shirati. It had really rained again the previous night, so we encountered lots of

mud and high rivers on the way. At Utegi, the Mori River was elevated and we waited more than an hour in the hot sun while the level slowly dropped by an inch to inch and a half before I ventured to cross it. We were still about twenty miles, and another river, the Merari, from Shirati.

The concrete Merari bridge was not covered with water this time, but a big lorry had driven too near the edge and broken off some of the concrete, flipped his truck onto its side, and dunked his load into the river. One of our nursing school students was returning to Shirati on that truck and her clothing and school fees were lost in river. The lorry was owned by the Indian businessman in Utegi who had helped Elsie and me when we got stuck in that same river last June. We finally got back to Shirati at 5:00 pm on Thursday, and I must say I was really glad to be home.

Sunday, January 27, 1963

Thank-you for the supply of pretzels, apples, and walnuts that arrived in good shape a week ago. It took them only two months to get here, which is rapid delivery for over the Christmas holidays. I put the pretzels into a molasses can and parked them on top of the refrigerator. (The kerosene heater not only works to cool our refrigerator but also doubles as a warming shelf on which to park our cereals to keep them fresh.) In Nairobi we can get puny yellow pretzel sticks with almost no salt, so these pretzels from home are vastly better. Hershey Leaman's parents occasionally ship him a big can of broken pretzels. His dad makes several holes around the edge of the lid and puts small bolts through them to keep the lid in place. He then puts his name on top and the battered can usually arrives intact. Once one can still lost its top, and its contents, before it got through New York City, so word was sent to the sender along with the battered can.

So much for pretzels! Last night I wrote about my arrival at Shirati on Thursday evening though my original plan had been to return from the court case by midday on Tuesday. At the various houses I unloaded the supplies I had brought back, then headed to my house to eat supper. I live with one of the nursing school teachers and she greeted my arrival with, "Can you teach tonight?" I promptly said yes. Because I went on holiday in September, I am behind on my schedule, so I now try to do at least three lectures per week.

Before I had finished the lecture that evening, Dr. Lester sent word for me to come see him afterward. I told him about the long wait for the court session, and he told me about a new OB admission who had previously had a C-section due to a small pelvis and was now in labor again. I took time to stop by my house to change into OR clothes and have a spot of coffee. The patient had been in labor for several hours, so I notified the Eshlemans. Dr. Lester had me deliver the husky seven-pound girl. The only finding of interest was that the mother had copious adhesions from the previous C-section. We do not do many C-sections here, because patients often come too late for us to use this procedure. I finally rolled into bed at around 1:30 A.M., after another cup of coffee with Anna Martin.

That morning I was a bit tardy for rounds. Some new admissions had come in during my absence, including a boy with heart disease and a patient with hepatitis. I saw a number of outpatients until almost noon. I then put some clean clothes into my safari bag and pulled out my medical bag to get ready for a weekend medical visit to Nyabasi. This visit had been scheduled several weeks ago but had been postponed by the court case at Musoma. Elsie Cressman went along to see her leprosy patients, and brought with her one of our leprosy patients. The patient got car sick on the three-mile ride from the leprosarium to our hospital and upchucked in the Microbus before we could get out of the hospital's front yard. At least the broom, water, and cleaning materials were nearby. I had hoped to get off at around 1:00 P.M., ahead of the rains, but we finally left at around 2:30. Fortunately it did not rain that afternoon after all. We arrived at Mara Hills School at around 6:00 P.M. We delivered to Edith Martin her barrel and trunk, which I had brought from Bukiroba, so she was very happy that we had come. She had not been told that her things were so close-by, so it was a surprise for her.

I found the work at Nyabasi to be as usual. I saw many outpatients, and some I advised to come to our hospital for surgery. Our two African nurses at Nyabasi are doing very well. The male nurse, who is married, works in the clinics with Mary Harnish, one of our missionaries, who is in charge of midwifery and OB-GYN. She also works in the dispensary.

Our first class of nursing school students recently passed their examinations, to our pleasant surprise; we plan to hire more midwives and nurses to reduce the workload of these faithful workers. We have already hired two nurses from other schools in addition to most of our own graduates. A nurse will also be sent to Mugango, where we currently have only uncertified nursing workers. Mary Harnish may be relocated at Kisaka later this year when Velma Eshleman goes on furlough.

So our nursing care is improving with the use of our nursing school students and the graduation of our first class, but there is more to do. And our scattered dispensaries need more supervision and training.

On Sunday morning, Elsie and I loaded up the Microbus with people and food, including nine bunches of bananas as well as potatoes, sweet corn, and onions. The Microbus decided to annoy us with water in the engine again, so I had several more cleaning sessions before we finally got home at 6:45 P.M. Now Dr. Lester will have a turn traveling around with this finicky Microbus while I stay at home a little. He is going for a court case tomorrow. I hope he has fun like I did last week!

Friday, February 13, 1963

The following material was originally written at the end of a meeting at the Tenwek World Gospel Mission and Hospital in late February 1963, but the events I wrote about preceded the meeting. I have placed them here in their proper order.

It was on Friday morning of the week before our trip to Tenwek that Orie Miller flew from Nairobi to Shirati to take me along on FDS to Musoma and Bukiroba. While we were there, Orie spent his time preparing for the upcoming special dedication of the Bible college at Bukiroba. Meanwhile, I saw some patients at Bukiroba. Then Gordon, the MAF pilot, flew me to Kisaka for the rest of the day. On Saturday, Gordon flew me to Kenyana, where I was welcomed by several patients who were quite sick and one who had sustained severe injuries to his one hand. I urged the injured man to come to Shirati for debridement and possible plastic surgery. But alas, he had no money and his home was far away in the bush. I shuddered to think of what could happen to him. If he managed to survive without a bone infection, his nerves and tendons would doubtless function poorly, so the hand could not do much work.

I got back to Shirati that evening by way of Musoma and saw patients. Dr. Lester had left that same morning by VW Microbus for committee work at Musoma. I made rounds of all our patients on Monday morning, then after the noon meal I took a fifteen-minute flight to Musoma to attend the dedication of the Bible college at Bukiroba.

This special occasion merited the attendance of all our missionary staff. Orie Miller was the guest of honor. The program was very nice. Various guests from other missions were also present, as were many local business and government personnel. Later we enjoyed tea under the trees, followed by a picnic lunch and an informal meeting with Orie. At seventy years of age he still gets around very well.

The next morning I was off early to return by plane to Shirati. Orie flew along to Entebbe and then on to Burundi to visit some MCC workers. Our African senior staff nurse, Kefa, welcomed me back enthusiastically to Shirati, for he had admitted several sick patients during my brief absence. He had consulted with me by radio on Monday evening about a mastoid problem. Later, another sick patient came in and then another decided to bleed, so he was kept quite busy. I felt that Kefa did very well with these problems, and I am especially pleased that we can take this nurse along to the Tenwek meeting this next weekend. Dr. Lester and some other medical personnel attended this special medical weekend in Kenya last year, so this year some other folks were invited. I look forward to it.

Saturday, February 14, 1963

Two weeks ago we had a special patient: a Catholic nun who is a medical doctor and stationed several miles south of Utegi. Several of us Shirati folks spent a night at their mission about a year ago, when we could not cross the Mori River, and they had treated us very kindly. Now their doctor had asked to come for an annual physical examination by me. She had also asked to spend the night on our compound, because the frequent afternoon rains and high waters could make the rivers impassable. We agreed, but frankly we Mennonites were unsure what to expect from her. She was very relaxed in our midst, however. She knew what to do and we got along fine. I soon discovered that she spoke the Luo tribal language whereas we used mostly Swahili. Luo is a tonal language and much more difficult to learn. The nun-doctor had been living among the Luo people for only three years, but she could speak it very well compared to our Shirati missionaries. I apologize that I do not now recall the doctor's name. She had an evening meal with the Eshlemans, then came along to our midweek missionary fellowship. That evening we listened to a tape of a 1960 EMBMC annual meeting.

Linden Wenger, a Bible teacher at EMC Seminary, spoke on the theme "We Would See Jesus." What our guest thought about this sermon was not revealed, but it did exalt Jesus and never mentioned the role of his mother, Mary, as a special avenue of access to God. Several of us single ladies welcomed our guest into our abode for the night. And we did not immediately put ourselves to bed.

The next morning, our guest stayed long enough to watch some surgery and make short rounds. She revealed that she had received specialty board certification in OB-GYN. After the nun-doctor gave her thanks and departed, the rest of us had some amusing conversations about our visitor. Some expressed surprise that she was so sociable and friendly and, well, not so stiff or pious that one could not talk with her about ordinary things. She could drink black coffee like me. She could joke and enjoy something funny. I'd had some contact with two Catholic nuns who were one year ahead of me in medical school. There may be more communication between Catholic and Protestant missionaries in overseas assignments than occurs in our infrequent contacts at home.

Two weeks ago we had another childbirth in our missionary group. This time the mother was Anna Ruth Jacobs and the father was Don Jacobs. Anna Ruth had arrived three weeks earlier from Bukiroba, and we surely enjoyed her presence. My only regret was that I was too busy to take advantage of her keen ability in teaching Swahili. She finally had little pains all morning without doing anything exciting, so I let her walk to Hershey's house for lunch. Well, whether it was the walk or the lunch or something else, she decided to forgo the dessert and return to the hospital—a rather long walk. The local car refused to start, so Anna Ruth walked halfway and stopped for a good pain. She was nearly conquered when Hershey pulled up on his *piki-pik*. Anna Ruth gratefully climbed aboard and rode the remainder of the way. She was most obliging in waiting to push until I was gowned and had draped her, and when I gave her the sign to go, she promptly delivered a squalling seven-pound son, Paul Evan—just twenty minutes after she left the dinner table. We soon had mother and baby in bed, and we all got our afternoon nap. It was very interesting to hear three-year-old Allen (who was here with his mother) report on the radio that evening to his father, brother, and sister that he has a brother "and he looks like me!"

I have been helping with surgery practically every OR day, which is Tuesday, Thursday, and Saturday, when Dr. Lester is here. In his absence I handle some minor cases, such as finger amputation, removal of a tumor behind the ear, and repair of an ankle tendon. Today I worked on an infected fallopian tube (the tube that goes from the ovary to the uterus) and removed it. Dr. Lester looked in several times to see how I was doing. Several weeks ago he helped me do a C-section. I want to get more experience on these procedures while he is still here.

Tomorrow I will go on FDS to Kisaka, and on Saturday I will go to Kenyana. I vividly remember my two other trips to Kenyana. I have packed my medical bag, which Velma Eshleman received from Dr. Merle Eshleman some years ago. Orie Miller is coming along from Nairobi to spend the weekend at Bukiroba in fellowship and consultation with church leaders and missionaries.

Tuesday, February 24, 1963

Greetings to you all from Kenya this time. The name of the place is Tenwek Hospital. It is near Bomet, which is twenty-five miles east of Sotik, which is between Kericho and Kisii on our route to Nairobi. Maybe that will help you find where I am on the Caltex map I sent you.

I have borrowed a typewriter, an Underwood machine, with small type. The owner is a friend from my medical school days. Frances Stine Campbell graduated from Woman's Medical College in 1961, one year after I did. She came to Kenya this past November with her husband. and they had recently moved to Tenwek after three months of language study. Mr. Campbell will teach in the secondary school, and Fran will be in charge of the forty-bed hospital when the other doctor goes on furlough at the end of March.

I had learned from the Woman's Medical alumni newsletter that Fran was coming to Kenya, but I had no idea when or what her final destination would be. She learned that I was coming to Tenwek for this annual meeting of medical missionaries (a time for fellowship and sharing of medical problems and concerns), so she arranged for me to stay in their home for the weekend. The medical missionary personnel of Tanganyika, Uganda, and Burundi are also invited. Last year, Dr. Eshleman attended the meeting with Hershey Leaman, two missionary nurses, two staff nurses, and our two midwives (one is in charge of maternity work at Shirati and the other is at Nyabasi). Anna Martin, Kefa, and others were in our current group.

We left for Tenwek on Friday morning in the VW Microbus. We spent forty-five minutes at Tarime, then several hours in Kisii, where we ate lunch. The total distance to Tenwek was about 150 miles, but only 30 were covered with tarmac. We were loaded rather heavily, and no one else asked to drive (one person even left their driver's license at home), so I was the understood driver for this trip. I got lots of work shifting gears to climb the hills—much like taking a heavy truck up Gap Hill back home. But I quite enjoyed the driving, as long as it was not in the cities with their confusing traffic circles.

We finally saw the sign for Tenwek and I made a hard turn to the right. Suddenly another VW like ours approached. We both stopped quickly and exchanged hellos before moving more slowly down the short approach to the compound, where we found the hospital buildings and facilities for the staff.

I was soon found by Frances Stine Campbell, who took me to their home. I enjoyed staying with them. She showed me their lovely forty-bed hospital, and we shared some of our East Africa experiences. They are still working on developing qualified nurses. The present doctor has done a number of surgical procedures, but he will go on furlough at the end of March. I could understand Fran's hesitation about being in charge of this hospital all by herself. I could appreciate her feelings about stepping into emergency surgery alone, and I prayed that both she and her husband would find wisdom and strength in each situation. It can be rather difficult for new folks to find their way in overseas mission work despite their best attempts to serve the Lord and minister to persons in need in an unfamiliar environment.

I soon discovered that about forty guests from various hospitals, mostly in Kenya, were attending the weekend. There were seven or eight doctors, including another one from Tanganyika, and both missionary nurses and African staff nurses. Folks were present from the various missions as well as from Britain and Scotland. Meals were served in the school's dining room, and our meetings were held in a classroom. The program consisted of both medical and spiritual topics. We heard about practical ways to administer anesthesia, both local and spinal. There were several case reports about special patients, and a midwife shared some interesting reports on her work. We toured the lovely hospital and discussed several of the patients. Last evening we shared a time of singing that was typical American style, with old familiar choruses interspersed with special numbers. The British, as you may know, tend to be more reserved and proper than we more "adolescent" Americans are, but these differences were rather minor here. We truly enjoyed the fellowship together, in song and otherwise.

This morning the hospital chaplain spoke to us from Mark 16 about obeying Christ and serving Him as commissioned disciples. The meeting has been a welcome interlude away from the work at Shirati, where things have been quite busy. We did get some free time before the evening meal on Saturday. I had noticed that there was a large building perhaps a quarter of a mile to the east. The area around it was open but the grass was rather tall. I was intrigued to explore, and I invited some other folks to walk along with me.

The building was made of stone. Seats were set up inside as though for a church service. Whether the windows were empty openings or contained window panes I do not remember. At any rate, the interior space could hold a rather large number of people. I do not recall the material or color of the roof, but it was a very attractive building, and I supposed it was the space they used for Sunday worship. I then noticed beyond the church a stream of water running to the south. The stream was more enclosed by trees and shrubbery, so I soon turned around and returned to the main complex.

All too quickly the weekend at Tenwek was over and we had to say good-bye to all our new friends. I thanked Fran and her husband for letting me stay at their house and wished them well in their new responsibilities at Tenwek. After the noon meal we slowly got into our vehicles, headed up the hill, and went our separate ways toward home, with many good memories in our heads and in our hearts. I hope we will meet some of these folks again.

Sunday, March 17, 1963

Greetings again from Shirati, where we are having rain and cooler weather. My old gray sweater felt really good last evening.

Our OB work has improved since Dr. Lester "started things" while I was at Tenwek. He recently explained to me, with tongue in check, that he had instructed the midwife to tie a rope around each prenatal patient who comes to the maternity clinic and then, when she begins labor, to yank on the rope and pull her into the hospital to deliver. Sorry, it is not that easy! But we are rating almost one delivery per day, with two deliveries on two different days in the past week, which is quite an improvement over only nine deliveries in the whole month of January this year. Last Friday, however, one mother did not make it to us for delivery. It is not clear whether they failed to get a lorry to bring her or she developed severe bleeding problems and died while on the way. But her five-pound daughter was in acceptable condition, so the family members arranged for our staff to give temporary care to the infant, then went wailing back home.

Now for some more pleasant news. Simeon and Edna Hurst have spent the past two weeks with us at Shirati. Simeon is providing leadership training for our younger men while Pastor Nashon is at Bible college in Bukiroba. Edna is quite a *fundi* (expert) in Swahili, so I asked her to give me some teaching. She gladly agreed, and we have spent seven sessions together. This has given me a real boost in learning some basic grammar. It also made it easier for me to get time for regular study; I could tell folks that I was having class with Edna and needed regular study and class time. I translated and read aloud some of the story of Joseph in preparation for my first Swahili exam.

Simeon and Edna will return to Nyabasi tomorrow to be there with their younger children for the Easter vacation. Edna invited me to come up to Nyabasi for a week to study and then take my first Swahili exam. I would love to do that, but I know that my time will be filled with FDS, Easter events, and maybe overland visits to other clinics, so my first Swahili test may need to wait.

I must tell you that I've been getting around a little faster this week. No, my legs did not grow two inches longer, but they now have two wheels that go faster, and a choice of four gears, all forward. This machine is naturally blue in color, and her name is Suzie, because she is female. Her brother, whose name is Zuki, belongs to Elsie Cressman. The father's name is Suzuki and he lives and works in Japan, but he has many children scattered around the eastern half of the world. Elsie has been busy at Shirati for several terms working several miles away at the leprosarium, but she comes to our main complex at night, so her Zuki will be very useful to her. Yes, the motors are rather small—I think the power is 55cc, but it is quite adequate as it says "buzzzz burpppp." The African folks call it a *piki-pik,* so I do not call it a motorcycle, but you may. It is a model for smaller ladies, so my feet easily reach the ground when I am on the seat. I rode down to see Elsie by the lake last Sunday, and have done some exploration around the hospital complex.

Dr. Lester seems to admire my Suzie too. The Eshlemans usually get around by bicycle, but last Thursday he borrowed a *piki* and rode it to visit a clinic that is forty miles away. When he returned from that safari, he still had enough energy to ride about a mile further to inspect the airstrip. As I returned from a spin over the back road, I saw Dr. Lester racing down the airstrip and I waited for him. When he came back, he admitted that he had even "tried to take off" but did not quite make it!

Every month we print a hospital news sheet that tells who visited where, the guests who came to us, a patient census, the number of surgery cases, the number of women-and-baby deliveries, unusual cases, and so on. I told Dr. Lester that I felt we could report a new and interesting disease at Shirati: *Piki* Fever! He really chuckled about that, then asked me how many such cases I thought we might have at Shirati. I was naturally thinking of him and myself, but he said he thought there might be four or five cases altogether. Several other women have expressed great interest in Suzie, so maybe the population will grow. I

have not yet written up a thorough case report on this "disease," but maybe I can do more investigation later.

During the several times she has worked here at Shirati, Elsie has used cycles of various types and then sold them when she went on furlough. Now she wanted another one and she talked to me about it. We had explored the possibilities when we were in Nairobi some months ago, and each of us had ordered a Suzuki. Eventually the bikes were shipped by train from Nairobi to Kisumu, then shipped south by boat to our small dock several miles from Shirati. Hershey Leaman drove one of the cycles back to Shirati, and another young man rode the other one up onto our porch, opened the front door, and parked my *piki-pik* right in the middle of our living room, smoke and all! Eventually I parked my machine on the front porch, with the key locked inside the house.

We use our *piki-pik*s mostly for short runs, but recently Elsie invited me to go with her for a ride north along the lake and across the border into Kenya. I made the mistake of not filling my gas tank, so I ran out of gas, but someone with a gas can came along and filled me up. Before we got home we got a run of rain and Elsie slid into a puddle in front of me. I could not control my amusement at her fall.

Simeon and Edna Hurst are still with us. This evening we started a series of doctrinal messages in English. Simeon spoke about Satan, about his downfall and his current state of deceiving men and women. Opportunity was given for folks to ask questions, and several students from the nursing school did speak up. So I hope this will continue as a valuable teaching series for these students.

Tuesday, April 2, 1963

I have not been "gadding around" recently, at least not on the ground, but I sure am flying up in the air a lot with our pilot, Gordon Marshall. Let me explain how it all came about.

Since I arrived in Tanganyika, I have kept my ears peeled for an introduction to Somalia before I go there to work for sixteen months. The two older children of missionaries Victor and Viola Dorsch have been going to Mara Hills School in Nyabasi and usually manage to go home to Somalia for the holidays. Sometimes they go by car and other times by MAF plane. I told Dr. Lester of my interest in Somalia some months ago. I also mentioned it to Gordon, and two weeks ago he wrote to say that he had room for me to travel home with the Dorsch children—James and Shirley—for Easter. (As thrifty Mennonites, we always try to plan a full load both ways in order to cut expenses.)

I wrote to Dr. Ivan Leaman at Somalia about my proposed visit and my attempt to get a visa. As you may know if you keep up with *Time* and the news, Somalia was recently rather peeved at Great Britain and Kenya because those two countries were not inclined to give a large part of northeastern Kenya to Somalia. A number of Somali people have scattered into the dry area of Kenya, but they still want to be part of Somalia. Consequently, Somalia broke off diplomatic relations with Britain (and thereby with Kenya as well, because Kenya has not yet received independence from Britain), and both the Somali consulate members and the British officials left Somalia. Thus I could not obtain a visa in Nairobi. Also, Gordon has a British passport, so for a time it appeared that even he would not be able to take the children home. I figured the trip was off.

But then things quieted down, and last Thursday afternoon I was informed via Nairobi radio that a telegram had been received from Harold Stauffer in Mogadishu. It said that visas had been cleared for Gordon and me and that it was "possible and desirable" for me to "come at this time." So I packed up a few things that evening (I was limited to twenty pounds), and made my hospital rounds as usual the next morning. That afternoon, Gordon brought several patients to us from Nairobi. We then went to the Mara mine, which has a longer airstrip than Nyabasi. The Nyabasi airstrip also gets soft during the rains, so for heavy loads Gordon uses the longer mine strip for takeoff. I stayed at the mine while Gordon went to pick up the Dorsch children and two teachers (Martha Jane Lutz and Miriam Buckwalter) who wanted to shop in Nairobi. As I waited, I practiced some Swahili on the curious Kuria folks who gathered around and asked me questions: Where did you come from? Where are you going? Have you been to Shirati? How many children do you have? and so on. I laughed at the woman who left her *debbe* (bucket) of water at a distance to come and talk. The nearby cattle and goats were quite interested in taking some water every time the woman turned her back! The woman ran after the animals several times to chase them away. Finally, she picked up her *debbe,* parked it on her head, walked over to a shade tree, and sat down to watch from afar. Another woman was fascinated by my plastic water bottles, so I gave them to her and said *kwa heri,* and she walked away happy.

At about 4:00 P.M. the plane came back from Nyabasi, so I climbed aboard and we were off. We flew over the Mara Valley and the *pori*—and did we ever see animals! There were big herds of buffalo, lots of hartebeests and other antelopes, giraffes, an ostrich, and even a family of lions—two males with several females and some cubs—parked under a tree. We almost missed them but for Martha Jane's sharp eyes. So Gordon circled very low—just several hundred feet above the trees—and we all got a good look while a disgusted male got up to walk away from our big noisy bird.

Upon arriving at Nairobi I was fortunate to get lodging at the Africa Inland Mission guesthouse even though I had no reservation. Lena Horning from Somalia was there too. After a long-soaking hot bath and a delicious dinner, I joined four teachers—Lena Horning, Helen Ranck, Miriam Buckwalter, and Martha Jane Lutz—in a Scrabble game, and made a stupendous score of 45! The next morning after breakfast I met with the Dorsch children, who had spent the night with Gordon's family. Gordon carefully loaded extra food, including fresh fruits and vegetables, and a few medications onto the plane.

We took off from Nairobi at 9:00 am and headed east. I enjoyed watching the countryside. Initially there were some hilly areas, but gradually the landscape became more flat and brown with a few villages clustered along the several "rivers," their tell-tale snakelike ribbons marking out their courses through the desert. We also had some headwinds and clouds that gave our flight some up-and-down variety. But after three and a half hours of flying between and above the fluffy white clouds, I was ready to touch ground at Kismayu, and James and Shirley were very excited to spy their parents and younger sister waiting in one of their Land Rovers. The customs police watched us transfer our goods to the vehicle, then we went into town for inspection and government clearance. We were eager to complete their business with us. It was 1:00 P.M. when we got into town, so naturally the officials had gone to lunch, so we did too. Eventually our inspections were completed, and we rode to our place of abode at Jamama.

Friday, April 5, 1963

I am typing from Shirati again but continuing the story of my visit to Somalia. I meant to do so promptly but the Cessna kept us moving right along.

We arrived at Kismayu just in time to catch the customs officer before he disappeared into an eating place. He did inspect our cargo of medicine and fresh fruits and vegetables. We then went searching for the immigration officer, and finally found an assistant who told us to leave our passports and the officer would fill out the necessary papers at 4:00 P.M. Victor Dorsch offered to stay to get the papers, and James stayed with his dad while Viola and their two girls and I flew with Gordon to Margherita. We arrived in fifteen minutes at 2:15 P.M. I was surprised that the towns in Somalia were much larger than Shirati and Tarime and other towns in Tanganyika.

Gordon had parked the plane at a safe place and Dr. Ivan Leaman was driving us to the mission compound in the mission's Land Rover when we had an unpleasant experience. The Leamans' house employee was standing in the rear of the open pickup and suddenly decided to jump off the moving vehicle. Her face was turned away and she jumped before any of the rest of us could stop her or ask the driver to stop. She landed stiffly on her feet like a stick then onto her buttocks and the back of her head. She was quite knocked out temporarily. Dr. Leaman examined her for any fractures or serious injuries, then took her to the hospital for further evaluation. Fortunately she seemed to recover OK, but she had a headache for some hours.

The weather in Somalia was not only hot but also quite humid, much like Philadelphia in the summertime. I think I sweat more in two days in Somalia than I did in a year and a half at Shirati. The Somali missionaries assured me that it was the hot season, and even the regular staff said it was hot. Being a mere ten to fifteen miles north of the equator and near the Indian Ocean, we should expect such weather. There are breezes from the ocean most of the time, but there has been no rain since August, so things are really dry and dusty, except for the green ribbon of vegetation along the Jubba River. The river is quite a marvel; its headwaters are in the mountains of eastern Ethiopia, and it worms its way down and across the desert miles of Somalia to empty into the Indian Ocean very near Kismayu. There is some irrigation along the lower end, with bananas being the major crop. Many shiploads of bananas are exported to Italy.

After a late lunch at the Leamans' house, I felt refreshed by a shower in warm salty water. (Wells are reportedly easy to dig in Somalia; they have to go down only ten to fifteen feet to get water.) That evening I joined Helen Landis and Dr. Leaman in a volleyball game with the school boys. I also had a peek into their hospital. I had supper with nurses Helen Landis and Miriam Leaman plus four girls who worked as aides in the hospital laundry. They were probably sixteen to eighteen years old and spoke English better than some of our Shirati staff nurses. Some of the Somali boys also spoke English, but in a very American vernacular fashion.

When Victor Dorsch and his son got back from Kismayu, Victor said that the inspector had refused to stamp our passports without seeing Gordon and me in person; the inspector had also sent a telegram to the Margherita police to tell them to be sure that we appeared on Sunday morning. So we took off at 6:30 A.M. by Land Rover and really saw some dust and sand. We did not fly down because of the high fees to land there plus the taxi fares and the time involved in getting from the airstrip to town. It was cheaper to go by car. The immigration official was courteous and served us some delicious tea with cinnamon. He also told us about the Muslim religion, then handed us our papers with dispatch. It took Victor another hour to finish the customs matters and get a receipt. This was all just ordinary red tape, and no one batted an eye at Gordon's British passport or asked a question.

We got back to Margherita at 11:30—in time for the tail end of Chester Kurtz's sermon. I then said a few sentences of greeting in Swahili from our Tanganyika Mennonite Church (TMC), and Gordon gave a greeting in Arabic (which he had used in the Sudan before coming to Nairobi). Somalia is a land of several languages. Somali is not well written or used officially, but it is spoken a lot. Italian has been very useful since the days of Italian occupation, and many Italians are still present. The Muslim religion and Arabic language are also widespread. The schools teach English early, and many Somalis speak it well. In southern Somalia there are many people who can also speak some Swahili. On Monday morning I enjoyed using some Swahili on my hospital rounds.

Before our noon meal on Sunday, I took another shower to wash off our travel in the dust to Kismayu. Our meal group included the Leamans as hosts, Barbara Reed and her children, several friends who had walked eight miles to attend the service, pilot Gordon, and me. While we were eating, a young Arab boy came to the door with a package that contained thirty-eight fresh shrimp. After we finished eating, Gordon supervised getting the shrimp into boiling water to make a tasty evening meal. Somali folks use charcoal stoves a lot, so I took a turn fanning the hot fire so that the bucket would boil for supper. We all enjoyed our evening meal of shrimp with hot tomato sauce at the Dorsch home. Later we had an English service at the Dorsch house, much like what we do in Tanganyika. If everyone can speak English, we use English, but otherwise the Somali language is spoken. Later that evening I spent more time with Ivan and Mary Ellen, but I will continue that story in my next letter!

Saturday, April 13, 1963

This is the belated end to my letters about Somalia. I will probably move there next February and work with Ivan for six to eight weeks before he and Mary Ellen go on furlough. Their four-year term will end in February, but they plan to stay on through the hot Somali season and not arrive back home in eastern Pennsylvania during the cold winter. I will be glad to work with Ivan for those extra months too.

Some things are done differently in Somalia than how we do them at the Shirati hospital, which is larger (with one hundred beds while Somalia has twenty-five). At Somalia, Mary Ellen does the book work and Ivan orders the drugs and does a lot of personnel management; at Shirati we have Hershey Leaman to do our administrative work. Somalia does not have a nursing school like Shirati does, so lessons must be provided for Somali students by trained nurses and doctors. Although there will not be nursing students to teach or FDS planes to take me to scattered dispensaries, there will be other things to keep me occupied, such as seeing outpatients five mornings a week in addition to seeing the inpatients. I am told that the robed pregnant Muslim mother must have special permission from her husband before any other man may see her, and that includes the male physician. Consequently there are relatively few maternity patients at the Somalia hospital, so the babies are delivered in the operating room. I hope these deliveries will increase some while I am there. The Leamans hope to obtain an X-ray machine before they go on their furlough.

In Somalia, the nurses spend many hours working with each patient every day, and the doctor sees each patient almost every day. This is rather different from Shirati, where African nurses are trained to treat most patients themselves and to refer only the more severe problems to the doctors. Shirati patients sometimes have to wait longer before seeing the doctor and getting treatment, or the Shirati surgeon may be absent for several days. In Somalia, Dr. Ivan takes more time to teach his patients how to care for themselves, such as how to prevent disease and avoid unnecessary hospital admissions, and how to care for a new-born infant. I would like to do at Shirati more of the preventive medical care that I saw done in Somalia. But I must be realistic about the heavy workload at Shirati compared with the smaller load in Somalia. There are other differences. For example, in Somalia there is the several-month period of warm humid weather to contend with. But the weather is what it is, and you sweat through it and make the best of it.

While I was at the hospital that Monday morning watching the staff at work, Gordon flew Mrs. Reed and her new daughter and two older children to Mogadishu, where they live with her husband, Harold Reed. Gordon returned before noon with Helen Ranck, David Miller,

and one Somali national. Helen accompanied us to Nairobi that same afternoon. Fortunately we did not need to return to Kismayu for exit permits but could instead stop at a small border town to get the necessary papers on our way back to Nairobi. As we were landing, we scared up a flock of guinea fowl who flew right into our path. One bird struck the posterior flap on the plane's wing (as it was turned down to decrease our speed in landing). Gordon ran back to investigate and found a lovely blue bird that was stunned but not dead. Gordon twisted the bird by its neck and placed it inside the plane to take along home for his wife to fix for supper that evening. As we waited for our papers to be completed, we huddled under the plane's wing during a shower. Although we had come unannounced, the papers were done with dispatch. We soon took off, and within a few minutes we were up in bright sunshine. We got to Nairobi at around 5:00 P.M. We were welcomed at the guesthouse with a good meal and time to chat with friends before sacking out in bed.

On Tuesday I did some shopping in Nairobi and some business for other Shirati folks. Some of them had been here the previous week, and I had gone on short notice, so I did not get a big shopping list. MAF was going to our area on Wednesday, with room for several passengers, so Miriam Buckwalter and I jumped onto the plane at 6:40 A.M. The clouds settled in, so we waited for takeoff until 8:00 A.M., and by 9:30 I was back at Shirati. I unpacked and got into patient rounds by 11:00 A.M.

So that FDS took about five hours one way by plane. By car on "good" roads (meaning rough dirt and lots of dust) one way could take three wearying days. So I was really grateful and I thank God that everything worked out for me to make this very meaningful visit to Somalia.

The news at Shirati is that Lake Victoria is rising even though we are not getting much rain here. Our pier at the lake was closed two weeks ago, so Elsie and my *piki-pik*s were delivered to us just in time! Now we will have more difficulty getting hospital supplies and wholesale orders from Nairobi. Elsie had to move out of her lake house (the place where I liked to study Swahili) and is getting fixed into an old house at our main station.

Saturday, April 27, 1963

Greetings to you from Shirati, where I have again "come home to roost." I suppose if for no other reason than high rivers and mud I will stay put for a while, except to venture out exploring with my Suzie. Several weeks ago Elsie with her Zuki and I with my Suzie went to explore the back road to Muhuru Bay. A rain came up as we were returning and we got sort of wet—drenched, actually. It rained so hard for a bit I could scarcely see the path, much less the holes and rough patches. At one point Elsie came to a mud puddle and did not get shifted back into low gear before she stopped. She put her foot down to start off in low, but she chose the soft side of the puddle to put her foot on, so she just laid over. It looked so funny from behind, and then she wanted me to come quickly to pick up her *piki* before the seat got into the mud. Soon after, we encountered more rain, so we were quite ready to wash properly when we got home, and I even found a good hot bath in another house. (I usually settle for a shower at whatever temperature it comes from the main storage tank-- sometimes delightfully warm and other times not quite so.)

Our Shirati pier was officially closed a month ago and we now have the problem of how to get supplies, so Elsie and I had gone to investigate the next pier north of us—a seventeen-mile ride one way. The rains have made travel by car impossible for the past week. Our *piki*s got through OK but our cars would have stuck. A local African has a lorry and has agreed to bring our supplies from there.

The next day, the padre from the nearby Catholic mission brought in a patient with "chicken pox," so I enlightened him that it was actually smallpox and he had real trouble. That opened his eyes a bit! I made hasty plans and that afternoon two staff nurses and a student went with me to their compound to vaccinate. The padre had a special service and then announced our "program." So as folks left the church we scratched their arms—four hundred in a little over an hour. We did more than a thousand vaccinations that week. Obviously we hadn't gotten everyone when we did those 1,200 vaccinations at Christmas. One day we set up a table by the roadside and as people came by en route to the nearby market, the staff nurse scratched their arms!

The three single ladies at Mara Hills invited the rest of us there for Easter. We left from Shirati on Friday afternoon and got into heavy rain just beyond Tarime. True to form, the roads got very muddy and we got stuck about halfway up a long hill. When the rains slacked off, four of us got out to push. After several attempts, the car reached the top, but now we pushers were somewhat muddy, so the driver consigned us to ride in the back of the VW pickup the remaining ten miles. We really appreciated hot showers and warm sweaters when we got to Mara Hills!

Besides the mud, the trip will always be remembered because on Saturday morning the president of Tanganyika, Julius Nyerere, came to Nyabasi to cut the ribbon at the official opening of the primary school, which is situated between the dispensary and Mara Hills School. After making rounds, I went with my camera and saw the doings. Several Nyabasi missionaries were in the official receiving line to shake hands with Nyerere. But we were even more delighted that our cameras served as "tickets": the police let us inside the roped-off enclosure to take pictures as he came out from tea. He seemed so astonished when all the cameras started popping. He smiled so pleasantly, so I hope I have some good pictures. I had more patients to see that afternoon, so it was not purely a pleasure weekend. But it was nice to go. We had some rain on the way back but did not get stuck this time, fortunately.

Tuesday, May 7, 1963

Today I did something I haven't done for a while: "I went to the river an' I couldn't get across / Oh, what a muddy day!" To elaborate: Hershey and I both had business at Nyabasi. Raymond Martin (who was visiting) wanted to go to Bukiroba, and others wanted to go to Tarime, so we left here at 6:15 A.M., waded through lots of mud from last night's rain, then turned around at the Merari River after watching four of our passengers wade through and start trudging along the three muddy miles to Utegi.

We got back here at around 9:00 A.M., and because I had not planned to work here today, I got busy and did some work in my two-room "suite" to straighten it up a bit, mended my old gray sweater, and fixed some lecture notes. I even almost got this letter to you started before I went to see an outpatient who wanted an appointment. Then there were other patients, so I was again late to dinner. It rained again this afternoon, so there were few admissions, and I did some more desk work tonight. Recently I am often at the hospital until 7:30 or 8:00 P.M.

I don't believe I told you about my last FDS. It was two weeks ago. We have been having "enough" rain lately, so I was quite impressed by all the water flooding the Mara Valley between Kisaka and Nyabasi. Many villages seem to be entirely surrounded and I wonder what the people do. We had planned to have clinic at Kenyana that afternoon, but when we flew over, we saw that half the airstrip was quite wet, with water standing at one end. And in the middle of the strip we saw a large X made of some light-colored material, maybe a tablecloth, that the village's leader, Naaman, had placed there. (His wife knows something about sewing.) The two nearby rivers had overflowed their banks, and it was apparent that patients were not able to cross the rivers to come to treatment. So we dropped a letter to Naaman (wrapped in an old cleaning cloth that the pilot found under his seat), then watched Naaman gather up his X as we left. As we had circled Kenyana I had been busy shooting pictures. I forgot about the young African dresser beside me, until I heard a familiar sound, looked over at him, and saw he had buried his face in a black plastic bag (which Gordon always had available, though I never had need for one).

We had lunch at Kisaka and even, as a bonus, got an afternoon rest before making ward rounds. The finance committee had requested an inventory of the various dispensaries, so that evening I helped inventory the hospital's stock of drugs. Wage increases required by law and having to give some trained workers higher pay has led to the medical program not making money (to say it gently), and the TMC still asks its dispensaries to be self-supporting. It is difficult for trained workers to provide good care and at the same time for special rates to be given to "special people" without getting a subsidy from somewhere.

After seeing outpatients at Kisaka on Wednesday morning, we went to Bukiroba, where I was very busy with students from our two schools and some folks from Musoma. That evening I went to bed early with a sore throat and a headache after taking chloroquine and APC (aspirin, phenacetin, and caffeine—a combination used in headache and cold remedies). But it was too late to avoid the malaria bug. I developed nausea with dry heaves plus fever. I finally got Velma Eshleman out of bed to give me chloroquine by injection. I slept late that morning and did not go along to Mugango as scheduled. Kefa, one of our Shirati staff nurses, who is very sharp and has diagnosed some difficult cases for me, was along on this FDS, so he saw patients for me at Mugango. I felt much better by evening and did go to Bumangi the next day. But it was Monday before I really got over it and felt like working again.

And it was high time, because on Saturday morning the Eshlemans left on the plane for Nairobi after dropping their children off at Mara Hills for their last school term before furlough; on Monday, MAF took them and Helen Ranck on to Somalia and returned with the Dorsch children. Dr. Eshleman went up to do some surgery with Dr. Leaman. They had wanted to go for a long time, and finally their plans did not fall through. Dr. Leaman had a number of patients waiting for major surgery, so I'm sure this safari will prove beneficial to many people in various ways.

Although I have had a month off from teaching, I have kept busy. I spent two entire mornings last week working in the OR, and it was not just little biopsies! Maybe I'll remember to tell you about that next time.

Friday, May 10, 1963

Last week we were privileged to have some guests from the Mennonite Church in America: Paul Erb and Joe Buzzard from Scottdale. They spent the week at Bukiroba and had planned to come to Shirati by car on Monday. Well, they got to the Mori River just a half hour too late. Hershey and Ray Martin had gone to the Merari River to meet them and walked on to the Mori, and Ray crossed it to go meet the guests in nearby Utegi. While he was gone the river suddenly rose, swelled by up-country flash floods, so the guests got to the river in time to see it run wild. It was much too deep and swift to wade across—and Ray was stranded without his shoes! So Elam Stauffer decided to try to get to Nyabasi, but they had to wait beside another swollen little river— a tributary of the Mori—for six hours before they finally got to Tarime, where they stayed with the TMC pastor.

On Tuesday morning, the two guests and Ray found a ride to Nyabasi. That afternoon, after MAF came in from Somalia with the Dorsch children, Gordon ferried the three men to Shirati. The two guests said they had enjoyed the experience, and Paul, who is gathering material for a book, said this will add to his impressions. I wonder if he is writing a "diary strip" for the *Gospel Herald*. I've always enjoyed his travelogues and articles.

We had informal fellowship that evening to get acquainted and hear some about their safari to visit Mennonite and related missions in Ghana, Nigeria, Congo, and Rhodesia in addition to their EMBMC work. We at Shirati appreciated their persistence in coming to see us here in the bush—or maybe I should say, in the mud behind the rivers! Sometimes flying visitors drop in at Musoma and Bukiroba, and if time is limited we in North Mara do not get to meet them. On Wednesday morning, after touring the hospital (they had seen the leprosarium and nursing school the evening before), MAF flew our guests back to Musoma, where they planned to meet with the executive committee for fellowship and sharing of ideas and concerns before moving on to Somalia and Ethiopia.

From Musoma the MAF plane went to Uganda to fly for ten days. There the pilot encountered a wet airstrip and was going to take off anyway, but either the load was too heavy or the strip was too bad and he decided to abandon takeoff. However, he was going fast enough that he could not stop before reaching the end of the strip, so the wheels hit a mudbank and unceremoniously flipped the plane over. The passengers were uninjured, but alas the plane's tail was badly mashed and its wings were crippled. The flip occurred on a strip near a mission hospital that, like us, has a radio connection to Nairobi, so we heard the news. The pilot was Gordon's assistant, Tony (Gordon had stayed in Nairobi). I have flown with both of them and they are both very capable. The accident resulted from a slight delay in making the right decision. It would have been much worse if he had not made that decision at all. I understand that the plane will be out of commission for two months.

It is now Wednesday morning, the 15th. We are hoping that Dr. Eshlemans get back this week, but I have heard nothing from them as yet. They may have difficulty getting the 240 miles from Jamama to Mogadishu if there are rains. They plan to come from Mogadishu by commercial airline because MAF cannot return them. I understand that a new MAF plane is to be ready by July 1, which is when Eshlemans leave and Dr. Housmans return. We expect D. Ralph Hostetters to come the following week.

Our rains are slowing down, we hope. Yesterday we had none at Shirati, so Elsie and I took Zuki and Suzie for a spin. We got through several mud puddles without any spills and got to see the deserted pier out in the lake appearing to hang on for dear life to its tiny thread of land. The lake is now five feet higher than its normal of a year and a half ago. It is right at floor level with Elsie's house, which she reluctantly vacated several months ago.

Mary Harnish hopes to go along today, to wade the river and find a way on to Musoma to meet Velma Eshleman and return to Kisaka before Velma leaves on furlough. Mary has been here since the end of February, for medical care and surgery, and has been trying to find a way back for the past month! Meanwhile, we have used her talents.

It is now 8:00 and I must fix my hair and go for rounds. Also, my friend Gati from Nyabasi is outside the window watching me type and waiting for me to finish so she can have a word with me, so *bas!*

Thursday, May 30, 1963

If you check the postmark on this letter you will see Dar es Salaam. How I got here is *not* a short story, but to *make* it short, UNICEF decided to sponsor a seminar on "Practical Problems of Obstetrics and the Newborn in East Africa." Dr. Eshleman heard whispers of it when he attended the surgeons meeting in Kampala last December, so he put in a word to get an invitation for me to attend. Months rolled by and suddenly a telegram arrived—a week after it was sent—inviting me to attend and asking for immediate reply. With high rivers and bad bridges, this was impossible. Then a second telegram arrived saying, invitation cancelled due to delayed response. So I thought, guess that chance is down the drain! But when Dr. Eshleman got back to Somalia, he felt we should try again. He radioed AMREF in Nairobi and asked them to telephone Dar es Salaam. On Wednesday at 4:00 P.M. I was told that my invitation was still good and that I could attend, with all expenses paid! I finished my ward work that evening and at 9:45 began packing.

The next morning Suzie and I left for Musoma. Hershey and Larry also *"pikied"* to the first small stream to help me across. Then I went on my way. Suzie was carried across both the Merari and Mori Rivers. I easily waded through the first one but went piggyback through the second. I got to Kinesi at 12:30, in time to catch a motorboat that was ready to leave, and by 1:30 I was in Musoma. I stayed at Bukiroba that night and went by mail plane to Mwanza the next morning. I visited the Africa Inland Mission there and on Saturday afternoon left by train for Dar es Salaam. It was a two-day safari on a slow train that stopped often. It was steam choo-choo much of the way but diesel for the last few hours. I arrived at 11:00 A.M. on Monday.

I am enjoying the seminar a lot, learning things, and meeting other East Africa doctors. I have been staying at the Salvation Army hostel outside of town and have visited with Mahlon Hesses and Raymond Martin. I plan to leave on Sunday morning by train and get to Musoma late on Tuesday, and perhaps on to Shirati on Wednesday. I hope to get a saltwater "bath" before I leave. The weather is lovely, with cool nights.

Time for a lecture to start, so *bas* for now.

Sunday, June 16, 1963

Greetings again from Shirati. I was listening to taped testimonies of missionaries given at an EMBMC board meeting, but the generator has now called it a day, so I'd better get on with this letter. I have not written since that note from Dar. I did enjoy that trip and the seminar was quite worthwhile. It is different riding a train here than at home. For one thing, the choo-choo merely walks along most of the time, and I saw one sign giving the speed limit as thirty miles per hour. One could almost get out and walk along when one gets weary of the ride. Because my fare was paid by UNICEF, I went first class and had a compartment to myself the whole way down. The trip was two days and nights from Mwanza to Dar es Salaam and I did sleep some of the second night after I got used to the poor locomotive snorting and coughing as if he was

about to blow his stack. Believe me, he did blow lots of smoke, and I have a picture to prove it.

I also enjoyed visiting with Mahlon Hesses and Raymond Martin. I saw where they plan to build a center and start a church. Some Mennonites have already moved from the lake area to Dar for work. On Sunday morning I attended a service in the home of two brothers whose father lives near Shirati. One of these men works for Shell Oil and is soon leaving on a company-sponsored trip to Britain and the United States to observe Shell operations. Mahlon preached that morning from Acts about the growth of the early church. This was only their second Sunday service and they are busy contacting Mennonites in the city to create a nucleus for organizing their witness. After church, Mahlon took me to the train and, to my pleasure, I was in a compartment with a Catholic sister—a doctor from near Moshi who had also attended the seminar—so we got better acquainted and compared notes about our work, problems of health education, and so on. Her ride ended at Dodoma early Monday morning and then I had the compartment alone.

I read two books on my safari. One was by Jomo Kenyatta (new prime minister of Kenya and former leader of the Mau Mau movement) about the tribal life and practices of the Kikuyu (a large and powerful tribe in Kenya). I enjoyed the book but do not "buy" all his conclusions about the influence of missionaries in breaking down tribal life. It is an interesting book from the standpoint of anthropology.

I got into Mwanza on Tuesday morning. I explored the town and purchased several *shukas*. Finally I bought a *Saturday Evening Post* and found a park bench on which to read for several hours before going to the plane and flying to Musoma.

On Wednesday came the real grind of the safari: going with Suzie to Shirati. The ferry left Musoma at 9:30 A.M., so I left Kinesi after 10:30 and got to Utegi soon after 12:00. I then had to find help across the rivers, which were not high enough for the usual crew to be there, but too high for my Suzie, whose motor is quite low-slung. But I did get to Shirati soon after 4:00 P.M., hot and red and tired. I also had developed several boils by the time I left Dar and could not get any proper medicine or apply hot soaks until I got to Bukiroba, so I was feeling a little rotten from that. And the aureomycin [antibiotic] I had started using at Bukiroba gave me nausea and diarrhea. But at least the boils got kicked by it and only faint marks remain. Reckon that's too much said about something that's all over, but it was a rather real part of my safari.

Here at Shirati, work continues to be plentiful. Last Tuesday I helped do a hysterectomy. Then on Wednesday evening we had a small birthday party for Naomi Weaver, who was thirty on Thursday. But *kumbe*, LeRoy Petersheim came at 6:00 P.M. with two patients, both with broken arms, so we examined and plastered them. We were late to midweek worship and left afterward for emergency surgery for a ward patient who had developed severe abdominal pain with bleeding from a ruptured pregnancy in her tube. (She is doing OK.) So we had the party on Thursday evening instead.

Wednesday, July 3, 1963

By way of statin' facts (rather than the unacceptable "complaining"), let me just say that for the past month I've been like the proverbial cat chasing its tail, and I still haven't gotten it! Or in plain English: I have been quite busy.

Maybe you remember that Dr. Eshlemans are due for furlough, so I've had extra calls as they do last-minute packing and visiting. Surgery continues to be busy, and I have been doing more cases by myself. In addition, the week before last was one of those terrible weeks in OB. I will spare you the gory details, but in summary it was like this:

On Saturday evening, the 22nd, a woman came from nearby after trying for four days to deliver her baby at home. She came in with the head visible and it was not difficult to apply forceps and deliver her stillborn infant. That did not end her troubles though. She had been in labor long enough with the head so low that she had worn a hole in her bladder. She is still far from well and keeps running a temperature of 102 despite various antibiotics.

On Sunday afternoon I was called out to see a patient brought from Nyabasi. She had been in labor for two days, they said. She was a very tired youngster who looked to be about fourteen, and it was her first baby. I gave her fluids and blood to resuscitate her. I got to most of church that evening to hear Lois and Lester's farewell messages, and I got to most of the special dinner and the speeches afterward and helped to sing our special arrangement of the mouthful "Oh where, oh where has my little dog gone?" Then I went out and did a "destructive" delivery to make the dead baby's head smaller so I could more easily deliver her. The mother was still in poor shape, so I continued special fluids and the digitalis I had started that afternoon, but she died before morning from sheer exhaustion. If only they could wait until physical maturity before getting married! She seemed like a nice girl and called her husband to come sit beside her when she realized she would leave him.

Then Tuesday afternoon I got another woman who needed help to deliver her first baby. She came earlier but had already worked hard. The baby's head was turned chin up, so I decided to help her with the forceps, but it was a tight squeeze and in the process she got a nasty vaginal tear and bled while I furiously sewed and mopped, trying to stop the red mess. Finally she cooperated, when I was about to haul her to the OR and call for general anesthesia. (I confess that her pain and discomfort were a minor consideration as I hurried to stop that leak, but she did not seem to hold it against me afterward; maybe she knew she was lucky to have a healthy baby.)

The next big trouble was Thursday night, when a woman had a miscarriage and bled a lot. I ordered some IV medicine over the phone and two hours later the staff called to say they could not start the IV because of her shock condition. I got out of bed and, behold, found the woman more dead than alive. So I revised treatment and several hours later she received her husband's life-giving blood. Meanwhile I had removed a large piece of placental tissue from her vagina, and thereby the cause of her bleeding. This case was all the more tragic because she had arrived in rather good shape after thirty-six hours of labor and no one realized how much she was bleeding until she went into shock, when she became very restless and thirsty.

Another emotional factor with me was that her teenage daughter has been in one of our main wards for several months with old osteomyelitis above one knee and I had operated on her two to three times to remove the dead bone. These cases take a long time to heal, so she has become sort of a special patient whom I can communicate with a bit. Fortunately her mother responded well to the blood transfusion and has since gone home.

That same afternoon, Sophia, the wife of a patient with an open fracture of the lower leg, was here cooking for him when it came time for her baby to come. (The man and a friend had started down the mountain in a Land Rover without brakes; the other man was killed but this one had jumped free.) This baby's chin was forward too, so I had to help her. It was not an easy forceps delivery, but her big daughter did OK after we thoroughly sucked her out. Guess who took her to meet Papa Francis for the first time?

On Saturday the hospital workers had a farewell tea for the Eshlemans and I did get there for part of it. The next morning I did abdominal surgery for an abscess and adhesions while the surgeon was in church, but I told him afterward what I did. He had been curious about why the generator was running. After dinner together at our house, they left. What a parting!

Tuesday, July 16, 1963

MAF is coming to take Anna Martin, Velma Eshleman, and Martha Jane Lutz to Nairobi on the start of their way home; later this week he will take them on to Jamama and Mogadishu in Somalia. It seems that going home is now sort of popular, with the Eshlemans leaving two weeks ago, Anna leaving tomorrow, and four more planning to leave (from Shirati, I mean) within the year. But then we get some replacements too. Dr. Housmans arrived at Shirati by plane last Wednesday morning. I said *jumbo* (hello) to Harold and handed over some notes about several sick patients, then said *kwa heri* and took off on FDS. I didn't get to greet Miriam and the children, for they were "marching" to the compound with the primary school band.

This FDS went as usual—quite interesting but not according to schedule. I did get to each place I was supposed to, although some stops were short. First we went to Nyabasi with a patient (leg in cast), his wife, and my newest namesake—Dorka—who was born here two weeks ago (during that week of OB problems I described in my last epistle). Next we stopped at Kisaka for the medicine box. Then Velma and her sister Esther, who traveled out with Dr. Ralph Hostetters, went with me to Kenyana. We saw a number of needy patients, and afterward had a wonderful African meal at Naaman's house (where Velma and I had stayed before walking to Kisaka more than a year ago) in honor of Esther's visit and Velma's going home.

The Hostetters, who had spent more time in Ethiopia, arrived in Musoma last Wednesday evening. I knew that daughter Kathryn would enjoy seeing a bit of FDS, so even though she knew nothing of our scheme, we took off from Kisaka before 7:00 A.M. on Thursday and buzzed the Stauffer house at Musoma. Elam Stauffer arrived promptly at the airstrip. We explained our wishes and he agreed. We gave Kathryn time to get her second foot out of bed, get dressed, and eat breakfast before we took off for Masinono at 8:00 A.M.

We arrived early for a change; too many times we were late or never got there at all. We set up our clinic in a nice shop three-quarters of a mile from the airstrip and, after a short service and introductions, got to work at 9:30. We saw many people with a skin infection called scabies, caused by a bug, and got rid of all our skin *dawa*. Altogether we treated nearly sixty patients.

At 1:00 P.M. we packed up and returned to the airstrip to await the plane, which in the meantime had been to Kisumu and other places. We waited with our backs to the sun until 3:00 P.M. Grace Stauffer had sent along bananas and water for Kathryn, but Mary Harnish and I did without until we got to Mugango. There were no trees at all nearby and I watched Kathryn's ears get red. Finally I decided that she and I had better find some shade. We had gone only a hundred yards when I saw the plane flapping its wings over the *pori*. We took a very sick child along to Mugango and started fluids for him before getting our late dinner of *ugali,* meat with juice, and rice. This was Kathryn's first African meal in Tanganyika and she ate more than I did my first time. Nowadays I do enjoy *ugali,* and rice I really like too, especially with curry.

At Mugango we saw twenty patients between 5:00 and 6:15. Meanwhile, the plane again went off for other passengers. We started out on foot for the airstrip because the station's car was not running. Before we got very far the plane flew over, so we walked faster and, *kumbe!* instead of landing he soon flew directly over us and dropped a letter wrapped in Velma's hankie, which landed in the path three steps in front of me. He was unable to return for us that evening, he said, so he asked us to arrange for a car to Musoma if possible. Things did work out: an Asian man took us, so we got to Stauffers' at 7:30 and had a late supper with the Leathermans at Bukiroba at 8:30. Kathryn, meanwhile, flew off to Nyabasi to join her parents and see the school.

If that sounds like an exhausting day, well, somehow I was relaxed through it and not nearly as tired out as by some other safaris. God does provide for physical needs too in times of special demands. If you think Kathryn got a free ride that day, let me tell you, she was as busy as Mary and me, for she was chief pill counter, change maker, and skin-ulcer washer.

Friday was a busy day too. We went to Bumangi and on the way back the car developed a terrible noise, so the dresser and I hopped a "taxi" ride to Bukiroba and left Mary with the car. Jim Mohler went out with some "glue" to close the radiator holes, straightened the fan, and poured water in so that Mary could drive the car home. We were reassured to know that this had happened before; the cause was loose motor "blocks" that shook loose on the washboard road and let the engine work forward into the radiator. The next day the car was "going" again. *Bas* for now.

Sunday, August 11, 1963

I am still at Shirati but in a different house, and I am "batching it." I left Cora and Naomi together in the nurses' house. It is interesting that Cora, Naomi, and I have each gained pounds since our arrival—on good food like Eleazar's fresh rolls, and rice and curry cannot be resisted. I reckon I must learn to cook the latter, for I cannot envision being without a rice and curry meal for longer than a week or so. The curry is a hot spice from India that is just delicious on chicken and other meats. I will continue eating noon meals in the nurses' house but will get my own breakfast and supper, although for the past week and a half I have made all my own meals because Eleazar has been off work. His father died in our hospital of diabetes mellitus with complications. He'd known for only around six weeks that he had diabetes. So I have had cabbage, carrots, potatoes, dried beans, lots of eggs, cold meat and cheese sandwiches, and fruits. I got along OK and managed to wash dishes once daily, but the house is "sorta dirty" because I haven't yet gotten anyone to clean it and it hasn't been swept since I moved in. Making my bookcase with boards and burnt bricks is dirty work. I made butter the other night and it took more than thirty minutes to get it yellow without streaks. I remember cranking our churn at home all morning as a girl—and I remember how tired I got of it too!

Among the highlights of the past month was the Hostetters' visit to us from Ethiopia, and Esther Eshleman. Elam Stauffer brought them to Shirati and showed them where the early missionaries stayed and how the work began. Mrs. Hostetter's sister was Elam's first wife; after her death from heart trouble, Elam married Grace Metzler, who had come as a single worker. It was very interesting to show the group around and to tell our African people about Brother Hostetter. He taught almost all of the doctors who have served here, as well as many others. One African said, "Truly he is a great teacher, for he has not only helped these people become doctors but he has also helped us through the services of these missionaries." They really were pleased to meet the *Mwalimu mkubwa* (great teacher) and *mzee* (a respectful term for an old man).

Two weeks ago tonight little Heidi Jean Housman made her appearance. Harold called me at 4:00 P.M. to say that Miriam was having some contractions, so I went over to check on her. I arrived just ahead of a group of middle school teachers she had invited for tea. Miriam said to me, "Stay for tea, and don't tell why you came!" So I had two cups of tea and helped a bit with the serving. I was glad to see all the teachers together and to get better acquainted with them. Afterward, when folks were supposed to be at the English worship service, Miriam and I walked out to the hospital, where nurse Cora Lehman was ready for us. Miriam made good progress and her seven pounds, ten ounces daughter arrived at 8:05 P.M., in time to get settled into bed after first being inspected by her brother Peter and her sister Ina Sue. Heidi has a lot of dark, straight hair and a round face. She is a nice-looking baby. Poor Papa Harold was on call and seeing patients while Heidi was making her appearance, so he did not witness it, but he came in soon afterward.

Friday, August 30, 1963

Greetings from Kisaka, where I have spent a week "loafing," that is, resting a bit from the Shirati work and bustle. I have just about recuperated from the hacky cough I had last week. I have slept late, seen a few patients at the dispensary, done some long-neglected sewing, and read a book entitled *Love and Conflict*—not a love story but a technical book about the stresses and problems facing the modern family in which the father is away all day. It is sort of difficult reading—the kind I don't get to do much of but which is good exercise. I have also written a few essential letters. The nights here are delightfully cool, so I have slept like a log under three to four blankets and not crawled out until around 8:00.

You asked about baby Susie (born last November). Once she weighed eight pounds and was nice and chubby, a nearby widow took her home to care for her. She wasn't there very long—maybe two weeks—when she was brought back with severe diarrhea. We did what we could but Susie died several days later. Recently we had four other orphans in our nursery: Alice, Jessca, Elizabeth, and Otonda (the last a boy, "all boy," to the last kinky hair on his head, but he is gradually learning a few manners). Recently Alice went to stay with the woman who took care of Susie and she is faring better so far. We have her on whole cow's milk, boiled each morning and evening. With Susie the formula had some water and the woman did not prepare it the same way, so I hope Alice does well. Jessca was brought by her father after the mother died at home. She weighed only four pounds, and when we asked her name the father said *Taabu*, which means "trouble." But she has not been trouble to us; she has done well and doubled her weight in three months. One of the midwives gave her the name *Jessca*, which means "God is watching." I am ready to let her go into a home too if we can find someone to care for her.

June was the month of OB problems. In July we had another record month in maternity, with thirty deliveries, and only one was complicated; the baby had severe heart trouble but did pull through, fortunately.

Today we have three guests with us from Ethiopia: Mary Ellen Groff (a classmate from LMS), Mildred Hiestand, and Lois Landis. This afternoon we will go to the Mara River to be met by Nyabasi folks and go there for the night. My vacation ends tomorrow morning because I am planning to see patients at the Nyabasi dispensary. We might return to Shirati tomorrow evening. Our visitors want to see a bit of big game before returning to Addis Ababa, so they will not spend much time with us. It has been good to hear about their work and to discover that there are some problems there that we don't have here. When one stays so close to the work, one can lose proper perspective.

Over a month ago I got the tapes you sent and have really enjoyed listening to your voices. Listening to all of these sweet heaven songs surely reminded me of Mother singing around the house when I was home. Only two or three are new to me, and I remember lots of words so I can sing along [*and still can in 2015*].

Sunday, September 8, 1963

Greetings to you all in the name of Jesus, "who personally rescues and delivers us out of and from the wrath which is coming upon the impenitent and draws us unto Himself" (1 Thessalonians 1:10 Amplified). Our Sunday school lesson last week was based on this chapter, and though I did not get a lot of what the teacher said in Swahili, I did get a personal blessing from reading it over in my New Testament. I was on Safari and had packed light, taking along my Swahili and Amplified New Testament rather than my RSV.

Now, more about that week of leave in Kisaka. Several months ago I talked to Alta Shenk about going along on one of their *pori* trips to visit some outstations and see more how and where our people live. It turned out that no *pori* safari was in the making until mid-October. By the time Dr. Housman left for the August FDS, I was beginning to cough, and Mary urged me to come to Kisaka "to rest a bit." I kept on coughing, so I was quite eager to go when Saturday, August 24 rolled around.

On Thursday afternoon of that week we drove over the hills to where a smaller river joins the Mara River and soaked our feet in the water. Mary assured me that the movement of the water would suck the cold out of me! After the hydrotherapy, she prescribed standing on hot rocks in the sunshine and skipping stones across the river. Sleeping in Clydes' trailer, my cold finally got loosened up. I had a red nose for several days, but by now I am finally over it.

That Friday afternoon we went to the Mara River, where LeRoy Petersheim, his children, and Clara Landis met us. On our way up the escarpment I saw someone I knew: Sophia, the woman who'd had a baby while caring for her husband, Francis, when he was in our hospital with an infected open fracture of both bones in the leg he'd broken while driving down the escarpment in a vehicle without brakes. Sophia reported that he had just gotten home the night before on crutches and had stopped at Mara Hills to ask LeRoy to stop by his village the next day to get a *zawadi* (gift) for the *doctari*. So we visited the village and chatted while a son led a young sheep to our car. The sheep was not as large as those at home, with brown hair rather than wool. I soon became attached to this baa-baa. He was a good little traveler, and a fine lawn mower for our backyard. Then, on Friday I let a boy kill it and helped to cut it up for eating. I didn't want to do it but I knew I had to sometime and it wouldn't be any easier later on. So tonight we all had roast leg of lamb. It was really good but I couldn't enjoy it much; I will long remember that sheep's gentle "baa" and innocent, trusting nature—and consider myself a butcher!

A letter awaited my arrival at Nyabasi that Friday. It asked me to come and see an OB patient, so after supper we went to investigate. I

found the woman in premature labor, with the baby in transverse position. I tried intravenous sedation first but it was inadequate. So I asked Lois Landis to pour ether, and then I was able to turn the baby without difficulty. The next morning when I went to check on the mother, someone went outside to ask her to come in!

That Saturday morning I had another OB problem. This woman had had eight children already without trouble. She'd also had surgery here last year for acute gall bladder disease, and I remembered her from that. Again I decided on surgery. With the woman under local anesthesia, I made an incision between the pelvic bones in front to make more room. I also gave her medicine for the pain, and she delivered a healthy five-pound, thirteen-ounce boy. We had thought of not leaving Kisaka until Saturday, but God arranged our trip so that anesthesia and a doctor were at Nyabasi when needed. Otherwise these patients would have needed to make a long trip to Shirati or Kowak for help.

On Saturday morning I did something different too. A neighbor reported that the baboons were eating the potatoes in his garden on the escarpment, so LeRoy went out and shot one! We then traipsed out to see the trophy and explore the hill a bit ourselves.

Sunday, September 29, 1963

Greetings to you from Shirati on a lovely Sunday evening. My typewriter had a too lengthy rest while I spent my spare time nursing a sore elbow. It is better now.

Two weeks ago we had guests here: Chester Kurtzes and Harold Stauffers from Somalia. This was the first time I had seen Harold and Connie since we left each other in Nairobi almost two years ago after flying there together from New York. Connie and I spent an hour or more one afternoon comparing notes on this period—how things were different from our vague anticipation of what our situation would be, and so on. Of course I was all ears to hear about their work, which will involve me in several months. According to present plans, I will transfer to Jamama around February 1 so I can work with Dr. Ivan Leaman for six weeks before their furlough. The medical problems will be much the same as at Shirati, but my work there will include administration and recordkeeping as well. At Shirati, Hershey takes care of ordering supplies and so on. At Jamama, Ivan's wife, Mary Ellen, helps him a lot with keeping records and preparing orders, but I'm afraid my wife won't be quite that efficient! But seriously, examining patients, writing orders, and doing some surgery is about all I get done here. Also, here I am the junior medical officer, and the senior medical officer does do more administrative and committee work, policy planning, and so on. In fact, at times I have felt like I know too little about what goes into making this hospital and medical program go—"Don't ask me what's going on; I just work here." I understand they will have an X-ray machine by the time I arrive, so I will need to learn how to use it. Here I have a staff nurse to do that. I am glad for this period of "internship" at Shirati before going to Jamama. I have learned a lot about parasites and have gained good experience and much more confidence in surgery. Perhaps by the time I go to the big city by myself they will have the interstation radio contact that we have here. But the specialist consultations provided by the Research Foundation are a unique arrangement between Shirati and Nairobi, and I will miss that up there. It is always so valuable to discuss difficult problems with a colleague.

Maybe that's enough about things that will surely turn out not exactly as I anticipate.

It was good to learn about the young church in Somalia. Perhaps you know about the recent requirement that in order for our schools to be accredited they must teach the Koran so that students can go on to government schools when they finish 8th grade. It appears that our schools will cooperate in order to continue this vital education service and maintain contact with young believers and interested friends. If we refused and the schools were closed, the mission would have less reason to stay and might be forced out by the zealous Muslim element, which puts pressure on the government to make Somalia a truly Muslim state. But some officials are very sympathetic and encourage our work.

I wonder what you would say if you saw me now—trying to peck away at this letter with my Tiger sitting on my lap and swatting at my arms. Oh, don't get scared. Africa does not have wild tigers (to my knowledge). My Tiger is a playful half-grown kitten—gray striped and hence the name. A year ago we had a female black Persian with a white face and paws. This is her daughter. So Tiger and I keep each other company. She is so playful and likes to tease but has learned there are a few things she must not do. She sits on my lap while I eat, but she must keep her head under the table. I do like living by myself. I have close neighbors and can hear Elsie talking in her house when a guest comes.

I can hardly see how one could be much busier than I have been for the past few months. I will be glad for leave in November; then comes missionary retreat, Christmas, and a visit from the Kraybills, then my move to Somalia.

Sunday, October 6, 1963

Last week I wrote about the visit of Harold Stauffers and Chester Kurtzes from Somalia. Let me bring you up to date on their safari, in case you haven't heard. On their way from Nairobi for the last lap of their journey home, they had a run-in with a giraffe. It seems the big ol' lummox was crossing the road as they came by and got his long legs tangled up in their Land Rover, clumsily crashed on top of it, and mashed in the roof. Mrs. Kurtz sustained a severe head injury and was unconscious for some days, and their daughter had some nasty lacerations. They were transferred back to Nairobi for treatment. It seems that Chester and the Stauffers were not injured. Do pray for these folks.

After hearing about the accident, someone here at Shirati said, "It surely seems that the devil is using every possible means to discourage and harass the young church in Somalia." I have also heard some of our folks say with relief, "I'm glad I was called to Tanganyika rather than to Somalia; the work is so difficult in that Muslim country, and our climate is much more pleasant too!" I can honestly say that I have enjoyed these two years at Shirati despite the volume of work and my failure to really get into the life of the church and feel a part of it. But I am also anticipating going to Somalia and consider it a challenge to prayer and deeper consecration so that God may be able to use me to glorify Himself in that needy land. Tomorrow it will be two years since I landed at Shirati. It does not seem long since I left you, but so many things have happened, so it seems long in that respect only. I have been lonely here sometimes because of the rush of work and too little time to just sit and talk with others. But (and I say this emphatically) I have not been homesick ever. In a way, it was harder for me to see Dr. Eshlemans leave here than it was for me to leave you all.

It's interesting that our staff generally assumed that after Eshlemans left, our surgery work would slow down a lot and our census would drop and we'd go begging for work. But it hasn't yet. In fact, we have kept the OR so busy, they really want a breather. I have done some hernias, removed some cysts of the ovary, and done some fracture work. Dr. Housman has done a number of eye operations as well as some general surgery too. Forgive me if this sounds like bragging but I understand that September was the highest income month in the past two years! If you visited our men's ward, you would know we did not lack patients; in a ward designed for twenty-six beds, we crowded in seven extra for two days. By now several of the extra beds have been moved back to the women's ward, which was not as busy. The other evening I was called to sew up a man who had been attacked by a leopard when he objected to the leopard's killing of a goat for its supper. He had nasty cuts on his chin, and several of his teeth had been knocked out. It took an hour to put him back together, and he is doing fine.

I plan to go on FDS this week and then to the *pori* to spend seven to ten days with Clyde Shenks visiting a number of small bush churches and doing evangelistic work. I will have equipment and medicine with me to examine and treat the sick. I am eager for this opportunity to get better acquainted and to see more how our people live.

You should see our two orphans! Jessca is getting so big and alert; she smiles a lot and coos a bit. Otonda is also big and more happy than when he came. They are both so interesting and are good teaching material for students on child growth and development. Otonda likes to bounce on his legs when I stand him up, but his head is still sort of wiggly. He was surprisingly good and quiet this morning when I took him along to our outdoor service for patients at the hospital.

The generator will soon stop but my kerosene lamp is lit and I'm listening to a good church program from Indiana with old familiar hymns like "Great Is Thy Faithfulness" and "I've Entered the Haven of Rest."

I enjoy getting Sis's letters from school; they bring back many memories.

Monday, October 21, 1963

I am writing from Chomongo in the Tanganyika *pori*. It will be two weeks ago on Wednesday that I left Shirati by MAF on FDS. Cora Lehman accompanied me this time. It worked out perfectly because Mary Harnish had gone home on short notice to help care for her mother. Thus there is currently no missionary nurse in South Mara, and it is usually the missionary nurse who goes with the doctor on these FDS visits. In fact, there were no missionaries at all at Kisaka while we were there, because Clyde Shenks had already left for the outstation tour. But Alta's house helper prepared food, and beds were made up, so Cora and I slept in Mary's house and the pilot slept in Clyde's house.

On Thursday we took along the staff nurse from Bukiroba to help us at Masinono and Mugango. It was a good safari, with needy people at each place. On Friday evening Cora returned to Shirati, and early the next morning the plane returned to Musoma and hauled me to Mugumu, where the pilot was scheduled to pick up some folks and return them to Kisumu. Mugumu is southeast of Kisaka, out near the Serengeti Game Area. There I met Clyde Shenks. We went six miles into the *pori* to their camp, near the game warden's camp—and did we see animals run! It has been rather dry (although the rains have begun in some areas) and the animals have moved nearer the rivers. We saw lots of zebra and wildebeest, as well as some deer. At night we heard the lions roar, and in the morning the children coming to school scared up the animals to run by our camp.

Clyde was helping to build a house for a church leader who plans to move there and develop a witness. Various folks from Kenya are moving into the area. A nice group attended the Sunday service in the small school and listened attentively. A song we have used to teach the gospel is the old German *Gott ist die Liebe*—in English, "God Is Love."

Since Tuesday we have been moving every one to two days to a new place. Clydes have been having communion services, baptisms, and so on at these places. We visited Matari, where I had gone on my first FDS. The airstrip had not been kept in repair, so this was the first time we could come back. We spent the weekend at Kenyana, where I felt quite at home because I have been there many times on FDS. I always enjoy visiting with Naaman's family.

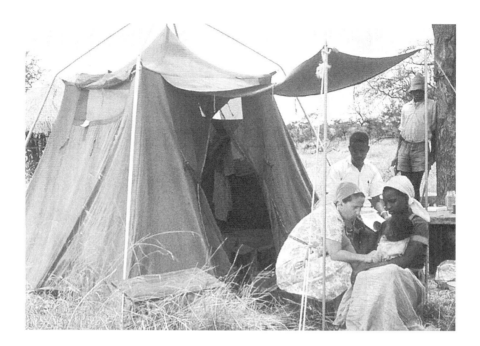

I didn't come on this safari merely for the ride and to see the animals and the countryside. I had two major motives: first, to see outstations of the TMC and learn more about where and how our people live; and second, to hear some nonmedical Swahili. I have enjoyed the more leisurely pace of seeing patients and trying to give a little health teaching along with the pills and injections—nurse the baby until he gets teeth, give young children eggs and milk, and so on. One dispensary worker has helped with giving injections, counting out pills, and collecting the cents. I have tried to order drugs in line with what each patient can pay. I have seen a number of people quite sick with malaria and anemia, several whom I think have tuberculosis, also two women with miscarriages who were greatly helped by injections and other medicines.

Yesterday we came to an area where we have no TMC witness but the Catholic influence is strong, so this place was different from all the other stops, where we had our own small nucleus of believers. Last evening, Clyde set up the small generator and we showed several film-strips of Bible stories—Daniel in the lion's den, Daniel's three friends, and the leper who was healed. Clyde told the stories in Swahili and wove together his own testimony and the gospel stories in a simple manner. The group was quite attentive and seemed to enjoy it. Today many folks came asking if we would show pictures again tonight, but alas, Clyde has been in bed with malaria. He is getting better and we plan to move on in the morning.

Our largest group of patients was fifty-five at Matari one morning. We saw thirty this morning and twelve this afternoon. Although we keep moving and often miss afternoon rest periods, the trip has been very refreshing to me, with a different kind of tiredness that feels good after doing some real physical work. I have been sleeping in Mary Harnish's tent and am getting my sleeping bag broken in good. On Wednesday morning we plan to get to the Musoma-Kisaka road, where I will hop a bus to Musoma and Clydes will head for Kisaka.

I mentioned wanting to hear nonmedical Swahili, or church vocabulary. Well, I did hear a lot and understood quite a bit at Kenyana, for which I thank God. I also read some of the gospel of John in Swahili.

Sunday, November 10, 1963

Greetings to you this time from St. Julian's, which is near Nairobi, or between Limuru and Nairobi, to be exact. It was three weeks ago that I last wrote. I was on that safari for two and a half weeks, then at Shirati for a week and a half. I left again last Wednesday for three weeks. Reckon that makes me sound like a gadabout. Well, sometimes I stay put for what seems like an age, so—the fact is, I am with Elsie Cressman and Martha Myer on annual holiday. We were together last year in September with others, so our leave is actually overdue.

To finish telling you about the safari: On the Tuesday morning after his bout with malaria, Clyde Shenk was tired but well over his symptoms, so we moved on to Masinki. I packed up the tent myself and helped Ibrahimu, the dresser, to load up the Jeep. At Masinki we examined 45 patients in a small house that the local TMC leader had built for this purpose. He also has a supply of medicines on hand to treat patients when other medical help is not available. We finished before 5:00 P.M. and hit the trail again, heading for the Kisaka-Musoma road. We arrived after dark and set up our tents. After we ate supper together, I did a little adding and found that we had examined around 850 patients in all. I had a box and two weighty tins of the "filthy lucre" to take along to the central office in Bukiroba.

On Wednesday morning, Clydes returned to Kisaka and I got on the bus to Musoma. It was rather old and the windows were "tinted" to effectively screen out much of the view of the countryside. After loading four two-hundred-pound bags of flour and several bicycles onto the roof, the seedy-looking driver crawled behind the big wheel and we took off. I'm sure he hadn't touched his hair for a month, it was so matted and brown with dust. But he knew how to handle the bus and sling us around the hills. He regulated the air conditioning by holding the windshield open with one hand at intervals while he drove; naturally the effect was best appreciated when he was going downhill at some speed.

I got to Bukiroba at noon, then went to Musoma to do some shopping and see several people. I had anticipated returning to Shirati that Thursday, but instead I was asked to stay in Musoma until Friday and then to go to Utegi by bus to meet Hershey Leaman and accompany him to Nyabasi for a medical visit. So that's how I managed to wash up all the dirty clothes in Anna Ruth Jacobs's faithful Maytag. And afterward I washed my hair. I finally got to Shirati on Saturday evening and took hospital calls on Sunday.

In retrospect, I believe the time I spent in rural Tanganyika will be THE highlight of my two and a half years here. I got to see some of our small "lights" in the isolated places, and how they appreciate our visits. I came to appreciate anew how poorly met their medical needs are, and the problem of getting to the hospital at Musoma or Shirati for help. I met several grateful patients whom I had treated at Shirati. One man had been gored by a buffalo and had nasty leg lacerations, which I had cleaned up and sutured. I had also done a skin graft over the shin bone. He proudly exhibited the perfect results and thanked God for our help.

I got to hear a lot of good Swahili—especially nonmedical vocabulary—and I understood more of it. Clydes speak it very well and use some grammar forms that I never picked up on at Shirati. I took only the Swahili pretest (while at language school in December 1961) and will not likely get to take any of the other three regular tests. However, I continue to listen, because there will be some Swahili-speaking people in Somalia too.

Another real treat was getting better acquainted with Clyde and his wife, Alta. One evening after washing some clothes, I returned something to the trailer, planning to go directly to bed (we often retired at 9:00 to 9:30), but Clyde suggested that I needed to have some coffee with them first, and I never refuse that, you know. So we got to talking and it was around midnight when I left. I thank God for that opportunity.

I was able to work at a more leisurely pace on this safari and I returned to Shirati feeling refreshed and not nearly as tired as I had been when I left. We all felt that the combined spiritual and medical ministry was blessed of God, and personally I could enjoy spending more time doing this type of work. One could really develop a teaching public health program (evening pictures, talks with patient groups during the day, and so on). It is a fascinating idea, but for now the path points elsewhere. In two, three, four years, God alone knows what will develop.

Tuesday, November 26, 1963

Greetings from Nairobi this time. We are winding up our three-week leave on a buying spree in Nairobi—you know, doing Christmas shopping for all our missionaries at Shirati and Bukiroba!

I want to tell you about a funeral—no, nothing like President Kennedy's, some of which I listened to, from leaving the Cathedral to the end in Arlington Cemetery after 11:00 P.M. The papers and radio have had a lot to say about it, and there have been lots of comparisons to Lincoln: both were involved with the rights of Negroes, which Africans appreciate.

No, this funeral was for a Christian from Shirati who lived across the street from the hospital. Many years ago, Rael (Rachel in English) was a famous witch doctor. But she received the message of salvation from the early missionaries. After getting rid of her "medical bag," she was employed in the hospital and developed into a skilled midwife. She had retired before my arrival but I met her several times and often saw her in church. Recently she was ill and then died rather suddenly a month ago, in the hospital. Pastor Nashon, Elam Stauffer, and other folks from South Mara learned about her death by station radio. A carload drove up for the funeral.

Rael died in the morning. Relatives removed her body to her village and placed it in the hut where she had lived. It was not embalmed, and a wooden box was prepared for it. The next morning, folks gathered in the village and some of the men dug the grave, about ten feet from her house. The box containing her body was then laid into the grave.

The service started at about 1:30 with several hymns in Luo and Swahili. Pastor Nashon "read the obituary," that is, he spoke about her life and her Christian testimony. Then Elam preached about the journey of life—that someday we will meet God: Are we ready? These talks were translated into Luo, and I was able to follow the Swahili fairly well. After the sermon and prayer, a young man, a relative, gave his testimony of how God brought peace into his life. Then Pastor Nashon spoke frankly to the group and urged the non-Christians not to perform their heathen funeral practices (driving the cattle over the grave, dancing and beating drums, bringing out the deceased's possessions to display over the grave, and so on). Various men then took turns closing the grave as the Christians sang hymns, mostly in Luo. As soon as the men stopped shoveling, several other men attired in skins and costumes began beating their drums and dancing. They threw spears, and some of the women sat down on the grave and wailed. The "band" soon left the village, then returned and put down their spears and drums to join in eating some food. There was not much noise thereafter. I was agreeably surprised that they did finally listen to Pastor Nashon's request, and I was thankful that he has such a good influence in the community.

On our leave, we spent four days just north of Nairobi; we went shopping one day and otherwise rested and read books (*The Savage My Kinsman,* by Elisabeth Elliot; and *My Several Worlds,* by Pearl Buck). We were served breakfast in bed at 8:15, and I think they woke me up every morning! We then went even further north to see the lovely Thomson's Falls. It was cold there, just several miles from the equator but 7,700 feet up! We drove near Mount Kenya and did see its ragged peak. We stopped in Nairobi for several hours to buy food, then drove more than a hundred miles toward Mombasa to Bushwackers Camp, where we spent nine days. Elsie was chief cook and Martha and I assisted as dishwashers, and so on. We were beside a muddy river, and there were lots of birds and monkeys around to add to the nature chorus. A crocodile sunned himself on the far beach of the river most mornings. We also saw numerous waterbuck, and the tracks of rhinos and elephants near the camp, but we did not meet their owners. We went "swimmin' and fishin'." What did I catch? I managed only two nibbles on the last evening. (The river was rather high and fish were scarce.) I didn't land either one. Martha got two and let two get away. So we had only one meal with fish.

We returned to Nairobi on Sunday and are now about ready to shove off for home. Elsie and Martha took a big load of food, clothes, and things for the nursing school and leprosarium to the MAF hangar for the plane to bring next week when it comes for FDS. The little VW was too full for me to go along. Tomorrow is Thanksgiving. If we were in town, we could attend a special service sponsored by the American Embassy here.

Tuesday, December 17, 1963

While my bath water heats up, let me tell you a little about the past several weeks.

Last month was as slow in OB as this one has been busy! (Did someone tell the women I was on leave last month? Only ten babies arrived. Most of those mothers had complicated labors. This month we already have fifteen.) I delivered a set of twins the other day at noon after "sleeping in" on the labor bed half the night in order to be near if she got in a hurry. The first baby was a boy, seven and a half pounds, feet first. His sister, six and a half pounds, also came feet first. They are a lovely pair!

Last Monday, after being at Nyabasi all weekend, I got back at 11:30 to find a lady who had arrived shortly before me after trying for three days to deliver in the village; the baby was lying crosswise. It was difficult to get it turned, even with general anesthesia. Before I finished with her, another woman arrived who had delivered her baby in the path and, *kumbe,* she had even tried to deliver the uterus! I had never seen an inverted uterus before. After due preparation, I was able to replace it into its normal position without difficulty.

Maybe that's enough about babies. To shift gears: last weekend we had our missionary fellowship gathering at Mara Hills. Dr. Housman was on FDS from Tuesday to Friday last week and we had graduation exercises for the nursing school on Friday morning, so I was rather busy. I managed to see every patient as well as attend most of the graduation. Elam Stauffer gave the commencement address, about joy in Christian service. After dinner I finished packing and left at about 1:30 P.M. We had some rain but passed through before the rivers got high.

The theme for the weekend was "Sharing the Living Christ." Various speakers told how they try to communicate the gospel in their work—at hospital, nursing school, secondary school, and so on. Pastor Zedekia and the TMC secretary also brought messages. Several speakers used John 4 as their base. Simeon Hurst stressed that despite the unfriendliness between the Jews and the Samaritans, Jesus must go through Samaria. He did not evade the unpopular and unpleasant things whereas we can make ourselves so busy with the things we enjoy that we are "too busy" or "too tired" to do that other important thing. Pastor Zedekia impressed upon us the fact that the woman came to fill her water pot but received the much greater living water from Jesus, whom she found sitting on the well. He asked us, what do the patients receive as we make rounds? Or what do we give to the village woman who comes to sell eggs at our door? Do they receive love from God in our dealing with them? Or are we too busy? Do we answer patients' questions and explain things? Do we show an interest in their problems, or do we rush off and tell the staff nurse to see what the relative wants? These several truths spoke to me, but rest assured that the whole weekend was worthwhile. Some of us "girls" stayed in the teachers' house, so we took advantage of the isolation away from the dormitories and families to sit up and talk. This sharing of questions and experiences was also very helpful.

[*Early one December evening of 1963, when I was thinking about supper and listening to a tape of Ernie Ford singing "My Jesus, as Thou Wilt" on my Wollensak tapeplayer, I heard a Hodi and saw Simeon Hurst at the door of my house. I invited him in and stopped the music. Simeon quickly got to the point: a cablegram had come to Musoma to inform me that my father was in critical condition with a blood clot and they would keep me informed. I'm sure that Simeon prayed with me before he left me alone with my thoughts. I reversed the tape and listened to the whole song again. I was admittedly surprised by this news. Dad had always been in good health and was an active man. Where was the clot? In his heart? In his brain? In his leg? If I had gotten such a message about my mother, it would not have been a sur-*

prise. But in the midst of my questions I also sensed a deep peace and the awareness that many friends back in the States had already been praying for Dad and our family in Pennsylvania and me in Tanganyika for some hours before I got the message. Several days later I got another cablegram saying that Dad's condition was more stable.

Two long weeks after the first cablegram, I finally got an airmail letter telling me that Dad had experienced a serious heart attack and was at home a number of hours with chest pain before he notified one of my brothers and got a speedy ambulance ride to LGH. My sister Anna Mary was a student at EMC, so only Mother was at home with Dad and he had basically been helping her. Dad stayed at Lancaster General for a month, then recuperated with Nathan and his family for a few more months. Slowly he regained his strength, then began helping my brother with some of the easy jobs on the farm. Sis, meanwhile, finished her first semester at EMC and returned home to help manage the household.]

Sunday, January 19, 1964

Greetings again from Shirati. This will probably be the last time I write from here, at least for a while. I will not be sorry if God brings me back here again, but that is for Him to arrange. I hope to finish packing this week and to make the rounds with FDS one final time. I want to send some loads with Paul Kraybill and Donald Lauver on MAF when they return to Nairobi on the 27th. I will fly by commercial air to Mogadishu later in the week. There are still several "ifs"—such as getting my tax clearance to leave this country, and getting my visa to enter Somalia. But I can use any extra time in Nairobi for catching up on letter writing.

Harold left the day after Christmas and got back from Nairobi and Jamama (where he went with the deputation and did some eye surgery) last Wednesday, so I am now relieved of hospital responsibility. (I hear that the deputation got a very warm welcome in Jamama, with a special meal and program planned by the nationals, a tour of a banana plantation, and nice speeches by local officials.) I have my filing cabinet in order now but have not done much else, so tomorrow the pots and pans will start flying into my barrel. I will not be taking much along with me by plane. My barrel, trunk, and filing cabinet will go by rail to Mombasa and then by ship. There is no lorry transport from Nairobi through the Northern Frontier District of Kenya into Somalia because the Somalis living there had been making numerous raids since the Kenyan Uhuru last month, until Kenya declared a state of emergency and prohibited most vehicle movement.

Two weeks ago, Dr. Keunen, a plastic surgeon from Nairobi, was here for two days and helped me to operate. He fixed up a boy who had a severe case of clubfeet, did several skin grafts (I still find them tricky; sometimes they take for me, sometimes not), and handled one messy abdominal case.

The other day I collected for myself an unusual souvenir. A young fellow came in with an arrow sticking out of his arm just above the right elbow. He said he had been hunting birds and saw one in a tree, so he shot at it and *kumbe!* the arrow went up into the tree, turned itself around, came back down, and landed in his arm. I didn't buy that story, but I did give him some Demerol and local *dawa* before enlarging the hole around the protruding shaft of the arrow. Eventually it was big enough for me to pull the arrow out of the bone. More than two inches had been embedded in his arm, and fortunately it missed major nerves and blood vessels. He let me keep it as my trophy, which I appreciated.

On two different days, six days apart, we delivered two sets of twins. The first set—a boy and a girl—was very premature and did not live. But the second set—also a boy and a girl—was quite healthy and a good size. The boys were the biggest, and both were breech, so I got more practice in waiting for a breech baby to arrive. Two girls from our first class of nurses have returned after their year of midwifery practice, so now we have four African midwives plus Elva Landis, so I get very few deliveries anymore.

After Paul Kraybill and Donald Lauver arrived, we singles had supper with them; afterward each of us had a personal interview to discuss anything "on our heart." My main concern was with future plans: How long would I be in Somalia? What after Somalia? They asked if I was interested in a second term, and would I care to return to Shirati? I'm sure you want to know the answers too. Two years. Probably furlough. Yes, I'd be delighted. I also reminded them that I hope to do some Bible work—possibly at the EMC seminary—as well as get more professional training in a hospital. So, if you all want to start dreaming a bit, go to it, for I'm doing it too, and we'll see what hatches. Do remember to pray much for these men, that they may have the physical strength and spiritual wisdom to understand the situation as they visit and be able to give expert counsel on the many questions asked of them.

Friday, January 31, 1964

Excuse me for writing by hand instead of typing but my pecker machine is buried in my suitcase. I wrote to you all a week and a half ago, but I suspect those letters were delayed due to the rumpus in Dar. We here

believe the trouble was not nearly as serious as it sounded. Mahlon Hess in Dar experienced no trouble at all. But there doubtless is "Red" influence, which President Myerere is concerned about.

I did manage to get my things packed and left Shirati after dinner on Wednesday. I'm doing a little shopping and plan to go on to Mogadishu tomorrow with Orpah Mosemann, a nursing teacher from Goshen College who visited Shirati. As we flew from Kisumu to Nairobi on Wednesday, we flew over White Highlands between Kericho and Nakuru—elevation eight to ten thousand feet—whose white Brits and South Africans have lovely farms, mostly wheat and some corn. I even saw a combine at work cutting a swath in a new field.

I will write from Somalia next time. I'm going with Psalm 138:8 ("You will do everything you have promised, / Lord, your love is eternal. / Complete the work that you have begun") and Psalm 27:14 ("Trust in the Lord. / Have faith, do not despair. / Trust in the Lord").

Friday, February 7, 1964

Greetings from the land of camels and donkeys! This morning I watched several camels getting their bath in the Indian Ocean; they willingly knelt in the shallow water and let the young man splash water over them, and waited while he went into deeper water for his own bath. And what was I doing? I was with Wilbert (Bert) Linds and Orpah Mose-

mann for breakfast on the beach. We took our charcoal fire along in a bucket and had pancakes and fried eggs with all the trimmings.

I arrived here in Mogadishu last Saturday with Orpah Mosemann. She is on leave from being director of the School of Nursing at Goshen College and is traveling around the world to find out what a missionary nurse is and to observe nursing schools. She spent five and a half months in India helping at Dhamtari. Then last month she spent ten days at Shirati doing a survey of our nursing school and hospital nursing service. A visitor with a background of teaching can often see things that we who are so deeply involved in the work can overlook. She shared some observations and concerns as well as suggestions. She also visited several dispensaries to see what the nurse does who is away from the hospital facility. She will submit her reports to the mission boards involved as well.

Our plane from Nairobi was delayed three hours. We did not know why but we were glad they told us the day before that our flight was at 10:30 rather than 7:15, so we could sleep later. When we got to Mogadishu at 1:00 P.M., I was surprised to see two KLM (Dutch) planes parked there. We learned that Chou En-Lai, the boss of Red China, had arrived in town at about 10:30 A.M. Most of the welcoming party had dispersed, but the Linds, Connie Stauffer, and Bertha Beachy were still waiting. Many banners around town extolled Somali-Chinese friendship, demanded a seat for China on the UN Security Council, and denounced imperialism. The big man left on Tuesday and I hear he will visit Zanzibar, but Tanganyika has cancelled his proposed visit there.

Dr. Ivan Leamans drove up from Jamama on Monday and he has been taking me to meet various medical personnel in town. Yesterday we visited an elaborate new hospital built by Common Market funds. It is not yet completely equipped, but it has some fancy gadgets that I wonder who will use and maintain. They have plans to get doctors from the same agency, but apparently have no plans for nurses and other personnel to care for the patients, so one hopes this is not a "white elephant" to compete with the secondary school being built by the Russians. There is as yet no nurse training course here, so Dr. Leaman is considering organizing a simple school at Jamama. Orpah Mosemann was able to give us some guidance in thinking about this.

Many things here do remind me of Tanganyika, but there are striking differences too. One, of course, is the Muslim influence—the regular prayer call (though not everyone stops to pray when they hear it), and Friday as their holy day, with most businesses and schools closed. The many camels and donkeys are a difference too. We had donkeys in Tanganyika, but not pulling trailer loads of water, straw, wood, and so on like here. And there are little scooters—three wheelers with a canvas top—that run around everywhere as taxi service. The mission is on a busy street and the lorries make a terrific noise as they grind past— sounds worse than on Gap Hill! I hadn't realized that Shirati was so quiet, but I suspect the Italians built their trucks to be noisy as well as huge and durable.

When I get to Jamama and among some Swahili-speaking persons, I will be delighted, for I find Swahili words popping out. And I hear some Somali words that are similar to Swahili, because both take some words from Arabic.

But first, the Leamans and I plan to go to Johar to see the school and to visit the clinic at Mahaddei; we will leave on Sunday and return on Wednesday. On Thursday we plan to go to Jamama—270 dusty, bumpy miles in the dry season.

Thursday, February 13, 1964

Greetings to you all again from Mogadishu. We are about ready to leave for Jamama. Time goes by fast and it doesn't seem like almost two weeks since I came here.

On Sunday evening I went with Ivans out to Johar and Mahaddei. These towns are sixty and seventy miles to the north. The road is tarmac all the way (or I should say was, for it has deteriorated at places— especially between Johar and Mahaddei—and is so rough that people choose instead to travel the dusty dirt road that threads through the bushes beside the tarmac), and it is something to travel that far on tarmac. The road runs to the border area and was built to facilitate access, so it is being used these days. We do not hear a lot about the rumblings to the north, except for the jets crashing the sound barrier overhead. Things are quiet here. In fact, last night the American embassy had a program in honor of Abraham Lincoln, with a good turnout. Some of us went and enjoyed seeing the two films. The first was from a documentary series on American history featuring the Civil War and Lincoln. The second showed the recent march on Washington. I enjoyed both, but especially the latter, with Martin Luther King Jr. speaking "I have a dream" and the orderly mixed crowd singing "I do believe we shall overcome someday!"

We got to Johar in time for part of the evening fellowship with Dave Shenks (Clyde's son and family), Dave Miller, Helen Ranck, and Anna Lutz. One Somali and one Bantu person were also present. We arrived too late for me to help them sing in Swahili; that will come at Jamama! We then went with Helen and Anna to Mahaddei, and the next day Ivan and I were in the clinic that Anna operates. I also visited the village with her and did minor surgery on an old lady with an infected arm to remove the necrotic (dead) tissue. This clinic is more than 350 miles from our hospital at Jamama, so visits from the doctor are not as regular as in the Shirati area. But Anna did appreciate our visit. MAF does not come to Somalia often, and sometimes the roads are impassable from mud, so the nurse at Mahaddei must be a doctor too, but fortunately she can usually get to Mogadishu without difficulty if necessary. So I will probably be more stationary here than I was for the past year.

The villages here are actually towns, some even with several thousand people, and cattle and gardens, whereas Shirati is a village consisting of only one family—a father with his wives and children and a few married sons—and seldom more than ten small houses enclosed in a fence of thorns or hedge. Cattle are often brought into this enclosure at night. In the Shirati area, one can drive for miles, it seems, without seeing any houses or people.

I have not traveled much by daylight in Somalia; it is cooler at night. We plan to leave at around 3:00 P.M. today and get to Jamama around midnight—dusty and ready to sleep. It is hotter with less wind than when I arrived, when it nearly blew one off the map! Hot season—March, April—is coming.

The Sunday morning service here at Mogadishu is held in a public chapel on the compound. It is more formal than at Shirati, with singing, scripture reading, and a message, all in English. Sudan Interior Mission (SIM) folks and local Christians attend, as do embassy folks sometimes. I met our ambassador on my first Sunday, and last week I met the embassy doctor, who had previously been a missionary doctor along Lake Victoria south of Kisumu in Kenya, so we found things to talk about.

The doctor from the SIM hospital was also visiting in town, so there were four American doctors present in our service that morning.

In addition to introducing me to doctors and other medical personnel, Ivan has also taken me around town to meet various government officials, drug suppliers, and others. He has been inquiring about the possibility of, after his furlough, starting a nurse aide and dresser training course, which he would want to have recognized by the government, and naturally such interviews take time.

When I came here last week, the only folks at our Somali mission whom I had not met previously were the Linds, but since I have been living with them in their house, for more than a week now, we have gotten acquainted. I have also had nice long talks with a number of others and I am happy for this time of getting to know one another before going to Jamama.

I have no illusions of becoming proficient in Somali, because it is much more difficult than Swahili, I am told, but I will study with Faye Miller as I have time until she transfers to Mahaddei in June, when Anna Lutz goes on furlough.

Bas is *bis* here—so *bis!*

Thursday, February 20, 1964

Greetings to you all from Jamama, where among other things I am trying to get my thermostat adjusted to a warmer climate. We—the Ivan Leaman family (including three-year-old Deborah and six-month-old David), Faye Miller, and myself—left Mogadishu a week ago today at 3:45 P.M. We had tarmac for the first forty miles, so that part went rapidly. Thereafter we bounced and ate dust, but never got stuck in it, though we slid a little several times—just like you do in snow. You can stick in sand and deep dust just like in snowdrifts.

At about 7:30 we stopped at a little place—some might call it a restaurant—for ravioli (an Italian pasta stuffed with cheese) and tea, plus tinned things. We were on the road again until about 12:30 A.M., when we finished our 270-mile trek and quickly collapsed into bed. I had gotten so tired of sitting during the last half hour of our journey that I rearranged myself into a partially horizontal position on my half of the seat.

I am staying in the Leamans' house and have had some meals with them. There are three houses and a garage apartment here. One is the doctors' house, the second is now occupied by the Dorsches but, when they go on furlough in August, the Harold Reeds plan to come here from Johar. The two nurses (Faye Miller and Miriam Leaman) and Lena Horning, a teacher, live in the third house. Chester Kurtzes use the apartment as their weekend headquarters between their trips to Noleye for an agricultural-settlement project among the Bartiri nomads. Ivans plan to leave here about March 10 and then fly from Mogadishu on the 13th, making visits to Ethiopia and Europe before arriving home a month later. Faye will probably move in with me after Ivans leave, but in July she will be going to Mahaddei to relieve Anna Lutz during her furlough. Then Miriam Leaman and I will be the missionary medical personnel for a while, though we hope that another nurse will be coming to help us before long. I am somewhat surprised to hear that nowadays it is easier to get doctors than to find nurses for missionary service, for surely there are still many more nurses than doctors in our constituency.

I don't imagine you ever made me out to be a lunatic, but you might have if you'd seen me last Friday after sunset, for I joined my neighbors in looking for the moon. If that sounds queer, let me assure you, it is mighty serious business for many people in the world—those living under the crescent. I've only begun learning about Islam, but it was quite interesting to arrive during Ramadan, the month when the faithful fast from sunup to sundown; some even spit out their saliva. They eat during the night, but you can imagine one gets tired in a hot climate while fasting all day and then losing some sleep in order to eat at night. One doctor in Mogadishu apologized for not walking along when we toured the new hospital, for he was fasting and wanted to save his strength.

Now, if you wonder what this has to do with the moon, I'm coming to that. The Muslim calendar is based on the moon, and the month lasts from one new moon to the next. For this reason, everyone was out looking for the faint sliver of moon after sunset, because it proclaimed the beginning of a new month and the end of fasting, so they could feast again, have guests, and go visiting. Fortunately, the sky was clear, so even I could see the moon and rejoice.

On Saturday morning I went visiting with Mary Ellen Leaman and Viola Dorsch and their daughters. We were treated to tea and tasty cookies. That afternoon I trailed after Miriam and Faye into some Arab homes, where I again managed to down their coffee—made with ginger. It is rather strong and I do enjoy the tea here more, with its cinnamon tang. I am told that the festivities were not as gay this year as sometimes because some people were involved elsewhere and could not join their families. The radio gives various reports and probably things seem worse than they are.

I already have a "son" here in Jamama. He arrived yesterday in a little rush, before Miriam had things ready, so I delivered all seven pounds and nine ounces of him in bed, and did he ever yell about that. His mother is so small, I surely didn't expect such a big baby.

Sunday, March 1, 1964

Greetings from Jamama on a lovely Sunday evening. You mentioned not being able to find Jamama on the map. Perhaps you can find Margherita, about half way between Mogadishu and the southern tip of Somalia—a bit north of Chismaio (also spelled Kismayu). Margherita was the name given to the village during the Italian occupation. After independence in 1960, the name was changed to the Somali one, Jamama, but many people still call it Margherita. Interestingly, our hospital was named Jamama Hospital even before the town's name was changed. It is just across the fence from the village, which has about a thousand residents. The hospital is still young—only three years old—and people often do not realize that we can help them, or they think of the hospital only as a last resort.

We do not have any church building here and do not publicly conduct services or witness openly. We missionaries gather in one of our homes on the compound for services on Sunday morning and evening. Some Swahili-speaking folks as well as village folks participate too. Sunday school meets at 10:00 and is bilingual—either English-Somali or Swahili-Somali (depending on who is leading it). And then there is a sermon. Sunday evening is more of a children's meeting with a flannel graph lesson or short devotional. Friday is the Muslim holy day, so it is generally an easy day at the hospital, with no clinic, so the ladies try to visit in the village on late Friday and Sunday afternoons—to see new babies, find out if a former patient is OK, and so on—just an informal visit around the teacups to get acquainted with our neighbors.

I just got my Somali driver's license today without taking a test—just the usual red tape of filling out forms and getting the appropriate signatures. Now all that remains is to become acquainted with the Land Rover—a heavy-duty four-wheel-drive vehicle, something like a Jeep but bigger—a British product.

Our "lawn" here is very brown and dusty now, with a few tiny trees and bushes struggling to survive the heat. But rains are soon due and that means good old gummy, sticky mud. It should also mean good juicy grapefruit from the nearby river farms. People who irrigate from the Jubba River can grow nice bananas, grapefruit, and so on. But do you know, they let water from this miles-long river sneak all the way across the country and run away into the Indian Ocean near Kismayu instead of using it for irrigation and developing agricultural projects.

It is now 6:30 Tuesday morning. I am trying to get myself into a different schedule—to rise a bit earlier and begin work before the sun gets so warm. We try to finish clinic around 12:30, and then I like to rest until about 4:00 P.M., before having language class with Faye Miller. But today we will have some surgery in the late afternoon. I prefer to keep afternoons and evenings as free as possible for study and letter writing and some reading.

Your prayers mean so much to us.

Monday, March 9, 1964

Greetings from Jamama, where it is letter-writing day. Tomorrow Ivans leave Jamama for Mogadishu. Many folks have been coming to give them good-bye greetings and it is apparent that they are appreciated in the community. On Saturday night the mayor invited the missionaries out to a local restaurant for supper in honor of Ivans. Faye and I missed it because of a truck accident. We were busy trying to help three seriously hurt patients. Two died within three hours of admission—one of a broken neck and the other of a skull fracture. The third man had a nasty concussion but is gradually waking up and should be OK. The dinner was to start at 7:30 but they delayed it until 8:30 and Ivan helped me a while. Chester and Victor made bed boards before they went.

Well, I keep doing things for the first time and this one may or may not surprise you. There are Swahili-speaking people here and on Sunday evening the Bible story is translated into Swahili for them. This past Sunday the children came but the young man who usually translates didn't—so I was drafted! The story was about the blind man. I translated rather freely and with many grammatical errors, I'm sure, but I think they got the gist of it anyway. But imagine translating for others before I even get organized to give a talk or teach Sunday school in Swahili, when I could at least prepare a bit and review vocabulary beforehand. I've had a fair number of Swahili-speaking patients and it's a real joy to work with them. I am studying Somali a bit with Faye Miller, and I do want to do some Swahili reading (Scripture mostly) to build up vocabulary. I am getting to the place, I think, where with a little effort I could really progress. During my last six months at Shirati I was hearing and speaking more without conscious effort (just from exposure). And the same was beginning with Luo; just from working in the hospital I was recognizing a number of medical terms and was beginning to use a few—to the immense pleasure of others. So I do hope to pick up some Somali too, so I can better understand what patients say.

Tonight the hospital employees had a dinner for Ivans and the rest of us missionaries were in on it too. The menu, which originated in Ethiopia, was *injera*—a very thin, big pancake that is torn into edible-size pieces and dipped into *wat*—a stew of meat, hard-boiled eggs, potato, and so on. A hot sauce can be added, which makes it really good.

Monday, March 16, 1964

Greetings on a rather warm evening with few breezes. It seems that winter is about to give way to more heat and welcome rain. I miss jumping on my Suzie to go for a spin down the airstrip or just out for a change of scenery. Here the large village is so handy, we make frequent trips there to buy something or just to visit. Folks here do a lot of visiting and I do enjoy getting into the homes. At Shirati I always felt like this important thing was being neglected because of more pressing duties.

Last Sunday I obeyed a biblical injunction in a way I can't remember doing before. The teenage boy who died from a skull fracture sustained in the truck accident I wrote about in my previous letter was the brother of Medina, one of our nurse aides. On Sunday morning the men attended the burial service at the cemetery. Women are not permitted to attend but they may go to the grave afterward. After the relatives returned to the home, Miriam Leaman invited me to go along to see Medina. I did not know her well but had worked with her a bit. We sat on the mat where they sat to mourn with those who mourn and weep with those who weep. Miriam naturally could talk with Medina, who sorely misses her only brother (who was en route to Kismayu to take a pre-admission exam for higher education when the accident occurred), but I just sat with the other women. We stayed for about thirty minutes, drank a bit of tea, and ate several dried dates before returning to the compound for our morning worship service. I know our presence was appreciated even though neither of us said very much.

This week has been busy. I enjoyed getting to the employees' farewell dinner for Ivans after missing the one given by the mayor the preceding Saturday evening. Ivans left Tuesday morning. Miriam and Sidi (a hospital employee) went along, so we were short-staffed, and I was still not well oriented to the routine. But somehow we got through despite much work. Miriam returned last night, so I hope things will be more normal this week. I plan to do surgeries for both an inguinal hernia and an umbilical hernia this week.

The generator has stopped and the bugs are crawling over my feet because my little lantern is now the only attraction. The bugs? They are brown, a half-inch long, mostly on the floor, love the light, come by spells, and usually die in the morning, leaving brown juice marks where you walk on the remains. The other night I was ironing and such a big spot there was in the middle of the kitchen floor when I finished! I hope to have Fatuma (who worked for Ivans) come in to clean up this place.

I wrote a complaint to *Time* magazine for not getting my address changed this time. Saw that President Nyerere is on the cover this week!

Monday, March 30, 1964

Warm greetings again from Jamama. Last Thursday (I think) there were dark clouds between us and the east, so Viola Dorsch got busy pulling the old dried up flower stalks from her flower bed and preparing for rain. We did get several little showers that morning, and some wind. But it hasn't rained since and it has been rather sticky and humid. This morning Chester Kurtz was out plowing the garden for the Dorsches with the red Massey Ferguson tractor and a two-bottom plow.

Chester is Christ Kurtz's son. With his wife and daughter he has been busy in the agricultural project at Noleye, about seventy-five miles northwest of here. A nomadic tribesman was interested in having his people settle along the Jubba River and become farmers instead of wandering around with their cattle and camels over the dry grazing land. So Chester spent much time there helping to teach the interested ones about farming. But the flood of two years ago, followed by drought, discouraged many of them and the group dwindled. Some months ago a tractor was purchased along with a plow and disk, a small wagon, and some other tools. Chester then did quite a bit of plowing of virgin soil along the river and helped work it up so that a few of the young men could plant sesame. Their first harvest was good, so they paid him to do more plowing. Meanwhile, several oxen have been gotten, so they can continue to work these fields without depending on the tractor.

The Noleye project was initially envisioned as a cooperative arrangement, but the man largely responsible for getting it started has recently gotten involved in other work, so for various reasons it was decided that Chesters should for now pull out of Noleye and see what is achieved without them. Chester will do some school building at Mahaddei primary school for several weeks, and then move to Johar to teach in the middle school (grades 5 to 8). Chesters had used Jamama as their base of operations for Noleye. Tonight we had dinner together—ham (tinned but very good), macaroni salad, cabbage slaw, and angel food cake (from a boxed mix). Today they loaded their old Land Rover to the top and started out for Mogadishu, hoping they won't encounter too much rain. Chester jokes about having become a nomad too! And they surely have not lived a settled life. But they do seem happy and I believe their work at Noleye was not wasted time.

Today was election day in Somalia. Locally everything was quiet. We saw some patients this morning but not the usual Monday crowd of a hundred! After voting, each person got a streak of red paint across the back of his wrist to show he had voted. Several came to the clinic with big blisters on the wrist; when they tried to rub off the mark, the acid mixed with the paint and caused a significant reaction and hurt enough that cheating was not easy.

It's after 11:00 P.M. and I promised to look up something on recurrent shoulder dislocations, so let me stop pecking for now and finish tomorrow morning before surgery—if I can wake up. Last night I didn't go to sleep for the longest time, and that isn't my style at all!

Wednesday, April 8, 1964

Greetings from Jamama, where the rains have come, and that's a welcome change to the cooler. The clinic census has dropped considerably. Folks are too busy digging gardens to come for pills. Along with the rain, however, come lots of bugs and, of course, mud—thick, gooey stuff that hangs onto the shoes and makes them feel like a ton. But if you walk on a path that has sand or stone, it's not too bad. When it's so wet, the traffic officials close the road to prevent the big lorries from plowing through and churning things up. Then nothing can get through.

The elections last week were quiet and orderly, at least here. One man elected to go to parliament in Mogadishu is a friend of the hospital; in fact, he helped to sponsor the farewell dinner for Dr. Leamans just before they left. Today there was a party to celebrate his victory.

Clinic work can be rather routine, with many of the same problems day after day: hookworm (gets into the intestines and eats blood until the person becomes very anemic and wonders why he doesn't feel like working), malaria with its chills and fever, bilharzia (a worm that gets into the bladder and causes infection with passage of blood and puss in the urine), tuberculosis, and so on. I am seeing a lady with a big ulcer on her face that I fear is cancer of the jaw with infection; it is improving, though, with penicillin, so maybe it is just a bad infection. I hope the latter, for she is a nice patient. She also speaks Swahili, and is so appreciative of my interest.

Last week one morning I did three operations: the first for appendicitis, the second for hemorrhoids, and the third for ulcers at the rectum. These men have all been discharged. The first man brought some lovely papaya before he left.

Tomorrow I want to work on a fellow who has some nasty ulcers on his leg. An orphan, he injured his leg fourteen years ago. It got infected and was never treated, so now he has some scar tissue and two big ulcers. I want to thoroughly debride the leg and remove the pound of flesh and most of the old scar. Later I will do skin grafting. The young man is twenty-two years old but has never had a good job or been able to feed and clothe himself properly, so he used to beg and visit the restaurants for food scraps. A hospital employee is now helping him with food, because I want him to rest in bed. Pray that he may come to understand something of Calvary love as we minister to his physical needs and try to give him a good, clean leg to walk on.

Last Saturday we had a hospital staff meeting. All employees except one cleaning girl met with the nurses, Victor Dorsch, and me. It was our first such meeting, so I made an introductory speech, then gave a "pep talk" on the team idea—you know: everyone is important in having a smoothly working hospital where patients can get good care. We also discussed some problems and areas of concern. It is important to have good communication with one another. Recently there have been several misunderstandings, but this meeting was helpful in clearing up those matters. I hope to have such meetings each month. They can be a good sounding board for new ideas, as well as a time to review our hospital policy on a given matter (such as visiting hours) and get more staff cooperation. The spirit exhibited by the employees this morning was good, and several of them shared their concerns about our hospital's "image" and public relations. I feel we really have a fine staff here.

Wednesday, April 15, 1964

Your most welcome letters arrived this morning while I was busy at the hospital with a very sick asthma patient. He's a little better now and I have the potatoes boiling to make soup, and the egg in a separate pot.

Now the soup is all eaten and I've had my rest. It is raining again, so it's the kind of day to make one lazy.

I discovered some months ago that Somalia personnel are usually assigned to four-year terms rather than five as in some other fields. Paul Kraybill visited Somalia before Tanganyika and, at the request of medical people here, tentatively arranged for me to be here about two years, working with Ivan the second year as he develops some sort of training program. When Paul came to Shirati and reported this at supper, I said nothing, but in our interview I indicated my interest in a shorter term, offering the following as my reasons: (1) Somalia workers have shorter terms. (2) A first-termer should perhaps have less than a regular five-year term. (3) Switching fields in midterm and facing many new things twice instead of once, with all the adjustments of culture, language, personnel, and so on, makes a four-year term long enough. (4) If present plans go through and Dr. Leamans return on schedule, I could overlap with them for three to four months while he does extra projects and I may do more language study, then aim for getting home for the fall semester of Bible work, with some time to travel en route. I can't quite see two doctors busy enough here to be content, especially after being at Shirati in what is sometimes quite a rat race. Our staff is being trained to take on more responsibility, and if we get another nurse in the dispensary, one doctor should be able to manage things.

Paul listened to me and indicated his willingness to consider my proposal, saying that the board is flexible in such matters. And I find almost everyone I talk to (both here and in Tanganyika) inclined to feel the same way. So, it isn't definite yet but daydream all you like about it, and best not to blow this around to anyone else yet. But you might ask EMC to send me a catalogue of courses to look at.

Friday, April 17, 1964

I got called out at 5:30 this morning for a delivery problem. After I finished, at 6:00, I came home. It was light but cloudy though the sun was not up yet. I hung out the wash I did last night. Then I got two biopsy specimens ready and wrapped to go to Kampala. And now it's exactly 7:30 A.M. So at least for today I got up more like your style—a little early. But even early it can be warm here, and there is little breeze at night. In fact, there's more often a breeze in the afternoon, so sleeping goes better then.

Yesterday the primary school here on the compound closed. Lena Horning is the missionary teacher and there are three Somali teachers. They have four grades and yesterday the first group of students graduated into fifth grade. Maybe next year they will begin an actual middle school so that these boys can continue their education here. Naturally the local officials, other important people, and the community in general were invited to the graduation ceremony, and a good crowd came. We were thankful it didn't rain and everything went OK. A number of students gave speeches—mainly in English but a few spoke in Somali and Arabic. They also sang in these languages. A group of boys performed their gymnastics exercises, and we observed a group in class with Lena as she quizzed them on geography, especially with reference to Somali imports and exports. Several teams of students also asked riddles of one another. Quite interesting to me was the Somali version of "Old McDonald Had a Farm"—"Jamal Ali had a farm. . . ." They seemed to enjoy singing it as much as American youngsters do.

My dear barrel, filing cabinet, and trunk are still in Mogadishu, where they have been since early March. There was some delay with papers before the stuff could be cleared through customs. So I am still wearing the things I carried with me and am trying to keep myself in clothes from one washday until the next. Thursday evening is prayer meeting and I also wash that night so I can hang it out on Friday morning, when I can spend more time at the house, because we have no clinic on Friday. I also aim to do my housework that day. A Swahili-speaking boy comes to help me. He sweeps out the bugs, scrubs the floors, and is learning to do dishes.

Tuesday, April 28, 1964

It's a sticky evening and I feel like stretching out, but I expect to have a chance to send post tomorrow, so I'll work at this. My recorder is playing "Sometimes I feel like a motherless child . . . a long way from home." I like the song but I don't feel especially lonely. I live in a comfortable apartment by myself except for some mosquitoes, land lizards, cockroaches, and some other species of bugs, plus millions of ants sometimes. Tonight a whole army was marching in the door and toward the refrigerator, so I bombed them good and scored a knockout! All that remains is a big pile of black dust.

My last letter left Jamama on, I think, Saturday the 18th and I'm sure it encountered a lot of mud between here and Mogadishu. A big lorry left from Mogadishu that Sunday with a load of people. One family had a number of children and live here in Jamama. The truck got stuck a number of times and after a day and a half their food was finished. The family sent a telegram to relatives here but the machine was broken, so no one knew of their planned arrival until Wednesday evening, when a Land Rover came by with a report that the truck and its hungry family were hoping to arrive that night. So the relatives prepared a lot of food and waited all night, but no one arrived. On Thursday at noon the relatives came by and asked Victor to go for the family by Land Rover. So Victor and James drove thirty miles and found the lorry stuck in the mud. The family was loaded into our vehicle, and were they ever glad to get to Jamama! The lorry didn't arrive until the next evening. At such times I am really glad to stay put or to go only as far as I want to walk.

On Saturday morning the Dorsch children and Faye Miller left for Nairobi. The pilot was hoping to get to Mara Hills yet that afternoon. They got to Chismaio at 10:45, but until the pilot went through customs, changed loads, and so on, it was after noon when the plane took off. I had sent two drug orders to Nairobi earlier and arranged for the pilot to bring them when he returned to Jamama. But one company didn't get the order filled, so the pilot filled the plane with apples, oranges, carrots, cabbage, cauliflower, potatoes, and tangerines. We have really enjoyed having fresh fruits and vegetables again. We can get delicious grapefruit here, also bananas and coconuts, but fresh vegetables are scarce. Potatoes are imported from Italy and cost about fifteen cents per pound. Large onions cost about that per piece, so I didn't buy any in the market the other day. They are sometimes cheaper. Prices go up during the rains, when it is difficult to get supplies in. This is true of sugar too.

Yesterday we were expecting the American doctor from Chismaio to come to do surgery, but he didn't show up. This morning at around 10:00 we got a telegram that he had sent at 8:30 yesterday morning saying that he had no car and asking us to reschedule the patient for

Wednesday. So you see a bit of our communication problems. It hasn't rained for several days, so the roads are well dried off. On Saturday afternoon, Miriam and I went to the village. I saw it was getting very black but I was buying some curtain material for my house and she was buying too, so we got wet before we got back to the hospital. Some of the employees saw us coming through the rain like drenched cats and thought this was funny. Getting soaked in warm Africa is different than getting wet in a colder climate, where a prompt change into dry clothes is important. Here one can often just dry off without danger. But I did change my top clothes after I got to my house.

On Sunday afternoon we women folks—five including Joy Dorsch—walked out to the camp where some of the German families live. A German company is building a tarmac road from Chismaio to Jamama. A number of the employees have families, so I see them at times in the clinic. We walked out to the camp to see little Hans Schopf, who is his parents' first child. I had seen his mother several times before delivery and she had considered delivering at Jamama but then chose to go to Nairobi, which was OK with me. So Hans arrived there on April 6 and came to Jamama two weeks later. The family was transported via the company's plane. Some of the German wives speak English quite well, and most of them understand some, but while we drank coffee and sampled delicious cakes, they got into speaking German. Everyone but Miriam could understand it. I still hear a lot, but let me try to think how to say something—and all that comes out is Swahili! But I think if I spent more time with them, I would pick it up again fast. And interestingly, when I began to study Swahili, my German really came back to me.

Friday, May 15, 1964

Greetings again from Jamama. You wrote about Dr. Frederick Brenneman and his work in India. Did you know he also served two years at Shirati as sort of a pinch hitter about six to eight years ago? I guess it was when Dr. Lester Eshleman's first furlough came up. But he first served in India and I suppose that was his family's second home, with Shirati being more of a stopover. I have never met them. They usually invited the Philadelphia Mennonite medical students out to their farm in the spring for a picnic. I never got there.

I'm not yet counting the time until I come home, but I think about it sometimes. It seems like everyone is doing it: Ivans and Victors leave Jamama this year, Miriam Leaman goes next year, and me—well, I don't know yet. I'm eager to wiggle my toes in the dirt again and to wind through the long rows of corn with the cultivator. Here I don't go barefoot, because I'm not that interested in having hookworms join up for a ride wherever I go. They burrow through the skin between the toes and then do such ugly things as run around in your lungs and give you a cough and chest pain. Then they settle down in your intestines and eat—not the food you eat but blood. Some of our patients with hookworm have only 20 percent of normal hemoglobin value, and they wonder why they are tired and their heart beats fast and their head hurts. Most of the time I wear sandals, which are cooler than shoes and do protect me from hookworm. We also have trees and bushes that have thorns and stickers to throw around, and I've encountered these often enough.

What I'm doing these days may be summarized by saying that it's mostly the same—seeing clinic patients, plus a few inpatients. I had a man in who had trouble passing urine due to a longstanding bilharzia infection, so I catheterized him and hooked him up to a bottle. When the catheter accidentally came out and he still had retention, I had more trouble. Bilharzia causes bleeding and I was conquered to get another catheter in, so I put a needle directly into the bladder through the abdomen and took out about a pint of urine that way. The next day I did get a catheter back in.

The other day his son came and decided that his elderly father had been here long enough and wasn't getting better anyway. He insisted on taking him home. I know he could have gotten better with time, but they were impatient and had decided he would die anyway. They had the patient all upset and afraid, and I could not persuade them to let him stay or to take him to Chismaio. So I had them sign a release and they left with him. He had gotten some injections in January but quit when he was only two-thirds finished, which was inadequate treatment.

When I see a case like this, when I try so hard to have them do the right thing so they can get better yet they refuse and glibly accept responsibility for the outcome themselves, then I have a little idea of how God must feel when we refuse His proffered salvation or (and this is perhaps worse), having tasted of His goodness, still hesitate to completely follow Him and still cherish our own childish whims. Salvation and medical help are alike in that you cannot help the needy one until he asks for help and is ready to accept it. Neither can be forced upon another against his wishes.

Monday, June 1, 1964

Some months ago, when Somalia was showing its neighborliness to Ethiopia, I wrote evasively about potential peekers misconstruing my meaning. Of course local Somalis insist that Ethiopia was the aggressor and so on. But it is well-known that Somalia claims a sizable chunk of land as grazing land for its nomads that Ethiopia also claims. Likewise, Somalia wants a huge chunk of the Northern Frontier District of Kenya and encourages its *shiftas* (bandits) to carry out raids. There are, of course, Somalis living in both areas, and I suppose many are content as they are. But Somalia wants all Somali people united in one country and agitates for these areas of Kenya and Ethiopia to have "self-determination" and to join the Somalia Republic. It must be admitted that for many years, before arbitrary boundaries were made by colonial powers, Somali nomads migrated with their cattle looking for water. It is also true that Somalis generally have a very exalted opinion of themselves, their army, their air force, their importance on the world scene, and so on. The Reds, of course, cater to the Somalis and send in plenty of stuff that looks great to people who don't recognize antique junk. There is a big pile of it next door—for some agricultural project, they say: several dozen Caterpillar tractors (one with a V-shaped snow plow!), four big cranes, and dozens of stake trucks. And yesterday a toy Turnapull chugged in; it really looks ancient beside LeTourneau workhorses.

A state of emergency was declared by Kenya in January (one month after their independence) and is still on as far as I know. No vehicle traffic goes between the two countries. Private planes have been grounded and private radio communication was banned for a short time. The Ethiopia border has simmered down with the help of anti-Christian Sudan. And in the Northern Frontier District, I suppose the "hit and run" continues in "normal" fashion.

Why am I writing all of this inflammatory material in such an open fashion now? Because I plan to have this letter posted in Nairobi when Miriam goes on leave, so the Somali postal authorities will not have the opportunity to censor what I say. Our folks are careful in what we write on touchy matters, such as the border problems, and our illegal witness in this land. Maybe these details sound a bit gruesome, but rest assured, none of us are sitting around chewing our fingernails and wondering "what if?" I have been impressed with the excellent relations we have with the Jamama community. This is their hospital and we are appreciated. Folks show it by bringing gifts of eggs, bananas, limes, chickens, and so on. And we are always welcomed into their homes and at their weddings. The Arab women (veiled in black *shukas*) especially marvel at our freedom to move about, and they especially appreciate our visits. Their lives are rather restricted, to say the least, and I have gotten into more homes here already than I ever did in Tanganyika. Why? Well, visiting is an important contact, plus one can make time for it here, and we do. We are of course not permitted to talk about Christ, but we do find opportunities to exchange ideas. One frequently discussed topic is marriage. In Somalia, husbands can engage in polygamy, and they often divorce a wife on the slightest pretext, so we frequently get to talking about what makes a good marriage and a good home.

It is now Saturday night, the 6th, and the big thought with us all is that we have lost another warrior. At 6:00 tonight we got word by cable that David Shenk was killed in a scooter accident at 2:00 P.M. today. Seems he got involved with a stupid camel! This is a shock, but we want to submit to God's will. Pray especially for his widow and two small daughters. They arrived here only in August, I think, but he was already in charge of our international school at Johar. What changes this will mean in personnel remains to be seen. Pray that through this all God may glorify Himself and somehow draw more to Himself. By our daily actions and attitudes may the persons we contact somehow sense His presence and desire to know more of Him. We thank God that some have bravely come asking for Bible classes in order to learn more about Christianity, and we pray that these hungry ones may go on seeking until they find full satisfaction in Him. I seldom write much about our believers or the fruit of our witness here, but there are some Somali as well as Bantu believers in our area. It is best not to ask or write about such matters in your letters to me, because of possible inspection.

MAF brought in an X-ray engineer today to install our X-ray machine. We had already gotten ready, which involved moving our drugs into another room so we could use the first room as a darkroom, to which we added curtains and water. We had also remodeled the former utility room, part of which became the drug room. It was a big job but we were about ready when MAF arrived at about noon. Victor, Harold, and the technician got the machine unpacked and assembled this afternoon.

The MAF plane will take off early tomorrow to go get Clyde Shenks and assist them in getting to Mogadishu to be with Grace in this time of sorrow. Davids had just returned from leave with their relatives and friends in Tanganyika two to three weeks ago. I'm glad they had this time together for Grace's sake.

Tuesday, June 9, 1964

The past ten days have really had variety, or maybe I should stretch it out to nearly two weeks. First, after the MAF plane took off for Nairobi and Tanganyika on Sunday morning, June 7, at noon we got a second cable from Mogadishu. It said that the previous cable had been in error— that it was David Miller, not David Shenk, who had been killed in the scooter accident the day before. David Miller was our builder. He was about sixty years old. His wife had died and his sons were grown and married, so he gave of his older years to the Lord's work in Somalia. We shall miss him, of course, but we know that he had a testimony with the nationals and we thank God for all the years he spent here. As he was building our hospital, houses, and schools, his workmen saw something of the love of God in his heart too.

Victor Dorsch drove the 270 miles to Mogadishu for Council meeting. It began raining the Wednesday night after he left, and it rained most of Thursday—more than five inches. I didn't leave the house until noon that day, and though I didn't wear a bathing suit, I could have used one!

I won't tell you how late I slept that morning, but after I got up I had a leisurely breakfast, then got out my carpenter tools and remodeled my closet. It seems that Somali missionaries are supposed to be tall, and I don't qualify on that standard, so I set about making my own. In the doctor's house I could touch the closet rod by standing on my tiptoes, but in my apartment there was no way but to jump, and I'm not keen on that, so I was living out of my suitcase and dresser, until it rained. Then I took the time to move the rod down four inches, put my clothes on hangers, and hang them up. Then I made another rod and hung a curtain across the opening to act as a door. I had previously made curtains from the same material for all of the windows, as well as one for the doorway between the kitchen-living room and the bedroom. Now I must make one for the transom above my outside door.

The next day, Friday, it was still wet, but I did get to the hospital once. Victor started back from Mogadishu that day, and the Reeds, with their two small daughters, also headed this way with their things to live here. Well, they all encountered rain and waterholes and mud. They got stuck numerous times, and Reeds once had to offload their barrels into water. When they reloaded, the barrels spouted water back at them. They broke several axles and had to get more parts, so they didn't get to Jamama until sundown on Monday evening. Fortunately they had been in towns on Saturday and Sunday nights, so they had set up their cots to sleep and had hot food. They arrived at Jamama very tired, and most of them took malaria treatment to get going again. All day Wednesday I helped Reeds wash all their clothes, and got sunburned in the process.

Yesterday the X-ray engineer mixed up the chemicals for developing X-rays, then taught Sidi and Combelo—two of our employees—and me how to take the X-rays and develop them. We did a tuberculosis patient first, then two of the patient's sons. One of them she had delivered last February, the week after I arrived in Somalia, so he is my first Somali "son," and the father told me recently that I am the boy's "grandmother." She and one son are taking streptomycin and the rest are getting prophylactic medication. Today we took pictures of some of the employees. Yesterday we also had a patient with a hand injury that turned out to be fractures of a bone in the little finger and of the bone in the palm going to that finger, so this morning I plastered that hand.

It hasn't rained for a week now and things are drying off, so maybe soon we will have post—I hope. Miriam Leaman is now on holiday, visiting our Tanganyika folks. Quite a crowd are soon going home from Tanganyika—Elam Stauffers, Jim Mohlers, Mark Brubaker, and Grace Gehman this month, and Petersheims and Simeon Hursts next month.

Monday, June 29, 1964

Greetings from Jamama, where frankly it is sometimes so cold when the wind picks up that I shiver to think about winter at home! Yesterday morning as usual I wore my sandals to church, and my toes got cold! So I have decided that Somalia differs from Shirati not only in that it is hotter here, but also that it is sometimes colder! In other words, there is more seasonal variation here. There is more wind too, related to the monsoons that blow from the northeast at certain times (January) and then other times from the southeast. We are having the latter now, interspersed with rain showers that come suddenly and last long enough to make you run to grab the wash, but about the time you have it all dumped in the basket, the rain is over. It's not the all-day rain of a month ago.

Today we got the EMBMC letter about Dave Miller's death and the memorial service at Salunga. It's fortunate that the news didn't get as confused at home as it was here. Apparently the person reporting the death to Mogadishu used only the name Dave, or Uncle Dave, and because Dave Shenk had been in Mogadishu that morning on his scooter, the assumption had been that the accident victim was Dave Shenk. Can you imagine the shock of the Mogadishu folks who went out to Johar that Saturday afternoon to give solace to Dave Shenk's wife? She was calmly peeling potatoes and insisted she wanted to help with the food arrangements. Then someone went outside and saw the supposedly dead man walking toward them!

I must tell you about the 13th. Talk about people flying around fast! Lena Horning left Shirati before the sun had his eyes even half open (6:30 A.M.), and Gordon, the MAF pilot, had already been to Musoma and returned with some passengers, so you know he got up in the dark. Lena flew to Nairobi and grabbed a different set of wings, and by 11:15 that morning she was flapping them at us. The plane made two loud buzz passes right over the hospital, and I was growling, "Yeah, OK, we know you're up there!" Meanwhile, all the patients evacuated outside and my helpers followed, so I went out too, and he flew over again. But before he was even near, he threw out a big red and yellow "butterfly," and I took off across the road to rescue it—right through the mud, getting my white shoes all dirty—and found that the "butterfly" had a bag of stones hooked to it. In a little pocket with a buttoned flap I found a letter from Gordon saying that he was delivering a patient from Shirati to Chismaio

and would someone go to meet her? We were quite surprised, for we had thought Lena would go only to Nairobi that day and not get to Jamama until the following week. So Victor went to Chismaio. After waving to us at 11:15, the plane didn't put its feet down at Chismaio for another fifteen minutes, and then the pilot didn't get home until after dark.

Lena brought lot of news from Shirati, including several letters, and even a bouquet of flowers (marigolds and zinnias, I think). They were drooping their heads so sadly, but I stuck them in a tin of water and the next morning they were standing up so bright that Lena and I had our picture taken with them after church. In all my years away at school and even leaving home to go to Shirati, I never felt homesickness like I did when Lena came with greetings and news from my many friends at Shirati. I really want to see them again, and Christmas seems like an awful long time to wait. It will surely be different to be at Shirati and not be on call!

Friday, July 10, 1964

Greetings on a chilly evening. We hear a plane from Mogadishu may be stopping by tomorrow to check the rainfall water gauges.

Last week included Independence Day not only for the United States but also for Somalia, on Wednesday, July 1. At midnight on Tuesday they relived hauling down the colonial flag and hoisting their own. I went to bed instead, though I did hear their twenty-one-gun salute. If they had been "civilized enough" to have fireworks, I would have been disgusted with myself for not going. But I did appear the next morning to hear several speeches and then watch the games. I enjoyed the latter—high jump, broad jump, tug-of-war, two-hundred-meter dash, and so on. That afternoon we were invited to the district commissioner's place for refreshments and a program of tribal dances. Some were very nice. They are nothing like the dancing we were taught against at home. Usually only the men dance, making music with drums and stamping feet, maneuvering a cane (or spear, originally), and so on. It was fascinating to see that some performers did well in staying together in their act, though I could detect little rhythm in the accompaniment to direct them when to fall or jump. Another interesting aspect of the celebration was the way ex-patriates were brought together. At the games the mission contingent was seated on benches with the German road-building group to our right and the Russian farmers on our left. We were also a bit conspicuous with all our camera activity.

I visited the Russians one evening when a young expat was sick. He recovered and I saw him at the games. His wife is with him and his two-year-old daughter is back in Russia with her grandparents, because they thought the climate here would not be healthy for children. A young woman in their group is a translator and speaks good English. She was entertaining Joy Dorsch for a while, so perhaps this will be the start of more contacts. Viola hopes to have the women over for coffee sometime. We had the German ladies here for coffee one Sunday afternoon. Yes, I baked a cake, and it wasn't even from a mix. It was a banana cake, and it was sort of good, I thought. I made a caramel icing; I hardly got it spread on the cake, it hardened so fast. But at least it tasted good, if I have to say so myself.

On Thursday and Friday afternoons there were "football" games—like our soccer—across the road. I watched parts of both games and really enjoyed it. Two players in one game got bruises, but they recovered overnight after a good dose of medicine for pain and sleep.

The other Independence Day last week (Saturday, July 4) was just another work day here, but not exactly an ordinary one. Bombelo is my right-hand man at the clinic—translating, taking histories, writing some orders—and he works afternoons in the lab. On Friday afternoon his uncle came in vomiting blood. We finally got two men to give blood for transfusion. I was with him until almost 1:00 A.M. and didn't sleep well after that, so I was tired on Saturday. The blood did the trick and he stopped bleeding. He did so well I let him go home on Tuesday, but with lots of medicine and instructions about food. I also asked him to get working on a visa so he could go to Nairobi for a complete workup and possible surgery to prevent another attack of bleeding.

We had seventy-eight patients this morning—quite a crowd compared to our usual thirty to forty during rainy season, but more folks are coming in from the bush and they are not as busy in their gardens now. Corn is quite available; I received two gifts of corn this week. A few days ago in the afternoon, Faye and I went to visit a garden beside the river. It was my first time at the Jubba River here at Jamama and I was surprised how wide it is. Our hostess gave us some mangoes, which are sort of flat, bigger than peaches but similar in color, and have a large cling stone, so we make do with them as peaches here (though sometimes we splurge on a few expensive imported peaches in Nairobi). They grow on huge trees, so a boy climbed up to pick them off and throw them down onto the grass.

Monday, July 13, 1964

MAF promised to give Faye a lift to Mogadishu tomorrow. She's been ready and on call to go for a week and has been living out of her suitcase. We will miss her here at Jamama, but she's rightly eager to get to Mahaddei to relieve Anna Lutz, who is going on furlough.

Paul Kraybill says that doctors are now available, so perchance my furlough will not be closely correlated with Eshlemans' leaving. With all its teaching and safari work, Shirati should have three doctors anyway. There was only one doctor at Shirati half the time when I was there (and that makes *much work*).

I am thinking about bringing a VW Bug along when I return. I will need transportation, I reckon, and that would be cheaper. I also keep dreaming about a safari to see more of the United States. Maybe you and I and someone else (like Esther Stover, though I've never daydreamed aloud to her) could travel comfortably in a Bug, take a small tent in which to camp, and of course sleeping bags, plus the cooler chest and the Coleman stove that went along to Colorado. I can think of many places to see and many friends to visit in a general westward direction, though I've not been to New England either, or to Canada.

I reckon the mid-1965 furlough and the safari are still indefinite, but let's daydream about it anyway. I have no idea if my furlough will be a year or adjustable. I definitely want seminary as first priority for a semester, or longer if I can also get at least six months in a hospital in OB and surgery. If I return to Shirati with Eshlemans gone and no other experienced surgeon available, I'd better learn more surgery and maybe skip the OB—just do surgery and gynecology (women's surgery).

Saturday, August 1, 1964

I suppose most of my colleagues are sleeping now. I'm not especially tired yet, at 12:45 A.M., despite not getting any afternoon rest today.

Last Sunday morning, after the sermon (the last in a series of messages on stewardship by Victor), the congregation discussed the matter and decided to begin giving offerings every second Sunday. This is a real step in faith, for our people do not have many financial resources, and some of their gardens flooded the other month. We do praise God for the courage of this step.

Dorsches are leaving tomorrow. The United States gave Somalia several airplanes to form Somali Airlines and the Dorsches are to be on its first flight from Chismaio. They are to be at the airport by 12:30 P.M., so we will have early communion and lunch before the hour's drive down. If no medical emergency shows up, I plan to go along—my first trip out of the Jamama environs since mid-April (three and a half months)! I'm ready to see something different—not that Chismaio is. I can now understand how Mother used to feel when she stayed home for several weeks on end and didn't get away. Frankly, I have gotten "buggy" more than once, especially when I thought I had arranged to go to Nairobi for several days on medical business and to see some different faces, but then was informed that this trip must be cleared through the director and so on—a real complicated deal, with the implication being that I had only come in February, so what was my trouble? And I miss my Suzie and can't go for those fast spins to clear out the cobwebs.

Some of the Smith Company folks (Americans building the port) came up yesterday to say farewell to Dorsches. Last evening we missionaries had a meal together and someone prepared a cake with "Good-bye and Hurry Back" in Somali written on it. This afternoon at 4:30 the Germans invited Dorsches and us single girls out for coffee and cake—and they always have the best cake! At 7:30 we were all invited by the employees of the school and hospital to the local restaurant for dinner, again in Dorsches' honor. It was all very nice.

It is hard to believe they are leaving. Reeds came back from holiday on Thursday afternoon, and Lydia Glick arrived yesterday to help in the school. (Both Viola and Victor Dorsch had been teaching.) Dorsches don't seem real excited about going home—maybe because it isn't their first furlough and they know that "home" isn't like it used to be, and in fact home is here in Somalia rather than in Canada. Even son James is very eager to return after furlough.

The mosquitoes have surely had a feast tonight; I must set off a bomb or get a different spray that will knock them out, for what I've been using doesn't seem to phase them, and they have established quite a community in my apartment. So maybe I'd better crawl under the sheets and cover all but my nose and tell them "enough" for one night.

Sunday, August 16, 1964

Greetings on a lovely Sunday. I spent a long afternoon in bed for a welcome change, so I reckon it is time to do something more productive, like write some letters!

On the day the Dorsches left, our Sunday morning worship began early and I missed the first half hour. Sunday school was omitted and, after several short talks, a sermonette, and testimonies, there was the communion service. Three new Christians participated, and we rejoice in this new fruit. Lena Horning, Lydia Glick, and I went along with the Dorsches to Chismaio. It was rather interesting to see them take off in a nice new blue and white plane. After they flew away, we girls went wading in the ocean, then climbed onto some rocks and recited poetry to each other while Harold Reed did a few things in town (like buy hot beef sandwiches for us). That was my first time away from Jamama since mid-April and I was so glad for the change of environment, even if it lasted only a few hours. I assure you, the Dorsches are missed here, for they really knew this community. But we are adjusting to the change. Lydia Glick was in Mogadishu her first year in Africa and transferred here on the Friday before the Dorsches left, to help teach school. Fifth grade was added this year; they call it intermediate school here. Lydia's presence is certainly welcome.

As for the hospital, I did two major surgeries in the past two weeks. I was doing that regularly during my last six to seven months in Shirati, but I hadn't handled any big cases here for so long, I actually felt a little rusty at it. The first surgery was for a lady who had an old infection with adhesions in the pelvis. I took out the old cheesy material and opened some of the adhesions. She is the wife of a member of Parliament, so someone rather important; they seem to be satisfied with her treatment. The other major surgery was a leg amputation. Why did I chop? Because he had a cancer just above the knee and it was too big to remove locally and it didn't go away with medicine, so the only thing left to do was to remove the leg and hope I did it soon enough. It took a little persuasion, because he was worried about how he will follow his cows in the bush with only one leg. But he had seen a plastic affair somewhere and wanted me to promise I would get him a plastic leg. I didn't promise but I agreed to try, and I feel we can get him a leg, though maybe more practical and less expensive than plastic. I will see what is available in Mogadishu and Nairobi. I did his surgery last Saturday and wasn't feeling so hot, so I treated myself for malaria and got through it OK. But one of my helpers fainted, so I got another to hold the leg. The patient, a young fellow, is doing OK. I appreciate his good spirits and uncomplaining manner, and I truly hope he gets a good result from my efforts.

I have learned that some patients here have definite ideas about their treatment (such as how long to stay in the hospital or how to care for a cyst of the eyelid and so forth) and proceed to make a big stink in town if the doctor dares to think otherwise. This has been a little hard to accept, for I try always to give good treatment. I have discovered that in this large village the men especially have lots of time to sit in the restaurants and drink tea or gamble, and of course talk. Talk is a major product, I'm convinced. So, while some patients are quite vocal in expressing appreciation for our services, others are just as loud in their disapproval or condemnation of our work. I do face a communication problem because I must rely on translators, who do a good job but I tend not to say as much or to explain in as great detail when it goes through another person, and they tend to fill in the blanks with certain "well-known facts." So patients do not always understand why I do something.

The other angle is that patients want everything "straight from the horse's mouth." But when seventy to eighty patients come to clinic in one morning, even if I gave five minutes to each patient it would take six hours to serve everybody. Plus some patients obviously need much more time. Thus, when clinic is busy and people are insisting that I write or supervise all orders instead of letting my assistant write for simple routine things, it means long days. Then lunch is late and the afternoon rest gets chopped off—especially when I get called out to have afternoon clinic for those who didn't come in the morning—and I become tired and—you can guess the rest. I would like for my assistant to manage some of this off-hours work, but the village people refuse to accept it, so what can I do? I would just like to go hide by the river with a book some afternoon and not have any hospital person know where I am!

For the past three weeks we have had two normal deliveries per week. It's so nice to have normal ones. Last night at 10:00 P.M. we had our first delivery for this week. The mother came in after being in labor for three and a half days, and she hadn't passed urine in more than a day. I delivered her stillborn baby and then sternly warned her to come earlier next time. She is so small and should have surgery in order to have a living baby. Her first was stillborn in the village after a long labor.

X-ray work is really tying up my evenings three to five nights per week. Sidi does the pictures but I check him on exposure and unusual positions, and naturally I must read them. We are up to ninety. In fact, we just did twenty in one week, so no wonder I get behind. Clinic is busy too, with sixty to eighty patients per morning—and dinner gets later and nap time shorter.

Friday, September 11, 1964

Greetings from Jamama on a warm evening. We had showers this morning, at noon, and tonight again. Despite that, the wash got dry by noon and we had a picnic this evening—the first real picnic since I arrived here. We went out to a grove of mango trees and Barbara Reed provided the eats: camel burgers, tomato-potato salad, pickled eggs, limeade, shrimp boats (similar to potato chips), and whoopies. I think these were my first whoopie pies in Africa, and they sure reminded me of home! The reason for the picnic was that tomorrow Galen Reed leaves to return to school at Mara Hills, on Wednesday Rhoda Buckwalter arrived to join us as a nurse, and last evening Raymond Martin, who spent more than a year at Jamama and Noleye before transferring to Dar es Salaam, arrived for a visit on his way home. He left Dar about two weeks ago and will travel some by boat to spend seven weeks with his brother Luke (Mary Kauffman Martin's husband) in Saigon before arriving home for Christmas. After the picnic we looked at some of his slides of Tanganyika and from a trip he took to South Africa.

We are expecting Dr. Housman to come along with MAF tomorrow to spend a week here again doing eye surgeries. So next week will be busy. We are happy that Rhoda Buckwalter is here to help. After next week, we plan to give her lots of time for language study.

I performed two surgeries again this week. One was for a man with a stone in his bladder that had passed partway out with the urine but had gotten stuck. I opened his bladder and managed, with some work, to get the stone back into the bladder and then to take it out. The other surgery was on a man who broke the corner off the upper bone of his elbow. I could not get it back in place by manipulation, so I operated and put in a screw to hold the elbow together. We did not have all the regular equipment needed for this procedure, so I went to the garage and found some screws as well as a drill and screwdriver. After boiling all of them, I got a satisfactory result, though I could have used a shorter screw, because this one went out the other side of the bone. So after the fracture has healed, I plan to remove the screw. It can get interesting when you have to improvise equipment like this! But if it works, it's a good test of using your head to make do with what you have.

Reeds are about ready to leave and I'm planning to go along for the ride, although there would be plenty of work to do here.

Sunday, September 20, 1964

The 20th, my birthday, is nearly past, and Monday, with all its work, is really bearing down on me. I'm cranking out letters to be posted in Nairobi. I'm running mainly on coffee and cookies, I think. Even the music on the radio has stopped, and Voice of America went off the air before the Phillies finished their game with the Dodgers. But at least the Phillies had a good lead. I'm getting pleasure out of following them in their pennant aspirations, and I'm proud of them.

Tonight the ladies had a little party for me, and afterward Lydia shared 2 Corinthians 9:8 ("God is able to make all grace abound toward you; that ye, always having all sufficiency in all things, may abound to every good work," KJV) as a promise for the coming year. In medicine I have faced situations where I did not know what to do, but God, from his bounty, brought together some principles learned in school, plus necessary wisdom to deal with the problem step by step. This was particularly true in surgery when I was still so green and inexperienced and lacked self-confidence, especially in emergencies when the surgeon was absent. God has assisted me in times like this when I was at my wit's end.

Friday, October 2, 1964

Someone said to me after I arrived in Jamama, "I'm glad you brought your sense of humor along to Somalia!" It's true: without the ability to see the funny side of life, things get depressing and monotonous. Things were too often that way when I was first at Shirati and seemed unable to share my feelings with anyone there. But eventually I did discover satisfying relationships and things got brighter. So I came to Jamama somewhat initiated into these things. Oh, sometimes I still let things disturb me, especially when I've stayed put for too long. I'm due a leave now, but I won't go until December.

I thank God for a Christian dad and for the fine example you have been to me. I still remember the awe with which I heard some Bible stories from your lips for the first time. Do you remember how impressed I was when you told me about Noah and the flood? I also recall when you first told me about Ruth; maybe I was ten years old, but it really fascinated me. And I remember how you told me, when we were going to meet the bus to New York at Maple Grove almost five years ago, that before my birth you had prayed that your child might be a missionary someday. That really impressed me, and I know that your prayers continue to follow me as I endeavor to reveal something of Divine Love as I deal with physical need. So just let me say THANK-YOU for being such a fine example for my young feet. And God bless you ever.

Dad, I was really thrilled to read about your meeting Elam Stauffer. You mentioned how he shook your hand in both of his. This is the African way of greeting a special friend or one who has been absent a while. So he was expressing pleasure in meeting you.

Saturday, October 10, 1964

I am in Mogadishu tonight for a welcome change. Carl Wesselhoefts from Mahaddei and Mary Gehman from Johar visited Jamama last weekend, so I hitched a ride back with Wesselhoefts to visit the clinic in Mahaddei. Faye Miller is working there now, and it's a shame how seldom the doctor from Jamama gets there to "supervise." I was there in early February with Ivan. When I saw the chance to come with Carls, I said *kwa heri* to all the work at Jamama and left with them on Tuesday morning.

It was a long, rough trip—6:45 A.M. to 5:00 P.M. and 270 miles to get to Mogadishu; then 75 more miles to Johar and Mahaddei, where we arrived at 10:00 P.M. My tailbone was about worn through, and the muscles in the middle of my back really hurt the next day. But it was worthwhile to see some more of Somalia by daylight. It really is bushy— that is, low bushes—in the bush. And there aren't nearly as many people as in east Tanganyika, and few signs of life, except cattle at times, and lovely, colorful birds.

I spent two days with Faye at Mahaddei. I had time to walk along the river there and enjoy the scenery. It was so relaxing—though I did fall into a well! I was standing on the main path along the river, aiming to take a picture of the bridge with my camera. I stepped backward to get a different angle, and abruptly disappeared! The well was nearly four feet deep and had water in it, so I got rather muddy—including my camera. I crawled out, took off my shirt, and swooshed it around in a big puddle before putting it back on and continuing our walk. I bumped and bruised my left palm in the fall, which is why I am scribbling this letter rather than typing it. The little finger refuses to work. I will get it X-rayed at Jamama tomorrow.

While in Mahaddei I also enjoyed roast goat at a local "restaurant" after watching them slaughter the chosen animal, cut it up, then put it into a huge outdoor oven after scratching out the fire (like old-fashioned bake ovens at home). After a half hour we had delicious goat with large rolls of bread.

On Friday we came to Mogadishu, where I've done medical business, and no shopping at all for myself—not even in the Somali market

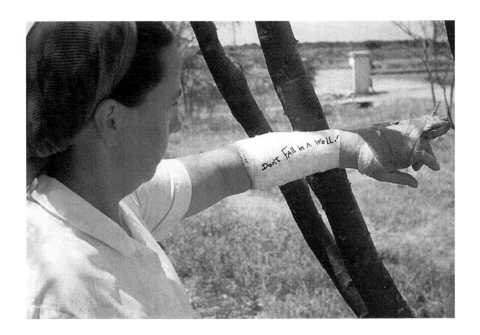

for fresh vegetables. I will fly to Chismaio early tomorrow morning and should get to Jamama in time for church.

Tuesday, October 27, 1964

I took an X-ray of my left hand when I got back to Jamama. When I fell into that well I was holding my camera in my left hand and the strap must have yanked on my little finger, because the bone in the palm leading to that finger is broken. Miriam Leaman plastered me up. At least I can still write and do some cooking, but I am glad for help with showers, and Rhoda Buckwalter does my braids. Miriam scrambled to help me do a difficult delivery last week. The baby wanted to "shake hands." It turned out to be twins and we got one living boy. I've had to postpone any major surgery for a month. I hope to repair a hernia and a few other things before I go on leave to Shirati in December.

Thursday, December 17, 1964

Greetings in our Savior's Name! Christmas is almost here and I am on holiday at Shirati. As I sit in Clyde Shenk's safari trailer, letting the morning breezes tease my hair and listening to a schoolboy play his homemade flute, I rejoice in being "back home" with my Tanganyika friends. But my mind also skips ahead to next year, when I hope to see you "at home" too. Plans were recently approved for me to begin my furlough in July 1965. Do pray that in all these plans I may know God's will. I want some formal Bible study. Can you imagine the irregular church attendance and erratic schedule of a medical student and intern added to several years of being in a country where you do not understand the language properly and so maybe get very little from the sermons? This is one missionary who has become barren and stale spiritually at times, as much work and numerous "good things" have robbed me of adequate time to pursue the "best thing." I want to do some hospital work too and have been strongly encouraged to begin a certified residency program in preparation for later board eligibility. I have always enjoyed maternity work, and in Africa I have developed much interest in surgery as well as in tuberculosis. So pray that I will find God's will as to what I shall study and where. I have given Bible study first priority for my furlough since even before I came to Shirati; in fact, I asked for a semester before coming, but there was not enough time. I still have much to learn about disciplining myself for systematic personal Bible study. As I consider all these questions, I claim again the promise of Paul in Philippians 1:16, that "the one who has begun his good work in you will go on developing it until the day of Jesus Christ." This word brings new courage to a fumbling missionary in times of discouragement, and bright hope for a young church in an unfriendly environment.

I rejoice that some who have known the Somali mission for a long time, either through employment or through our adult education programs, have come to believe in Christ. Pray also for those small groups of believers who are scattered in various places, that they may grow into a beautiful Bride of Christ. Already some locals have considerable understanding of biblical truth, and four have been chosen by the group to be leaders. One of these young men is in high school and longs to become a doctor. Pray that God may direct him in his further education, because it is not available in Somalia. He probably will have opportunity to go to Russia, and perhaps to the United States as well.

[When I knew that I would be returning to Tanzania (in October 1964 the country was renamed Tanzania to represent the April 1964 merger of Tanganyika and Zanzibar) for the 1964 Christmas holiday season, I asked if some of the Shirati folks were going on a hunting-camping trip in the Mara Valley and, if so, could I please go along? That is how I got to go on my one and only hunting-camping trip in East Africa.

It was so neat to sit by the fire in the evening and listen to the sounds of the pori while chatting with whoever else came to sit by the fire. One

day Dr. Lester shot a topi (a member of the gazelle family), so we had fresh meat from our "grille" that evening. Then he gave me the hide, which I cleaned, then got tanned—and I still have it! (My name, Dorcas, means "gazelle.")

I suspect that most trips to the pori *have* some sort of adventure or mechanical problem to make it memorable. This trip went well until we started our return journey and one of our two vehicles overheated. It was discovered that the oil level was quite low. Of course we had no extra quart of oil among our luggage, and we were still in the bush and had a steep escarpment to climb to reach Nyabasi. The only remedy was to take some oil from the other engine for the limping one. We also reduced the load on the limping vehicle. I seem to remember that a number of us walked up the escarpment. I don't remember if the limping VW Microbus got up on its own power or if the other vehicle had a chain and provided some pull-power to help it up the hill. I know we were all glad to arrive at Nyabasi, where a satisfying meal awaited us. Then we sacked out in the Mara Hills School dormitory for the night.

The next morning we spread out our wet tents in the schoolyard so they could thoroughly dry and not mildew. When the group talked about how to get our VW Microbus to Musoma for a thorough checkup and repairs, David Clemens offered to pull it with the school's Land Rover, and because I had no need to hurry back to Shirati, I volunteered to steer the Microbus. We decided to go the following day, which gave me time to keep tabs on how the numerous tents were drying out, and later that afternoon I rolled them up for their return trip to Shirati. It also gave me time to clean the inside of my topi skin.

The next day we had an early lunch. Then David Clemens produced two portions of chain plus an old tire. He ran one chain from the back of the Land Rover to the tire, and the other chain from the tire to the front of the Microbus. The tire was supposed to take up some of the slack when David accelerated without jerking me forward too quickly. With practice, I learned how to use my brakes when David slowed down or we descended a hill so that I did not get too close to his vehicle. We stopped at Tarime for gas, then proceeded down the dirt road through Utegi, where a side road goes off to Shirati. Finally we got to the Kirumi ferry, which could carry two passenger cars across the Mara River, so we did not have to unhitch the Microbus and cross with it separately.

Now we were on the final leg of our approximately one hundred mile journey, and it was late afternoon—just the time for a sudden rain shower. Most of the dirt road was firmly packed, so the rain was no problem. Then, as we came out of the rain and were just a few miles from our destination, we suddenly came upon an area where some roadwork had been done. This work consisted not of concrete or macadam patches but of loose red dirt that had been shoveled from the ditches and sides of the road up onto the driving surface. When I saw the wet dirt, I hit the brakes to slow down. But David, who was less familiar with this kind of mud and did not want to get stuck in it, kept moving, and my vehicle began to bounce up and down. I quickly got off the brakes, and fortunately all my wheels came down again. But the windshield was plastered with mud! David did slow down soon, *and after we were through the mud, he stopped and apologized pro-fusely for dragging my passenger, Danny Shenk, and me through the mud like that. We tried cleaning the windshield, but with little success. I did suggest to David that next time he came upon wet soft dirt like that he could shift down a gear or two for a slower but steady pace through the mud—please! This isn't my only "dirty story" from my Tan-zania days, but it is still good for some laughs whenever the Clemens family and I see each other.]*

Wednesday, January 13, 1965

Greetings from Jamama, where the wind is really blowing. It's winter, but still quite warm. Also dusty.

My furlough is no longer a secret! And now that I know it's coming, I'm getting sort of eager. I'm not sure exactly when I'll arrive; that de-pends on whom I have as travel companions and when we leave. If I travel with Helen Ranck (a schoolteacher at Mahaddei, more than three hundred miles from here; her sister Ethel went along with brother Paul and me to Alabama in 1953), who is due home in time for EMBMC orientation the first week of July, I will have time to do a few things this summer. But if I travel with John Leathermans, who can't leave until mid-July, it might be mid-August before I arrive. That means I can't be definite yet about my proposed US safari. I won't be very rich after my arrival, and I possibly won't have the time. Another factor is whether I bring a car. And then there is the question of whether my furlough will be one year or longer. After Paul Kraybill comes here next month, these questions of timing should be cleared up and I'll begin serious work on travel plans.

Week after next we are having a three-day missionary conference at Johar. If it is anything like the ones we had in Tanganyika it will be refreshing and stimulating, and an opportunity to get better acquainted. We Jamama folks are rather far removed from the rest, so we are espe-cially eager for it.

This is the month of Ramadan, when obedient Muslim people (except the sick, pregnant women, and nursing mothers) eat nothing from sunup to sundown, then have a big meal after dark. Some em-ployees come to work late, and patients are late too, and the census has dropped markedly—only thirty-four this morning. But it gives me a chance to do some other necessary things, including book work.

Friday, January 29, 1965

Greetings to you all from Harold Stauffer's dining room table here in Mogadishu. All of us except Miriam Leaman have forsaken Jamama for a week and left her with the stuff. We took off in the Land Rover on Sunday after dinner and bounced ourselves to Mogadishu in around eight hours. The road was dry but rather bumpy and rough at the lower end. Rhoda Buckwalter and I got to do some driving, and that helped me. It is something how tender the bottom of the spine gets when you bounce around on it for several hours; mine felt like it needed the tip filed off a bit, but I didn't have a file along and was too tired to make one, so I just "rutsched around" and survived. After driving a while and leaning a bit forward over the wheel, I did feel better. And I feel fine now!

On Monday we went shopping here in Mogadishu for some tinned things and some cheese to take along. After an early supper, we went out to Johar, where we spent the next three days in a missionary conference. In several sessions we thought about Christianity and Islam: what they have in common, the contrasts, and how we can best approach the Muslim to share information and learn from each other as friends— more like "how to win friends and influence people" rather than a direct, formal witness approach. I recognized how woefully ignorant I am of the religion of Islam, and I found these sessions very helpful. We also had a very thought-provoking book study on Philippians. I was impressed again that Christ is all I need. I may think that what I need is a more effective prayer life, better Bible study habits, more patience, and so on (or a semester of Bible study during furlough). But this is all beside the point. All I need is Christ—to open myself and let Him be all to me. ("But my God shall supply all your need according to his riches in glory by Christ Jesus," Philippians 4:19; and "For to me to live is Christ, and to die is gain," Philippians 1:21.)

Last evening we had a communion service that was quite impressive. First, Dave Shenk spoke about Christ being the Bread of Life, from John 6. Then each person gave testimony as to what Christ is teaching us, followed by communion and feet washing. It was wonderful just to be together, get better acquainted, and have fun and fellowship. I even played some Ping-Pong. I also enjoyed an auction for Dave Miller's things that were not sent home. I was delighted to get a travel iron, which will be useful for coming home and for any other safari that might materialize.

We plan to return to Jamama tomorrow. I do hope I'll find some mail. There has been a noticeable increase since I announced my forthcoming furlough, and I am enjoying it. Folks here have encouraged the idea of buying a car, and it would be nice for travel in Europe, and cheaper. Helen Ranck and I, who are thinking of traveling together, are interested in the same itinerary, except she doesn't want to cross the

Atlantic by boat, and if I find no other companion, I just might agree to fly along with her rather than go by boat by myself, because I can't see any special pleasure in that.

Friday, February 12, 1965

I reckon you've heard that cousin Nora has offered to finance a VW for me, so I am making plans to get a Bug. I haven't decided on the color yet. By this time next week I should know just when I can leave. I hear that Ivan Leamans are returning to Jamama in May, but I see no need for a lengthy overlap after they arrive. If this trip materializes, I hope to get back earlier than mid-August so I can have a little time at home and get ready for the safari and for school and not dash off directly after my arrival. And if I fly across the Atlantic instead of coming by ship, I will need to wait several weeks for the car to arrive in the States; if so, maybe the car pickup can be combined with seeing the World's Fair.

I got involved in a big fight on Sunday night after church, and I have the black and blue marks to prove it—even bled some too. I got the worst of the bargain from my small but vicious opponent; in fact, I did not see any bruises on Tammy. The thing was, she wasn't very receptive to my idea that she move herself and her family to a new abode, and she literally fought it tooth and nail. She even tried to run away, leaving her family with me, but I grabbed her and in desperation plunged her into a basket and rolled the top down like the end of a paper bag over a loaf of bread. I then carried her into the bedroom and, after preparing a nice home for her family (who were carried in another basket and thus escaped the fight), I set the basket on the floor and quickly pulled the door shut behind me as I retreated to the bedroom. This fight occurred right on Main Street in Jamama, but it was after dark and the street lights were few, so I hope the fight wasn't too public. She is still suspicious, but she's been outside twice, and tonight she came in eagerly by herself as I held the door open with one hand and a squealing kitten in the other. Yes, Tammy is a pretty yellow, gray, and white cat whose previous owners moved away on Monday. The family included a fine teacher from our school, and a valuable dresser-translator-laboratory assistant from our hospital. We really do miss this fine Arab family.

Friday, February 26, 1965

I've just cleaned the globe, trimmed the wick, and filled the tank of my you-know-what, so I should be ready for the generator to call it a day.

Today I did a number of things, like boil up another pot of drinking water and change my bedding (Friday is our "Saturday" for household chores). I went to the village to "look around" but didn't buy anything—and I slept this afternoon and woke up before I intended to get up, so I read a while. And I didn't get my hair washed, and it surely needs it.

Tonight we had supper together at Reeds' house. (My contribution? Ice cubes and a good appetite! But this is to be a turn-about affair, so my turn will come.) Afterward we had a prayer meeting in which we shared requests from our other stations and prayed for our own needs.

I did something else today too: I started sorting out my stuff, planning what can go into a barrel *now* to go home and what will be packed later for when I return to Tanzania and what I will want to travel home with. Miriam Leaman and I are packing a barrel together, with our sewing machines and recorders and so on. My recorder has a hum and needs to have the Somali dust cleaned out of it, so it may as well go home, although I do hate to give it up already as I have been enjoying listening to tapes.

Tentative plans are for me to travel with Helen Ranck and arrive home in time for the firecrackers on the 4th of July. But it's not the firecrackers we're looking forward to so much. We are aiming to attend orientation at Salunga on July 5th. I think this is really an opportune way to get oriented to being back in the States and to decrease the culture shock of wearing nylons and those hot, restrictive girdles, and in general trying to look like and be a "good Lancaster County Mennonite" again—if such a thing is at all possible or feasible. To start my furlough in the company of other furloughed as well as newly appointed missionaries will be a treat. I have sent in my application to go to EMC next year and I'm really looking forward to that, even though I know it will be far different from ten years ago.

The summer is still pretty much open, except I have been invited by Dr. Samuel Bucher to spend a week at Harman, West Virginia, while he and his family take a short vacation to visit family in Pennsylvania and to rest. (Of course it would give me a little do-re-mi.) And maybe I can get to the Mennonite Medical Association meeting. And I've been invited to visit Sam Millers; if I go, I'd like to stay a little longer this time. And of course there are reunions—especially the Stahl reunion.

Sunday, February 28, 1965

About ten days ago—Wednesday before last—Paul Kraybill flew into Chismaio in the morning with an import license so that we could retrieve from customs the medicines that MAF had brought from Nairobi on January 2. We have waited patiently all these weeks for these medicines, and when Paul arrived we finally got them! Harold Reed met him there and they got back here at noon. Meanwhile, the Mission Council members and Dave Shenks were traveling overland and got here at about 5:00 P.M. It was nice that Paul came by plane; it gave him time to visit before the others arrived, and he was less tired.

So, Wednesday evening was interview time and mine was scheduled for 5:00. I marvel every time how Paul makes his visits so refreshing and meaningful, how he is so interested in each of us personally—as if nothing or no one else in the whole world mattered. He naturally wondered how I like Somalia, how it compares with Shirati, and so on. I admitted that it had been very nice to be back there for Christmas. But I have enjoyed Somalia too. As I see it, there are two major differences: clinic work here is mostly routine and without the diversity of inpatient problems to stimulate and challenge one in dealing with new situations. I was never enthused about clinic anyway, especially when most communication must go through an interpreter. Also, there is no safari work here to break the routine and provide that welcome chance to get away and see something and someone different. I have gotten used to it by now, but I told him that from mid-April to August 1 I was not away from the Jamama environs, so I get "buggy" sometimes. And I had no Suzie to take me for a spin and clear the cobwebs from my brain. If I go back to Shirati I will surely need another Suzie!

We also talked about my furlough plans and proposed residency. He encouraged me to take a year at EMC (not just a semester as I had hesitantly hoped) to study Bible. He also said I should investigate residency work and keep him informed, and he felt I should count on at least a year for that. They will probably get another doctor to replace Eshleman, so I could have even longer, until Housmans are due for furlough again. We also discussed furlough travel, how Helen Ranck and I are interested in the same places, and so on. She is due home for orientation whereas I was given permission to leave in July, but Paul said that Ivans are returning in May and would need no detailed introduction to the work, so we need not overlap much. So, if Council agrees, I can travel with her. I also felt I should go to orientation this year too, because if I get into a residency the following July, it will doubtless be impossible to attend orientation then.

After talking about the hospital work, we kept on going. He asked about my folks. I showed him a recent picture of you all with Ruthie, and one of Anna Mary and Leonard. He surely does remember people! I did tell him that one wonderful thing at Jamama that Shirati was often short on was friends who took time to talk and listen when a person is "buggy" instead of letting a person stew until the lid blasts off. Truly, the privilege of venting frustration as well as joy and plain frivolity is precious! My sense of humor was pretty shriveled at Shirati for a long time. Nonetheless, I look forward to returning to Tanzania.

After our chat, we toured the hospital with Wilbert Lind and Harold Reed. We have remodeled some since Ivans left, especially by the re-arrangement to accommodate the X-ray room, making, I think, more efficient use of our space.

On Friday morning I entertained Paul and Bert for breakfast—grapefruit, scrambled eggs, toast, and coffee. Fortunately I had received a gift of eggs the day before; I used them all that morning and haven't gotten any since. So I've been eating shredded wheat that I brought along from Nairobi, but that will soon be finished. If I ever get eggs again, I can have fried eggs with fried potatoes. Don't worry! I'm not getting as skinny as I'd like to be yet! We received a lot of limes the other day, so I'm drinking limeade often.

Saturday, March 6, 1965

The work here is quite routine these days. I did do a big hernia repair last week and hope to do several small knee operations this week. One boy has had pus draining from above his knee for two years! It is not a usual bone infection and may be caused by tuberculosis.

So time passes—only three months to go! Ivans return sometime in May, and then Miriam Leaman, Harold Reeds, and I all go on furlough this summer. We are working to pack up several barrels of stuff to send soon by boat. I do not relish this work!

The days are getting warmer here and there are some clouds around but not rain yet. I reckon it will get hotter first because the winds stop before the cooling rains come and the bugs arrive. It will be nice to drink rainwater again; the "city water" from the reservoir is so salty that the salt settles out to the bottom after I boil a pot of it for drinking. Nowadays we are receiving limes as gifts and drinking lots of limeade, which hides the salty taste quite well.

It's Monday morning now and I must finish this letter before running off to work. The weekend was busy. On Friday afternoon I was tired but went along to visit in the village anyway. On Saturday afternoon an Italian lady was to bring her baby for a three-in-one shot but didn't come, so I did other stuff and then helped with several X-rays. A visitor from MCC in Indonesia came to spend the weekend with Lydia Glick, so I was over there to see her pictures. We finished off the evening with some games and coffee, plus Somali cake to celebrate Lena Horning's birthday.

I had planned to sleep in yesterday morning but an Italian man fell out of a tree and came in with a sore back. I also relieved a man who was having difficulty passing urine. Thus I missed Sunday school. After dinner I took two X-rays of the Italian man's back and found, as I'd thought, no fracture, so I gave him pills and such. In the afternoon I didn't really sleep but was able to read a bit. I got up at 4:00 P.M. to hear the Mennonite Hour from the Philippines and then made mint tea for our picnic out under the mango trees near the river. And before I got off to church last evening, a lady came to deliver a tiny baby. She had not felt movement for a month and was only seven months pregnant, so it did not take long for her to deliver. I did miss out on our guest's talk about MCC's agricultural work in Indonesia, which I am told was very interesting. I arrived soon after church had finished and was able to look at slides. I crawled into bed at 9:45 and read for a while. After I went to sleep I was awakened by someone biting me, so I got out the torch and bomb spray and finally found him in the upper corner of the net. I let him have a blast, then went back to sleep.

Friday, March 12, 1965

I've waited for a letter from Menno Travel Service. The worst possibility is that someone stole the stamps and ditched the letter, so I just wrote another one, asking for definite information on paying for the car.

I am daydreaming a bit these days, when I have a chance, about our summer plans. This week has been busy for a change, with more X-rays, lots of teeth extractions, and even three deliveries. One of those was a little stillborn child who died sometime before the onset of labor. The other two babies are quite healthy, though one of the mothers would have had great difficulty if she had not come to the hospital, because even with special injections and forceps we both had to sweat a little to get her little girl out.

Monday, March 29, 1965

At long last, a letter again from me. I'm playing hooky from clinic for a while to do this. We are busier these days, with surgery and X-rays keeping my afternoons full. Plus there is that never-ending job of packing! If I had another barrel I could fill it. I already have one full one waiting at Shirati, and I need the second one to put my kitchenware in and send to Shirati too. Others have generously offered room in their barrels but, as I expected, the space left was only about a quarter of what was promised. So I have stuff scattered in barrels and in a box belonging to two people, plus a wooden box of mine that I filled with books. I also started some parcels and have two ready to go, with my tape recordings and my brown overnight bag, sleeping bag, and so on. The other two parcels are begun. I have sorted out well what clothes I will use to travel home and what will be returned to Shirati. I'm wearing my old clothes already and I'll have a heap of rags by the end of May! But I'm not even throwing away rags at this point, because I can use them to pack my dishes and such. I'm trying not to think about how I will get all my stuff rounded up again, especially because the others won't get home until late August, when I'll be on safari and then running off to school. I have been accepted at EMC into the seminary's missions course, and I am really looking forward to it!

Yesterday was one of those days! I even got up a half-hour earlier than I usually do on Sundays because a really sick woman—in shock and vomiting—was admitted the night before. When I came to see her she was so-so, and we finally got a blood pressure we could hear last evening. I also had to do a finger dressing on Sunday that I could not do on Saturday night because the boy went to sleep before I got around to him at 9:30 and I did not have the heart to wake him up and hurt him! A week ago he had gotten the third and fourth fingers of his right hand caught in a cog wheel that had nicely chewed up the ends. This work plus checking on a new maternity patient made me miss half of Sunday school and Mzee Elisha's teaching from the Sermon on the Mount. I always enjoy hearing him teach in Swahili.

Before I got dinner on my plate after church, a bushman came with some things to sell, so I bargained with him for a while. After dinner I went out again and checked on the OB patient (her first baby but she's a fat woman who doesn't exercise any). I ruptured her membranes to try to speed things up a little. Just then a man arrived with the end of the fourth finger of his right hand chopped off. I cleaned it up carefully, then swiped some skin from his upper arm and sewed it over the bare end of his finger. I finally got to go to my house for about a half hour to work on packing. I gave up trying to listen to the Mennonite Hour (terrible static for the first time in a long time). I went back to the hospital and had to resort to giving injections to the fat lady to get on with having her baby. She finally delivered at around 6:00 P.M. but wasn't yet finished. She decided not to clamp down her uterus and instead gushed blood at me several times. We gave her more injections while I mashed on her tummy. She was telling me to get out but I finally put some cloth packing in and she stopped bleeding—or at least I couldn't see anything red. Before we got her back to bed, a young boy who had gotten his heel caught in the wheel of a bicycle was brought in. I cleaned him up—he didn't like that; nor did he like the injections I gave him for pain, so we had some four-year-old music for a while. Finally, after 8:00 P.M., I had some supper, painted my address on the box of books I had prepared to ship, and invited myself to have some coffee. But before the coffee was poured, the hospital called to say that our fat woman had a blood puddle in her bed, so I went out and mashed her tummy again (which she still didn't appreciate) and ordered more injections. Then, naturally, I went back to my coffee. I was tired when I got home but did finish the packages I was preparing before calling it a day at about 12:30 A.M.

Sunday, April 11, 1965

Somehow tonight as I try to concentrate on writing this letter, my mind prefers to daydream instead. Daydream?! Yes! Because, well, it's like this: I'm trying to imagine what it will be like to be "home" again. To renew old friendships and meet new relatives. To face the whirl of so many things to do and places to go. To anticipate meeting my sister and our friend at Red Lake, Ontario, in mid-August and then meandering across the West together for three weeks. To return to Eastern Mennonite College for some solid Bible study. To shiver delightfully in a silent snowstorm, and even to hope I get snowed in again! To later begin residency training—probably in OB-GYN, although general surgery may be a possibility. And eventually to return to Africa and be more effective in treating the medical and spiritual needs of my patients.

To be more specific about my plans, Helen Ranck and I expect to leave from Mogadishu around June 12. We plan to visit in Ethiopia, then pick up my new VW at the airport in Germany, then go sightseeing in Germany, Switzerland, and Holland before arriving in New York and traveling by train to Lancaster late on Saturday, July 3rd—just in time for the fireworks and to attend orientation week at Salunga. Maybe you thought orientation is for folks who are about to leave for an overseas assignment, and that is basically true, but I suspect that this week at Salunga will measurably ease the jolt of returning home, because Shirati and Jamama have also become home to me. And I will discover that some changes have occurred in Lancaster County during my absence. And I will probably have forgotten some details of how things were when I left, so I should prepare to make some adjustments in dealing with new and unfamiliar situations at home. But I am confident that just as God has directed me through various unfamiliar situations in the past, so He will continue to lead me in the future.

Regarding our work here at Jamama, our clinic census has recently dropped even though the local rains have not yet begun. Fewer patients are coming in from the bush. But several weeks ago I had a different experience. I was in the midst of our morning clinic when I received a message from a believer who lives ten miles down the road toward Kismayu. His daughter was having trouble with the birth of her first child. He was unable to find someone in their village with a vehicle to bring her to our hospital, so he asked if we could help. Miriam Leaman prepared the emergency kit with supplies, and Rhoda Buckwalter and I were soon on our way in our Land Rover. We greeted the men outside the house and were ushered inside. Someone opened the one tiny window in the fairly large room; I was then able to see that the mother was being supported in an upright position by two women, one on each side, and the village midwife was seated at the mother's feet.

We greeted all of the women. I then asked if the mother might lie down on the bed, and they agreed. My examination revealed that the baby's head was presenting, so I decided to attempt my first at-home delivery. I asked Rhoda to give the mother an injection to improve her contractions. One of the women kept incense burning by the window. As we waited, I chatted with the older women in Swahili. I explained that when the mother's membranes ruptured before she was in active labor, the umbilical cord had slipped down into the vagina in front of the baby's head, and the baby would be stillborn. The village midwife agreed with my prediction. When delivery was imminent, Rhoda opened the sterile supplies and I pulled on a pair of gloves. The midwife watched closely and gave her verbal encouragement as I delivered the infant. She was rather surprised to see me use some local anesthesia to make an episiotomy and later repair it, but she accepted my explanation that this was to protect the mother from lacerations and prolonged labor and to ensure good healing.

After I had managed to stand up straight again (the bed was quite low so I'd had to do some bending), we packed up the used instruments and supplies. We washed our hands and gave the patient our sympathy on the death of her firstborn son. We were then invited into another room, where a recently married sister of the patient served us delicious tea and some lovely Somali cake. We said good-bye to everyone and as we left we thanked God for this opportunity to be with our friend and his family in this time of need. We were also grateful that the village women had accepted our suggestions so that we could help the mother at home and spare the family the expense of hospital care.

[*More than forty years later, let me explain something about this letter. I deliberately did not name the father of the mother whose baby I delivered in their village home. Instead, I identified him as a believer without using his Christian name because I had been warned that our outgoing letters might be "inspected" by the local authorities to see if we were trying to proselytize their people. I probably should not even have said he was a believer—I could have called him a friend—but I knew the folks at home would get it.*

This father—we knew him as Elisha but in the village he used a tribal name—had been led to faith in Christ by Swedish Lutheran missionaries who had begun working in eastern Kenya along the Jubba River in 1896, and he had remained a believer. The family lived in the town of Zunguni, just east of the Jubba River and ten miles south of Jamama. This area was ceded to Italian Somaliland by the Treaty of Versailles in 1925, but the Lutheran missionaries continued their ministry until Mussolini, Italy's fascist premier, expelled them in 1935.

Our first Mennonite missionaries, Wilbert and Rhoda Lind and their young son Daniel, arrived in Mogadishu in January 1953. Faye Miller and Caroline Plank arrived two months later. Schools were soon developed north of Mogadishu at Mahaddei and later at Johar. Then, in July 1957, Victor and Viola Dorsch and their family along with builder Roy Shirk and his wife traveled in a convoy of three vehicles 265 miles south of Mogadishu. They moved into rented quarters in Margherita, now Jamama. The Dorsches soon began teaching English classes in the town and made visits to the riverine villages of the former Swedish missions. In July 1958, a five-member deputation team of Tanganyika Mennonites visited Jamama to explore teaching in Swahili-speaking villages.

A garage apartment, three houses, a clinic, and a three-room school were built over the next year and longer. The Dorsch house, with its fairly large living room, became the site for the Sunday worship services. A few Somalis, including Elisha and his wife, and two Bantu couples from Mofi, which was three miles from Jamama (if the boat is used to cross the river) often attended the service. The Dorsches obtained copies of the Swahili Songbook Tenzi za Rohoni to use with Tabitha and the other Bantus as they met under the mango tree near the river. When I came to Jamama in February 1964, I got to know all these folks as my brothers and sisters in Christ.]

I ask you to pray that in our contacts with our few scattered friends we may experience a deepening fellowship of walking together in the light that Christ brings to us. Words cannot express what your prayer support has meant to me personally during the years I have spent here in Tanzania and Somalia. I will appreciate your continued prayers that during furlough I may ever seek His will and be a faithful steward for my Lord. I look forward to seeing you all again in several months

Sunday, April 18, 1965

Voice of America has a good program of Easter music on as I type; they just sang, "Sing alleluia, the Lord is risen!"

We have been sweltering this past week. The rains are late. There has been some rain in the area, and we even got the smell of fresh rain-washed air the other morning, and a little patter on the roof several days ago, but there has been no rain worth talking about yet. Last night it was so hot and quiet that I woke up around 4:00 A.M. and slept very little thereafter. It's not common for me to sleep a whole night nowadays without waking up at least once, or more. But the wind really blows at midday, so I really sleep in the afternoon—*if* the men aren't too noisy building the piece onto my apartment to make it big enough for two people, and if I get finished in clinic before so late.

The past week was busy. Tuesday was a holiday in memory of the death of Mohammed, the Muslim prophet, so we closed clinic and let several Somali nurse aides take care of the hospital while we all took off for Chismaio. Just off the shore of Chismaio is an island that can be walked out to during low tide. An American company and the US government have built a road to the island and are constructing a big pier off the far end of the island into the deep water so that larger ships have a place to dock and unload their cargo. This port will really put Chismaio on the map. Even Mogadishu has much less port potential because it has no natural island or sheltered area for ships, so they must unload way out in the ocean using baskets to transfer the cargo onto smaller boats. During certain seasons (December to January), when the strong wind is from the northeast, they often cannot unload for several weeks because of the rough seas. But the island off Chismaio will be a sheltered place for ocean ships.

After we arrived, we picked up a lady from the port construction project, went down the coast, and went shell hunting on a lovely beach all by ourselves. When the tide started coming in, we packed up and returned to Chismaio, where we went swimming on the wide sandy beach across from the island until lunchtime. After we ate with our hostess, we sat in her air-conditioned kitchen and played Scrabble.

On Wednesday a man came to Jamama hospital with a broken collar bone and broken left upper arm. On Thursday a man came with a broken leg, so I fixed up the big overhead frame bed for him. On Friday another man came in with a broken upper arm. So this has been orthopedics week. In addition, on Thursday morning I operated on a boy who had polio with weakness of the left leg that was so bad he had been crawling around on his hands and knees, and his knee tendons had gotten tight. After exercising him for two weeks to stretch things, I operated to lengthen the tight tissues and applied casts. Well, he decided to swell and his casts got tight, so I made windows in them. But his feet continued to swell and frankly yesterday I was worried. I had thought his feet would be OK, but the previous night I had split the cast to two inches from the top and found that his feet were still cold and blue. But he is getting more color and warmth in them today. He still has much swelling in the knee of his good leg, opposite the operation side. I really prayed for him, because chronic lack of good blood supply for some hours can have dangerous results. His left leg is still weak, but I hope to get him walking with crutches or a cane. I helped a girl with a similar contracture of just one knee from a tuberculosis infection and she walked again, so I really hope things will turn out OK for Abdi.

So, with the heat and all the bone problems, plus a slight cold and loss of sleep, is it any wonder that I felt pooped all day today?

On Friday afternoon I went with Reeds and the teachers to Chismaio again. There are a few families there who meet on Fridays for worship and at their request the Reeds go once a month to conduct the service for them. I had gone one time before. There were two couples plus five men in attendance. Afterward, we went down to listen to the ocean, then to a southern couple's veranda for a delicious supper of cold sliced gazelle meat, stuffing, tossed salad, potato salad, cranberry sauce, and banana butterscotch pudding. As we ate we watched a gorgeous full moon rise out of the ocean. Beautiful!

We had Easter service today with communion and were very happy to have a believer from Mogadishu with us. I really slept this afternoon and have a little more oomph tonight.

Sunday, May 2, 1965

Greetings to you on a warm, quiet evening. At times a cool breeze meanders in the window, but we're not having the cold rainy spring weather yet. It was very hot over Easter. I almost thought I'd melt. It was too hot to sleep right, and I had no appetite, and no oomph either. We did have two lovely showers last week and a little rain yesterday—only enough to cover the bottom of the rain barrel. But I had collected from the first rain, so I could boil up drinking water.

Sometimes it has been hard to write letters from Jamama, because the work is so much the same from day to day and folks may get tired of hearing how many people come to clinic. And there's no safari work and very few visitors, so there's not much to write about—though recently I can write about coming home! I can hardly believe it's only two months away. I am really looking forward to it.

Our group here at Jamama is quite small these days since the two teachers and Rhoda Buckwalter went on holiday, leaving only Miriam Leaman and me here with the Reeds. We are still seeing around fifty clinic patients daily, and our inpatient census has been higher than usual the past month. In one week, three people came in with broken bones—two arms and one leg. I've also done a few hernia and hemorrhoid operations. Several Arab ladies have decided to have their operations done before the man doctor returns! Which reminds me: Leamans are planning to leave New York today, to arrive in Nairobi on Wednesday and then in Mogadishu on Saturday. I haven't heard what day they will come to Jamama, but they will doubtless spend several days up north. We will certainly welcome them back.

I am in the throes of packing and hope to get moved over with Miriam within several days so that the men can start tearing around in this apartment. They have the walls up for the new bedrooms and bath, but not the roof yet. They need to put the kitchen into what is my bedroom, and to make a new window in the living room. And they have to have it ready soon for the nurses to move in. But there will probably be five of us girls in a tiny four-bedroom house for a bit after the girls return from holiday and until I shove off for Mogadishu.

Friday, May 14, 1965

Greetings on a lovely evening. It's been a busy day and I'm tired. It's supposed to be the rainy season but we haven't gotten very wet yet—not enough to make the grass green or to sprout the trees. In fact, they got the men to come in again to haul water by donkey cart to the trees. At least the wind isn't blowing from the south and east, so the weather is bearable. When I get home I'd really like to help with the garden again, as well as eat the produce. We don't get many fresh vegetables here, and I've almost forgotten what a tossed salad is like.

Ivans will be heading north to help organize a famine medical team for several weeks until the MCC team arrives, so they probably will not get to Jamama until about June 4. I could probably go to Mogadishu by car on June 3, but I reckon I'll stay until after Ivans arrive, to give him a tour around the place (we women changed a few things, there are new employees, the X-ray machine was installed, some remodeling was done, and so on). Then I will probably fly to Mogadishu on June 7 and maybe visit the Sudan Interior Mission stations before leaving with Helen Ranck on the 13th—which is only a month from yesterday! And when I get home, I hope the weather is nice on the 4th so our family can have a picnic in the woods. And I'm hungry for sour cherry pie and homemade ice cream. And green beans and ham. And fresh peaches come August!

These years in Africa have been good ones—though not everything was easy. Anybody who worked with me knows the frustrations and failures, but I have learned some things too about how sinful I am and how much I need to depend on the Lord for everything rather than assume that I am capable of dealing with a given situation by myself. The time has not been long as I think of being separated from you all, for I was busy in my new relationships. But as I think of all that has happened in this period and the many experiences of living in two quite different communities, it has been a very educational and broadening experience to see how others live. I realize that things have not been at a standstill at home either. I hope I don't get dizzy trying to integrate myself into home affairs and EMC school life.

Thursday, June 17, 1965

I am writing from the Nazareth station, sixty-two miles southeast of Addis Ababa, Ethiopia. I have just made rounds with Dr. Vernon Kratz, whom I knew in Philadelphia and at EMC. His wife is Elizabeth Nolt, who taught at LMS.

I want to tell you about leaving Jamama. Dr. Ivan did drop in for a weekend visit. He arrived on June 4 and on Saturday morning I showed him around, including the X-ray room and new drug room. I even got him to see some clinic patients. We had a business meeting on Saturday afternoon to discuss new contracts for our employees, then had a staff meeting with the employees to welcome Dr. Ivan back and to introduce the new employees; we'd had a large turnover, with one man going to Aden (in Yemen), another going to nursing school, and another running off to elsewhere in East Africa. We had also hired five new people, which brought us to thirteen.

After all the introductions and business, they made speeches for my departure! It was sort of amusing; when one leaves, the Somali people can lavish on praise for one's work even if they sometimes felt otherwise and if the praise was not completely deserved. But it did make me feel rather good to hear them express appreciation and welcome me to come back again.

On Saturday night we missionaries had dinner at the restaurant, which was nice. On Sunday afternoon I finished reading all the X-rays and completed all the chart work. I managed to discharge all but five patients before I left (including a girl with tuberculosis of the hip who had been there almost a year; she did not want to go). I also arranged to transfer one patient to Chismaio for future surgery. He'd been bitten by a snake one month before admission and had been getting sulfa powder from a dresser, but the foot had started smelling bad, so he came looking for different treatment. I had removed the large bones going to the toes and cleaned the foot, but it was not definitively ready for surgery to close the wound so he could walk.

On Sunday evening we had a picnic and enjoyed hearing Ivan tell about their trip home through Europe—which made me feel rather eager to go. Later that evening, because there were guests, we could not have church, but we girls felt like singing anyway, so we borrowed the organ from Reeds and made a joyful noise for a while.

On Monday morning, June 7, I did several dressings and drew some tables for X-ray, which I'd meant to do months ago! So I was at it until nearly noon. After lunch, Rhoda accompanied Reed and his daughter Grace and I to Chismaio to meet the plane, which was late. The rains had finally started about a week before, but the odiferous carcasses of animals were still evident along the road. (Several weeks before, Reed had gone to our local airstrip to meet a plane from Mogadishu and had found several weak cows on the airstrip, obstructing it so that the plane could not land. A man was nearby and Reed asked him to move the cows. He replied that they could not move. Sure enough, the cows made feeble attempts to stand but were unable to do so. Finally, with the assistance of a third man, they managed to roll the cows like sausages to get them off the strip so that the plane could land. I had never quite realized before just what a gift rain is, or how dependent a country like Somalia is on rain.)

The plane arrived at Chismaio and in the midst of a quick shower I got on it. Within an hour and a half, thanks to a strong tailwind, we touched down in Mogadishu. Danny Wert had arrived the preceding Saturday and would not be moving on until Friday, so he and I left on Tuesday at noon to go to the Johar and Mahaddei stations. I was glad to see Ivan's wife, Mary Ellen, and children at Johar. We returned to Mogadishu on Thursday at noon. I did some laundry and wrote some essential letters.

Ivan stayed at Jamama until Wednesday the 9th. Dr. Housman and his wife and daughters were due to arrive the next day by MAF. I was so sorry they could not come sooner so that I could orient them to the Jamama ropes, and chat with Miriam again.

On Saturday evening the Mahaddei folks were in Mogadishu and we had a pizza supper together on Harold Stauffers' porch. Afterward, we looked at some slides of Helen Ranck's and mine. The next morning I was up at 4:30. (Imagine! Honestly, I still do not enjoy getting up at such horrible hours, and I still get teased about it. But I can manage to do it if I *must!*) By 5:30 we were off to the airport and we took off soon after 6:30. It was a big Italian jet—my first jet ride—and very nice. Shortly after 8:00 A.M. we landed in Aden, Yemen. Aden is across the gulf from Somalia where the Red Sea and Arabian Sea meet. It is an important shipping post, especially for oil from the Arab world. A bustling city, it is quite dependent on British businesses to keep its economy booming. It is hot here and much like Somalia, with camels even on the main street. We walked across the street to watch the ships unloading. That night at dinner on the top floor of our air-conditioned hotel it was really something to see the lights of the ships in the harbor, the airport lights in the distance, the car lights crossing the causeway of the harbor, and so on.

We were met at the Aden airport by two brothers, Muhsin and Bombelo, who used to live in Jamama and were employed there by the mission. If you are a faithful reader of *Missionary Messenger,* you may remember Lena Horning's article published several months ago about a teacher named Muhsin. Bombelo was my right-hand man at Jamama—translating in clinic, writing some orders, pulling teeth, doing lab work, and helping in surgery. The brothers are Arabs and left Somalia in February after the government threatened to withhold merchant licenses from shops and businesses that did not have Somalis in them. Of course many of the Arabs in Somalia are shopkeepers, and a number of them left the country as a result. I had written to tell Bombelo we were coming. After taking us to the hotel (provided at the airline's expense), they took us to visit the big hospital (four hundred beds) where Bombelo is working in the lab and learning many new tests that he had never heard about at Jamama. We also saw the clinic and met a lady doctor who kindly took us to visit the children's ward. It really is a nice hospital—air conditioned in many areas—and I enjoyed seeing it.

I had hoped to do some shopping in Aden but there wasn't enough time. We did, however, get to see where the brothers and their families live. I was pleased to meet Bombelo's wife, whom he married in Mogadishu after he left us in February. I also especially enjoyed meeting their lovely mother, and Bombelo's four children. They all live together in a rented double house of concrete with a flat roof that has high side walls so that they can eat in privacy on the roof. As you may know, Arab women must wear their black *shuka* and veil over their face when they go outside or if a man who is not a family member comes by. Naturally they are leery of having their picture taken too, but because the walls around their roof are so high, they let us take several pictures, to my great pleasure.

On Monday morning we took off at 10:00 (a more sensible hour, though it was already very hot by then) for Djibouti in French Somaliland, and after a short layover we flew on to Dire Dawa in Ethiopia. The Ethiopian missionaries had had their annual conference in Addis Ababa that weekend. One nurse had stayed at the Deder hospital, and Robert Garbers were to return there on Monday to properly welcome the area governor, who had sent word that he would visit their hospital and school. So it worked out that they waited in Dire Dawa for us and we went together to Deder—a lovely two-hour drive into the mountains on good roads with lots of hairpin turns (which really reminded me of Virginia and northern Pennsylvania). Deder is over eight thousand feet above sea level, so it's wonderful for sleeping, and I had a chance to wear my corduroy coat again—like seeing a long-lost friend.

The governor arrived about an hour and a half after we did and was a big man. The nurse and the Garbers were honored to attend a feast in his honor that evening (Monday). On Tuesday evening the other nurse and Rohrer Eshlemans returned from conference. It was good to see the Eshlemans again; they had come to fill in while Dr. Burkholders were on holiday. We all ate together and afterward Rohrer ostensibly wanted to talk with me about medicine in Africa. So, first he went to the nurses' house and helped put the children to bed. Then he came back and we spent all but maybe ten to fifteen minutes of two hours talking about their conference. Don Jacobs had been a guest speaker and God had blessed the messages. I rejoiced to hear about it. You know, missionaries are expected to be models of Christian behavior, of fellowshipping together, but we "ain't all that way" sometimes. It is so easy to get busy with good things and thereby ignore the best, or to feel that the other person doesn't appreciate our work or isn't doing his or her share, and so on. Thus barriers arise and one's work becomes barren and routine. I have experienced too much of this. I was thus glad to hear about new lessons in brokenness and sharing among God's people. I enjoyed that news more than "shop talk."

Yesterday morning we returned to Dire Dawa, where we eagerly chatted with Mary Gehman, who is passing through en route to Jamama, where she will teach. We also walked around town a bit and looked into their nice shops, including the Mennonite bookstore. Last evening we (Mary Ellen Groff from Deder, Helen, and I) got on the train before 8:00 and traveled all night to Nazareth. We arrived at the mission at 6:15 A.M., in time to get them out of bed! We rode second class and slept in sleeping bags, one of us on each of the compartment's two facing benches and I on the floor. We all slept some. In fact, I don't feel nearly as tired today as I did yesterday.

After breakfast this morning I washed up from top to bottom (except for my hair), then went to the hospital to tag along with Dr. Kratz on rounds. I also visited the clinic and was impressed with how efficient it is compared to the two others I am familiar with. The hospital itself is a converted warehouse and nothing spectacular in terms of layout, but it has lots of light. The clinic is rather new and well planned for efficient movement of many patients. After coffee, I returned to the house and helped myself to Millie Hiestand's typewriter to compose this long-overdue letter.

It is now 4:15 P.M. We visitors had dinner with Nathan Gingrich (a brother to Mrs. John Brennemann). I've also had a wonderful two-hour sleep and plan to go out soon to visit the Academy. I just watched a real dust wind go by. Somalia can be very dusty and windy, but I never before saw the two combined to kick up such a mess!

We have just hatched plans to visit the P. T. Yoders. He preached my farewell sermon about the prophet's mantle and is a brother to Amos Yoder. P. T. and his wife and four children live three hours back along the railroad track toward Dire Dawa. We plan to leave here at 11:00 P.M. with our sleeping bags, to arrive at Awash by train at 2:00 A.M., and then to return here tomorrow afternoon. P. T. also spoke at Mary Ellen and Helen's farewell, so they too are eager to go. I am really looking forward to this. It is best that we came on to Nazareth last night and will go back to Awash tonight or we could have missed seeing the students here because they have a picnic scheduled for tomorrow. We plan to get to Addis Ababa on Saturday, to see Mary Ellen Umble and the rest. On Monday we fly on to Frankfurt and pick up the Bug.

Sunday, June 20, 1965

P. T. Yoder had made plans to make a bush safari the day after our visit to Awash. The other two women decided against it, but I jumped at the chance. P. T. is especially interested in working with the Danakil people, who are related to the Somali people; even their language is similar. They are mainly cattle herdsmen and nomads; they also have camels. P. T.'s bush clinics reminded me of our FDS trips in Tanzania. But traveling by Land Rover is better, I think. Of course a plane goes faster, but that's the trouble: you don't have time to get acquainted with the people. After we had clinic at the plantation, P. T. drove us around through the bush. He stopped to greet people, and we went into villages to see patients or just to visit a bit. The houses in these villages are like the Somalis'—very portable—and I got some pictures. I had never gotten to visit a bush home in Somalia. I really enjoyed being with P. T., not only to see his safari clinic work and compare it with Tanzania's, but also to talk over medical missions in general.

That evening I had a short nap at the Yoders' house, then went out at 1:30 A.M. to meet the train back to Nazareth. I slept in the sleeping bag and managed to wake up without an alarm to get off the train at 5:30 A.M. After breakfast at Nazareth we came to Addis Ababa.

Saturday, June 26, 1965

Greetings from Bienenberg Bible School in Switzerland. This is the Mennonite school you probably read about in a recent *Missionary Messenger*. It is on a high hill overlooking the city.

Yesterday morning at this time we were on the train, climbing the mountains to see the famous Jungfrau summit. The weather was clear and cold at the top—very enjoyable. Dad would really have liked it—except I suspect he would have wanted the train to stop more often and longer so he could look around more.

Germany and Switzerland have both been lovely. We stayed at a village farm near Frankfurt the first two nights, so naturally we walked along the fields too. That made me homesick. Such big, strong horses! And the women work in the fields too. I think with more practice on my German I could really be at home here! I am getting along fairly well with my rusty German, and enjoying it.

Today we want to drive up along the Rhine River, visit a castle, stop in at Zweibrücken, then get to Saarbrücken by evening and go to church with Omar Stahls in the morning.

The VW is doing OK; I've put more than seven hundred miles on it already—up mountain and down. It is due at Amsterdam by Wednesday afternoon next week, so we are pushing our trip a little faster than we had planned. Next week at this time I won't be writing to you, but probably will be counting the hours! ✠

Homecoming

After twenty-seven months in Tanganyika/Tanzania followed by sixteen months in Somalia, I arrived in New York City on Saturday, July 3, 1965, at 4:00 P.M. after a long-enough eight-hour flight from Amsterdam. I took the 7:00 P.M. train to Lancaster and arrived at 9:40 P.M. Brother Paul, brother Nate and his wife, Mother, Dad, cousin Nora, and Sis's Leonard had come to the station to meet me. Once home, we enjoyed ice cream, pretzel sticks, cheese crackers, and chips. By then I was hardly enthusiastically sociable. It had been a very long day and my yellow timepiece told me it was 4:00 A.M. So I went to bed after turning my watch back to 11:00 P.M. In the morning I was invited to speak at church in lieu of the sermon, so I "apologized" for not preparing, then spoke off the cuff for thirty minutes—to my mild surprise.

On Monday morning I washed clothes, and it rained. I picked green beans for dinner (served with hot dogs; really good). At 2:00 P.M. I left for Salunga and orientation. It rained hard, so I pulled off the road and let it pour for a while. The Ford felt like a big boat after driving my little Bug around Europe! Orientation ended the following Monday. A couple of days later my brother Paul and I went by train to New York City to get my VW Bug, which had arrived there on Sunday.

My sister Anna Mary and our friend Lois Stoltzfus had spent the summer working in Red Lake, Ontario, and I had agreed to pick them up so we could go see the West. Dad was available to travel with me to Red Lake, but Mother preferred to stay at home, and my brothers Paul and Nate lived nearby so that was workable. We stopped at Laurelville in western Pennsylvania the first night and at Goshen, Indiana, the second night. On the third night we camped at Virginia, Minnesota. (I'm not sure how well Dad slept without a real bed.) The last two days we covered about five hundred miles each day.

After arriving finally at Red Lake, we stayed for several days, and I got to fly on a pontoon plane to Poplar Hill. We then packed the car with luggage for four, both inside and on the roof rack. On our way south we stopped at International Falls, Minnesota, and used my tent and our sleeping bags. Because the local airport did not have good connections to Philadelphia, we drove further south—all day as I remember—to Minneapolis, where Dad bought a ticket for a direct flight to Philadelphia. After we had seen him off, I found a pay phone and called brother Paul and asked him to head for Philadelphia to pick up Dad.

Then we three single girls headed west. We had a great time, but none of us kept much of a written log of our journey. We did, however, take some photos, so I will let a few of these tell you a little more about our adventure.

We arrived home just before Labor Day, in time for Sis and Lois to start teaching in a small Christian school in Juniata County, and for me to pack up and head off for a year of seminary at EMC. I really needed a break from medicine, with its often hectic pace, especially in the overseas setting. I also wanted spiritual nourishment and stimulation after

"hearing" church services in Swahili and Luo and Somali but failing to understand most of them because of my limited knowledge of those languages. And I really looked forward to returning to my alma mater and working with some of my previous professors. ✝

My Year in Seminary

The 1965–1966 school year developed into one great experience after another for me. It began with the roommate assignments in the dormitory. I was assigned to a large with Ruth Westenberger (later known as Mrs. Wilbur Lentz) from Elizabethtown, Pennsylvania; and Luella Moshier, a nurse from Lowville and Syracuse, New York. A room with three occupants can spell difficulty, but we soon learned to enjoy each other. Sometimes a group of Ruth's friends from her church in Steelton, Pennsylvania, near Harrisburg, would come to visit when they were attending a fellowship meeting near Harrisonburg, and that is how I first met Betty Shaffer, Violet Gibney, Kathryn Hertzler, Nancy Frey Longenecker, and others. I enjoyed all of these women, but I especially clicked with Betty. Little did I know what a precious friend and mentor she would become to me a few years later when I moved to the Harrisburg area—but that's getting ahead of my story.

One of the first things I did in seminary was to register for the classes I wanted. I remember that Linden Wenger offered to help me and suggested that I take homiletics. I was taken aback and asked, "But why?"—the unasked question being, "Why should I, a woman, study preaching?" He persisted and I finally agreed to sign up for a class taught by J. Otis Yoder, a skilled orator and a rather conservative Mennonite. I wondered how he would respond to having a woman in his preaching class.

We met in Room 48 of the old administration building, just to the left of the big clock in the main entrance hallway. The door of the room opened into the front and swung to the left, and the seats faced the front, of course. I vividly remember going to class a bit early the first day and sitting in the first seat of the second row so that the open door would protect me from being seen until a person was completely inside the room. Several other students (there were maybe nine of us altogether—eight young men and myself) came in, said hello to me, and sat in seats near the window. Then Brother Yoder entered. When he pulled on the door to close it, he saw me sitting behind it. Without saying a word he turned around, calmly pulled the door open again, walked out, and closed the door behind him. We students sat quietly and said nothing. A bit later Brother Yoder opened the door again, came inside, closed the door, went to his table, and without further ado launched into his introduction to homiletics.

As the weeks passed, I learned a lot about Brother Yoder's methods for making the Scriptures live and for outlining a sermon so that its hearers could better remember it. I enjoyed doing sermon outlines and learning from the other students. As second semester approached, we were told that each of us would be presenting a sermon or two to the class, and somehow I felt hesitant to do so in front of a group of men and Brother Yoder. As it turned out, I found another class to take, so I did not do the second semester of homiletics. Still, I remember very clearly that my brother Paul attended Minister's Week at EMC that January and I was able to introduce him to my homiletics teacher. Brother Yoder was so pleased to meet Paul and, in a teasing manner, as if telling him a secret, whispered to Paul loudly enough that I could hear him too, of course, "You know, your sister here, why, she does better in homiletics than some of the men do!" And I admit that his class was very useful to me several years later when I returned to Shirati, where I was frequently asked to speak at our Sunday evening vesper services. So I have thanked God more than once that Linden Wenger and J. Otis Yoder were used of God to prepare me for a meaningful ministry during my second term at Shirati Hospital in Tanzania.

During my year at EMC Seminary, I felt real acceptance from professors and students alike, and I made some good friends among the college women. I learned more about the ways of God both in class and from the individuals who shared their lives with me. Fairly early in the year I met Mrs. Edith Yoder, who worked in the counseling department, and I quickly made it a habit to stop by her office to chat once a month or so. Our times of fellowship were such a blessing to me. We enjoyed sharing Scriptures that had become meaningful to us. I remember how blessed I was by Philippians 2:13 in the Living Bible: "For God is at work within you, helping you *want* to obey him, and then helping you *do* what he wants." Another time it was Philippians 1:6 in the Living Bible: "And I am sure that God who began the good work within you will keep right on helping you grow in his grace until his task within you is finally finished on that day when Jesus Christ returns."

One of the college women who lived on my hall, Dorothy Wissler Zehr, soon became a special friend as well. Sometimes we went to an upstairs prayer room to talk and share our spiritual journey. I vividly remember when I was trying to decide whether I would go home for Easter vacation or accept the invitation of Dr. Bucher to cover his medical practice for a week so he and his family could have some time away. As I struggled with this decision, Dorothy and I prayed together, and God made it clear that I really did not want to go home, that I did not want to spend my vacation with my mother, that in fact I really did not love my mother the way a daughter should love her mother. As the prayers and confession and tears came spilling out, I found myself feeling a deeper love for my mother and a willingness to go home for Easter. Dorothy prayed with me in a very supportive and understanding way and never chided that I—a missionary, no less—had been rather distant from my mother all those years. That was a humbling and very precious experience for me. I informed Dr. Bucher of my decision and went home. I don't recall much about that vacation except that I spent more time with Mother and was at peace.

Another special friend from my seminary year was Grace Delp Jones. She always listened carefully when someone had a pain to share, but she also overflowed with joy and was a vivacious person. We enjoyed each other immensely. She often wrote me short notes of cheer and affirmation. She was so willing to share about her spiritual journey, and that helped me to be more honest about my struggles and failures. Too often I wanted to look like a "good missionary" instead of revealing my warts and faults. I remember the time we were planning a seminary tour to Marion, Pennsylvania; Franconia Conference area; and New York City. I was asked to take along another female student as a companion. I approached Dorothy and I think at least two other ladies, but no one was available to go. So Linden Wenger suggested that I ask Grace, and she said yes. It was a wonderful trip on which she shared, among other things, how she came to walk in the Spirit. That helped me to understand so many things I had wondered about but, as was natural for me, had not opened my mouth to ask about! Grace and her family remained special friends to me for many, many years.

Sometime during that year in seminary, God hit me with another message from my Living Bible, this time from 1 Peter 1:22:

> Now you can have real love for everyone because your souls have been cleansed from *selfishness* and *hatred* when you trusted Christ to save you; so see to it that you really do love each other warmly, with all your hearts.

Well, that really got my attention. Peter was implying that the reason we don't love others is that either we hate them or we are too self-centered to care about others who are different from us in some way, and we assume we are superior to them. Well, I did not want to admit that I hated others, because I knew that Jesus said in Matthew 5:21–22 of the Good News Bible:

> You have heard that people were told in the past, "Do not commit murder; anyone who does will be brought to trial." But now I tell you: whoever is angry with his brother will be brought to trial, whoever calls his brother "you-good-for-nothing" will be brought before the council, and whoever calls his brother a worthless fool will be in danger of going to the fire of hell.

The Good News Bible also says, in 1 John 3:15, "Those who hate others are murderers, and you know that murderers do not have eternal life in them." And in the next chapter, 1 John 4:20, I read, "If we say we love God but hate others, we are liars. For we cannot love God, whom we have not seen, if we do not love others whom we have seen."

These verses left me facing the charge of self-centeredness and self-ishness, and I realized with a shock that it was true. I just did not want to share my time with some people, and I caught myself having negative feelings toward others without any reason, such as the time I went to the optometry office to pick up my new glasses. As I sat and waited and looked around the room, I noticed a middle-aged man with a small child. He was somewhat overweight and not well dressed, and he seemed a bit frustrated by the wait and needing to entertain his child. My mind had begun developing a negative resume for him when God suddenly entered my thoughts and challenged me to do something positive instead. So I silently prayed that God would grant the man peace and patience and whatever else he might be in need of. I also thanked God for catching me in my negative thoughts that day. On subsequent occasions, God has also prompted me to communicate with Him silently when there is a special need, such as a hectic situation in the emergency room, or if I did not feel like loving a colleague, or when the anesthesiology staff had difficulty getting an IV started so we could do emergency surgery for a patient in dire straits.

During that year in seminary I was privileged to speak at a number of churches and to various groups. Sometimes I spoke about my experiences as a missionary, but sometimes I spoke more personally, about the things God was teaching me during my seminary year. One day, Ira Miller asked me to speak in chapel. That was a more difficult assignment, especially to prepare a speech that would be finished just before the dismissal bell rang. But again God was faithful. In my "Confessions of a Missionary," I told some personal experiences, and finished just before the bell rang. Afterward, as we met briefly in the dining hall, Grace said to me, "Well, Jesus really helped you in chapel this morning!" And I responded, "Yes, He really did!" Brother Yoder gave me a special compliment on the content and delivery of my talk too.

I must mention another incident that happened soon after I started seminary. I planned to get residency training after my year in seminary, so I had applied for a slot in general surgery at my other alma mater, Woman's Medical College of Pennsylvania. Several weeks later, Paul Kraybill came to EMC and asked to see me. He advised me that EMBMC was more in need of someone trained in OB-GYN and if I pursued training in surgery they might not have a position for me in East Africa. Well, that really put me in a tailspin. I tried to pray, but finally it was as though God pinned me to the rough wall of my dorm room and said, "Do you remember that verse you put on your prayer card, the one from Psalm 138:8, 'The Lord will fulfill his purpose for me; thy steadfast love, O Lord, endures forever. Do not forsake the work of thy hands'?" Well,

God seemed to be asking, "Are you letting me fulfill my plan and purpose for you? Or are you telling me you want to do surgery when EMBMC is asking you to do OB-GYN? Are you insisting on your own way? Or are you willing to accept my plan for you?" I squirmed for a while but finally said, "OK, OK, God! Have it your way!" His peace promptly flooded over me and I soon fell asleep.

I kept praying, and several weeks later I got word that I had been accepted into the surgical residency program at Woman's Medical College Hospital beginning July 1, 1966. So I assumed it was God's plan for me to do surgical training after all. But then, in February 1966, Paul Kraybill called and asked if I could possibly work in their hospital in Ethiopia for several years, starting after my year in seminary was finished. I replied that I was willing to go but it was contingent upon the residency program being willing to release me from my surgical residency contract. If they refused to release me, I did not want to unilaterally break the contract. As I prayed about this situation, God gave me another message, from Philippians 4:6–7 in my Living Bible:

> Don't worry about anything: instead, pray about everything: tell God your needs and don't forget to thank him for his answers. If you do this you will experience his peace, which is far more wonderful than the human mind can understand. His peace will keep your thoughts and your hearts quiet and at rest as you trust in Christ Jesus.

So I rested in His peace, knowing that God would reveal His will for me in His time. I set up an appointment with Dr. Cooper in Philadelphia about the surgical residency situation. I also realized that I was no longer so eager to work in the surgical residency; in fact, I would have been ready to forget all about it. Talk about a change in one's thinking!

Later, when I explained the situation to Dr. Cooper, he responded that he felt it was unfair of EMBMC to ask me to accept their assignment to Ethiopia on such short notice and he was unwilling to release me from my contract. So I thanked him and said I would do my best in surgery for the coming year. As I traveled from Philadelphia back to Harrisonburg, it almost seemed as though God was laughing and saying to me, "Hey, you wanted this surgical residency so badly last fall. Now you don't want it. But here, have it anyway!"

So, from July 1, 1966, to June 30, 1967, I got a lot of good experience in general surgery, neurosurgery, and orthopedics at the Woman's Medical College Hospital. It was a busy year, with open heart surgery being performed at WMCH for the first time. Within a few months of beginning the residency, however, I realized that although I enjoyed working in surgery, I did not want to spend the rest of my medical career, after my commitment to EMBMC was finished, working in general surgery. I did not think I would enjoy the hectic pace of a surgical practice in the United States. OB-GYN was looking more attractive to me. So I began exploring OB-GYN residencies in Harrisburg and central Pennsylvania. At Christmas I got an acceptance letter from my second-choice hospital but had not yet heard anything from my first choice. Then I remembered, with a shock, that I had not actually asked God to provide a speedy reply. Well, I began to pray, and let me tell you, the enemy got busy telling me *not* to expect an answer until sometime in the new year. But I continued to pray, asking God to provide his confirmation, and in two days I had received my acceptance letter from Harrisburg Hospital! So, with peace and joy in my heart I expeditiously wrote two letters, one to decline the first offer, from Geisinger Medical Center, the other to accept the offer from Harrisburg Hospital.

Several months after I started my surgical training I arrived home one Saturday afternoon to find that Mother had experienced a probable stroke or mini-stroke several days earlier. She was having trouble walking and was staying upstairs rather than trying to navigate the stairs. Our family physician had been unavailable for a week or so and for some reason Dad had taken Mother to see another doctor, who was not familiar with her medical history. That doctor had decided to give her an intramuscular medication (I think it was a hormone preparation), and the next day she had these new symptoms. I don't remember what other problems she had (such as with speech), but I think it was after this episode that she had more trouble with her vision. Her walking did improve and she again used the stairs. But she was unhappy about not being able to see clearly and to read. Some years later I read reports about the use of certain hormones in older women being associated with a higher incidence of heart attacks and strokes. Mother's eyes were examined but cataracts were not found, nor the need for new glasses. Rather, her condition was described as a vessel problem of the eyes for which no treatment was currently available.

Meanwhile, Dad's hearing was declining and his memory was failing him at times. But he did fairly well at maintaining his sense of humor. When Mother would sometimes complain about her poor vision, Dad would gently say, "Well, if you will just listen for me and my deaf ears, I will look out for you and your weak eyes!" And he did look out for her, and he often took her hand when they were walking outside.

That's how things went for several years. Sis married Leonard Groff and joined him in Vermont, where he was serving his I-W (1-W) service (an alternative to military service). Their first son was born there. Eventually they returned to Pennsylvania and resided in the parsonage of the Coatesville Mennonite Church. Later they offered to come live where our parents were living if Mother and Dad would consider moving into the trailer beside the farmhouse. ✝

My Life in the Harrisburg Area

I arranged to meet one of the OB-GYN residents in June to look for an apartment. The first complex we went to had no vacancies, and it was on the eastern edge of Harrisburg whereas the hospital was on Front Street, facing the Susquehanna River. We went next to an apartment complex on the western shore that was still building new units, and there I signed a contract for a basement apartment with drapes and new furniture for $139 per month. I was not eager to buy my own furniture and then have to store it, or sell it, three years later. On July 1, 1967, I moved in with my clothes and books and began my new position as a resident in OB-GYN at Harrisburg Hospital.

Easier than finding an apartment was deciding where to go to church. Near my apartment was Steelton Mennonite Church, a growing congregation in which my former roommate Ruth Westenberger was a member. I visited one Sunday morning, was warmly welcomed, and soon made new friends. I also got to know some already casual friends in a deeper way, including Betty Shaffer and some of the other women she spent time with. It seemed inevitable that Betty and I began calling each other and visiting, sometimes at my apartment and sometimes at her house. I came to enjoy her family as well.

As Betty and I got to know each other better, she shared with me some of the pain of her childhood—how as a girl, maybe ten years of age, she had watched her mother hemorrhage to death during the birth of premature twins, who also died, at home. Betty was the oldest child in a family of girls. After their mother's death, Betty and some of her siblings were placed in foster care in Philadelphia, where they lived for several years. Betty did not have a close relationship with her father, but he remarried at some point and had a second family that Betty did not meet, or even know existed, until many years after the wedding. Betty married and had three sons. She later divorced. She finally came to faith in Christ, married again, and had a daughter. She attended the local church regularly and made many friends.

As she shared with me the pain from her childhood, I finally shared with her my own abuse history and my subsequent confusion about the meaning and function of sexuality. Betty gradually helped me to understand that God intended sexuality to be a special relationship between husband and wife, but sin had corrupted it into something hurtful and "dirty." She helped me to understand that God wanted me to accept myself as a woman, as one of his daughters. Well, that was news to me. Granted, I had heard of "self-acceptance," but when I looked at myself I saw a girl who was too short, too fat, and too freckled. And my reaction was, why would anybody like *me?* Especially because I did not even like myself very much. My mother did not seem to know how to teach me to be a woman. Granted, she tried, but she had grown up in a different era, and her own mother had died when she was only seventeen years old, and her father five years before that, so she had probably raised herself. I was pretty much on my own too, and I had really been floundering at being a woman, let alone "a daughter of God," until God sent Betty into my life.

Betty was very down to earth and practical. In time she made suggestions about my attire and the way I "carried" myself, so I learned to wear shoes with "some" heel and to be more ladylike. I even changed my hair a bit, by moving my part to the side.

Betty even challenged me to believe that God might have a companion for me sometime in the future. She shared some of her experiences as a wife and mother, and sometimes I let myself think about what it would be like to have a husband and be in a long-term relationship. But to think about becoming a mother was really "way far out" for me. After all, after I finished my postgraduate work in mid-1970, I was probably going back overseas to serve for another three or four years. So marriage was probably at least five to seven years in the future, maybe more, I thought. And by then I would be in my early forties. But Betty did live to see me become a bride, and then a mother too.

Betty and I came to find prayer together very meaningful, not only in person but also over the phone. My devotional life became more vibrant, and I developed special relationships with some people I met in my daily work. I was able to share my testimony for God in an effective way with several persons. It was an exciting period of my life in which God was at work changing me and touching others through me. During the three years in which I lived near Betty, she helped me in so many ways to become a more mature woman and to feel good about myself.

In time I met a number of Betty's sisters, and several became good friends of mine as well. One day I was doing an admission history and physical on the fifth floor of the hospital. Somehow we must have gotten "off the subject" and I quoted to the patient a part of the opening sentence from the *Confessions of Saint Augustine,* where he says, "Thou hast made us for thyself, and our souls are restless until they find their rest in thee." There was a woman in the other bed. Her head popped up and she looked at me and asked, "What are you, a preacher or something?" So I told her who I was. She then told me that she was Betty's sister Dolly. As we became comfortable with each other, she invited me to visit her and her three children and common-law husband at their home. She then began going with me to church at Steelton. One Sunday when the pastor gave an altar call, I could tell that Dolly was deeply moved by it, but she made no outward response. After the service, instead of taking her directly home, I drove us up to the hospital and parked my car. It was a lovely summer day, not too hot, so we crossed Front Street, walked over near the Susquehanna River, and sat down on the grass. I let her tell me how she was feeling. Then I affirmed to her that God was inviting her to become one of his children. She was ready to accept Jesus, so I led her in a prayer of confession and repentance. I then assured her that she was now a member of the family of God. As time passed, it was a real privilege to watch her grow, to see her rejoice in answered prayer and in finding precious truth in the Word of God. Dolly had struggles too; she especially wondered how to find the blessing of God on her marriage. She was also diabetic and used insulin. I knew she longed to be healed from her diabetes. Several years later, after I had returned to Tanzania, Dolly was released from her diabetes and physical limitations, and I felt like a precious sister had gone to be with Jesus.

Another patient who became special to me was Anne. She was a young single mother who was born when her own mother was only fourteen. Her parents later married, but it was not a happy marriage, and Anne's mother never loved her. She even wrote Anne a letter describing her dislike for her daughter and how she wished she could somehow have had a miscarriage instead of giving birth to Anne. So Anne did not know the security of a stable family with loving parents. She sought love and acceptance in church, but even there it seemed elusive. I tried to love her too, as a sister, but was sometimes rather exhausted by the effort. It seemed that because of all the misery Anne had suffered, and all the negative messages she had received from her mother, it was hard for her to believe that God really loved her and that she was valuable to Him. Eventually her son was placed in foster care. At one point she made plans for marriage, but she probably was not ready for that either. I tried so hard to help her get into a better lifestyle, but with little result. Sometimes I tried to help her climb out of her depression. Years later, after I myself had gone through the deep waters of depression for several years, I visited Anne again, and after we had talked for an hour or two, she finally said to me, "Now you understand what it's like to be depressed. Now you have been through it too, like I have been." And she was right. I was not just using theoretical jargon but was instead sharing feelings that were similar to her own. Unfortunately I lost contact with Anne after I got married and was too busy working and learning how to be a wife and stepmother to keep up with writing letters to my scattered friends.

I also met Jay while I was in Harrisburg. His wife Marie was a patient I helped to care for in the hospital. She went along to church with me sometimes and showed some spiritual hunger. They had some marital problems, and Jay visited the bars regularly. One night, Marie was so unhappy she walked out onto a bridge that crossed the river and stood by the rail, trying to decide whether she wanted to climb up onto the rail and jump off or not. The next thing she knew, a person, or perhaps it was an angel, was by her side and invited her to walk back home. When she told me later about this experience, I was ill prepared to help her. I'm not even sure if I referred her to a pastor or a mental health center for further counseling to help her deal with her problems. I wish I had been more helpful to her.

I met Jay different times when Marie was an inpatient at the hospital. On one occasion I invited him to have a cup of coffee with me in the snack shop, and he accepted. As we talked I felt led to share with him what it means to be a complete person as I had heard it explained by Bill Gothard in his Basic Youth Conflicts seminar, first in New Jersey and some years later in Baltimore, Maryland. In short, a person is somewhat like an onion and is made of three major layers: body, soul, and spirit ("May your spirit and soul and body be kept strong and blameless until that day when our Lord Jesus Christ comes back again," 1 Thessalonians 5:23).

- The *body* is the external, physical portion. It has the capacity to see, taste, hear, feel, and smell.
- The *soul,* or *psyche,* is our psychological being. It has the capacity to think and reason and remember, the ability to discern various emotions, and the ability to make choices and exercise the will.
- The *spirit,* or *pneuma,* is the innermost part of our being. It has the capacity to comprehend the essential nature of God, the ability to discern right and wrong (conscience), the capacity to discern the basic meaning of life (wisdom), the ability to be sensitive to the spirit of others, the capacity to be creative, and the ability to develop basic drives and emotions.

I tried to make it simple for Jay by asking, "When you say you know someone, what do you mean?" I explained that he could tell me whether his friend is tall or short, young or old, handsome or not, puny or athletic, has lots of hair or is bald, and so on. And how does he know these things? It is by what he sees in his friend, what he hears him say, what he feels, and perhaps smells. But these are all external things that do not reveal much about the inner person. Some people get very preoccupied with their external physique. They exercise vigorously, follow certain diets, and work to have a strong, muscular body. But if a person concentrates only on his physical body, he is a truly incomplete and poorly developed person.

As we observe a person and get to know her better, we discover she has a psyche, a soul, that can think and reason and remember things. She can express a variety of feelings and emotions, and she can make choices and exercise free will. These qualities separate humans from the animals around us, who obviously can learn certain behaviors but cannot communicate their thoughts and emotions as human beings can. We can learn from past experience and become less prone to repeat our mistakes. Men and women and children enjoy being together and working together and playing together for the good of each other. Some persons can become preoccupied with developing their psychological being with excessive education or perennial use of counseling and therapies to allay their symptoms of anxiety.

Finally, there is a deeper and often unrecognized core to the human being: the pneuma or spirit. This is the innermost part of our being, which God put within us so that we can learn who God is and why He made us. Our spirit also lets us know what is right and what is wrong, and what life is all about. It helps us to be sensitive to others and gives us our creativity to be and do special things and to develop basic drives and emotions. God wants His Spirit to live in our spirit, to lead us and empower us to become His kind of people. Without this relationship with God, our lives have an empty, aching hole inside that is wanting to know God's purpose and plan for our life.

I explained this to Jay as we sat at a table with our coffee mugs. He listened quietly as I talked. Then I asked if he wanted to invite God into his life, and he said yes. I said to pray after me, and he did, right there in the snack shop. I believe that Jay walked out of that snack shop a new man, a baby believer in Christ. I later gave him a copy of *Letters to Young Churches,* a paraphrased version of the New Testament Epistles. I also contacted one of the men at Steelton and asked him to follow up on Jay. I gave him Jay's phone number, and he met Jay outside a bar for their first chat. I'm not sure what happened to Jay and Marie, because I left Harrisburg soon after that. But I sometimes think it is easier to get that initial commitment to Christ than it is to nurture people into mature Christians and help them grow through the trials and rough places that life throws at them.

Meanwhile, I was enjoying OB-GYN a lot. Even though there was only one woman physician among the staff who did deliveries, and even though all the other staff people and residents in the department were men, I felt at home with them and, with only a few minor exceptions, enjoyed good working relationships with everyone. Those exceptions were related more to my own impaired communication of my intentions and wishes rather than to their picking on the female in the group! And I really enjoyed working with the patients, in both obstetrics and gynecology. I especially enjoyed sitting with patients during labor. More than once a patient asked me, "Hey, Doc, how many kids you got?" And I always replied, "Oh, lots of 'em. Just none of my own." Being there to usher in a new life was such a great experience, usually. Once in a while the baby did not survive despite all our medical efforts. Then I sometimes had to accept responsibility for things that might have been done differently, with perhaps a better outcome; and I learned to sit with the disappointed parents and offer comfort in their time of grief. Working with maternity patients often provided contact with other family members as well. A number of my patients became personal friends.

The nurses and doctors at Harrisburg Hospital were a good group of people to work with, and my three years there passed quickly. One of the last things I did as a resident was to give an interview to the local newspaper about my work in Africa and my plans to return to Shirati Hospital in late July 1970. ☩

Saying Good-bye to Mother

I had been in the States for about five years and was about to finish my OB-GYN residency when I was asked to return to Shirati Hospital. Mother did not drag her feet about my going to Tanzania this time. And I felt ready to return. After my farewell service in late July 1970, brother Paul asked me a potentially difficult question: "You know, our parents are getting older, and if one of them should pass on, what do you want us to do? Do you think you would want to come home for the funeral?"

My answer, though not premeditated, was prompt and clear: "Try to get the word to me quickly. I will then make a decision and inform you if I'm coming or not." Over a year later, that question became reality.

Christmas Day 1971 came on a Saturday. The rest of my family gathered for a lovely Christmas dinner at the home of my brother Nate. Everyone had a lovely time together, and as they were preparing to return home, brother Paul had a clear premonition that our Mother would not be with us much longer. But she seemed to be fine and had enjoyed the day.

Mother and Dad went home and that evening they enjoyed a pleasant visit from some longtime neighbors who brought along a lovely fruit basket. After the neighbors departed, Mother admired their gift and asked Dad to open it so she could have a sample. Dad, who was not feeling very hungry because of their big noon meal, replied, "Oh, it is so pretty, but I'm not really hungry. Let's wait until tomorrow." So Mother didn't push the matter further, and they soon went into the bedroom and got ready for bed.

But before either of them had fallen asleep, Mother turned to Dad and said, "Would you get me one of my nitroglycerine pills, please?" He went to the medicine cabinet and brought the bottle to her. Soon she said, "Maybe you should call Dr. Beacher." Dad replied, "But you haven't given the medicine very much time to work." He could tell she was still uncomfortable, so he invited her to go out to the living room, where it was warmer and she could sit in her favorite chair. He extended his hand to her. After she was seated, he did call Dr. Beacher, who promptly answered the phone. Dad explained that Mother was having pain and the nitroglycerine did not seem to be helping. Dr. Beacher said, "I am expecting another patient to arrive within minutes with an emergency. As soon as I take care of that patient, I will come to see your wife." Dad relayed this message to Mother, who replied slowly, "I'm. So glad.

You're here. With me." She took several deep, slow breaths, then her head relaxed onto the soft back of the chair, and she was gone. It was about 10:15 on Christmas night.

Dad was sure she was gone, so he tried calling other family members, but in one place a phone extension was off the hook and in another there was no answer. Dr. Beacher arrived about fifteen minutes later and agreed that Mother was gone. He offered Dad his sympathy, then wrote up the paperwork. Meanwhile, my brothers and Sis received the message and arrived at the trailer. Before he left, Dr. Beacher gave them information for contacting a funeral director.

One of the next things Paul did, after calling the funeral director, was to contact Eastern Mennonite Missions to find out how to get the word to me. They decided that Paul should telephone Hershey Leaman in Nairobi and ask him to get a message to Musoma by phone and then by shortwave radio to me at Shirati. So Hershey tried to call Musoma but their phone was out of order. And the AMREF radio from Nairobi to Shirati was on a schedule of certain weekday call times with no service on weekends. And because East Africa time is eight hours ahead of US eastern standard time, in Nairobi and Shirati it was Sunday morning, December 26.

Hershey quickly went to plan B. He remembered that a family visiting from Goshen, Indiana, had spent several days in Nairobi and had left an hour ago to drive overland to Shirati. Hershey told his wife, Norma, about his urgent mission, made sure his vehicle was filled with petrol, then took off to the west. He went out over the escarpment and down into the broad valley past Naivasha to Nakuru, then turned south and began climbing into the highlands. When he finally saw the vehicle he was chasing, he easily flagged them down and explained that he had an urgent message for them to take to me at Shirati. He tore out part of a page from a ringed tablet and wrote this note:

> Dear Doctor Stoltzfus,
>
> Your brother Paul called me at Nairobi to say your mother died of a heart attack at 10:15 Christmas night. *Pole sana.* Please let us know your plans and how we can help.
>
> Hersh

He gave the note to the family and wished them a safe journey to Shirati. Then he turned around and headed back to Nairobi at a slightly more leisurely pace. (Hershey was always very proper and addressed me as Dr. Stoltzfus rather than as Dorcas, even though we had graduated from LMS together in 1951.)

At Shirati we had experienced a good Christmas holiday. Some of our folks had family members visiting from the United States (including Cora Lehman's parents and a sister-in-law), and we'd shared a lovely candle-lit meal in the large dining-living room in my house. We ate ham brought by our guests, who also brought frozen (or was it canned?) minced meat in their luggage. It was good timing for me that we had our feast before Christmas, so I did not miss it. I think this was also the year that Elsie campaigned for us ladies to wear our nylons to dinner!

Anyway, the day after Christmas, Sunday, was special that year because Pastor Nashon's only daughter, Loyce, was being married to the son of Eleazar, an employee of the hospital and a respected man in the Christian community. Because I hoped to enjoy the festivities, I had arranged that one of the other doctors would take calls for any hospital emergencies that Sunday. The wedding ceremony was held at the Shirati church that morning, with many guests, including Bishop Zedekia Kisare from Musoma.

The reception was held in the village of the bridegroom and his parents, just across the street from the hospital. We gathered with many friends in midafternoon and were served delicious food at outdoor tables. As some folks began to wander away, I was thinking of returning to my house too when I noticed a student nurse in her green uniform coming toward me. I assumed she had a question about a patient, and I fear I was a little too quick to tell her that I was not on call that day. She softly replied, "But no, this is a message especially for you, from your family." Then she handed me the note that Hershey had written to me that morning. I read it and murmured a quiet "thank-you." The student nurse replied "Pole sana" before she turned and went back to the hospital ward.

The rest of that evening is somewhat of a blur. I remember telling Nurse Okidi about it, and of course my fellow missionaries. Because Bishop Kisare was also at Shirati, it was easy to tell him in person, *Mama yangu amekwenda mbinguni usiku was Chrismas* ("My mother went to heaven on Christmas night"). He asked me what I wanted to do and I said I would really like to go home for the funeral. He gave me his blessing to do that. Later, Clyde and Alta Shenk drove into the compound. Somehow the message had finally gotten through to Musoma, so they had driven the seventy miles to Shirati to ensure that I had gotten the message too.

I could sense the prayers of God's people in both the United States and East Africa as I made hasty plans for this sudden trip. I remembered that our missionary car had just been serviced and was ready for a safari. And within the past month I had also renewed my Kenya visa in Nairobi. On Monday morning my fellow missionaries contacted our Nairobi staff to get me a flight to Philadelphia for Monday evening. They also got word back to Paul that I was coming and when to meet me in Philadelphia. Several people went along to drive me to Nairobi, including one of our guests, a sister-in-law of Cora Lehman. Alas, I don't remember who the others were on that trip.

We left early Monday morning and got to Nairobi by mid-afternoon. I did have a late afternoon siesta but did not sleep. It seemed unreal that Mother was actually gone. I remember Don and Anna Ruth Jacobs coming over to pray with me that evening before I left for the airport around 10:00 P.M. I did not get off the plane when we stopped in Cairo, and my fall coat could have been warmer against the cold night air as the workers came in to clean and service the plane during our stop. I had to change planes in London, and after waiting in the passenger lounge for several hours, I was glad to embark for the last leg of my flight. However, when I was shown to my seat near the front of the plane, I found a young mother with an unhappy infant plus an older child to entertain. Of course they did not understand my English, or my attempts to comfort the infant so the mother could entertain her older child. Fortunately for me a stewardess came along and took me to a different seat where I relaxed and even fell asleep. But I woke up suddenly when I heard the sounds of the staff bringing trays of food. I needed no other reminder of the fact that I had not bought any lunch in the London airport (with my foreign money), and I don't remember if I was served breakfast before I arrived in London. Anyway, I did enjoy that afternoon meal as we crossed the Atlantic Ocean. As we flew west, following the sun, our flight stretched into a very long afternoon.

When I arrived in Philadelphia it was only 4:00 P.M. but my body felt like it was midnight! And I found Dad, my brother Nate, and I don't remember who else waiting to receive me. Before we left the airport I called Viva Reedel (a good friend from my Philadelphia days who had also become a good friend of Mother's and Dad's) to tell her of Mother's death. Then, as we traveled home, Dad told me all the events surrounding Mother's death. He seemed so concerned that he had not agreed to share the fruit with her before they went to bed on Christmas night, so I said, "But Dad, I'm sure Mother does not hold that against you. And besides, now she has everything she could ever want with Jesus. So please, don't worry about it, because I'm sure she isn't!" And I think he accepted what I said.

That evening, I think I went to bed fairly early, for it had been a long day for me. But the next day, Tuesday, as our family met in the farmhouse on Gap Hill, talking about our memories and preparing for the funeral scheduled for Thursday, I came up with the idea of writing a tribute to Mother, so I did. I felt sure, however, that I would not feel up to reading it at the funeral service, so I asked my brother Paul to read it for me.

On Wednesday evening we had a public viewing at the funeral home in Atglen. I was so blessed by all the friends who came to visit, share some memories, ask about my trip home, and offer their sympathy.

Among those who came and waited until most of the others had greeted us were Betty Shaffer and Nancy Bruaw, who had become my close friends during my years of residency training in Harrisburg. Betty had become like a mother and Nancy like a sister to me, so their friendship was very meaningful and it was great to visit with them for a while.

The funeral was held on Thursday afternoon. Again many friends came to express their sympathy. Before the service Paul asked again if I wanted to read my tribute to Mother myself, and again I said I wanted him to do it.

Tribute to Mother
by Dorcas L. Stoltzfus, MD
December 30, 1971

One of the first things I remember is Mother going to the barn early and late to help with the milking the winter that Dad had hepatitis. I also vividly remember that after Dad was feeling better he would wash the supper dishes and then read *Heidi* to me or tell me a Bible story while Mother was out milking.

As a girl, Mother did housework for various families. At one place she often had many, many dishes to wash and dry by herself, so she determined that if she ever had daughters, she would not make them do dishes alone. And she kept her word. Usually she would wash the dishes and I would dry them. When I was a boarding student at LMS, Mother and I often had our best talks as we did the dishes together on Friday evening while Dad and my brothers did the milking. Many times on Sunday afternoon we would all sit around the table talking for an hour or longer after the meal until Mother would say, "All right, girls. Let's get these dishes done." After Sis was old enough to help, Mother would sometimes ask the two of us to do them. And because we were both so used to drying, we would invariably say in unison, "Sis is gonna wash!" Either way, the dishes got done. Thanks to Mother, doing dishes was not an unpleasant chore or a punishment at our house.

As a girl, Mother learned to work hard, and she persisted in that habit as long as she was able. Her father died when she was only twelve years old, and her mother passed away five years later. So Mother learned early in life to "hoe her own row." She never did get an opportunity to become a practical nurse like her mother had been. But when I hesitantly revealed my desire to become a doctor, she encouraged me to return to school and pursue my dream. She knew I felt this dream was far beyond my ability to attain, so she quietly cherished it with me but seldom spoke about it. After I finished high school she encouraged me to enter college. And she accompanied me when a cousin drove me to EMC that first time in September 1951. On my occasional trips home I usually came with a bag of laundry that Mother washed and sometimes even ironed on Saturday while I was doing other errands. I doubt that I always gave Mother advance warning when I brought a college friend along, but she gladly accepted my friends and made them feel welcome.

Later, while I was attending medical school in Philadelphia, I met some girls who were too far from home to join their families for the holidays. So we sometimes had a girl from North Dakota, Oregon, Washington State, or Guam sharing Thanksgiving or Christmas with us. These friends expressed deep appreciation for the informal but warm welcome of Mother's kitchen, with its inviting wood stove and her well-laden table of delicious food. I was happy to spend more weekends at home too. And Mother gave me extra incentive to come home: in addition to doing much of my laundry, she knew I was "pinching pennies," so she always made sure that I had a box filled with milk, cereal, bread, and other food essentials to take back to school with me. And when I finally received that M.D. degree in 1960, the whole family shared my joy. But Mother's joy was extra special because she had helped me fulfill my dream after having been denied her own.

I don't remember Mother complaining about all the things she did without for the sake of her family. She missed many church services to stay with Ruthie as long as she was able. Her childhood training, followed by living on a farm during the Depression years, never let her spend money foolishly. And some of the lovely gifts she received were put aside to be saved for some "special occasion" that didn't always arrive. She gladly gave of herself and her resources for others, but she did not expect others to do endless things for her. After she lost her sight in 1967, she often wished that she could see again to read and sew and cook and write letters. She had spent her life doing such things for her family and friends, and it was rather hard for her just to sit or to content herself by listening to music while others were working. But with time she did learn to enjoy just being with people and she would often request from Dad to go visiting on Sunday afternoons.

While Mother was not the most vocal person in talking about her faith, we children knew what she believed. Often as we were going away for the evening she would say, "Remember who you are." And we knew what she meant. And many times as I was leaving to drive back to Philadelphia or Harrisburg by

myself, she would assure me of her prayers as she bid me good-bye. "May the Lord protect you, and may He keep us safe too," she would say.

I thank God for the wonderful husband He gave to Mother—a man who has also worked hard for his family and who deeply loves his Lord. Dad learned to cook and "keep house" after Mother could no longer do it. And he even got around to writing letters—with his own special kind of humor—after Mother could no longer write to me. And I thank God that Mother could spend Christmas Day with the family at Nathan's. And the visit of several neighbors that evening was much appreciated too. I am really glad that her departure was a quiet one without a prolonged terminal illness. Mother never wanted to be a care to anyone or to cause anyone extra work. So I thank God that He honored her wish and took her to Himself in the way He did.

When I kissed her good-bye on July 28, 1970, I knew I might not visit with her again. And although separation hurts, I do not wish to have her back. She lived a full life serving her Lord and her family. She knew her share of illness and hard work. And although the tears come forth as I remember the many blessings she brought into my life, inwardly I rejoice that God let her become my mother and that He has now in mercy received her from this earthly life to be with Himself in glory.

I do not remember who gave the sermon, but it was likely Reuben Stoltzfus, who was not only our pastor but also a friend who had rented my dad's farm for a number of years. When Paul read my tribute, it may have been the first time a family member had done so for a funeral at Millwood. Some folks expressed their appreciation, and I later gave a copy to be published in the monthly newsletters of Millwood and Maple Grove.

My round-trip ticket was good for twenty-one days. The time passed rapidly as I took Dad to visit family friends. I also visited Mary Harnish from Shirati, who was recuperating from major surgery, and we arranged to return to Shirati together. Sis and Leonard took me along to Juniata County to visit the daughter of Donald Lauver and her family. Donald and his wife, who had visited Shirati, shared the evening meal with us, which I recall as a pleasant experience.

I also helped Dad get a birth certificate and apply for a passport so he could accompany Reuben Stoltzfus on a tour with Reuben's brother Abner to see the Holy Land. Reuben and Dad also made plans to come to Tanzania to visit Reuben's son Don and me, and to meet our coworkers and friends, which he was eager to do. And in February 1972 he indeed flew with Abner and Reuben Stoltzfus to Israel. They then flew to Nairobi, where Judy, Don's wife, and I met them. We drove them to Tanzania, where they stayed for two weeks. ✞

A Second Term at Shirati: My Experience with Depression

When I returned to Shirati Hospital in early August 1970, I naively thought I was ready for whatever lay ahead. After all, I had already served at Shirati for two and a half years, so I knew many of the people. I had observed the local culture and learned *some* Swahili (though clearly not enough). During my extended home leave, at seminary I had learned to be more honest about my needs, and God's Word had become more alive and precious to me. I had also gotten more medical training—a year in general surgery and three years in OB-GYN.

I arrived at Shirati to find a renovated hospital with new buildings for maternity, a dispensary, the laboratory, medical records and offices, the operating room, central supply, and a wing of semi-private patient rooms. There were now three doctors on staff, with one assigned primarily to leprosy and public health services. Our hospital administrator was Mr. Matiku Nyatambe, a young Tanzanian man who had earned a master's degree in hospital administration in the United States. Our five missionary nurses were busy teaching in the nursing school, managing central supply, and making prostheses for leprosy patients.

Things seemed to go fairly well for eight months or so. Then Dr. Glen Brubaker went on furlough, from late February 1971 through July 1971, and Dr. Leo Yoder and his family terminated their service on March 31, 1971. Dr. John Keiser came in for six months (from mid-February 1971 through July 1971), but for three months, from April 1 until Dr. Brubaker returned in August, there were only two doctors on staff. This situation had a special impact on me. Dr. Yoder had been Medical Officer in Charge (MOC). Who would his successor be? Sure enough, after the medical board of the hospital had its next meeting, I was informed that I was the new MOC. But no one had spoken to me about it beforehand, nor did anyone ask if I had any questions or input.

The biggest issue for me was that I was still rather limited in my ability to understand Swahili, and far from fluent in expressing myself in Swahili. But as long as I could work with Mr. Nyatambe and discuss things with him, I figured I could be comfortable with the arrangement. After Dr. Yoder's departure I also did most of the surgery, which I usually enjoyed but sometimes felt poorly qualified to do, which was very stressful for me. But to refer patients to Nairobi, Mwanza, or the new Kilimanjaro Christian Medical Centre involved many miles and much expense for the patient, so we tried to do all we could for them at Shirati.

One of the situations I had to deal with early on as MOC was the matter of Mr. Ayoo's employment. Mr. Ayoo had completed medical assistant training and had come to us in February 1971 asking for work. Neither Dr. Yoder nor Mr. Nyatambe knew much about him, but we were shorthanded, so they decided to hire him for a probationary period of three months before offering him a permanent position. Within weeks we recognized his lack of medical experience as well as some personal problems. We prayed and discussed our options. This decision was not an easy one to make, because we saw little hope of getting another doctor when Dr. Keiser would leave us at the end of July. In fact, I seem to remember that EMBMC was searching for three doctors that year, with poor prospects of finding even one.

As I prayed about whether to hire Mr. Ayoo, God seemed to say clearly to me, "Look, if you will only release this incompetent man and let him go, then I will show you what I can do." At our next medical board meeting, the members talked at length about this matter and offered various opinions. Then I shared what I felt God had said to me. The board agreed to release Mr. Ayoo. Some weeks later we learned that Dr. Roger Unzicker and his family would transfer to us from Machame Hospital in mid-August. Their family was such a blessing to us during their year at Shirati, and we often thanked God for their help in our time of need.

I cannot pinpoint when I began to feel depressed, but I was really feeling the pressure that spring when there were only two of us doctors at Shirati. Early on I noticed a change in my appetite. Initially I gained some weight, which I did not need. But after some months my appetite decreased and I lost weight, maybe ten pounds. I also was not sleeping well, and sometimes I took something to help me sleep. But then I would sleep through the calls from hospital staff trying to reach me at night, which was a problem. If I did manage to sleep without taking medication and then heard the phone ring, whether for me or for someone else on our party line, I often could not go back to sleep until it was about time to get up. Is it any wonder that I became irritable and demanding at times?

I usually did not share my feelings with my colleagues or other staff, but I brooded a lot and at times would abruptly make a harsh comment that caught others by surprise because they had little clue as to what I was thinking before my sudden outburst. I remember one painfully vivid example of when I was quite unreasonable in my expectations of our staff. When I made postoperative rounds I felt annoyed when I saw that staff had removed the dressings and exposed an incision only a day or two after surgery. I had been taught to keep the incision dressing intact for five to six days, until the doctor removed the alternate sutures. Granted, they put a sterile towel over the area, but curious eyes and hands could move the towel to inspect the incision and perhaps introduce foreign bacteria.

One morning as I made rounds in a "touchy" frame of mind, the young Tanzanian nurse removed the towel so I could observe the incision of a patient whose abdomen I had opened and closed two days previously. Well, I felt so annoyed that I spoke in obvious anger and told her I did not want the bandages removed from my patients until the fifth or sixth day after surgery. She stepped back from the bedside, clearly surprised and frightened by my outburst. She did place a new dressing on the incision, and I don't recall any further incident during rounds that day, but I was very embarrassed by that outburst, and I hope I had the grace to apologize to her, though frankly I can't remember if I did.

Sometimes a patient did not receive the loving care from me that they should have received in a mission hospital. I did not like the way I felt, but I seemed helpless to change it. I did trust, however, that God knew all about my pain, and I never lost hope that He would somehow get me through it all.

But things got worse. In August and September we lost three faithful nurses to other hospitals, including our very capable Nursing Officer in Charge (NOC). Five newly hired nurses also soon moved on to other positions. The morale of our Tanzanian staff was low, in part because some of them were not committed to the discipline code of the TMC. There was also marked turnover among the missionary staff that year; only four missionaries were present at Shirati for the entire year, and fifteen expatriates came and/or went during the year.

Then, in November, Mr. Nyatambe submitted his resignation as hospital administrator in order to accept a better position, with two weeks' notice. This was a severe loss for me, for he was so good at working with people, sorting out personnel problems, dealing with government matters, and meeting the public. But God had given me a message to help me through this loss. I had recently spoken at our Sunday evening English vesper service (as I often did because we had very few men who were prepared to preach) about Jesus calming a storm in Mark 4:35–41 and John 6:16–21. My two major points had been that the boat would not sink when the Lord of the universe was on board, and our boat would safely reach its destination when Jesus was in command. When I was told of Mr. Nyatambe's resignation, I instantly remembered that sermon, and it became the basis of my speech at the farewell party for him. I offered hope that Jesus was still with us and that our Shirati Hospital "boat" would not sink or flounder while Jesus was on board.

But more changes and uncertainty followed. Mr. Okidi, who had upgraded to Grade A nurse in mid-1970 and then was promoted to NOC in September 1971, was named acting hospital administrator in December 1971. So now the question was, who was ultimately in charge? Did the acting administrator have the same authority as the prior trained administrators? And was the MOC now responsible to the NOC, who was also acting administrator? Both the staff and the missionaries were confused, and many questions were asked.

Although I was so glad for my time at home with family and friends after my mother's funeral, I did not get much rest, and I was still tired when I returned to Tanzania in January 1972. There I found that some staff were asking that no new administrator be appointed. Some supported the idea of developing a new organization plan for our hospital and medical services. They asked to present their concerns to the Medical Board of TMC. The board met at Shirati in February 1972 and spent several hours with the hospital staff. Subsequently, the Medical Board seemed to agree that the MOC rather than the acting administrator should have final responsibility. Several weeks later we were rather startled to learn that the Executive Committee of TMC had appointed an administrator for us: Pastor Naftali Birai. They indicated that his position would be beneath the MOC. Although Pastor Birai was not trained in administration, with his cooperative spirit and readiness to learn a new job he proved to be an asset to our medical community, and gradually our staffing situation did improve.

In March 1972 my Dad and Reuben Stoltzfus came to visit me in Tanzania. That was a special time, but I was still so tired and still depressed. Sometimes I was tearful, and sometimes I would ride down to the lake on my *piki-pik* with my tape recorder so I could talk out my feelings and frustrations and send the tape to my trusted friend Betty.

Sitting in our monthly Medical Board meetings for a whole day, including several hours after the evening meal, made those days very long for me. It was tiring to try to understand everything and then to add my own comments when I felt I had something to say. After our April 1972 meeting, Mennonite Mission Director Victor Dorsch came to talk with me. He knew I was struggling with depression and asked if I wanted to go on medical leave for a month or so. I replied that I would like to do that but as MOC I had felt I could not make that decision on my own. He authorized me on the spot to go to Nairobi for a medical checkup followed by several weeks of rest, and he told me not to worry about who would take care of things while I was gone. I took the next few days to do several surgical procedures I had already scheduled, including the amputation of the severely infected forearm of a leprosy patient (whom I found waiting to say good-bye to me when I returned from my leave). Then I hitched a ride to Nairobi with some other folks who were going there from Shirati—so convenient for me.

The doctor in Nairobi found my blood pressure elevated, which did not surprise me. He gave me a low-dose sedative to help me sleep and

asked me to return in two weeks. I then spent a week at St. Julian's, where the ladies liked to pamper overworked and stressed-out missionaries with breakfast in bed. One morning they even brought me mid-morning tea in bed! Elevated above Nairobi, St. Julian's had cool nights and good visibility to the south. Another morning I happened to go out on the south lawn and was surprised to spy Mount Kilimanjaro many miles away—an exciting sight to behold. So I ran inside for my camera to shoot a picture before the clouds hid its flat, snow-covered top.

I had long enjoyed collecting stamps but had gotten behind, so I brought along several stamp albums and a lot of stamps that I had cut from the corners of letters and packages I had received. During my stay at St. Julian's, I made a routine of soaking a pile of the stamps in the sink until they easily slid off the paper. I then put the wet stamps on a towel to dry overnight. The next day I put the clean stamps into my stamp albums and put another batch to soak in the sink. This was a very relaxing project for me to work at during this time.

My blood pressure was better when I got back to Nairobi, so the doctor did not prescribe medication for it. Several days later, Naomi Weaver, a nurse from Shirati, met me and we traveled in a vanlike vehicle from Nairobi to Mombasa and spent a week plus at a resort called Two Fishes, enjoying the ocean and the beach. We played a lot of Dutch Blitz on our veranda, though Naomi was a much better player than I was.

When we got back to Nairobi I was sleeping better and feeling better. I was less irritable too. I even looked forward to getting back to Shirati—

the major reason being that Julius Nyerere, the President of Tanzania, was coming to cut the ribbon for the official opening of our recently expanded and renovated hospital. Don Jacobs was going to Shirati for the big celebration and asked me to ride along. We rode the hours away talking about many things and listening to the soundtrack of *Jesus Christ Superstar*.

The weather was perfect for our big day on June 5, 1972, with clear blue skies, bright sunshine, and refreshing breezes off Lake Victoria. President Nyerere and his entourage arrived on time. The audience assembled outside listened to speeches by local officials, church leaders, and special guests. Then President Nyerere took the scissors and cut the wide ribbon across the entrance to the new administration building. He was prepared to sit down when someone asked him for a speech. He protested mildly, "But I was only asked to cut the ribbon!" But he did offer a few words of congratulations. Afterward he was led by designated staff members on a tour of the hospital to visit each ward and greet many of our patients, including our orphaned twins Donna and Dorka. He also met many of our staff members. Then all of our guests went into the nursing school and were served a typical African meal of vegetables, rice, and meat with *chai*. Too soon it was over, and the president and most of the guests departed. But we Shirati folks were left with a treasure of happy memories that climaxed a number of years of dreams and hard work to get a better and bigger hospital in our corner of Tanzania beside Lake Victoria.

Dr. Brubaker and his family returned on August 1 and relieved me of most of the surgical workload, giving me more time to do business correspondence. But I realized that I was still depressed and sometimes still expected too much of my staff and colleagues. When I began writing the annual medical report for 1972 and compared it to the report of 1971, I was rather surprised to find that there was significant progress on most of the goals I had set for 1972. I was still stuck in my depression and had been quite oblivious to the good progress being made.

My depression lasted at least two years. But as I reflect now on my years at Shirati, I realize that I sensed the most personal fulfillment as I shared the Word in our Sunday evening vesper services. I chose various stories and Bible passages that ministered to me. I remember a time when I was feeling so gloomy and did not know what hope or light to share with the group, so I read portions of a variety of Psalms in which the writer verbalized feelings akin to my own but also dared to hope that God would answer his cry. I still remember that several colleagues came to me afterward and offered me their own hope and comfort that God did understand and was still in control of the situations surrounding me.

When I look back now at my second term at Shirati, I see clearly that my depression seriously interfered with my ability to be an effective physician and missionary. There were many contributing factors: the increased turnover of missionary and African staff, my elevation to MOC without being consulted about it beforehand or being trained for the job, the resignation of our hospital administrator and the questions about who would take his place, the death of my mother and my three-week trip to the United States for her funeral, and my limited knowledge of Swahili, especially at the monthly Medical Board meetings, where I struggled to understand everything said in Swahili and to say in Swahili what I felt needed to be said. When I left Shirati in late January 1973, I was eager to get out of a very painful situation in which I often failed to be who I wanted to be, but I was not really eager to get back home and work on my depression. Still, over a period of months, God did slowly bring healing and new purpose into my life. Praise His name!

That was not my only experience with depression, but at least the second one was not as severe or prolonged. Several years after my marriage, one of my stepchildren experienced depression and received repeated psychiatric care. At times many negative feelings were expressed, which was hard for me to deal with. I obtained counseling at that time, which helped me to express my own feelings as well as to listen to what my stepchild was saying. We have grown to enjoy each other as friends, but it took years of both of us working at it. I now thank God for my good relationships with each of Ted's children and their families, as well as with my son and his family.

One real blessing I find in all of these depression miseries is that they enabled me to come to know what depression is like from the inside and thus to relate and minister better to other persons who are suffering from depression. Eventually I even got training in psychiatry, and for eleven years, until my retirement in early 1998, I worked at Norristown State Hospital, mostly with geriatric patients. ☦

Part Two
Theodore Eggleston Morrow

I met Ted Morrow in the early fall of 1953 when I went with a friend to visit my first-year college roommate, Catherine Roth, and her family at their home in western New York State. Ted and Catherine married in November 1955 and I was a member of their wedding party. Eighteen years later, Catherine died of metastasized breast cancer, and in August 1974 Ted and I became husband and wife. I have already told the story of my own life before our marriage. I would now like to share with you about Ted's life up to that point. Some of the material in this section was written by Ted himself; the rest of it I composed on the basis of what I learned from thirty years of conversation with him and his children.

The House That Wanted to Burn

Ted wrote this story in January 1946 while a student at the University of Rochester, as part of an autobiography. He attempted to write in an Irish English voice, which I have not edited.

There lived in the land of Ireland a man whose name was John. He had three sons: his firstborn, Robert; the second, James; the third, Thomas by name.

John was a weaver of fine linens by trade, and prosperous in all his undertakings. Now, it came to pass that John thought to himself, "Behold, I am increased in goods and have much wealth; therefore will I build me an new house, that I may contain all that I have." And this he began to do in those days.

And in those days, in that part of the country, which was Caven County, there abode a fierce band of robbers, who had for their chief one whose name was Mulreeney. And they were a terror to all who passed by, insomuch as there was a large reward for him who would bring them forth to justice. And all were filled with fear at the thought of them.

But Robert, being a lad of fifteen years, said within himself: Shall I now arise and capture these crafty thieves? Do they not trouble the lands of my father? And he began to search diligently wherein they might be found.

And, lo and behold, he discovered wherein they hid their spoils, and he said, now will I lay in wait for them, what time they shall appear. And in the second hour of the morning did the robbers return. And Robert watched, and beheld their goings out and their comings in.

And one day Robert arose early in the morning and went forth alone to meet them, thinking to capture them by divers wiles. But the thieves pounced upon him and took him prisoner.

Then there arose a controversy among them, for some said: Let us utterly destroy this troubler, lest he bring upon us great mischief and we be undone. But others said: Nay, but he is a mere lad; he deserveth not to die. Let us straightly swear him to secrecy and suffer him to depart, lest his blood be upon our hands.

Then did the chiefest among them arise, and he said: Brethren, hear me when I speak. The one in our midst is of tender years; shall we find great pleasure in the blood of such innocence? Nay, men, but rather let us do this: Shall we not seek vengeance upon his elders, who have made this lad our adversary by the teachings of their mouth? Are they not our foes? And they released him.

Not many days hence it came to pass that three of the robbers were taken and were cast into prison. And Mulreeney and his men were very wroth. They came to the home of John and they laid hold upon the new house, being partly built, and razed it to the ground.

And John mourned many days for his loss. But then he arose and built anew his house upon the old foundations. And all those about marveled and said: Is any like John, who has built again upon the old wastes?

But soon after he did, the thieves again set fire to the house and it burnt utterly to the bareness of the earth. And John said: Where now shall I turn? I have suffered great loss, and my life, is it not even in great danger? We are all as dead men. But later he gathered around him his household and said to them: Fear not, but let us arise and go to America. Surely shall we find there great peace and plenty.

And in eighteen hundred twenty and two did John arrive in New York. From thence did he journey up the Hudson River, and from the Hudson did he go up the Mohawk. And from the Mohawk he made journey to Watkins Glen, and from Watkins Glen to Mud Creek, to Bancroft Lake over against Bath, in the county of Steuben. And there bought he an hundred acres of land, on which he settled, and there he prospered greatly and bought land and built houses for his sons.

And John slept with his fathers, being four score and three years old at his death. And his sons buried him in Grove Cemetery in Bath. Behold, his sepulcher may be seen to this day.

And these are the generations of John who was surnamed Morrow: John begat Robert and James and Thomas. And Thomas begat Robert and John and Alec and Joseph and Thomas and Charles and Henry. And Henry begat Olin and Floyd and Irving and Mildred of May Belle of the house of Yost. And Olin took to wife Alice of the tribe of Eggleston, and she conceived and bore her firstborn and named him Theodore, which means, being interpreted, "gift of God." ✝

Ted's Birth

The following account was written by Ted when he was in his late sixties, in the voice of his mother, who died in 1976.

Nowadays they talk so much about being "pro-choice" or "pro-life." I was thinking about it just recently: Which am I? It was hard to decide. Finally I thought, maybe both. At least that was true at one big moment of my life, when I was giving birth to our first child. It was a double header in more than one way. It was in the same room where I myself had been born twenty-four years earlier, in my parents' farm-house. In those days you didn't worry about going to the hospital to have your baby. You just stayed home and the doctor came to help—if you could afford to have a doctor. Otherwise, you might just have a couple of neighbor women come in to help with it.

Well, it sounded reasonable enough. And I understood that mothers had been doing it that way for a long time. In those days, back in 1928, who could afford the luxury of a hospital room? That was for rich people.

So I was ready to do my best. It was a warm August day and I looked forward to being unburdened of the heaviness in my tummy. Even when the pains started, I was relieved at first, as I thought, "Soon this will all be over!" But time went by, and it wasn't getting over; the pains just got harder and closer. It was more than I could stand. So this was what they meant by labor pains!

Then I heard someone say, "We'd better call Doc Rice, quick." I began to wonder what was wrong. Of course, just about everything seemed to be wrong at that point. Then the Doc arrived, a bit ruffled about being called for an "emergency case," as usual. He began to feel my tummy, but he didn't say anything for a while. Then he straightened up and said, "We'll have to call in Doc Jensen, if he's available. You all have got a big problem here." Meanwhile the spasms of pain came closer and closer together, and I was thinking, "It will be a lot of extra expense, and we have so little money. But it will be worth it if I can just get rid of this terrible pain." Marriage had been a rough start for us, with a husband who had such poor prospects for a job just then. He was a university graduate and a high school teacher, but he had lost a good job. These were supposed to be "good times," but for us they were a financial disaster.

Doc Jensen soon arrived and more examinations followed. Then he looked around at the worried folks in the room and said gravely, "You people will have to learn that it is better to have babies in a hospital, where there is equipment to deal with situations like this. This mother's pelvic area is just too small to have a baby of this size. If we had seen her earlier, we could have done a C-section, but now her labor has progressed too far."

If I was panicking before, my panic now multiplied. I know I wasn't thinking sensibly at that point, but my emotions surely were working full-time. I remember Mama looking Doc Jensen in the eye and asking, "But can't you do something?"

Doc Jensen shrugged his shoulders, looked at the other doc, then grumbled, "Well, we'll have to do our best. But I really think the easiest way now would be to deliver the baby in pieces."

In my pain I had not been following much of the conversation, but I did hear the words "in pieces." My incoherence and misery cleared for a moment and I heard myself saying, "This is my baby and I've been carrying it for these nine long months!" Was all this to be in vain? "Wait," I blurted out, "if my baby can't live through this, then I don't want to live either!"

They tried to reason with me, which wasn't exactly easy, in the condition I was in. But nothing they said convinced me to change my mind. "If I can't have my baby, let me die too," I kept saying over and over, until finally the docs said, "OK, let's try!" They rolled up their sleeves and scrubbed as well as they could in that farmhouse with no running water. Then they began the attempt to deliver the child, hopefully in one piece and alive.

As hopeless as the situation had seemed, and some might even call it a miracle, eventually we heard the faint cry of a new baby and Doc Rice gave a happy yelp of relief, "It's a boy, and he's alive!" Then everything around me went black for several minutes.

When I came to, everyone was smiling, happy and relieved. Someone brought the new baby to me, and he looked so perfect that I felt like shouting, because our son was born alive and well! But some of the women advised me to save my energy and take time to rest after my long labor. I was so relieved it was all over and that our son was alive. Though I had only a limited idea of what lay ahead in my new role as a mother and of what would be involved in caring for our new son, I was too tired to think much about anything, except that my long labor was over and that we could thank God for our living son. I was too tired to eat much, but I sure was ready to sleep after all that labor and all that worry about whether our baby, and I, would survive and be healthy after this ordeal.

[*Sometime in 2004, while speaking with Ted's sister, Katherine (a redhead who preferred the nickname Pinky), I asked what she knew about his birth. She thought the doctors did use forceps, which proba-*

bly indicates that open-drop ether was used as anesthesia. In mid-2005 I found Ted's "baby book" with a pale blue cover. It showed that he was born on Wednesday, August 22, 1928, at 9:30 P.M. and weighed six pounds and four ounces, but it did not mention the length of labor or the doctors in attendance. I have delivered a number of babies and Ted was certainly not a large baby, but maybe his head was not flexed enough to facilitate an easy delivery.] ☩

Naming the Son

Ted wrote the following story in his mother's voice too, using a fictitious name for himself and for his father, and a fictitious outcome, intending it to be a Christian fiction elaborating the story of Jabez found in 1 Chronicles 4:9–10. But the facts of the story, as I heard it more than once, are good reading too. So, because I intend this book to be a biography of things as they happened rather than a fictional account—even if sometimes we wish the facts had been somewhat different—I have used real names and events.

Now that our baby had arrived safely, and it was a boy, a new crisis came up. We hadn't talked about a name for him. Of course it was OK in those days to delay the naming of a new child for a period of time, even for a week or more. But we were eager to give him a good name. My husband, Olin, could have gone for some family name like Henry or George, but I just wasn't satisfied with some "common" name for my baby. My interest in history made me insist on some "famous" name such as Woodrow Wilson or Grover Cleveland. But Olin said those names were bad baggage to put on a child. And I could visualize the little guy's playmates teasing him to death about his name, so I backed off.

Then I tried to explain to Olin, "I'd like him to have a distinguished name, something that could go with his being an ambassador someday, or maybe even a president. I don't want him to be some ordinary Tom, Dick, or Harry. You know, Papa had this evil friend named Harry and whenever they got together they would get drunk and Papa would come home and beat everybody up. I don't want any of that for *our* son. I want him to grow up to be somebody. Do you understand?"

Olin didn't say anything for several minutes, but I could hear the wheels turning inside his head. Finally he said, "Well, I'd really like him to have a name that would fit in with my family. I would not want him to be a stranger. My family is poor, you know. You said it yourself, that you could hardly stand the way we lived up there on Bonny Hill, saving the dishwater for the pigs and—"

"Well, the pigs got a little more soap when I washed the dishes! But what do you want to call him? You're better educated than I am, with your university degree. Not that it's done you all that much good, though, when it comes to keeping a job!"

I knew that would get to him. You see, I had been a good student until I got into high school. My trouble seemed to start after I fell down the stairs when I was twelve years old. After that, my eye muscles didn't work right and my eyes would jump around on the page when I tried to study my lessons. I knew better than to ask papa to pay for me to see an eye doctor. And that old principal at our high school just didn't seem to understand me and my problem. Then, during my second year in high school, I had a quarrel with him about getting credit for one of my courses. He said I had not done all the work, and I said I had. I got mad and told him that if I didn't get credit for my work, well, he could have his old high school. And I quit. After that, I was through with education.

Olin thought some more, then mentioned some famous names that I had never heard of. I kept saying, "No, not that one," until I could see he was really getting tired of it all, and I even began to feel a little sorry that I had made things so hard for him. He was trying so hard to please me, but he didn't want to give up his own ideas either. He had mentioned the name Theodore several times and it was no secret that he admired President Theodore Roosevelt. But I had objected because I figured with that name my son would get the nickname Teddy, and in my circles Teddy was a name for a dog, or even for some of the larger farm animals. Anyway, Olin tried the name Theodore again, and I thought a while this time. Olin spoke up again, "We could call him Theodore. Yes, Theodore Eggleston, for your family name. Would that make you happy?"

Finally I said, "Well, I guess I can live with the name Theodore, but I still don't like Teddy!" Olin breathed a big sigh of relief and soon was beaming all over. For my part, I was sure I would always address him as Theodore, no matter what others might call him. But at least our baby now had a name. I think we all slept better that night.

Several weeks later, when I was able to travel, we went to the little Presbyterian church I had attended as a girl, and our son was christened *Theodore Eggleston Morrow*.

Later, as my son grew up, he preferred the name Ted when among friends, but for business matters he went by Theodore E. Morrow. And as his mother I always called him Theodore (which means "Gift from God" when translated from Greek into English), as I had promised I would. ♱

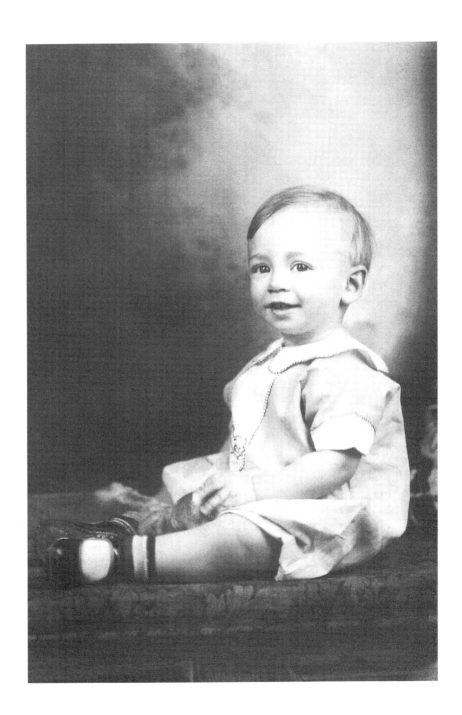

Ted's Early Childhood

This story too was written by Ted as he felt his mother would have told it.

We had made it through the difficult labor, and we had chosen a name for our son. He had seemed so perfect when he was born, but we soon discovered that our son was not as perfect as we had thought, and we quickly learned that being parents could be a demanding job. It seemed like he was only a few days old when he came down with a mysterious illness; he had breathing problems and bouts of fever. We tried so hard to keep his fever down, because otherwise he might develop convulsions. We tried to protect him from even a slight draft lest the fever start all over again. We did not want to take him to the hospital, especially because of the expense involved, though at least one time we did take him there when we were afraid he would not "pull through." Somehow he managed to weather each crisis, and our hopes would begin to rise again. But it seemed like any slight problem, like letting the front door stand open too long in the summer or letting his feet touch the cool floor, would trigger the illness, whatever it was, to reappear.

Along with the frequent episodes of illness and the needed care for our son, it was very hard for my husband and I to get enough rest and sleep. The first three years were very difficult, made much worse by my husband's struggle to get employment after the Depression of 1929, as well as by his worrying for the health of his son. I remember so vividly that one night he tried to comfort me by saying, "Please don't worry, my dear! If something happens to this son, we could try to have another one." That didn't comfort me at all! Instead of being "cheered up," I was furious at the way he said it. For one thing, I couldn't bear the thought of losing our little fellow. And frankly, I was not at all sure that I wanted to go through any more "labor pains" like I had experienced with our firstborn son!

But after a time I let my anger subside, for I knew that my husband and I both needed all the strength and cooperation we could muster between us if our family was to survive. And my husband needed to be alert and resourceful if he was to find a job that would support the three of us.

It was the early 1930s and it seemed that Hammondsport was not a good town in which to find employment, so we began looking in Bath, where my husband grew up, five miles south of my home. It was a bigger town, so hopefully there would be more job opportunities. Several times we left our son with my parents so we could explore Bath. But it seemed that no one was hiring, and people who had a job clung to it tenaciously, no matter how menial and poor-paying it was.

There was one possibility, however: the local post office. Olin arranged to take the Civil Service exam and scored more than 100 percent, thanks to the extra points he could claim as a World War I veteran. It seemed almost inevitable that he would get some kind of job. But time passed and other persons with lower civil service scores were hired, and Olin was still waiting. I soon figured out that the problem was "politics." Postmasters received their positions through political appointments, and to some extent the politicians could decide who to choose for open positions. This was a big blow to my husband, who couldn't understand this way of doing things.

I thought a lot about this situation of how to get a job for Olin. Granted, I wasn't as well educated as he was, but I remembered that one of his relatives had previously served as the mayor of Bath and that he still wielded some influence with the Democrats, who were in power at the time. I suggested to Olin, as gently as I could, that we might pay a visit to this relative. We went and were graciously received. After listening attentively to our problem and then sitting in silence for a few minutes, he asked several questions, beginning with "Which political party are you registered to vote with?" Olin freely admitted that he was a Republican. The relative thought some more, then said, "OK, I'll take care of it. But meanwhile, do me a favor and don't talk about your admiration of Teddy Roosevelt and your political sympathies."

It wasn't long before Olin was called for an interview, and he did keep his mouth shut when it came to politics. The result was that he was hired as a "temporary substitute." He soon knew all the train routes for the towns in the state and which mailbag to throw the mail into to get it to its destination. Eventually he became the unofficial "dispatcher and information man" for the Bath post office staff, and finally he was promoted to the position of "regular substitute" for the postal service, and his family had a major celebration. He remained a valued employee of the postal service until his retirement in September 1956. ✝

Ted Goes to Haverling Elementary School

According to Ted's baby book, he gained weight normally after his birth, reaching fifteen and a half pounds by five months, but then his growth slowed down. He began experiencing episodes of respiratory problems, and sometimes lost weight. At one year he weighed eighteen and a half pounds; at two years, twenty-four pounds; at three years, twenty-seven pounds; and at five years he was a small thirty-three pounds.

Childhood diseases were common in those days before immunizations were available. The following illnesses were recorded in Ted's baby book:

Whooping cough	*June 1931*
Tonsils and adenoids removed	*June 1934*
Measles	*December 1934*
Mumps	*February 1942*
German Measles	*1943*

Ted turned five years old on August 22, 1933, and in spite of his small size, ten days later his mother walked him across the street to first grade at Haverling School. Was she perhaps in a bigger hurry to get him into school than he was to get there?

The indented portions of the following account are from Ted's own work on his memoirs; the other paragraphs were written by me.

As reported previously, Ted was not a healthy child but was prone to recurrent bronchitis and pneumonia, sometimes with fever and even seizures. This was before the advent of penicillin and other powerful antibiotics, so when Ted got sick it often took weeks for him to recover. He also had abdominal problems and often did not eat well, which is why he was small for his age.

Haverling School was a large three-story brick building where all of the students in grades 1 through 12 (Kindergarten had not yet arrived) in the metropolis of Bath, New York, were educated. I can picture Ted's mother walking him the half-block down their street to the main thoroughfare, where they would turn left and cross the street to arrive at the school's big front doors. I can also see the bigger children watching them come, and then laughing at Ted and teasing him after his mother had gone back home. Ted describes it thus:

> At school, all the boys were bigger than I was. One fellow in particular, named Eddie, was not only big but also well built. Unaware of the potential consequences, I one day said something to him that aroused his wrath. Eddie quickly landed his powerful fist into my face and sent me home with a bloody nose! It was a very painful experience, and for a long time afterward I was a very timid young man, never sure when someone else might decide to do the same thing to me.

So Ted learned that he was no match for Eddie, at least not with his fists; but he also learned to use his mouth to come up with some retort for his tormentors. In time he seemed to gain some respect from his classmates by what he said; and they seemed to tease him just to see what he would say in response.

Ted continued to have bouts of respiratory illness during elementary school, but he still made acceptable-to-good grades. In fact, he became identified as a boy who liked books. He was rather clumsy in sports and was frequently ridiculed by the other boys for his lack of athletic ability. He admitted that he sometimes wanted to run away from the games to where no one could find him, but of course there was nowhere to hide. This little guy who was no good at sports and liked to read books—no wonder he did not make many friends among his classmates. And his mother would not let him play with the neighborhood children, for fear that he might "catch something" from them. But some of Ted's teachers were fond of him and encouraged him in his academic interests.

In later years Ted wrote this:

> With the athletic world closed off to me, my intellectual curiosity developed rather early. In fact, by the age of three and a half I had started to read books, and I became well acquainted with math and astronomy at an early age too. This of course did not help my popularity in school, as I later came to understand that no one likes a "smart aleck." As a result, I became withdrawn and had almost no friends. And my parents seldom invited dinner guests to our home, so I had only limited opportunity to develop appropriate social skills.

I can believe that Ted was not exaggerating his early reading ability and his early exploration of math and astronomy. I suspect that his father, Olin, had similar abilities. Ted continues in his memoir draft:

> My father had taught in high school before he was married, and he kept a lot of his old schoolbooks. I discovered those books at an early age and was especially interested in his language books. I began reading some of his easier German readers. I was still fairly young when my dad brought home a copy of Friedrich Schiller's *William Tell,* written in German. At the time I was recovering from another bout of illness, but the sight of the book aroused my interest, so I got out of bed, found some paper and a pencil, and began trying to make an English translation. I didn't get very far with it, because the subject matter was much too difficult, but it was a harbinger of things to come when I reached adulthood.

Ted also showed an early interest in music. His parents had an upright piano in the alcove of their living room, so they started him on private lessons. Unfortunately for Ted, he took sick again in third grade and missed a month or more of school. During this time of illness, Ted was too tired to practice on the piano. When he felt better and returned to school, he asked his parents when he could resume the piano lessons. His mother tartly replied, "You had your chance!" His father apparently said nothing to support Ted, because he was afraid of the backlash from his wife. So Ted was left to gaze longingly at the piano that he so much wished to learn to play. That pain never left him. When he and Catherine had their family, though money was not plentiful for them they did have a piano in their home. They often sang together, and the children had access to a variety of music lessons (piano, violin, string bass, viola) and two of the children were music majors in college. Ted did play the piano some, but mostly in only one or two keys. As an elderly grandfather, he obtained a portable keyboard that he enjoyed playing.

When Ted was in fourth grade, Professor Oldfield discovered Ted's interest in music and spoke to his parents about resuming private piano lessons. Ted's mother insisted again that he'd had his chance to study piano and, besides, it was too expensive for their tight budget. After all, Ted's baby sister had recently been born with bilateral cleft lip and cleft palate and needed surgical repairs. So Professor Oldfield did second best for Ted: he started a group class for students to study violin and invited Ted to join the class. So Ted studied violin through tenth grade, then opted to join the choir, because he also had a good tenor singing voice. Ted later played violin in the orchestra at Houghton College, and

years later he dug out his violin and played with the worship team at the last two churches we attended. He never claimed to be a great violinist, but he did practice diligently, and we all enjoyed the music he shared with us. ✝

On Growing Up in Bath

I grew up in what is known as the Finger Lakes region of western New York State. My great-great grandfather John Morrow, his wife, and their six children came there after leaving their home near Carrigallen in the County of Caven in northern Ireland in 1822. After a rough voyage of forty-seven days, they landed in New York and traveled up the Hudson and Mohawk Rivers, then over the hills to Mud Creek (which originates from the eastern shore of Lake Keuka, traverses Waneta Lake and Lamoka Lake, and winds southwestward to join the Cohoctan River near Savona; the Cohoctan River then heads southeast to Corning, changes its name to the Chemung River, and continues to Elmira and Sayre, where it is joined by the eastern branch of the Susquehanna River). John bought a hundred acres of land south of Bancroft's Lake in the vicinity of Mud Creek at five dollars per acre.

Some maps of New York State show a row of eight deep but slender lakes running in a north-south direction, with the largest lakes in the middle and the Y-shaped Lake Keuka on the left. Other maps show additional lakes scattered to the south and west of Lake Seneca, as far west as the area south of Rochester. Most of the lakes have Indian names. Hammondsport lies at the southern end of Lake Keuka, and Bath is five miles or so further south. The topography of western New York State consists of a southern tier of small cities (Olean, Corning, Elmira), a northern tier of larger cities (Buffalo, Rochester, Syracuse), and a lot of rolling farmland in between. The village of Bath, named after the city of Bath in England, is small but it is the Steuben County seat, and its schools, stores, and other businesses serve a wide expanse of varied agricultural communities that have produced lots of grapes and wines, potatoes, and maple syrup.

John Morrow was of Irish and English descent and traced his ancestry to the Orangemen clan. He was also described as a very religious man, an Episcopalian who actively supported the Episcopal Church in Bradford, located at the southern end of Lamoka Lake. John was born in 1779 and died in 1865. His wife, Margaret Mathews, was born in 1779 and died in 1861. They are both buried in the Grove Cemetery in Bath, New York, along with their son Robert and daughter Barbara. My great grandfather was Thomas Morrow, the third son of John Morrow. He married Sarah Place and they had nine children, of whom my grandfather, Henry Daniel Morrow, was the youngest child. Thomas Morrow and his family first lived on Mount Washington (southeast of Hammondsport), then went to Canada for three years. After their return to New York, they lived on Bonny Hill, a few miles southeast of Bath. Henry Morrow married May Belle Yost. They had three sons—Olin (my father,) Floyd, and Irving—and a daughter, Mildred, who died at nine years of age of a congenital heart condition. Henry and his family also lived on Bonny Hill. It may have been a "bonnie hill," as the Irish like to say, but it was also a dry, windswept hilltop that was not blessed with enough rain to ensure adequate income for a farmer.

As I have written, I was a sickly child, and the smallest boy in my first grade class. On the day that big Eddie proved he did not like me by socking me in the nose and giving me a real nosebleed, when I got home from school my mother asked me, "Did you see stars?" I replied, "No, but I saw sparks." I know this because my mother recorded it in my baby book. It was episodes like this encounter with Eddie that colored my view of myself for many years to come and led me to think of myself as a tiny ant surrounded by big giants who were ready to step on me. I therefore tended to ignore the other students and instead devoted my time and energy to intellectual pursuits. I learned to cope with the forbidding world around me by withdrawing into myself and concentrating on reading and exploring new things—projects that I could do by myself.

My parents were not very helpful when it came to helping me learn social skills. Because I was a sickly and frail child, they felt I needed to be protected. They discouraged me from associating with other children lest I "catch something." I was forbidden to participate in any sports or other activities that might be dangerous. I never got to go camping, for example, until I was drafted into the US Army, and that was not usually meant to be fun!

In addition, it was a prevailing idea among parents in that era that they should not offer compliments or say anything that might cause their child to become "proud." So if my parents were pleased about some accomplishment of mine, they would not tell me so, but they might mention it to a friend, who would *perhaps* later relay to me what my parents had said. This was also the era when parents were not skittish about using physical punishment. My mother in particular found abundant opportunities to avoid "sparing the rod"! [*This comment agrees with Pinky's report to me that when she was a child her mother often struck her across her lower legs with Olin's razor strap, and Pinky believes that this beating accounts for her difficulty in walking today. I do not remember Ted ever saying that his mother was physically abusive to him, but this comment seems to indicate that she did mistreat him, in spite of his frail physique and health problems as a child.*]

The first real friend I had was a boy named Wayne. We enjoyed playing Monopoly and other table games together. And we talked about

lots of things. I wasn't used to having a friend who was my age. I soon came to admire his knowledge of a bigger world that was so foreign to me. We were in seventh grade together and he got me interested in writing short plays. Then he would get permission from the English teacher and she would let us act out our plays for the class. This was such an exhilarating experience for me and helped me to expand my horizons. As I continued into high school I became fascinated with writing short rhymes, and eventually classmates would ask me to write "poetry to order" for specials occasions such as birthdays.

My parents began attending church regularly soon after we moved to Bath. My dad liked the local Methodist church while my mother preferred the Presbyterian church in Hammondsport. Some things about church mystified me for a long time. For one thing, my parents always managed to get us there late for the morning service and I wondered what happened before we arrived. It wasn't until I was in high school that I awoke early one Sunday morning and sneaked off to church ahead of my parents so I could see how the service began. The other mystery to me was, what happened when everyone bowed their heads during prayer? Did the Almighty make an appearance while our heads were bowed? The question kept bugging me; however, I was afraid to investigate further for fear of some reprisal that might be visited upon me. But my curiosity finally got the better of me, and one day when everyone's head was bowed I opened my eyes and looked straight up at the ceiling. To my disappointment, I noticed nothing unusual. But for a long time afterward I kept wondering if I would be punished for my curiosity.

For several years during high school I delivered the Sunday newspaper. When I got the delivery route, the fellow who had previously delivered the papers would not hand over his list of subscribers to the boss, so I contacted all the residents on the assigned blocks and got more subscribers than the previous carrier had. Initially I used an old bike with wooden wheels and a big basket on the front to deliver the papers. Talk about an antiquated conveyance! One day as I was doing my deliveries, with the basket full of papers, I hit a stone in the street and the front wheel collapsed, so that was the end of that bike. My dad then decided to help me deliver the papers, but he left me in time to attend Sunday school, after the church service, while I made my collections and did my record keeping for the boss. Eventually Dad became Sunday school superintendent. Meanwhile, I was missing both the Sunday morning church service and Sunday school, but I did attend the Sunday evening youth meetings at the local Methodist church. The pastor and his wife at that time related well to young people and had an effective ministry, and I enjoyed attending their services.

One of the truly positive experiences of my childhood developed after my parents established contact with a "distant cousin," Charles W. Egleston, and his wife, Clara. Actually, Charlie was a first cousin of my grandfather, George D. Eggleston, and yes, Charlie used only one *g* while grandfather George used two *gg*s in his surname! Cousins Charlie and Clara lived about thirty miles from Bath at the upper end of Lake Keuka, near Penn Yan, but my parents enjoyed being with them, so we visited them several times a year. I was especially impressed by my cousin Clara. She was a most unusual woman, unlike anyone I had ever met before. To Clara, life was a constant companionship with the Christian God, and I found myself strongly attracted to that way of living. One summer, Charlie and Clara invited me to spend several days with them, and remarkably my parents agreed. Those were some of the happiest days of my childhood, when the world outside was somehow eclipsed and I could just enjoy being in their unique atmosphere. The simplicity and strength of their way of life became permanently stored in my memory. ✝

Ted's Dad

During much of my youth I held some very negative ideas about my father. To begin with, he was short, bald, and not especially handsome. But more than that, I was uncomfortable sitting beside him in church, because although he couldn't sing on pitch, he loved to sing—very loudly.

For many years he played violin in the Sunday school orchestra, but he wasn't any better at that either. He couldn't get the rhythms right, and he hit a lot of sour notes.

Dad was poor at making speeches too, but nonetheless he accepted many opportunities to do so. He also strongly resembled the character Caspar Milquetoast in Harold Tucker Webster's cartoon series *The Timid Soul* in that he seemed to be deathly afraid of my mother.

None of this evidence matched up very well with what I knew about his early life. Although he came from a very poor farming family, he attended Keuka College for two years, then transferred to the University of Rochester, where in 1917 he acquired a bachelor of arts degree in a class of forty-four men. He once explained to me that he had earned some money by delivering flowers for a Rochester florist, which he had accomplished despite the fact that his mother had contracted polio when he was still a boy and was basically confined to a wheelchair for the rest of her life, and her three sons were expected to help with the housework as well as work on the farm.

After graduation, Dad served in the US Army. After discharge, he teamed up with a teacher friend and the two men worked as teacher-administrators in small rural high schools scattered throughout New York State. That job lasted until 1927, when the love bug bit him and he married my mother. I was born a year later, just one year before our country entered the Great Depression. Teaching jobs then became "as scarce as hens' teeth," and despite a very high score on the civil service exam, for a long time Dad was unable to find a job to support himself and his family. But finally he did get a position as a dispatcher in the local post office, and from then on Dad dreamed about becoming wealthy, or at least comfortable enough not to worry.

Eventually I came to realize that Dad was an unusually good calligrapher, with a very clear and forceful handwriting style. I also discovered that he was very accomplished at lettering in Old English characters. He never used tobacco, alcohol, or profanity, and on at least one occasion he described himself as "an old-fashioned Methodist."

When I was old enough to read, Dad started the daily practice of family Bible reading. We would gather in the living room after supper and sometimes read a few verses and discuss them and other times read several chapters. I especially remember how much I cried when we

read the story of Joseph in Genesis, especially the part where Joseph revealed himself to his brothers, who had thought he was long dead. Even today I can't seem to read that story without my eyes clouding with tears.

Dad had a lot of mementos from his school-teaching days. When I discovered his treasure trove of high school textbooks, I began to study math on my own, years ahead of studying the subject in school. I also got into his library of German, Latin, Greek, and Spanish language books, and that was the birth of my interest in languages. I also discovered astronomy and became fascinated with that topic too.

During my second year of college I came to know Jesus Christ as my personal Savior and Lord. When I told my parents about it, their first reaction was fear that this was some sort of fanaticism. But they soon became restless in their own church and started to visit other churches.

One Sunday during one of my summer vacations from college, Dad asked me to accompany him to the Sunday evening service of a church in town. "I've developed a fondness for the pastor there," he told me. "He's an outstanding scholar and a good preacher." So I went with him, and was not disappointed. The church—a tiny building compared with every other church in town—was at the other end of what was the most celebrated thoroughfare of our small town. The islands in the middle of this impressive mile-long avenue were lined with streetlamps like those along the Champs-Élysées in Paris.

Attendance was not all that great—just a handful of poorly dressed people. The highlight of the service was the eloquent sermon of the young minister, and the piano performance of his wife. The sermon was so compelling and powerful that, as we went home, Dad and I compared notes and discussed the sermon's implications for our lives.

When we arrived at the house, we sensed tension in the air. Initially we did not understand what it was about, but my mother soon explained what had happened. Two policemen had come to the door and asked for my dad. My mother told them she was sorry but her husband and his son had gone to a church service. The two officers snickered, then said, "That's OK. We'll come back later. And," one of them added ominously, "we have a warrant for your husband's arrest."

When my mother said this, I wondered out loud what had brought this about. So she explained: "Your father and I were out on the front lawn one day, resting, and next door a kid from another neighborhood had a cap pistol that he was showing off. He grew more and more daring, until finally he came into our yard and menaced us up close. This got me very upset and finally I said to your dad, 'Could you please do something about this?' Because your dad is such a mild-mannered man, I guess I didn't expect much to happen. But he suddenly jumped up, ran after the boy, turned him over his knee, and gave him a sound spanking. Then he tossed the cap pistol into the yard next door."

"So that's what this is all about?" I asked.

"And apparently his father went and swore out a warrant for my arrest," Dad replied. "It's for third-degree assault, I think."

"So, what do we do now?" I asked.

"Well, for my part, I'd like to go to bed," Dad said, yawning.

So that's what we did. It was around midnight when the policemen showed up again. Dad and I both got dressed and accompanied them down to city hall.

"There's a problem here," Dad told me. "Your mother doesn't quite understand what's going on. If they ask for bail, I don't dare pay it, because your mother thinks that would be admitting I was guilty."

I didn't say anything because, well, I was no expert in such matters. When we arrived at the police station, we were met by the police justice, as they were called there, and he read the charge. Everybody in the room knew my dad. When the magistrate asked for ten dollars for bail, my dad just sat there and said nothing.

"Look, Oley, I have to have something to hold you from skipping town," the justice said with a smirk, knowing full well that my dad was not apt to run away. His reputation in town was good and everyone knew he was a responsible person.

Dad still had nothing to say.

"Oley, don't you have ten bucks on you?"

Dad shook his head.

"Don't you have a watch or something you could use as a deposit?"

Finally Dad said, "You don't understand. I promised my wife that I would not pay any bail. I know it's not an admission of guilt, but my wife doesn't understand that."

"Oh, come on, Oley, couldn't you just tell a little white lie?"

At that point it seemed like Dad suddenly stretched up to about ten feet tall. "I don't tell lies," he said firmly.

The judge frowned. "Well, then, I guess we'll have to lock you up." A policeman came forward reluctantly, finding it hard to believe that Dad would take such a stand with so little money involved. But Dad had nothing more to say. The cops took him to their paddy wagon and whisked him off to the county jail.

I returned home by myself, my thoughts jumbled, and went to bed but slept poorly. The next morning I went to work for the farmer who had hired me for the summer. I was still processing the events of the night and the farmer could tell something was bothering me; I wasn't usually that quiet. He kept talking and asking questions, and finally I told him what had happened.

Bert, the farmer, was rather shocked by my story, and he promptly said, "What fool would do something like that to a man as honest as your dad? That boy should have gotten another spanking when he went home!" Then he reached into his pocket and pulled out a ten-dollar bill. "Here, take this over to that jail and get your daddy out of there. I won't start work here until you get back."

More startled than ever, I went to the jail and presented the money, then went back to see how Dad was doing. He was sitting in his cell looking very dejected, until he noticed me. He was so relieved that I had come for him. "This is a terrible place," he said. "I couldn't sleep all night, and the food they brought me was so awful I couldn't eat it."

Dad never forgot his night in jail, and neither did I. Somehow I had seen a facet of his personality that I had not recognized before, and his night in jail had crowded out all the negative feelings I had been harboring against him. I came to see him as a man who had dared to pursue his dreams as a youth and who had enjoyed teaching as a young man but later learned to accommodate himself to the needs and wishes of his family rather than insisting on his own goals. In later years I often wished he had told me more about his early life and his dreams, for I found myself sharing his love of languages, of teaching the Bible, and of mathematics and science.

In his later years, Dad still remembered his jail experience, and he became quite interested in jails and prisoners. In fact, this interest developed into a ministry that was to last the rest of his life. He also was active in speaking to various groups about the Gideons and in placing Bibles in various public facilities. ✝

Life After High School

It was 1945. High school was over. My days of sparring with Miss Barnes in English class were over. But I clearly remember the satirical essay I had once written about the "old maid" teacher in which I said that "Miss Barnes is one for whom wedding bells never toll," and she had castigated me before the entire class for not knowing that "bells never toll for a happy occasion such as a wedding!"

I also remember Miss Hanson, the new English teacher who arrived the following year, and how she sparked my interest in writing with the assignment to write our autobiography. I was late getting mine finished, but I enjoyed writing it, and she liked my work too. Next thing I knew, she got me working on the school newspaper as proofreader, headlines editor, and then writer of some poems and feature articles and maker of crossword puzzles. Then Miss Hanson even convinced this very shy student to enter a speech contest—she just would not let me say no! And guess what: I even won—to my surprise. It was a boost to my low self-esteem when teachers and fellow students gave me their congratulations.

Graduation was over too. I'd had several years of science, math, and foreign language study. I'd also received some musical training and been introduced to journalism and writing. I had the highest GPA among the boys in our class, but a girl ranked above me, so she was valedictorian for our class. I did receive the bronze Bausch + Lomb medal for the highest average in science, and the prize for the highest average in foreign languages. My yearbook was now filled with autographs, including one that really baffled me. Signed by Miss Hanson, it merely said, "John 3:16." I puzzled over that reference for a long time and kept looking it up in my Bible for several years before I finally discovered what it meant.

It now seemed that my education was over. I had no clear idea what I wanted to do next. I did not have money to go to college, and my parents could not pay my way either. And if I did go to college, what would I study? What I really enjoyed most was languages, but I enjoyed music too.

The obvious thing to do was to get a job and earn some money. One of our town's major sources of employment was the nearby Veteran's Administration (VA) facility, which included a large hospital and a separate "domiciliary ward" for fifteen hundred veterans who were not necessarily sick but were so accustomed to military life that they felt insecure living "on the outside." I got a job in the kitchen, which fed the domiciliary veterans three meals every day of the week. I started working there in the summer of 1945 as World War II was winding down in Europe, with the Far East engagement to be completed some time later.

I had been on the job for a month, or maybe longer, and was enjoying the work and the employees when one day something unusual happened that really made an impression on me, even though it did not make much sense to me at the time. My work shift was over and we fellows had just changed back into our street clothes. Everyone else had finished and had already left the locker room, leaving me alone. Suddenly I sensed the presence of an unseen person, who spoke directly to my mind: "You are now becoming of age. Your life has so far been controlled by others. You have lived a life of obedience, but mainly that was because you knew that misbehavior would result in punishment. But from now on you must learn to be a responsible person, making decisions on the basis of what is right and wrong." The bearer of this message was invisible, but compellingly real.

Several weeks later, in August 1945, another startling surprise came my way. I received a letter from the New York Board of Regents informing me that I was one of five people to receive a four-year scholarship to a school of my choice, provided it was on their approved list and that I was accepted to begin classes that fall. Well, I had not given serious consideration to attending any college, so this was really short notice for me.

So my dad began talking up his alma mater and strongly recommended that I consider it. He then offered to drive me the seventy-odd miles to the University of Rochester, and because I had no driver's license and did not know my way around, I accepted his offer. When we got to the admissions office, we discovered that the director of admissions had been at Rochester at the same time as my dad. This fact seemed to influence the director to accept me into the school for the coming fall semester, and he even granted me an additional scholarship from the university.

So I returned home with a school catalog. All I had to do was choose the courses I wanted to take and see if I could fit them all into my schedule. I was enrolled in the River Campus, which was predominantly a campus for men to study science. The women's campus specialized in liberal arts. The River Campus at that time was heavily controlled by the Naval Reserve Officers Training Corps (NROTC) and was operating on a three-semester school year. Because the fall semester did not begin until November 1, I had two extra months to earn more money at my VA job before starting college.

Choosing my major and the courses I wanted was the hard part. I really wanted to study languages, and I had that prize for language proficiency from high school. But my dad insisted that a degree in science would earn more money than a degree in languages. He strongly urged me to take the optics course, because, he said, the university was closely tied in with Eastman Kodak and Bausch + Lomb, the two major optical industries in Rochester, and if I got an optics degree I could surely hope to get a good-paying position afterward. So, my decision boiled down to these two options: either do what my dad, with his awareness of the Depression and the value of a good job, recommended; or pursue my love of languages even though I was not sure what I would do with such a degree. As I looked over the optics major, I was impressed by the fact that it included several years of German study. I also noticed that I had studied enough high school math and science to let me sign up for advanced chemistry and calculus in my freshman year. So I finally, and reluctantly, conceded to my father's wishes and signed up as an optics major, but not for the right reasons. ✞

University Life

My life in Bath had been a very sheltered and protected one, and I came to university with quite limited social skills and limited ability to fend for myself, so I had many things to learn when I arrived on the University of Rochester campus in early November 1945.

One of the first things I encountered in the dormitory was the diversity of the students, who came from many different backgrounds and countries. The NROTC still dominated the dormitories, except for the fraternity houses, which became available to civilians. One of the occupants of my "house" was a black man from Waco, Texas. Soon after my arrival, the proctor came to me and asked if I would mind accepting him as my roommate, because the person to whom he had been assigned refused to accept him. I saw no reason to refuse, and Ike proved to be a delightful roommate. In fact, he knew more about social graces and etiquette than I did, and I learned some things from him. In time, Ike counted me as his closest confidant at the university.

I enjoyed the opportunity to make new friends. Because I had missed out on Sunday morning church services while I was carrying the Sunday paper route in Bath, I was happy to attend a small Methodist church in Rochester. Soon I was singing in their choir. Among the students who became my friends was Lenny, a young Jewish man from the Bronx who was a Zionist and introduced me to his Zionist friends in the area. I soon became convinced that there would be a Jewish state for the people of Israel, even though it was not yet a reality.

I began to form my own ideas about religion. I saw Christ as only one of a host of outstanding moral teachers, and Christianity was only a part of the great "world religion" that would someday sweep all men into a common brotherhood of peace and goodwill. I decided to dedicate my life to this ideal, so I began to read the scriptures of Buddha, Mohammed, Confucius, Lao-Tzu, and Zoroaster so that I might see what my own beliefs had in common with theirs. My friends came to include a Chinese graduate student who followed Confucius, a Polish Catholic who was into psychoanalysis, and a Hawaiian musician who believed in reincarnation.

As my first year wore on, the Navy vacated more and more dormitories, so I moved into one of them. Later I moved to the stadium dormitory, because the rental fee was less. My room was probably the smallest I have ever lived in, with just enough space for a desk and a locker. Residents of this dorm slept in a common room in another part of the building. One advantage to this arrangement was that many graduate students were housed here, including a student from Shanghai, China, who taught me a little Chinese.

I started off by making the dean's list in the first marking period, which made me feel good. The only problem course was engineering drawing, which proved to be exceedingly difficult for me. By midyear I had completely flunked the course, a most unusual experience for me; but undaunted I repeated the course during the second semester—and flunked it again. And because the drawing course was a requirement for the optics major, I decided to change my major to physics, which also included science, math, and German in its requirements.

Meanwhile, the university had hired a young Presbyterian minister as campus chaplain. Under his leadership, a dozen of us organized what came to be known as the Student Christian Association. I joined in heartily to formulate the creed of the new group and to map out plans for its future. We soon began working with a similar group from the women's campus and sponsored joint social projects. Our major project in 1946 was an international festival with a stage show of various national dances, booths that displayed other aspects of national cultures, and an intercampus Sunday morning church service featuring a number of guest speakers from the city. One of my accomplishments for this festival was to introduce my friend Lenny and several of his Zionist friends to the festival's chairperson. Lenny and his friends wanted to make a presentation at the festival too, but the committee felt they were merely representing a religion, Judaism, and not a nation. The Zionists were not so easily dissuaded and eventually prevailed. As a result, they presented a performance that proved to be one of the highlights of the evening. It was groups like Lenny's that developed into the Friends of Israel Gospel Ministry, which is still well known today. And of course in 1948 Israel was recognized—by most of the non-Muslim world, at least—as a nation.

I threw myself into these activities with such fervor that my studies began to suffer. By the end of my freshman year I had forfeited one of the two scholarships I was holding, because of the drop in my grades. But during the latter part of my freshman year, my studies could no longer hold my attention. There had arisen in my heart a deep hunger that I could not satisfy, although I sought to gain relief by plunging into more and more activities. I realized I was not satisfied with the church I was attending, so I found another Methodist church with a young pastor who used every device possible to attract young people. The Sunday evening program was built around lively entertainment, and on Friday nights there was a big party, complete with games and dancing, both square and round. This whirl of worldly glitter was initially attractive to me and I threw myself into it with great gusto. However, as time went on I began to realize that pleasure was the main goal and real spiritual nourishment was lacking, and my hunger for real heart satisfaction became more acute.

It was at about this time that I began to receive letters from my cousin Clara, wife of my Eggleston grandfather's cousin Charlie. In her letters, Clara often said that when she went to bed the Holy Spirit would come upon her in great power, and she would find herself praying for my spiritual condition. It all sounded very strange to me at the time.

As my freshman year was coming to an end, I learned that I could arrange to stay in the stadium dorm during the summer. Through some university contacts I also got a job at Kodak Park, working in the building where their light-sensitive emulsion was made. I was part of an entry-level gang of maintenance workers, which was not very inspiring work but was a source of income.

A week later, Paul, a pre-ministerial student and freshman classmate, moved into the stadium dorm. He had just returned from a leadership training course sponsored by the Student Christian Association at a summer camp and was bubbling over with his experiences. He invited me to share a time of evening devotions with him. I decided to give it a try. We met at 10:00 P.M. every night to read a chapter from the Bible and then offer a prayer to God. Now, reading the Bible was not new to me, because we had done that at home, and I had heard enough long eloquent prayers, adorned with flowery phrases, and learned enough theological gymnastics that I figured I could pray too. But as to understanding the Scriptures? That, for me, was like wandering through a dark and dense jungle. Inside I was groping for the light, but I was still only dimly aware of it.

After several weeks of regular devotions, Paul told me about another student, Pete, who also lived in the stadium dorm and might attend our devotional sessions, "if we are careful not to step on his theological toes." Pete joined the group and became a special friend of mine after Paul moved into a fraternity house in the fall. After we had finished reading the Gospel of Mark, Pete suggested that we try 1 Corinthians. This was less familiar territory for me; I knew much more about the Bible's stories than about the Apostle Paul's theology. I discovered that Pete was very skillful at comparing this epistle with other passages in the Bible. I also found that the opening chapters of 1 Corinthians had a lot to say about the wisdom of God and the foolishness of man. I had never thought of it that way. Are human beings really so foolish in their reasoning? I began to have second thoughts about my project of studying all the world's religions and extracting from each of them what I considered to be best and combining them to make my own religion. This line of reasoning troubled me deeply, and I had difficulty sleeping at night as I tried to reconcile the conflicting ideas I was having. And the 10:00 P.M. meetings continued.

In my sophomore literature class that fall I grew rather troubled by the teacher's skeptical attitude toward Scripture. He presented the Bible as an allegory, as something we no longer take seriously. One day someone knocked on the classroom door and gave a note to the teacher. It announced that a Bible study was to be held later that afternoon in the library. Almost everyone was amused, and some openly expressed their contempt. But I went to check it out. I discovered that it was sponsored not by Chaplain Crary nor by the Student Christian Association. The leader was an older man and he was expounding from Isaiah 6. Beside him sat my friend Pete, looking very contented. I knew none of the other students. The leader referred to the Bible as the "Word of God" and talked about the virgin birth of Christ and the Resurrection as though they were actual facts of history. I thought that only ignorant and superstitious people had such credulity as that, and I became quite confused. When the leader later gave opportunity for questions, I spoke up: "Sir, you speak of the biblical miracles as things that really happened. Is this a genuinely scientific attitude?"

The Bible study leader listened calmly, then said, "If it's a matter of being scientific, just remember that the God who made creation and the laws that govern it has had perfect control of the situation and is quite capable of handling miracles just as readily as the more ordinary things we find in the stories."

When the Bible study was over, I learned that the leader was the pastor of the local Christian Reformed Church, and my friend Pete's pastor. That explained why they seemed to be such close friends! Well, I went home with new questions and new ideas to mull over in the days ahead.

Several weeks later I met Don, a friend of Pete's. Don sometimes visited our 10:00 P.M. Bible readings, and he always brought several other students along, so the room was packed. Don really impressed me when he prayed and addressed God as "Father." He really seemed to know God as his father, and he brought the peace of God into our room. Despite a speech impediment, Don talked freely about God to others. My inner turmoil became worse; I had more difficulty sleeping and sometimes walked the streets at night for several hours, asking God to show me the light. And I could not concentrate on my studies.

One evening when studying seemed impossible, I decided to hunt for Gloria, a high school student whom I enjoyed talking to about religious topics. I learned that she had gone to a youth meeting, so I went too, and discovered that it was a Youth for Christ (YFC) meeting. I had heard bad news about YFC from my Student Christian Association, so I basically tuned out the speaker while a storm raged within me. When the invitation to learn more was given, for some inexplicable reason I went to the inquiry room, but instead of praying for myself and talking to a counselor, I mostly found fault with the prayers of those around me. When I got up and left, I was still a proud Pharisee.

Several weeks later, in mid-November, I found myself sitting in church and this time I was listening with my heart as well as my ears, straining to find a secret in the pastor's words. Several times I thought he was about to disclose it, but at the last minute he would veer away, and I would feel disappointed. I headed home very unsettled and discouraged, but promptly ran into my friend Pete, who invited me to go with him to hear a guest speaker, Dan James, that evening. After the meeting, we met with Dan and talked a while on a street corner. Then Dan invited us to his apartment, so we hopped onto a bus that took us to the southwestern part of the city. We talked casually for a time, but I was quiet and lost in thought, and Dan sensed it. Finally he turned to me with a smile and asked, "Well, Ted, tell me, are you a Christian?"

That little question turned the focus onto me, and I shuddered as I realized it, and half rose to my feet in terror.

"Well, Ted?"

"No, Dan, I'm not a Christian as you define it, and please, I've got to settle this thing. Could it be done tonight?" Dan jumped to his feet and beckoned Pete and me to the bed, where we knelt together, with Dan on my right and Pete on my left. Dan pulled out a New Testament, turned to Romans 10:9, and asked me to read these words: "If thou shalt confess with thy mouth Jesus as Lord and believe in thine heart that God hath raised him from the dead, thou shalt be saved." Then he said, "Now, let's pray."

I began to pray. Ordinarily I started with "Father in Heaven." When I began to pray that way this time, a voice in my head seemed to say to me, "But God is not your father and you are not his child."

I cried out, "Oh, Lord!" But the voice said, "No, He is not your Lord, for you are not his servant."

At last I cried out in great desperation, "Oh, God, be merciful to me a sinner!"

A sinner! Ah, that was it. That was the word that broke open the fountains of the deep in my heart. Before when I had prayed, I had been Ted Morrow the Pharisee. Before I had known a few things *about* God and His Word. But now I was Ted Morrow the lost sinner, pleading for mercy before the throne of God. I kept repeating those words, over and over, and all the pride and self-righteousness were vomited forth from my heart. Then there came a great calm and peace inside me.

Dan said to me, "Ted, you have confessed your need. Now tell him that you believe he saves you."

So I did, and a few minutes later Dan asked me, "Ted, did he do it?"

"Oh, yes, Dan. There's no longer any doubt."

I felt Dan's hand close over mine. "Then praise the Lord, Pete, for He has won!" I rose to my feet feeling as relaxed and refreshed as after a good night's sleep. When Pete and I left Dan's place a few minutes later, it was as if I was stepping into a brand new world. I realized later that it was the same old world, but I had become new—a new creation in Christ.

I continued to marvel at the new sense of life I had experienced. God had done a perfect work, and I knew that neither man nor devil could prevent Him from bringing that work to completion. I knew that someday I would be able to stand in His presence, not because I had earned that privilege, but because the Lord Jesus Christ had paid for it with his blood on Calvary.

Now Jesus Christ was more to me than a historical figure, more than a great teacher of ethics and religion. He was my Savior, my Friend, my Life, my Strength. I had found that I could trust Him not only for my eternal salvation but for my every need of every day, whether for wisdom or physical stamina or money or courage for a fierce trial. If I lacked anything, I knew it was because I had failed to ask for it and to believe that He would supply my every need. I was no longer a modernist, for I had found the living Christ. ☩

The "New" Student

When I awoke the next morning, I felt as if I had really slept, for the first time in months, and I felt so refreshed. I was at peace inside instead of carrying a heavy burden of worry and frustration. I had never experienced this before. I went to my usual classes, but it all felt different to me. The university world around me felt different. But I came to understand that the world was still the same and the difference was inside me, because I was now a new creation in Jesus Christ.

That day at noon I decided to skip lunch so I could spend time with the New Testament. I was amazed to find that it was now a completely new book. It now made sense to me. In fact, sometimes as I read, rings of light seemed to encircle the words to highlight the meaning. Sometimes I felt like dancing around the room as I finished a paragraph. This was a real change from the scholarly recluse I used to be.

The 10:00 P.M. Bible readings continued. Soon a third fellow—another Paul—joined Pete and me. This Paul was a graduate student in nuclear physics. He had been a Christian but had lapsed in his faith after his girlfriend, June, involved him in many questionable activities that drew him away from his earlier commitment to Christ. Paul had changed direction and had started taking June to places and activities of his own choosing. Then a crisis came up between them and everything seemed lost, until one evening June too became a Christian, and a new life began for them.

Then a new problem developed. June's mother became very antagonistic to June's relationship with Paul and began opposing it. For some weeks we continued to pray for them. Then one evening June's mother came to a meeting with them, and she too experienced a real change of heart. She now opened her home to youth gatherings and Bible meetings. I once traveled somewhere with the three of them, and as we delivered her back home I commented on what an alive person she now was. Her face beamed as she replied, "Why wouldn't I be? After all, I'm born again!"

We were soon joined by a fourth person, a freshman named George. After attending our Bible readings for some weeks, he too accepted the invitation to become a Christian.

As our little Christian community grew in numbers, we also experienced growth in other ways. When one person was in need of cash, the rest of us chipped in to help the needy person until he received enough money to pay back what was owed. We also found out just how vital and meaningful prayer was to our daily lives. For example, one day a member of our group found that someone had taken the wrong coat from our cloakroom, and the coat contained a set of keys he needed that same day. The coat was returned in a dramatic fashion soon after we finished praying about it. Sometimes one of us would be asked to do something "out of the blue." And sometimes the answer to our prayers would be so sudden and unexpected that we would burst out laughing.

It was only a few weeks after I came to Christ that I was asked to lead a Bible study on the first chapter of John for a youth group. I did not know much about the Gospel of John at that point, but I began to study it as I had opportunity, and again I sometimes had the sensation of seeing rings of light around certain passages. And when I presented that first Bible study, I was conscious of clear insights appearing in some of the passages. Afterward, a more experienced student of the Word complimented me on my comments, then asked if I had read several "commentaries" on the chapter. I was puzzled and innocently asked him, "What is a commentary?" So he explained to me what a commentary is and where to find one.

Over the winter of my sophomore year (1946–1947) things went fairly well so far as my Christian life was concerned. But my life as a student was less encouraging, and my grades continued to drop. In fact, by the end of the school year I realized that it would be hopeless to continue as a physics major. My heart just was not in physics, or even in science in general. I applied to get my job back at Eastman Kodak, and I continued to rent the stadium dorm room. I registered for geology, first-year French, and statistical math for the fall semester. These were all subjects that I enjoyed and knew I could do well in. Meanwhile, I was hoping and praying that somehow funds would arrive so I could continue my studies. I began my new courses and kept praying about the money. Two weeks passed and I was up against the deadline. I had to make my payment for the new school year either by borrowing from some source or by using some other fundraising method.

I made an appointment to see Dean Lester Wilder to discuss my situation. I poured my heart out to him. "I have no more money to continue in school, and I don't feel I should borrow the money because I am wondering if I am even supposed to pursue science as my career." We agreed that I would completely drop out of school for a time to clarify what course I should pursue. He arranged for me to go back to work at Kodak, and to get room and board with a Jewish family who lived across the river from Kodak.

When I notified my parents about this new development, they were very unhappy over what they considered to be a rash decision and immediately drove up to the River Campus to discuss the matter with Dean Wilder. The dean listened to their emotional entreaties for a time as my mother sobbed. I began to feel as though maybe I had made a big mistake. Dean Wilder then asked to speak to me by myself. He said, "Young man, when you were here the other day, I thought you had made the wisest decision of your life so far. How much can your parents help you with your continuing education?"

"They have nothing to offer me," I told him.

"Then stick to your guns," he said.

So my disappointed parents drove back to Bath. I guess that was the first time I had ever defied their wishes. ✝

University Dropout

So I collected my books and belongings from the Stadium dormitory and moved in with the Dankoff family for several months, until they asked to terminate our arrangement for some reason. They did, however, refer me to another Jewish family, the Korens. I later recognized this as part of God's providence for my study of languages. The Korens were an interesting family, consisting of the elderly parents plus their daughter and son-in-law. The son-in-law had an interesting one-stringed musical instrument that he would sometimes play along with the radio. And his wife was personal secretary to Rabbi Bernstein, whose name I had heard mentioned at the university by my Jewish friend Lenny.

Meanwhile, I sometimes felt lonely. I especially missed my buddies and our 10:00 P.M. Bible reading and prayer time together. I began to wonder what had happened to my happy experiences of the previous winter. Decades later, as I have looked back on my life, this dropout year has registered as the most unhappy year of my life, despite the many other unhappy experiences I have had. But it was also a great time for self-examination and for sorting out what my goals were for my life.

My job at Kodak was in the same building as before, and again it was not very interesting work. I helped to transport bags of various chemical products to the upper floor, from where they were dispensed back to the lower floor as needed through large duct pipes to be mixed and dispensed for photographic use. As one of the slender guys on the gang, one of my occasional jobs was to climb inside the duct system and clean it. It's good that I was not claustrophobic! I clearly see now that if I had stayed at Eastman Kodak, I might have advanced into a much better position, with good job security too, especially if I had gotten a university degree. But my heart was not in photography production, and if I had stayed, my life would doubtless have followed a very different path.

One day as I was walking to work, another man, older than I, drew up beside me. I had seen him before but did not really know him. As we walked and talked, I noticed that he kept looking down at my feet. Finally he said, "I'm curious and excuse me for asking but what size shoes do you wear?"

I did think it was a strange question, but I replied, "Oh, a size eight, triple E."

"Well," he said, "maybe I can help you out with a pair of new shoes. They were purchased for my father but they are not a good fit for him. Maybe you can use them." We arranged to meet several days later, and then he did give me a pair of quality work shoes. They were indeed my size and fit me to a T. I thanked him profusely as I put my old and well-worn shoes into the box. I walked to work in the new shoes that my heavenly Father had provided. He had supplied my needs via a new friend without my even asking for new shoes.

I think it was during those dark times that I attended a Pentecostal camp meeting on the shores of Lake Ontario. I really did not want to go. For one thing, I was dating a lovely lady who was scared to death of Pentecostals, and the last thing I wanted to do was rock the boat with her or her mother. They both had warned me not to have anything to do with these weird people. But I had an invitation to go from a very good friend of the family, someone I admired very much, and after walking the streets of Rochester agonizing over the decision and deciding a hundred times that I couldn't go, I finally went anyway.

I arrived at lunchtime, and afterward there was a siesta time before the late-afternoon activities began. The camp was like a ghost town, so I walked over to the tabernacle and found myself strolling down the center aisle to the altar, uncertain what I was doing there but feeling an inner peace. I knelt by the altar and prayed by myself, with no real objective in mind, when suddenly I realized that I was praying in words I did not understand. This was completely new to me and I was rather mystified by it.

I did attend a few Pentecostal church services after that. One evening, when I asked the pastor about being baptized, he arranged for me to be baptized by immersion that very night. But I never became a member of the Pentecostal church. Their style of worship did not really appeal to me. I preferred a more reasoned approach to preaching and less emotionalism in worship. And I did lose the girlfriend after that experience, but what I gained from that episode of praying in an unknown tongue was a heightened ability to work with foreign languages thereafter. I cannot explain this phenomenon, nor can my professional colleagues of the past thirty plus years, most of whom are better educated and more widely traveled than I am, but they seem to have a genuine respect for my "gift of tongues" and my ability to translate from a variety of languages into English.

Mr. Koren subscribed to a Yiddish newspaper, and naturally I peeked at it. One day I finally asked him to read the title for me. He promptly said, "Der Tag," which I instantly recognized as German for "The Day." My curiosity was piqued, and soon afterward I purchased a Yiddish New Testament from a Christian organization that ministered to Jewish people. At that time I had no grammar of the Yiddish language, but I did locate a small New Testament with Psalms that also contained a list of the letters of the Hebrew alphabet. I made a table of the letters and their names, which I assumed would be clues to their pronunciation. I then began deciphering a familiar passage from the Yiddish New Testament, and was fascinated to discover that most of the words were also German words, though some of them were spelled a bit differently. There was also a sprinkling of other words that I assumed were Hebrew. That was my earliest experiment in using a foreign-language Bible and a dictionary for that language along with a familiar language Bible, usually English, to study a new language (and later I would add to the mix a grammar book for the foreign language).

This method became my way of studying languages throughout my life. Sometimes I listened to language tapes to get better pronunciation. Each new year I would choose a new language to study for the coming year. When the next year rolled around, I would start over again in Genesis in another language and see how far I could get by the end of that year. Eventually, as a freelance translator I made written translations from about twenty-eight languages into English. After I was basically retired from translation work, I continued studying a new language each year, just for my own enjoyment. In 2002, for example, I studied Swahili, because we had some Swahili speakers at our church, and the following year I worked on Arabic.

During the year I worked at Kodak (1947–1948), I began to attend the Christian and Missionary Alliance Church in Rochester on a regular basis. I found their services to be more compatible with my temperament and approach to Bible study, and I appreciated their ministry. One of their customs was to invite missionary speakers to give weekend conferences several times a year. And once a year they had a pledge drive to gain support for their mission programs for the following year. At that time I was not thinking very far ahead, at least not so far as any further education was concerned. I only knew that I had a job at Kodak, and I figured it would last for a while. So I made a rather substantial pledge for the coming year.

As the year wore on, I did make my pledge payments as they came due. But I also became restless and finally realized that I was not ready to say that my college education was finished. I began to wonder if I should be saving more money for college and if I had made too big a pledge to support the missions. But I also believed that my pledge was a promise to God, and that God could provide a way for me to finish college if I kept my pledge to Him. So I paid off my total pledge with peace in my heart.

Meanwhile, in the spring of 1948 I was invited to attend the Intervarsity Christian Fellowship weekend conference to be held at Cornell University that summer. The conference appealed to me immensely because my friend Pete had been involved in this ministry since coming to know Christ as an undergraduate student at the Massachusetts Institute of Technology. So I went, and among the many folks I met were some students from Houghton College in western New York State, about sixty miles west of Bath. Though most of the students who attended the conference were from secular colleges, Houghton College was a Christian college operated by the Wesleyan Methodist Church, and its students represented the affiliated organization, the Foreign Missions Fellowship, which was a special branch of Intervarsity Christian Fellowship for those planning to engage in or support foreign missions work. As I talked with some of these Houghton students, I began to think that Houghton might be the place for me to complete my college education.

As I was preparing to leave Rochester in the summer of 1948, sadness came to the Koren household. For years Mrs. Koren had delighted in making baked goods for her family and her guests, but she was diabetic and had a weakness for sampling her sweets. One morning she went out to water her flowers and collapsed into a coma that took her life. The family invited me to attend her funeral service at the synagogue. This gesture touched me deeply as an indication of their acceptance of and friendship toward me, a Gentile. ✞

Ted Goes to the Poconos

Ted told me the following story on several occasions, but I could not find an account of it in his memoirs, so I have written it as I recall it, with some feedback from other family members.

No one seems to know exactly why Ted decided to go to the Poconos. Maybe he was having another "problem" with his mother and just wanted more space. Or maybe he just wanted a change of scenery. Maybe he thought the Pocono area would be a better place to earn some money over the summer months. Nor is anyone sure when this bike ride took place. It seems clear that Ted did not tell his parents about his plans, because they would have forbidden him to go, and as a high school student he would not likely have been assertive enough to make such a trip without his parents' approval. During the summer break after his freshman year at the University of Rochester, Ted worked in Rochester. He also worked there for a year after his sophomore year at the university.

So it was most likely a summer morning in 1950, after his junior year at Houghton College, that Ted got on his bike with just the clothes on his back and a little change in his pocket and took off. He rode through Bath, then pedaled down US Route 15 along the Cohocton River toward Elmira, New York. For several hours the trip was mostly downhill and easy going. Where Route 15 turned south, at Corning, the river's name changed to the Chemung. From there Ted basically went east and a bit south to Elmira, then to South Waverly and Sayre on the Pennsylvania side of the New York–Pennsylvania state line, where the Chemung River turned south and was met by the eastern branch of the Susquehanna River. Here Ted turned to the south too and followed US Route 220 for thirteen miles to Towanda, where US Route 6 intersected it on its transverse journey from Ohio to the northwestern corner of Pennsylvania, our Keystone state, and continued into southeastern New York. (*I clearly remember that on one of our trips to Houghton College for one of Ted's class reunions, we decided to travel along the Chemung River until it met the Susquehanna. I don't remember whose idea it was, but I do remember that I was driving, as I usually did. And I know we both enjoyed going this scenic route. Whether on that particular day he was reminiscing about his bike ride of years ago, I don't know. But I do know he mentioned US Route 6 on various occasions and had vivid memories of its many hills.*)

After Ted got onto US Route 6, the going was slower, and then night came. When he met a steep hill he would walk and push his bike, hoping for a nice long coast down the other side. He did not look for a motel where he could sleep for the night, but he sometimes found a park bench where he could relax for a half hour before resuming his journey. The next morning was cloudy and cool, so he stopped at a diner to "use their facilities" and have breakfast before resuming his journey. By afternoon a heavy rainstorm moved in. With no raincoat to protect him, of course Ted got drenched, but he just kept pedaling along and pushing his bike up the steep hills. After several hours the rain stopped, and before sunset some sunshine appeared to dry his awful-looking clothes. He also discovered that his trousers needed to see a tailor.

But he kept going, although he was getting rather tired, and somewhat hungry too. That night he napped a bit on another park bench, and after another diner breakfast he again hopped onto his bike. He was glad, finally, to see several signs for Pocono area resorts some miles ahead. So he knew he was getting closer to his destination. Whenever he passed through a town, he looked for a tailor shop or a seamstress's sign, and finally, by midafternoon, he saw one that read "John the Tailor: I Give You Fits." He pulled off the street, parked his bike on the porch, and went inside. There he saw a man seated at a Singer treadle sewing machine. He asked the man, "Are you John?" Upon receiving an affirmative reply, Ted explained that his trousers needed some repair work, so John directed him to the powder room, where Ted removed his trousers, handed them out the door to John, and waited until John gave the mended trousers back to him, twenty minutes later. While he waited, Ted washed up a bit, then sat down on a somewhat more comfortable seat for a while, though frankly he was tired of sitting after riding his bike for more than two days. When Ted came out of the powder room, he politely asked for the bill. John looked at his soiled clothes and sunburn, then generously said, "Oh, give me a quarter." Ted gladly handed over a quarter. Then Ted decided to seek more help from the kind tailor. "Sir," he said, "I've come to this area hoping to get work for the summer. Is there a church nearby or some church people who could maybe help me find a job and a place to stay for the summer?"

"Oh sure," John replied. "There's a church just over the next hill. And the pastor and his wife and daughter live in the parsonage next door. They are nice folks and they can probably help you." Ted thanked John again for all his help and hopped back onto his bike. He arrived at the parsonage at about 4:00 P.M. and knocked on the door. The pastor himself came to the door and listened to Ted's story, then excused himself and went back inside to speak with his wife. They both soon returned with an invitation for Ted not only to share dinner with them and their twelve-year-old daughter, but also to spend the night in their home. Ted gratefully accepted. He clearly did not have enough money in his pocket to buy some fresh attire, but the pastor's wife was able to provide a complete change of clothes so that Ted could enjoy a leisurely shower and put on clean clothes before joining the family for dinner. As they ate, he told them about his spiritual journey and his hope of finding a summer job. They agreed that it should be easy to find work in a food establishment during the summer, and they gave him the names of several resort restaurants in the Pocono area. They also invited him to join them for church services whenever it was feasible.

After a refreshing night of sleep in a comfortable bed and a good breakfast, Ted thanked the family for their generous hospitality, hopped back onto his bike, and went to check out some of the nearest Pocono restaurants. A Hungarian establishment caught his eye, so he parked his bike in the bike rack, went inside, and asked to speak to the owner. A well-nourished middle-aged woman came out of the kitchen and greeted him with a noticeable accent. Ted explained that he was an experienced dishwasher, so she agreed to see what he could do, starting immediately. Ted applied himself well and she was satisfied with his work. The hours were long and included every day of the week. Ted did, however, ask to be excused from work on Sunday evenings so he could attend the youth meetings at the church where the pastor and his wife had been so helpful to him. The owner agreed, so the Sunday evening youth meeting became his "evening out" event of the week.

I'm not sure if Ted rented a room for the summer or if his Hungarian boss had a little room somewhere that she let him use. I feel pretty sure that he got his meals on the job. I think a reason that Ted was attracted to this specific job was that he hoped to hear some Hungarian. Well, he did, and when he tried using what he had heard, the other young fellows at the restaurant laughed at him and explained that this was not the kind of language they used but rather curse words and dirty jokes. But when they realized that he was genuinely interested in learning some Hungarian, they began to teach him simple phrases, which really pleased Ted.

At some point, Ted contacted his parents, probably by letter, to let them know they need not worry, that he was OK and had a dishwashing job for the summer. He told them that because he worked every day and seldom went shopping or to a movie, he was saving almost everything he earned. When his parents learned where Ted was, they immediately drove to the Poconos, located the restaurant, and tried to talk him into returning home with them for the rest of the summer. Ted refused, and he stayed with his dishwashing job until it was time to return to Houghton for his senior year of college. His parents then made a second trip to the Poconos, to collect him, his bike, and his few belongings and transport them back to Bath, and a bit later to Houghton. ☩

Experiences at Houghton College

I was so impressed by the students from Houghton College whom I had met at the Intervarsity Christian Fellowship conference that I proceeded to send a transfer application to Houghton along with the necessary transcript of my credits earned at the university. I had lost a year of my four-year Regents scholarship because I had dropped out of university after two years, but I decided to try to salvage the final year of the scholarship. I wrote to the Board of Regents, and they replied that I should send them my award certificate for endorsement. Alas, I was unable to find it among my papers. So I wrote again to the Board of Regents, and they replied that I should send them a notarized statement to the effect that I had lost the certificate. They also requested a transcript of my grades at Rochester.

Meanwhile, the registrar at Houghton replied promptly to my application and said they could not possibly admit me to Houghton because it would violate their long-standing precedent of not accepting a student on scholastic probation. The registrar went on to suggest that I return to Rochester and raise my grades above the probation level. So I headed back to Dean Wilder's office, showed him the letter, and asked if I might be readmitted to the university for this purpose. After reading the letter he said, "They shouldn't reject you like this! Will you permit me to write this woman a letter?" I readily consented. Shortly afterward I got another letter from the registrar at Houghton: "Dean Wilder has given you a high recommendation. He says that if you were to be admitted at Houghton, he is certain that you would quickly improve your grades and come off scholastic probation."

So I arrived at Houghton College in the fall of 1949, in time for freshman week and the new students orientation. I understood that I was beginning on probation as a sophomore and would have to raise my grades to a more acceptable level before I would be classified as a junior.

One of my first surprises at Houghton was to find an old friend at the desk in the library. Yes, it was Miss Hanson, my favorite English teacher from my high school days, only now she had a married name, and her husband was a student at Houghton too. It was so good to see her again and to tell her about my spiritual journey. She was still modest about her own accomplishments and it was months later that I learned that not only was she a Houghton graduate but she also was valedictorian of her class!

I originally planned to complete a German major at Houghton, because I already had two years of German. But I soon discovered that Houghton did not offer enough German for a major. Then, early on, I met Professor Gordon Stockin, a Greek professor. I warmed up to him immediately and decided to major in Greek. I started with first-year New Testament Greek and third-year German for my first year at Houghton. I really got into my studies and was pleased to see my name on the dean's list for the first marking period—which took care of the scholastic probation issue. Although I still did not know what I wanted to do with my life, at least I was finally studying Greek and German, and enjoying it. In my senior year I took the second year of New Testament Greek as well as a course that surveyed classical Greek literature, from Homer and Herodotus through Lucian, who wrote in the sixth century A.D.

So things were going well. Then there was another unusual happening, somewhat like the episode in the locker room at the VA hospital the summer after high school. One day as I was ready to go to lunch, I had a sudden urge to fast and pray instead. I always enjoyed going to meals and chatting with other students, so the idea of fasting for even one meal caught me by surprise. But the urge persisted, so I found myself going to an empty classroom and sitting down at one of the desks.

Almost immediately I was again aware of that invisible presence; it was so strong that I felt unable to resist it. I was clearly told, without audible words, that on the following Saturday I would receive a very disappointing letter, and as a consequence I would need to take a trip home for the weekend. As I thought about it, I remembered that I had arranged for a first date with a certain girl, so I would have to cancel that if what I was hearing came to pass. I also remembered that I had an appointment to give my testimony over the campus radio that same weekend. Normally it would have been very difficult to make two such cancellations on the same weekend, but this message was so strong and compelling that I saw no alternative but to obey.

When Saturday came, I went to the campus post office and found my box empty. I was rather puzzled by this, but as I prepared to leave I noticed that my name was on the package list, indicating that there was a registered letter for me at the main post office in the village. I went there directly and signed for my registered letter. It was from the New York State Board of Regents in Albany and it said that there was a problem with my claiming the last year of my scholarship and the funds had been awarded to another applicant. This was indeed very disappointing news, because I was counting on those funds to help pay my school bill.

Then I remembered that I was also told to go home that weekend. I had neither a vehicle nor even a driver's license, so I could not ask to borrow a friend's car. I had very little cash for public transportation—but there were very few buses in rural New York state anyway. I could not call my folks because they had not yet installed their own phone.

And I was not about to call a neighbor and ask them to deliver a message to my folks that I needed a ride home. So I told a friend I had an emergency and needed to go home. Then I began walking and hitchhiking the sixty miles to Bath. I reached home on Sunday morning as my folks were getting up. I showed them the letter and had breakfast with them. They then suggested I go to bed and sleep while they went to church. So I did.

I joined them for Sunday dinner, and as we were eating, Dad said, "I'll tell you what we will do. We'll go see Dr. Cole this afternoon and show this letter to him. Maybe he can help us." Dad explained that Dr. Ernest Cole, a long-time resident of Bath, was now retired but had previously been the chairman of the Board of Regents. He also had a son who was serving in the US House of Representatives. When Dr. Cole finished reading the letter, he immediately said, "They can't do this to you. Listen, I'm going to Albany this next week on business, and I'll talk to them about this."

We all went back home, and then my parents decided to drive me back to school. Well, I had done what had been so vividly impressed upon me to do, but I was uncertain what would happen next. Christmas was drawing near, and after that would come a new semester, and new school bills.

When Christmas vacation time arrived, I still had no news from the Board of Regents. So I went home for the holidays, and while I was at home I decided to look up Dr. Cole to ask how his meeting with the Board of Regents had turned out. When I arrived at the house I could sense tension in the air. I rang the bell anyway, and after a minute or two Mrs. Cole came to the door. Her face was red and wet from crying, and she looked at me in a sort of daze, but she remembered me. "I'm sorry," she said, "I have no information on your scholarship. My husband has just died and I'm in no condition to give you any answers." I mumbled, "I'm sorry," and beat a hasty retreat as she closed the door.

After the holidays I returned to school, feeling rather perplexed and very unsure about the future. But a week later I finally received a letter from Albany. Actually, it was a copy of a letter that the Board of Regents had sent to the president of Houghton. The good news part of it was their explanation that a mistake had been made in withdrawing my scholarship and giving my money to another applicant. The bad news part of it, for Houghton, was that my money would have to wait for a special act of the state's legislature to authorize the funds for me, because the money originally intended for me had already been paid out to someone else. The funds eventually were received, and everyone was satisfied.

Meanwhile, I enjoyed school life at Houghton, even though it was located in a very rural area, in sharp contrast to Rochester. I participated in the college orchestra with my violin, and I enjoyed singing in the college chorale. We did some wonderful programs by classical composers such as Bach, Beethoven, and Handel. We also had guest performers come to campus, and one of my major regrets was that I did not come up with the ticket price to take my girlfriend and myself to hear the Trappe Family Singers when they came to Houghton while I was there. But spending money was almost nonexistent for me during my Houghton years.

During my senior year, I took more time for social activities and eased up a bit on my studies. After dating several girls, I met one who became extra special. After several months of dating we were really seeing each other a lot and I had met some of her family. But both of us began having trouble keeping up with our studies. Finally, some good friends suggested to us that maybe we needed to slow down a bit on our relationship and focus more on our studies. We discussed it and agreed to heed this advice. Eventually we decided to put a halt to our "being a couple," and though we remained on a friendly basis for some years after college, in time we both also met and married other companions.

Finally, it was the spring of 1951 and graduation was approaching. I thought that everything was in order, so imagine my dismay when we were gathered for our graduation rehearsal and someone came to me from the dean's office and informed me that my grade on a certain required course was recorded as an incomplete. I would be permitted to participate in all the formalities of graduation (the cap and gown and the processionals, and I could even receive the diploma holder for my bachelor of arts degree), but I would not receive my actual diploma until the required coursework was satisfactorily completed! Well, this was rather embarrassing, to say the least, especially because some of my classmates knew about it. But I did participate in graduation, and afterward I got to stay at the now-forsaken Houghton campus for several more days to spend time in the library and finish the required work. Then I left my completed work at the office for the professor and went home.

Several weeks later I received my diploma and congratulations in the mail. Now, the next major item in my life was the reality of the Korean War and the fact that "Uncle Sam" would surely draft me into the US Army without delay. ✞

The Korean War and My Battle

Early September mornings are usually raw and nippy in western New York State, especially during those hours when most people are in bed. That was the kind of morning it was when this story begins.

Induction and Life at Fort Devens

It was September 1951 and a little group of us were waiting in front of the dingy old courthouse in Bath, watching our breath make little white balls in front of us.

Dad was there too—faithful Dad, passing out Gideon New Testaments as he always did. Only this time it was different, for now his own son was entitled to one too.

While I was trying to keep myself warm by thinking about all of the good breaks I'd had in life so far, the bus pulled up to the curb. One of the draft board officials called the roll, then gave one of the inductees a packet of orders and told us to pile in. I stiffly shook hands with Dad and we said good-bye, both of us trying not to show our emotions. I climbed aboard and watched Dad wave, and noticed a little moisture beneath his lower eyelids. And I felt some little shivers that weren't just from the cold. I knew that a new, strange battle lay ahead and I had to face it alone. Dad couldn't help me much now.

After a two-hour ride we arrived at the induction center in Rochester. It was a long and tiring day—standing in lines, answering questionnaires, having physical exams. I tried to combat the boredom and fatigue by thinking about the good wishes of my friends and family. I thought about the job I had been promised with a small business when I got back home. Here I was, young, single, with no dependents and no real plans for my future. All I had to do was give my two years to the government. Besides, I was a Christian and I knew God had promised to keep his sheep safe, no matter what He asks them to go through. It was nice to think about that, and before I knew it we were boarding our train to go from Rochester to Fort Devens, Massachusetts.

We traveled all night and awoke in the damp, foggy old town of Worcester, Massachusetts. It was only a few more bumps and jolts by bus to our camp.

I had assumed that our "processing" was done. What a mistake! Here at Fort Devens there were more exams, more quizzes, more questionnaires, and longer and longer waiting lines. I began to think that there's no war more nerve-racking than the ones you fight with paper.

We then began to learn what military life is all about. Actually, it can all be put into one word: *discipline*. We didn't have any "military tradition" in our family. Granted, Dad had spent some months in boot camp just before the end of World War I, but he did not talk about it, so I had to find out for myself what army life was like.

Army discipline shocks a bit at first. They wanted us all to dress alike, act alike, talk alike; they even expected us to think alike. There was a gory job to do and in order to do it we had to stop being ourselves and learn to be someone else. That bothered me, because I was used to being myself and doing as I wished. But now for two years I would have to lay aside my rights, swallow my pride, and become a floor mat for fellows I didn't care two hoots about so I could eventually return to civilian life and insist on my rights again. How is that for a paradox?

Besides, I was a Christian. A Christian learns to be different by the way he loves others, even his enemies. He turns the other cheek, goes the second mile, and prays for those who hate the very footprints he makes in the sands of time. He lives a life of love and trust; he overcomes evil with good.

The big problem was that Uncle Sam didn't get very excited about overcoming evil with good. It was clearly "yellow" and "unpatriotic" not to do your duty for your country and serve your time. I figured that serving my country was being a good witness; by being consistent in my personal life I could still live the Sermon on the Mount and win souls and all that. And Uncle Sam could worry about the rest.

I won't say much about all the routine marching and "police duty" they put us through at Devens, because you would get as bored as I did. It wasn't easy to be "an example of the believers." I had to stuff a lot of grumbles, complaints, and angry thoughts inside me while my civilian personality was being reshaped and blistered into that of a soldier.

It wasn't too bad until the day I pulled KP (kitchen police) duty. We had been up later than usual the night before and the KP staff had to roll out of their bunks at 4:30 A.M. Well, that New England chill was even more damp and raw than the New York kind, and the cold stung me all over. Worse yet, I just couldn't seem to get awake. The early morning hours seldom found me at my best anyway, but this seemed to be my record for fighting the blues. They herded us under cover of darkness to the kitchen and turned us loose on the huge stacks of mess trays and garbage that we had to battle with the whole day, accompanied by the hum of the dishwasher. My morning stupor persisted and I was as mean, as sour, and as cynical as I had ever felt. What's more, I was really disgusted at myself for feeling that way. I chided myself that

I was not a fine Christian when I got so upset, and all over a little KP duty. My feelings of resentment against Uncle Sam and his organization began to have a tug of war with my other feelings of shame for not acting more Christlike. As I continued to dump what seemed like tons of discarded food and to put hundreds of trays into the dishwasher, my back ached and my head pounded. My bones were trying to recover from the early morning chill. You can imagine my relief when I heard that there was only a half hour more to go. Finally the mess sergeant growled, "Okay, you guys, carry these stacks of clean trays to the other room out there. Then you can report to your barracks." I reckon I looked rather happy when I picked up my skyscraper of metal trays and headed for the door.

Suddenly another "noncom" (noncommissioned officer) appeared in the doorway. "Just a minute. We've got a little extra job in here. You last five men just volunteered to help us with it." My built-in arithmetic machine quickly told me that I was one of the fatal last five. I won't try to tell you the thoughts that ran through me like red-hot lava at that moment. I was standing fairly close to the guy who dispensed the "special job"—a gray-haired sergeant whom I would have been scared to death of in my right mind. But that day I looked him straight in the eye, then crashed that big pile of steel trays onto the concrete floor. It just about split everyone's eardrums. The old sarge just stared at me for a minute, probably trying to figure out what sort of illness I had. And frankly, I was wondering what made me do it too. Old Sarge, however, found his voice more quickly than I did.

"Just a minute, Son. Nobody acts like that around here. If that's the way you feel about it, OK. But you get an extra hour of KP too."

I helped the other four fellows with the special job for which I had "volunteered," which lasted all of five minutes. Then the others went their way while I was given the job of peeling onions for the next hour. I guess all those ugly feelings I'd had must have landed beneath that pile of trays as they hit the floor. Anyway, the world became a more friendly place again, and I even got into an interesting conversation with the other rookie who was sharing my job with me. And I forgot to watch the time, so when Old Sarge poked his head into the room and announced that my duty time was finished, I was surprised. "But Sir," I grinned, "would it be all right if I worked a few more minutes? I think these onions are helping me get over my cold."

Old Sarge snorted. "In the first place, don't call me Sir. I'm not an officer. And if you aren't satisfied with your punishment, I can do better, or worse, as you prefer." He bristled and walked away. I peeled enough more onions to complete my discussion, then took off my big rubber apron and headed for the barracks, whistling a happy tune as I went. Sure, I was ashamed of myself, but hey, hadn't I also gone the second mile?

These many years later I do not remember very many of my buddies from Fort Devens. But there was one unforgettable character: Jerry, a Jewish man from Boston. At six feet and five and a half inches tall, if he had been a half-inch taller he would not have passed his physical exam. As it was, he caused the army a lot of headaches. They had no uniforms that fit him and no shoes big enough for his large feet. Therefore, while special uniforms were being tailor-made for him, he marched around in his "civvies" while everyone else wore army clothes and boots.

But Jerry was no shrinking violet. Instead of being embarrassed by his height, he delighted in embarrassing his superiors. One day a new drill sergeant bellowed at him, "Well, soldier, what happened to *your* uniform?"

Jerry just smiled and looked down at the sergeant from his almost-six-and-half-foot observation tower and cracked, "Oh, excuse me, I must've wandered into the wrong place!" Jerry had a cynical but good-natured kind of humor and, as I watched him or thought about him, I sometimes wondered, "Maybe it's not half bad living as a misfit." But later I changed my mind.

Life at Schofield Barracks in Hawaii

One day they called us out of our barracks and lined us up in formation again, and for the several dozenth time we listened to orders being read. But this time it was different, because my name was on the list to go to Schofield Barracks in Hawaii for sixteen weeks of infantry basic training. Several days later we boarded an airliner, which was a first for me, but I soon got tired of all the ups and downs as we stopped at Youngstown, Ohio; Indianapolis, Indiana; Kansas City, Missouri; Amarillo, Texas; Albuquerque, New Mexico; Prescott, Arizona; and finally Oakland, California, where an army bus took us over the steep brick streets to Camp Stoneman, my last lodging place on the mainland, where we waited for our boat to Hawaii.

Someone remarked to me that he thought Camp Stoneman must have been built by some of the earliest Spaniards to arrive in northern California, and I had to admit that there was sort of an ancient aura around the place. I also found out how many times you get a needle jabbed into your body before you travel overseas for Uncle Sam. I felt like a guinea pig crossed with a pin cushion.

There were all kinds of fellows in our ranks, of all sizes and shades. The one I noticed especially was a young black man who was reading his Bible as the waiting line slowly wound its way down the street toward the medical building. When our line got near the building, I tossed over a remark about how wisely he was using his time. He responded with a big grin and said he was glad someone appreciated his reading tastes because most of his buddies clearly did not. The thing that startled me most, when I got close enough to see clearly, was that it was a Roman Catholic Bible. I later learned that Carl too was Roman Catholic, and an ardent one.

Before we got too attached to Camp Stoneman, they put us on a ferry to cross the bay to the San Francisco harbor, then crammed us into a troop ship bound for Honolulu. My residence for the trip was a large steel-floored and steel-walled compartment lined with five-decker bunks. I squeezed myself and my duffel bag into one of these bunks and that was my "stateroom" during the voyage. There was a large wash-room on the next deck, and we could usually roam the open decks above, so it wasn't too bad. As we got to the warmer latitudes, nobody cared to stay in his hot stuffy compartment anyway. Long after mid-night, the top deck still had lots of inhabitants. During the day, the ship's store (the PX, in army lingo) was open, and if you cared to wait in line for an hour or two, you could buy a little candy or tobacco. At night there was usually a free movie, and once a day there were Protestant and Catholic religious services. The rest of the time you could play checkers, chess, or poker, depending on your recreational tastes and your game partner.

The trainees were already organized into battalions and companies, and Hawaii had sent along several training instructors to escort us to our new home. One of these men, a heavy weapons instructor, announced that there would be a Bible study in the mess hall on Sunday evening. A handful of us showed up. The leader introduced himself as Pat and pro-ceeded to lead us in a pretty good Bible study. Then he told us about the "spiritual emphasis" at Schofield Barracks. The Schofield chaplain, he explained, was a modernist and a tolerant sort of person. He didn't object if evangelistic meetings were held, provided somebody else did the preaching. Pat and the chaplain's assistant, also an evangelical, had organized the Sunday evening meeting. Along with some other enlisted men, they led the meeting while the chaplain sat at the rear of the chapel to provide his official approval. But then Pat lowered his voice and got very serious. "There's just one hitch to this whole business that I don't like," he told us. "My partner in this deal, the chaplain's assistant, is a CO."

"What's a CO?" I inquired innocently.

He was surprised by my question. "A CO is a conscientious objector. Some COs won't even wear an army uniform. This fellow cooperates with that part, at least. But he won't carry a weapon or participate in combat. And it sure spoils his testimony. Some guys shy away from him because they think he's just plain yellow."

"It's funny," I interrupted. "I always thought pacifists were Jehovah's Witnesses, or maybe modernists."

"Not in this case," Pat said with one of those you-haven't-been-around-have-you smiles. "He's a real born-again believer, far as I can tell. This funny idea he has about war just sort of spoils the whole business."

Honolulu harbor gave us a big welcome five days after we left San Francisco. Even the sun wore a big smile for us, and the palm trees waved. The band played and the hula dancers performed for us. I used to think that Hawaii was just a flat little patch of grass with a palm tree pushing up through the middle, like you see in ads and cartoons. It was a real eye-opener to see big mountains crawling up out of the ocean with the city of Honolulu hanging onto their backs. It was hard to find a really flat bit of land anywhere. (Our fiftieth state, Hawaii consists of four major islands, four smaller islands, and a large number of islets and coral reefs. The largest island, which Hawaiians call the Big Island, is about the size of the state of Connecticut and gives the name Hawaii to the island chain. But Oahu, the third largest island, ranks first in political, commercial, and military importance. The state capital, Honolulu, is located there, as well as Pearl Harbor, America's preferred naval base. And in the center of Oahu was Schofield Barracks, our largest army outpost, and my destination.)

As usual, waiting for us were those bumpy buses that whizzed us inland over some really modern highways. We passed some "cornfields," but they turned out to be sugar cane. And what I thought were potatoes turned out to be pineapples.

We pulled into the big bustling military post and stopped in front of a neat quadrangle of six white cement dormitories. The quadrangle would house our battalion, with one company in each of the six dormitories. Each company was divided into four platoons of forty men who shared one large room as our sleeping quarters. This was to be my "home" for the next six months. Right away they showed me my furniture—a bunk and a foot locker. And I discovered that the Bible-reading black Catholic was my next-door neighbor. He told me his name was Carl, and he seemed to be as pleased as anything to have me as his neighbor. The next morning the "cadre" woke us up and gave us five minutes to jump into our clothes and race down to the front lawn to stand for reveille. After everyone had reported "present" or "accounted for, Sir" to the company commander, we grabbed our breakfast. After a minute or two to scratch our noses or yawn a little, we reported in front of the building again. Then they marched us off to our first training class. That was the way it was from then on.

They gave us lectures, some dull, others not as much; but it really didn't matter if the speakers were not interesting, because they provided sergeants to wake up the sleepers. We drilled, we hiked, we shot M1 rifles, and did a lot of other things. The army was packing a lot of training into the long Hawaiian days to make us into crack infantrymen, ready for frontline duty.

I knew the chances were good we would be shipped to Korea; after all, we were already well on the way to Asia. We were always outdoors, and soon our bodies became tough enough to take almost anything. I rather liked the climate in Hawaii; it was like a vacation in the South Seas. I did not miss the cold winters of New York and New England at all. And frankly I did not have much time to worry about going to Korea.

In the evenings we spent our time getting ready for the next day. We scraped the red mud off our boots and polished them to a mirror shine. We cleaned and oiled our M1s until the barrels glistened. Sometimes we even talked about home and wondered if we'd ever get back there again. In time we became fairly close-knit and learned to work together, even to the point of exerting pressure on those platoon members who stepped out of line and jeopardized the reputation and privileges of the whole platoon.

Most of the guys in our platoon were young local Hawaiians with whopping names like Yamamoto and Wakabayashi. Our company's first sergeant was a full-blooded Hawaiian named Kahihikolo. Our company commander was Captain Lum. He was Chinese-Hawaiian and liked to quote Chinese proverbs and lecture us on the wonders of nature. I heard it said that he was a pretty unusual company commander and might have done better as a company chaplain.

On the post we had a handsome chapel, a big movie theater, a bowling alley, and a recreation center. There was also a good library, a room for listening to classical music, ping-pong tables, a pool, and, well, just about anything I could have wished for to amuse myself.

The chapel services were like my friend Pat had said: a nice, thin, watery Sunday morning service, then an evangelistic meeting in the evening. I saw right away there was trouble between the two leaders—Pat, the weapons instructor, and Ezra, the chaplain's assistant, who was a "CO." After what Pat had told me about him, I was curious about Ezra. So I dropped in on him one evening and quizzed him about his beliefs. He was a true-blue, born-again Christian all right. It's just that he was kind of, well, sad about something. Sometimes we talked about our girlfriends back home, and we got to be good buddies. Was Pat disgusted about that? I wondered. Pat seemed to delight in nursing a grudge against his Christian brother.

For my part, I didn't want an argument with either of them. For one thing, I wasn't sure where I stood anymore. And I was a long way from home and needing Christian fellowship—badly. And I didn't want these petty ideas about war to spoil my friendships with the few Christians in my company.

My black Catholic neighbor got to be a buddy of mine too. Oh, sometimes we would fight the Thirty Years' War all over again. I'd quote a verse and say it proved that the Protestants were right. He'd quote another verse and say it proved transubstantiation. We talked louder and louder and got more excited all the time, but after a while we would yawn a little, finish cleaning our rifles and polishing our boots, and crawl into our bunks. Then we would say good night to each other like two retired generals who had just finished a tied game of checkers.

One night I especially remember was when we were sitting on the big lanai getting our equipment ready for a big inspection and he began telling me about his childhood. When you're a long way from home you sometimes think about those things. He said his dad used to send him to a Protestant Sunday school and maybe that's where he started to read his Bible. But his mother was a Catholic who died when he was still a young boy, and she had asked him to be a Catholic when he grew up, and he had promised that he would. He sometimes found it hard to keep that promise, but he felt he had to keep it for her sake. Now, whenever he began to think about going to the Protestant Sunday school, he would see his mother on her deathbed and remember his promise. And he just could not bear to trample over her dead body.

"After a while it got easier," he sighed, "after I decided I'd have to go through with it. Maybe deep down in my heart I'd still rather be a Protestant, but I know it's not God's will for me."

Well, I wasn't really sure what to say, so I tried to mostly listen as he shared his feelings.

[*Two pages of Ted's draft memoir are missing at this point and I do not know what material was lost in those pages. But I do remember two stories he might have told and I include them here.*

One night without moonlight, the men were gotten out of bed at midnight to go on a single-file hike in the dark, across the invisible terrain, in silence, to some "enemy destination." Well, Ted was not the most "fleet of foot," and somehow he lost contact with the man in front of him. Suddenly he and the group behind him were lost. I doubt that he was allowed to call for help, because that would attract "enemy attention." But maybe the man in front of him realized that Ted and his group were not following, and somehow he reestablished contact with the stragglers.

Another of those midnight dead-silence adventures involved climbing up a steep hill, or perhaps even a mountainside, that was covered with loose stones and probably some rocks too. Again, Ted was not very sure-footed, and as he was climbing he slipped on the loose stones and began to slide, or roll, down the hill. Fortunately a buddy, or perhaps even an angel of God, grabbed him and stopped his rough descent toward the river below.

Although I do not remember that Ted ever explicitly said so, he may have suspected, just not verbalized it, that God had intervened to spare his life on both of these occasions, not so much for some specific role in his army career as for some divine purpose in his life after his military service was over.

Where Ted's story resumes he is writing about his infantry train-
ing, specifically on the use of the bayonet. It is fair to say that he was
not enthusiastic about using such a weapon, or even about learning
how *to use it, as he explains here.*]

Well, I would go through the motions and hope I was fooling the instructors. I would look as fierce as I could and do whatever they told me
to do. Then some sergeant would come along and growl at me: "Look,
soldier, that's no way to use a bayonet! You've gotta have your heart in
it! Come on, just imagine there's a man on the other end of that steel!"
I guess he thought that would fire me up, but it did just the opposite. A
man on the other end! Another man who was fighting for *his* country
just like I was fighting for mine. Maybe the poor fellow didn't like it any
more than I did. The thought would give me a sinking feeling. Then the
sergeant would say that if I snuffed out that other guy's life before he
got mine, the world would be a safer place again. So I'd screw up my
face into a real hideous look and go charging at my "enemy."

Sometimes, though, I would remember all those wars they had in
the Old Testament and wonder, if God told his people back then to go to
war against their enemies, then why did it seem so awful now? Maybe I
was just being silly and squeamish. This was no time to be sentimental,
I thought, so get with it, soldier!

Confronting the Korean War

After some weeks on the post they began giving us weekend passes. Of
course we all made a mad dash for Honolulu. The first time I rode into
the city I saw a newspaper lying on a seat of the bus, so I grabbed it and
looked over the church announcements. One ad for a little community
church said, "We preach the old-fashioned Gospel." So I got directions
and went to check it out. The church was located in a quiet middle-class
neighborhood known as Kaimuki, which in Hawaiian means "toward
the mountains." The church was small but the friendly group welcomed
me. The preacher, Mr. Boone, was an excellent Bible teacher and I was
surprised to learn later that he was a layman who was only filling in
until a full-fledged pastor was found. This church became my church
during my time in Hawaii, and to paraphrase a quote from my history
book, "I came, I stayed, I was conquered."

At Christmastime we were given a few days off from training and
passes for the weekends and holidays. I visited my friends in Honolulu
and drank in as much of civilian life as I could while I had the opportunity.
By then I was really thinking hard and long about Korea. Its shadow was
too close already and I was ashamed to admit, even to myself, that I
was scared. But deep inside I knew I was plain terrified of going to Korea.

I began to think about Officers' Candidate School (OCS). I knew that if you made the grade they sent you back to the States, and suddenly I really wanted to go back home instead of to Korea. I had already passed the preliminary tests for OCS. I could sign up if I wanted to. So I did.

To get sent to OCS, a number of hurdles had to be gotten over. The next one was a physical exam. It didn't take much physical health to get into the army, but it took quite a bit, I learned, to become a second lieutenant. We spent a whole day at Tripler Army Hospital, where specialists went over us with a fine-tooth comb.

Then I waited. The next step would be to appear before a board of officers for a grueling oral exam. I tried not to be too happy about being an OCS candidate. I didn't want my platoon to know how much I longed for the homeland, for anything that would take me eastward instead of across the Pacific to the west. But a few of my buddies must have read my mind. Some said, "Hope you make it"; others said, "It's safer in the States."

I waited, and waited some more, but the army was silent. There was no summons to appear before the board of officers. Nor was there any explanation, so there was still room to hope.

Vacation with Ray

When our sixteen weeks of training were finished, they had a big parade and gave us diplomas. I was pleasantly surprised to see my pastor, Mr. Boone, on hand for the ceremony, along with a number of other folks from the church. When the formality was over, Adelina came up and placed a lei around my neck. It was such a thrill to have a dozen orchids thrown over my head, even knowing that orchids are as common and plentiful to Hawaiians as dandelions are to mainlanders. The thoughtfulness of their presence plus the lei were very meaningful to me.

The following week we could roam about as we wished. A few brave souls flew home to the mainland. But I still thought I might somehow go stateside before long anyway. And if officers' school passed me by, I might just get assigned to Germany, especially because the army knew that I had studied German for several years in college. Then at least I would be going in the opposite direction from Korea.

But whether I went to Korea or not, I decided I would see Hawaii. After all, some folks paid a small fortune for a short vacation there, but I was already in Hawaii, and Uncle Sam was footing the bill.

I was joined at the Honolulu YMCA by Ray, a fellow in another company of my battalion who until now had been only a casual acquaintance. He had decided that he and I should see the sights together. First we looked around Honolulu itself. We visited Kapiolani Palace, from which the Kamehameha kings had ruled until they decided it was safer to become subjects of the United States than to remain independent. We saw the huge banyan trees, and the rare birds and animals, and we visited several Buddhist temples. One of these temples so terrified Ray that he wanted to leave immediately. "It's so spooky, I can't stand it," he said. I guess he was really overwhelmed by the huge golden image of the Buddha and the intricate tapestries and other wall hangings.

As we made our departure, he sighed deeply. "You know," he said confidentially, "I'm glad I'm a Christian."

"And what is your definition of being a Christian?" I asked.

"Well, you know—well, what I mean is, I'm glad I'm not a Buddhist. What did you think I meant?" said Ray defensively.

By this time we were beginning to run low on cash. Ray, who was a heavy smoker, had spent his cash on cigarettes and I knew that sooner or later he would ask me to buy more weeds for him. I took the precaution of making sure that both of us had return tickets to Schofield. Then I announced that whatever money we had left was reserved for food. As it was, we did skip several meals, and Ray resorted to checking the public ashtrays for cigarette butts when he got desperate for a couple drags of nicotine. One day a man on the street must have recognized our hunger, for he suggested that we "join ourselves" for an hour or two to an outdoor picnic at a nearby church, so we did.

The next day we left Honolulu and walked up through the Nuuanu Pass to the Poli, where there is a breathtaking view of the ocean and the fertile fields of Oahu. We then headed for Laie, on the northern end of the island, where there is a famous Mormon temple, sometimes called the Taj Mahal of the Pacific. Finally an army truck came by and offered us a lift. We gladly climbed into the back and rode with the luggage. As we sped along toward the north, one of the two GIs happened to turn around and with a silly grin said, "Oh, there are some extra sandwiches in the bag back there, in case anybody's hungry." We tried not to appear too anxious as we dug into the sandwiches with obvious delight.

Nightfall found us back in Honolulu, where we roamed the streets, watching the lights shining from the hillside homes. At that moment, Korea seemed far away. Then I discovered that Ray was still thinking about that question I had asked him—about what it means to be a Christian. He began to open his heart, and I could see he was longing to be at peace with God.

Somehow, however, I seemed unable to offer him much help. Salvation seemed so simple to me, but how could I help a fellow who was in the grip of multiple bad habits, who had even joined the army as an alternative to serving a prison sentence? Ray was asking me how to leave all that behind and start walking with Christ. It staggered me.

In that crucial hour of opportunity, I felt I had failed Ray. Strapped by my own fear and anxiety, I sidestepped the task of leading him to a personal faith in Christ and instead took him to my pastor, Mr. Boone, [*And right here, in mid-sentence, the story breaks off. I have no idea if Ray came to know Christ, nor how many pages are missing. I have added several other stories from Ted's Korean experience that I remember him telling on several occasions. I have written them as he told them. The letters he sent to his family from Korea contain many other tales, but they will perhaps appear in a separate volume someday.*]

Life in Korea

When we arrived in Korea we were greeted by sacks of mail that had finally caught up with us. Before we were herded onto the train, I collected my stash and sorted through it to pick out the goodies to read en route. There were several letters from home, and another one from my cousin Clara. I always enjoyed Clara's letters, even though I did not agree with her on the matter of military service. She had talked and written to me about the nonresistant position more than once, but I just didn't buy it and thought she was off base. So what is she saying to me this time, I wondered? I opened her letter first and read her message of love and concern. She expressed her disappointment that I had not asked for noncombatant service, for she felt very strongly that a Christian should not kill his fellow man.

But then she really shocked me. She went on to say that because I had not asked for noncombatant service, she had prayed to God that He would protect me anyway, and God had *told* her that I would not see any combat. I was dumbfounded by her audacity. Here I was, headed for the front line. I had no special training; I was just an ordinary infantryman. I did not even have a driver's license, and she clearly believed I would not be involved in combat? What did she think I was going to do: sit in a corner somewhere and watch while my buddies marched to the front and gave their lives to defend our country? I really wanted to laugh; my precious cousin was so naive about this military expedition. Of course I was going to the front, where I expected to be "cannon fodder" for our war. But I respected cousin Clara too. She was a Christian who lived a beautiful life, and deep inside I probably suspected that my story was not yet finished.

Soon we were packed into a train and carried to the front. Now we could hear the sounds of war, especially when our camp got quiet at night. A day or two later, as we were receiving some last-minute instructions at the regimental headquarters, which was a scant mile from the front, an officer called out my name. When I reported to him, he told me to pack up my duffle bag and belongings, because I had been "misassigned" and was being sent back to the rear! I got no further explanation as I waited at the Replacement Company for someone to decide my fate. Finally I got tired of sitting around, so I asked the officer, "Sir, if I ask to go to the front, they have to send me, right?" I knew the army *always* accepted volunteers for the front line.

Well, he hemmed and hawed for a bit. Then, to my surprise, he asked me to wait another day or two before making that decision. And sure enough, the next day he offered me a position as a supply worker, and for the next two months I dispensed supplies and equipment to other soldiers as they came through on their way to the front. After that, I was given a position at the PX warehouse, which was the closest thing to a civilian job that the army could offer. It was located even further away from the front. Now I did not even hear the sounds of the battlefield as I issued clothing and all sorts of supplies to army personnel. Basically, I worked by myself and managed all the supplies. I also traveled by train to the coast every month to get boxcar loads of new supplies.

The Korean children often came by to watch me at the warehouse, so I gave them sweets. I would also try talking to them. Somewhere I found a Korean New Testament, and in my spare time I worked on learning their alphabet and simple greetings. Some of the young Korean men would sometimes come by in the evening. They knew some English, so I learned more Korean from them. Sometimes they even serviced and cleaned my rifle for me. They sure did it much faster and better than my clumsy hands could.

I would sometimes also give them small gifts, because the gifts did not cost me anything. The army could be a rather wasteful organization at times. Soldiers did not always have the time or the facilities to wash their clothes, so often the dirty stuff was put on a heap, then a match was put to it. The GIs would then turn their backs while the Koreans ran in to rescue the dirty clothes before the flames devoured them.

I did join up with three other soldiers who were also professing Christians to form a men's quartet. We often sang at the Sunday evening services. We sometimes assisted in other ways too, under the chaplain's supervision. I was not ashamed to be known as a Christian, but I also felt I was doing my duty for my country.

One night I was sleeping in our tent when I was awakened by some loud talking. I got awake enough to realize that the noise was coming from two of our sergeants who were approaching our tent, obviously drunk. They were also apparently looking for mischief. They came into our tent and headed for my cot. "Come on," said one of the men, his speech slurred. "Let's take him out and throw him into the stream. We'll see what kind of Christian he is then!" They then grabbed me, still tucked inside my sleeping bag, and clumsily pulled me out of bed.

When I realized they really meant to give me a cold bath, I decided to help them! "Wait a minute," I said. "Don't mess up this good sleeping bag. Let me unzipper it first." So I pulled down the zipper, stepped out of the bag, and marched right into the cold stream before they even got themselves organized enough to throw me in! Well, that did rather spoil their fun! I then suggested that they might want to go to their bunks too. They were both decent men who did not often resort to such drunken behavior, especially not in front of us regular soldiers. That episode was one of my early experiences of learning what it means not to resist one who is evil but instead to turn the other cheek and do good.

One of the highlights of my military service was my week of R&R (rest and recuperation). The chaplain gave me some information about visiting Tokyo, including several names, addresses, and phone numbers of people I might contact. So I got in touch with a young Japanese lady and had several "dates" with her. One evening she showed me some of the sights of the city, then surprised me by inviting me to come to her home the next evening for dinner. I accepted with some trepidation, not sure if I knew the proper protocol. She graciously led me inside when I arrived and asked me to sit in the kitchen and watch as she prepared the meal. When it was ready, she explained what the various foods were and the proper etiquette for eating the delicious meal. Too soon it was all over. I thanked her for all her kindness to me and finally said goodbye. I headed back to my lonely warehouse in Korea with so many good memories. When I told the chaplain about my wonderful R&R, he was amazed and said, "How did you rate that you got invited to her house and she cooked you a special meal? I've never heard of any other guys getting treated so well by that Japanese young lady!"

Before I knew it, I had served most of my time for Uncle Sam, and I had an armful of rotation points for serving in the combat zone. But I had not used my weapon to kill anyone, I had not participated in any combat—and I had not even seen anyone die! Thanks be to God, who answered the prayers of my cousin Clara!

It was on the thirty-four-day ocean trip from Asia via the Pacific Ocean and the Panama Canal to the East Coast that I finally had time to really think about war and military service and the concerns that cousin Clara kept writing to me about. I managed to find a few quiet places on the ship where I could read, meditate, and even do a little writing again. By the time I arrived back in the United States, my thinking about serving in the military was going in a different direction.

We arrived at Fort Meade, Maryland, on June 22, 1953. I had figured it would take several days for all the discharge paperwork to be completed. But that was before my parents and sister appeared! They did not plan to wait around for several days. My dad knew a few things about military protocol, so he asked to talk to one of the top officers. When he got his opportunity, he explained that they had driven from New York State to pick up their son and they needed to get back home, so could he please expedite matters? The officer acquiesced, and an hour later I received my honorable discharge.

While we were driving back to New York and catching up on news about each other's lives, my parents dropped a surprise in my lap. They had met a Mennonite family the previous summer and had ended up visiting a Mennonite congregation at Alden, New York, some ninety miles one way from Bath. The real shocker of their story was that these people had a four-hundred-year history of conscientious objection to war! Now my folks wanted me to go along to visit these "different" people, to see if I thought they were "for real." Well, yes, I was ready to go meet these people and ask them some questions. I was eager to hear a logical and reasoned defense of nonresistance. And I wanted to know how to reconcile the use of war in the Old Testament with the New Testament teachings. ✝

The Morrows Discover the Mennonites

I have recorded this story as I remember Ted telling it.

I'm not sure whose idea it was but it could be that Katherine, who was going on sixteen years of age, had discreetly suggested to her father that it would be so nice if the Morrow family (she and her parents; Ted was busy serving with the Army in Korea) could go see the Smithsonian Institution in Washington, DC. Well, that was a big piece of pie to ask for. After all, it was 1952, before interstate highways and turnpikes where drivers zip along at sixty to seventy miles per hour without stoplights and city traffic to impede their progress. For example, the Baltimore Harbor Tunnel, with its toll collectors, did not open until 1957, when it provided better traffic flow from places like Philadelphia to Washington. And the Baltimore Beltway did not form a complete freeway loop until 1962, and the Outer Harbor Crossing over the Francis Scott Key Bridge was not completed until March 1977 and expanded to four lanes in 1981. But all of that was still only a dream when the Morrows began thinking about going to the Smithsonian.

One day, Olin sensed that his wife, Alice, might just be in a receptive mood, so he bravely broached the idea with her. They discussed the pros and cons. It was three hundred miles one way, but it was something all of them could enjoy. And if they left really early and avoided some of the traffic and midday heat, and if they packed a picnic lunch to eat on the way, then returned home instead of spending money on a motel that night, well—they would be really tired afterward, but it seemed like it could be done, and even be fun.

Olin picked up some road maps at the gas station (they were free for the asking in those days) and proceeded to study them and map out the best route. He also asked for a Friday off from his post office job so he would have the following two days to recuperate after the big trip. He even took his car to the mechanic to have the tires, fluid levels, and so on checked over before starting their trip. This was one time when the three of them were all looking forward to the same thing together. More often, the parents made the plans and the children went along without a lot of input.

When the long-awaited Thursday night arrived, they went to bed early but were probably a bit too excited to sleep well. The alarm clock was set, and by 1:00 A.M. everyone was awake and eager to go. Pinky had the back seat to herself, so she made herself comfortable and announced, "I'm gonna get some beauty sleep." From Bath her dad headed southeast on Route 15 to Painted Post. He stayed on Route 15 as it turned south into Pennsylvania, where they passed through small towns, such as Mansfield and Blossburg, and larger cities, such as Williamsport, where they met the west branch of the Susquehanna River. Further south, at Northumberland and Sunbury, they met the east branch of the Susquehanna, which included waters from the Cohoctan River that had originated in the highlands northwest of Bath. The river was now much wider but still shallow on their left as they continued south to

Camp Hill, just across the river from Harrisburg. Here Route 15 veered away from the river, which headed southeast, but Olin stayed on Route 15 as far as Dillsburg, where he briefly followed route 74 until he met route 194 south of town and followed it to Hanover. At Hanover he found route 94 and followed it across the Mason-Dixon line, where the route number changed to route 30 and eventually merged with route 140, which took them into Baltimore.

By this time Katherine was awake, and wondering if they would soon reach Washington. This was getting to be a rather long ride! Her dad sensed her curiosity and told her they had already traveled 225 miles, that they were in Baltimore and still had 70 miles to go. Then Alice mentioned lunch, so Dad pulled off at a gas station and pulled the lunch basket out of the "boot" of the car. (Yes, the Morrow family liked to connect with their British ancestry, so they insisted on talking about the "boot" and the "bonnet" of the car instead of the trunk and the hood.) They finally got through Baltimore, found the Baltimore-Washington Parkway, and began watching for the sights of the city. Dad was the first to spy the tall Washington Monument. Then they came upon the Capitol building, and the other big government buildings, followed by the mall with the large reflecting pool between the Lincoln Memorial and the Washington Monument. Such a big city!

The Smithsonian Institution, beginning just across the street from the Washington Monument, was big too. First they needed to find a place to park. Then they would have to decide which building to head for first, and which door to enter. Each of them was eager to see a lot in the six hours they had to look around. And hopefully they would all enjoy seeing the same things, because they had agreed to stay together so no one got lost in the crowds of people.

Katherine doesn't remember much about what they were looking at when suddenly her mother said, "Oh! Look at those people over there. They're wearing different clothes. The man is wearing a black hat, and the women—I guess it's his wife and daughters—one is wearing a black bonnet and the other two have white hats on their heads." Katherine looked helplessly at her dad, hoping he could somehow keep Mother from going to talk to the strangers. After all, they had come to see the museum, not to talk to people who were wearing odd-looking clothes!

But Olin was unable to distract his wife from her curiosity. "Come on," she said. "Let's go talk to them and find out who they are." Reluctantly Dad and Katherine followed Alice as she threaded her way through the other museum visitors. They were both hoping she would not embarrass them and spoil their day at the museum.

Alice marched up to the family and came straight to the point. "Excuse me. I see you are rather different from the rest of us here and, well, I'd like to know who you are. Are you some special religious order? What do the special clothes mean? And where do you live?" Finally she stopped for a breath of air. The family smiled, as if they had been asked similar questions before. They looked at one another, waiting to see who should speak first.

The man started: "I am Victor Rife. This is my wife, Bessie Rife, and our two daughters, Ruth and Janet. We live in the Chambersburg, Pennsylvania–Hagerstown, Maryland area. And we are members of the Mennonite Church. We wear a different style of clothing because we believe that our clothing should be modest rather that stylish and expensive. Many of our wives sew their own dresses, using simple patterns without elaborate collars or a lot of buttons."

At this point, Alice interjected, "I see. I like to sew too. I make my own dresses. And I have done seamstress work and have made several of my winter coats too."

Mrs. Rife then spoke up: "Well, I don't sew winter coats like you do, but we do have special sewing shops to make the 'plain suit,' as we call the dress suit that the men wear. This is another way we show that we are different from the world. We do not want to be proud of our clothes. We want to show we are Christians by the way we live and act, not just by our clothes. When we are working on the farm, my husband wears regular denim bib overalls like other men do."

"But why do you ladies wear the black bonnets?" Alice wanted to know.

Mrs. Rife spoke again: "We believe the Bible is our guidebook for life. Do you folks know what the Bible is?"

"Yes. I'm sorry. I didn't even introduce our family before I asked my questions," said Alice. "I am Alice Morrow and this is my husband Olin Morrow, and this is our daughter, Katherine. Yes, we are Christians and we go to a Baptist church. But we have never heard of Mennonites before."

Mrs. Rife continued: "Well, in 1 Corinthians, chapter 11, the Apostle Paul teaches us about the divine order, which is God is the head of Christ, then Christ is the head of man, and man is the head of woman. A man who prays or prophesies with his head covered or wearing a hat dishonors Christ, but the woman should veil her head when she prays or prophesies in order thereby to honor her head. If she does not cover her head, she may as well cut off her hair. Our women wear a white net prayer veil on our heads, and when we are in public places we older women wear a protective black bonnet too. Long hair is a glory to a woman, but for a man long hair is a shame."

"About the Mennonites," Mr. Rife picked up. "Our church dates back to the time of the Reformation of Martin Luther and other reformers. Our ancestors wanted to follow the Bible as fully as possible. Rather than baptizing babies, they felt baptism was only for believers who had a personal relationship with Jesus. They believed that Jesus wanted us to love one another, even our enemies. They were not popular and suffered much persecution. But William Penn invited our ancestors to come to Pennsylvania and enjoy religious freedom. Many of our young men have asked not to participate in the war efforts and instead have worked as volunteers, without pay, in other programs that are of benefit to our country, such as being smoke jumpers, or orderlies in mental hospitals, and working in conservation programs and on public health projects. Sometimes we are called 'the quiet in the land' because we don't say a lot about our beliefs. But when people ask us questions, we try to give an understandable and biblical answer."

Katherine, meanwhile, was not terribly interested in the adult conversation. But she did notice that both the mother and the daughters were wearing long-sleeved dresses of an unusual pattern, with a second piece that covered the bust and shoulders from the waistline up. The girls wore their hair in some sort of bun on the back of their head covered by a white hat with narrow white strings, about ten inches long, attached to the lower corners just behind their ears. What were those strings for? At least on the mother's black bonnet the wide black ribbons had a purpose; they were tied in a neat bow under her chin to keep the bonnet on her head. And the father's suit was rather old fashioned, with buttons running all the way up the front to the neckline.

Katherine decided to communicate via her body language that she was rather bored by all this Bible discussion, that she wanted to see more of the museum displays, and could her mother please speedily wind up this conversation? So Alice did. But first she had a final question. "Could our daughters please exchange names and addresses? Maybe they could be pen pals. It would be nice to stay in touch with you—if that is all right with you, of course."

"Yes," the Rife family said in unison. Someone produced some paper and addresses were exchanged as the Morrows murmured, "Thank-you." Then everyone said good-bye.

As they parted ways, more than one person wondered what might be the long-term results of their "chance" meeting at the Smithsonian that summer day in 1952. Olin had not said much during the conversation, but he had listened carefully and had some new ideas to think about as they headed back to the display cases. ✝

The Morrows Learn More About the Mennonites

After they returned home from their trip to DC, the Morrow family continued to talk about these "different" Mennonite people. Eventually the Rife daughters, Ruth and Janet, sent a letter to Katherine. Mother Alice was more interested in the letter than Katherine was, but with some encouragement from her mother, Katherine eventually sent a letter back to the Rife girls.

At some point, probably in the fall of 1952, the Rife family invited the Morrow family to come visit them on a weekend and attend church services with them. This invitation conveniently coincided with the fact that Olin had recently traded in his older car on a more recent model and was eager to try it out on a longer trip. It was also the weekend that a visiting Mennonite minister was speaking at the Rifes' church, and both Morrow parents were admittedly eager to learn more about the Mennonites. Katherine was less enchanted with the idea of visiting the Mennonite family, but she obediently went along because her parents would never dream of letting her at home alone for a weekend.

Their new car performed well on the trip down to the Chambersburg area that autumn Saturday. They arrived at the Rife home at around 4:00 P.M., in time to get more acquainted before the evening meal. After they ate, the Morrows went along to hear the visiting Mennonite minister from eastern Pennsylvania speak at the Rifes' church. He was a short, older man of slender build with piercing eyes, thin gray hair, and an intensity of speech and facial expression that communicated a deep love for his Lord. His sermon was solid Bible teaching and easy to understand. The Morrow family was also impressed by how they sang the old hymns in four-part harmony without piano accompaniment.

After the service, the Morrow parents spoke with the visiting minister, who introduced himself as Elias W. Kulp from the town of Bally, some miles northwest of Philadelphia. He proceeded to answer their questions about Mennonite history and beliefs. He also suggested that if they wished to visit a Mennonite congregation in the future, they might want to check out the Alden Mennonite Church, located maybe twenty miles east of Buffalo, New York. He explained that Alden was only half the distance from Bath that Chambersburg was. I assume that the Morrow trio spent the night with the Rife family, attended the Sunday morning service, and had dinner with the Rifes before giving their thanks and saying good-bye. They traveled home to Bath with lots to think about.

Elias Kulp had given Ted's parents the phone number of Dave Beachy, pastor at Alden Mennonite Church, so they called and arranged to visit him on a Saturday afternoon. Pinky—who was not eager to leave her friends at the Baptist Church in Avoca to go to another church where the people wore such obviously different and conspicuous attire—was not really interested, but of course she went along. While the adults talked, she occupied herself with the younger Beachy children—two girls and a boy. The Morrows returned to Bath that evening, but several weeks later they got up early on Sunday morning to go visit the Alden Mennonites. It was a ninety-mile drive one way, which took a good two hours in good weather. They drove to the Beachy home, then followed the family to the Alden Mennonite Church, a simple white building in a country setting.

They got to the church a bit early, so the Morrows sat in their car and watched as other folks arrived. An older couple pulled up in a VW Beetle and noticed the visitors sitting in their car. They promptly got out, approached the visitors, and introduced themselves. The man said he was Joe Roth and the woman was his wife, Salome. The Morrows accepted the Roths' invitation to enter the church and sit with them. The Roths soon learned that the Morrow family had traveled up from Bath that morning, so they promptly invited the Morrows to come along home with them for dinner. They also assumed responsibility for introducing the Morrows to other families as they arrived for church. And they explained where the different Sunday school classes met, where to find the restrooms, and so on. When the service was over, the Morrow family met more Alden families, with such names as Beachy, Bontrager, Kypfer, and Baer.

Then the Morrows followed the Roth Beetle to the Roth farm near Corfu. Joe and Olin sat down to talk while Salome and Alice prepared dinner, and Katherine decided to do some exploring around the farm. She soon found some cats near the barn, but they were not really friendly, to her disappointment. She also saw the cows in the pasture. Meanwhile, Olin and Alice were learning that Joe and Salome were of Amish background, and Joe had been the pastor of a small Amish congregation nearby, but when the group disbanded, he and Salome decided to worship with the nearby Alden Mennonites. They had ties with the Beachy Amish and sometimes attended the Weavertown Beachy congregation near Lancaster, Pennsylvania. The Roths also explained that they were unable to have children, so in the late 1920s they had taken in as foster sons two brothers from the Amish Mennonite Children's Home in Grantsville, Maryland. Then, in 1931, they had adopted a daughter, Catherine, from the same home, and the following year they also took in her older brother, Albert. Catherine, their youngest child, had finished two years at Eastern Mennonite College and was currently teaching in a one-room school near Wooster, Ohio. The conversation continued to flow freely as the two families sat around the table and enjoyed the delicious meal. Afterward, the ladies did the dishes while the men continued talking. When Olin said it was time to "hit the road," the Roths encouraged the Morrows to come to Alden again, and to their home again as well. And the Morrows responded that they would indeed like to come again.

I don't know how often they went to Alden that first year, but clearly they were made to feel welcome. They appreciated the Sunday school and preaching, and got to know many of the families in a meaningful way. Katherine even became friends with some of the young folks and enjoyed attending some of their events. Sometimes the Morrows drove to the Alden area on Saturday and stayed with a family overnight so they could attend a Saturday event as well as the Sunday morning service.

When Katherine Morrow met Catherine Roth I do not know. But Catherine doubtless came home from her teaching job in Ohio for Christmas and may have met the Morrow family then. Though Catherine Roth was seven years older than Katherine Morrow, the two young ladies became good friends. At some point as they were getting acquainted, Katherine mentioned to Catherine that she had an older brother, Ted, who was serving with the US Army in Korea.

By the spring of 1953, after having visited Alden Mennonite Church for perhaps six or nine months, Ted's parents were thinking about becoming members. Ted was expected home from Korea in a few months, and his parents were eager to get his impression as to whether or not these Mennonite people were "for real." ✝

"KOREA" IN KOREAN—Pfc. Theodore E. Morrow of 5 Elm St.
Bath, is home again after 15 months service in Korea. Although
glad to be home, he values the experiences he had abroad, especially
the opportunity to further his hobby of language study. He learned
to write and speak basic Korean. Here he writes "den hon" (both
vowels soft) in the Korean language. Syllables are written top
bottom.

Ted Transitions into Civilian Life

Soon after Ted's homecoming, he did go with his family to meet the Alden Mennonites. Within weeks he had accepted nonresistance as a biblical position, and soon afterward he asked, with his parents, to become a member of the Alden Mennonite Church.

A few days after Ted arrived back in Bath, a local reporter contacted him and arranged for an interview and photo for the local newspaper, the *Steuben Advocate*. The photo shows Ted standing at a blackboard that has several Korean words written on it. The article mentions his love of language study and that he had learned basic Korean during his military service. As for his future plans, he hoped to continue his studies, with the possibility of combining missionary work and business administration with his knowledge of languages in a civilian position overseas. The article also mentions that while Ted was in the Army he took correspondence courses in business law and accounting.

A few weeks later, Ted applied for a driving permit. He also checked to see if the sales job offered to him before he left was still available. The job meant visiting stores in the eastern part of New York State and collecting orders for future deliveries. Driving wasn't exactly Ted's forte—he was rather easily distracted. After he got his license and then a car, he decided to check the map after he had already started down the road. Unfortunately he missed seeing the upcoming bend in the road and totaled his recently purchased car. But at least he was not hurt.

Another car was purchased and Ted began his job as a glove salesman. As the weather got cold and it snowed, the glove sales did not improve. One morning when he climbed into his car and sat down, the plastic seat cover shattered, to his great surprise. So he began thinking about finding a different job, maybe in a different part of the country.

Meanwhile, through his new Mennonite connections, Ted learned about an opening for a male attendant at Brook Lane Farm, an MCC facility for persons with mental illness near Hagerstown, Maryland. He was accepted for the position and worked there for maybe two months before agreeing with his supervisor that this was not the ideal employment position for him. He then learned about a school teacher position in Greenwood, Delaware, so in the spring of 1954 he went there and submitted an application. Meanwhile, he had gotten a temporary job selling chicken feed and talking to farmers about their chicken problems. When he learned that the teaching position had gone to another applicant, he decided to head west to Ohio to attend a Conservative Mennonite Conference gathering. He had been boarding with the Slabaugh family, and when Mr. Slabaugh heard of Ted's plans, he suggested that Ted stop at Scottdale in western Pennsylvania and visit Mr. Slabaugh's brother Lorenzo. "And you really should go see the Mennonite Publishing House while you are there."

Well, Ted never did make it to Ohio on that trip. When he got inside that publishing house and saw all those people and what they were doing, he was impressed. And the person taking him on the tour was also impressed with Ted, because he knew German and was a writer, proofreader, and so on. I can imagine those staid Mennonite managers getting into a huddle after their coffee break that morning to talk about this novice Mennonite who had these excellent skills, especially in German, which they needed sometimes, and wondering, should we offer him a job or are we being too hasty? Well, they did offer him a job, and he accepted. In time he worked in a variety of positions—linotype operator, proofreader, German translator, editorial of Sunday school and worship materials, and writer of numerous articles, poems, stories, and children's crossword puzzles. The work was rewarding and he enjoyed most of his colleagues, who soon discovered that if they received something they did not know how to read because it was in another language—whether a handwritten letter, a magazine, or a Bible—they could give it to Ted to decipher and he would enjoy the challenge of producing a translation for them. ✝

Ted and Catherine Meet, Then Separate

Ted and Catherine met in Alden in July 1953 on his first visit to the Roth household. He was immediately attracted and had soon trailed her to the barn to "help" with milking the cows (though he knew nothing about cows or farming). It didn't take him long to realize that Catherine could be his love companion for life. He enjoyed being with her, and Catherine enjoyed being with him too.

Catherine had spent the previous year teaching in a one-room school in Ohio. For a while she had dated a farmer's son and even considered marrying him, but he was his parents' only child and, Catherine perceived, too attached to them and their plans for him, so she concluded that he was not the man for her. After the breakup and at the end of her first year of teaching, she decided that she was ready for a change of scenery, even if it was just going back home to the Roth farm in New York. She was also thinking about taking a break from teaching, especially in a one-room school.

In a letter to her parents while she was still in Ohio, Catherine had suggested the idea of going to Germany with her parents for their next term of service to refugees displaced by World War II. Her father, Joe Roth, had gotten his first taste of this work when he went on a cattle boat ride to Europe in the late 1940s. When he arrived home, he was no longer satisfied with just farming in New York. So Joe and Salome went back a year later, under the auspices of the MCC, to work for two years with refugees, some of whom were German-speaking Mennonites.

During one of her parents' overseas terms, Catherine was a student at Eastern Mennonite High School in Harrisonburg, Virginia. There she met another student who introduced herself as Ruthie Ravenscroft. Well, Catherine's ears really perked up when she heard that name, so she said, "Oh? Who is your father?"

The girl said, "His name is Arley Ravenscroft."

Catherine responded with obvious excitement, "I think he might be my older half-brother! Where do you live?" Ruthie told Catherine that Arley had been adopted by the David Yoder family of Greenwood, Delaware. As a young man, he had maintained contact with his birth mother and family. After attending his mother's funeral in 1931, he had decided

to resume using his birth name, Ravenscroft. He spent most of his adult life living near Newport News, Virginia.

Of course Ruthie told her father about meeting Catherine, and in due time Arley arranged for Catherine to come home with Ruthie for a weekend to meet the rest of the family. Ruthie had at least two siblings, Joe and Betty. Catherine was impressed by Joe's artistic ability. She also wanted to know more about her birth mother. She learned that Arley was the oldest of five sons (Arley, Elmer, James, Hillary, and Abbott) born to Hattie Duckworth and Harvey Ravenscroft between August 20, 1909, and September 12, 1916. Harriet later married Oscar Rouch in 1926. Another son, Albert, was born on March 2, 1927, and finally a daughter, Catherine, arrived on August 19, 1929. Catherine also learned that her father, who worked in the mines near Lonaconing, Maryland, was a Cherokee Indian. Hattie had died in Lonaconing on April 13, 1931. Two weeks later, on April 27, Oscar surrendered Albert and Catherine to the Amish Mennonite Children's Home in Grantsville, Maryland. Two months after that, on June 29, Catherine was taken home by Salome and Joe Roth. Her brother Albert followed in March 1932.

Catherine was ecstatic to have discovered her birth-family siblings, and she visited them as often as she was able. But she also had a strong bond with her adoptive parents and with their Amish roots and rural life values. She enjoyed working with children and she hoped to marry and have a family someday. She liked working with her mother in the house, but she was also ready to help her father milk the cows and do outside work when needed.

After they had begun dreaming of a future together, Catherine revealed to Ted her intention to go with her parents to Germany that fall, and their plan to be there for two whole years. It seemed unreal that the fulfillment of their dream would have to be postponed for two years. They discussed the prospect with their parents and with trusted friends, and after much prayer and input, Ted and Catherine decided that because Catherine had made the commitment to go with her parents to Germany in good faith, she should indeed go. They would write letters to each other (in the days before computers and e-mail), and if they still felt the same way about each other when she and her parents returned in the fall of 1955, they would get married around Thanksgiving time.

As Catherine and her parents prepared to go to Germany, Ted and Catherine treasured the time they could spend together before her rapidly approaching departure. ✞

The Roths Go to Germany

All too soon the day arrived. Catherine's diary shows it was foggy when she and her parents left Corfu, New York, at 4:00 A.M. on October 14, 1953. They arrived at the Morrow residence in Bath at 6:20 A.M. Catherine writes that "Cal's brought us"—meaning it was Calvin Beachy who drove the Roth family and their steamer trunks to New York City. The Morrow family followed in their car. Catherine notes the covered bridge on which they crossed from Pennsylvania into New Jersey.

They must have spent the night of October 14 in or near New York City because Catherine mentions that she and Ted went to Staten Island on October 15. What a logical place for a young couple with limited finances to go, especially when they would be saying good-bye for two long years! How could they resist the Staten Island ferry, with its nickel fare for the ride, or ten cents each for the round-trip. (I remember going on that same ferry ride and passing by the Statue of Liberty in the spring of 1960.)

Catherine mentions in her diary that "George Bylers and a group from there" were present. She may have been referring to a group from the Weavertown Beachy Amish congregation near Lancaster, Pennsylvania, where the Roths had many friends. In those days, when folks were leaving by boat to serve in Europe or in other foreign mission fields, it was customary for a large group of friends to travel to New York, board the ship, and conduct a farewell service with the departing missionaries before their boat left the dock. Ted and Catherine wandered off to a less public corner for their own special farewell. Catherine later wrote in her diary that "parting from Ted was hard, but when Christ sends comfort we know it is only for a little while." Then the foghorn sounded and all of the guests were asked to leave the passenger ship.

Many people stood on the dock with Ted and his family waving good-bye as the ship inched away from the dock, and some lingered to wave handkerchiefs and watch as the big boat crept further and further away. Finally, Ted turned from the shrinking ship, let his family know he was ready to leave, and drove with them to Pennsylvania, where they hoped to spend the night with friends in Lancaster County. Meanwhile, Catherine's diary for that day records, "Left promptly at 4:00 P.M. Beautiful day. Turned clock ahead one hour."

It had been a long day for the Morrow family, especially for Ted, who was exhausted and emotionally drained. It was late afternoon with rush-hour traffic as the family headed for Pennsylvania and Lancaster County. They did stop to eat and finally circled around the northern perimeter of Philadelphia, but by the time they got to Paoli and started heading west on Route 30, they all agreed that they were too tired to push on to Lancaster County. They began looking for a motel and soon saw a sign announcing that the Brackbill cabins for overnight lodging were coming up on the right. They noticed the Harry Brackbill produce market as they turned into the lane and found several cabins secluded from the highway. Ted went to the main house to inquire if lodging was available. The owner's answer was affirmative: a two-bedroom cabin was open. The family lost no time in getting to bed.

When they went to check out the next morning, they discovered that the owner was Milton Brackbill, pastor of the nearby Frazer Mennonite Church. Milton promptly invited the Morrow family inside to share more of their journey into the Mennonite Church. His wife, Ruth, soon appeared with coffee and fresh cinnamon buns. An hour later the Morrow family departed for Lancaster County, carrying with them a deep appreciation for the friendship shown to them by the Brackbills.

As the family traveled west on the Lincoln Highway (Route 30), they stopped at our farm on Gap Hill, which was right beside the highway. I remember that I offered Ted some instant coffee, but our electric stove was slow in heating up the water, so the coffee was "not quite" hot. I don't remember if the Morrow parents slept in our guest room or if Ted used it, but I do remember that Pinky and Erma Lapp (a friend we had invited to join us for the night) and I sat around the kitchen table for an hour or two until Erma got tired and went to bed. Then Pinky and I talked some more, but mostly Pinky talked and I listened. I'm not sure what time we went to bed, but it could have been 3:00 or 4:00 A.M.

The Morrow family arrived back home "late Sunday night," then sent my parents a postcard on October 21, 1953, to thank them "for your hospitality to us and to Katherine. Hope to see you again." Pinky and I stayed in touch by letters, and she did write interesting letters. One outcome of our conversation that night at my family's kitchen table was that Pinky's parents agreed to enroll her at Eastern Mennonite High School for the 1954–1955 school year, her last year of high school. She lived on the second floor, where Catherine Roth and I had roomed together in my freshman year, and she made lots of friends there. That year I lived one floor above her, so we ate in the same dining room and saw each other frequently.

That fall, Pinky invited Edna Hoover, a classmate of mine, and me to spend our Thanksgiving vacation with her and her parents in Bath. Alice and Olin came to meet us at Selinsgrove, Pennsylvania, because we were able to get a ride that far with an EMC college student from

Juniata County. Ted was at home some of that weekend too. I remember that the family took us around to see some places that were important to them, such as Houghton College, Letchworth State Park, and the town of Morris, where a Derrick cousin had died in the tuberculosis sanatorium. We also visited a cousin named June Eggleston, who lived above her millinery store in Perry, New York, and a cousin named Edna Derrick and her mother, Olive Derrick. These were all relatives of Pinky's mother.

On Sunday we spent the whole day at Alden, though I cannot recall where we ate and what we did that afternoon. I know it was late when the six of us traveled home. We three girls had the back seat and Ted was in front beside his mother. We girls were tired and had stopped talking, so it might have appeared that we were asleep, but Edna and I were both awake (I checked with her later). I don't remember that I ever asked Pinky if she was awake or not. Anyway, Ted's dad was driving and at some point Ted's mother began talking to Ted about something he should have done differently. I can't remember what the issue was, but she was speaking to him as though he were a small child rather than a twenty-six-year-old adult who was a college graduate and had served in the US Army in Korea and received an honorable discharge. Ted just let her "rant and rave" and did not try to defend him or answer her harsh accusations. He probably knew better than to respond. But Edna and I were appalled that a mother would talk that way to her adult son. ✞

Catherine's Service in Germany

What Catherine expected during her overseas assignment is not specified in her diary. Her comments are often terse, but they contain many facts about her two years at Espelkamp, which I have tried to summarize here.

Catherine, Salome, and Joe Roth traveled by ship from October 15 to October 24, 1953, with several rough days and some sea sickness. There were stops at Ireland (where Catherine "noticed the beautiful green to the shore"); at Le Havre, France (where it was "foggy and misty" and "everything" was "done in such a backward way. Funny-looking cars, railroad cars, people"); and at Southampton, England ("Don't know when we left—sleeping. Saw large Esso refineries. Saw large hospital") before they disembarked at the German port of Bremerhaven. Their final destination was Espelkamp, a town in the Minden-Lübbecke district of North Rhine-Westphalia, approximately one hundred miles due south of Bremerhaven. After World War II, this former site of a German munitions dump and poison gas factory was occupied by the British Army, which intended to destroy it. But a clergyman of the Church of Sweden named Birger Forell intervened and the town was instead transformed into a home for refugees from East Germany and other parts of Europe and eventually other parts of the world (such as South America and the Soviet Union). The MCC opened a voluntary service camp at Espelkamp in 1948, and this is where the Roths would spend the next two years.

The next morning, the Roths attended a Mennonite church whose congregation Catherine described as "a very cold group." The service that evening, however, featured a farewell service for a couple named Mary and Henry who were leaving the following Friday, and a "welcome for us" that included "very nice talks by four pastors" and several musical numbers played on a flute.

Catherine promptly became involved in the camp's housekeeping chores. She cleaned and waxed floors, changed feather ticks (the coverings of down comforters and feather beds), washed clothes and dishes, ironed clothes, and fixed meals. She prepared many Bible stories for the children, often using flannel board illustrations. She worked with the youth in Bible studies and discussions, and helped them present plays. She was involved in music programs and informal game times with these groups as well. Catherine also did a lot of typing for these teaching projects, and she typed up notes for her father for a series of lessons on nonresistance. She mentions preparing financial records that she transferred to other staff persons on a regular basis. She also wrote frequent letters to Ted.

I get the impression that at first Catherine kept a detailed diary in order to document what she did throughout each day in case someone were to ask what she was doing. For the first three weeks her entries are very short. Then, beginning just three weeks after her arrival in Espelkamp, there is a lapse of approximately a year before she resumes regular reporting, with longer entries as she comes toward the end of her term.

About halfway through her term she went on holiday to Italy, Greece, Israel, and Egypt. The trip had been encouraged by her mother, who had written to inquire whether there was still an opening for Catherine to join the group. Catherine was feeling a bit strapped financially and was thinking of her future wedding expenses, but she finally decided to go anyway. As it turned out, this was her one and only trip to these countries. She listed the purchases she made in these places, such as material for her wedding dress bought in Jerusalem, a linen bedspread purchased in Damascus, a wall hanging bought in Cairo, a dresser scarf from Jericho, and china plates found in Athens, as well as a tablecloth she had bought in Austria.

Catherine did have some adjustment problems after arriving in Germany, as do most people who are transported into a foreign culture. She had learned some German and Pennsylvania German from her parents, but she also took German lessons from a Frau Hedebreckt and became fairly fluent. She seemed to make many German friends, but her relationships with coworkers could wear her down. Several times she mentions a lady I will call Martha. In her first diary entry after not writing for a year, Catherine admitted that she felt "quite tired" and "quite discouraged. How I long that Martha and I could agree more often. It just seems to take an awful lot of love to work with her. I don't know what to do anymore—guess just pray all the harder. I really long to cooperate with her." She then writes a prayer in quotes: "O Lord show me the right way to deal with her. Be it my fault, purge me of all sin. Help me to see myself as I am and to walk as you would have me walk. Give me a clear path so that I know more how to meet the barriers that stand ahead. Give me a strong will to do the right no matter how much I may be wronged. Grant me a will to do thy will. Amen."

Several days later, Catherine and Martha had another misunderstanding, but Catherine continued to pray. Two weeks later, Martha and Catherine traveled to Lübbecke, where Martha was seen by an eye doctor, who told her she had an infection and needed to be admitted to the hospital. She seems to have remained there for several weeks, which added to Catherine's responsibilities at Espelkamp. Six months later,

Martha made a new commitment to Christ during a series of evangelistic meetings, and Catherine said, "Praise God."

During Catherine's two years at Espelkamp, her parents were often assigned elsewhere in Germany, but Catherine seemed most happy when they worked at Espelkamp for several months (from December 5, 1954, through June 20, 1955) before going to Berlin for two months. They were at Espelkamp again briefly before returning to the United States to begin preparing for their only daughter's wedding two months later. The Espelkamp women had a farewell party for Salome Roth on Saturday evening, August 13. Catherine, of course, escorted her mother. The ladies had made a lovely cake and arranged for instrumental and vocal music by Frau Schopke, stories by the girls, and lots of lovely flowers. Many tears were shed. It was a very special time for both Catherine and her mother. The next evening, August 14, a farewell service was held at the church for Joe and Salome. The choir sang two special songs: "With the Lord" and "Don't be Afraid." Again tears were shed as Joe shared stories about the love of Christ at work among them. Catherine was sad to see her parents preparing to go home without her.

The next day, August 15, the Espelkamp group had a farewell supper for Joe and Salome. Afterward, many friends dropped in to wish them well. The next morning, August 16—just three days before Catherine's twenty-sixth birthday—Pop and Mom Roth "left at 9:30 for Luxembourg," and presumably traveled from there to the coast to board a ship that would carry them to New York. On the eve of her birthday, Catherine wrote in her diary, "Cried because of homesickness." And on her birthday, August 19, she wrote, "Today I've been very lonely at times," yet she praised the Lord "for bringing me safely through these 26 years and [who] in spite of my many, many sins still loves and cares for me."

On September 1, Catherine went to Lübbecke by bicycle to get her passport renewed and to purchase traveler's checks. Later she asked a staff member for someone's mailing address, but after he had looked several places for it, he said to her, "I have no records of any kind to go by. Joe never kept any records on paper! It was all in his head!" Catherine was so upset by his remark that she went to her room and bawled. "I shall not soon forget it," she later wrote in her diary. She wrote her dad a letter about the incident "and told him everything." That night she let someone else wash the supper dishes and she went to bed "at 7:30 P.M. with a furious headache."

The next day, September 2, she received "a very interesting and encouraging letter" from her parents, as well as an "encouraging" letter from Ted. "Even tho' the going may be rough and life seems tough— never forget that the Father cares," she wrote that evening in her diary. Catherine had no apparent doubts about her relationship with Ted and was totally committed to him, as he was to her.

Ten days later, on Monday, September 12, Catherine wrote that "time is drawing closer to my departure from Germany. It will be with mixed feelings that I leave. Met many dear people here. . . . God has worked wonderfully. Praise his name." On Thursday September 15, she recorded, "I see that it is only four weeks until our boat pulls out. I'd better hurry." Then she asked God to help her find a particular letter that her mother had sent. "He showed it to me almost immediately altho' I had looked my letter holder over very good. Praise His Name." During those four weeks her diary entries frequently ended, "Tired but happy."

On October 3 she discovered "it would be quite expensive to ship" her bicycle "to the USA," so she sold it to one of her coworkers for one hundred Deutsche Marks. On October 4 she packed her trunk and duffle bag and bought a suitcase. During her final days she was given many gifts to take with her, including a silver cookie dish, several teapots, a cream pitcher and sugar bowl, a tablecloth, bouquets of flowers, and cash. On October 7, beginning at 10:00 in the morning, she "went visiting and said good-bye to many friends in twenty-four different homes"!

On Monday, October 10, the day before her departure, Catherine helped to peel pears and can twenty-three liters—nothing like working up to the last minute! She went to friends' for supper and stayed up late talking, until 12:45 A.M. Then, on Tuesday, October 11, she arose at 6:30 and finished packing. After a noon meal of liver, mashed potatoes, and date pudding, she left Espelkamp with her travel companions at 1:30 P.M. and traveled by way of Herford, Dusseldorf, and Aachen, then "spent the night at the Hotel Hindenburg." In the morning they left the hotel at 7:45, arrived at the Belgium border at 8:30 A.M., and at around 2:00 P.M. crossed the border into France, where she "had to show my ship ticket to prove that I wasn't selling what is in big box." They continued on to Rouen, where they spent the night at the Hotel d'Angleterre. The next day, October 13, at 12:30 P.M. they arrived at Cherbourg, from which they left by ship at 5:10 P.M. ✞

Preparations for THE DAY

The ship finally docked at New York City on Tuesday, October 18, at 7:00 A.M. It took Catherine three hours to pass through immigration, retrieve her luggage, and exit the pier. "My heart beat real fast as I saw Ted," she later wrote in her diary. "Such a blessed feeling of knowing that Ted and I still loved each other and that love was really deep. After getting things in the car we hightailed it out of NYC by way of the Holland Tunnel." Ted drove west to Scottdale, where they arrived at 8:30 P.M.

The next day, October 19, Ted gave Catherine a tour of the Mennonite Publishing House, where she "met oodles of faces." On October 20 they looked at a house they thought they might live in after they married, and they were "very much pleased with it. We told Joe we'll take it for $5,000 if we can get someone to finance it." That afternoon they packed up the car and headed north to their home state, where, Catherine wrote, it was "so good to see Mom and Pop."

On Friday, October 21, Catherine and Ted had their pre-wedding blood tests done, then went to visit Dave Beachy, the bishop who would perform their wedding ceremony. "He is in favor with our plans," Catherine recorded in her diary. "When we arrived home, Mom and Dad Morrow were there. It was so good to see them. They showed us some slides. Pop showed some slides too. I was really tired when I got to bed, but I also was so happy to be at home."

On Sunday, October 23, Catherine and Ted went to the Alden Mennonite Church with her parents. "Good to see the people again," she wrote. That afternoon, Ted left to return to Scottdale. "We both prayed, so glad that we can part from each other in Christ."

On Wednesday, October 26, the results of the blood tests arrived: "All OK," Catherine wrote. On Thursday, October 27, she received a letter from Ted "with wedding invitation. He forgot to put 2:00 P.M. on them." On Tuesday morning, November 1, Catherine went to nearby Batavia to get her eyes examined, to buy "clothes for wedding" and to order napkins. That afternoon she went with her parents to "see about dishes." On Wednesday, November 2, she ordered her wedding cake. On Thursday, November 3, Joe Roth drove his daughter to Scottdale to visit Ted and to see the house they wanted to buy. "Pop quite well pleased," she wrote. And he turned over a check for the down payment.

On Friday morning, November 4, Catherine bought a stove for the house for $25, then "planted roses and took down the For Sale sign." In the afternoon, she and Ted went to the bank, where they were approved for a loan. After supper, Ted, Catherine, and several other people headed south to EMC. They arrived in Harrisonburg at 10:45 P.M. Catherine stayed with Ted's sister, Pinky, and they talked into the wee hours. I was a senior at EMC that year. The next day, Saturday, Catherine and I spent some time together, and she asked me to be her "stand by," or bridesmaid. Of course I said yes! Pinky would be her maid of honor.

On Sunday, November 6, Catherine and Ted went to church with Pinky in the morning. After a late dinner, they left Harrisonburg at 3:20 in the afternoon to head north to Scottdale. They went by way of Lonaconing, Maryland, the small town tucked between the mountains southeast of Grantsville, Maryland, where Catherine had been born and where her older half-brothers Henry, Elmer, and Abbott Ravenscroft still lived. Catherine and Ted arrived in Scottdale at 9:00 P.M., then left immediately for Pittsburgh, where Catherine boarded a bus that departed for Corfu at 1:00 A.M. on Monday morning. When the bus got to Corfu at 11:00 A.M., Joe Roth was there to meet her. After a long, busy day, she was asleep that night by 11:30.

On Wednesday, November 9, Catherine's parents drove her to Bath to spend a few days with Ted's parents, and to give Ted's mother opportunity to begin sewing Catherine's wedding dress out of the fabric that Catherine had purchased in Jerusalem. "I tried on one of Pinky's dresses and it fit me to a T," Catherine recorded in her diary, "so we decided to use that pattern, only altering the skirt a little." On Friday evening, November 11, "at 8:30 P.M., Ted pulled in. Oh so happy to see him." The next day, Saturday, Catherine and Ted drove northwest to Corfu, stopping along the way to visit some of Ted's relatives, including his uncles Floyd and Irving Morrow and his aunt June Eggleston. They also stopped at the VA Hospital where Ted had worked for several months before starting college, and at Letchworth State Park "for a few minutes walk." They arrived at the Roths' at 3:00 P.M. The next day, Sunday, at Alden Mennonite Church, the couple was "published to be married." Ted left at 6:15 that evening to return to Scottdale.

On Wednesday, November 16, Catherine "helped to load two cows. One very stubborn." She washed and packed the dishes that would be used for the bride's table, and washed and ironed tablecloths and "sheets to be used as tablecloths." Later in the day there was "rain and terrific wind" and Catherine wondered aloud "what the wind will blow up now." Pop Roth replied, "Likely a wedding." On Friday, November 18, some sixty friends threw a wedding shower for Catherine and Ted (though Ted was not in attendance).

On Thursday, November 24, Ted arrived and the final preparations for the wedding began. That evening they went to Bishop Dave Beachy's to finalize the program for the wedding and get "any further info that he might have for us. He read the vows for us. These are only a few minutes but are for life," Catherine wrote in her diary. The next morning they took Ted's car to a garage in Batavia " for greasing and cleaning." They left it there while they went "to different stores, bought groceries, clothes, gifts and what have you." When they went back to get the car, they discovered that "Ted was playing tricks again" and had "walked off with the keys" and "of course the garage man wasn't a magician. So we waited till the job was done." While they waited, they "studied the map over quite well" for their honeymoon trip.

On Saturday, November 26, Catherine and Ted spent the morning and some of the afternoon at the church hall setting up the tables and decorations and making other preparations for the wedding and reception. At 6:00 that evening there was a "practice at church. Very interesting. Gave one a funny feeling," Catherine wrote.

Finally, THE DAY—Sunday, November 27, 1955—arrived, and "what we dreamed for years came true." Catherine did not record anything more about THE DAY in her diary, but I was there, and this is what I remember.

The day began with a regular Sunday morning service at Alden Mennonite Church. After lunch, the bridal party and guests assembled at about 1:30 P.M. The attire of the bridal party was "plain," that is, there were no floor-length gowns or tuxedos. The bride wore the dress her soon-to-be mother-in-law had made—a regular "plain" dress that fell below her knees and had a cape and a two-inch flat collar. The bridesmaids were invited to provide their own dresses, so one wore a pink nylon dress that later was worn for her college baccalaureate service and many other times, and the maid of honor wore a light blue dress that was also worn on many other occasions. The bridegroom and his attendants wore plain suits. The service featured a sermon on the blessings and responsibilities of marriage, after which the bishop read the marriage vows and the bridegroom and bride pledged their lives to each other. They were then introduced to the congregation as Mr. and Mrs. Ted Morrow, after which they led their attendants to the rear of the church to greet their many guests.

A number of folks had excused themselves early to go to the reception hall to make final preparations for the reception, for which there were about two hundred guests. The food was plentiful and delicious, with both chicken and beef as the meat entrees and a variety of pies and cakes for dessert. When the guests were all satisfied, we all went upstairs to the assembly hall, where Ted and Catherine received and opened a variety of gifts. A few of the guests took photos, but there was no professional photographer that day. Some time later, Ted and Catherine did go to a photographer and get professional pictures taken of themselves in their wedding attire. Despite their Amish background, Catherine's parents did not object to pictures being taken; both Catherine and her father had taken many photos and slides while they were in

Germany. But they did get some "flack" about it from some of their Amish friends in the United States.

After all of the gifts had been inspected, the guests gradually said their good-byes and left. Pinky and I stayed overnight somewhere in the small Roth house, and Ted and Catherine spent their first night together as husband and wife in her bedroom. During the night it began to snow. Before we left on Monday morning, Catherine's mother gave Pinky and me some of the leftover reception food to take along to Virginia. We drove out of the snow by late afternoon and were really glad to arrive at EMC at around 10:00 P.M.

Ted and Catherine had originally wanted their honeymoon to be a trip to Kentucky to visit some of the Conservative Mennonite Conference ministries there. But Catherine's mother at some point offered them some Amish motherly advice. It went something like this: "Look, both of you have been so busy these past few months getting ready for your wedding and you are both tired. You really should not go on a long trip and be visiting a lot of people and places. You should take time just to relax and be together. Also, you don't have a lot of money to spend on motels and meals. Why don't you instead spend the nights at our house, have some meals with us, and go on some short day trips nearby?" This was the Amish way: to invite newlyweds to various homes for meals and lodging after the wedding. Ted and Catherine accepted her advice. They spent a day at nearby Niagara Falls and visited friends in the Corfu area for a week before traveling off to Scottdale with their belongings and moving into their new home. ✝

Catherine and Ted Begin
Their Life Together

Even though they did not have much furniture or many belongings, Ted and Catherine's new house seemed small. But it was adequate for the two of them. Soon after they got settled, they were visiting friends and having guests to their home, which they both enjoyed.

It was several months before Catherine again wrote in her diary, on February 3, 1956—and she had something exciting to report! "Doctor Bucci says we are awaiting a 'little one.' May God bless this growth abundantly. Have been feeling quite nauseated of late and suspected it was so." She and Ted were both pleased about the pregnancy despite their less-than-affluent financial status.

A couple of months later, Joe and Salome Roth left for another tour of service in Germany, this time with Amish Mennonite Aid. Their timing was hard for Catherine, who would have liked to have her mother's help during her pregnancy and after her child was born. And that child would be nearly two years old before they got to see him or her. But Catherine remembered that it was not easy for her and Ted to be separated for two years, and they had survived, so she knew that God would help her and her parents through this next period of separation.

Catherine's diary says that the Roth parents arrived at their home in Scottdale at 8:00 P.M. on Tuesday, April 17, 1956. The next morning it was snowing, and after changing a flat tire and putting luggage into Ted's car, they all left together at 10:00 A.M. They arrived in Lancaster County at 5:00 P.M. After supper, they went to a farewell service at the Weavertown Beachy Amish church.

The next morning, Thursday, April 19, Joe Roth left with Dan Stoltzfus for New York City while Ted, Catherine, and Salome visited with Ted's family, who had come down to Lancaster to meet them. They did some shopping, had lunch at Dairy Queen, then left for New Jersey, intending to arrive in New York City the next morning. But on the way Ted's car broke down just beyond Conshohocken, so they were towed back to Conshohocken, where they called Markley Clemmer, a well-known Mennonite pastor in Norristown. Markley came and picked them up at the Conshohocken garage while his wife made sure the beds were ready for occupants. The mechanic would not be able to get the necessary parts to repair Ted's car until the next day, so it would not be ready for an early morning departure. So Markley consulted his wife, then offered to drive the Morrows and Roths to New York City himself. They got up at 3:30 A.M. on Friday, April 20, and got on the road soon after. They stopped for breakfast at a Howard Johnson's in New Jersey—where they were surprised to find the occupants of two charter buses that were carrying friends from Lancaster County to see the Roths off in New York City! "Mom and Pop got a big laugh" out of that, Catherine wrote in her diary. They transferred the Roths' luggage onto one of the buses. Ted, Catherine, and her folks arrived in New York City soon after 8:00 A.M. and found a good parking space.

After all of the Roths' guests were on board the ship, they "met in the theater for the farewell service," Catherine wrote. Before the service, one of the Weavertown ministers had approached Markley Clemmer and asked if he would provide a speech and farewell blessing in English, because the Weavertown Beachy Amish ministers were not comfortable preaching in English. Of course Markley was happy to oblige, even with little advance warning or time to prepare. Ted and Catherine were so blessed by his provision for their multiple needs—a place to sleep, a ride to New York (so early in the morning!), and then a meaningful send-off speech for her parents.

The boat pulled out at 11:00 am. It was hard for Catherine to see her parents leave again, but she knew they were in the will of God. Ted then called the garage about his car and was told that it would be ready to go that afternoon. Markley drove them back to the garage by 4:30. The car was indeed ready to travel, so they paid the bill ($44.55 for a secondhand alternator) and thanked Markley again for all his help and hospitality.

Ted and Catherine then went into nearby Philadelphia to visit her brother Albert, who had not been at their wedding because the invitation Catherine had mailed had not arrived. They stayed overnight. The next morning, Saturday, April 21, they all slept late. Then Albert, his wife, Frieda, and their daughter, Peggy, showed Ted and Catherine some of the city. They "paid 59 cents for a new dress for Peggy. She will be five years old on Monday, April 23. She is attending kindergarten." Frieda served them "a very nice dinner" before they left at 2:30 P.M.

From Philadelphia they drove to Baltimore, where they intended to visit her half-brother James Ravenscroft, but Catherine had forgotten to bring the address. Yet "here we see God's leading," Catherine wrote. A possible address finally came to her mind, so they went to that block of South Pulaski Street. "Ted walked up the street, saw a woman in the window and asked her if Ravenscrofts live close by." "Next door," was the prompt reply. The Mennonite Mission was on the same street, so they stopped there briefly as well. That night they stayed with James and his family. The next day, Sunday, April 22, they attended church

and Sunday school. They left Baltimore at 2:30 P.M. after a "scrumptious dinner." At 4:30 they stopped at Brook Lane Farm, the mental health facility near Hagerstown, Maryland, where Ted had worked as an attendant for a couple of months after returning from Korea. It snowed as they crossed the mountains, and when they arrived back in Scottdale at 10:00 P.M. they were glad to be there. On Monday morning, April 23, Ted went back to work. ✝

The Morrow Family Expands

After Catherine's nausea subsided, she tried to do more things inside and outside the house, but by the hot summer months she was into her last trimester and was tiring more easily. She missed her parents and eagerly read their letters for news about people she knew. She and Ted talked about possible names for their child and decided to use the first names of both grandparents; that is, if the baby was a boy he would be named Joseph Olin after his grandfathers, and if it was a girl she would be named Alice Salome after her grandmothers.

The day finally came when the contractions began and the doctor said it was time to go to the hospital in nearby Mount Pleasant. On September 14, 1956, Joseph Olin was born. He was only a few months old when Catherine conceived again. This time the baby was a girl. She arrived safely on November 30, 1957, and as planned they named her Alice Salome. Their little house was bursting at the seams, so at some point they found a larger, two-story house on North Scottdale Avenue and bought it. And again, like clockwork, fourteen months after Alice was born, sister Mary Katherine arrived on January 25, 1959.

Having three children three years of age and younger kept Catherine rather busy with changing diapers, feeding the children, and keeping them out of mischief. Then, several months after Mary's birth, Catherine was pregnant again, and this pregnancy somehow did not feel the same as the others. The doctor was concerned too. Early on the morning of November 19, 1959, Catherine went into premature, difficult labor and delivered by breech presentation a stillborn little girl with multiple congenital deformities. Ted's sister, Pinky, came up from Harrisonburg, Virginia, to care for Joey and Alice that night while a family friend cared for Mary. The tiny infant was given the name Rhoda Ann and the dignity of a graveside service and burial in a Scottdale cemetery the same afternoon. Many friends shared in the parents' grief by visiting them, telephoning, and sending sympathy cards.

A caring friend suggested to Ted and Catherine that they might try using a diaphragm to space their pregnancies, because breast-feeding was not popular in those days and contraceptive pills and intrauterine devices were not yet available. Married couples in past generations sometimes used abstinence to space their pregnancies while others used breastfeeding, nature's way, to space children to around every two

years. But for couples who were quite fertile and preferred to bottle feed rather than nurse their babies, pregnancies could come close together.

Ted and Catherine did use the diaphragm, and it worked, until their last daughter, Rita Joy, was conceived. She was born on August 16, 1963. ☩

Ted's Adventures in Faith and Employment

When Ted suddenly moved to Scottdale in the spring of 1954 to be an employee of the Mennonite Publishing House, he was stepping into a new world. Granted, he was familiar with the Mennonites at Alden, New York, and he had met Mennonites in Lancaster County and Ohio. But now he was working with some of the leaders of the Mennonite church where the church's publications were produced.

Still, Ted was not able to limit his interest to the Mennonites. He read widely, and somehow he heard that a Bruderhof community had purchased the Gorley's Lake Hotel, a former summer resort, outside Farmington, Pennsylvania, in 1957. Ted learned that these folks were sincere Christian believers who practiced the "community of goods." They had been expelled from Germany in 1937 because they did not say "Heil Hitler" or support his military regime. After spending three years in England during World War II, they met Orie Miller, who helped them obtain refuge in Paraguay. Later they explored the United States, and in June 1954 they bought the property that became Woodcrest Bruderhof in Rifton, New York. The property near Farmington was their second US site. They named it Oak Lake, because it had a big lake in front. It was located thirty miles southeast of Scottdale via routes 119 and 40.

One Saturday afternoon, Ted and Catherine loaded the children (Joey and Alice and possibly Mary; the precise date of this trip is unknown) into the car and drove down to check out their "new neighbors" at the Oak Lake Bruderhof. They had not made an appointment. They came into the house through the main entrance and found someone inside ready to welcome them. Ted introduced his family and indicated that they were Mennonites from Scottdale and were interested in knowing more about Bruderhof life. The receptionist answered their questions and invited the family to come back at a future time, perhaps over a long weekend or during a vacation break, to experience life in the community and meet more of its members. Ted and Catherine expressed their thanks and indicated their intention to return.

Later they did stay at the Bruderhof for perhaps a week. They were made to feel welcome and were shown to a room where the whole family was to sleep. Then they were taken to the dining room, where the whole group shared most meals. They were also introduced to the kindergarten room for preschoolers, the child care center for infants, the school for elementary students, a workshop where Community Playthings (wooden toys and other play equipment) were made as a source of income, and other shops for construction and maintenance.

Catherine and Ted were asked to work on separate projects while others cared for their children. They met a lot of new people and, despite the busy schedule, which included evening meetings, they managed to form a significant, lasting friendship with another family, the Dunlaps, whose children were similar in age to the Morrow children. Maybe it was the relief from providing total care for their small children, or maybe it was the stimulation of meeting so many new people, or the joy of letting others do the cooking and wash the dishes—in any case, the Bruderhof succeeded in making Ted and Catherine feel at home, and by the end of the week they were thinking about staying. Someone suggested they leave their children there, return to Scottdale, collect their belongings, and put up their house for sale—just like that! Of course Ted would have to resign from the Publishing House.

Apparently Catherine and Ted did leave the children in the care of the Bruderhof and drove back to Scottdale. But as they traveled home they both realized they had been so busy the past week that there had been little time just to talk about what they were experiencing. After they got inside their house they prayed together, and they realized they had also been too busy to pray together much. Catherine finally said, "Ted, let's go back and bring the children home—right now!" So they did. (Ted told me this story more than once, but his older children do not remember the experience, and when I told them about it they were dumbfounded that their parents would leave them at the Bruderhof, even for a short time, while they went home.)

At the Mennonite Publishing House, Ted also worked with some persons of the Catholic faith and from them he learned about a group of Catholics who met for Bible study in their homes on a regular basis. The Morrows became regular attendees. Ted also spoke about visiting the Greek Orthodox church down the street from their house and conversing with the priest. And not far from Scottdale, in Latrobe, Pennsylvania, was Saint Vincent Seminary (founded in 1846 by a Benedictine monk from Bavaria), which had given Ted the privilege of checking out library books for study and self-education.

Among Ted and Catherine's friends were Henry, a former Catholic priest who had sought release from his vows, and Florence, a former Catholic nun who had also obtained release from her vows. But Henry and Florence had not met one another, so the Morrow matchmakers got busy and invited both of them to dinner. Eventually the Morrows received a wedding invitation, and sometime later the newlyweds took all of the Morrow family to see the movie *The Sound of Music,* a very special treat for everyone.

Ted sometimes took the family to the Catholic church in Scottdale. He also learned about the Focolare, a Catholic ecumenical "movement" founded in northern Italy in 1943. Its goal was to fulfill the longing that Jesus expressed in His prayer recorded in John 17:21: "that they may all be one." Ted formed some lifelong friendships with members of this group. Several times over the next decade he took the family to the Focolare's summer gathering, the Mariopolis (city of Mary). The publishing arm of the Focolare, New City Press, produced an Italian Catholic renewal magazine and a number of the articles were translated and published in an English edition, *Living City,* produced in New York City. Ted was hired to translate some of these articles. Then, after Pope John XXIII died in 1963 in the middle of Vatican II, New City Press hired Ted to translate a biography of the deceased Pope. They flew him to Rome and the Vatican for a week to prepare him for the work. The trip gave him the chance to practice his spoken Italian, and it turned out to be his only trip outside the United States beyond his military service.

The timing of this trip was difficult for Catherine. Not only did she have three children six years old and younger to care for, but she was also eight months pregnant. The Focolare sent a young Italian "Focolarina" named Rita Muccio to stay with Catherine and the children while Ted was away. Rita made such an impression on Catherine and Ted, and they were so grateful to her, that when their new daughter was born they named her Rita. Daughter Alice, who at the time was five going on six, clearly remembers the older Rita gathering the family around the dining room table and teaching them how to pray using the Rosary. For a time Ted and Catherine considered joining the Catholic Church, but they did not follow through on that idea because of negative pressure from their parents. But twelve years later, as a freshman in college, daughter Alice did become a member of the Catholic Church.

When Rita was born, Ted was employed in the editorial division at the Mennonite Publishing House and his income was enough to provide for his growing family. Still, he was not completely satisfied with writing and editorial work. Then, in mid-1965, he learned that Slavia Press in Pittsburgh had a job opening for a typesetter that required proficiency in German. Pittsburgh was about an hour's drive from Scottdale, and the pay was not as much as he was making at the Publishing House. But it was language work, so he decided to try it. Reluctantly he resigned from the Publishing House.

Alas, the commute to Pittsburgh was a real drag, over back roads with lots of traffic. Ted did not really enjoy driving, and there was no car pool. He also missed going home at noon to have a hot meal with his family. And after he had paid for gas and a noon meal, his take-home pay was considerably less than what he had been earning at the

Publishing House. Finally, after he spent two hours driving each day, he was quite tired when he got home and did not have the energy to do much language study or to tackle a freelance translation project. So, in January 1966 Ted quit that job and tried to make a go of freelance translation for the New City Press.

He and Catherine soon realized that they could not survive in this arrangement. Catherine was full-time wife and mother for their four living children, and Ted still wanted to do translation work. So he began looking for translation jobs. In mid-1966 he learned of a job opening at Fortress Press, a Lutheran publisher headquartered in Philadelphia. They wanted an in-house person to translate a German book about controlling family size. Ted inquired and was invited to Philadelphia for an interview. He was hired, and soon afterward the whole Morrow family came to the city in their VW Beetle to look for a house to buy. It just so happened that I was living in Philadelphia at that time because I was a resident in surgery at Woman's Medical College of Pennsylvania, and their trip included an evening visit with me. They moved into their Germantown residence on Columbus Day 1966.

In search of a church community, they initially checked out the quaint old Germantown Mennonite Church and the Mennonite mission churches at Diamond Street and Norris Square. But they also visited some Lutheran churches and finally decided to attend Ascension Lutheran Church at the Lutheran Seminary in nearby Mount Airy. All four of the children were baptized there in 1967. Eventually a colleague at work suggested to Ted that the family visit Trinity Lutheran Church, which was closer to their Germantown home and had good preaching plus a strong program for growing children and teenagers. So they attended one Sunday morning, and stayed.

Fortress Press was only fifteen minutes from the Morrows' new home. Ted applied himself to his translation project, but it went rather slowly. He soon discovered that the librarian at Fortress Press knew a lot about foreign dictionaries and could refer him to the sources he needed. He also enjoyed getting to know the other employees in this big establishment. The book he was translating had been written by a German doctor who in 1964 had written in his first preface, "Special attention will be given to two matters which in my judgement have not been adequately treated until now, at least on the popular level. It will be our purpose first to discuss the ethical questions involved in planned parenthood, and second to impart the factual information that is essential for regulating conception." The book was so well received that, according to the preface to the second edition, published in 1965, it was reprinted after the author considered the thoughtful criticisms of his readers: "their criticisms and requests for expansion have been taken into account, and new findings considered, to the extent that this could be done without making the book too technical for the general reader."

Ted was quite interested in this book. After all, his first three children had been born at fourteen-month intervals, and he and Catherine had been using a diaphragm since little Rhoda Ann was stillborn. Wrage's book was written after the contraceptive pill for women became available in the early 1960s. The author presented his material in a very methodical way, and Ted tried to translate it so as to make it understandable to the average person.

Ted completed his translation of the book in mid-1967, but the Press did not expedite the process of getting the book printed and out into the stores. Instead, revisions were made so that the translation was much more technical and scholarly than Ted's version. Ultimately the book was not published in the United States until 1969. I do not know how well it sold. Ted had hoped that this book would serve as a display piece for his work as a translator, but he was so disappointed by the final version that he added a disclaimer to the copyright page verifying that the book was a translation by Ted Morrow that had been revised by his employer.

After completing his work on the book, Ted worked for Fortress as a copy editor and assistant book editor until August 1968, when he was relieved of his position. He promptly found work with a translation agency in downtown Philadelphia owned by Frank C. Farnham, whom he worked with from September 1968 to late 1969, when Mr. Farnham cut back his staff. Ted promptly found a temporary job at Biological Abstracts, which was looking for people who could handle a variety of languages and both translate titles and provide short abstracts of foreign-language articles. Ted enjoyed the variety of languages he encountered there, but the job was indeed temporary.

One day Catherine surprised Ted by asking him, "Why don't you do freelance translation work here at home and I will type it for you?" They talked about it and agreed that they could make a small office for Ted in the alcove of their bedroom, and Catherine could park the typewriter on the kitchen table because the family ate their meals in the dining room. So, even before the Biological Abstracts project was finished, Ted began contacting translation companies to search for jobs. He emphasized that he could translate a number of languages instead of just one or two.

Thus Ted and Catherine's home business began, early in 1970. Ted soon came up with a name for it: Morrow Multilingual Services. Initially he would write out his translations by hand and Catherine would type them on their portable Hermes typewriter. As their business grew, they invested in a used set of Stenorette dictating and transcribing machines. These tools made the work go faster for both Ted and Catherine. Ted would mention all of the punctuation marks, capital letters, new paragraphs, indentations, spellings of unusual words, and so forth in his dictation, which was really helpful to the typist.

Their work as a husband and wife team went rather well for a number of years, with jobs coming from various clients in New York, Philadelphia, and even Washington, DC. Again Ted and Catherine upgraded their equipment by investing in a new Hermes office-size manual typewriter and a new set of Sony dictating-transcribing machines. Some months later a New York customer asked Ted to get an electric typewriter and arranged a payment plan to help finance the purchase. The electric typewriter made the work even easier for the typist, and improved the appearance of the finished product. The family business was prospering nicely. ✢

Begin by Loving Again
by Theodore E. Morrow

The Lord sometimes gives
And sometimes takes away
There's happiness followed by pain
But when hearts are breaking
There's joy for the taking
In learning to love once again

Chorus
Begin by loving again
Begin by loving again
When all that once mattered
Seems ruined and shattered
Just begin by loving again

When Jesus was taken
And tried for his life
And Peter so fearful of men
Ran away from beside him
And cursed and denied him
He was told to start loving again
Chorus

Sometimes we are happy
and God is so real
But sometimes we are
Conquered by sin
When the world has gone sour
The need of the hour
Is to start by loving again
Chorus

When you have been spited
And hurt and betrayed
By someone you thought
Was your friend
There's strength in forgiving
And then you'll start living
With love in your heart once again
Chorus

Part Three
Begin by Loving Again:
Our Life Together

Saying Good-bye to Catherine

I returned from my second term at Shirati Hospital in Tanzania in February 1973. I traveled alone via Dar es Salaam, Moshi, Nairobi, and Zaire (now Congo). Soon after coming home, I moved back to Steelton, near Harrisburg, where I had obtained two part-time jobs. Thus I could partially arrange my work schedule.

In May of that year, Anna Martin and I drove to Florida, where Anna visited her brother and his family, and I attended the annual meeting of the American College of Obstetricians and Gynecologists and visited a cousin's family. Anna and I took a lovely day trip to Key West, then we traveled a more inland route on our return trip to Pennsylvania. We visited my cousin Aquila Stoltzfus and his family in North Carolina, and stopped at several Appalachian Regional Hospitals (ARH) in Kentucky and Virginia, because I was seriously thinking of working in a needy area. After I got back to Pennsylvania, however, I lost interest in an ARH position, and a year later I understood why.

That summer I took the written half of the OB-GYN exam, and passed it. In December I prepared a Christmas form letter for my scattered friends. Several days after I mailed it, Catherine Roth Morrow called me. I hadn't heard from her for several years, and at that time the family had been thinking of relocating to Oklahoma so that Ted could take a translation job there. But they were still in Philadelphia. Then Catherine told me that she was being treated for cancer of the breast.

So, several days after Christmas, I took off and went to Philadelphia to spend some hours with Catherine. We talked about a lot of things, and then she fixed hamburgers for us for lunch. I clearly remember that she gave her burger to Ted, so I figured her appetite was not very good. The children were at home too, but they kept themselves occupied upstairs as Catherine and I visited in the dining room. She seemed so glad to see me. When I was about to leave, I stood up and gave her a big hug and kiss. I assured her of my prayers for her and her family. Then she said to me, "I'm not afraid to die. I know that God loves me and will take care of me." It meant a lot to me to hear her say that.

I remember it was a bright winter day when I left Catherine to head back to Steelton. I had traveled only four blocks down Chelten Avenue from the Morrow house when my VW abruptly died. So I found a phone (before the era of cell phones!) and called Ted about my dilemma. He came, then contacted his VW mechanic, who promptly came and pulled me and my car to his garage. He put in a new alternator and by late afternoon I was again on my way back to Steelton. As I rode out the expressway and up the Pennsylvania Turnpike, my thoughts were with Catherine and her guarded prognosis. I also thought about Ted and each of their children, and prayed that God would meet their every need during this time of Catherine's illness.

Several weeks later I visited with my sister and her family on Saturday evening and stayed overnight. I returned to Steelton on Sunday morning in time to go to church there. I stopped by my apartment to drop off my bags and was surprised to hear my phone ringing. When I answered it, Catherine greeted me, with a question. She said something about having cramps with her menses. I discovered that she still had her ovaries, and I knew that the ovaries are often removed in breast cancer patients who are still having menses, so I urged her to ask her surgeon about it. Sure enough, Catherine was soon scheduled to have her ovaries removed.

Catherine and I talked on the phone a number of times and I sensed she was not improving. The family had gotten a hospital bed so she could sleep downstairs. I made another trip to visit her in mid-March. She was expecting me and was glad to see me. She lay in bed the whole time I was there, but I could tell she had lost more weight. I don't remember what we talked about, but I visited with her for an hour or more before praying with her and then bidding her farewell.

As I departed, I knew this was probably my last visit with her. I clearly remember that after I got on the expressway, I began praying aloud for Catherine and her family. I asked God to somehow minister to Catherine and to each member of the family during her final days with them. And I asked God to provide for Ted and each of the children after Catherine was released from her cancerous body. I did not have any thought that God would use me to answer my own prayer for the Morrow family!

Several days later, on March 19, 1974, in midafternoon, Ted called me to report that Catherine had gone home to be with her Lord and Master. He also told me that not only had I been her last visitor, but soon afterward she had lapsed into sleep, or a coma, and had subsequently had no meaningful conversation with any of the family members. The family arranged for friends to view the body on the day preceding the funeral in the living room where she had spent her final days. Ted invited me to spend the night at their home before the funeral. I slept in a bedroom with one of the girls.

The service was held the next morning at Trinity Lutheran Church. The undertaker service was provided by Kirk & Nice, and the body was placed in a blue-covered wooden coffin. Family members had prepared the funeral service, choosing appropriate songs and creating original artwork for the announcement and program. The body was buried at Ivy Hill cemetery in northwest Philadelphia. The family and guests then returned to the church for a meal prepared by folks from Trinity and the Germantown Mennonite Church.

As I drove back to Steelton that afternoon, my thoughts stayed with the Morrows, and the idea came to me to write a personal letter to each member of the family, with the goal of sharing some personal memories of Catherine. So I did. I did not mail them all on the same day, and I did not tell them all the same things. Ted's letter got to be the longest, because I could tell him about my last visit with Catherine. I printed by hand my letter to Rita, who was only ten years old and loved animals and outdoor things. I don't remember if any of the children replied to me, but Ted did.

One day during the week before Easter, I got a phone call from Ted. He said that the children had some time off from school and someone had come up with the idea of escaping the city for several hours—to come visit me! Well, I had promised to visit a friend in Carlisle early that afternoon, but I figured I could be back in time to meet the Morrow family at the Highspire exit of the Turnpike at 3:30 and let them follow me home.

Meanwhile, I began planning what I could fix for supper to feed three teenagers, one adult, and a ten-year-old. I had some rice, several cans of tuna, some peas, and maybe some ice cream for dessert and perhaps some cookies. I met them as planned, then found enough chairs for all of us to sit in the large living room and talk. Seventeen-year-old Joseph admired my record player and record shelf arrangement. Sixteen-year-old Alice admired several of my records. Fifteen-year-old Mary noticed some of my books. And ten-year-old Rita went out to the backyard to play with my dog, Pepper. Supper went OK. No one seemed to mind my array of odds-and-ends tableware, silverware, and chairs for around my small table. Somehow all six of us got to sit down at the same time and everyone seemed satisfied with the food. Afterward we sat for a while in the living room again. Then we slowly wandered into the backyard with Pepper and talked some more. Finally the children began edging toward the street, where their car was parked. Ted and I were still in the yard when he suddenly announced, out of the blue, while looking my way, "Well, who knoweth whether thou art come to the kingdom for such a time as this!" I was too amazed to say anything, but I surely remembered it, though years later when I reminded Ted of it, he claimed to have no memory whatsoever of making that statement!

It had become clear to me that the family was under considerable stress. The girls were struggling to plan and fix evening meals, Ted was not doing much translation work, and he now had no in-house typist. He would sometimes call and tell me of his frustrations. And we continued writing letters to each other, because phone calls could get rather expensive.

Then, early one morning, perhaps in mid-May, he called and said he had something urgent to tell me. He felt confused because Catherine had died only two months previously and now he was feeling attracted to me, and he wanted to know if I had similar feelings toward him. I admitted that I did, and that I was somewhat frustrated that he had not waited to tell me of his feelings in person. After that phone call I did not get back to sleep for a long time, and I suppose he did not sleep for a while either.

Ted then made opportunities to talk with each of his children individually about his interest in me and to ask them how they felt about this. No serious objections were offered. He also consulted several trusted friends, most of whom had met me at Catherine's funeral but did not know me very well. One exception was Ted's translator friend Miroslav, who had provided transportation for me to the church and the cemetery, so we had talked. I had also met the Lenny Szczezniak family, who were very special friends to Ted and his children.

Our first date was a picnic in the Valley Green area of Fairmount Park in northwest Philadelphia. Before I left Steelton, I called my sister and mysteriously asked her about borrowing a thermos with meadow tea "enough for two." When I stopped at Gap to pick it up, my dad met me at the door and asked point-blank, "Are you going to see Ted?" I admitted that I was. When I got to Ted's place, I gave him the keys to drive my VW Bug to Valley Green. He absent-mindedly headed northwest rather than southwest until I mentioned it to him. So I learned that he was not the most alert driver, and we got to Valley Green eventually. On our first picnic I learned that he did not care as much for chew foods like carrots and celery as I did. But afterward we walked a while in the park, and exchanged our first kisses.

Sometimes Ted came by train to Harrisburg to visit me and we attended a fellowship meeting at the home of someone from my church. Sometimes I drove to Philadelphia and went to church with Ted and the children. Dating was a new experience for me, but at some point in our relationship I told him that what I wanted in a husband was someone who would be the head and leader of the family and receive the honor and respect of his wife and children.

When we began talking about marriage, I soon indicated to Ted that I felt we should marry before the onset of the new school year so the children could begin the year focused on their studies. Three of the children would be high school seniors (Mary was a year ahead, Alice was in the grade expected for her age, and Joseph was a year behind), and the youngest, Rita, would be entering sixth grade. I did not want to uproot them from their schools and friends, and it would simply be much easier for me to move from my rental apartment into the home that Ted was buying than it would be to find a new place for all of us to live in together in the Harrisburg area. So we settled on August 4, 1974, so that we could have our honeymoon and get me moved in before the new school year began.

In June of 1974, just three months after Catherine's death, Ted's father died at the VA hospital in St. Petersburg, Florida. Both of Ted's parents had lived in Sarasota for many years, until Olin needed more care in his final months. When Ted learned of his father's death, we decided that he and Rita would fly to Florida for Olin's funeral, then Rita would stay with Ted's sister, Pinky, in St. Petersburg until Pinky and her two boys accompanied her home for our wedding in August. While Ted was absent, I stayed with the three older children to keep things in order—or at least try to. He was gone for about five days. I also offered to finish a project he had been asked to do: to prepare a week of worship readings for family meditation for a Lutheran worship booklet. I called Ted to see if he agreed with what I had written, and he did.

As planned, our wedding ceremony was held on Sunday afternoon, August 4, at Steelton Mennonite Church, where I was a member. I had invited a number of my relatives, college friends, and overseas coworkers. Ted had invited some of his translation friends as well as his sister and her two sons from Florida. We sang old familiar hymns, such as "God Moves in a Mysterious Way" and "O God, Our Help in Ages Past." We also sang a new song, "Begin by Loving Again," which God had given to Ted several days before the wedding. The sermon was given by Gerald Studer, and my brother Paul officiated at the wedding covenant as we lit the unity candle. Our concluding song was the familiar "We Are One in the Spirit." As it was being sung, we rearranged the platform furniture and went into the congregation to bring our family members together onto the platform. After Ted and I were formally introduced as husband and wife, we went to the rear of the sanctuary to greet all of our guests. We then moved to the basement for a lovely meal of ham and cheese sandwiches and other mostly cold items, perfect for a hot afternoon. Many people shared advice and memories on the open microphone.

When we left the church to head west for our honeymoon, we learned that at some point the Morrow children and Ted's sister and her sons had fastened a "JUST MORROWED" sign on the back bumper of my car, along with some tin cans that dragged on the road behind us as we drove off. Needless to say, we soon disposed of the noisemakers.

We spent the first night of our honeymoon in Carlisle, Pennsylvania. On Monday we visited a friend of mine in Carlisle, then spent the night with other friends in Chambersburg. On Tuesday we visited briefly at Brook Lane Psychiatric Center, near Hagerstown, Maryland, where Ted had worked for a couple of months many years earlier (when it was called Brook Lane Farm). We then went to Harrisonburg, Virginia, and spent almost a week of relaxation and fellowship with Harold and Grace Jones, good friends from my EMC days. Next we spent several days in Scottdale,

Pennsylvania, where Ted had lived and worked for twelve years. In fact, we were at Scottdale when Gerald Ford was sworn in as president of the United States. The Scottdale folks had a lovely reception for us one evening. Someone had fixed up a box to look like a kitchen stove that featured a slot where folks could deposit their cards and monetary gifts for us. We certainly appreciated that thoughtful idea. Of course there were refreshments too as we spent the evening with so many of Ted's friends, some of whom I had met previously as well.

I had packed up a lot of my things before our wedding, but I finished packing in the afternoon after we got back from our honeymoon. The next morning, my sister Anna Mary and her husband, Leonard, and our brother Nate arrived with a small rental truck into which we loaded my stuff. We then traveled the one hundred miles east to Philadelphia, where we arrived in the early afternoon. Imagine our surprise when we found an empty house with no young helpers to unload the stuff! They had left a note for us saying that Pinky had taken them and her two sons to Washington, DC, for the day to "see the sights." So we three men and two women unloaded the truck and carried everything up the stairs and into the house.

After I had returned from Tanzania in January 1973, I had needed to furnish my Steelton apartment, so I had purchased a new bedroom suite that included a double bed, a three-section dresser with a large mirror, and a smaller chest of four drawers. I had also bought a used wooden office-size desk with two deep drawers on each side. Moving that bedroom furniture into the Chelten Avenue house was not too bad with the drawers removed, but the desk was very heavy even with all the drawers removed. But somehow our crew got it up all the outdoor and indoor stairs (the first floor had eleven-foot ceilings) and into the bedroom. All of this furniture initially went into the large front bedroom, which also served as Ted's office, and the desk replaced the very small desk that Ted had been using. Several years later we moved our bedroom suite into the smaller middle bedroom.

The children's note also said that the kitchen sink had sprung a leak—welcome back to Earth! Yes, the piping where it attached to the metal sink was done for and beyond repair. Well, it was an old sink in an old house. Sis offered to look in the Lancaster newspaper for a used replacement sink. Meanwhile, as needed, I would check the plastic bucket that had been put into place and empty the water into the commode off the closed-in back porch.

Our helpers left late that afternoon to return their rental truck to Lancaster and go home, and we waited for Pinky and the children to return. They hadn't arrived yet at midnight. Ted really worried about them, but I was so tired and just wanted to sleep. They finally got back at around 2:00 A.M. and we all promptly went to bed.

And that is how we started our married life! ☦

Getting Oriented to Married Life

We were still tired the next morning and not in a hurry to get out of bed and face the new day. But we finally got up and took time to hear about the children's trip to Washington, DC, and we told them about our honeymoon trip, especially our visits with many friends of the Morrow family at Scottdale. Pinky and her sons stayed around only a day or two after our return, and we were grateful that she had provided some degree of supervision until we got back.

The following day, Sis reported that a used sink had been advertised in the Lancaster paper, but when she called she learned that it had already been sold. However, the salesman said a friend of his had a metal sink with matching cabinets for sale. So I asked her to call the second man and ask him to hold the whole set until we could come see it and make a decision about it. The next day Ted and I drove to Gap, picked up Sis, then drove into Lancaster, where Sis knew her way around and easily found the seller's store. The sink and cabinets were in good condition, so we decided to buy the whole set. When we stopped at Sis's house, I called my brother Nate to ask if he could pick up our "new" kitchen equipment with his ten-foot-bed truck and deliver it to us in Philadelphia. I also called Earl Graybill, pastor at Coatesville Mennonite Church, which I had formerly attended. He was an experienced carpenter and builder, and he agreed to come with Nate. I also invited Dad to join them so he could see where we Morrows were living in the City of Brotherly Love. Everyone agreed to come and help fix our kitchen.

The following week the three men brought the sink and cabinets to us. I had already decided that we would install only the sink that day, because I hoped to later do more renovations to the kitchen, including dropping the eleven-foot ceilings by three feet, redoing the walls, and putting in new overhead fluorescent lighting. I would then install the large inverted U cabinet above the stove and the other two cabinets on the wall beside the hallway. The three cabinets were temporarily stored in our basement.

Another urgent concern in the early days of our marriage was the issue of a job for me. As God arranged it, one Sunday morning when we attended Germantown Mennonite Church we met Arline Zimmerman, a nurse supervisor for the School District of Philadelphia. When she heard that I was a physician and wanted less-than-full-time work, she suggested I apply to the school system. So I did, and was accepted and assigned to District 6, the district in which we lived. My hours were 9:00 A.M. to noon and I mostly did health exams for students in first, sixth, and ninth grades. A few parents attended when their child was examined. If a questionable finding was detected, a report recommending further evaluation by the family's physician was sent to the parent. Special exams were given to high school students applying for driver education. The stipend for me was rather low initially, but later it became more substantial. And rather good medical coverage was provided.

After the children went back to school, a month after our wedding, and as I was getting oriented to my morning job with the school district, Ted and I got into a routine of having a late lunch at around 1:00 P.M. It soon became my habit to make us a soup, often using leftovers from the previous evening's supper. I would then have several hours to work in the house before the young troops arrived home at around 4:00 P.M.

I began "inspecting" the house, which was more than a hundred years old, on the first day the children were elsewhere. I quickly realized it did not have much closet space. There was a coat closet on the first floor under the stairs. The second floor had a small diagonal closet across one corner of the middle bedroom, where Rita slept, and Joseph's bedroom at the back of the house had a closet that was maybe four feet long but only a foot deep. There was no closet in the front room, where Ted had his office and that we used for a while as our bedroom. The third floor had a large clothing closet in the front room, which was Mary's space, and a nice enough closet in the middle bedroom, the abode of Alice, but there was only a pantry closet in the back bedroom, which at some point before the Morrows moved in had been made into a "grandmother's" kitchen with running water, a sink, and a gas stove. We eventually moved the stove out and put in a single bed so that Rita could move upstairs with her sisters. We placed an old wooden wardrobe in the hallway for her to use as her closet.

One day I wandered into the dark closet in the first floor hallway. I found a chain to pull for some light—and what did I see? Such a shock! The taller end of the closet, on the left side of the door and next to the stairway to the basement, had a rod about three feet long that could hold some coats, but a big pile of clothes and coats were laying on the floor. To the right of the door were shelves where a number of small boxes of Christmas decorations were stored along with boxes of board games and some other items. I removed everything from the floor and hung the coats on the rod. I would need to find out who would claim the clothes before I washed them or took them to a secondhand store.

At some point, I also took a long look around the basement, where there was a clothes dryer as well as a number of clotheslines. (The washing machine was upstairs on the closed-in back porch.) There was an array of "stuff" down there, including a crib, a baby buggy, and other things that were no longer used or maybe beyond use, such as a tall

Victrola phonograph cabinet. But what piqued my curiosity most was a large wooden cupboard that was about seven feet tall and six feet long and three feet deep. It had junk inside and old green paint smeared on one end. But what I really wanted to know was HOW did anyone get that cupboard around the upper corner, down the narrow cellar steps, then around the bottom corner into the basement? I will tell the rest of this story a little later.

Now that I was Mrs. Morrow, I was in charge of the cooking, so I went along for grocery shopping. Cooking for a family of six was a new experience for me. I had done very little cooking at home when Mother was there, and in my apartment I had cooked only for me, with very few exceptions. I tried to provide balanced meals. I had access to the *Mennonite Community Cookbook* and several other cookbooks that had been Catherine's. I learned to make a good spaghetti with meatballs, meatloaf, chili con carne, scalloped potatoes, candied sweet potatoes, and a few other dishes. Eventually I could also make a good apple pie from scratch.

When the children returned to school I learned that they were in the habit of having supper when they got home at around 4:00, because they'd had an early lunch at school. But I, after having such a late lunch, was not in a hurry to leave my house projects to start preparing supper before 6:00 P.M. So the children had to adjust their schedule a bit that first year. The following year three of them were in college and on different schedules, and usually only Joseph and Rita ate supper at home, so there was less pressure to eat early.

I sometimes asked one of the older children to fix the evening meal. We got a few surprises! One evening we were treated to a casserole that featured macaroni with peanut butter, and the dessert was a pudding with peanut butter. I probably needed to provide more supervision! I must say that when I made requests or suggestions, the children were cooperative and did not complain—at least not in my hearing. They enjoyed baking cookies, especially at Christmastime, and I clearly remember taking some cookies along to Middlebury, Indiana, in December 1975 when we visited their Grandma Salome Roth, Catherine's adoptive mother.

There were a variety of other things for us to learn during the early months of our life together. It clearly was hard for Joseph and his sisters to lose their mother, and it quickly became clear that there were many things I did not do in the same way as Catherine had done them. For example, that first year we encountered many special days that brought up memories of how Catherine made those times special for her family, including birthdays (Catherine's, Rita's, and Ted's in August; Joseph's in September; Alice's in November; and Mary's in January). I just was not accustomed to what they expected to happen on those days. As Christmas approached that year, we were all thinking about how different it would be for the family. On Christmas eve, we shed some tears as all of us (except Alice, who was dating a Catholic college student and spending the evening with him and other friends at Temple University's Newman Center) gathered together in the living room and shared our feelings about how it felt to be there without Catherine. The next morning I fixed something a bit special for breakfast. Then we talked some more about Catherine (this time including Alice), before opening the small gifts that Ted and I had purchased for each of the children. At noontime we ate a simple Christmas meal together, then spent the afternoon playing games.

As the weeks and months progressed, I found many other things to do around the big old house. During the winter months I repaired plaster cracks and did interior painting by brush, which I preferred to a pan and roller. I bought new green and yellow drapes that transmitted the sunlight into the living room and dining room much better than what had been there before. During the summer months I worked on the outside of the house. Rita would often help me; for instance, she would guard the ladder as I caulked around the windows and painted the frames. I noticed that the frame to a basement window was badly rotted, so I took it out and used other wood to make a "new" frame for the window. The most dusty job I took on was repairing the front of the house. I parked two stepladders on the porch with a plank between them six feet above the floor. I stood on the plank and brushed off the peeling paint. With a big old hat on my head I was prepared for the resulting "snowstorm"! It surely improved the appearance of our house when I finally applied new paint to the ceiling, the front banister, the repaired porch floor (done by a real carpenter), and the wooden latticework beneath the porch. Slowly this house was becoming more of a home to me. (For more about my adventures with ladders, see the Appendix at the back of this book.)

I hired a carpenter to do a variety of other jobs to improve the house, including new steps up to the back porch and kitchen renovation, which included dropping the ceiling from eleven feet to eight feet, installing a two-by-eight-foot fluorescent ceiling lamp in the new kitchen ceiling, hanging the steel cabinets we had bought above the stove and on the wall by the hallway, and redoing the walls around the bottom four feet of the kitchen. The room was so much brighter now, and much warmer in the wintertime too. Ted and I now enjoyed having breakfast and lunch in our kitchen. The carpenter also redid the wall covering in the third-floor bathroom. At some point, Ted and I moved our bedroom into the second floor's middle room. I hired the carpenter to install some bookshelves with room for my tape player and tapes in one corner of the office. I watched how he made it, and later I built similar floor-to-ceiling shelves behind Ted's desk for his language reference books, foreign Bibles, and other books.

By the time I was "finished" with my repairs to the house, I had done all of the outside work, with some help painting the gutters at the third-floor level. I had also removed wallpaper, filled cracks with caulk, and painted the first floor, the stairway to the second floor, the second-floor rooms and hallway, and the third-floor rooms. I did not strip the paper from the stairs to the third floor.

During my first year in the family, I had to apply for financial assistance for the three older children, who would all be starting college the next school year. Ted was a freelance translator and I was a first-year part-time worker, so our income was rather skimpy. But at least the federal financial aid office was generous in those days, and we were able to provide assistance for transportation and other incidental expenses.

Early on in our courtship, Ted had invited me to share Sunday breakfast with the family before going to the 9:30 "contemporary" service at Trinity Lutheran Church. I arrived at the Morrow home at 8:30 that morning to find Joseph preparing to fix pancakes for us. The rest of the family soon appeared and we did justice to breakfast. We then traveled the short distance to Trinity in two cars. The contemporary service featured music accompanied by guitar, string bass, and acoustic piano. All of the church's pastors were good preachers, and communion was an integral part of each service. After the service that day, I was made to feel welcome. Then the Morrow children scattered to their Sunday school activities. While the children were occupied, Ted and I drove up Germantown Avenue to visit the Germantown Mennonite Church.

After driving fifteen blocks on cobblestones, we spied the small stone church with its 1770 cornerstone resting beside an equally old cemetery. The service had already begun, so we entered quietly and sat in the last row of its five or six rows of benches. Maybe twenty-five persons were present, mostly young white adults, plus an older couple who I learned were Roman and Marianna Stutzman, the live-in caretakers of the nearby Wyck House. Roman also served as pastor of the church. Ted knew some of these folks already and was not shy about meeting strangers, as I tend to be. He had of course worked with many "old" and conservative Mennonites at the Mennonite Publishing House in Scottdale and at the Alden Mennonite Church in New York State. And I had grown up in the Lancaster Conference and attended "old" Mennonite schools and college, but I had also spent six and a half years in East Africa and attended services there with both Mennonite and other mission groups, so I was comfortable with things that were different from what I had grown up with. Yet despite our deeply rooted Mennonite connections, when Ted and I later expressed our interest in becoming members at Germantown Mennonite Church, after attending there for a year or so, they were openly hesitant but finally accepted us after a rather extensive interview.

We maintained contact with Trinity Lutheran Church while the older children were still living at home. They often played basketball before Sunday school, participated in Luther League on Sunday evenings, and attended an annual retreat. We enjoyed going together to the Christmas Eve service, which was especially geared to children but we parents enjoyed it too. I also appreciated the Good Friday service, which focused on the events of the cross. Once her older siblings were in college, Rita mostly went to church with Ted and me. She eventually attended and graduated from Christopher Dock Mennonite High School.

While we were members at Germantown Mennonite, we assisted with the two-week summer Bible school, which was attended by a nice group of neighborhood children. We worked with some of the classes to put on skits for the closing-day program. Afterward, a few of the children who had participated in the summer school began attending the church's Sunday school. A boys' club was started by two single fellows and a girls' club by two of the younger ladies. But after three years it became painfully clear to Ted and me that our goals and priorities did not mesh with those of most of the Germantown folks, so we began visiting other churches and finally, in early 1978, withdrew from Germantown Mennonite and began attending Frazer Mennonite Church in Frazer, Pennsylvania.

Now let me return, finally, to the puzzle of the cupboard. Some months after I discovered it in the basement, some friends of mine from the Harrisburg area were visiting and I showed them most of the house, including the basement, where I showed them my puzzle. One of them quickly said, "I think that cupboard comes apart. Get me a flashlight and let me look inside." So I got a flashlight, and she showed me where the upright ends were bolted to the bottom section, and there were similar bolts at the top. Wow. Now I knew how to take it apart—eventually. I mulled it over for a number of months and visualized how I would do it. I also visited several paint stores to check their supply of varnish and finishing oils. Then, finally, I took it apart, removed the paint and original lacquer, and began working to make it a new creation.

At some point I learned that the official name of this piece of furniture was *armoire*. When I had covered it all over with a shiny cherry luster, I asked Rita to help me carry the eight pieces up the two flights of stairs to Ted's and my bedroom. We put the two upright ends on the bottom support and inserted the big bolts in each bottom end. I had decided to put a sturdy piece of one-inch-wide metal pipe through the length of the armoire, so Rita and I inserted the pipe in a transverse position near the top of the middle piece and the two upright ends. Next we put the two posterior upright panels on the back and inserted their screws. We then set the heavy decorative piece on the top and inserted a single big bolt at each end. The last step was to put on the lovely front doors, one of which someone had marred by cutting out a chunk along the margin, presumably to open the door. I did nothing about that blemish. I just fastened each door to its lateral wall support, and we were done! I was *so* pleased that Ted and I now had a closet in which to hang our clothes, and such a pretty closet it was too.

In the fall of 1975, after Mary went off to Eastern Mennonite College and Alice and Joseph began attending Temple University, the house became more quiet. Alice and Joseph were still living at home that year, but they primarily just slept there and shared some meals with Ted, Rita, and me. In the fall of 1976, Alice moved into a dormitory at Temple, then transferred to the University of Scranton in the fall of 1977. Joseph spent the summer of 1977 working in a resort at the New Jersey shore, then roomed with some other students for the fall semester before transferring to Houghton College. With only Rita still at home, there was even less activity at 617 East Chelten Avenue. ✞

Our Son

Before Ted and I got married we of course talked about many things. We needed to learn what was important to each of us and that we were in agreement on the major issues. We were both satisfied that his four children were enough for our family. I was almost forty-three and Ted was almost forty-six when we married. I knew I was on the older side so far as becoming pregnant was concerned, but I still had menses every month. My mother had died of a heart attack at sixty-six, and her older sister and older brother both had severe strokes in their mid-sixties, so I was not eager to take birth control pills at my age due to the potential for blood clots and heart attack. But I was willing to have an intrauterine device inserted as a deterrent to pregnancy. So I discussed the matter with the OB-GYN physician I was working with part-time in Harrisburg before I got married, and I asked him to insert the loop. He agreed and did the insertion shortly before our wedding. Some weeks after our wedding I discovered that the loop was no longer in my uterus but was residing in my vagina. Well, a lot of protection that loop was giving me! So I removed it and stored it in a safe place for many years before I finally discarded it. I did not go for another type of protection, and my periods continued to come every month.

The three older children were in college and Rita was a sophomore in high school when, in the spring of 1978, I developed some strange symptoms. I just did not have much energy to climb those twenty stairs to the second floor of our house. And then I had an unusually light, spotty period. I attributed it to being perimenopausal, but I made an appointment anyway with Dr. Laufer, who had been a resident training in OB-GYN when I was a student at the Woman's Medical College of Pennsylvania fifteen to sixteen years earlier. I had enjoyed working with her, and she had once complimented me on the reports I had written on a patient's chart to document her progress in labor. When I appeared at her office, she greeted me warmly. She asked the usual questions, did a complete examination, then asked, "Do you think you might be pregnant?" Well, I don't think I had even considered the possibility! But I did sputter out an answer: "I don't know!" She said my uterus was enlarged, which could occur with a pregnancy, or it could indicate a benign fibroid tumor. She asked me to get a pregnancy test.

I'm not sure Ted and I talked much on the way home that day, but that evening as we sat at the dinner table with Joseph and Rita, we shared with them the results of the examination—that I might have a tumor, or I might be pregnant. It was clear that no one wanted me to have a tumor—not after their mother had died of breast cancer.

The next day I collected a urine specimen and took it to Germantown Hospital for the pregnancy test. (Reliable at-home tests were not yet available.) Several days later Dr. Laufer called to say that the results were positive. She did ask me to take another specimen to be tested at the Medical College of Pennsylvania, just to be sure. So I did, and that test was positive too.

I had already started a taped letter to Mary at EMC about some things I wanted to share with her, but there was still room on the tape for me to tell her about this new development. A letter was written to Alice in Scranton. She promptly responded that she had already sent us a letter telling us that in a private conversation with one of her sisters during the recent Christmas break she had shared her intuition that her father and I would have a child. This affirmation from before my conception occurred (in early February 1978) was very special to us.

The next test that Dr. Laufer ordered, in May, was an amniocentesis, which involved going to Jefferson Hospital in Center City Philadelphia to provide some amniotic fluid to see if there was any evidence of genetic defects (because I was older and because my youngest sister was a severely impaired Down Syndrome person). The first test was not very revealing, though my abdomen was sore for a day afterward (maybe they hit a nerve on the way in!), so I had to return for a second test. Ted went along that time, and everything went OK. The results showed no evidence of genetic defects—and I could expect to deliver a son!

Soon after I learned that I was pregnant, the School District of Philadelphia decided that if they trained nurses to be clinical nurse practitioners, they could get the same services from nurses for less money than the doctors were being paid. We doctors helped to train the nurses for their elevated positions, and then in mid-1978 most of us received our "pink slips." So as soon as school ended, in late June, I joined the lines applying for unemployment compensation. I had to return every month to report in person that I was still unemployed and still able to work. When my first unemployment check arrived, the man who delivered our mail commented that it was rather rare for a doctor to receive unemployment compensation. I continued to receive such payments until my son was born. Then I abruptly stopped showing up at the unemployment office.

One afternoon that summer I got a long-distance phone call from a Lancaster Mennonite School classmate who lived in Juniata County. He and his wife had several healthy children and were now expecting another. They'd had amniocentesis done and had been told that there was a high chance of significant defects, and the doctor had suggested that they terminate the pregnancy. They wanted my opinion as a Christian on what to do. I don't know if they knew that I was pregnant too, but I frankly revealed it. I also told them about my sister Ruthie's severe Down Syndrome, that she had never learned to talk but had communicated in her own way and had slowly learned to do things for herself. I said that we had involved Ruthie in all our activities and that everyone in our family felt that Ruthie's life had meaning despite her significant limitations, and despite the fact that Mother had suffered depression after Ruthie's birth, because she had not been prepared for a child with such difficulties. I must have talked with this couple for at least thirty minutes. Some years later I met them at a school reunion, and they thanked me for having shared with them. They told me that their daughter had some limitations but nonetheless was an important member of their family.

That summer I did not do much work around the house. On warm days I preferred to rest quietly in the cooler back bedroom. I went to see Dr. Laufer frequently that fall. My expected date of delivery was November 7, and my weight gain and girth were about as expected. In mid-September, however, I developed a chest cold that persisted as a hoarse cough, so an antibiotic was prescribed. The croup persisted and I could scarcely talk until after our son made his arrival.

On Friday evening, October 20, Ted asked me to go with him to a prayer meeting at the Main Bible Institute in North Philadelphia, where he taught two classes every week. I said that I really preferred to rest at home, so he told me that the folks had planned a baby shower for us. So I went, and the folks gave us a lot of very useful baby things.

After we got home, rather late, I got ready for bed and dug out our vaporizer to help me breath more easily. It was after midnight when I finally got to bed and could relax. But before I could drift off to sleep, I suddenly realized that I had released fluid—without coughing! That meant I had ruptured my membranes and released amniotic fluid instead of leaking a bit of other liquid. Well, my suitcase for the hospital and the baby's suitcase had already been packed some days earlier. So I put on some clothes, called Dr. Laufer, then woke up Ted. We got to the emergency room at the Medical College of Pennsylvania at around 4:00 A.M. An OB resident checked me and confirmed that I had ruptured my membranes, but I was not having contractions yet. They admitted me to a labor room and because I had not slept at all that night, they let me sleep several hours before they started an IV of Pitocin to stimulate some contractions. They also put a clip near the baby's head to monitor his heart rate. Meanwhile, Ted called home to tell Rita that we had sneaked out of the house while she was asleep and come to the hospital.

By 2:00 P.M. my contractions were hard enough to make me uncomfortable and they gave me something for pain. The next thing I knew they were wheeling me into the delivery room and telling me to push. So I did, and promptly little Benjamin Isaac arrived, at 4:46 P.M.

on Saturday, October 21, 1978. He weighed in at five pounds and seven ounces, having arrived about three weeks before full-term.

Ted got to hold our son first, while my episiotomy was being stitched up. Then I was wheeled out to a bed, in time for supper, but I was mainly thirsty rather than hungry. Ted said good night and went home to tell the children about Benji's arrival. Later, the nurses brought little Benji to me. They told me he was almost a perfect baby but had several minor abnormalities. Number 1, he had a half-inch threadlike skin tag in front of his left ear. Several days later a surgeon came by to see him. He tied a tight thread around the tag near Benji's face; several days later the tag fell off, and that was the end of that!

Abnormality number 2 was more obvious: his face and body were yellow. Tests showed that the bilirubin level was elevated. It was not due to the dangerous RH incompatibility, which would have required removal of the baby's blood and transfusion with new blood of a certain type. Rather, his blood reaction was due to the ABO difference between Ted's and my blood types. The treatment was more simple: he was to be exposed to a special fluorescent lamp a number of times a day, in the nude except for a diaper. This treatment required a longer hospital stay to give him time to lose his yellow color. It also gave me more time to improve from my chest cold and to develop some skill in nursing Benji. The nurses had been giving him formula in a bottle before they brought him to me, so he was not very interested in nursing with me. Breast-feeding was just coming back into vogue in those days, but some medical folks were opposed to it. I kept trying to nurse Benji, and I did later attend some meetings of mothers who were breastfeeding their infants.

Abnormality number 3 was an inward deviation of his right foot. I took him to an orthopedic surgeon several times and she showed me how to exercise his foot into a proper position throughout the day. Those exercises did the trick for him without further treatment. My son probably didn't know that he had these minor defects as a baby—until he reads this book!

Benji and I stayed in the hospital for a week. The staff would have sent me home a day or two earlier without him, but I refused to go home without my son. They wanted his bilirubin level to come down some more, and I wanted to stay near him so I could nurse him regularly. In retrospect, Benji's extended stay also gave the nursery staff more opportunity to give him bottle formula feedings and to work against my desire to breastfeed him. But I knew it would be my only opportunity to bond with a child by breastfeeding him. Oh well, that was more than thirty-five years ago.

Ted visited Benji and me every day, and one afternoon two of the Main Bible Institute ladies came in to see us. Another afternoon a nurse asked me to demonstrate to a group of other new mothers how to bathe my son, without discussing with me first how to hold a newborn baby and keep him warm. I suspected that I was being tested as an alumna of the Woman's Medical College of Pennsylvania to see if I was fit to care for my son!

Saturday was a sunny but rather cool day to go home and for Ted and I to begin to face our new life together with Benji. I remember putting Benji into his new little green outfit, and he promptly pulled up his legs and waved the empty leggings around. I don't remember if they put a knitted cap on a newborn's head in those days, but I do remember that I held him in my lap as Ted drove us the few miles to our Germantown home. Car seats for babies were just coming into vogue, and we did get one for him when he was several months old. Then I could carry him in the back seat on the right side, which was safer than carrying him in my lap in the front seat.

I had a lot of things to learn, and Benji had a few things to learn too. I continued to try to nurse him, but I seemed not to have enough milk to satisfy him, so I had to supplement with formula, including several times at night. Feeding him by formula meant going to the refrigerator and warming the milk on the stove, and nursing meant bringing him to my bed, then putting him back in his bed when he was finished. I felt no more satisfaction feeding him one way rather than the other. And I lost some sleep. But at least for several months I was not working away from home. I had a baby scales at home so I could monitor his weight regularly, and I often wished he were gaining more rapidly. After he began eating store-bought baby foods at several months of age, I also introduced some table foods that I had put through a pediatric food grinder. He finally began gaining more weight, and even became rather chubby before he began to walk around.

Soon after Benji was born, the School District of Philadelphia invited its doctors to return. Many had found positions elsewhere, but I had not, so I figured I had best find a sitter for three hours every morning and keep my school board employment intact for the time being. My first sitter was a young mother who had two preschool children, the youngest one being some months older than my son. Eventually I enrolled Benji in the morning preschool program at Trinity Lutheran Church. And after he was in grade school, I enrolled him in their after-school program so I could continue to do work on the house. ✝

My Circuitous Journey to Psychiatry

My Grandpap was an avid reader and received many magazines in the mail. After his death in September 1944, some of those magazines came to our house and somehow I found the big 1946 issue of *LIFE* magazine that contained photos and reports about the treatment of patients at a number of state mental hospitals. It made a deep impression on me that these people could be so neglected and mistreated. The same article told about a number of Quaker and Mennonite conscientious objectors who were working at Philadelphia's Byberry State Hospital and had been instrumental in improving the care and treatment of this hospital's patients. I was thus given an early awareness of the mental health situation in our country.

Then there was Dad's older brother, Harry. He had symptoms of mental illness after several children were born. I remember when his barn was struck by lightning in September 1937. Uncle Harry tried without success to douse the fire with buckets of water. Afterward he was distraught and hid in the nearby woods for several days. Relatives cleared the rubble and helped build a new barn. I clearly remember that my parents, brother Paul, and I were present on that warm sunny day. After dinner, Mother and I walked the four miles home on a dirt back road, with me probably in my bare feet while lucky Paul, who was a year and nine months old, rode in the baby buggy. As we got closer to home we stopped at Lavina Fisher's house and she gave us fresh water to drink.

Soon after the fire, Uncle Harry was placed into Embreeville State Hospital. Dad visited him regularly on Sundays, taking along some of us children or other relatives. Dad made sure to go promptly after our noon meal because Uncle Harry left at 3:00 P.M. to help milk the hospital's herd of cows. Over the years Dad could see some improvement in Uncle Harry's condition, and with time our family started calling him just Uncle instead of Uncle Harry.

Dad began asking permission to take Uncle for a short ride. Then he asked to take Uncle to our home for a short visit. Later Dad got permission for Uncle to spend the night at our home. After more such visits, Uncle was permitted to stay indefinitely at our home. He slept in our largest bedroom in a single bed while my two brothers shared a double bed. After some months, Dad spoke to Uncle's power of attorney about buying a small used trailer so that Uncle could live alone and fix his own meals. This arrangement worked well until a fire destroyed the trailer some years later. Uncle eventually moved to the Tel Hai Rest Home in Honey Brook, and he died there on October 23, 1967, at seventy-three years of age.

As I wrote in my chapter about medical school, after my third year, ten of my classmates and I took a summer elective at a nearby mental hospital. I enjoyed doing admission histories and daily follow-up visits. New medications such as Thorazine were just being introduced for use in psychiatry. It was an interesting summer.

After I resigned from the School District of Philadelphia (following a second round of pink slips), I was left to wonder, what should I do now? I was *not* ready to return to OB-GYN with all its night calls, because I now had a son to care for. I learned that the medical residents at Norristown State Hospital were on call three weeknights and one Saturday or Sunday per month, and that schedule seemed workable to me. So I applied to enter the next class for residency training in psychiatry. The doctor in charge stalled somewhat on admitting me, probably because of my age. But eventually they let me join the group. I enjoyed the work, and it *was* work, with lots of reading and classes. It was not always easy for me to keep up with everything. There was even talk at one point of letting me go. But one of the teachers spoke well of me and they let me stay. I thanked her more than once for her assistance. And I did complete my three-year program in psychiatry.

By early 1987 I was thinking about moving, and Ted agreed, for a number of reasons. It was now only the three of us—Ted, Ben, and me—rattling around in that big three-story twin with five bedrooms and an office. The third floor was unoccupied. My psychiatry residency would be finished at the end of June and I had been invited to stay on as a staff psychiatrist at Norristown State Hospital, primarily in geriatrics. I accepted the position because, when I was ready to retire, my pension would be combined with the credits I had accumulated with the School District of Philadelphia. I was so ready to stop commuting to work from Germantown, and Ted and I wanted to live in a better community so that Ben could attend a better school and develop good friendships. Because Ted worked at home, as long as he had office space for his books and equipment, the address was not so important for him.

So I began driving around in various communities near Norristown and watching the real estate ads. In July we enrolled Ben at Penn Christian Academy in Montgomery County for the coming school year. In August we located a colonial split-level house with a large upper-level room for Ted's office in Blue Bell, a nice community one mile from Ben's school, four miles from my job, and convenient to many services. Our offer was accepted. We put our Germantown house on the market, and it promptly sold.

I started to sort and pack, but on Labor Day I just did not feel like working. I awoke in the middle of the night and could not get back to sleep because I was so uncomfortable. I finally called 911. The police transported me to the hospital so that Ted could stay at home and let Ben sleep. I suspected appendicitis, but the ER doctor told me I was too old and that my white blood cell count was too high. I did not believe him. After three days of tests, IVs, and antibiotics, I finally remembered that as a medical student I had been told that I possibly had a retro-cecal appendix, meaning that it was not in the usual position. The next day they removed my ruptured appendix and, sure enough, it was located behind the cecum, so the infection had been kept more localized. I went home a week later and my family came to pack up our stuff while I answered questions and "gave orders." We moved into our new home ten days later, on September 30, 1987. The buyers of our old residence met a delay in settlement, so we had an extra month in which to clean out the old place. We also had to get an emergency "swing loan" to cover the income we had expected to make from the sale so that we could close on our new home and move in as scheduled. I was off work for six weeks while my incision healed, and I slowly did some unpacking and arranging of things in our new home. I went back to work half-days for several weeks before resuming full-time work. The copious leaves from the maple trees in our new half-acre yard didn't get raked up until the next spring, when I also developed an incisional hernia in my appendectomy scar. It was repaired that summer without incident.

In mid-1989 I was asked to move from geriatrics to the admissions unit of Norristown State Hospital for two months. I did not refuse, but I was not happy, especially when it stretched into three months. Also, despite my complaints, I was expected to do a physical exam on my admissions patients, just like a resident, whereas the staff psychiatrists in the other units did not have to do them. I applied for a part-time position (all day on Mondays and Wednesday afternoons) at the Penn Foundation, a behavioral health services provider in Sellersville, and gave Norristown State notice of my decrease in hours to three days (60 percent time). At this point they found someone to do the physical exams on my admissions. They then invited me to transfer to Building 9, which was to house geriatric men, for whom I had previously cared. Building 9 was more relaxed than building 52, so I agreed to the transfer, which took place in late 1989. After about a year of driving in winter weather and paying part of my medical coverage at Norristown State, I returned to full-time hours there in October 1990.

Meanwhile, hospital officials learned that the beds in Building 9 were not Medicare certified, so the geriatric men were shuffled back to Building 53, and I ended up with young male patients with such problems as drug and alcohol abuse, elopement (running away), fire-setting, and other behaviors related to mental health issues. These cases were not as interesting to me, but I did enjoy working with the nursing staff.

Then, in the spring of 1991, I was invited to return to Building 53 and its geriatric patients, and I accepted.

Before I left Building 9, Ted and I signed up for the Slim-Away program at Montgomery Hospital. He dropped out but I continued to walk and ride the exercise bike—until I developed edema of the lower legs and feet, followed by shortness of breath and fatigue. I went to the ER on February 11, 1991, and was admitted to coronary care. My echo-cardiogram and EKG were OK, but the stress test was not, so I was transferred to Medical College of Pennsylvania on February 14 for cardiac catheterization, which showed evidence of previous hypertension and ventricular changes. I was discharged on February 16 with a prescription for Calan, which my doctor promptly changed to Cardizem. I continued to have bouts of fatigue, so I decreased and finally stopped the niacin I was taking.

In the mid-1950s, when Edna Detweiler was my roommate at EMC, I had gone home with her at least one weekend, during which we attended the Worcester Mennonite Church, a little white church somewhere out in the Pennsylvania countryside and a long ride from her family's home. At the time I had no idea it was only a few miles from Norristown. After we moved to Blue Bell, Edna occasionally sent a note inviting us to visit Methacton Mennonite Church some Sunday. We finally went in the fall of 1994, and I immediately recognized the building as the former Worcester Mennonite Church. There we found a friendly congregation and an active youth group. The following spring, Ted and I transferred our membership to Methacton. Ben enjoyed the youth group and participated in three or four of their weeklong summer work camp projects. Ted served on the worship committee and as a song leader. Sometimes he also presented a violin piece. I was asked to help with the Sunday school. First I taught the 3rd to 5th grade class for a year, then the youth class for two years, using stories from Genesis. Later Ted and I team-taught Genesis and Exodus to a mixed class of Tanzanian folks and Methacton regulars for a couple of years, until the Tanzanian folks went back to Tanzania and two of the other participants began teaching a class for children. Depending on who was present, we used Swahili or Luo Bibles as well as English Bibles in that very enjoyable class.

Back in Building 53, things had gotten even busier. We were expected to write more copious notes in the patients' records, which resulted in my having less time to actually talk with the patients. In early 1998, because I was already at retirement age (sixty-six, though I had previously thought of working until age seventy), I said enough was enough and went home to spend more time with my husband and teenage son. My final day was January 16. The staff had a nice farewell luncheon and gave me a lovely clock and gift certificates to Strawbridges worth $200—a surprise! ✝

Saying Good-bye to Dad

My father died unexpectedly in his sleep at eighty-five years of age on December 27, 1985. His funeral was held at Millwood Mennonite Church. Ben was just over six years of age at the time, but when he learned that his Pop Pop had departed from us to be in heaven, he said, "Pop Pop can just fly!"

During the funeral I sat between Ted and Ben, and sometime during the service Ted leaned toward me and asked if I had any paper that he could write on. I pulled out an old notebook from my purse and gave it to him. He began writing, made only a few changes, and soon was finished. Later, when opportunity was given for family and friends to speak about my dad, Ted was ready with this poem, hot off the press!

After we got back home, Ted found a photo to go with his poem, then made a copy of it for each of Dad's children.

In Memoriam: Christian G. Stoltzfus, 1900–1985

Some say, "the quiet in the land!"
With a pitying tone, with condescension to a brother
Who had not met the hosts of evil
In dark, suffering city streets
Or on the mountains of Afghanistan
Or where men shout and shake their fists.

No, he was quietly turning the soil,
Working oh so gently with the crumbly earth
And tender heifers;
A man who smiled with simplicity
And seemed aloof to all the conflict
That tears men apart
And causes them to hate.

In quietness was his strength,
And his battleground the place of prayer.
Here was the hero at his best,
Overcoming evil with good,
With a smile of unsung victory
Claiming what the Lord of hosts has promised:
Peace at last. ✞

Saying Good-bye to Ruthie

In late December 1996, my sister Ruthie, who had tolerated several surgical procedures and reached fifty-one years of age, became ill again and was found to have an internal hernia. Surgery was performed, but Ruthie's liver function was so impaired that she was unable to rally after the procedure. Several days later, on January 1, 1997, three of her siblings and a niece gathered at her bedside to say good-bye to Ruthie. We told the doctors to keep her comfortable but to stop the lab tests and heroic measures. We sang several children's songs for her. Sometimes she responded by pulling up her knees or raising her hands as if waving to someone. When I gently opened an eyelid and saw her big brown eye, I felt a real connection with my special sister again. We prayed with her and kissed her before we left late that afternoon. At about 3:00 the next morning, my sister Anna Mary was notified that Ruthie had died.

Sis called me that morning with the news before I left for work. After I had arrived and was seated at the nurses' station checking the report book, one of my patients with paranoid schizophrenia approached me and said, "Dr. Morrow, I thought you died last night!" I slowly replied, "No, John, it was my sister who died last night." How did he know?

As our family discussed funeral plans, I made two suggestions. I proposed that Earl Graybill preach the sermon because he also had a "special sister," who had spent a number of years at Laurelton State School in Laurelton, Pennsylvania. I also asked if we could sing the song "I'll Fly Away," which I had been reminded of when Ruthie waved her hands during our final visit with her.

The funeral was held at Millwood on a winter morning following a viewing and burial. I was amazed at how many friends and relatives came to share their memories of Ruthie and offer their sympathy; it really meant a lot. A number of Ruthie's caregivers from Hamburg also came for the viewing, service, and luncheon afterward, which was very special.

Dad had provided for Ruthie in his will a fifth share just as he had for the rest of us, except for the farmland and ground, which he had divided among his four older children. He also provided in his will that after Ruthie's death the remainder of her share should go to EMBMC.

Several weeks after the memorial service, the Hamburg folks invited our family to their own memorial service for Ruthie, which was also meaningful because we met a number of Ruthie's friends and care-

givers. Their chaplain gave a nice talk and someone handed each of us a rose. They offered us her belongings, but the only thing I took was a picture of Ruthie from her bulletin board. ✝

Ted and I Slow Down

Ted and I had both dreamed of doing some traveling after I retired, but the big trips never happened. Ted's major dream had been to see Venice and then write the novel about some early Christians, either Huguenots or some other conservative believers, that had been in his head for years. But we never got to Venice, or to western Europe, and that novel did not get written. We did make smaller trips, such as a refreshing week on Cape Cod in September 1999. We also enjoyed the East Africa Connections reunion at Kidron, Ohio, on July 26 to 28, 2002. There I met many colleagues from former years and made new connections. Even driving west on the Turnpike with all the traffic was no problem, until we hit a heavy downpour of rain on the mountains near Laurelville, so I pulled off the road and just let it rain for a while.

At our local community college (Montgomery County Community College), special rates were offered to senior citizens to attend classes after regular degree students had registered for them. So, in the fall of 1999, Ted signed up for a course in English literature and I signed up for a weekend course on computers. Then, in the spring semester, we attended an evening course on memoir writing together, and both enjoyed it. The next fall, Ted took a course in creative writing while I attended a class on ancient history that I thoroughly enjoyed. I did all the extra assignments and library reading too, and offered some comments in class. At some point I also took a class on word processing, which was very helpful. As time went on, other classes were offered that I could have enjoyed, but the prices were going up and somehow I was becoming less inclined to exert myself physically or intellectually. And Ted was slowing down as well.

Several times Ted and I visited Landis Homes in Lancaster County for special events, and we liked what we saw. The prices there were less than at similar places we visited, so in the spring of 2000 we contacted the admissions office and submitted our application for an apartment with two bedrooms or one bedroom with a den. We knew it could take several years before such an apartment would became available.

Ted had been diagnosed with Type II diabetes when he was about fifty-four years old and had been on twice-daily insulin shots since January 1988, shortly after we moved to Blue Bell and changed doctors. He did well for some years but was rather casual about what he ate; he especially loved ice cream but abhorred the sugar-free version! Then, one day in February 2001, Ted and I visited my brother Nate and his wife Esther near Gap. Ted was unusually tired, so we went home early. I offered to contact his doctor, but he just wanted to go to bed. Two days later he agreed to see the doctor, who put him in the hospital for tests. Nothing showed up at first. He was put on a water pill. A later EKG finally showed that he had suffered a "silent heart attack." One tablet of Lasix daily was added to his medications. His energy continued to decrease and he no longer campaigned for translation work, but he continued his daily reading in his foreign-language "Bible of the year," with dictionary at hand.

Meanwhile, my legs were not working well, especially when going up stairs, and I began to experience transient vision disturbances, and weakness in my left arm and leg, which remained. Later I wondered if these problems may have been the result of a stroke. At any rate, I had handrails installed on our outside steps, which made it easier for me to carry groceries to the house from the car, and railings along the inside stairs.

Then, in December 2001, I began to have episodes of rapid heartbeat (supraventricular tachycardia, from 150 to 160 beats per minute) instead of my normal 60 to 70 beats per minute. Despite treatment with Toprol and Digoxin and multiple trips to the ER, where I was often given IV medication to slow my heart down, the episodes became more frequent. Finally, in June 2003, I had three episodes and went to the ER each time. Twice while I was in the ER it decided to race again—once while the cardiologist was with me. For him that was enough, so he sent me off to Lankenau Hospital, where on July 2 they did a catheter-type procedure to locate the position of the extra electrical trigger that was setting off the tachycardia, then "zapped" it. I had a miserable night lying flat on my back after my late-afternoon surgery, but I survived. The next morning, Ted and Joseph came to see me, and that afternoon Ben came in and took me home. I have had no more runaway heart rate since then, praise be to God!

In retrospect, I am so glad that God arranged for me to get my racing heart taken care of before Ted got into his more serious health problems. Though his diabetes had been diagnosed well into his adulthood, in some ways he responded more like a Type I diabetic. His blood sugar could fluctuate rather wildly, especially as he got older, and he sometimes had episodes of severe hypoglycemia (low blood sugar). I never could convince him to take less insulin when he was not hungry. Then I would set my alarm, because I am a sound sleeper, to awaken me soon after midnight so I could check to see that he was OK and not unresponsive from very low blood sugar. At least five times I found Ted unresponsive in the early morning and called the paramedics to come give him intravenous glucose to bring him back to me when he was unable to take anything by mouth. Sometimes his blood sugar was down below

30 and he had seizures. But when they started the IV glucose he promptly woke up, and probably wondered what the strange men were doing in our bedroom. I don't believe that Ted remembered anything the next morning about the night visitors, and I never asked him about it. Eventually he was also treated for high blood pressure; for heart, thyroid, and kidney troubles; and for pain in his feet.

Ten days after I returned from the hospital, Ted developed a cough and fever overnight and was unsteady on his feet. In the morning I called the paramedics to transport him to the ER, because I was not about to take him down the stairs by myself. His temperature was 103 and the diagnoses were congestive heart failure and pneumonia. He was in the hospital for ten days receiving IV fluids and antibiotics, and an up-and-down course of medications for orthostatic hypotension, pleural effusion, anemia, and the congestive heart failure. He was still weak and unsteady on his feet when they wanted to discharge him, and I knew he was not ready to use the stairs in our house. So he was admitted to a nursing home for short-term rehabilitation to improve his walking. The rehab was helpful, but the meals were not always attractive and were sometimes late and rather "cooled off" too. Combined with Ted's poor appetite, this situation led to him having two episodes of low blood sugar (just before a noon meal and around 2:00 A.M.), and both times he was taken to the nearby ER for treatment with intravenous glucose. A pair of almost new pajamas never returned from the laundry despite my inquiries. After two and a half weeks of less than ideal care, Ted was nevertheless walking better with a walker and I asked to bring him home. The walker and cane came along for him to use as needed. And six years later I found new uses for them.

That fall, Ted's heart was literally wearing out. He had returned home from the hospital with even more medicines to take, and we were kept busy visiting the family doctor plus three specialists. Ted did fairly well initially, so the doctors prescribed some outpatient rehabilitation exercises. After several weeks of this regime, he began to have bouts of dizziness and unsteady gait, so in late September they readmitted him with the diagnosis of low blood pressure, especially when he got up to walk. They slowly adjusted his medication dosages, and later they resumed his outpatient rehab therapy. Sometimes Ted got so tired during this therapy that he did not finish the whole hour.

In the midst of all this, in October we were finally invited to inspect an apartment at Landis Homes. It would be available in late January 2004. When we arrived in the early afternoon of a sunny day, I asked for a wheelchair for Ted because it was a long walk down to the far end of Harvest View. The apartment was empty but lovely, facing south, with a view of the neighboring farmland, plus a veranda and shade tree, walk-in closet in the bedroom, washing machine and dryer in the bathroom, bathtub that could accommodate a shower seat, and a small den that would hold multiple bookcases, three file cabinets, my computer, plus books, boxes, and general stuff. Of course there was a nice living room and a compact kitchen. There was also the option of buying the window dressing in the living room from the previous tenant. What more could we want? I sent in our notice of acceptance several days later.

Soon afterward, one cold and windy day when we went to see the doctor, Ted suddenly became obviously short of breath before we got inside the hospital building. He was no better when he was seen again two days later, so he was admitted as an inpatient. The diagnosis now was a pleural effusion (fluid in his left lung). On October 30, a thoracentesis was done, that is, they used a needle to withdraw a quart of liquid from his chest, resulting in some improvement. He came home with two oxygen machines, one to use at home, especially at night, and one for smaller tanks to use when we left the house to go to the doctor and so on. Initially he complained about dryness of the nose and throat from the oxygen, but in time he came to realize that the oxygen did help him to breathe more easily and to rest better.

In the past Ted had been treated several times for anemia. Iron shots in 2002 had led to improvement, and he had received Procrit injections in the spring of 2003, again with improvement. But after the pneumonia and heart failure were diagnosed in July 2003, the shots were discontinued, because they involved traveling to Phoenixville Hospital, which was thirty minutes away. Later we were asked to see the hematologist (blood specialist) again, and he ordered iron shots every two weeks. ✟

Preparing to Move Again

Now I really had to start making plans for where all of the belongings in our Blue Bell home would go. How could I get everything done in three months? And stay very attentive to Ted's needs as well? It really was rather overwhelming for me. But at least we could count on a place to move into when we moved out of Blue Bell, which had been our home for fifteen years. And we would need to sell our house, quickly. At least we could ask our neighbor Carole Pine to be our real estate agent, knowing that she would do a good job of getting a buyer for our home. The "For Sale" sign promptly went up in the front corner of our yard.

One evening Carole Pine came by to see me, as real estate agents do when one is selling or buying a house. After we covered the business and how Ted was doing, Carole popped me a different question: "Do you have a Bible?" she asked.

"Yes, I do—more than one," I replied. Carole explained that she had just gone to a funeral for a friend who apparently was a Christian and the minister had spoken about Psalm 23 and she wanted to read it again. So I went from our dining room down to the living room, where I had been sorting books and where there were a number of new and scarcely used Bibles in various translations. I brought one up and handed it to her. I don't remember which translation it was but it seemed very unfamiliar to her. I showed her where Psalm 23 was located and gave her the Bible to keep. Some months after Ted's death, I invited Carole to join me at Methacton Mennonite Church. She accepted my invitation and came with Emerson Verden, a fellow translator and friend of Ted's who also lived fairly close to us. That morning some of the Morrow family put on a skit about the life of Joseph that had originally been prepared by Ted and me for our adult Sunday school class.

Soon after the "For Sale" sign went up, a number of folks came to look at the house. We finally accepted an offer in early December, even though we would have liked a higher price for it because we had made a number of repairs and put in almost all new appliances and a new roof and spouting. The most expensive addition had been a system installed beneath the basement floor to pump out the water that otherwise settled on the floor whenever it rained.

On December 4, 2003, Ted was scheduled for an iron shot. Usually a wheelchair was parked just inside the hospital door and I would bring it out to the car to give Ted a ride into the doctor's office. But this time

no wheelchair was available, so Ted slowly walked himself inside as I carried his oxygen tank. His hemoglobin count was still low, below 9 grams, so the doctor gave him the shot but also asked us to return the next day for a blood transfusion. Ted was really tired when we got home that afternoon, so I helped him up the stairs to bed. When I called him for the evening meal, he took his insulin and came downstairs, but he was too tired to eat very much. As it turned out, that was the last meal—what it was I do not remember—that Ted had in our home with me.

That winter would be one of multiple snowstorms, and the forecasters had told us to expect a heavy snow during that night. Neither Ted nor I wanted to travel back to Phoenixville Hospital the next morning with, or even without, snow. And because Ted had not eaten much supper, I knew there was a good chance he would have another low sugar episode during the night. So I suggested to Ted that I take him to the ER that evening so that their staff could manage his care. Ted agreed, and they gave him a transfusion during the night in the ER and admitted him to a bed in the morning. And we did get the forecast snowfall that night.

While Ted was being cared for elsewhere, I started to sort our belongings into boxes in the living room—family items for our children in one area and things to go to Landis Homes in another. Items to go to auction were sorted into the family room. There were shelves of books to be sorted, some to be kept, some to be given to family, others to be donated to the Bookworm Frolic at the Lancaster Mennonite Historical

Society. I rented a dumpster for trash and other useless items. I got no takers, not even for free, for the upright piano that had served our musical family for many years, so I sadly assigned the piano to the dumpster. I was happy, however, to be able to rescue baby car seats and a stroller, which went into a pile for the flea market at Norristown State Hospital. After sorting and packing in the earlier part of each day, I would visit Ted in the late afternoon. Afterward, on the way home, I often stopped by a fast food joint for a sandwich or a cup of chili.

After Ted had been in the hospital for ten days and was making slow progress, I kept listening for the word *discharge*. It came on December 18, one week before Christmas. Ted's daughter Alice and her husband, David, who were located in the Washington, DC, area (the other children lived within eighty miles of us), had come to visit. I remember the call I received from David the morning before: "This is your son-in-law David calling. We will soon be arriving at your home." After a quick lunch together, I went with them to visit Ted at the hospital.

Ted was pleased to see them but was still rather weak and tired, and unusually quiet. I soon suspected that his blood sugar was low, and sure enough he had not eaten much of his lunch. I asked the nurse to check him. She did and soon brought some sweet liquids to him and—Bingo!— Ted became more talkative. Later the social worker came in and told me that the doctors were ready to discharge Ted. She also said that the Rittenhouse Pine Center in Norristown had a bed available for him, and it had a reputation for good nursing care. When I opened the subject with Ted, he naturally wanted to come home, but I gently said that this was not really feasible. I told him this was a different nursing home and that our doctors had assured me it provided much better care than the one he had been in previously. He repeatedly asked to come home, and each time I quietly said that this was not possible. Finally I said that I would not decide for him, and I prayed for him to peacefully make the right decision. After some minutes of quiet, he said he would go there. And within minutes I had gathered his belongings and we were ready to go. ✝

The Different Christmas Season

Exactly one week before Christmas Day 2003, I followed the hospital vehicle carrying Ted two miles down the street to the Rittenhouse Pine Center. We went upstairs to a room on the second floor and were introduced to the man who was to be Ted's roommate, who was in the bed beside the window. I put Ted's belongings into his closet and kissed him good night. It had been a busy day for both of us.

When I came to visit the next day, Ted soon volunteered that the nursing care there was better than the service had been in the previous facility. The staff were more available, and he liked his room. It was bigger than the room at the other place, which had seemed more like a dungeon and was located at the end of a long hall and rather far removed from the nurses' station. In addition, here Ted could look out the window and see people coming and going, whereas at the other place he could see nothing out the window except an occasional car passing by. I don't recall Ted offering any complaints about the care he received while he was at Rittenhouse Pine.

The doctors still wanted him to do some physical therapy to improve his walking with the walker. I watched him working with the PT supervisor one day; he quickly tired and asked to stop. In retrospect, I have to wonder if that PT was of any value to Ted, or did it just hasten the failure of his weary heart?

When I was with Ted on Christmas Eve, I asked a staff member if she would arrange for me to have Christmas dinner with him at noon the next day. She agreed. On Christmas Day I arrived by 11:30 and found Ted in the lounge by himself, near the Christmas tree. We sat together and talked as we looked out the window toward the east and waited for our meal to arrive. It was not a traditional Christmas meal with all the fixings, but it was Christmas and we were together. Afterward Ted said he was tired, so I pushed him and his chair back to his room. The nurse came in and put him to bed. I kissed him good-bye and went back home to my sorting.

On the day after Christmas, Alice headed north from DC to join Rita and me in some more sorting. But those plans got rearranged, because God has a special way of revealing His love to us and answering our prayers.

The girls had not yet arrived when I got a call from a nurse at Rittenhouse Pine. She told me they had gotten Ted ready for breakfast, but later when they went to check on him he was not responsive. They promptly sent him to Mercy Suburban Hospital and notified me. I hurried to the ER and waited a while before they invited me inside to see him. I watched the monitor as his blood pressure dropped to 69/45 with a heart rate of 54 beats per minute. The staff had tried to start an IV in his arm in five or six places before they finally put it into his neck vein. The doctors were unsure whether to push fluids and try dopamine to raise his blood pressure, because it might overwhelm his weak heart. But his blood pressure did come up some and he opened his eyes several times. Ted was moved to the intensive care unit that afternoon, but the doctors warned us that this improvement was only temporary.

It did buy enough time for some healing to take place. Ted and I had always maintained contact with all of the children—but rarely were all of them at the same place at the same time. We had hoped and prayed to become a whole family again, and Ted lived long enough to see those prayers answered, at least for a while.

That evening, Rita and Alice drove to Philadelphia and brought Mary; her husband, Leslie Farrell; and their two daughters, Cathy and Virginia, out to the hospital in Norristown. Joseph and Ben, both of whom lived nearby, joined us. The children took turns meeting with their father in the ICU. At the staff's suggestion, Joseph spent the night with his dad. At one point, Joseph was called away to answer a phone call, and just that quickly the IV was dislodged from Ted's neck. But a new IV was inserted without any difficulty. As the night passed, Ted regained his coherence.

The next morning I went to Methacton for the Sunday morning service, during which I shared the latest information about Ted's condition. Meanwhile, Rita and Mary went to visit Ted that morning. When they arrived, Ted announced, "I missed the Big Guy last night." Neither daughter was sure what he was talking about, so one of them said to him, "Well, no. You didn't miss him. Joseph was here with you all night long." But Ted said it again: "I missed the Big Guy last night." Later, as the girls were leaving the hospital and returning to Rita's car, it suddenly dawned on them that Ted was telling them he had come close to the pearly gates and God had said it was not yet his time to come inside.

When I arrived at noon to visit Ted, he was sitting up in bed and feeding himself. This was quite a surprise to me. That evening he was transferred downstairs to a regular room. Several times during the week that followed, Ted spoke about the day he "could not remember."

That week, Ted's daughter Mary and her two daughters were off from work and school, so Mary spent most of the week and each of the girls spent two days helping me. Mary and Virginia helped me take some old tires and metal to a junk yard. In the process, I picked up a nail in a rear tire, so by the time I got a rubber plug inserted at the garage, no change was left from my junk-delivery profits. When Cathy was with us, I had Mary contact some used clothing places and arrange for them to pick up clothing and coats that were no longer needed. I also had Mary prepare cards with my change of address and phone number on them. I asked Cathy to pick out a foreign-language Bible for each language that Ted had learned and a dictionary to go with each one. These I intended to keep until Cathy, who shared her grandfather's interest in languages, was ready to care for the collection herself. ✝

Our Last Month Together

After New Year's Day I got more help for moving, from my brother Paul and his wife and from my sister Anna Mary Groff. Paul worked first in our garage, which had never been a home for our vehicles. Instead, we had used it to store our ladders, lawn mowers and other yard equipment, and an assortment of other things. Paul picked out some tools and supplies that I might need at Landis Homes. The rest he delivered in several loads in his pickup to the auction house near Hatfield. Paul's wife, Mary, sorted out clothing for me to keep; the rest went to second-hand shops. Sis sorted out and inventoried family possessions for Ted's children, including things that had belonged to their mother, and lots of things from Ted's parents (china, crocheted tablecloths that his father had made, dresses that his mother had made, afghans, old books including Bibles, bedding, towels, and so on). After the death of Ted's mother early in 1976, Alice and I had flown to Florida, rented a truck, and driven all of these things back from Sarasota to Pennsylvania. Now it was time to share them with the next generation.

On the afternoon of Saturday, January 17, we gathered around the big makeshift plywood table in the living room and, beginning with the oldest child, the children took turns picking items from a given category until that category was finished. If a person did not care for a certain category, he or she could pass up that group of items. Everything was distributed in an orderly fashion, and I was blessed to watch the family members choose objects without any arguments. We got tired and hungry before we had finished dividing everything, so we quit at 6:30 and drove in several cars to Country Buffet to eat. While we were there, it began to snow—*again!*

After dinner, we went to see Ted. On our way, the group in my car sang, like they did when they traveled with Ted and Catherine as children. Ted was awake when we arrived, as if he was waiting for us to come. I pulled up a chair beside him and sat down. The children plus Ben's wife and daughter gathered around Ted's bed and I said to him, "I want you to really look at what you see here. *All* of the children are with you tonight, and you and I have not seen everyone together like this for a number of years. But we are all here tonight, and we are going to sing together for you." And sing together we did. We began with "Faith of Our Fathers." Next we sang "My hope is built on nothing less than Jesus' blood and righteousness." We then tackled number 606 from the orange hymnal, "Praise God from Whom All Blessings Flow," which Ted had really enjoyed leading at Germantown Mennonite Church some thirty-five years earlier. Next we sang "Jesus Loves Me," for three-year-old Skylar. Then I asked for a Christmas carol, so we sang "Joy to the World," our finale. I watched Ted mouthing the words to every song as we sang. I know he really enjoyed that singing, even though he could not sing loudly enough for us to hear him as we had so often heard him sing in years past. Then I got up from the chair and let everyone take turns sitting next to Ted and talking with him. I went over to his roommate's side of the room for several minutes, and was blessed that he expressed appreciation for our beautiful singing. I really believe that God gave Ted that extra month on Earth with us so that he could see the answer to our prayers for more unity in our family.

One evening in early January when I came home from the hospital, I found the screen door locked and was unable to enter our house! So I walked over to my helpful neighbor Adele's house. She called the police station and explained my plight. An officer soon arrived. He had me write and sign a statement explaining what had happened. He then pulled out a heavy hammer and applied it to the glass of the front door, which flew into pieces. I carefully inserted my hand inside the hole and pulled on the inside lock. The door opened. I stepped inside and headed for a dustpan and brush to clean up the mess and deposit it in the trash. When Paul arrived the next day, I asked him to measure the door for a new glass, then go to the nearby Sears hardware store to buy the new glass, and then install it for me.

By January 16 it became clear to me that despite all the help I had received from the children and from Sis and my brother Paul and his wife for several busy weeks, I would *not* be ready to make settlement by January 20. And because I had another week before we were due to occupy our residence at Landis Homes, I decided I had better use it. I asked the movers to take our furniture, clothes, books, computer, and other "stuff" to the apartment at Landis Homes on Wednesday, January 21, and then to collect our armoire, bookcases, and other items for auction on Friday, January 23. That would leave the delivery to the Norristown State Hospital flea market for Monday morning, January 26, after which we could do cleanup and make settlement for the house that afternoon. I felt that this schedule was attainable, but I learned that God's schedule was somewhat different.

On Wednesday, January 21, I put kitchen supplies into my car and Sis and I left ahead of the moving truck to get to Landis Homes by noon. After lunch we unpacked the kitchen things while the movers brought in the furniture, clothing, bedding, books and bookcases, office things, and other boxes. Director of Admissions Virginia Musser stopped by. I told her that Ted was not doing well and I did not know if he would make it to Landis Homes. By 4:00 the movers were finished, so I locked up and we went our separate ways.

When I arrived back at the nursing home at 6:00, Ted was alert and I told him that everything had arrived safely at our new apartment, including his treasured violin and his foreign-language Bibles and dictionaries. I explained that the boxes were not yet unpacked except for the kitchen things. Then I said, "And when everything is unpacked and ready for us to move in, will you be ready to move in?" And his clear answer was, "And why not?" Ted had really looked forward to coming to Landis Homes. He always brightened up when I spoke about it.

Ted's "And why not?" was the last thing he said to me that I clearly understood. The next morning I spoke to Virginia Musser and reported on my visit with Ted the evening before. She said that a Medicare bed was now available either for the next day (Friday) or for Monday. When I explained our schedules for both those days, she said, "Well then, lets go with Tuesday."

On Thursday afternoon when I arrived to visit Ted, he was very tired. For several weeks I had been encouraging him to eat soft foods from his tray, but lately he was eating very little. Then I had tried to give him liquids to drink, but each day he seemed to take less nourishment. Ted had been a faithful reader of the Bible. He would begin with Genesis and work his way through the entire Bible, reading one of the Psalms each day. When he finished Revelation he would start over again in Genesis. Since he had gone into nursing care, I had begun reading to him from the middle of Numbers. I would also use his electric shaver on his face every two to three days.

The nurse had asked me to come see her that afternoon. My brother Paul came with me. The nurse explained that Ted was taking only minimal liquids, so the doctor had discontinued his insulin and his oral medications. Ted took only a small sip of juice for me while I was there. He made no verbal communication. I knew the end was coming soon, so I prayed a new prayer aloud with him. I not only thanked God for the loving father and husband he had been to our children and me, but I also released him to go home to God in heaven, in His good time.

When I offered to shave his face that Friday, Ted shook his head: no, he was too tired. Later that day I told the rest of the family that the time had come for all of us to release him to go to his family and friends who had preceded him to heaven.

On Saturday afternoon the children gathered again to finish dividing the remaining family objects. Afterward we went to the Country Buffet again and then to see Ted. He was very tired and weak and his skin was very dry. We tried to sing again, but this time it was very difficult. But we tried, and Ted even managed to open his eyelids just a slit several times to let us know that he knew we were there with him.

On Sunday morning the weather forecast was for snow that night. On Friday Paul had already loaded my car with things to go to Landis Homes, and by Sunday morning I had not yet moved it. So I asked Rita if we could load more things into her car and then drive both cars to Landis Homes (forgive me for skipping church that morning!) while Alice and David returned to Washington, DC, with a large piece of furniture. Alice was now employed at the National Cathedral in DC, so she needed to be back that evening. So Rita and I drove our loads to Landis Home, unloaded them, and ate dinner with Laura Kurtz, a friend from my Tanzania days. There were perhaps two dozen folks at Landis Homes whom I had served with in Tanzania, plus a few from Somalia, as well as folks I knew from my childhood days in the Gap area.

I remember that I was tired and fought fatigue as Rita followed me back to Norristown to visit Ted at around 3:00 P.M. Ted was resting quietly and appeared to be sleeping. On the stand next to his bed I saw a note from Pastor Dawn Nelson, our lead pastor from Methacton Church, who had stopped in after the morning service. She too had assumed that Ted was sleeping. This time Ted seemed unaware of our presence, so I prayed in thanksgiving for his life and his many gifts to us, his knowledge of the Word of God, the many things he had written and left to us, the poems and stories and songs that God had given to him. As I prayed, I told him that I believed his work on Earth was about finished and that God would soon take him to rest in heaven.

When I finished praying with Ted, I stepped near the window to speak to Ted's roommate. This time his wife, whom I had not met before, was present and she greeted me. When I told her that Ted was very low, she stood up and hugged me close to herself. She comforted me and prayed for me. I failed to write down her name, nor did I write down her husband's name, but she really ministered to me in that one contact.

After we got back to the house I asked Joseph and Rita to load some small desks, some tables, and a set of shelves onto my pickup truck and take it into Philadelphia to their sister Mary and her family. I helped secure the stuff with clothesline and they left at around 7:30 while I stayed at the house to do more packing. At about 9:00 P.M. the nurse at Rittenhouse called to tell me that Ted had passed on. He had been my husband for more than twenty-nine years. Now his struggle with diabetes and heart failure was over and he was at home with his Lord Jesus Christ.

Now that Ted had gone to his eternal home, I went into a different gear. First, I called my next door neighbor Adele, who had lost her own husband in the previous year. Within minutes she was at the door. I also called Dawn Nelson, who later arrived with Bill Kull, a member of the pastoral team, and his wife Susan. They offered me sympathy. I also told them that delivery of things to the flea market at Norristown State

Hospital the next morning was still on, so the Kulls, with the assistance of Don McDonough and a number of high school students, took over management of that delivery. I also called our real estate agent, Carole Pine, to tell her of Ted's demise. I asked her to arrange for our house buyer to postpone the settlement for a week, and Carole gladly took care of that detail.

It must have been near 10:00 P.M. when Joseph and Rita got back from Philadelphia with some late supper for us. The pastors prayed with us, then left. Did we take time for supper before we went to Rittenhouse Pine? Maybe, or maybe not. In any case, we got there at about 10:30 P.M. We went to Ted's room and pulled aside the curtain around his bed. It was immediately clear to me that Ted had left us and only his body remained. His cheeks were already cold. I gathered up his clothing and personal belongings. Then I went around the screen to talk to the roommate. I told him that Ted had left his body of pain and misery. I also told him how much I had appreciated meeting his wife that afternoon and the kindness she had shown to me. We next stopped by the nurses' station to give them the undertaker's information. I had chosen Kirk & Nice, who had provided the same services for Ted's first wife, Catherine, after her death in March 1974. They now had a new facility northeast of Norristown. ☦

Saying Good-bye to Ted

How many times have I said this? The night Ted died it *snowed again!* And there was enough snow to close many local schools the next day. Fortunately a man at Norristown State Hospital agreed to open the back entrance of building 53, a former patient building where I had worked some years prior, on Monday morning, January 26, to receive our stuff for the flea market into the rear hallway even though the flea market volunteers had decided to stay home because of the snow. The pickup and delivery went as scheduled, and by noon the house was looking quite empty and forlorn. Only a few food items remained in the refrigerator. Sleeping bags were spread out on the floors of the otherwise empty bedrooms, and several three-way floor lamps had been kept behind to light the rooms. Now we needed to prepare for the funeral.

On Monday afternoon, Ben and his wife and daughter drove Rita and me to Rita's home in Lebanon so that she could collect some clothes and other items to bring back to Blue Bell. She had arranged to be off work for the rest of the week. Then we headed to Landis Homes. It was after 4:00 when we arrived and it was getting dark as we looked for clothes and some of Ted's writings to use at the funeral. Ben picked out a good suit and other clothes for Ted's body while I checked other hangers in the closet for clothes for myself. I found a suitable dress but I could not find the suitcase that contained my slip or my dress shoes. Pastor Dawn later bailed me out with a pair of her shoes. They were a bit long, so I pushed some newspaper into the toes. There was no lamp or flashlight available in the den, but I had recently looked through the file cabinets and remembered where Ted's writings were that I wanted for the funeral. It was 5:30 by the time we located everything we wanted and took it to Ben's vehicle. We then went to the dining room for supper, but the Landis Homes crew was already removing the food, so we just went home without supper, and we survived. Maybe we weren't really hungry anyway.

On Monday evening I slept in my sleeping bag on the floor of my empty bedroom at Blue Bell, which was rather hard, so I did not sleep very well. Rita slept on a sleeping bag too. On Tuesday morning Adele asked where I had slept, and when I told her she invited me to her house to sleep in an upper-level bedroom for the rest of the week. She also gave me a warm winter nightgown to use, and at the end of the week she sent it home with me, and I still use it.

On Tuesday morning, January 27, Joseph, Mary, Rita, Ben, and I went to the Kirk & Nice funeral home to make the funeral arrangements. Alice was on her way up from DC, but the funeral director opened the phone so she could hear the conversation and offer her comments to us as she drove. We decided to have the service on Thursday evening, January 29, at 7:00 P.M., to be preceded by the viewing beginning at 5:00 P.M. The burial would be at Millwood Mennonite Cemetery on Friday morning, January 30. Finally, we went to see the many caskets and selected a nice wooden box. Adele had a good lunch ready for us when we got back to her house at noon.

On Tuesday afternoon, the pastoral team from Methacton—Dawn Nelson, Bill Kull, and Luke Beidler—arrived. We—myself, the five children (by then Alice had arrived), and the pastoral team—met around Adele's dining room table. I read aloud some of Ted's writings that I felt would be appropriate to share at the funeral, and we eventually agreed to make Ted's service a celebration of his life and to use the materials he had written, including the song "Begin by Loving Again" that he had written for our wedding. We were told that the church ladies would prepare a light meal and serve it to the family before the viewing began at 5:00 P.M.

On Wednesday morning, January 28, Alice did a major job of preparing the program for the funeral, with Ted's photo on the front and the order of the service inside. While she did that, Ben took me to our nearby Walmart store, where I found a dark slip to wear with my funeral dress. Later I got busy writing what became a five-page story of Ted's life to be read at the funeral. It was nice to have a Staples store nearby to do our printing and copy work. We relied on Adele for meals, for as many as six of us at a time. She also served a lot of her special humor to break up the weariness and tension that we sometimes felt. She was like a mother to us and we appreciated it a lot.

Thursday was the big day, when we would say good-bye to Ted. That afternoon my brothers and some of my nieces went to the auction house where some of our things were being sold and bought some of the things that had been ours, including some of our heavy-duty bookshelves. We also sold the antique armoire that I had restored and used as a clothes closet in Germantown and then as a closet for our winter coats and boots in our Blue Bell residence. After the auction they came to the funeral.

Friday, January 30, was a bitterly cold and windy day. Pastor Dawn Nelson, the Morrow family, and Stoltzfus relatives met at Millwood Mennonite Church. After Ted's body was buried there, next to my sister Ruthie and my parents, we had lunch and spent the afternoon together at the home of my niece Joyce (oldest child of my brother Nate) and her husband, Cliff Blank.

Ted's Translation of 1 Corinthians 13

Translated from the Greek for the wedding of Alice S. Morrow
and David C. Rowan, October 9, 1993, San Francisco, CA

Yes, it is good to desire the spiritual gifts, but there is one that is better than all the rest. It is the way of love.

If I could actually speak all the languages of men, and even of the angels, and love was absent, then I would be like an orchestra that had only cheap tambourines and cracked bells. If I could be a prophet and know all secrets and everything there is to know, and if I had such faith that I could tell mountains to move, yet all this without love would mean nothing. Oh, and if I could give away all I own to others and could let my body be burned at the stake, and did none of this with love, then it would all be wasted.

What is this love? It is always patient and always kind; it is never jealous nor arrogant; it never lacks consideration for others; it is not self-seeking or hypersensitive; it does not hold grudges. Love is not happy when others are hurting, but only when truth prevails. Love can put up with anything; it keeps on believing and hoping and enduring no matter what.

Yes, love is forever! There are times when prophecy is silent, and there are no more messages in tongues, and even the word of knowledge is not to be found. For even what we know is incomplete, and the prophecies we speak are flawed. But the perfection of love will dispel what is imperfect.

I was once a child, and it was normal for me to think as a child. I spoke and thought and reasoned like a child, but then I grew up, and what was childish I abandoned. The way we see things now is like the dim reflection from an old mirror, but there is a time when we will see reality face to face. My knowledge now is incomplete; then it will be full knowledge, with as clear a vision as of the One who sees me, the One who loves completely.

So there you have it, the three things that last: your faith, your hope for the future, and love, but of these, my friends, it is love that matters most.

The day after the funeral, Saturday, January 31, we loaded up the remaining stuff from the Blue Bell house into my pickup truck, Alice's car, and Rita's car, and formed a caravan to Landis Homes. Joseph was in the middle of moving things into his own new apartment but did not want us to leave him behind, so Alice made room in her car, then drove him back that evening so he could finish his move.

We arrived at Landis Homes in the late afternoon, had supper in the Garden Room, then unloaded the cars. The children left after dark as I watched through the porch window and cried—my first night at Landis Homes. I got up early the next morning and went to Methacton for church. There I saw a photo of Ted on the front table and nearly lost control. That night I stayed with Adele. She was so helpful. ☩

Life After Ted

After my official move into Landis Homes on February 2, 2004, I was so glad to be here. Many friends from my East Africa days were also here, as were many folks from the Millwood and Maple Grove area where I grew up, and they were all very supportive. So many services are available on the Landis Homes campus, and there are many activities in which to participate, such as music programs, missionary speakers, dramas, bingo, quilting, exercise, and so on. During my first years at Landis Homes I attended two different writing groups. In one group I shared my writing about my own life, and in another I shared about Ted's life. Fortunately he had worked on his memoirs, so I had a lot of material to use. I also enjoy working on jigsaw puzzles, and we usually have one in progress at the end of our hall.

Over the years I've enjoyed some special events off campus too, such as a bus tour of the early Amish settlements in Berks County, the auction at the Nicholas Stoltzfus homestead, the bookworm frolic at the Lancaster Mennonite Historical Society, and the Rough and Tumble Threshermen's Reunion at Kinzers. I've attended concerts at Lancaster Mennonite School and minor league baseball games in Harrisburg and Lancaster, and I've walked with a group around the Landisville Campground, followed by breakfast in Mount Joy. I've been to the Landis Valley Farm Museum and, with my sister, to Long Green, Maryland, a rural community near Baltimore, a bit north and east of the big city, where a set of our Amish great-great grandparents are buried, to attend an annual meeting of descendants who care about preserving the Amish Mennonite cemetery at Millwood. Another special treat was spending two days one October at the Delaware shore, just below Rehoboth Beach, with two stepdaughters and three other female friends. It was such fun to watch the sun rise from the ocean twice, and to see the full moon rise over the water. I did not go swimming, but I did get wet and sandy up to my knees when I turned my back to the ocean to pick up a shell and was caught by a wave. I went kerplunk onto all fours in the wet sand and could not get up, so I crawled about twenty feet to the boardwalk and pulled myself erect using an upright post. I managed to knock most of the sand off my jeans. Oh well, it was fun, and I'd love to go again.

I have visited the hospital too since I moved in. The first time was a few months after I arrived. I attended an open house at the new Heart of Lancaster County Regional Medical Center, located just south of Lititz. The new buildings and equipment were quite impressive. I really was not planning to return there anytime soon, but things can happen suddenly, as they did on September 10, which you can read about in the next chapter, "Soup in a Bread Bowl."

Two months later I had two episodes of bilateral pain over my anterior lower rib cage, accompanied by nausea. I was referred to the Heart of Lancaster emergency room and admitted for heart studies (stress test and echocardiogram), which were normal. I had no more pain so they let me go home after two days and an omelet breakfast. I went to my writer's group that afternoon, but my appetite was not up to par for the rest of the day and I was rather tired. I went to bed earlier than usual and slept well until 12:30 A.M., when I awoke with upper abdominal pain. Going to the bathroom did not help, and neither did a Tylenol, nor getting rid of the soup I'd had for supper. After several hours I got back to sleep. In the morning I reported to the nurse, then went to see the doctor, then went to the hospital for more blood tests. I still had no appetite. Early on Friday afternoon I was told that my pancreatic enzymes were "markedly elevated" and I should be admitted to the hospital promptly. Later that afternoon I had an ultrasound, which showed several small stones in my gall bladder and swelling in the lower bile duct, which was compatible with my having passed a stone fifteen hours or so previously after a period of blockage by the stone, which accounted for the pain and nausea. I was started on IV fluids and my enzyme levels came down promptly. On Monday morning I had my gall bladder removed by laparoscopic surgery, and on Wednesday, November 17, I came home. A month later I was feeling back to normal, trying not to gain back the pounds I had lost, and so glad that I was living indoors and had no concern about snow and severe weather. Incidentally, that was my first ever gall bladder attack, but I guess we doctors like to have nonroutine medical problems. ✝

Soup in a Bread Bowl

It began like any other day. I woke up, yawned and stretched, then decided to relax for another ten minutes. Eventually I got up, brushed my teeth, showered, and got dressed. I took my pre-breakfast medication and sat down to watch the latest news about Hurricane Ivan on TV as I also scanned the morning newspaper, with special attention to the Phillies three-game winning streak over the Braves. After eating breakfast and taking the rest of my morning medication, I went to the exercise room for my routine workout on the machines and stationary bicycle. I did one special thing too that morning: I went to hear MCC storyteller Ken Sensenig talk about the Mennonite couple who helped care for wounded soldiers at the Ephrata Cloister during the Revolutionary War. After dinner I happened to meet Ken's mother-in-law (a lady I knew from my LMS days) and told her how much I had enjoyed his story. I checked my mail, did some reading, and rested a bit before going to my computer to do more writing and revising on my current memory writers' club project, which I had titled *Learning About Ladders* (see the Appendix at the back of the book).

I was looking forward to stepdaughter Rita coming to visit that evening, so I printed out a copy of what I had written so she could read it. Rita called at about 6:00 P.M. to tell me she was ready to leave her home in Lebanon. We hadn't really talked about what we wanted to do for the evening meal, but I had been thinking about Oregon Dairy Restaurant and the delicious soup in a bread bowl that I had enjoyed when a group of us went there two months before. So I suggested Oregon Dairy to her and she replied, "I was thinking about that too!" I said, "OK, and it's my treat this time." Rita and her friend Chris had taken me to Hoss's in early August to celebrate what would have been the thirty-year wedding anniversary for Ted and me. They had also invited me to a steak barbecue on Labor Day weekend, so my turn to treat was overdue.

When Rita arrived a bit before 7:00 P.M. I offered to drive us in my pickup, because I'm more comfortable in my 1991 Ranger than I am in most low-slung cars (which hers was). At the restaurant we were promptly seated in a booth beside a window that overlooked the parking lot. I looked over the menu for several minutes before I found the bread bowl soups. Then I had to select from among five or six options. Finally I chose the potato soup with bacon and cheese. When it arrived I realized that I should have chosen something with more vegetables and less cheese and less bacon (for the sake of my cholesterol). We gave thanks and began to eat. The thick, delicious soup tasted so good, and after I had eaten more than half of it, I began to cut away at the bread bowl and eat it too, as I had done on previous occasions.

What Rita and I talked about as we ate I frankly don't remember, but suddenly some bread got stuck in my throat. I could not get it to move. I stood up and asked Rita to hit me on the back. Maybe that was not the best thing to do, but at least it made other persons aware that I was choking. A man came up behind me and asked, "Shall I do the Heimlich?" I'm not sure if I gave him a verbal response or just nodded, but the answer was affirmative. I remember him applying a sudden compression to my lower chest. At some point I blacked out and was unaware of what was happening. However, Rita told me later that the Heimlich maneuver was done at least three times, and my lips were getting blue. At any rate, I woke up to find myself on the floor with a number of helpers around me, and I heard a woman say, "I asked if anyone had swept the back of her mouth." She apparently was then given a surgical glove, after which she dislodged the bread from my throat with a finger. I am not positive but I think I also heard her say that she was outside passing by our window when she saw someone inside doing the Heimlich maneuver, so she quickly came in to see if her help was needed. I also remember the release of my bladder control, perhaps as I was going down to the floor.

Meanwhile, the paramedics had been called. They arrived promptly. My blood pressure and heart rate were elevated, but they returned to normal levels within minutes. I decided anyway to accept the invitation to go to the emergency room and get checked out. After I got on the stretcher, though, I remembered I had told Rita that our meal was my treat. When I mentioned this, however, a restaurant staff person replied, "No, it's on the house." I do hope I remembered to thank him! (A couple of weeks after the incident I did write and send a thank-you letter to the manager of the Oregon Dairy Restaurant.) Rita handed my purse to me and I retrieved my truck keys and gave them to her, then told her how to get to the Heart of Lancaster emergency room.

The ER staff examined me and got a chest X-ray. No problems were found, so they gave me a sheet of instructions about preventing a repeat episode of choking. Then Rita drove me home, where we arrived at around 10:00 P.M. I left a message for the nurse on call to tell her what had happened and that I was very tired but seemed to be stable. I promptly fell asleep and slept well, as I usually do. The next morning I called Rita and gave her my morning report: teeth brushed, shower, breakfast, morning medication, and laundry all done. I also told her that I had discovered some aches in my rib cage from the Heimlich compression. And I assured her that I was very glad that I was still here to *feel* that pain!

Later, as I thought back over the whole experience, I remembered that it had happened so quickly that I really did not have time to panic. But afterward I realized how quickly my life could have been snuffed out! And I knew it would have been such a devastating blow to all the children to have me snatched away so abruptly when they had just lost their father seven months before. I also thought about my unfinished goals—the writing I wanted to do about Ted's life and mine, both of which I had begun after arriving at Landis Homes. I also wanted to type up the materials we had used in our Sunday school class on Genesis and Exodus, and to do some traveling. I had a supply of Bibles and reference books that I wanted to dig into again. But most important, I wanted to grow into a deeper life with my Lord through personal study of His Word and through prayer for family members and other persons who need such support.

As I continued to think about the events of September 10, 2004, I marveled that God had spared my life. I told my sister Anna Mary about it the next morning as we began a trip to Long Green. When she sent me a birthday card and a lovely letter a week later, she told me she was very glad that she had not seen my name on the obituary page of the Lancaster paper. And when I was speaking with Rita about it more recently, she said that as she watched me pass out and not respond to the Heimlich maneuvers, she began to wonder how she would tell the rest of the family that I was gone. Well, thank God He brought me back! And I do want to make my remaining days—hopefully years—count for Him.

The following passages from the Psalms (Good News Bible) express some of my feelings about my experience of almost choking to death. I share them here as more praise to God for sparing my life.

Rescue me from death, O Lord, that I may stand before the people of Jerusalem and tell them all the things for which I praise you. I will rejoice because you saved me. (Psalm 9:13c, 14)

You take notice of trouble and suffering and are always ready to help. The helpless commit themselves to you; You have always helped the needy. (Psalm 10:14)

Protect me, O God, I trust in you for safety. I say to the Lord, "You are my Lord; all the good things I have come from you." I praise the Lord, because he guides me, and in the night my conscience warns me. I am always aware of the Lord's presence; he is near, and nothing can shake me. And so I am thankful and glad, and I feel completely secure, because you protect me from the power of death. I have served you faithfully, and you will not abandon me to the world of the dead. You will show me the path that leads to life; your presence fills me with joy and brings me pleasure forever. (Psalm 16:1,2, 7–11)

How I love you, Lord! You are my defender. The Lord is my protector; he is my strong fortress. My God is my protection, and with him I am safe. He protects me like a shield; he defends me and keeps me safe. I call to the Lord, and he saves me from my enemies. Praise the Lord! The Lord reached down from above and took hold of me; he pulled me out of the deep waters. He rescued me from my powerful enemies and from all those who hate—they were too strong for me. He helped me out of danger, he saved me. You save those who are humble, but you humble those who are proud. This God—how perfect are his deeds! How dependable his words! He is like a shield for all who seek his protection. O Lord, you protect me and save me; your care has made me great, and your power has kept me safe. The Lord lives! Praise my defender! Proclaim the greatness of the God who saves me. (Psalm 18:1–6, 16–19a, 27, 30, 35, 46)

I will always thank the Lord; I will never stop praising him. I will praise him for what he has done: may all who are oppressed listen and be glad. Proclaim with me the Lord's greatness; let us praise his name together! Find out for yourself how good the Lord is. Happy are those who find safety with him. Good people suffer many troubles, but the Lord saves them from them all. The Lord will save his people; those who go to him for protection will be spared. (Psalm 34:1–3, 8, 19, 22)

I waited patiently for the Lord's help; then he listened to me and heard my cry. He pulled me out of a dangerous pit, out of the deadly quicksand. He set me safely on a rock and made me secure. He taught me to sing a new song, a song of praise to our God. You have done many things for us, O Lord our God; there is no one like you! You have made many wonderful plans for us. I could never speak of them all—their number is so great. Lord, I know you will never stop being merciful to me. Your love and loyalty will always keep me safe. (Psalm 40:1–3a, 5, 11)

Praise the Lord! With all my heart I will thank the Lord in the assembly of his people. How wonderful are the things the Lord does! All who are delighted with them want to understand them. All he does is full of honor and majesty; his righteousness is eternal. The Lord does not let us forget his wonderful action; he is kind and merciful. (Psalm 111:1–4)

I love the Lord because he hears me; he listens to my prayers. He listens to me every time I call to him. The danger of death was all around me; the Lord saved me from death; he stopped my tears and kept me from defeat. And so I walk in the presence of the Lord in the world of the living. What can I offer the Lord for all his goodness to me? I will bring a wine offering to the Lord, to thank him for saving me. In the assembly of all his people I will give him what I have promised. (Psalm 116:1–3a, 8, 9, 12–14) ☦

A Letter to Ted

I began the following letter to Ted on August 27, 2006, while on retreat with other Methacton folks at the Jesuit Center in Wernersville, Pennsylvania, using a BIC pen on a steno pad; I finished it on September 20, 2006, on my new (as of January 2006) Dell computer.

My Dearest Ted:

For more than two years I have thought about writing this letter to you, especially when our anniversary and your birthday have come around.

On your last birthday you would have been seventy-eight years old, if you were still with us. But of course you are in your eternal life and I assume that our earthly years are not as noteworthy to you there. It's hard to imagine what it is like where you are, but I'm sure you don't get bored by things that are uninteresting to you. In a perfect place like heaven there should be no problem with boredom or irritable neighbors. I'm sure you don't get tired or have to worry about your diabetes, finger sticks, and insulin injections. My own health is fairly good, although I have more backaches. Also, I had laparoscopic surgery to remove my gall bladder in November 2004; maybe I was getting too much cheese in my noon meals here, but I like their food. I seldom take dessert, however, even though they have sugar-free ice cream in several flavors that taste good, including peanut butter brickle and sometimes butter pecan, which is my favorite.

The other folks in our group for the silent retreat were George Azari, Greta Mast, Vicki Ball, Erma Schnabel, Mary Wycof-Kolb, and Dawn Nelson. The Jesuit Center has acres of well-manicured grass on rolling hills. However, it was a drippy day, so I stayed mostly indoors. Delicious meals were eaten in silence. Dawn provided several handouts and Scriptures to think about, but she said we could do whatever we wanted—even sleep! But we were *not* supposed to just read all afternoon. Maybe that would be a little hard for you, huh? It's hard to imagine you coming here without your bag of books to peek into.

I am enjoying Landis Homes a lot and keep making new friends. I am also enjoying writing for the two writers' groups. Martha Stahl, Omar Stahl's widow, leads both groups, but one group is geared to pursuing commercial publication while the other is focused on writing stories for our families, with photos if we wish. With my new HP Photosmart Three-in-One printer I can scan photos and print out color copies. I can also scan slides and negatives, plus crop and enlarge them. It is a lot of fun to bring old photos into new life.

In the commercial group I am working on *your* memoirs, and I must thank you for preserving your writings, in a file cabinet and stashed in boxes. As I have sorted through the boxes and the file cabinets, I have found so many interesting things, including your "Korea Battle." I also found your testimony from the University of Rochester, *From Modernism to Christ*. Those yellowed pages apparently were given to your parents soon after you wrote it, and they accompanied your parents to Harrisonburg, Virginia, and then to Sarasota, Florida. Unbeknownst to me they then came with Alice and me to Germantown in 1976, hidden in the bottom of a box that contained odd pieces of plywood and your mother's patterns for making wooden animal decorations for the lawn. That box stayed in the basement until we moved to Blue Bell, when it got parked in the garage. When Paul cleaned out the garage for our move to Landis Homes, I gave the box of wood scraps to Rita, so it went to Lebanon. Rita found the yellow papers in the bottom and showed them to me. As soon as I saw the title I knew what it was, and I thanked God for preserving it for our family. I retyped it and made a few minor editorial changes, and have since shared it with other family members. I was also glad to find your "Korea Battle," even though it was partially handwritten and some pages were missing. Because I had heard you tell some of those stories several times, I decided to "fill in the blanks" as I hope you might have done.

The written testimonies that you shared at Frazer and Methacton also helped to fill in the blanks about how you found your way into translation, that is, how you figured out that Yiddish was related to German and how to read it, and how you got into studying foreign languages by using your English Bible plus the foreign Bible and a dictionary and perhaps the foreign grammar. You really were a *fundi* ("expert" in Swahili) in foreign languages! So, thanks again for not throwing out your writing because it was only a first draft, because maybe what we found was the *only* draft!

In your memoirs I am up to where you meet Catherine and the Roth family. In my own autobiography I have just finished eighth grade, although I have already written many segments of my later life too. I really hope both of these books will find a commercial market, and in fact I did show what I have done on your book to Levi Miller, currently the top man on books at Herald Press, and offered them first chance at publishing it.

I think of you every day and have often thought of writing you a letter, but somehow it was hard to get started. And even now some things are hard to say and my eyes get wet. But I have finally turned to it again on September 20, 2006, which also happens to be my 75th birthday. I pulled out the stenography pad on which I had written my first draft and finally began typing this version.

I especially remember the special times, like our wedding anniversary and our birthdays, when we always went out for a nice meal somewhere. You were in Towne Manor West for our twenty-ninth wedding anniversary on August 4, 2003, but we did go to Olive Garden for *your* seventy-fifth birthday on August 22, 2003. I remember we had a quiet table in a corner, facing the sunshine, and we both enjoyed a delicious meal and the fact that you were home again after being in the hospital and in the rehab program for a long four weeks. When our server brought our check, he also gave us a comment card, so I wrote on it, "Thank-you for making it such a special birthday!" Little did I know then that this would be the last birthday you would spend with me on this Earth.

Well, that birthday was more than three years ago, and you have been enjoying heaven for more than two and a half years. I am so glad that God took you to be with him. As I watched the life energy slowly ooze from your body, you became unable to walk and to eat solid foods that you formerly enjoyed, and finally you could not even sip liquids. I saw the weariness overcome you, and I rejected the offer of sending you back to the hospital for IV fluids that would prolong your "life" by only a few days at most.

I cherish the memory of our whole family singing together a number of your favorite songs the weekend before your death, just like you and Catherine did with the children when they were much younger. The following weekend, when we all came again, you were much weaker and unable even to drink liquids. But tired as you were you managed to open your eyes just a slit to let us know that you knew we had come again. Thank-you! That meant a lot to all of us! The next night I got the call that you had departed for your better home before 9:00 P.M., and I was glad you went at that time, just before my move to Landis Homes, so that we could have Kirk & Nice for the funeral and have the service at Methacton. The time of your leaving us to go to Heaven was a time when our remaining family was drawn closer to one another.

We planned the funeral to be a celebration of your life, with two songs you had written, several of your poems, and your article about the impact of Catherine's death on you. I shared about your early life and your journey to faith in Christ. Others shared memories of you too, and we sang a number of congregational songs. I hope you liked it.

Although I miss you often, I could never wish you back into your frail physical body with your diabetes, episodes of low blood sugar, and congestive heart failure. I have adjusted fairly well to "living alone" again, but that does not mean I have not missed you, for I have felt a deep loneliness at times. I remember the way we talked about our shared Sunday school class on Genesis and Exodus; you wrote the skits, with very few exceptions, and I led the class discussions, but we often talked about the lesson at meal times and discussed information from nonbiblical sources too. I really enjoyed that. And I appreciated your input during the class sessions too. I still miss that.

I have many friends here, some of whom I have known since my teenage years, others from my work overseas, and others are new friends. I feel you would have enjoyed it here, but surely heaven surpasses this, and someday I plan to join you over there.

I still love you, and I look forward to seeing you, Catherine, and many others, later on.

Love,
Dorcas ☦

Saying Good-bye to Dorcas

It was at the beginning of October 2014 that Dorcas and I (Alice, her oldest stepdaughter) began working in earnest to prepare this book for publication. For six weeks I arrived at her apartment every weekday just after lunch. For those six weeks I read aloud to her all of the material she intended for the book. Some of it she had printed out and placed in thick three-ring binders; more was stored on her computer. And then there were the letters she had written to her family while she was in Africa; many of them she had already typed onto her computer and edited; others I eventually typed for her. She told me what she wanted to include in her book, and what she wanted to leave out. She admitted that there was much she hadn't written down before her memories and abilities faded, but she was relieved and happy that she had captured so many of her memories before losing access to them in her own mind.

I had already heard or read some of what Dorcas wrote in the first decade of her eleven-and-a-half years at Landis Homes. For nine of those years I lived just a few miles away, and we had many adventures together during that period, beginning with her invitation, less than two months after I moved to her neighborhood, to accompany her to an Eastern Mennonite Missions East Africa reunion at Goshen College in Indiana. We shared the driving both ways, and on the way home we made a few detours. First we went to Scottdale, Pennsylvania, to visit the Mennonite Publishing House and wander around the town where my parents, Ted and Catherine, had spent the first decade of their marriage and where I and three of my four siblings had begun our lives. Then we went to Grantsville, Maryland, to visit the archives of the children's home from which Catherine had been adopted as a baby. Finally we visited Lonaconing, Maryland, where Catherine had been born. That journey was our longest road trip—except for the first one we made together, in 1976, when I was eighteen. After the death of Ted's mother, we drove a U-Haul truck loaded with my grandmother's things from Sarasota, Florida, to Philadelphia. I don't remember if Dorcas asked me or told me to go with her that time, but it was the beginning of a friendship I never imagined.

As the years passed in Lititz, I gradually spent more and more time with Dorcas. I don't remember exactly when I started joining her for Sunday dinner and afternoon puzzling every weekend, but it was after I realized she needed more help but often didn't ask for it until I was there, because, as she said, she didn't want to bother me. I learned that it had become difficult for her to navigate the humanless telephone-answering machines at offices and businesses (if you want this, press 1, if you want that, press 2), so I offered to make phone calls for her to schedule appointments or get information. At some point I began taking her to those appointments, and on shopping trips (and in the wintertime I would shop for her), especially after she stopped driving and gave her pickup truck to her brother Paul. Sometimes while we were out we would stop and have lunch at the Kingdom Buffet, a sort of Chinese smorgasbord, or at the Oregon Dairy Restaurant. These are just a very few of the places we went and things we did together.

In mid-November 2014, Dorcas fell backward while playing shuffleboard, which she had been doing nearly every Thursday morning for many years, even after she needed to lean on a cane and then on a walker. Nothing broke, but she was bruised and in pain. After receiving a call from a nurse, I came and stayed with her for the rest of the day. It was that evening that I learned the extent of the help this strong, independent, generous woman had come to need and, finally, want. Thereafter I was with her for part or all of nearly every day of the rest of her life, which I did not allow myself to imagine would come so soon.

The winter of 2014–2015 was a difficult one for Dorcas. She gradually recovered from her fall, but in mid-January, just before she was to move out of the apartment she had called home for eleven years, she became ill with the flu, which was followed by several other health problems over the next month and a half. She moved into nursing care and her physical health improved, and then it began to sink in for her that she would not be going back to her apartment.

I came every day Monday through Saturday at suppertime and stayed with her until bedtime, and on Sundays I arrived in time to go with her to a church service and stayed until suppertime. One evening in early March we went, as usual, to her room after supper. She was feeling rather low emotionally and expressed to me how hard it was that she was no longer able to do the things she used to do. She felt she was no longer needed and she wondered, apologetically, if "this" would "soon be over."

I told her she did still have a purpose, a mission to complete for God: I needed her to help me finish publishing her book. I could almost see the wheels turning in her head as she considered this information—and then she seemed happy again. Every day after that, in one way or another I reminded her of our project and kept her apprised of its progress. I continued to read to her from the manuscript as I edited it and designed it into book pages. She seemed to grow stronger and to have more energy. She wanted to walk, so after dinner we would wander the halls of the east campus of Landis Homes. And when real spring weather finally arrived, we wandered outside. We found a few places that became favorite spots in which to sit and observe nature, and we would often stay until it began to grow dark.

In early June, Dorcas moved into another nursing unit at Landis Homes. Her new room looked out onto a lush courtyard filled with trees, plants, and flowers that was often visited by small creatures—an assortment of birds (including ducks and ducklings), squirrels, and a black and white cat. My sister Rita set up a bird feeder outside the room's big windows, which led to hours of enjoyment not only for Dorcas as she watched from inside, but also for her neighbors, and me, as we spent many an afternoon and evening sitting with her in that courtyard.

Dorcas and I continued to enjoy long walks both inside and outside until the last couple of weeks of her life, when she tired more easily. Because she had rallied before, it did not occur to me that this change was anything but temporary. She'd been blowing her nose more often and experiencing occasional postnasal drip, which seemed to be an allergic response because she had no fever and had a history of seasonal allergies. I assumed that her fatigue was related, and the staff kept close tabs on her. We continued to enjoy our hours together, reading, talking, working on puzzles, and watching Phillies games on the TV in her room. She was so excited that they were winning more often, and she would sometimes stay up an hour or more past her usual bedtime to see the outcome of a game. One weekend evening in late July we went to an EMM East Africa reunion in the Harvest Room, which Dorcas agreed to attend as long as she didn't "have to get up and say anything." She enjoyed the fellowship and food at that gathering very much, including meeting the current medical director of Shirati Hospital, Dr. Bwire Chirangi. I am so grateful that Laura Kurtz thought to invite us to that gathering.

On Friday, August 7, 2015, I arrived at Landis Homes at about 5:00 P.M. Dorcas was seated where she always was when I arrived for supper, at a long table in the dining room. I could see that she had eaten a bowl of soup, but an intact sandwich remained on the plate in front of her. She communicated that she was still a little hungry but just wasn't sure how to proceed. She talked about returning to the smaller unit she had lived in before moving to her current location, because she felt she would soon be needing more help and she remembered that most of the residents there had needed help with just about everything. Dorcas had moved two more times after leaving her apartment on February 2, but I made a mental note to contact the social worker about her concerns the following Monday.

After supper we walked to Dorcas's room, where I told her how that morning I had uploaded the files for her book to the printer. It's finished, I said. We did it! For the next couple of hours we sat at the card table in her room, on which we had started a new puzzle the night before, and looked at the book's cover and pages on my computer. I read the back cover to her again, and the entire table of contents. We looked at every photo, and I read aloud the bits of text that the photos illustrated. She nodded and laughed and launched into telling the rest of the stories as she now remembered them.

When we were finished, she turned toward me and said, "I couldn't do it, so you did it for me."

"But you wrote it," I reminded her. "I just organized it and put it all together so that others can read and enjoy it."

"I appreciate everything you've done for me," she continued. "When you are here I can make sense of things, because you take the time to help me think things through. But I know you can't be here all the time, because you have many, many other things to do."

As I've recalled those words again and again in the weeks since, it has seemed to me that she wasn't just telling me I needed to go home and wash the dishes and clean the bathroom. Now her words seem like a release, a well-done, a "Go forward!" (see the meditation by Chaplain Jim Leaman at the end of this chapter), a good-bye.

Dorcas then wanted to work a little more on the puzzle, so we played for about a half hour, until she said she was ready for bed. I rang the bell for the nurse to come and help her prepare.

During the first four months that Dorcas lived in nursing care, I would leave for home after someone had come to help her get ready for bed. I would hug her good night as they headed into the bathroom. The second night of Dorcas's stay in the last room she called home, she asked if I would wait to leave until she had gotten into bed. "Of course," I said. When she came back from the bathroom, she apologized for asking me to do something more when, according to her, I already did so much for her. I told her it was nothing at all to stay five more minutes, and I did so thereafter without being asked. I would wait for her just inside the room, and when she returned with the nurse I would give her a hug before she crawled into the bed. Usually I would have to ask her, "Can I have my good-night hug?" to get her attention. The nurse would then tuck her in and read to her the two scripture verses we had stumbled upon a few months before when she was having trouble sleeping:

"When I lie down, I go to sleep in peace; you alone, O Lord, keep me perfectly safe." Psalm 4:8

"And God's peace, which is far beyond human understanding, will keep your hearts and minds safe in union with Christ Jesus." Philippians 4:7

Dorcas would always close her eyes as these verses were read, then she would say, "Thank-you." I would say another good-night and leave the room, followed by the nurse, who would pull closed the curtain that separated her "semi-private" room from the foyer of the suite she shared with another resident—a woman with whom she had graduated from Lancaster Mennonite School many years before.

That last night, when Dorcas came in from the bathroom, I was still over by the window, putting my computer into my backpack. I turned to look at her and instead of heading for the bed she had stopped and was looking at me as though to say, "Where's my hug?" I got up quickly and obliged. She hugged back. After the rest of the bedtime ritual was carried out and before the nurse left, Dorcas asked for an additional blanket. She was cold. We covered her with the warm fleece blanket that usually hung over the back of her rocking chair—a blanket I had brought to her apartment one night during the winter when I had stayed over. I had left it there and she had found it and put it on her own bed.

I was about to turn and leave the room when Dorcas got my attention. The nurse left and I went to the head of the bed to hear better what Dorcas was saying. She asked if I could leave a little extra light on in the room. I turned on the night-light on the lamp next to her bed, but she said it was too much. I adjusted the digital picture frame on the window seat across the room, and she said that helped. I told her I would also leave the curtain open to let in a little extra light from the hallway. I then leaned down and put my forehead next to hers and said, "Good-night, Dorcas. See you tomorrow." I did not know that I was really saying good-bye.

Two hours later I received from the nurse the phone call I had never allowed myself to imagine.

We—family and friends—said our formal good-bye to Dorcas at a funeral service held in the West Bethany Chapel at Landis Homes on the morning of Thursday, August 13. Dorcas's son Ben, my "little" brother, gave one of the tributes. Her sister Anna gave another. With their permission I have shared their tributes here. A third tribute was read by a representative from Eastern Mennonite Missions, and that too is included. A condensed version of the message that Chaplain Jim Leaman gave closes the chapter.

Mom: A Tribute
by Ben Morrow

When my sister Alice asked if I could write out the tribute I gave to my mom at her funeral service, I was honored and glad she asked. Unfortunately, because I use just a rough outline when I speak, it can prove difficult to recapture what I said once it

*has been released upon the world. I will try my best to stay
true to the tribute I gave to Mom at her funeral, but I ask that
the reader forgive me if it is not exactly as I said it that day. I
hope that what I write here captures the spirit of my tribute
and honors Mom. So, without further rambling, here it is.*

Today I want to celebrate and honor my mom's life. This is a time of
sadness because we have lost a wonderful person. To deny our sadness
would be to deny that Mom meant much to us. We do have hope,
though, because we know that death is not the end, but only another
step in our journey, and that Mom is in a better place now.

I am grateful for the time I had with my mom. Your perception of
your parents changes as you get older, especially when you become a
parent yourself. You start to see your parents as human beings who are
not perfect, just like you. Up to a certain point in my life Mom was just
that: Mom. It wasn't until I grew up that I really started to learn more
about this special person I call Mom. I am still learning, and I will be
forever grateful for this book about her life, so I can continue to get to
know her.

One of the things I remember most about Mom was her love of jigsaw puzzles. I remember many Stoltzfus family get-togethers when
puzzles were pulled out. This love of puzzles must skip a generation,
because I never could understand what was so interesting about them.
Mom loved putting puzzles together even as she grew into the twilight
of her life. Many times I would call her, get no answer, leave a message,
and get a call back that started with, "I was at the puzzle." I think a jigsaw puzzle is a great metaphor for life. We are all part of this great big
puzzle that God is putting together. We may not know all the other
pieces in the puzzle, but we are all connected. One piece of the puzzle
can touch many others.

Mom's life touched many lives. There are many stories that could be
told. Mom was a good storyteller. She seemed to be at her most ani-
mated when she told stories, like about one of the horses on her childhood farm, Roy, who stepped on her foot. I don't know many of the
stories that others know about my mom, and I am not much of a storyteller myself. However, I am pretty good when it comes to concepts. So,
for my tribute to Mom I want to look at some Scripture and see how
Mom embodied that Scripture.

> "For God so loved the world that he gave his only son,
> that whoever believes in him shall not perish but have
> eternal life. For God did not send his son to condemn
> the world but to save the world through him." John
> 3:16–17

This is one of my favorite scriptures. It speaks of God's love for all he has created and it speaks of eternal life. Now, when I say "eternal life" I do not mean what happens after you die. Jesus spoke many times of eternal life as something that starts here, now, in this place, not in some far-off place after we die. Life is about so much more than the absence of death. Mom brought life to this world in many ways. She brought countless children into the world as a missionary in Africa. She brought healing and restoration to a family that had lost a wife and mother. She brought dignity to elderly people with mental illness—many of whom were forgotten or abandoned because of their age or illness—while working at Norristown State Hospital.

God chose to save the world by coming to it in human form. Mom let herself be used by God. She went to serve those who were less fortunate, those in need , and those whom the world forgot about or discarded.

I also think of Mark 8:11, where the Pharisees ask Jesus for a sign that he is who he says he is. I once asked God for a sign. Many of us do. We just want something to show us that God notices us, that he cares about us. The thing is, God rarely speaks to us through a burning bush or through miracles. God does, however, send people into our lives to show us that he sees us, cares about us, and loves us more than we know. God sent his son. God sends people to be his sign to the world. God sends us to be his miracles. God sent Mom to be a sign to all those around her that God uses little things to do great works. Mom may have been small in stature, something I reminded her about frequently, but that never stopped her from being used by God in big ways.

So now that Mom is gone and we are left with the memories, how do we celebrate and honor her life? By being part of the jigsaw puzzle, realizing that no person is an island and that we are all connected. By being that sign from God to those around us. By doing small things with great love, because, like Mom, little things can make a big difference.

My Sister and I
by Anna Mary Groff

Dorcas was twelve years old when I was born into the Stoltzfus family. There are two brothers, Paul and Nathan, between us. Two years after I was born, our little sister, Ruthie, joined the family. She was a Down syndrome child but lived fifty-one years—until 1997.

My first memories of Dorcas are of her being a dorm student at Lancaster Mennonite School. I remember eagerly going along with Pop to LMS on Friday afternoon to bring Dorcas home for the weekend. After her graduation from LMS in 1951, when I was seven years old, she was off to EMC and then to Woman's Medical College in Philadelphia, when

I was a grade school girl. And then I went to LMS too. My junior year was not a good one, and I wanted to drop out of high school. It was Dorcas who encouraged me to keep going. I did, and graduated in 1961. I'm glad I finished high school—thanks to my Big Sis, although by that time I was taller than she was! And then, about the time I was becoming mature enough that we could relate to each other as adults, she flew off to Africa. She had just turned thirty years old. So then we communicated *not* by e-mail but by airmail. I'm not sure when we started calling each other Sis, but our letters to each other began "Dear Sis."

Our biggest adventure together was in the summer of 1965 after she came home from Africa for her first furlough. Sis, a friend, and I traveled to the West Coast in the blue VW Bug she had bought in Europe and shipped to the United States. We were at some of the national parks and also visited some of Sis's many friends. And we camped. The tent fit on the roof rack, and there was a place for everything—three sleeping bags, a one-burner stove—and everything had to be in its place! What a trip!

I was the first to be married and to become a mother. After her second term overseas, Dorcas married Ted. It was 1974 and she was forty-two years old, and she immediately had a family of three teenagers and a ten-year-old! The following years were busy ones for both of us, and trips between Gap, where I lived, and Philadelphia, where she lived, were not frequent.

After Ted's passing and her move to Landis Homes in 2004 (and here I am skipping over several very significant chapters in her life), our calls and visits were more frequent. We both enjoyed putting jigsaw puzzles together and working on family history and genealogy. I would often call her with a question about someone or some event in the past. We were both amused when people here asked us if I was her daughter. We'd chuckle and say, "No, we are SISTERS!"

Several years ago she said she was having a problem with a "forgetter that really works." And it gradually became worse, to the point that she did not remember the names of her family members. I don't remember when she last addressed me as Sis or Anna Mary. But when I'd come to visit her, I'd say, "Hi, Sis," and I'm sure she knew who I was.

Last Friday was a beautiful day. The sky was so blue with some white, puffy clouds and the temperature was comfortable. I came to visit her after noon. She was sitting in her room with a heavy sweater on and a blanket across her lap. She was cold. I suggested that we go outside—she always loved the outdoors. So the staff helped her into a wheelchair and I pushed her outside. There were several other ladies outside. Dorcas was calm and quiet that afternoon—and she did get warm enough to open her sweater! We talked about the beautiful blue sky and I sang a song I had taught to little people: "Blue, blue sky, oh, I can see the sky. God gave me eyes so I can see the sky." Sis did not know that song. Then I started singing, "Come, we that love the Lord, and let our joys be known. Join in a song with sweet accord." One of the ladies joined me in singing and I heard Dorcas humming along as we sang, "We're marching to Zion, beautiful, beautiful Zion." I had not heard her hum or sing for quite a while! Late that evening when Alice called and told me of her passing, I wondered, did Sis know she was that close to Zion, "beautiful, beautiful Zion?"

The most important thing my Sis did for me was back in the mid-1950s. David Thomas was the evangelist at tent meetings near Parkesburg. Sis and I were there together, and she sensed that I was being convicted. I was such a timid girl and just did not get up from my chair. She encouraged me to stand and accept Jesus as my Savior. And I did.

I thank you, Lord, for my sister and her influence on my life.

Meditation

The following tribute is adapted with permission from words spoken by Landis Homes Chaplain Jim Leaman at Dorcas's funeral service.

Precious in the sight of the Lord is the death of his saints. Precious in the sight of the Lord is the death of his faithful servant, Dorcas Leah Stoltzfus Morrow.

As I was beginning to work on these remarks, one of Dorcas's neighbors from Harvest View stopped by my office to ask whether I knew Dorcas loved to put puzzles together. "Dorcas would complete puzzles that others had given up on as being too difficult," she told me. "She was persistent."

Perhaps persisting with puzzles is illustrative of Dorcas' life. She persevered in her walk with the Lord, in her dream to pursue a high school education, and to keep going until she had graduated from college and medical school, served as a missionary doctor, and later trained as a psychiatrist. She figured out the challenges of education and medicine just as in recent times she figured out the challenges of jigsaw puzzles. She went far beyond her country farm girl roots. Later in life she married the widowed husband of college roommate Catherine Roth and took on the role of stepmother, mother, and grandmother.

The family gave me three Scriptures for the service this morning, all of which were meaningful texts to Dorcas. The first is **Psalm 138:8,** *The Lord will fulfill his purpose for me; your love, O Lord, endures forever; do not abandon the works of your hands.* The second is **Exodus 14:13–15,** *Moses answered the people, "Do not be afraid. Stand firm and you will see the deliverance the Lord will bring today. The*

Egyptians you see today you will never see again. The Lord will fight for you; you need only to be still." Then the Lord said to Moses, "*Why are you crying out to me? Tell the Israelites to move on.*" The third is **Philippians 1:6,** *Be confident of this, that God who began a good work in you will carry it on to completion until the day of Christ Jesus.*

As you listened to these three Scripture selections, perhaps you noticed a theme—that God has a purpose for our lives, God wants us to pursue that purpose, and God plans to complete that purpose as we anticipate the great day of the Lord.

Psalm 138 begins with these two verses: *I will praise you, O Lord, with all my heart; before the gods I will sing your praise. I will bow down toward your holy temple and will praise your name for your love and your faithfulness, for you have exalted above all things your name and your word.* This psalm is a prayer of praise to God, who is steadfast in love for God's people. "Steadfast love" is the translation of the great Hebrew word *chesed.* It is mentioned in verse 2 and again in verse 8. It is often translated as "love that endures."

The love of humans is fickle and often unreliable. God's love is steadfast, enduring forever and consistent and faithful. People often ask as a greeting, "What's new?" If you can't come up with something, tell them, "God's mercies are new; every morning God's mercies are new and fresh!" God's steadfast, faithful love is the foundation for our depending on the Lord who gives us a purpose for life.

Dorcas grew up as a farm girl. She worshiped with the Millwood and Maple Grove Mennonite Churches to the east of Lancaster. It was not expected that she would attend high school. She received a work permit so that she could discontinue going to school. But Dorcas had a dream. She had been inspired by the story of Dr. Ida Scudder, who as a teenage had observed that the husbands of women in India often did not want a male doctor to attend their wives at childbirth. Ida had decided that the Lord wanted her to go back to the United States, go to medical school, and return to India as a doctor. When Dorcas heard that story she too heard a quiet voice within giving her the vision of going to medical school herself and becoming a missionary doctor. It was not easy, but she persevered in what she believed was God's purpose for her life. Probably more than one person doubted that Dorcas would be able to fulfill that vision, but accomplish it she did, by the help and grace of God.

Now to Exodus 14—the Scriptural text of a sermon preached by a minister who was influential in Dorcas's life. She had committed her life to Christ under his evangelistic preaching. On one occasion he preached from the verses in Exodus 14 where Moses tells the Israelites, when they were thinking it would have been better to have remained in Egypt than to die in the desert, that they should wait, be still, and trust in the Lord to deliver them from the Egyptians. Even Moses might have been swayed by the people's despair.

But the Lord said to Moses, "Why are you crying out to me? Tell the Israelites to move on!" Another translation puts it, "Go forward!" It was that imperative phrase that caught young Dorcas's attention. Like the Israelites, Dorcas could have succumbed to fear and given up in despair. Probably she was tempted to do that at times. But she heard God say, "Go forward!" And "go forward" she did as she pursued God's purpose for her life.

Dorcas leaves us with the challenge from this text and from her life to "move on; go forward" as God leads us too, trusting God to provide whatever is needed to fulfill God's purpose in us. What God calls us to pursue will be beyond what we can do by our natural abilities; it can be accomplished only by the power of God at work within us. We serve in humility so that our little light shining will point people to see God at work through the Spirit of Christ. That, I believe, was Dorcas's desire.

The third Scripture text is Philippians 1:6—*Be confident of this, that God who began a good work in you will carry it on to completion until the day of Jesus Christ.* Some of you may remember the little buttons that some persons wore pinned to their shirt or blouse years ago that had a bunch of letters on them that stood for this sentence: *Please be patient; God is not finished with me yet.* Dorcas knew that God was not finished with her yet, even in the later years of her life. Paul knew that God wasn't finished yet with the young and growing Philippian church, but Paul was convinced that God's Spirit would continue expressing in these believers the character of Jesus Christ and the fruit of the Holy Spirit. And one day these believers would reach maturity, either at the day of Christ, when the Lord would return, or when they were called to their heavenly reward.

The day that Dorcas died she was part of a devotional group. One of the participants made a comment stating his wish that the Lord would soon return or that he could soon go to be with Jesus. Then Dorcas spoke, echoing those words and expressing her own desire to go home to heaven. That was on Friday morning, and that night God called Dorcas home. She had fought the good fight, she had finished the race, and she had kept the faith.

Dorcas had pursued God's purpose for her, by the grace of God, and God's plan for Dorcas's life had been completed. Jesus would say to Dorcas, "Well done, good and faithful servant; enter into the joys of your Lord."

We are yet running the race. The call of God and the example of Dorcas Stoltzfus Morrow challenge us to pursue God's purpose for us, to let God's purposeful plan be fulfilled in us too.

The following letter was read at the funeral by a representative of EMM:

August 12, 2015

Dear Morrow Family,

Greetings in the name of our Lord and Savior Jesus Christ. On behalf of Eastern Mennonite Missions I would like to express our sympathy and condolences in regard to the homegoing of Dorcas L. Stoltzfus Morrow, M.D.

At Eastern Mennonite Missions we hold a deep appreciation for the seven years of service that Dr. Stoltzfus Morrow gave to the Kingdom of God through EMM's program. Dorcas served as a missionary doctor from October 1961 to July 1965, first in Shirati Hospital in Tanzania, and completed her term at Jamama Hospital in southern Somalia. After seminary and an OB-GYN residency she returned to Tanzania in July of 1970 to work in the Shirati Hospital and devotedly served until December 1973.

We give thanks to God for Dorcas's life and ministry. We would like to share with you that her contributions in the past continue to impact the work of God in the world today through EMM.

Our thoughts and prayers are with you as you adjust to this season of separation from Dorcas. May the peace of God which transcends all understanding guide your hearts and minds in Christ Jesus.

Sincerely,

Eastern Mennonite Missions
Nelson Okanya
President ✝

Appendix
Learning About Ladders

I don't remember my first encounter with Dad's forty-foot wooden extension ladder. You see, I was only two or three years old. But Dad told me about it, more than once. The story went something like this:

There was a big cherry tree along the fence row in our meadow, about halfway up the hill, and there were three smaller cherry trees along the fence row below the bigger, older tree. Dad had noticed that the bigger tree had a lot of ripe cherries waiting to be picked, so one sunny morning he got out his big extension ladder. I followed close behind as he carried the ladder out past the springhouse and into the meadow, around the orchard, and halfway up the hill to the big cherry tree. He let me carry the gallon King Molasses can for him. He also brought along an old hook to put on the can handle so he could hang the can on a rung of the ladder and use both hands to pick the sweet cherries. I watched him lean the ladder against a part of the tree that had good strong limbs. He also found a stone to place under the leg of the ladder that was on the lower side of the hill so that the ladder would stand level. Then he pulled on the ladder's rope to extend the ladder up to a height of about thirty feet. He checked again to make sure it had good support. Then he climbed the tree, pulled a short piece of binder twine from a pocket in his bib overalls, and tied the ladder to a supporting limb so it would not shift position. I watched as he came back down, put the hook on the handle of the molasses can, then went back up the ladder to pick the cherries. It did not take him long to fill his can and come back down the ladder. We ate some of the delicious cherries as we walked back to the house, where we gave Mother the can of remaining cherries.

Dad went back to the barn to do some more work, but apparently I didn't trail after him this time. Later, when he came in for the noon meal without me, he discovered that I was not with my mother either!

Dad was pretty sure I wasn't out at the barn, and I wasn't in the house, so he headed off through the meadow, taking fast strides with his long legs. As he rounded the corner of the orchard, he looked up and saw the yellow of my cotton dress among the green leaves of the cherry tree. I was about twenty-five feet above the ground! As he quickly covered the hundred yards to the ladder, he realized that he should move quietly lest he frighten me and I lose my grip on the ladder. Gently and slowly he climbed up the ladder without speaking to me, and just as he was two steps beneath me and about to reach up, I apparently suddenly realized he was there and without any warning abruptly let go of the ladder and dropped into his arms! Fortunately he hung onto both the ladder and to me! Then he got us both down off the ladder. I'm sure he must have told me not to climb a ladder like that by myself again until I was older and knew how to do it safely.

I think I can safely assume that we had cherry bread soup for supper that evening. During the Depression we often had bread soup (bread torn into small pieces with cold milk and a bit of sugar) to which we would add whatever cold fruit was available—sweet cherries, sliced peaches, strawberries, raspberries, wine berries, blueberries, and so on. In fact, bread soup became a favorite meal for warm summer evenings, and it was so easy and quick to make.

My next encounter with a ladder was when I was about nine years old. I can date it fairly closely because my youngest brother is seven years and three months younger than me and he was probably just over a year and a half when this event took place.

Dad and the hired man had been gathering hay with the hay loader, a machine hitched to the back of the hay wagon that picked up loose hay as the wagon pulled it astride the rows. It carried the hay upward and dropped it onto the rear of the wagon so that Dad and his helper could pack it into the wagon. When the wagon was loaded, they pulled it to the barn and onto the left barn floor and beside the haymow. The hired man got down into the mow to spread the loose hay around while Dad stayed on the wagon. The barn had a track attached to the ridge-pole (the highest horizontal timber of the roof, to which the rafters of the two big sections of roof were attached like an inverted V). There was also a series of pulleys: one on the track above the barn floor, another anchored at the far end of the track by the stone wall—the east end of our triple-decker barn—and two more that carried the long end of a rope across the mow from the east barn wall to the barn floor near the big barn doors. The other end of the rope was attached to a three-foot-long hay hook with a four-inch tip on the bottom end that could be turned from a vertical to a horizontal position after the hook had been pushed down into the loose hay. The distal end of the rope ran thru a pulley by the barn door and had a heavy metal ring attached to it. A team of horses waited nearby on the barn bridge with their double tree hitched to the ring on the rope. When Dad said he was ready, I replied with a "giddyap" to the horses and we walked over the barn bridge and down to the bottom of the incline while the rope and hay hook carried the pile of hay upward to the barn roof, then along the track above the mow. When I said "Whoa!" the horses stopped. I unhooked the rope and said "Whap!" They turned to the left and we returned to the barn bridge. Meanwhile Dad had given a strong tug to his end of the rope to trip the hay hook, and as the tip returned to its vertical position, the hay dropped into the mow. Dad then pulled the hay hook back along the track until it stopped above the wagon, where he pulled it down to himself. We repeated this cycle a number of times. It was interrupted only by trips to the hay field to gather more hay whenever the wagon got empty, or perhaps to enjoy some cool meadow tea that Mother sometimes brought to us from the springhouse. I was having a good time. I enjoyed working with the horses, and I was glad I could be a helper on the farm.

On this particular day my youngest brother came to watch us. I'm not really sure who was supposed to be watching *him*. He did have a way of getting around by himself. In fact, he began walking when he was only nine months old. Maybe my other brother, Paul, who was going on five years of age, was with him, but I don't remember. Anyway, at some point Dad had parked his short ladder against the big log beams between the two barn floors. There was a deck above the other barn floor and sometimes Dad stored something up there, then used the ladder when he wanted to retrieve it. That day, when I was walking the horses back to pull up another hookful of hay, I happened to notice that little Nathan was climbing up the ladder, so I said "Whoa!" to the horses, then quickly went to the ladder and climbed up about ten feet, scooped him into my right arm, and held tightly to the ladder with my other arm as I carried him down and off the ladder. As Dad watched me rescue my little brother, I'm sure he was remembering the time he rescued me from the cherry tree. And I have no doubt he thanked God both times for protecting his children from potential harm.

When I was twelve years old and in fifth grade, Dad decided to downsize and moved us to a smaller farm because during World War II it was difficult to keep reliable hired help to run a 107-acre farm. At his late-winter sale in 1943, Dad sold many of his cows, two horses, his McCormick-Deering 10-20 tractor, the old hay wagons, and some other major equipment, but he kept one team of horses, Mike and Roy. He soon got a new rubber-tire flatbed wagon, and a week later we used it to move most of our household furniture to our new house, only three miles by state road or one mile over the hills by dirt road from the old place.

Dad gradually renovated the "new" barn; he put in a second barn floor, enlarged the cow stable, and built a new milkhouse. He slowly added more cows from his own stock, then installed DeLaval milking machines like the ones we had at the old place. Within a year he was convinced he needed a tractor, so he bought a new John Deere H. Later, when my brothers were old enough to help on the farm, he bought more land from a nearby farm. Later he got a John Deere B with corn cultivators, and I spent many happy hours in the cornfield with that green "put-put-put" machine. Eventually I noticed that I was being relegated to jobs like milking cows, mowing the lawn, and helping in the garden, and one of my brothers even had the audacity to tell me, "You can stay in the house now and help Mom. We will take care of the farmwork!"

But Dad still found outdoor jobs for me to do, even if it was hoeing weeds in the cornfield. We had a cherry tree near this house too. Dad had sold the forty-foot ladder but later got a shorter one for our smaller barn. When the cherries got ripe, Dad hauled out the new extension ladder, set it up, and secured it. Then I climbed up and picked cherries to my heart's content. Afterward I often made cherry ice cream in our eight-quart freezer for our evening meal.

As I gained more confidence in using the ladder, I asked Dad for some paint so I could paint our old gray barn. The side with the barn doors, which faced our house to the southwest, was less than twenty feet high, so that paint job was easy. But the side facing the southeast, with its attached chicken house and pigpen with steeply sloped roofs, was more difficult. Granted, I could get up on one of those roofs and paint what I could reach from a standing position. But the top of the barn was a lot taller than I was, and how could I raise a ladder on those steep roofs? Well, I never did get that end finished, but at least it faced away from the highway, so my incomplete paint job was not so conspicuous.

I did finally tackle the opposite end of the barn, facing northwest, in spite of two problems. First, it was a long way up to the center of the roof and, though our ladder was long enough, I needed someone to "anchor" its bottom as I climbed all the way to the top. The other deterrent was the steep bank that rose from the middle of the cowbarn, where a door exited directly to a small parking area beside the old highway to permit deliveries to and pickups from the lower barn. This steep slope to the right of the door was basically parallel to the barn's foundation, and just as it was not easy to mow, it was also *not* an easy place on which to park a ladder! I was able to prepare a stone platform on which to rest the left foot of the ladder and create a level base position for it. My brothers then provided strong hands to hold the ladder steady, especially as I climbed up and down with the paint bucket in one hand and my brush and paint rag in the other. If there was any wind blowing or a threat of rain, the painting was postponed. That end of the barn received light green paint. I suspect that the only paint our barn had seen before was the old Mail Pouch tobacco sign that hung on the northeast side of the barn for many years as an advertisement to those who traveled the old Lincoln Highway. Dad eventually had that side of the barn, and the old sign, covered with gray siding.

Dad also got around to improving the house with a new kitchen and more windows, a nice sunporch plus a small room that connected the sunporch to the kitchen, and a rear entrance. He also had a bathroom built upstairs and took out the stairs from the kitchen to the bedroom above it. When the carpenters began working to make a connection from the old house to the room above the kitchen, which clearly had been built later, well, surprise! They found solid logs filling the wall. When they cut the door hole into the wall—surprise again! The floor in the bedroom above the kitchen was about twelve inches lower than the other upstairs rooms, so they put in a step down to that bedroom, and a short door, so tall people had to stoop to enter that bedroom. Before the renovations we had no idea that we lived in a log house, because it was covered with clapboard.

Meanwhile, something strange was happening, to me. My love of farm life was being "adjusted" by a dream of returning to school and becoming a medical missionary. Despite a number of obstacles, that dream became reality when I got my M.D. in 1960 and flew off to Tanganyika in October 1961. After a first four-year term of missionary service in East Africa, a year in seminary, four years of graduate medical training, and another two-year term in Africa, I learned that God had an even broader plan for my life than I had ever imagined. In the spring of 1974, the friend who had been my roommate during my freshman year of college died after a yearlong battle with breast cancer, leaving behind her husband and four children. I had known Ted since before their marriage and had visited the family whenever I could. My life now took a major turn as on August 4, 1974, Ted and I were married.

I joined the family in their big hundred-year-old, three-story twin house with a basement and unfinished attic in the Germantown neighborhood of Philadelphia. The first-floor ceilings were eleven feet high. Each child had her or his own bedroom, and we had two and a half bathrooms. Ted's office was in the alcove of the largest second-floor bedroom, but as his dictionary and other reference book needs increased, and after he got first one computer and then a second, we moved our bedroom into the middle room and let his office take over the front room, after I had finished painting it a pale blue. I kept finding patches of loose wallpaper, stains, and multiple cracks in the plaster throughout the house—and plumbing problems. The kitchen sink sprung a serious leak even before

Ted and I got back from our honeymoon, and my sister helped us find a used sink with wall cabinets to remedy that emergency. The outside front and back walls of the house were crying for paint, and the front porch too. So, after I got myself oriented to all my new responsibilities and routines, I began doing some indoor repair work. I took off old wallpaper, washed the walls, learned to fill in the plaster cracks, used sealer paint to cover the stains, and gradually painted a number of the rooms and most of the hallways. I found that a stepladder and a sixteen-foot extension ladder could be quite useful; I figured out how to prop the extension ladder against a side wall, put the stepladder in the middle of the room, and place a sturdy plank between the steps of the two ladders; then I could easily reach the upstairs ceilings. For the first-floor ceilings, however, I covered the dining room table with an old sheet, parked the stepladder on the table, and asked my tall stepson to work on the middle area of the ceiling while I used my short ladder to work on the edges. The living room and dining room looked really nice with their bright paint and new curtains. Later the kitchen got treated to a dropped ceiling (making it much warmer in winter), new floor, new linoleum, new sheets of tile-board on the bottom four feet of the walls, new fluorescent lights above the table, and light green paint on the remaining wall surface. It was now a cozy place for Ted and I to have breakfast and lunch together when the others were gone for the day. The third-floor bathroom also got treated to new tileboard and paint.

Then I got a forty-foot aluminum extension ladder and began working on the outside of the house. Rita, my youngest stepdaughter, helped me manage the ladder from the back porch roof so I could sand and clean the rust spots on the metal wall outside her third-floor bedroom and upward to the top of the attic. After covering the spots with Rustoleum paint, I put Sears Weatherbeater paint on the whole back of the house, and it looked so much better.

Next, Rita helped me walk the upright ladder around to the front porch. We parked it on the sidewalk, climbed it to the porch roof, and pulled the ladder up. We raised it into an upright position against the front wall of the house. I was so glad that the front of the house outside the attic and third-floor front bedroom was covered with large white shingles so I had no metal rust spots to scrape and sand and could just paint the wall, then work on the windows. Over the course of several years, I worked outside during the summer, then in the fall afternoons after I went back to my school physician job, until the weather got too cold.

I next worked on the lower windows, putting new glaze on the panes and applying caulk around the frames as needed before I painted the window sash. I enjoyed the painting, but I had learned from Dad that it was important to prepare the surface beforehand. In fact, preparation seems to be in order before starting almost any job. I was really glad that the side wall of our house was brick, with a mansard-style slate roof that angled down from the attic to the bottom of the third-floor rooms. That meant less painting for me! However, there were two full-size dormer windows in the mansard walls that were not easily accessible. But I kept thinking about them and figured out that by sliding both windowpanes down, then sliding both of them up, I could work on the outside of the windows from inside the rooms. But I couldn't reach everything that way. I found that the foot-wide ledge gutter that ran along the brick wall just below the mansard roof would support me, so I brought my short ladder out the window and laid it against the mansard with its foot in the gutter. Then I stepped through the window and went up the ladder and painted the dormer frame. I repeated the process on the other side and thus finished the window from the outside. Later I used the same approach with the other dormer window. I admit I was relieved when those high areas were all painted. I did ask two young men from church to clean and paint the ledge gutter, because that was up just about as far as my big ladder would stretch, and it was a job that required two people (one to hold the ladder) because the walkway between our house and the neighbor's house was not exactly level.

The last major project was the front porch. The paint was peeling from the ceiling, and when I applied my "elbow grease" and wire brush to it, the old paint swirled around me like snow. The fancy wood decorations along the edge of the roof were not easy to clean either. Some upright supports had to be put back into the porch railing, and the lattice-style gate beneath the porch, which could be removed when I needed to put my big ladder into the basement through the window under the porch, needed some new lath slats. I replaced the rotted frame of another basement window that had hinges at the top, and I was rather pleased with the result even though it took me a while to measure and fit everything, more than once, until it fit "just so." Finally the repairs were finished and the painting was done. It was so good to see the house looking better and to know that it was in better shape.

Some years later I pulled my big ladder out of the basement again to put a new coat of paint on the back of the house. I had some other project in mind too, so I left the ladder in the back yard, because it was such a job to take it into and out of the basement by myself. (By that time Rita was no longer at home to help me.) Some days later when I went out back I realized that my ladder was no longer there. Frankly, I did not get too upset about it; after all, I was the one who had left it in the back yard. But I had left it outside so often before and no one had bothered it.

In 1987 we decided to leave Germantown and settled on a home in Blue Bell, Pennsylvania, a nice community located a mile from Ben's new school and four miles from my job. We moved in on September 30, 1987. Getting settled took some time and the copious leaves from our three big maple trees never saw a rake until the next spring. In Germantown we'd had only a small, shaded back yard that was easily managed with a push mower. Now we needed more equipment. We settled on a power mower to do the trim areas, and a Craftsman tractor mower to do the "easy" part. Later we added an electric hedge trimmer and a Weed Wacker grass trimmer. I really enjoyed working in the yard and did some major trimming of some overgrown bushes. I also dug up some heavy sod in the back yard and made a nice vegetable garden.

I soon discovered that in order to clear the gutters of all the leaves and maple "nose-pincher" seeds, we needed a ladder. Fortunately the roof of this house was not very high, so a twenty-eight-foot aluminum extension ladder was more than adequate. And the roof had a very gentle slope, so it was no problem to sit down on it near the gutter to scoop out the leaves and junk with one hand while managing my five-gallon bucket with the other hand as I inched along beside the gutter. When my stepson was available I sent him to the roof on the ladder propped up against the gutter (rather than against the chimney side of the house). He would stand on the ladder to clear out the part of the gutter he could reach, then climb further up the ladder, step onto the roof, and take the upper end of the ladder while I carried the lower end as we moved the ladder another four feet to the right. That maneuver cleaned gutters more easily and quickly than my one-person way.

Some winters we got little snow and other years it seemed like we got snow every week. One morning I discovered we had water dripping from the ceiling into our living room, not far from the wood-burning stove installed in front of the fireplace. The emergency fix was to put a five-gallon bucket beneath the drip, then call our church folks to see if someone could help. The problem, we discovered, was that melting snow in the mid-afternoon had left moisture along the edge of the roof just above the gutter (the roof did not extend out over the side wall to the gutter) and the water had frozen overnight. In the morning the heat rising through the side walls from inside the house melted the ice at the edge of the roof and capillary attraction carried the water further up the roof while the gutter remained frozen solid. The water then came down inside the wall and trailed along the ceiling four feet into our living room.

A friend from church soon appeared and cleared the snow off the roof, and the dripping soon stopped. Thereafter I kept a wary eye on the roof whenever we got snow, and on various occasions I propped our ladder against the chimney and got onto the roof to sweep off the snow. If the snow had partially melted then frozen again, it could be slick. I admit that my feet went out from under me once, or maybe twice, but I tried to be very cautious.

In our later years in that house my legs did not have their former strength, so I had handrails installed outside for the steps to our driveway and for the inside stairs to our second floor. I also resorted to going up one step with my stronger right leg, then bringing my left leg up to join the right one, then repeating the process. And when I went up the ladder, I now carried only one item with me instead of two so I could use both hands to pull me up the ladder instead of relying on my legs to lift me up. When I moved to Landis Homes in 2004, my ladder days came to an end, except for the step stool I used to reach the top shelves of my bookcases. Now I no longer use even that.

To wind up this long tale about the ladders in my life, I guess I should admit that I never was afraid of climbing a ladder, probably because Dad was not afraid of ladders. He taught me how to use a ladder properly and safely. One thing he sometimes did when he wanted to have both hands free on the ladder was to put one leg over a rung of the ladder then bring it back underneath that rung and hook his foot onto the next rung below. But his legs were longer than mine, so I did not often try that anchor method. Sometimes I put my arms around the ladder, other times I put one arm between the rungs. Dad also told me it is very important to have the proper angle when leaning a ladder against a building or tree so that your weight pushes the ladder into the tree or building. Having an excessive angle between the ladder and tree or building could be a problem too, because it increases the stress on the ladder. I know that some persons are not comfortable climbing ladders, so I have tried not to ask someone to help with ladder work if they are not comfortable doing it. I hope I have never made anyone feel inferior if they have declined to climb a ladder.

There are many ways a person can get hurt on a farm because of all the animals and heavy equipment. Trees and ladders can be vehicles of injury too. I often rode our horses bareback, and one time when I was riding Mike I carelessly slid off, but he stopped immediately and let me pick myself up from beneath him. Another time I was leading Roy, our big bay horse, to the watering trough. When I stopped close to the trough I guess he thought he was supposed to stop too, even though I had not told him to stop. The only problem was that when he stopped he put his big foot down on my little bare right foot! And he stood there for what seemed like forever as I pushed at him and told him to move. When he finally did I hobbled away to the nearby walnut tree and sat down for a while as Mom and Dad finished milking the cows. My foot swelled up and stayed that way for several days. But it got better, without even being checked by a doctor. Soon I was running around again in my bare feet, just like old times. Anyway, I thank God for protecting me from danger and possible injury on various occasions, throughout all my years on the farm, on the road, and everywhere I've been. ✞

Acknowledgments and Credits

I am grateful to my family for helping me to share the story of my life and the life of my husband, Ted. I am thankful to all of the Morrow children—Joseph, Alice, Mary, Rita, and Ben—for their love and support and for the information they provided over the years as I wrote what has become this book. I am especially grateful to Alice for making my dream of publishing this book a reality, and to my sister Anna and her husband, Leonard Groff, for the many kinds of support they provided to Alice and me in the process. (Anna proofread everything at least twice.) I also thank my sister-in-law Pinky, Ted's sister, for the help she gave me in writing about Ted's childhood and family of origin, especially in March 2007, when Anna and Leonard took me to visit her at the Villas of Casa Celeste in Seminole, Florida.

I am grateful to Reuben Bigelow at Landis Homes for reading and reviewing an early copy of the manuscript. [*Editor's note: Thanks is also due to Dorcas's niece Joyce Stoltzfus Blank for reading the proof copy and offering much helpful feedback.*]

An assortment of photos have been used to illustrate this book. Many of them (including the one used for the front cover) were originally slides that I took, or that others took while with my camera, in Africa and while I was traveling. I am grateful to Leonard for scanning all two thousand plus of those fifty-year-old slides into his computer, and to Alice for cleaning up and enhancing some of them for use in the book. The following table contains as much information as I am able to provide about the book's photos. I am sorry that I do not recall the names of everyone who appears in the pictures, nor do I know who took many of the ones that were not taken by me. I ask your forgiveness for what is lacking.

Page	Photo Information
1	Me in 1961
2	Me in Somalia, 1964 or 1965
13	My parents, Elizabeth S. Stoltzfus and Christian G. Stoltzfus in 1928
17	From left to right: Anna Mary, Paul, Nathan, Ruthie, and me in 1945 or 1946

Index

Brunk Brothers (George and Lawrence): **63**
Bucher, Dr. Samuel: **74, 277, 302–303**
Buck, Pearl (*My Several Worlds*): **236**
Buckwalter: Miriam, **192, 206, 207, 211**; Rhoda, **267, 270, 275, 282, 286**
Buddha: **358, 389**
Burkholder, Dr.: **290**
Buzzard, Joe: **215**
Byler, George: **409**

California: Camp Stoneman, Pittsburg, **382**; Oakland, **382**; San Francisco, **383, 384, 481**
Caldwell, Miss (Mrs. Barley): **32–34**
Calverley, Dr. Eleanor T.: **177**
Campbell, Frances (Fran) Stine: **201, 202**
Catholic: mission at Kowak, **111, 161–162, 198, 212**; missionaries, **200, 232**; Newman Center, **444**; nun-doctor, **198–200, 218**; Polish, **358**; Pope John XXIII, **428**; in Scottdale, **427–428**; in US Army, **383, 384, 385–386**; Vatican II, **428**
CCH (Chester County Hospital): **xi, 82–83, 85–87, 94, 160**
Cemetery: Amish Mennonite, **484**; Arlington, **235**; Christ's Home, **94**; Germantown Mennonite, **445**; Grove, **331, 345**; Ivy Hill, **437, 438**; Millwood Mennonite, **3, 480, 483**; Scottdale, **424**; Shirati, **249**
Cesarean section (C-section): **82, 133, 144–145, 167, 170, 172, 189, 196, 200, 334**
Chaplain: assistant Ezra, **385**; Crary, **361**; Hamburg State School, **462**; Jim Leaman, Landis Homes, **498, 499, 503**; in Korea, **391, 392**; Schofield Barracks, **383**; Shirati Hospital, **202**; University of Rochester campus, **359**
Charles, Raymond: **131, 134, 148**
Charlotte, CCH switchboard operator: **85, 86**
Chicago: **4, 88, 92**
China: **100, 242, 359**
Chinese: friendship with Somalia, **242**; graduate student, **358**; Hawaiian, **385**; language, **359**; smorgasbord, **496**

Chirangi, Bwire: **497**
Chou En-Lai: **242**
Christian Medical School for Women, Vellore, India: **7**
Christian Medical Society: **92, 173, 176**
Christmas: 1935, **15**; 1944, **45**; 1949, **376**; 1951, **387**; 1952, **401**; 1956, **81**; 1960, **86**; 1961, **118, 125–129**; 1962, **190–193, 195, 213**; 1963, **229, 235, 239**; 1964, **261, 267, 270–272, 278**; 1967, **306**; 1971, **313–316, 319**; 1973, **435–436**; 1974, **443–444**; 1975, **443**; 1977, **450**; 2003, **468, 470–472**; during medical school, **318**; jobs, **xi**
Christ's Home, Warminster, PA: **94**
Christopher Dock High School: **94, 446**
Church: Ascension Lutheran, **429**; Baptist, **397, 400**; Brethren in Christ, **159**; Bukenya, **161**; Christian and Missionary Alliance, **369**; Christian Reformed, **361**; Episcopal, **182, 345**; of God Mission, **175**; Greek Orthodox, **427**; Mara Hills, **162**; Methodist, **347, 348, 349, 358, 359**; Mormon, **389**; Pentecostal, **368**; Philippian, **505**; Presbyterian, **337, 347, 359**; Quaker, **9, 454**; Seventh-Day Adventist, **161**; of Sweden, **413**; Trinity Lutheran, **429, 436, 445, 446, 453**; Weavertown Beachy Amish, **400, 409, 421**; Wesleyan Methodist, **370**. *See also* Catholic; Mennonite Church; Millwood Amish Mennonite Church; TMC
Clemens, David: **273, 274**
Clemmer, Markley: **421, 422**
CMS (Church Missionary Society): **102, 103, 145**
CO (conscientious objector): **383, 385, 393, 454**
Coble, Arabella: **87**
Cole, Dr. Ernest: **376**
Colorado: **88, 89, 92, 93, 94, 97, 263**
Combelo: **259**
Conference: Conservative Mennonite, **404, 420**; Franconia, **303**; Lancaster, **95, 96, 445**
Confessions of Saint Augustine: **308**
Confucius: **358**
Congo (Zaire): **123, 139, 215, 435**

Ontario, Canada: **11, 92, 93, 109, 138, 518**; Poplar Hill, **295**; Red Lake, **282, 295, 518**
Oregon State: **318**
Oregon Dairy Restaurant: **485, 486, 496**
orphans: **165–166, 251**; Alice, **224**; Daniel, **363**; Donna, **326**; Dorka, **326**; Elizabeth, **224**; Jessca, **224, 230**; Otonda, **224, 230**; Susie, **189, 191, 224**
Overkamp, Corrine: **176, 177**

Page, Dr. William B. and Alice Thut: **96**
Palestine: **134, 143**
Panama Canal: **392**
Peachy, Paul: **74**
Pellman, Hubert: **72**
Penn: William, **53, 398**; Christian Academy, **455**; Foundation, **456**
Pennsylvania: **75, 83, 110, 118, 187, 210, 239, 277, 290, 295, 306, 398, 399, 404, 409, 410, 435, 473**; Atglen, **9, 14, 38, 316**; Bally, **399**; Blossburg, **395**; Blue Bell, **455, 457, 463, 467, 479, 480, 482, 491, 514, 520**; Bridgeport, **98**; Byerstown, **12**; Camp Hill, **396**; Carlisle, 437, **439**; Chambersburg, **55, 69, 397, 399, 439**; Christiana, **9, 10**; Coatesville, **38**; Cochranville, **38**, 174; Conshohocken, **421**; Dillsburg, **396**; East Petersburg, **169**; Elizabethtown, **41, 301**; Ephrata, **11, 49, 75, 109, 147, 485**; Farmington, **426**; Frazer, **99, 446**; Frog Hollow, **9, 10**; Germantown, Philadelphia, **21, 84, 429, 445, 455, 480, 491, 512, 514**; Hanover, **396**; Harrisburg, **301, 306, 307, 309, 311, 317, 318, 396, 435, 438, 439, 446, 449, 483**; Hatfield, **473**; Honey Brook, **455**; Kinzers, **483**; Lansdale, **94, 139**; Landisville, **483**; Latrobe, **427**; Laurelton, **461**; Lewistown, 174; Lititz, **484, 495**; Malvern, 174; Mansfield, **395**; Marion, **303**; Morgantown, **13**; Mount Gretna, **105**; Mount Joy, **483**; Mount Pleasant, **424**; Norristown, **327, 421, 455, 457, 469, 471, 476, 477**;

Northumberland, **395**; Paoli, **410**; Paradise, **109**; Parkesburg, **39, 503**; Pittsburgh, **418, 428**; pretzels, **130, 195, 196, 295**; Salunga, **90, 96, 97, 99, 124, 146, 182, 260, 277, 282, 295**; Sayre, **345, 371**; Scottdale, **92, 93, 215, 404, 417, 418, 420, 421, 423, 424, 426, 427, 428, 439, 440, 441, 445, 495, 520**; Selinsgrove, **410**; Sellersville, **84**; South Waverly, **371**; Spring City, **50**; Springville, **109**; Steelton, **301, 435, 436, 437, 438, 440**; Sunbury, **395**; Towanda, **371**; Turnpike, **86, 92, 436, 437, 463**; Umbletown, **14, 53**; University of, **75, 84**; Warminster, **84, 94**; Wernersville, **490**; West Chester, **xi, 16, 82, 85, 99, 138**; White Horse, **12, 31, 33**; Williamsport, **395**; York, 159. *See also* Gap; Lancaster; Philadelphia
Pennsylvania Dutch/German: **11, 16, 19, 178, 414**
Pepper (dog): **437**
Persian Gulf: **176**
Petersheim: LeRoy, **99, 129, 160, 219, 226, 260**; Mary, **90**
Philadelphia: **xi, 16, 21, 77, 83, 84, 85, 208, 288, 295, 305, 307, 315, 316, 318, 394, 399, 410, 422, 429, 430, 431, 435, 440, 441, 471, 476, 477, 495, 501, 502, 512, 520**; Center City, **450**; General Hospital, **82**; medical school, **75, 76, 173, 255, 318**; North, **451**; Northwest, **437, 438**; School District of, **441, 442, 450, 453, 455**; Shibe Park, **87**; Valley Green, Fairmount Park, **438**; West, **80**; Zoo, **21**
Philippines: **280**
Phillies: **87, 268, 485, 497**
piki-pik: **125, 185, 200, 204, 205, 212, 216, 217, 219, 249, 264, 278, 324**
Pine, Carol: **467, 477**
Pinocchio: **32**
Plank, Caroline: **284**
pori: **114, 150, 168, 207, 222, 226, 230, 231, 271, 272**
President, US: Cleveland, Grover, **336**; Ford, Gerald, **440**; Kennedy, John F., **235**; Nixon, Richard, **89–90**;

26163549R00305

Made in the USA
Middletown, DE
20 November 2015